DISCARDED

MASTERPLOTS II

AMERICAN FICTION SERIES,
REVISED EDITION

MASTERPLOTS II

AMERICAN FICTION SERIES, REVISED EDITION

5

Plu - Tel

Edited by

STEVEN G. KELLMAN

The University of Texas at San Antonio

SALEM PRESS

Pasadena, California   Hackensack, New Jersey

Editor in Chief: Dawn P. Dawson
Managing Editor: Christina J. Moose
Project Editor: Robert A. McClenaghan   *Research Editor:* Jeffrey Jensen
Acquisitions Editor: Mark Rehn   *Research Assistant:* Jun Ohnuki

∞ The paper used in these volumes conforms to the American National Standard for Permanence of Paper for Printed Library Materials, Z39.48-1992 (R1997).

Library of Congress Cataloging-in-Publication Data
Masterplots II. American fiction series / edited by Steven G.
Kellman.—Rev. ed.
    p.   cm.
Includes bibliographical references and index.
    ISBN 0-89356-871-6 (set) — ISBN 0-89356-872-4 (v. 1) —
ISBN 0-89356-873-2 (v. 2) — ISBN 0-89356-874-0 (v. 3) —
ISBN 0-89356-875-9 (v. 4) — ISBN 0-89356-876-7 (v. 5) —
ISBN 0-89356-877-5 (v. 6)
    1. American fiction—Stories, plots, etc. I. Title: Masterplots
2. II. Title: Masterplots two. III. Title: American fiction series.
IV. Kellman, Steven G., 1947-   .
PS373 .M37   2000
809.3'0097—dc21   99-053295

First Printing

PRINTED IN THE UNITED STATES OF AMERICA

LIST OF TITLES IN VOLUME 5

MASTERPLOTS II

AMERICAN FICTION SERIES, REVISED EDITION

PLUM BUN

Author: Jessie Redmon Fauset (1882-1961)
Type of plot: Social realism
Time of plot: From 1900 to the 1920's
Locale: Philadelphia and New York City, specifically Greenwich Village and Harlem
First published: 1929

> *Principal characters:*
>
> ANGELA MURRAY, the central figure, a young black woman who can pass as white and who changes her name to Angele Mory
>
> VIRGINIA (JINNY) MURRAY, her younger sister, who has brown skin
>
> ROGER FIELDING, a rich white man who, thinking that Angela is white, wants her to be his mistress
>
> ANTHONY CROSS, a sensitive black man who can pass as white but chooses not to, and who is in love with Angela
>
> RACHEL POWELL, a young black woman who is a fellow art student of Angela
>
> MARTHA BURDEN, a young white woman who is a friend and fellow art student of Angela
>
> JUNIUS and
>
> MATTIE MURRAY, the parents of Angela and Virginia; the father is dark-skinned; the mother can pass as white; both die early in the novel

The Novel

Most of the narrative focuses on the life of Angela Murray, from her early childhood in a black, working-class area of Philadelphia to her late twenties, when she achieves some success as an artist in New York City. The novel is divided into five parts, each part based on one portion of the well-known children's verse: "To Market, to Market/ To buy a Plum Bun;/ Home again, Home again,/ Market is done."

In the first part, "Home," the Murray family is introduced: a father, a mother, and two daughters, living on Opal Street in Philadelphia, a residential area of small, cramped houses. The race of the family immediately becomes an issue as the focus moves to Angela, the older daughter, who feels at a very young age the constraints placed upon her life by the fact of the family's color. Angela, like her mother, has a "creamy complexion" and can pass as white; Virginia, like her father, is dark. Angela's youthful yearning is for freedom, and she very soon realizes that she and her mother, when in the city alone, have access to the rewards of life, the glamours and pleasures of the marketplace, that are closed to her father and to Virginia. Mattie Murray often plays at being white and finds it a pleasant pastime, but she always professes her color when principle demands it. Angela, however, is keenly aware of the disadvantages of color and deeply hurt by the rejection of her white friends when they learn that she is black. The family is a close and caring one, but the tensions brought on by color are only relieved on Sunday afternoons, when they are alone and isolated from the color-conscious world of the city.

The two sisters are left truly alone, however, when both parents die within weeks of each other. The father dies of a heart attack, seemingly brought about by a racial confrontation in which he has to deny his husbandly relationship to Mattie. Mattie dies shortly thereafter, her heart more with her husband than with the tribulations of the world. Angela's inheritance, three thousand dollars, is, she believes, her golden opportunity for freedom; she flees Philadelphia for the glamour and promise of New York City; Virginia decides to stay with her inheritance, the parents' home, in Philadelphia.

In part 2, "Market," Angela becomes an art student in New York City, changes her name, establishes herself in Greenwich Village, and, after some inner debate, determines, as she did in Philadelphia, that to refrain from announcing her race will afford her the freedom to reach for the riches and pleasures of life. In New York City, she can rely on the fact that nothing will betray her race; she can even hope to marry a rich white man who can give her the entrance into the good life she so desires.

Angela is drawn to the simplicity and the values of the other art students, particularly Martha Burden and Anthony Cross; she is especially fascinated by a young black woman, Rachel Powell, who quietly and persistently develops her art. The entrance of a rich young white man, Roger Fielding, is more alluring, however, and Angela determines to make him her husband. Roger is attracted to Angela and pursues her, but only with the intention of seducing her: He is not about to marry a girl out of his own class, even though she may be white. The climax of this section occurs when Virginia decides to come to New York; Angela, caught between Roger and her sister, denies the sisterly bond, initiating an estrangement with Virginia that will last until the closing section of the narrative. Virginia is always a reminder to Angela that, unlike her mother, Angela does not acknowledge her race when principle is involved.

In part 3, "Plum Bun," Angela appears to be well on her way to achieving her goals—she has taken Roger as her lover with the hope of future marriage; she is persuading herself that she loves Roger and he her; she is succeeding in her art. Yet the life of her friends and her sister persists in intruding—Anthony Cross, who is in love with Angela, attracts her because of his sensitivity and his sympathy with the struggles of black people; Martha Burden offers her a straightforward, sensible view of the world, an open, honest friendship; Rachel Powell reflects a pride in race and in talent that in Angela's own self has been submerged; Virginia's delight in the life of Harlem, the sustenance and joy she draws from living among blacks, presents Angela with the reality of the happiness possible within the black community, a reality that Angela has evaded since her childhood. Roger grows restless under Angela's possessiveness, and the third section of the novel closes with the end of their affair and Angela's growing awareness of the superficiality of her desire to be white and rich and free.

In part 4, "Home Again," Angela attempts a reconciliation with her sister and tries to recapture the closeness and the caring of their earlier life together. Angela is awakened, by a series of incidents involving her friends and Virginia, to the fact that she in her self-absorption has been blind to the developing selves of the others. Hoping to regain Anthony's love, she learns, by his confession, that he is "colored," and that he and her sister are engaged. This relationship has evolved over a period of time and has, as Anthony tells Angela, been partially a result of his own struggle to overcome the temptations of "passing" as white. Anthony, still thinking that Angela is white, is unaware of her relation to Virginia. Anthony's confessions prompt an empathetic confession from Angela—she, too, is "colored."

Angela's awareness of the ironies of her life, her decision never to see Anthony again, her recognition of the strength of her race, as evidenced not only in Anthony, Virginia, and Rachel but also in her new perceptions of blacks who have moved briefly through her life, lead into the last section, "Market Is Done." Here, Angela confronts her own racial consciousness and announces her heritage publicly, primarily to defend Rachel, who has been refused an art scholarship because of her color. Angela realizes how much her own scholarship was a matter of color and not simply of talent and so identifies herself with those who have been rejected, ostracized, and humiliated because of race. After a series of acknowledgments by all the major figures, Anthony and Angela are reunited, and Virginia returns to her first love, Martin, and to Philadelphia. There is common agreement that happiness cannot be achieved by a denial of one's race and cultural heritage.

The Characters

The continuing focus on Angela allows the development of the duality in her character—her inner sympathy with her race, her external rejection of it. The characterization allows, on one hand, for the reader's questioning of Angela's materialistic external values and, on the other, for the reader's understanding of the inner evolution of Angela's self-esteem and race identification. Most of the other figures are, in some way, parallel with Angela, and they serve symbolically as reflections of various, often contradictory, aspects of Angela's self. Mattie Murray, for example, is the Angela who can pass as white; Mattie has achieved a balance between this external "white" self and the black self she really is—Angela's progress throughout the novel is to achieve that same kind of balance, only in a more complex world than that of her mother. Virginia is the external reminder to Angela of that black self that should be publicly acknowledged; Angela's warring with Virginia is symbolic of the war between her own white and black selves. Anthony's struggle with his racial consciousness parallels Angela's, and his emotional confrontations with his own actions bring to life authentic passions in Angela. Thus, the black Anthony and the white Roger represent the conflict within Angela between a true expression of love for others and a false passion based on selfish ends. Rachel is symbolic of the unity possible between self and art, a unity that Angela must struggle to achieve. Angela's art cannot be true until she is true to herself and to her race.

The characters are all established in realistic settings, in the context of descriptions of their homes, their clothing, and their physical interaction with the varied events and things of the marketplace. This depiction of the external world reinforces those aspects of character that are formed by physical and social realities. For example, Junius and Mattie's withdrawal to their home and their eventual deaths reflect their decision to isolate themselves as much as possible from the pain that the larger society provides. The descriptions of Harlem and of the people actively and intensely involved in that bustling community help to reinforce the characterization of Virginia, who accepts her race and finds within it joy and affirmation. Throughout the novel, Angela's developing character is reflected in the homes and apartments in which she lives—her sense of being cramped is reflected in the smallness of her room at home; the apartment rented by Roger is filled with material objects that have no human connection. The realistic description in the novel reflects how much the characters, and Angela particularly, are tied to the external world. Angela, Anthony, Virginia, and Rachel all achieve a sense of freedom and of freedom of choice once they have confronted truthfully the realities of a larger society that has defined their limitations and constricted their movement.

Themes and Meanings

One of the major themes of the novel and the one concept that Angela has much difficulty in accepting is that color is a matter of paramount importance in the American social system. The characters are caught in a fallacious social construct that stretches appearance far beyond being. To appear white is more important to the marketplace than any quality of being, so friendship for whites, for example, can be created only if the participants are white or are willing to pass as white. Angela could maintain her friendship with her white childhood friends only for as long as she "appeared" white; once the appearance was assaulted by the truth of being, the friendships ended.

This book, like others of the Harlem Renaissance, touches not only on the racial prejudices of white America but also on the color-prejudice involved in denying one's race, as Angela does, because she can pass as white. Through Angela, Fauset shows how those who deny their race also deny their own being; they are both victims of the social system that sanctifies appearance and victimizers of their blood sisters and brothers who do not have the "safety" of a white appearance. Moreover, those who pass as white lose the opportunity to do good for the entire race; Angela can defend Rachel against the injustices of the system only after she decides to announce publicly her own racial bond.

Fauset also suggests that society as a whole can claim its identity if it can reject the powerful myths of the white social system. The myths of the marketplace tempt and seduce Angela. She creates and re-creates her identity only after she overcomes the belief that the pleasures of the white world are more satisfying than the life that can be created on the foundation of values not dependent on appearance. The life of Harlem and the life that Virginia creates come from a love of human worth, diversity, and talent, not from the myth that initially attracted Angela—that the combination of white skin and wealth will provide happiness and freedom.

Critical Context

   Plum Bun is generally considered to be one of Fauset's best novels. Fauset, however, has been valued more for her social and journalistic contributions to the Harlem
Renaissance than for the considerable literary and cultural value of her fiction. Her
fiction has also been misjudged by those who claim that, as an upper-middle-class
black woman, she had more sympathy for white American values than for the values
of black Americans. A careful reading of *Plum Bun* reveals that Fauset is, indeed, in
sympathy with black American values. Her point is that blacks in cities such as New
York can find their identity only when they can work through the myths and social
constructs of the dominant white culture. Fauset chose Angela rather than Virginia as
her protagonist, not because she wanted to promote the values of the marketplace but
because she wanted to depict both the internal and the external struggle that is often
necessary in order to achieve black pride.

   With the recent emphasis on feminist criticism, Fauset's work is receiving the comprehensive attention it deserves. She is no longer dismissed as a writer who wanted,
through the novel of manners, to promote the values of a white, class society. By focusing more on the techniques that Fauset used to present the struggle of her major
women figures, contemporary critics can separate Fauset's views from those of her
characters—for example, no longer is there the simplistic assumption that Fauset validates such beliefs as Angela articulates through most of the narrative. What Angela
does admire and value at the end—authentic emotional expression, the bonds of sis-
terhood and talent, the enhancement of a culture through the vitality of its members—is humanistic values that are not class-dependent, nor are they very evident in
the white society that dominates Angela's life. These values are, however, as in the
community of Harlem, able to have their impact on cultural growth, both within the
black community and perhaps, with even more struggle, within the entire American
culture.

Bibliography

Allen, Carol. *Black Women Intellectuals: Strategies of Nation, Family, and Neighbor-
    hood in the Works of Pauline Hopkins, Jessie Fauset, and Maria Bonner.* New York:
    Garland, 1998. Allen devotes a chapter to Fauset and details the theme of family,
    home and creativity in Fauset's works.
Draper, James P., ed. *Black Literature Criticism.* 3 vols. Detroit: Gale Research, 1992.
    Includes an extensive biographical profile of Fauset and excerpts from criticism on
    her works.
Foreman, P. Gabrielle. "Looking Back from Zora, or Talking Out Both Sides My
    Mouth for Those Who Have Two Ears." *African Literature* 24 (Winter, 1990):
    649-666. Foreman analyzes the black women's literary tradition with a focus on
    Fauset's *Plum Bun.*
McClendon, Jacquelyn Y. *The Politics of Color in the Fiction of Jessie Fauset and
    Nella Larsen.* Charlottesville: University Press of Virginia, 1995. McClendon ex-
    amines Fauset's *Plum Bun* and compares it to *Quicksand* by Nella Larsen. Both au-

thors exhibit a subversive element in their novels. McClendon also explores how Fauset and Larsen reinvent and transform the stereotype of the "tragic mulatto" into the concept of doubleness of the African American experience.

Sylvander, Carolyn W. *Jessie Redmon Fauset, Black American Writer.* Troy, N.Y.: Whitston, 1981. A critical and interpretive study of Fauset's life and works.

Wall, Cheryl A. *Women of the Harlem Renaissance.* Bloomington: Indiana University Press, 1995. Wall profiles Fauset in a chapter-length discussion and places her in the context of the Harlem Renaissance. Wall evaluates Fauset's contributions and impact on black women's literature.

Rosalie Hewitt

THE PLUM PLUM PICKERS

Author: Raymond Barrio (1921-   )
Type of plot: Social criticism
Time of plot: The 1960's
Locale: The Santa Clara Valley, California
First published: 1969

>   *Principal characters:*
>   RAMIRO SANCHEZ, the protagonist, a Chicano farmworker who fights
>   exploitation by the growers
>   MANUEL GUTIERREZ, a Chicano farmworker from Texas whose endless
>   labor barely keeps his family alive
>   LUPE GUTIERREZ, his wife, who dreams of a middle-class life
>   MORTON J. QUILL, an overseer who is murdered
>   FREDERICK Y. TURNER, the owner of the Western Grande migrant
>   compound
>   JEAN ANGELICA TURNER, his wife, a delusional failed actress

The Novel

Detailing the daily lives of Chicano migrant farmworkers trapped in low-paying, dead-end, back-breaking roles within the corporate agricultural system, *The Plum Plum Pickers* protests their exploitation and degradation. While exploring the hierarchy of oppression, the novel attacks the greed, racism, and injustice leveled against workers and reveals the unfulfilled hopes of the workers, who suffer from self-deception, disillusionment, and self-destruction.

Written with a loosely framed narrative but carefully designed coherent structure, the novel consists of thirty-four chapters that are like fragments in a collage of episodes, broken by graffiti, picking instructions, newspaper articles, radio broadcasts, popular songs in both Spanish and English, and government announcements to the pickers. The reader not only receives a complete description of daily routines in the migrant compound and of the pickers' futile labor in the fields of plums and tomatoes but also feels immersed in the emotional tension between hope and despair and engulfed by the juxtaposition of a lush landscape with the brutality of harsh, racist exploitation.

As the novel opens, Morton J. Quill, the Anglo manager of the Western Grande migrant compound, receives an anonymous death threat. Quill, behaving more like a merciless plantation overseer than a competent manager, fears the ruthless power of his boss, Frederick Y. Turner, the compound's greedy owner. Blind to the squalor in which the migrant children live, Quill measures his success by the number of boxes of fruits and vegetables; the less overt resistance from the pickers, the greater Quill believes his status to be. To insulate himself from confrontations with the pickers, he relies on Roberto Morales, his Mexican assistant.

Much of the novel proceeds not so much by plot as by unabashed—even didactic—social protest that documents migrant pickers' routes from state to state, their desperate and self-deceptive dreams, their self-destructive conflicts among themselves, their increasing entrapment by the growers and their political allies, and their increasing rage. Manuel and Lupe Gutierrez recall their brutal treatment at the hands of the Texas Rangers and try to believe that their life in California's Santa Clara Valley is really better. Manuel works himself to exhaustion and fears never being able to provide his wife and three children with a stable life of human dignity and worth; Lupe, however, dreams of a bigger house, regular schools, and greater opportunity for her children. Although she can sustain her fantasies of freedom and security during her own daily grind amid the harsh conditions, she must often be awakened from nightmares of seeing her children plowed alive under the earth by the noisy tractors.

When the pickers seek a Saturday night escape at the Golden Cork, their frustration, fueled by alcohol, erupts into a near brawl. Zeke Johnson, an Anglo mechanic and sometime picker from the South, provokes Ramiro Sanchez, a vocal critic of the system from Texas, with racist taunts. He passes out before fists fly, and Sanchez's crew unceremoniously carries him outside and dumps him in the garbage.

Throughout the narrative, Manuel and the other pickers move closer to embracing the collective bargaining power of the farmworkers' union and the threat of strikes. Turner and his cohorts, such as the bigoted, right-wing radio announcer Rat Barfy and the governor Howlin Mad Nolan, continue to assert their paternalistic delusions that they are preserving the freedom of the pickers and their right to work without government interference. Any reform, in their minds, would mean the arrival of communism.

Meanwhile, Turner's wife, Jean Angelica Turner, becomes trapped in her own isolating fantasies of a career on the stage. To hold back the stark reality of suffering that surrounds her lonely mansion, she "acts" as an organizer of the rich growers' wives to provide hollow deeds of charity.

When Quill, his ego inflated by a meager raise, decides to confiscate some of the pickers' few possessions to pay off their food and rent debts, his own nightmare of death becomes reality. Seized by unidentified vigilantes during the night, he is lynched behind his own apartment. When Turner arrives at the compound, he is greeted by Lupe's scream announcing discovery of the body twisting in the sun. Despite the workers' rage, little has changed, save that their nightmare existence has emerged into daylight.

The Characters

Barrio balances fully rounded characters with stock types in order to integrate his themes with the psychological development of his strongest characters. The novel achieves its significance and power more through skillfully constructed characters than through the elaboration of a linear plot. Barrio relies heavily on a combination of precise description, blatant polemic, and insistent dialogue. These elements find common ground in the speech patterns of characters and the third-person narration.

Reproducing rhythmic dialect of his protagonist pickers, highlighting the bark of clichés from Barfy and Turner, and crafting the affected diction of menial workers in the compound who have deceived themselves into thinking that they have improved their lives because they no longer depend on picking for their low wages, Barrio uses parallel syntax, arranging English in a typically Spanish word order, and provides immediate translations of Spanish words and phrases. His switching between Spanish and English within paragraphs or even sentences echoes the larger thematic conflict between Chicano pickers and Anglo growers.

Manuel, an innocent man who believes in the dignity of his labor but struggles with despair, internalizes this conflict. When Morales pushes Manuel's crew to the brink of collapse, Manuel resists by proclaiming himself a man like any other in the hierarchy—owner, overseer, crew boss, or picker. Setting the tone for eventual resistance to exploitation, he wins the respect of his crew and realizes his own qualities of leadership. Turner's system permits no development of Chicano leaders, for that inevitably would mean reform and an end to his profiteering at the expense of human lives.

Ramiro is Barrio's spokesman. He is willing to engage in any resistance rhetoric and to give it flesh in any revolutionary act. He knows that Turner's greed has made slaves of his people and that such enslavement not only diminishes their present lives in their exploited poverty but also degrades their heroic heritage and robs their children of the future. He is often keenly astute in his analyses of the exploitive system, but he seldom indulges in revolutionary jargon, preferring ordinary language of authentic change.

Pepe and Sarafina Delgado, having escaped the picking crews to become custodial attendants at the compound, embrace the stereotypes of Turner and Barfy. They believe that the pickers are lazy and ungrateful, pursuing only a good time through alcohol, marijuana, and meaningless sex, yet Pepe embodies the stereotypes more than any of the pickers. The Delgados serve as the deceptive model that Lupe Gutierrez hopes to imitate: They have a house, their children go to school, and they maintain the pretense of upward mobility.

Morton Quill, the manager, regards Turner alternately with awe, as the outlaw hero Black Bart, and fear, as his own sense of vulnerability wakes him with every sound in the night. He is as likely to ignore acts of vandalism by the pickers as he is to test his derived power by directly challenging such resistance. Most of all, he fears that the death around him will become his own; by the novel's end, his body has replaced the straw effigy of Black Bart that twists ominously from the hangman's tree in the compound.

Against these rounded, complex characters, Barrio juxtaposes several type characters. Zeke Johnson represents the poor Southern white man who depends on his presumed racial dominance for his higher sense of place in the pecking order of the pickers. He abandons his wife's illegitimate child in a stark gesture of his own inhumanity. Similarly, Chuck and Olive Pope, in an ironic reversal of the stereotype they seek to perpetuate, are too lazy to work, too ignorant to change, and too inept to pursue any trade but selling drugs on the compound. Phyllis Ferguson, the compound prostitute whose fat body but alluring seductions both repel and attract Quill, represents the objectification of the exploiter and the exploited. She easily seduces the young pickers out of their money, but she becomes a sobbing, dirty object in her own eyes as she pursues her "easy" money.

Themes and Meanings

The Plum Plum Pickers closely parallels the historical exploitation of California farmworkers, whether Mexican, Chicano, or Anglo. Both the fiction and the history testify to the paradox of abundance that buries the humanity of those who have the least and are exploited the most. Barrio strips the mask from the face of a ruthless capitalism that crushes the pickers and proclaims its own benevolence, convincing those businesspeople and politicians who are prone to believe in their own racial superiority that the agricultural corporate combines are the guardians of lesser human beings than themselves. The owners of plum and apricot orchards or of vast acres of tomatoes see only the green of profits, denying the reality of rotting human lives in deference to the appearance of a lush green paradise. They convince many of the pickers either that their lives are meant to end in futility or that their salvation rests in copying the corrupt success and fraudulent goodness of the rich.

What the greedy owners do not see is their psychological and spiritual self-destruction. Quill lives in suspended terror, never sure whether he is alive and dreaming of death or instead living death and dreaming of having a life that he can call his own. Despite his power and influence, Turner isolates himself in fantasies of his days as a Hollywood extra in cowboy roles, obsessively constructing his own false reality by turning the Western Grande compound into an absurdly "authentic" old Western town, complete with false fronts on the migrant shacks.

In the process of revealing that slavery inevitably leads to revolt, Barrio shows that the pickers, once forced to act against their enslavement, achieve a higher human dignity and self-worth than any imagined by the owners. In their struggle to overcome physical misery, the Chicano pickers find humanity precisely in the struggle for a self-determined identity and a fragile existence. They see themselves in the cycles of life and death that surround and threaten them. Their unshakeable faith is symbolized by Lupe's careful watering of the avocado plant she nurtures in her shack. Their faith in themselves is defiantly symbolized by Lupe's refusal to accept Jean Turner's old dresses and her implicit condescension.

The novel does not indulge in blind optimism, for although hope may survive, it does so in the ambiguity of Barrio's principal symbol of the omnipresent summer sun. The symbolic sun is both destruction and resurrection, reality and appearance, futility and hope. Rising with the sun, Manuel feels the hope of a new day, but he knows the reality of the searing sun that waits in the fields. That ambiguous reality is too dark to accept fully but too bright to deny completely.

Critical Context

Having its origin in Barrio's friendship with a migrant family that he met in Cupertino, California, *The Plum Plum Pickers* failed at first to reach publication. Although

Barrio wrote at the time that César Chávez's movement to unionize farmworkers was making national news, every major publishing house to which he submitted the novel rejected it as too didactic, too narrow in its topic, or too regional in its significance. He was forced to publish it himself. Only after the novel had sold more than ten thousand copies through five printings in less than two years did Harper and Row inquire about purchasing publishing rights. The novel emerged as an underground classic, its impact spreading largely by word of mouth.

The Plum Plum Pickers serves as a foundation in the development of the Chicano novel over the next twenty-five years. The first Chicano novel to explore social issues through literary innovation and experimental techniques, its forerunners are the North American proletarian novels of the 1930's, the literary extravagance of the Beat poets in the 1950's and 1960's, and the early 1960's Magical Realism of South American writers. Now widely acclaimed and more anthologized through brief excerpts than almost any other Chicano fiction, the novel is one of the first issued in the Chicano Classics series published by the Bilingual Press. Despite its favorable reception in brief reviews, the novel has received scant in-depth analysis and focused critical attention.

Barrio has continued publishing, though none of his subsequent works has gained the reputation of *The Plum Plum Pickers*. His interest in the visual arts resulted in a collection of essays on art, *Mexico's Art and Chicano Artists* (1975). In *The Devil's Apple Corps: A Trauma in Four Acts* (1976), he cast Gore Vidal as the public defender in a mock trial of Howard Hughes, perhaps the industrial parallel to the fictional Turner. Barrio makes it clear that he remains a harsh critic of those who exploit the rank and file of American workers. His editorials in *A Political Portfolio* (1985) consistently attack exploitive figures from all professions; among the pieces in this collection are three selections from the novel *Carib Blue* (1990). That novel further develops, in broader contexts, the potential for aesthetic experimentation to reveal the exploitation behind the masks of the practical approaches to resolving social issues.

Bibliography
Geuder, Patricia A. "Address Systems in *The Plum Plum Pickers*." *Aztlán* 6 (Fall, 1975): 341-346. Geuder explores the complex relationships among the Chicano pickers and between them and the Anglo bosses through a classification of the ways in which characters address one another.
Lattin, Vernon E. "Paradise and Plums: Appearance and Reality in Barrio's *The Plum Plum Pickers*." *Selected Proceedings of the Third Annual Conference on Minority Studies* 2 (April, 1975): 165-171. Lattin argues that the essential tension in the novel, both within the characters and between them, is the juxtaposition of the bountiful landscape against the squalid realities of the pickers' existence, supporting this thesis through analysis of Barrio's techniques of characterization and symbolism.
Lomelí, Francisco A. "Depraved New World Revisited: Dreams and Dystopia in *The Plum Plum Pickers*." Introduction to *The Plum Plum Pickers*. Tempe, Ariz.: Bilingual Press, 1984. Lomelí extends and elaborates Lattin's premises by detailing the

living conditions of migrants and the self-deceiving strategies of both Chicanos and Anglos.

McKenna, Teresa. "Three Novels: An Analysis." *Aztlán* 1 (Fall, 1970): 47-56. Although minimal in its assessment, McKenna's study does seek to place Barrio's novel in the historical moment. She notes the promise of social realism to detail migrant conditions and comments on the aesthetic difficulties in reading the work, implying that Barrio's novel may suffer from its aesthetic experiments.

Miller, Yvette, E. "The Social Message in Chicano Fiction: Tomas Rivera's *And the Earth Did Not Part* and Raymond Barrio's *The Plum Plum Pickers*." *Selected Proceedings of the Third Annual Conference on Minority Studies* 2 (April, 1975): 159-164. An interesting comparison of the different ways in which the two authors approach social issues and protest.

Ortego, Philip D. "The Chicano Novel." *Luz* 2 (May, 1973): 32-33. Ortego claims that Barrio mediates his social protest with fantasy constructions that collapse back into social realities. He notes the dilemma of the Chicano writer in finding a medium between Spanish and English, applauding Barrio's ability to shape both into a coherent fictive whole. He also realizes that Barrio has established a new artistic direction for the Chicano novel.

Michael Loudon

PNIN

Author: Vladimir Nabokov (1899-1977)
Type of plot: Fictitious biography
Time of plot: 1950 to 1955
Locale: Waindell College, New England, and a nearby mountain resort
First published: 1957

> *Principal characters:*
> TIMOFEY PAVELOVICH PNIN, the protagonist, fifty-two years old, a
>   professor of Russian and a naturalized citizen of the United States
> DR. LIZA WIND, his former wife, a psychologist
> VICTOR WIND, fourteen years old, her son by Dr. Eric Wind
> DR. HAGEN, the head of the German Department and Pnin's boss
> THE NARRATOR, a Russian scholar

The Novel

Timofey Pavelovich Pnin has taught Russian at Waindell College for several years; his odd ways, his restlessness, his difficulty with the nuances of the English language, and his gnomelike features make him the brunt of endless cruel anecdotes and imitations. The story laid out for the reader, however, is one refashioned after the fact from these unkind stories, by the narrator, a scholar who replaces Pnin at Waindell College and who makes of the anecdotes a sympathetic biography of a true humanist, in love with the infinite variety of life and its ability to give pain, in love with his simple surroundings, constantly changing, and impervious to cynicism and incapable of ill will.

The novel follows a series of displacements as Pnin moves from dwelling to dwelling in the college community, first displaced by a returning landlady's daughter, again by a mistaken sense that permanency is on the horizon, and finally by loss of his position at Waindell, when he is replaced by the narrator, who assembles from a residue of anecdotes a portrait of Pnin himself. Pnin's restlessness is an externalization of his own inability to adjust to any circumstance, an outward sign of an inner discomfort with his situation. Having begun his adulthood with exile and emigration, Pnin seems destined to continue it past the novel's last page.

Three incidents give the novel a structure based on human contacts made and broken: Pnin's former wife Liza returns to him briefly but turns down his timid offer to regain their lost affection, breaking Pnin's heart once again. Her son Victor, by another marriage, visits Pnin and establishes a relationship despite the clumsiness of Pnin's efforts to anticipate his pleasures. Pnin's final separation from his friends and colleagues, stemming from his loss of his position, ends the novel on a depressing note; the reader learns in Nabokov's *Pale Fire* (1962) that he finally earned tenure at another college. A bucolic interlude at The Pines, a retreat for Russian immigrants in the mountains, shows a different side of Pnin, a side that, had his ingrained restlessness not taken him away, would have given the reader a happier, more successful story to hear; swimming with friends, Pnin is self-confident, even brave, and on the croquet course he is a force to be reckoned with. His return to the American college atmosphere returns him to timidity. A "house-heating," as Pnin calls it, turns sour when Dr. Hagen, his superior, informs him of his release; the unnamed narrator comes to the campus only in time to see Pnin drive out of town in a wreck of a car.

The Characters

Pnin is an Old World scholar misplaced in a New World academic community; his charming scholarly habits go unappreciated among his colleagues, most of whom are inadequate to their tasks (the head of the French Department cannot speak French and believes that Chateaubriand was a great chef). It is a mistake, however, to label Pnin as a typical absentminded professor. The narrator describes him as overconscious of his surroundings, attentive to details, inconveniencing only himself as he struggles to adjust to the bewildering world of reality. His digressions on details of information constitute an attempt to be helpful, and despite his confusion over the American idiom, he knows intuitively when his help is needed.

His former wife, Liza Wind, every bit as restless as he, moves from husband to husband as Pnin moves from place to place, living a desperate version of romance, possibly begun by a brief affair with the narrator in their youth. On the surface unworthy of Pnin's affection, she is equal to his ardor because her quiet intensity, aimless but complete, echoes Pnin's own aimlessness and intensity. It is appropriate that her son by the man who stole her from Pnin should appear, like a gift, in Pnin's life just when it is most inappropriate and, at the same time, touching.

Young Victor, unsporty, part-orphan, awkward in Pnin's presence, shy and gracious at the same time, shares an uncanny resemblance to Pnin without sharing blood, as though they were related by mutual disappointment. Victor sends Pnin a delicate crystal bowl, a pointless gift that is as accidental and wonderful as his visit; in the most poignant scene in the novel, Pnin drops a nutcracker into some soapy suds and hears a heartrending crack. Has the beautiful crystal bowl broken? It has not, just as Victor's fragile link to Pnin is not shattered by their separation.

Of the faculty at Waindell, Dr. Hagen comes closest to wisdom, although he gives Pnin the bad news of his termination with more insensitivity than one might expect. Regretting the necessity of dismissing Pnin, he offers to keep him on through the spring as the least painful severance procedure, an offer which Pnin declines. Hagen's own change of venue ironically signals Pnin's next, forced exile. The narrator, about whom very little biographical information is given, presents himself modestly; he is apparently a more responsible scholar and a rather more celebrated figure, a neutral observer whose life touched Pnin's at undramatic moments and whose final tribute is the linguistically adroit rearrangement of the cruel anecdotes into the story of Pnin's life.

Themes and Meanings

"Displaced" by the circumstances of his youth, Pnin spends his life trying to find a little corner where he can be comfortable with his books, his eccentricities, his loneliness. Nabokov indicts much of the academic community in this portrait (he was a professor at Cornell University when he wrote the novel), sparing individuals who harbor Pnin from moment to moment, but exposing the callousness and political self-preservation of the majority.

Oddness is never popular, but in theory a liberal arts institution should have a corner or two for the more fragile souls who seek refuge in the academic world. Nabokov's delightful sensitivity to words gives the reader a metaphor for Pnin's more universal difficulty with communications of all kinds; he can understand a squirrel's needs, but not his own. Among the recurring motifs is the presence of a squirrel on certain occasions of Pnin's loneliness, a symbol, according to some scholars, of his lost love, a victim of the German concentration camps. One particular squirrel anecdote adds a special clarification to the reader's understanding of Pnin's dilemma. He holds the water fountain faucet down so that a squirrel can take a drink. The squirrel drinks and goes off without gratitude, and that detail speaks for the thematic thread of Pnin's life: The nurturing and nourishing Pnin finds only ingratitude from those whose thirsts he tries to quench. Every time Pnin looks at an out-of-date timetable, shoves the wrong notes into his pocket, or otherwise relies on an unreliable permanence, the theme of miscommunication that runs through the novel is reinforced. Even Pnin's anguish is untranslatable: "Emitting what he thought were international exclamations of anxiety and entreaty," he lives his life from misunderstanding to misunderstanding, until it is knit together by the narrator.

Nabokov's narrative style is uncommonly complex. Eschewing the simple omniscient narrative form, the narrator assumes, gathers evidence, projects possibilities, and invents isolated incidents based on conjecture, in a complicated style that complements the themes of the novel itself. The author's own remarkable control of the English language, a language he learned under circumstances similar to Pnin's, adds a final layer of irony and pathos.

Critical Context

Although Nabokov's reputation rests in large measure on the successful publication of *Lolita* two years before he published *Pnin*, the later novel offers special pleasures to his readers that the more self-conscious and lustier best-seller lacks. Termed a "fictitious biography" by critic H. Grabes, who discusses the English novels of Nabokov independently of his novels in Russian (which Nabokov himself later translated into English), *Pnin* is distinguished by a narrative strategy that can be traced to the eighteenth century novel, though Nabokov gives it a modern twist. The narrator of *Pnin* falls between the omniscient narrator of traditional fiction and the so-called unreliable narrator of William Faulkner and his imitators; by inserting his own character into Pnin's story, the narrator deliberately limits his knowledge of the man and, unlike a true biographer, selects from truth and fancy those elements that seem to illuminate his subject without undue attention to accuracy. By depicting Pnin as a concentration of central traits, the narrator seeks to show the "real life" of Pnin rather than the true one. While almost all biographers claim accuracy and neutrality regarding their subject, a fictitious biographer is bound by no such stricture, and can paint in whatever strokes and colors best present his fictitious invention.

The reviews of Nabokov's novel about the life of the exiled professor did not accord Nabokov unqualified praise. Some critics thought *Pnin* a slight accomplishment after *Lolita*. *Pale Fire*, on the surface a more ambitious work, followed close after and gave the character Pnin a tenured position as "professor of Russian." In time, however, it has become apparent that the novel's charms, like the those of Pnin himself, are more enduring than the attractions of some of Nabokov's flashier books, which gained a cult following for reasons unrelated to their own literary excellence. Close textual studies of *Pnin* have turned up all manner of obscure literary and personal references, etymological oddities, hidden allusions to other novels, and the like, but no amount of superficial "scholarship" of the kind Pnin both practiced and transcended can obfuscate the book's basic charm and grace.

Bibliography
Appel, Alfred, Jr., and Charles Newman, eds. *Nabokov: Criticism, Reminiscences, Translations, Tributes*. Evanston, Ill.: Northwestern University Press, 1970. A good introduction to Nabokov's writing, including a varied sampling of material about the man, about the writer, and about his several unique works. Perhaps a hodgepodge, but an early collection that contrasts dramatically with later criticism, which suggested that Nabokov was a humanist if also a kind of verbal magician.
Bloom, Harold, ed. *Vladimir Nabokov*. Essays on Nabokov's handling of time, illusion and reality, and art. There are separate essays on each of his major novels, as well as an introduction, chronology, and bibliography.
Boyd, Brian. *Vladimir Nabokov: The Russian Years*. Princeton, N.J.: Princeton University Press, 1990. The first volume of the definitive biography, fully researched and written with the cooperation of Nabokov's family. Boyd has an extraordinary command of the origins of Nabokov's art. This volume includes a discussion of Nabokov's years in Europe after he left Russia.
_____. *Vladimir Nabokov: The American Years*. Princeton, N.J.: Princeton University Press, 1991. Boyd concludes his masterful biography. As with volume 1, his work is copiously illustrated with detailed notes and an invaluable index.
Field, Andrew. *Nabokov, His Life in Part*. New York: Viking Press, 1977. An intimate portrait written by an author who was often very close to Nabokov during the latter part of Nabokov's life. The book may also suggest to would-be biographers some of the difficulties of writing a biography while enjoying an intimate relationship with the subject. Follows Field's critical work, *Nabokov, His Life in Art: A Critical Narrative* (Boston: Little, Brown, 1967).
_____. *VN: The Life and Art of Vladimir Nabokov*. New York: Crown, 1986. Not as definitive as Boyd, but still a very important biographical/critical study of Nabokov. Field has been called the "father of Nabokovian studies. Includes illustrations, detailed notes, and index. The best one-volume biography of Nabokov.

Foster, John Burt. *Nabokov's Art of Memory and European Modernism*. Princeton, N.J.: Princeton University Press, 1993. Burt divides his study into three parts: Nabokov's early years in Russia, his period in Europe, and his prolonged period in America. This is a more specialized study for advanced students.

Pifer, Ellen. *Nabokov and the Novel*. Cambridge, Mass.: Harvard University Press, 1980. Uses as an epigraph Flannery O'Connor's "All novelists are fundamentally seekers and describers of the real, but the realism of each novelist will depend on his view of the ultimate reaches of reality" to develop a critical dialogue about Nabokov's technique, not surprisingly including realism. Ends in a discussion on Nabokov's humanism. Robert Alter called this book "poised and precise," and it is excellent for serious, critical readers of Nabokov.

Thomas J. Taylor

POCHO

Author: José Antonio Villarreal (1924-   )
Type of plot: Bildungsroman
Time of plot: 1923-1942
Locale: Santa Clara, in the Imperial Valley of California
First published: 1959

> *Principal characters:*
> RICHARD RUBIO, the only son of Juan Manuel and Consuelo Rubio
> JUAN MANUEL RUBIO, a soldier in the Mexican Revolution who
>   becomes an itinerant laborer and conflicted family man
> CONSUELO RUBIO, the wife of Juan Manuel, the mother of eight
>   daughters and one son
> JOÃO PEDRO MANÕEL ALVES, a Portuguese aristocrat and poet who
>   befriends young Richard
> RICKY MALATESTA, Richard's Italian American school friend
> THOMAS NAKANO, a Japanese American schoolmate of Richard who is
>   sent to an internment camp
> ZELDA, a neighborhood tomboy and bully who becomes Richard's
>   girlfriend
> MARY MADISON, Richard's Protestant friend and fellow enthusiast for
>   reading and writing

The Novel

Pocho recounts the lives of Mexican migrant farm laborer Juan Rubio, his wife, and their nine children as they attempt to hold their family together, survive the Depression, and adjust to American culture. As family bonds disintegrate, the only son, Richard, defines himself against both Mexican and American cultures and affirms his determination to become a writer. The first of eleven chapters introduces Juan Rubio, a colonel in Pancho Villa's army, and depicts his grief over the Mexican Revolution's failure, his flight from Mexico, and his resettlement in California; the chapter ends with the birth of Juan's only son, Richard. Richard's background and development from childhood to young adulthood in chapters 2 through 9 strongly resemble experiences of José Antonio Villarreal's own life. The division of each chapter into two or three sections emphasizes the tensions, conflicts, and multiple perspectives associated with the construction of Richard's personal identity: family, church, school, language, sex, friendship, career, money, prejudice, injustice, and, most important, dual cultural allegiances. Dramatic events of chapters 10 and 11 (including Juan's leaving home, Richard's high-school graduation, and his enlistment in the U.S. Navy) move Richard to the brink of adult responsibility and an uncertain future as a man and as a Mexican American.

As early as age nine, Richard is aware of his attraction to books and his interest in writing. In contrast to his soldier father, he shrinks from fights and sex and finds shelter in reflection and escape in reading and imagination. He is in love with words, words such as "sundries," which is painted on the window of his home, an abandoned store, and he shifts easily between English and Spanish as his context requires.

As Richard matures, he consciously rejects large parts of his Mexican heritage, including some of the "macho" privileges offered him by his father, his mother's faith in God, and obedience to religious dogma; at the same time, he rejects pressures in Anglo culture to devalue his own intelligence, neglect his own education, and settle for menial and meaningless labor. Such negations are in fact affirmations of his own self-worth and his own aspirations to be a writer. Free of many of the ideological constraints of both cultures, he may at last be able to write his novel and his life.

Although Richard's liberation of consciousness as man, Mexican American, and artist is in the foreground of the novel, the backdrops to his personal growth include the dissolution of the traditional Mexican family, the chaos of a nationwide depression, a vast panorama of social unrest and prejudice, and, finally, world war.

The Characters

Richard Rubio, whose development is the central focus of the novel, is presented in a third-person-omniscient narration that seems reflective, distant, neutral, even blandly indifferent to characters' struggles. This mode of presentation is a strange contrast to the frequent episodes of passion experienced by the hero and his family. This portrait of the artist as a young man is more typical, however, in its depiction of its writer-hero as a sensitive child, a contemplative, curious, and voracious reader, observant and self-conscious. It seems *Pocho* is this boy's own story and testament to the successful realization of his boyhood dream to write. Richard's movement away from traditional values and roles contrasts vividly with his father's conscious clinging to connection with his homeland and native culture. Richard is last seen entering war, not on a horse but on a ship, motivated not, like his father, by patriotic fervor but by desire to escape his own fierce inner conflicts and sense of personal loss.

The Juan Manuel Rubio shown in chapter 1 is a famous colonel in Villa's revolutionary army. He is also a cold-blooded killer and a ruthless exploiter of women who is callous to the pain he causes. Yet he weeps profusely and grieves deeply when told of the assassination of his idol Villa. After flight to the United States and reunion with his wife and children in California, Juan appears to be a different man. He gives up gambling, women, and violence for manual labor, family closeness, and generosity to those in need. The patriarch of the Rubio family is a man of contradictions, but in one thing he is consistent: He never relinquishes the romance of return to his homeland, even while buying a house in California. As he sees his wife and children assimilate, he is at last driven to abandon them entirely and reaffirm his ties to Mexico.

Consuelo Rubio, loving and dutiful wife and mother of nine children, discovers that American law protects her from physical abuse and, even more surprisingly, finds that she loves her husband and enjoys sex. The novel suggests that these new awarenesses lead directly to new freedom, new jealousy, and new demands on her husband that culminate in the disintegration of her marriage and her family. She dotes on Richard and indulges him totally, but she is ashamed of her own inadequate education and her inability to guide him in the world and respond to his intellectual needs. Abandoned in midlife by her husband, she is bitter; she refuses to divorce to spite him and seems destined to a lonely and sour old age.

João Pedro Manõel Alves is a forty-year-old social outcast, scorned by his aristocratic Portuguese family for apparent sexual indiscretion. Living reclusively in Santa Clara, he has only two friends, the boy Richard and twelve-year-old Genevieve. Richard is shocked and grieved by the accusation that Alves impregnated the girl and by Alves's commitment to a hospital for the insane.

Ricky Malatesta, Richard's best friend in school, differs in values and goals. His character is a foil to Richard's and helps to distinguish some of Richard's unusual qualities. Ricky is a scrapper, an egotist, a charmer, a pragmatist, and a materialist.

Thomas Nakano is a Japanese American schoolmate whose internment dramatizes the prejudice and racial fear that pervade American society.

Zelda is one of the few females in Richard's social existence. As a child, she is a cruel bully who dominates the boys with violence and willfulness. At adolescence, she suddenly becomes the object of their sexual exploitation. Richard claims her as his own sexual object in his teens, and she is submissive and docile.

Mary Madison is three years younger than Richard and enjoys the same passion for reading and writing. She has a teenage crush on him and declares that she intends to marry him, though she and her family are moving out of town.

Themes and Meanings

Three concerns dominate *Pocho*: What is a "man"? What does it mean to be Mexican in American society? How does a writer come to be? For Richard Rubio, answers to each are found in negations. Richard finds his manhood not in the esteemed tradition of fighting but in feeling and weeping, and he finds his male dignity not in acts of valor but in reading and thinking. To define himself in an alien culture, he negates the macho tradition of his father's world, refuses the comforts of insularity in a Mexican barrio, rejects the reassurances of religious faith, and opts for joining the "melting pot." As a writer, he immerses himself in the books and the language of Anglo culture and relinquishes dependence on the language of his forefathers. Yet he rejects as well Anglo social pressure to make do, to leash his dreams and settle for the life of a welder or a policeman. Without support or encouragement, he affirms for himself the less conventional aspiration to write, to labor with head and heart rather than hands. Ironically, Richard seems less a Mexican American than a man without a country. What is, after all, the origin of a man's nationality? Is it the accident of his place of birth or the geography of his residence? Is a man's nationality determined by his past, by his present or by his future? What physical or mental borders separate a Mexican from an American identity? Shedding gender, familial, religious, linguistic, and social skins, Richard slowly builds a liberty of mind and perception that frees him to be an artist.

The title *Pocho* suggests one of the major themes of the novel: the complexity of the immigrant's dual existence in language, culture, and values. The term *pocho* has many resonances. Among loved ones, it can be a term of affection acknowledging the practical and emotional difficulties of surviving as an alien in an alien world. Used by a stranger, the term is an ethnic slur or a shaming label suggesting a Mexican who is a would-be gringo. As a descriptive term, it can mean the hybrid language used by the immigrant or it can mean the man himself, a kind of hybrid, who lives with simultaneous powerful attachments to two cultures. This one word and Richard, the *pocho* of the novel, represent the many tensions in personal identity that exist in a man undergoing the metamorphosis of acculturation.

Although Richard is a *pocho*, a man who thinks in two languages and lives in two cultures, the language of the novel itself is very much English, a relatively formal and academic English at that. Richard the writer was never Ricardo, and the language of his novel is never *pocho*, never hybrid. Its language bespeaks total assimilation.

The dominant tone of the novel is elegiac. An adult evokes his lost youth, innocence, parents, and culture. This is a tale of exile characterized by a profound sense of loss. Loss of homeland, loss of culture, loss of language, even loss of family, faith, and friends, pervade every chapter. It is small wonder that lamentations, profuse weeping by men and women alike, occur repeatedly. Richard's personal sacrifices and negations of his heritage are only a solitary, individual portion of one family's disintegration, of Mexico's impoverishment, of America's panoply of social ills and racial fears, and of worldwide poverty, prejudice, and cataclysmic violence.

Critical Context

Pocho is widely recognized as a literary landmark; it was the first novel in English written by a Mexican author about the Mexican experience of the United States to be printed by a major publisher. At its publication in 1959, however, the novel received little attention and went quickly out of print. After the social activism of the 1960's, the novel was reprinted, and discussion focused on the book's social and political import.

Pocho was Villarreal's first novel. His second, *The Fifth Horseman* (1974), takes Mexico for its setting and deals with interpretation of the Mexican Revolution. While in that work Villarreal decried the excesses of the Mexican Revolution and affirmed its spirit, in *Clemente Chacón* (1984) he showed how high the cost of success in the United States can be for the Mexican immigrant.

Bibliography

Bruce-Novoa, Juan. "*Pocho* as Literature." *Aztlán* 7 (Spring, 1976): 65-77. Claims that *Pocho* deserves careful literary analysis instead of the sociological, historical, and political responses given it for fifteen years. Argues that the book's literary stature arises from its exploration of themes that are not culture-bound but are of universal appeal: the individual's struggle for identity, search for moral direction, and need to contribute to the world.

Grajeda, Rafael F. "José Antonio Villarreal and Richard Vasquez: The Novelist Against Himself." In *The Identification and Analysis of Chicano Literature*, edited by Francisco Jiménez. New York: Bilingual Press, 1979. Asserts that the significance of *Pocho* lies in its historical status as the first novel by a Mexican American depicting the cultural identity of Mexican Americans. Perhaps because of this, it is in fact an unmistakable "failure"; obvious, sentimental, flat of character, and stylistically "flaccid."

Luedtke, Luther S. "*Pocho* and the American Dream." In *Contemporary Chicano Fiction: A Critical Survey*, edited by Vernon E. Lattin. Binghamton, N.Y.: Bilingual Press, 1986. An exploration of the social context of this "typical American story" follows an excellent summary of the novel. Luedtke offers many insights into the mythos of the immigrant experience in the United States and the literary powers of *Pocho*.

Myers, Inma M. "Language and Style in *Pocho*." *Bilingual Review* 16 (May/December, 1991): 180-187. Myers evaluates the contribution of Villarreal's novel to the development of Chicano literature in English. She gives a plot synopsis, explores the use of Chicano English in the book as a stylistic recourse, evaluates whether the novel gives the reader a true insider's view of Mexican American life, and discusses the use of Spanish words and direct translations of idioms in the book.

Paredes, Raymund A. "The Evolution of Chicano Literature." In *Three American Literatures: Essays in Chicano, Native American, and Asian-American Literature for Teachers of American Literature*, edited by Houston A. Baker, Jr. New York: Modern Language Association of America, 1982. A tracing of the origins of Chicano literature that acknowledges the historical importance of Villarreal's work. Asserts that though *Pocho*'s subject is important, its treatment of issues such as abuse of women and the role of Catholicism is oversimplified.

Tatum, Charles M. "Contemporary Chicano Prose Fiction: A Chronicle of Misery." In *The Identification and Analysis of Chicano Literature*, edited by Francisco Jiménez. New York: Bilingual Press, 1979. Discusses how Villarreal's novel portrays the *pocho*, the Mexican male who retains connection to tradition while adapting to and integrating into Anglo culture, in a positive light.

Virginia Crane

POSSESSING THE SECRET OF JOY

Author: Alice Walker (1944-   )
Type of plot: Psychological realism
Time of plot: The 1930's to the 1980's
Locale: Africa, the United States, and Europe
First published: 1992

Principal characters:

> TASHI (EVELYN JOHNSON), an Olinka African woman executed for killing a tribal medicine woman
>
> OLIVIA, the child of African American missionaries to Tashi's tribe and friend of Tashi
>
> ADAM, the child of African American missionaries, Tashi's husband and Olivia's brother
>
> M'LISSA, a tribal wise crone whom Tashi murders for her part in performing female circumcisions
>
> LISETTE, the white French lover of Adam and mother of Pierre
>
> PIERRE, the son of Lisette and Adam
>
> MZEE (The Old Man) Lisette's uncle, a Swiss psychiatrist who treats Tashi
>
> BENNY (BENTU) MORAGA, the learning-disabled son of Tashi and Adam
>
> RAYE, Tashi's American female therapist, who helps her identify the real source of her madness
>
> AMY MAXWELL, a Southern white American "lady" whom Tashi meets in a mental hospital

The Novel

When their missionary family arrives at the tribal village of the Olinka, young African Americans Adam and Olivia Johnson see Tashi, the main character of *Possessing the Secret of Joy*. They observe the six-year-old girl weeping silently alongside her mother; readers later learn that Tashi's favorite sister, Dura, has just died from complications of a ritual clitoridectomy, performed on all village girls as they approach puberty. The novel weaves back and forth between the early memories of Tashi, Adam, and Olivia, cycling forward as Walker chronicles Tashi's later American/Western European life, her madness and struggle to accept the horror of female mutilation. While the Johnsons work as missionaries to the African Olinkas, Tashi recounts folktales of female power and plays with Olivia. In Tashi, Adam meets the woman whom he will later make his wife.

The novel pieces together fragmentary reminiscences of the main characters, stories that move toward Tashi's eventual murder of M'Lissa. *Possessing the Secret of Joy* does not provide a straight chronological narrative, only fragments of a story seen from the perspectives of different characters. Not until the novel's conclusion, when

Tashi has returned to her native Olinka and is executed for M'Lissa's murder, does the story make sense in a traditional way.

When Adam makes Tashi his bride, she changes her name to Evelyn; she undergoes a gradual external transformation into a Westernized black woman. Much of Tashi's story—and, by extension, the stories of her husband, his lover, and the other main characters—serves as Walker's means of telling Tashi's interior story, her confrontation with the source of her madness: the excision of her external genitalia, including the clitoris and labia, which was done to her as part of a tribal rite when she was a young woman.

As Evelyn, Tashi seeks help to recover from the trauma induced by the death of Dura and her own mutilation by becoming the patient of a European disciple of Sigmund Freud; this doctor sees her "madness" as an aberration caused by repressed or "unnatural" sexual appetite. Interwoven with the European doctor's and Tashi's accounts are observations from Adam, Lisette, and the two boys, Benny and Pierre. These fragmentary narratives provide additional insight into the difficulties Tashi experiences in articulating the sources of her "madness." Furthermore, the voices of the others show how Adam deals with his damaged wife: by seeking companionship with Lisette, a white French woman. In part, at least, his long-term affair lets Adam abandon not only his fragile wife but also their son, Benny, who needs Adam as much as Tashi does, since he suffers from moderate mental retardation.

Ironically, Pierre, the son of Adam and Lisette, tries to unravel the mystery of Tashi's pain. The young man works as a cultural anthropologist, taking as his subject female circumcision. Raye, Tashi's second psychiatrist, a woman, also helps Tashi to name her wound and explore the forms of psychic circumcision that the physical surgery and death of her sister have caused her. While in a psychiatric hospital, Tashi meets a white American woman, Amy Maxwell, who had been circumcised as a treatment for her "excessive" sexual curiosity. It is at this point that Tashi begins to understand the extent to which women, and not just black African women, have had their identities cut away from them; Tashi begins to see clitoridectomy and infibulation as a means of controlling females. Tashi's anger turns outward, finding as its focus M'Lissa, the Olinkan woman who circumcises the female children of her tribal village.

Returning to Olinka, Tashi at first nurses M'Lissa and then murders her. The book ends with Tashi's execution; she is accused of destroying a great cultural hero, M'Lissa, who fought alongside the males of her village as they struggled to throw off European oppression.

The Characters

Tashi/Evelyn, the central character, is a woman caught between the world she knew as a child—tribal Africa—and the European and American cultures. As a woman who symbolically bridges these two worlds with her marriage to Adam, Tashi cannot cope with nor understand what has been asked of her as a woman of the Olinka tribe: to give up her sexual identity through the removal of her clitoris and labia, a ritual that was meant to bond her to her tribal sisters but that also separated her from her complete self through the erasure of her ability to respond sexually. Nor can Tashi fully transform herself into an American black woman, because she carries her Africanness with her in ways that her American-born husband cannot fathom. Her madness stems not only from her circumcision but also from her situation in an alien white culture that cannot understand who she is. In changing her name to Evelyn, Tashi attempts to become another woman, to cut the Africanness out of herself, thus denying herself full expression as a black African woman. Tashi's strength comes when she sees what she and her two cultures have done to her; her solution is to choose to kill M'Lissa, the woman who circumcised her. The murder enables Tashi to recapture her femaleness by obliterating the person who destroyed its outward symbols.

Like his wife, Adam is a person caught between worlds. As an African American, he represents the legacy of slavery. His time in Africa as the child of missionaries introduces him explicitly to his blackness, and he seeks in the African Tashi a reconnection to that heritage. Ironically, Tashi has been circumcised so that she could be the wife a tribal African male would prefer. It is clear, however, that Adam is a split person, divided forever from his Africanness by his slave heritage and by his acculturation in a predominantly white society. Adam's desire to become truly blended with the white culture that has oppressed him expresses itself in his liaison with Lisette, the young, white Parisian woman with whom he strikes up an ongoing sexual relationship that endures for decades and produces Adam's illegitimate son, Pierre. Like the other characters in the novel, Adam eventually learns to "see" Tashi for the complete woman she is and to understand and value her because of her identity—as black, as a sexual female, as African, as libidinous, as circumcised against her will.

The two half-brothers, Benny and Pierre, represent the outcome of Adam's and Tashi's forced blendings. Benny (whose African name is Bentu Moraga) is the product of Adam's insistence on returning to the Africa inside himself. A gentle, retarded young man, Benny will never survive alone. Ironically, it is Pierre who comes to his rescue; like Benny, and like Adam before him, Pierre (ironically named after Lisette's father) is a person who does not "fit." His blackness is muted; he has fair skin and hair, and it is the knowledge of his difference that drives Pierre to become a cultural anthropologist. Furthermore, both young men bear the stigma of their mothers' sexuality: Benny is something other than what the dominant culture would define as an adult male; he retains an emotional and sexual innocence that will, like Tashi's literal circumcision, forever keep him from realizing his full potential. Similarly, Pierre's mixed racial heritage will keep him forever between the African and the white worlds.

The roles of the village crone, M'Lissa, and the male psychoanalyst parallel each other. Both persons serve to maintain their "tribe's" status quo: M'Lissa by rendering women docile through the removal of their source of sexual joy; the male psychiatrist by defining depressive, sexually unsatisfied, or frigid women as mad, thereby removing them as sources of power.

It will take the female psychiatrist, Raye, and a white, female victim of circumcision, Amy Maxwell, to facilitate Tashi's healing. Both women can be seen as more fully realized aspects of Tashi herself: Women who have recognized exactly what female circumcision does to and takes from a sexual woman. Most powerfully, it is the white American Amy who helps Tashi to name her oppression. Until well into her adult life, Amy did not even realize what had been done to her, did not even remember that she had been circumcised; thus, she had been removed from the company of fully sexually expressive women and not even known it. By talking to Amy and hearing her story, Tashi learns to name her own pain and is empowered to choose a path by which she can make herself whole again. The path she takes is the murder of M'Lissa, who symbolizes Tashi's oppression.

Themes and Meanings

Possessing the Secret of Joy is foremost an exploration of female sexuality and the way that that aspect of a woman's self-identity is managed on a grand scale—not simply in Third World cultures but also in supposedly progressive societies in Europe and America. Walker equates the position of women in every culture with that of a castrated male; female circumcision is the equivalent to castrating a male, since both surgeries destroy a person's ability to attain sexual release. In the case of the female, one of the chief locuses of sexual pleasure, the clitoris, is excised. The circumcision of Tashi stands for her personal enslavement to a patriarchal world. In such cultures, women's needs and women's desires are not only passed off as unimportant but also considered to be unhealthy aberrations. This is certainly true in the case of Amy Maxwell, whose mother had her young daughter circumcised for masturbating.

Possessing the Secret of Joy is an angry novel. Walker focuses her attack on European colonialism, in its metaphoric castration of Africa and the silencing of Africanness in slaves excised from their mother countries. She also condemns the excision of femaleness from every woman that is performed by patriarchal cultures. Walker clearly parallels these two lines of argument by drawing all of her female characters as needing strong or oppressive males for their validation. For all the women, these relationships diminish their capacity to become complete, independent, strong women. In the case of Lisette, for example, her father dominates her young life, treats her like a fragile blossom, and prevents her from becoming a fully realized, independent adult. In Tashi, the parallels are obvious, but they also exist for M'Lissa, the Olinkan medicine woman who circumcises the female children of the village. Although circumcision itself is repugnant to Walker, the male Olinkan rebels co-opt and use even this person, the strongest tribal female, for their own purposes. M'Lissa cooperates to gain their protection and approval during the rebellion; she cannot exist as a woman alone. M'Lissa must allow herself to be used by the men of her tribe.

The metaphoric relationship between African and European cultures creates a similar master/slave dependency, which can be interpreted as a metaphoric castration, clitoridectomy, or rape. Even though the Olinka have gained their freedom, they have, like the mutilated women, lost their integrity—that of their culture. The forced imposition of European Christian values has irreversibly altered their culture; this shift can be seen, for example, in the tribe's adoption of European dress. A more telling form of castration is the excision of the Olinkas' African names: M'Lissa renames herself during the fight for independence, taking as her new name a contracted form of the European name Melissa. She has cut out her female as well as her Olinkan identity—first literally, because she has been circumcised, but also metaphorically, because she has cut off her given tribal name. The same set of circumstances surround Tashi, and, because she physically relocates herself by marrying an American and living in his home country, her loss is more extensive. Unlike M'Lissa, Tashi loses all of her Africanness, her roots as well as her femaleness.

Critical Context

The purpose of *Possessing the Secret of Joy* is not only to indict the practice of female circumcision but also to make the physical removal of the clitoris a metaphor for many other forms of oppression and diminishment. Walker's novel is a powerful feminist expression as well as a forceful consideration of tyranny, no matter what shape it takes, and is equally applicable to both genders. As such, it deserves to be read from both perspectives.

Walker earlier explored the nature of being black and being female in such novels as *The Color Purple* (1982). Of equal importance in her fiction is the black struggle for identity in a white-dominated culture, a theme taken up not only in *Possessing the Secret of Joy* but also in her earlier novels *Meridian* (1976) and *The Third Life of Grange Copeland* (1970). In *The Temple of My Familiar* (1989), Walker examines African American spirituality, a theme that in part also informs *Possessing the Secret of Joy*. Throughout Walker's distinguished career as a writer, women and women's roles, ambitions, psyches, and sorrows have occupied a central place in her vision. In her nonfiction analysis of the African American female literary tradition, *In Search of Our Mothers' Gardens: Womanist Prose* (1983), Walker seeks to identify the many women whose voices inform hers and those of other contemporary African American women writers.

Bibliography

Benn, Melissa. Review of *Possessing the Secret of Joy*, by Alice Walker. *The New Statesman and Society* 5 (October 9, 1992): 36-37. Offers an analysis of the rite of female circumcision. Also makes the point that Walker is really looking at human barbarism, no matter the culture: in Africa, in the contemporary psychiatrist/witch doctor's office, or in the symbolic circumcision rendered by male infidelity.

Buckman, Alyson R. "The Body as a Site of Colonization: Alice Walker's *Possessing the Secret of Joy*." *Journal of American Culture* 18 (Summer, 1995): 89-94. Buckman explores the contradictions regarding the practice of clitoridectomy as portrayed in Walker's novel: both as a way for the ruling class to gain power over women's bodies and as a way for women to resist domination by the colonizers. Because Tashi submits to the ritual in order to keep tribal traditions alive in spite of the British colonizers, she transcends the status of victim and becomes an agent for change.

Hospital, Janette Turner. Review of *Possessing the Secret of Joy*, by Alice Walker. *The New York Times Book Review*, June 28, 1992, p. 11. Points out the nature of the taboos Walker includes in her fiction and the various strategies she selects to structure her text. Interesting consideration of the ways in which the narrative structure of the book shapes it as myth and archetype rather than as a conventional novel.

Souris, Stephen. "Multiperspectival Consensus: Alice Walker's *Possessing the Secret of Joy*, the Multiple Narrator Novel, and the Practice of 'Female Circumcision.'" *CLA Journal* 40 (June, 1997): 405-431. Addresses both the negative and positive comments concerning Walker's novel. Although some critics have found the novel racist and its characters poorly developed, Souris argues that Walker has actually advanced the technique of the multiple narrator, as well as the feminist opposition to patriarchal oppression.

Watkins, Mel. Review of *Possessing the Secret of Joy*, by Alice Walker. *The New York Times*, July 24, 1992, p. B4. Discusses the novel as a feminist clash with racism and sexism. Describes the book as mythic in tone and structure, in particular because of its use of multiple narrators and shifting points of view. Characterizes the novel as a polemic against female genital mutilation as well as other forms of sexism and racism.

Melissa E. Barth

PRAISESONG FOR THE WIDOW

Author: Paule Marshall (1929-   )
Type of plot: Psychological realism
Time of plot: The 1940's to the 1970's
Locale: Tatem, South Carolina; Carriacou, a small island in the Caribbean; White
   Plains, New York
First published: 1983

> *Principal characters:*
> AVEY (AVATARA) JOHNSON, a widowed, middle-aged African American
>   woman
> JEROME (JAY) JOHNSON, Avey's late husband
> CUNEY, Avey Johnson's great-aunt
> LEBERT JOSEPH, the proprietor of a bar on the island of Grenada

The Novel

In *Praisesong for the Widow*, Paule Marshall explores the dynamics of the West
Indian cultural landscape as well as its African heritage. The title of the novel reflects
the author's attempt to celebrate both cultural transition and African continuity.

Praisesong for the Widow is a novel of healing, as its structure emphasizes. Dedi-
cating the work to her ancestral figure, Da-duh (Alberta Jane Clement), Marshall divides the book into four parts that delineate the journey from disease to health for
those affected by the contradiction of being "old" in the "New World."

In the first section, "Runagate," named for African American poet Robert Hayden's
poem about the flight of a runaway slave, Avey Johnson feels the burden of being a
slave to materialism when, on her annual cruise to the Caribbean, she dreams of her
great-aunt Cuney. In this first section of the novel, as throughout the work, Marshall
uses ritual as an opening to a hidden worldview that is antithetical to the values proclaimed by the elite of the Americas. "Runagate" recalls slavery times, when threats
of corporal punishment precipitated slaves into flight.

The first section of the novel opens with sixty-two-year-old Avey Johnson, the protagonist, a black woman widowed one year previously. Avey is frantically packing her
six suitcases for flight from her luxury liner, barely five days after setting sail on a
two-week cruise in the Caribbean. Agitated and bewildered, she has no concrete reason to offer for her behavior. She can hardly recognize her own image in the mirror. A
self-doubt triggered by her daughter's criticism of the cruise has escalated into hallu-
cinations after a vision of her long-dead great-aunt Cuney, who seems determined to
force Avey to confront her past, her roots, and her heritage. Cuney directs Avey to the
highly symbolic Ibo Landing in Tatem, which is a key to that heritage. At the end of
this section, Avey misses her flight back to New York and stays at a hotel on the island
of Grenada instead.

In "Sleeper's Wake," Avey, in a dream, recalls her husband, her marriage, and the events leading to its spiritual death. In this section, "wake" represents both a ritual of death and an awakening. Literally, it might be the wake for Avey's husband, Jerome Johnson. More likely, it is a wake for Jay Johnson, the man Avey married, whose spirit died unnoticed—along with the marriage—one Tuesday in 1945. It could also be a wake or funeral for the close relationship between Jay and Avey, which was killed off by their materialistic ambitions. "Sleeper's Wake," in another sense, refers to the awakening of a sleeping Avey—from the stupor of her bourgeois mentality to a sudden realization of all that she has lost, all that she and her late husband had sacrificed in terms of happiness and life-giving values in order to acquire a house in a white neighborhood.

In "Lavé Tête," the next section, destiny intervenes in the form of Lebert Johnson, the proprietor of a local bar on the island of Grenada. He convinces Avey to take a brief excursion to the annual festival of the "out-island" people—people of the smaller island, Carriacou—who live and work in Grenada. The excursion back to their native land (Carriacou, and, by way of myth/ritual, Africa) is in fact their annual rite of rejuvenation, their rite of the eternal return, their form of communication with the African past and its sacred forces.

This section of the novel chronicles a cleansing ritual, a head washing, as well as a shedding of false image or worldview. The sudden awareness and tragic sense of loss that make Avey mourn Jay's death force her into a violent confrontation with the root cause of the loss: her bourgeois values. The rejection of those values is rendered symbolically and dramatically through Avey's excruciating vomiting fits. Ironically, it is in her moments of greatest weakness that she finds the greatest sympathy and moral support from her fellow passengers. None is repulsed. Their support of the purgation reveals that the process is natural and even anticipated. This communal support echoes the African communal involvement and deep empathy with young initiates during their rites of passage.

"Beg Pardon," the final section, is, as the title implies, the final stage in the growth process of awareness, when Avey, the cultural prodigal, comes home to beg the pardon of her offended ancestors. In preparation for the feast and celebration that mark all initiations, Avey is thoroughly bathed, oiled, massaged, and dressed. Psychologically, she is now ready, willing, and eager, and is no longer persuaded or coerced. Avey has finally understood the significance of her heritage.

The Characters

Avey Johnson, affluent and ready for retirement from her supervisory job at the state motor vehicle department, lives in a fashionable section of New York. Her late husband, Jerome, literally worked himself to death to attain this affluence. The novel relates an experience on the level of the psyche toward which Avey's whole life has been pointed. The movement of the novel is a gathering together, the achievement of linkages in time and place, linkages of the disparate elements of the individual self as it merges with the collective self.

In her journey, Avey fulfills the promise of black women in the twentieth century. In *Praisesong for the Widow*, Marshall emphasizes that the fulfillment of promise cannot be achieved without a true understanding of the past. In the character of Avey, myth and history, place and consciousness unite in her struggles to become fully human.

Jay Johnson, Avey's late husband, is depicted as a hardworking, dependable family man who spends time with his family and whose wit and sensibility keep the love between him and Avey alive. The novel makes it clear that the confidence and contentment in this marriage comes from acceptance of self and one's roots. The schism between the couple starts with a slow but steady movement away from all the rituals that held their family life together. Endless work demanded by new ambitions takes Jay away from his family and away from love. The yearly trip south to their relatives and heritage is forgotten, as are old friends and values. At this point in his life, Jay insists on being called Jerome. He cuts himself and his family off from their roots. Avey's journey will bring her back to those roots.

In gaining an understanding of the past, Avey is guided by two elders. The first is her great-aunt Cuney from Tatem, South Carolina, long dead before the action of the novel begins. When Avey was young, her great-aunt used to take her to a place called Ibo Landing, where slaves were said to have walked across the water back to Africa. Avey's dream of her great-aunt and of the place takes hold of her consciousness in such a profound way that past and present unite in her spiritual journey. On the island of Carriacou, Avey finds her roots as a member of the Arada people of Carriacou and accepts her identity as "Avatara," the name her great-aunt had insisted she use as a child. Her discovery prompts her plan to sell her house in White Plains and move to her girlhood home in Tatem for at least part of the year, so that she, like her great-aunt before her, could instill in her grandchildren the history of their people.

The second spiritual guide on Avey's journey is Lebert Joseph, the proprietor of a bar on Grenada who lives in Carriacou. He plays a leading role in redirecting Avey's journey and is Marshall's artistic reincarnation of the Yoruba deity Legba, the liaison between man and the gods. He is vital to numerous rituals, both in West Africa and in the New World. In this role, Lebert Joseph links the spiritual and the physical worlds, the ancestors with the living and the unborn. Lebert meets Avey at her crossroads and firmly but gently leads her back to her roots, to a unified African worldview. Avey soon begins to remember the oral narratives and folk tales she heard as a child from her great-aunt, and she joins in the islanders' dances and rituals.

It is precisely because Avey responds to the call of her spiritual guides, because she undergoes her physical and spiritual journey, that she comes to deserve her praisesong. Only then can she recognize her true name and become an elder whom others can respect and from whom others can learn.

Themes and Meanings

In *Praisesong for the Widow*, Marshall suggests that the journey through the African diaspora must be rooted in an understanding of the past, which must be continually sung, continually reiterated in the present. The novel is about a woman reclaiming her story in a context in which storytelling becomes part of a larger project of self-actualization.

For Africans, a praisesong is a particular kind of traditional heroic poem. Sung in various communities over the entire continent, praisesongs embrace many poetic forms but are always specifically ceremonial social poems, intended to be recited or sung at public occasions. When sung as a part of a rite of passage, they mark the advancement of a person from one group or stage to the next. This novel, therefore, celebrates for the widow her coming to terms with her widowhood—a reconciliation that has greater implications than coming to terms with the loss of an individual husband alone. The entire narrative in itself acts as a "praisesong" for the widow, with the narrator as the griot (the oral historian/genealogist/musician of traditional African society). The title also refers specifically to the communal song and the dance of the "beg pardon" at the end of the novel, which itself becomes a praisesong for the widow in homage to her homecoming. Through the healing of one of Africa's lost daughters, a scattered people are made whole again.

In this work, storytelling is not only a metaphor for cultural self-possession and wholeness but also a literal injunction. The quest on which the widow is embarked culminates in her taking upon herself the burden, bequeathed by Cuney, of telling the story of the African slaves at Ibo Landing. This story serves in the text as the representation of spiritual understanding and the will to survive and triumph. In taking it upon herself to perpetuate the story, the widow finds a meaning to her own personal journey, which then also transcends the self and the family. Storytelling, like singing, becomes a cultural metaphor and the carrier of cultural meaning. This is Avatara's true inheritance and legacy.

Critical Context

In her first novel, *Brown Girl, Brownstones* (1959), Marshall felt compelled to make a spiritual return to her sources, a return she believes is necessary for all African Americans. At the end of the book, the heroine, Selina Boyce, leaves the United States in order to return to the Caribbean. In her second novel, *The Chosen Place, the Timeless People* (1969), Merle Kinbona completes the voyage to the Caribbean only to depart for Africa at the end of the novel. Those two novels, together with *Praisesong for the Widow*, in which Avey Johnson also makes the mythic return to the Caribbean, form a trilogy.

In a note to a reprinting of her 1967 story "To Da-duh, In Memoriam," Marshall explains that Da-duh is an ancestral figure who appears in various forms throughout her work—from the character Mrs. Thompson in *Brown Girl, Brownstones* to Cuney in *Praisesong for the Widow*. Like Alice Walker and Toni Morrison, Marshall believes in the significance of ancestors and celebrates them in her fiction; they are the ground upon which she stands.

In focusing on such an unlikely heroine as Avey Johnson, Marshall once again charted new territory in the area of African American women's literature. Older women, such as Eva in Toni Morrison's *Sula* (1974) or Miss Hazel in Toni Cade Bambara's story "My Man Bovanne" (1978), had been represented in fiction. In the 1980's, moreover, African American women writers—for example, Toni Morrison in *Tar Baby* (1981) and Gloria Naylor in *Linden Hills* (1985)—had increasingly approached the question of class schisms in contemporary African American society. Yet no writer had fashioned a "praisesong" for a character such as Avey Johnson, whose life journey explores issues of age and class in relation to the racial, cultural, and political issues of her society.

Bibliography
Dingledine, Donald. "Woman Can Walk on Water: Island, Myth, and Community in Kate Chopin's *The Awakening* and Paule Marshall's *Praisesong for the Widow*." *Women's Studies* 22 (March, 1993): 197-216. Dingledine explores the symbolism of the female protagonists in Chopin and Marshall's novels.
Konan, Amani. "Paule Marshall: A Conradian Praisesong." *Critical Arts* 9 (1995): 21-28. Konan presents an analysis of Marshall's *Praisesong for the Widow* and Joseph Conrad's *Heart of Darkness* (1900). He discusses the characters' reactions, location, the connotation of darkness, treatment of the double, and narrative strategies.
Locke, Helen. "'Building Up from Fragments': The Oral Memory Process in Some Recent African-American Written Narratives." *College Literature* 22 (October, 1995): 109-120. Lock explores the memory process generated by oral cultures through a close reading of *Praisesong for the Widow* and novels by Toni Morrison and David Bradley. She argues that remembering is not merely a textual representation but also a reconstruction where readers "hear" the voice within the text.
Mills, Glendola A. "The Image of Dance in Paule Marshall's *Praisesong for the Widow*." *Sage: A Scholarly Journal for Black Women* 8 (Fall, 1994): 27-31. Mills explores the use of dance in Marshall's novel, asserting that dance plays a significant role in the lives of Avey Johnson and her husband Jay. The descriptions of the dance and dancers demonstrate how the rhythms of African dance revitalize people and make them feel more youthful.
Olmstead, Jane. "The Pull of Memory and the Language of Place in Paule Marshall's *The Chosen Place, the Timeless People* and *Praisesong for the Widow*." *African American Review* 31 (Summer, 1997): 249-267. Olmsted analyzes Marshall's use of female characters in her two novels to portray the struggles of African Americans against racial oppression. She compares the deep-seated resistance of Merle Kinbona to the colonial invasion of her native island to Avey Johnson's liberating experience of returning to one's roots.

Genevieve Slomski

A PRAYER FOR OWEN MEANY

Author: John Irving (1942-   )
Type of plot: Bildungsroman
Time of plot: 1952-1968 and 1987
Locale: Gravesend, New Hampshire, and Toronto, Canada
First published: 1989

   Principal characters:
      JOHN WHEELWRIGHT, an expatriate who recollects his youth in
         Gravesend, New Hampshire
      OWEN MEANY, John's childhood friend, whose death gives John faith
         in God
      HARRIET WHEELWRIGHT, John's eccentric grandmother, a small-town
         matriarch
      TABITHA WHEELWRIGHT, John's loving mother, whose one brief affair
         resulted in John's birth
      DAN NEEDHAM, John's stepfather, an amateur drama coach
      HESTER EASTMAN, John's cousin, who loves Owen Meany and becomes
         a rock singer famous for songs related to Owen's death
      LEWIS MERRILL, John's father, a guilt-ridden minister

The Novel

   A Prayer for Owen Meany is the story of John Wheelwright's relationship with his childhood friend Owen Meany, a midget with a high, squeaky voice, whose life and death move John to have faith in God. Despite his size, Owen has a commanding presence that directs John's life. Owen comes to symbolize a moral intensity that John finds sorely absent from American life.

   In 1987, John Wheelwright, a forty-five-year-old English teacher living in Canada, is finally able to write about his experiences with Owen Meany in the 1950's and 1960's, when they were growing up in Gravesend, New Hampshire. John's narrative is disjointed and nonsequential, oscillating between past and present, intermixing current news events, historical statistics, and cultural commentary with personal recollections. Unable to adjust to Canadian life and outraged at the moral malaise in the United States, John is drawn back to his youth in New England. His recollections focus on his illegitimate birth to a single mother, his mother's marriage and untimely death, and his close relationship with Owen Meany.

   Tabitha Wheelwright, John's mother, had an affair during one of her overnight trips to Boston that resulted in John's birth. She never tells John the identity of his father. Tabitha rises above town gossip and rears John in the stately house of her mother, Harriet Wheelwright, whose ancestors go back to the *Mayflower*. Tabitha is devoted to John. She later marries Dan Needham, a Harvard graduate and a teacher at Gravesend Academy. During Tabitha and Dan's wedding, an ominous hailstorm breaks out. As

Tabitha offers a ride to Owen, whom she loves almost as much as her son, a hailstone hits her on the head. Owen apologizes for the accident.

This part of the wedding scene carefully mirrors the scene of Tabitha's death. During a boring Little League baseball game that is already lost, Owen hits a foul ball that strikes Tabitha on the head, killing her. This scene propels John on his quest for his father. John believes that his mother was waving to his father when she was hit. The baseball, which the local policeman calls the murder weapon, mysteriously disappears. Owen is convinced that he is God's instrument. Overcome by a sense of destiny, Owen believes that he frightened the angel of death away from John's mother one night and thus was ordained to be the instrument of her death.

Owen Meany's father owns a granite quarry that primarily engages in manufacturing tombstones; his mother is reclusive and unstable. Owen becomes a dominant figure in the life of John and his family. Although a diminutive young man with a screechy voice, Owen creates an overpowering presence. He directs the Christmas pageant, stuns the audience with his performance in the role of the Ghost of Christmas Future in *A Christmas Carol*, and becomes the leading spokesperson for student rights at Gravesend Academy. Brilliant, attractive to women, and able to beat off bullies, Owen helps John through school, stays back with John when he repeats the ninth grade, teaches John how to read, inspires John to become an English major, practically writes John's master's thesis, amputates John's finger to keep him out of the Vietnam War, and tells John to go to Canada to escape America's moral exhaustion.

Owen Meany also directs John on his quest to find his biological father. Owen, who sees everything and forgets nothing, leads John to discover that his mother was a supper-club singer called "The Lady in Red." After Owen's death, Owen's spiritual voice directs the Reverend Lewis Merrill to pull the missing baseball out of his desk drawer and to admit that he is John's father. Merrill waved at Tabitha during the fatal baseball game and wished her dead; when she was killed, he wallowed in remorse and guilt. Owen, however, kept Tabitha's dressmaker's dummy with her red dress. John uses it to convince Merrill that he is seeing an apparition of Tabitha and to shock him into a renewal of his faith.

Owen himself directs the key plot line of the second half of the novel. As a young boy playing the Ghost of Christmas Future, he sees his own name and the date of his death on Scrooge's tombstone. Later, in a dream, he sees himself bloodied and wounded after saving a group of Vietnamese children. Owen joins the Army so that he will be sent to Vietnam. Instead, he is appointed as casualty officer with the task of delivering bodies to bereaved families in Arizona. He invites John to Phoenix to spend some time with him. Owen promises that no harm will come to John but becomes concerned as the day of his heroic death (July 8, 1968) approaches. On that date, he is not in Vietnam but in a Phoenix airport. As a group of Vietnamese orphans deplanes, the nuns with them ask Owen to take the boys to the airport's makeshift restroom. Dick Jarvits, a drugged and deranged young man wearing military fatigues and contraband weapons, throws a grenade to John, who throws it to Owen. Within seconds, John lifts Owen up to a window as the grenade explodes. The children are saved, but Owen loses his arms and dies. John realizes how elements fit into place: Owen's lightness that tempted people to lift him, his undeveloped voice that matched the voices of the children who listened to him, and Owen and John's game in which John lifted Owen to slam dunk a basketball. All these attributes and skills were ordained for a purpose. Realizing now that Owen had foreseen his own death, John becomes a believer.

John realizes that Owen Meany was a man of faith living in an age of doubters. The older John, struggling with his own faith and disillusion, asks God to give him Owen Meany back.

The Characters

Owen Meany is both a realistic and a symbolic character. His diminutive size and screechy, undeveloped voice contrast with his powerful presence. As his name, Meany, implies, Owen believes that all actions and objects have meaning. In an indecisive world that has lost its sense of purpose, Owen sees all actions as purposeful. He processes all information, forgets nothing, and saves everything. He believes in strong moral leadership in a country of flawed leaders and morally righteous hypocrites who value public relations above human relations.

Owen is also a Christ figure. In Sunday school, he endures the other students raising him overhead. He is hung on a coat rack like a crucified Christ, and his parents tell him that he is the result of a virgin birth. Playing the Christ child, he disturbs the complacent churchgoers. Owen's life also focuses on death and resurrection as he absorbs appropriate quotations from Scripture, hymns, and the works of William Shakespeare. He carves gravestones and later delivers the bodies of dead soldiers. Owen knows that he must sacrifice his life to save others, both physically and spiritually. He also proclaims the resurrection of the dead. Raised overhead as a young man, elevated as a Christmas angel, lifted up to slam dunk a basketball, and thrown up to a window to shelter children from a grenade, Owen is connected with resurrection even in the moment of death, as he sees himself raised above the palm trees. Owen is a Christ figure and a hero in an age that has lost its belief in heroes.

John Wheelwright is the disciple of Owen Meany and creates gospel versions of Meany's life and death, highlighting Meany's words in capital letters. John, however, is not heroic. Outraged at political scandals, he criticizes American foreign policy from a safe distance. Owen casts him in the Christmas play as Joseph, a witness to the miraculous but not a participant. John is an alienated, detached parade-watcher who has escaped real suffering. When lost for words, he proclaims what Owen would have said. A detached and celibate Christian, he clings to his faith in Owen. Both are victims of the Vietnam era, Owen as a heroic martyr and John as an alienated defector.

Minor characters symbolize family life, politics, and religion. Harriet Wheelwright, the *Mayflower* aristocrat, holds on to her antiques and her preserves as she and her generation drift into senility. Fathers are also significant figures. Dan Needham is a caring stepfather who shows John the meaning of friendship. Paul Meany cares for Owen, but is a detached father. The victims of the Vietnam era include Hester Eastman, a rebellious and promiscuous girl who turns into a street revolutionary proud of her scars and becomes an aging rock star, converting her suffering into a mixture of sex and violence. Harry Hoyt, bitten by a poisonous snake, dies in front of a Vietnam whorehouse. Buzzy Thurston takes drugs to dodge the draft and kills himself in a car accident. A variety of members of the clergy are satirized. The novel thus features a broad range of eccentric characters separated into several social and religious configurations.

Themes and Meanings

The novel principally concerns faith and the ability to hold on to it in a collapsing world. It is about young Americans growing up in an age of innocence and faced with the terrors of war abroad and senseless violence at home. The novel also chronicles the history of a lost generation and the failure of American leadership. At each New Year's celebration, John rolls through the death count in Vietnam. When Defense Secretary Robert McNamara says that America is winning a war of attrition, Owen comments wryly that such a war is not the kind that one wins. In some ways, America's guilt goes deeper than Vietnam. As he dies, Owen recalls the name of the Indian chief who sold his land to John's ancestors, thus connecting Owen's death to the genocide of the Indians. Owen also connects the fate of America to the abuse of women. Like Marilyn Monroe, America has become the plaything of powerful men.

Set in a world in which leadership is breaking down, the novel is also about the absence of the father. This theme is brought to the fore in the novel's climactic scene. Dick Jarvits, a crazed and violent teenager whose father is dead, throws a grenade to John, a young man who does not know who his father is. Owen Meany, a truly fatherless young man who believes he is the result of a virgin birth, saves John and a group of orphans.

The novel also depicts a cultural wasteland in which television renders disasters entertaining and Liberace turns serious music into kitsch. Biblical epics turn religion into soap opera while rock videos present a mindless mixture of sex and violence. Owen uses the term "made for television" to comment on any absurd incident.

Critical Context

A Prayer for Owen Meany is postmodern in its approach, blending the grotesque and the comic with the mysterious and the realistic. It views a declining civilization through the eyes of an alienated narrator. In the tradition of American novelist Kurt Vonnegut, Irving reduces minor characters to short biographies, forecasting their ironic deaths, such as Harry Hoyt's death by snakebite in Vietnam. Like Vonnegut, Irving mixes statistics and historical events with the lives of characters, even pointing out the ironic fates of real people. Although Liberace supposedly died from acquired immune deficiency syndrome (AIDS), for example, the official press release said that he overdosed on watermelons.

Despite its modern tone, the novel is closely connected to the traditional romantic American novel. It is heavily weighted in the New England Calvinist tradition of predestination. John is named for John Wheelwright, the rebellious Puritan who believed in justification by faith and the grace of the Holy Spirit. The novel's secret sins, fated destinies, search for the father, mysterious dark-haired women, biblical allusions, and prominent symbolic objects all could come straight from the works of Nathaniel Hawthorne or Herman Melville. The novel clearly mirrors elements found in Hawthorne's *The Scarlet Letter* (1850). Tabitha Wheelwright, the good woman, is called "The Lady in Red," and her red dress becomes the symbol of her illicit sexual relationship with the Reverend Merrill, a guilt-obsessed minister who eventually confesses to John. Even the scandalization of the town matrons at Tabitha's wedding and their belief that divine justice had been done at her death reflect the Puritan wives in *The Scarlet Letter.* Hester Eastman, a dark-haired, primitive woman, resembles Hawthorne's Hester Prynne. The Christ figure with the speech problem resembles Herman Melville's Billy Budd. Even the novel's interconnecting symbols are in the tradition of the classic American novel. The armless totem of the Indian chief who sold his land, the declawed armadillo, the armless dressmaker's dummy, and the statue of Mary Magdalene with her arms sawed off all reflect Owen's martyrdom when a grenade blows his arms off, just as the statue of Joseph with his missing hand forecasts the amputation of John's finger.

Bibliography

Campbell, Josie. *John Irving: A Critical Companion.* Westport, Conn.: Greenwood Press, 1998. Offers a brief biography of Irving's life, as well as an overview of his fiction. Devotes an entire chapter to *A Prayer for Owen Meany,* which includes discussion of plot and character development, thematic issues, and a new critical approach to the novel.

Kazin, Alfred. "God's Own Little Squirt." *The New York Times Book Review* 94 (March 12, 1989): 1, 30-31. Gives a detailed summary of the novel. Focuses on the political commentary. Praises Irving's craftsmanship but finds the book devoid of irony and sees its religious message as somewhat juvenile.

Page, Philip. "Hero Worship and Hermeneutic Dialectics: John Irving's *A Prayer for Owen Meany.*" *Mosaic* 28 (September, 1995): 137-146. Page demonstrates how Irving's novel plays with differing hermeneutical dialectic of William James and Paul Ricouer. He analyzes the novel's central character, John Wheelwright, and shows how Irving offers an alternative way of knowing: the use of common sense.

Reilly, Edward C. *Understanding John Irving.* Columbia: University of South Carolina Press, 1991. Chapter 8 gives a thorough analysis of Irving's characterization and symbolism and a brief summary of critical reviews.

Shostak, Debra. "Plot as Repetition: John Irving's Narrative Experiments." *CRITIQUE: Studies in Contemporary Fiction* 37 (Fall, 1995): 51-69. Shostak's examination of *The World According to Garp* and *A Prayer for Owen Meany* focuses on Irving's use of repetitive phrases and images that become motifs within and across his novels. She sees the narrative as a "psychic entity" and argues that Irving's repetitions can be read as "plot determinism."

Wall, James M. "Owen Meany and the Presence of God." *Christian Century* 106 (March 22, 1989): 299-300. Sees a profound theological message in the novel that secular critics are not willing to approach.

Paul Rosefeldt

THE PRINCE OF TIDES

Author: Pat Conroy (1945-   )
Type of plot: Family
Time of plot: The 1940's through early 1980's
Locale: Coastal South Carolina and New York City
First published: 1986

> *Principal characters:*
> TOM WINGO, the narrator and protagonist
> SAVANNAH WINGO, Tom's twin sister, a famous poet who is psychotic
> LUKE WINGO, Tom's older brother, a courageous idealist
> HENRY WINGO, the father, violent and abusive
> LILA WINGO NEWBURY, the mother, obsessed with social status
> SUSAN LOWENSTEIN, Savannah's psychiatrist, with whom Tom has an
>   affair

The Novel

The Prince of Tides is a long novel of twenty-seven chapters framed by a prologue and an epilogue. Strewn with autobiographical overtones, the novel recounts the life of the fictional Wingo family of Colleton, South Carolina, as seen through the eyes of narrator and protagonist Tom Wingo. Through his attempts to help a psychiatrist save Tom's suicidal twin sister, Savannah, by telling the family story, he learns to face and accept his past and thus begins to set his own life in order.

In the prologue, Tom's ambivalence about both his birthplace and his parents emerges in his recollection of his childhood as "part elegy, part nightmare." He proclaims that his entire life has been dominated by the South Carolina low country tides and marshes and by his warring parents.

The novel then begins with news from Tom's mother, Lila Wingo Newbury, that his sister Savannah, a famous poet, has tried to kill herself again and is in a psychiatric hospital in New York. Tom is struggling to survive himself, having suffered a nervous breakdown following the death of his older brother Luke. He has lost his job as a high school English teacher and football coach, and he realizes that his marriage to his college sweetheart Sallie, now a successful physician, is falling apart. Nevertheless, Tom leaves immediately for New York to help Savannah. A visit from him disturbs Savannah severely, however, and her psychiatrist, Susan Lowenstein, forbids additional contact and urges Tom instead to assist in Savannah's recovery by telling her everything about Savannah and the Wingo family. Seemingly in no particular order, Tom begins to pour out the stories of his and Savannah's past, stories that reveal a violently abusive father and a mother obsessed with social position and appearances. Tom does have happy memories of hours the three children spent with their father on his shrimp boat and of magical moments when their mother took them out to see the sun set and the moon rise almost simultaneously. Most of the stories, however, focus on an almost implausible series of events that Tom justifies by maintaining that "extraordinary things" happened to the Wingo family.

The most traumatic event, withheld until near the end of the novel, occurs the summer after the three Wingo children are graduated from high school. Three escaped convicts force their way into the Wingo home and rape Savannah, Lila, and Tom. They are saved from death by Luke's arriving at the right moment and releasing their pet Bengal tiger to attack and assist in the violent killing of all three rapists. Lila then insists on burying the bodies, cleaning up the mess, and pretending nothing ever happened. Three days later, Savannah attempts suicide for the first time.

Dozens of other episodes fill the novel, as Tom recounts a childhood filled with pain and unhappiness but with a strong bond of love among the three children. Among the stories Tom tells are those that are obviously family legends—the marriage and separation of his grandparents, the dramatic events of his and Savannah's birth during a hurricane, the story of his father's escape from Germany during World War II. Many episodes may seem at first to be digressions, but all serve to provide a broader understanding of Tom's background. Several focus on the paternal grandparents, perhaps the most grotesque characters of the Wingo family. Every year on Good Friday, Grandfather Amos Wingo carries a ninety-pound cross through town and gets arrested for obstructing traffic. Additionally, in his late seventies or early eighties, he begins to have difficulty driving his car, and a patrolman tries to revoke his license. Amos then water-skis for forty miles to prove that he is still capable of driving. An equally fascinating character, Grandmother Tolitha Wingo left her husband Amos when Henry was a young boy, spent years married to another man and, following his death, traveled around the world for several years before finally returning to her first husband. In one of the most humorous episodes in the novel, Tolitha decides to choose her coffin, crawls into the coffin to try it out, and subsequently scares a town busybody into hysteria by sitting up unexpectedly in the coffin.

Among the innumerable tragic events in the life of the Wingo family, the one that has pushed Tom and Savannah into their current state of despair is Luke's death and their mother's indirect role in that death. Lila turns the family island over to her husband, Reese Newbury, who sells it to the government for use by the Atomic Energy Commission. Luke, with his love for the shrimper's life, begins a one-man rebellion against the government that leads to his being shot by a government agent.

Interspersed with Tom's stories of his and Savannah's past are sections devoted to the present time and the growing romantic relationship between Tom and Susan Lowenstein. As Tom reveals his own suffering, he becomes aware of Lowenstein's unhappy marriage and of her sense of failure as a mother. At Susan's request, he begins coaching her bitterly unhappy son to play football. The growing relationship with Susan enables Tom to see himself again as capable of love, and his success in working with her son Bernard resurrects his love for coaching and his belief in himself as a teacher. Despite his love for and desire to remain with Susan, Tom also feels a strong commitment to his wife and three daughters back in South Carolina, and when Sallie calls and asks Tom to return, he does so. The epilogue suggests that Tom's return to his wife and children and to teaching and coaching have been successful, and in the final lines, he pays tribute to Lowenstein for making this renewed life possible. A reunion of Savannah, Tom, and Henry provides some possibility also for family reconciliation.

The Characters

Because Tom is the narrator as well as the protagonist in *The Prince of Tides*, all the characters are developed through his eyes and become significant primarily as they affect him. Scarred by the traumatic events of his childhood, Tom finds his life coming apart as the novel opens. His attempts to aid his psychotic sister, however, enable him to come to grips with his past and provide him with the self-confidence to face the future. At the end of the novel, he is able to say truthfully that he is a survivor.

Savannah, Tom's highly intelligent and ultra-sensitive sister, has apparently suffered the most psychological damage from the repression of reality practiced by the Wingo family. Three days after the rape, which Lila makes the children swear never happened, Savannah first attempts suicide. Soon thereafter, full of bitter hatred for her parents and for the South, Savannah leaves South Carolina for New York. Although she establishes herself as a poet, Savannah cannot escape her past. Following Luke's death, she first assumes a new identity, that of a lesbian friend who has committed suicide, and then she again attempts suicide herself. With Tom and Susan Lowenstein's help, she moves toward recovery.

Luke as a child assumes the role of protector for the younger twins. Compassionate, courageous, and a loner, Luke is a physically strong outdoor person who wants to spend his life as a shrimper. When the government takeover of Colleton County threatens to destroy that life, Luke singlehandedly battles governmental officials and temporarily delays the project, but he is ultimately killed by a government agent.

Henry, although he occasionally gives evidence of love for his children, is generally violent, unpredictable, and cruel. Physically abusive to both wife and children, he is nevertheless desperate for Lila's respect. His repeated commercial ventures invariably fail, however, and elicit bitter scorn from Lila, the least sympathetic character in the Wingo family. Seemingly protective of her children against their father's violent temper, Lila actually contributes instead to the dysfunctional nature of the family with her hypocrisy, selfish manipulations, obsession with social prominence, and repression of the truth. After divorcing Henry, she manipulates Reese Newbury, one of the county's wealthiest and most prominent citizens and the Wingo family's bitterest enemy, into marrying her by nursing his first wife until her death from cancer and by using the Wingo family island, which Newbury has long coveted, as bait.

Susan Lowenstein is a successful professional who feels like a failure as a wife and mother. Through her relationship with Tom, however, she regains a sense of self-worth and self-confidence.

Themes and Meanings

The major theme of *The Prince of Tides* is the damaging effects of denial and repression and the need of the individual to understand and accept the past in order to function in the present. Lila stands out in the novel as the prime instigator of denial in her constant demands that the children never talk about family problems. Henry is also guilty, even managing to convince himself that he has never abused his wife or children. Such repression leads the Wingo children to feelings of inadequacy, self-doubt, guilt, and anger, and manifests itself ultimately in self-destructiveness. The novel suggests that release occurs only through acceptance and confession of reality. While the ending of the novel does not suggest that Tom and Savannah will "live happily ever after," both seem to have experienced significant healing and to have reached a level of self-acceptance that provides a sense of hope and peace.

Another theme that emerges in the novel is racism. Amid classmates who are hostile and cruel to Benji Washington, the first black admitted to Colleton High School, Tom is bullied by Savannah into befriending Benji. Ultimately, through Tom's work with Benji on the football field, Benji gains acceptance in the school and the community.

Conroy also uses *The Prince of Tides* to demonstrate a love for land, sea, and nature and to attack those who destroy nature in the name of progress. Reese Newbury, the greedy land-grabber and seller, stands in remarkable contrast to Luke, the prince of tides, who sacrifices his life trying to defend the takeover of the island by the government to build plants to manufacture nuclear weapons and nuclear fuel. On the whole, the novel seems to reflect Conroy's discontent with the twentieth century and with its destruction of place, innocence, and family.

Critical Context

While *The Prince of Tides* has clearly been Pat Conroy's most popular success, a book widely read and hailed by the public, its critical reception has been mixed. Most of the negative criticism has centered on the novel's ornate style and the melodramatic, sentimental, and implausible elements of the plot. Other critics, however, have celebrated it as a continuation of the southern gothic school and have praised the novel for its power, its excellent storytelling, and its affirmative conclusion. Pat Conroy has acknowledged working in the tradition of Thomas Wolfe and William Faulkner, mentors whose achievements Conroy fails to reach in this novel. Nevertheless, it is a worthwhile novel that has become firmly entrenched among popular fiction.

The Prince of Tides is Conroy's fifth book; like all of its predecessors, it is set in coastal South Carolina and grows out of his own experiences. *The Boo* (1970), Conroy's first book, is a memoir of a college teacher; *The Water Is Wide* (1972), alternately referred to as both nonfiction and as a novel, covers Conroy's experiences teaching poverty-stricken black children on Daufuskie Island. With *The Great Santini* (1976), Conroy began revealing family secrets in fictional form. *Lords of Discipline* (1980) furthered Conroy's move into fictionalized autobiography with its expose of the sexism, racism, and harsh discipline he experienced at the private school the Citadel. Both *The Prince of Tides* and *Beach Music* (1995) reflect Conroy's continued use of autobiography in his fiction, though the latter contains less overt family history.

Bibliography
Burns, Landon. C. *Pat Conroy: A Critical Companion*. Westport, Conn.: Greenwood Press, 1996. The first full-length study of Conroy's work. Chapter 6 provides a detailed study of the novel's plots, characters, and themes.
Toolan, David. "The Unfinished Boy and His Pain: Rescuing the Young Hero with Pat Conroy," *Commonweal* 118, no. 4 (February 22, 1991): 127-131. Brief analysis of Conroy's works, with emphasis on the way Conroy's rejection of Catholicism influenced his writing and a discussion of each protagonist's attempt to find purpose in life.
York, Lamar. "Pat Conroy's Portrait of the Artist as a Young Southerner." *Southern Literary Journal* 19 (1987): 37-46. Argues that Conroy's first four works function as autobiographies of a writer.

Verbie Lovorn Prevost

THE PUBLIC BURNING

Author: Robert Coover (1932-   )
Type of plot: Magical Realism
Time of plot: June 17-19, 1953
Locale: Washington, D.C.; Sing Sing Prison in Ossining, N.Y.; and New York City
First published: 1977

   Principal characters:
      UNCLE SAM SLICK, a personification of the United States
      RICHARD M. NIXON, the vice president of the United States
      ETHEL ROSENBERG, a convicted spy

The Novel
   The Public Burning is an exaggerated fictionalization of the actual execution of Julius and Ethel Rosenberg, who were convicted of passing atomic secrets to the Soviet Union. Much of the book is narrated in the first person by a fictional version of Richard Nixon, but there are also folklore-like accounts of Uncle Sam, a larger-than-life mythic figure, in a life-and-death struggle with the Phantom, who symbolizes world communism, as well as actual documents from the Rosenberg case and contemporary news accounts, often adapted into the form of free verse or play scripts.
   The novel begins with a prologue detailing the arrest, conviction, and sentencing of the Rosenbergs. This is the first indication of the book's mixture of folklore and fact, as an accurate account of the historical workings of courts and law-enforcement agencies is counterpointed with a folk song about a groundhog hunt. As in history, the Rosenbergs are sentenced to die; in this version, their execution will take place not in the privacy of Sing Sing Prison but rather on a public stage in Times Square as part of a show-business performance.
   The story proper begins on Wednesday, June 17, with Vice President Nixon's account of the day's events. Supreme Court Justice William O. Douglas has issued a stay of execution for the Rosenbergs, so President Dwight Eisenhower orders the Supreme Court into session to overturn the stay. Nixon encounters Uncle Sam at the Burning Tree Golf Course. Nixon knows that in this book's mythic version of politics, Uncle Sam actually incarnates himself in the president, and Nixon longs to be the vehicle of that transformation. Nixon has no idea how that is done; he curries Uncle Sam's favor and hopes to find out. This account of the events of Wednesday and Thursday is followed by an intermezzo, a mélange of quotations from Eisenhower's public statements set as free verse.
   On Friday morning, Nixon is chauffeured into Washington. Traffic has been all but stopped by the crowds, so he decides to walk. He finds himself in the middle of an angry mob, which frightens him until he realizes that it is on his side, cheering for the upcoming execution. He finally makes it to the White House, where Eisenhower announces that the Supreme Court has overturned the stay so that the Rosenbergs can

die that evening. A second intermezzo presents Ethel Rosenberg's plea for clemency and Eisenhower's denial of it as a dramatic dialogue.

Nixon then takes a taxi to the Senate office building. The cab driver, who regales him with jokes and stories, is a mysterious figure. At first, he claims to be an old friend from Nixon's World War II Navy service, but he gets stranger and more menacing; Nixon finally flees. Nixon is puzzled by the case: He does not understand the Rosenbergs, and he is by no means entirely convinced of their guilt. He is particularly fascinated by Ethel, whose background in some ways resembles his. As he ponders her story in his office, his thoughts grow lewd, and he may be about to masturbate. Uncle Sam catches him and orders him to go to Sing Sing Prison to speak to Ethel and perhaps find out the truth about the Rosenbergs.

After the final intermezzo—remarks of the Rosenbergs and Sing Sing's warden presented as an opera—Nixon is admitted to Ethel's cell. Ethel spurns Nixon's offer to spare her and execute only her husband. Finally, Nixon makes a pass at her, and they kiss. She encourages him and even opens his belt, but before they can actually have sex, she says she hears the guards coming; she leaves him frustrated, his pants around his ankles.

Back at Times Square, the public burning is about to take place. There is a nationally televised warmup for the execution, led by Uncle Sam himself, and performers such as Jack Benny and the Marx Brothers do comedy bits about the case. Then Nixon arrives, his pants still down and the words "I AM A SCAMP" on his bare buttocks, written there in lipstick by Ethel. Nixon manages to turn this embarrassment into a public triumph, urging everyone to drop their pants for America. At the height of the excitement, there is a blackout, but the power is restored by Uncle Sam himself, and the Rosenbergs are electrocuted.

In the epilogue, Uncle Sam performs the ritual recognition of the future president in his usual fashion—by sodomizing Nixon and telling him, "You're my boy." Nixon finds the pain almost unbearable but finally says, "I love you, Uncle Sam."

The Characters

The one character readers see most closely is Richard Nixon, presented through a continuing internal monologue that shows him at his worst and at his best. Throughout the book, he displays a single-minded pursuit of the presidency and a morbid concern with how he is being perceived. In a revealing moment, he muses on the fact that both he and Eisenhower had wanted to be railroad engineers when they were children, but he had done so merely because he knew that America considered such an ambition praiseworthy, while Eisenhower would actually have been willing to waste his life in such an unprestigious job. He is both fascinated and repelled by sex, and he is unwilling to face his feelings about the matter.

Yet for all these skillfully presented flaws, the book's Nixon is by no means an entirely unpleasant figure. He is, within his limits, a person who cares about his family and generally wants to do good as he perceives it, so long as it will not interfere with his ambitions. His desperate efforts to understand his situation give the reader a certain sympathy for him. Coover skillfully weaves into the narrative actual writings of Nixon's, from the explanations of public events Nixon included in his autobiographical *Six Crises* (1962) to a letter he wrote to his mother when he was a child in which he took on the persona of a long-suffering dog.

Uncle Sam is presented as mythical, if not actually Godlike. Like a trickster god, he creates bounty but often victimizes those who try to seek it. He is presented in his public statements and his conversations with Nixon; in both, he speaks less like an actual person than like a character in a tall tale. He is vulgar, trashy, grandiose, and boastful. Uncle Sam's rival, the Phantom, who personifies communism as Uncle Sam personifies America, is an enigma. Appropriately enough, he makes no open appearances in the text, but it is suggested that the taxi driver Nixon encounters is really him.

Ethel Rosenberg is also distantly presented. She is encountered primarily through melodramatic public discourse, phrased in the rhetoric of the left. Readers get no view within her, no knowledge of whether she actually did what she was charged with having done. Even when she appears onstage and interacts personally, she speaks mostly in political rhetoric, and readers cannot be sure whether her near-sexual encounter with Nixon actually arouses her or is merely part of an effort to embarrass him.

Themes and Meanings

The Public Burning is a satirical and mythical heightening of America's view of itself at a particularly dramatic time. Coover ransacks the entire history and folklore of the nation for images of Uncle Sam, personifying the nation's flaws and its greatness. He also gives readers the American image of the communist Phantom as an utterly evil and destructive foe equipped, as America is, with that seemingly ultimate weapon, the atom bomb. In the official version of events, the Rosenbergs and others treacherously handed the bomb to an enemy that might not have had it for years without their assistance. The book, though, mentions that there were questions about whether the Rosenbergs were involved and whether the Soviets needed much help in completing a bomb.

The book is also about the process by which news is reported and becomes a part of history. *Time* magazine (referred to throughout as "the Poet Laureate of the United States") and *The New York Times* are extensively quoted. Actual news reports, of everything from baseball scores to the death of a centenarian, are counterpointed against the central story, but these are mixed with invented comedy routines about the case. As with much of the book, the richness of detail adds greatly to the reading experience.

Nixon's pursuit of the facts is a harrowing tale with many of the elements of a bad dream, from the taxi driver's apparent changes of persona to Nixon's own recurring inability to pull his pants up. It concludes with an ambiguous sexual encounter that brings him what he most wants and most fears, while his questions of what really happened are left unanswered. The reader likewise has been given a tale with a multitude of tellers, with no indication of whom to believe. In this work of fiction, readers are given no ultimately authoritative statement of what to believe, any more than they are when they read news or history.

Critical Context

The Public Burning was Coover's third novel, following *The Origin of the Brunists* (1967), which satirically detailed the founding of a new religion with marked similarities to Christianity, and *The Universal Baseball Association, Inc., J. Henry Waugh, Prop.* (1968), in which a lonely man playing a tabletop baseball game of his own invention may have succeeded in bringing to life his imagined players and their world. He was also known for experimental short stories, including those collected in *Pricksongs and Descants* (1969). The audacious imagination, verbal and stylistic invention, and sexual explicitness of *The Public Burning* were unsurprising to those familiar with Coover's early work, though all these qualities may have reached their peak in the novel. In *Whatever Happened to Gloomy Gus of the Chicago Bears?* (first published as a novella in 1975, revised version in book form 1987), Coover imagined another Nixon, one who failed in politics but found success in football and sex, both of which he mastered through sheer repetitive effort despite a lack of aptitude for either. This Nixon meets a sad end when he mindlessly follows one of his old football signals at a political demonstration. Other Coover novels, like the complex mystery *Gerald's Party* (1985), have their admirers, but *The Public Burning* is generally deemed Coover's masterpiece.

The Public Burning came out in 1977, three years after Nixon had been driven from the presidency in disgrace. Some saw the book as further picking on a defeated figure, while others thought the book and the recent events shed light on each other. The book was praised by some critics for its inventiveness and condemned by others for its sexuality and alleged leftist bias. The guilt of the Rosenbergs was still a controversial topic in 1977. Later evidence, including apparent Soviet spy records, makes the case for their guilt stronger, but questions about the case remain unresolved.

Bibliography

Anderson, Richard. *Robert Coover.* Boston: Twayne, 1981. This thorough presentation of Coover's work for a prestigious American literature series includes a remarkably condescending treatment of *The Public Burning* (Chapter 4, as part of a general discussion of "the later works"), grudgingly praising its inventiveness but accusing it of lack of emotional range.

Cope, Jackson I. *Robert Coover's Fictions.* Baltimore: The Johns Hopkins University Press, 1986. This study relates Coover's work in general, and *The Public Burning* in particular, to Mikhail Bakhtin's theory of the "dialogic novel," in which the single authorial persona of traditional fiction is replaced by a multiplicity of voices, with the reader left to choose among them.

Gordon, Lois. *Robert Coover: The Universal Fictionmaking Process.* Carbondale: Southern Illinois University Press, 1983. A detailed study of Coover's methods. Chapter 4 looks at mythical, linguistic, and social aspects of *The Public Burning.*

Viereck, Elisabeth, "The Clown Knew It All Along: The Medium Was the Message." *Delta* 28 (June, 1989): 63-81. As the subtitle suggests, this essay applies Marshall McLuhan's theories to the view of the media presented in *The Public Burning*.

Arthur D. Hlavaty

THE PUTTERMESSER PAPERS

Author: Cynthia Ozick (1928-   )
Type of plot: Magical Realism
Time of plot: The late 1980's
Locale: New York City
First published: 1997

> *Principal characters:*
> RUTH PUTTERMESSER, a lawyer and Jewish intellectual, later mayor of
>   New York City
> MORRIS RAPPOPORT, Ruth's married, middle-aged lover when she is in
>   her thirties
> XANTHIPPE, the golem Ruth creates from the dirt in her potted plants
>   and endows with life; she is named after the philosopher Socrates's
>   shrewish wife
> RUPERT RABEENO, Ruth's lover when she is no longer employed and is
>   in her fifties; Rupert is a painter and copyist of the paintings of the
>   Old Masters
> EMIL HAUCHVOGEL, the boyfriend from her youth whom Ruth marries
>   in the novel's fantasy of her life after death

The Novel

The Puttermesser Papers is divided into five parts, which are further subdivided into several short chapters that trace the life history, including the life after death, of the novel's feminist, Jewish, intellectual lawyer-heroine, Ruth Puttermesser. An amalgam of comedy and social satire, the book also includes supernatural fantasy derived from Jewish folklore, literary parody that inverts the conventions of historical sagas of great men who run for high public office, and a serious psychobiography of three famous nineteenth century figures. As a result, The Puttermesser Papers divides its energies among various genres of literature and social critique ambitiously and sometimes, to the reader, perplexingly.

The first part, "Puttermesser: Her Work History, Her Ancestry, Her Afterlife," presents a brilliant but frustrated thirty-four-year-old lawyer who has quit a prominent Wall Street law firm, where both her gender and her ethnicity were barriers to advancement, to work for the Department of Receipts and Disbursements in New York. While working for the city, she also visits her Uncle Zindel for Hebrew lessons in which the reader learns that the name Puttermesser means "butterknife." In this scene, Cynthia Ozick refuses to allow the reader to take her character seriously when the narrative voice erupts with "Stop. Stop, stop! Puttermesser's biographer, stop! Disengage, please. Though it is true that biographies are invented, not recorded, here you invent too much. A symbol is allowed, but not a whole scene: do not accommodate too obsequiously to Puttermesser's romance." Telling readers that Puttermesser is not "an artifact" but "an essence," Ozick ends the chapter with the direct challenge "Hey! Puttermesser's biographer! What will you do with her now?"

The second Puttermesser Paper answers this question. Ozick turns to Jewish folklore for her answer, and Ruth Puttermesser creates a golem. In folklore, a golem is an artifically created human being supernaturally endowed with life, and Ruth's is made from the earth in her apartment's houseplants. Fantasy and allegory merge in this part of the novel, as the golem, Xanthippe, sets out to cleanse New York of filth and municipal problems and to elevate Ruth to the office of mayor. Part perfect daughter and part monster, the golem quickly grows into a sexually insatiable giantess who sleeps with every man in Ruth's administration until the mayor is forced to uncreate her.

The next section, "Puttermesser Paired," follows Ruth in her fifties as she falls in love with Rupert Rabeeno, a young painter and copyist of great European art. Here, life again imitates art as Ruth introduces Rupert to the works of the nineteenth century woman writer George Eliot and Eliot's romance with George Henry Lewes. Rupert develops an unusual thesis about Eliot, Lewes, and Johnny Cross, Eliot's younger husband after Lewes's death. In a bizarre twist of fate, Rupert ends up acting out his thesis in his Platonic romance with Ruth, and he abandons her.

The fourth section, "Puttermesser and the Muscovite Cousin," examines how political and artistic idealism associated with the term "Russian Jew" became debased into vulgar materialism during the period of *glasnost* as communism began to dismantle itself in the late 1980's. Ruth's cousin Lidia emerges as a caricature of the Jewish intellectual in her crass commercialism.

The last section, "Puttermesser in Paradise," recounts Ruth's ugly death at the hands of a burglar who breaks into her apartment, murders the retired woman in her sixties, and then proceeds to rape her. In heaven, Ruth's youthful dreams come true as she marries a childhood sweetheart, Emil Hauchvogel, and gives birth to the son she lacked on earth. Yet for human experience to have meaning it must be linked to duration, or time, and heaven is, by definition, the realm of timelessness; thus, Ruth's bliss is condemned to fade. "The secret meaning of Paradise is that it too is hell," she learns. The book concludes with a plaintive poem that both laments and ridicules the dilemma of the childless intellectual whose hopes for life, literature, and love have been bitterly ignored by reality: "Better never to have loved than loved at all./ Better never to have risen than had a fall./ *Oh bitter, bitter, bitter/ butter knife.*"

The Characters

The characters of *The Puttermesser Papers* are less novelistic creations who grow and change in the course of the novel than they are static and one-dimensional figures in Ozick's fantastic allegory. With the exception of Ruth Puttermesser, whom readers come to pity more than admire, most of the characters function as figures serving Ozick's purpose of social satire. An alter ego for Ozick herself, Ruth made her first appearance in 1962 as a character in story published in *The New Yorker* magazine that later became the first chapter of *The Puttermesser Papers*. About once a decade afterward, Ozick revisited Ruth to add another chapter to a character who came to life at age thirty-four, then entered successive decades as Ozick herself entered them. The first two chapters of Ruth's saga appeared in *Levitation* (1982).

The second chapter, "Puttermesser and Xanthippe," confirms Ozick's reputation for outrageous inventiveness when Ruth creates and animates the golem. A fantastic Frankenstein-like creation, Xanthippe, named after Socrates's wife, aids Ruth in her revenge upon the political machine that fired her and helps her in her "Plan for the Resuscitation, Reformation, Reinvigoration & Redemption of the City of New York." Then, as Frankenstein raged against his creator, the golem utterly destroys Ruth's achievements as mayor. This plot also resonates with echoes of the Book of Genesis, in which God creates man out of earth; the name "Adam" means "clay" or "earth." While Ruth imitates God the creator, she also imitates Ozick the writer, who is made a writer by the characters she creates, as Ruth is made mayor by the golem she creates.

The third chapter, "Puttermesser Paired," returns to the question of art, imitation, and their relationship to life when Ruth falls in love with the painter Rupert Rabeeno. She first meets him at the Metropolitan Museum of Art, where he is painting an imitation or "reenactment" of *The Death of Socrates*. Here Ozick engages in subtle symbolism in her second allusion to the philosophic tradition and to its central Socratic tenet, "The unexamined life is not worth living." By the end of the novel and of Ruth's life, the irony of such a belief will be clear to the reader.

The fourth chapter, "Puttermesser and the Muscovite Cousin," is, in contrast to earlier chapters, the least richly imagined and fantastically described. It returns to Ozick's central preoccupation as a writer with questions of Jewish identity and its relation to community.

The fantastic returns in the last chapter, "Puttermesser in Paradise," where Ozick indulges her satirical antiutopian impulse and manages to negate much of what the reader has learned about Ruth in a paradise that quickly becomes hell.

Themes and Meanings

The novel is in many ways a meditation on mortality and the transience and ephemerality of human striving. Ozick announced in an electronic interview that *The Puttermesser Papers* can best be thought of in connection with William Shakespeare's *Hamlet*. Where Hamlet believes that "readiness is all," Ozick is interested in the moment after readiness; if one does not devour life or act decisively, then one decays. If, indeed, decay is all, then one is driven to confront the human condition and mortality. In Ruth's tragicomedy of disappointments and thwarted dreams, she struggles mightily against meaninglessness, only to find herself engulfed by it at novel's end.

One of the novel's strongest motifs rests in its allusions to Socrates and his philosophic project. Socrates probably held the doctrine that human error is based on ignorance and that no one desires to do bad things; that it is worse to do injustice than to suffer it; and that human excellence is a kind of knowledge. While Ruth's ethical idealism and dispassionate commitment to higher ideals seem to confirm her enlightened status in the novel, the end result of her sacrifices and sufferings point toward the vision of the world laid out in Ecclesiastes.

Critical Context

Ozick's publications, beginning with the novel *Trust* (1966), range among collected poems, short stories, essays, novels, and plays. They include *The Pagan Rabbi and Other Stories* (1971), *Art and Ardor: Essays* (1983), *The Messiah of Stockholm* (1987), *Metaphor and Memory: Essays* (1989), *Epodes: First Poems* (1982), *The Shawl* (1989), *Portrait of the Artist as a Bad Character and Other Essays on Writing* (1994), and *Fame and Folly* (1996). Ozick has received numerous awards, among them a Guggenheim Fellowship and a Mildred and Harold Straus Living Award from the American Academy and National Institute of Arts and Letters.

Ozick rejects the term "woman writer" as a significant category to describe her achievement, but she embraces "Jewish writer" as a category of civilization, culture, and intellect, a heritage she affirms that always informs her fiction. Many critics found her first novel, *Trust* (1966), unreadable because it was heavily influenced by the example of Henry James. Once she abandoned Jamesian influence, however, Ozick's fiction became preoccupied with questions of Jewish identity, particularly the meaning of the Holocaust. In her short story "The Shawl," she creates a powerful and moving account of life and death in a concentration camp. *The Cannibal Galaxy* (1983) concerns the spiritual struggles of a survivor of the Holocaust who becomes a headmaster of a school in the American Midwest. *The Messiah of Stockholm* (1989) raises questions of identity and authenticity important to a writer as morally serious as Ozick. It also reflects Ozick's interest in the ways in which art can interfere with life, as it does in the third chapter, "Puttermesser Paired," of the *The Puttermesser Papers*. For many of her characters, assimilation of Jewish identity to that of the dominant culture is impossible, since it entails the disappearance of what is distinctively Jewish in the characters' makeup.

Bibliography

Cohen, Sarah Blacher. *Cynthia Ozick's Comic Art*. Bloomington: Indiana University Press, 1994. States that Ozick writes comedy of character that exposes the flawed nature of her protagonists. Places her in the context of other Jewish writers and the tradition of rabbinical wisdom.

Finkelstein, Norman. *The Ritual of New Creation: Jewish Tradition and Contemporary Literature*. Albany: State University of New York Press, 1992. Only one chapter discusses Ozick, but she is placed in elite company with Harold Bloom, George Steiner, and Walter Benjamin as one of the twentieth century's leading Jewish intellectuals.

Friedman, Laurence S. *Understanding Cynthia Ozick*. Columbia: University of South Carolina Press, 1991. A good general introduction to her fiction. Useful on the tensions between assimilation and separateness as they relate to issues in Jewish identity. Good on the role of fantasy and the golem in Jewish tradition.

Kauvar, Elaine M. *Cynthia Ozick's Fiction: Tradition and Invention*. Bloomington: Indiana University Press, 1993. Good discussion of the role of Socrates, fantasy, and the *Doppelgänger* in Ruth Puttermesser's adventures. An impressive study of Ozick's achievement, especially in her short fiction.

Victor Strandberg, *Greek Mind/Jewish Soul: The Conflicted Art of Cynthia Ozick*. Madison: University of Wisconsin Press, 1994. Excellent on Ozick's biography and its connection with her art.

Roberta Schreyer

PYLON

Author: William Faulkner (1897-1962)
Type of plot: Modernist realism
Time of plot: Mid-Depression, during Mardi Gras
Locale: Primarily New Valois, Franciana, a transparent reference to New Orleans, and Ohio
First published: 1935

    Principal characters:
        LAZARUS, the reporter who covers the air show and becomes the book's major protagonist
        ROGER SHUMANN, a pilot and the leader of a flying team
        LA VERNE, a companion of Roger Shumann and a member of the team
        THE BOY, LaVerne's son
        JACK HOLMES, a member of the team and a parachutist
        JIGGS, an airplane mechanic
        HAGOOD, a newspaper editor

The Novel

    Pylon was William Faulkner's eighth novel; he wrote it at the height of his powers, just before *Absalom, Absalom!* (1936) and not long after *Light in August* (1932). The novel is, above all, about flying and the motivation of those who fly. The "pylon" of the title is the tower or steel post around which a pilot must turn as he competes in a race at an air fair. The term figures prominently in the jargon of competing pilots; they "turn pylons" with their planes on each lap—they "take that pylon" and try to "fly the best pylon." Because of its subject matter, the novel is less well known than other novels Faulkner wrote during this period, yet it would be a mistake to think that it is "just about flying"; many of the themes closest to Faulkner's heart receive full, complex treatment in this neglected novel. *Pylon* is also one of Faulkner's most exciting books, set near and in New Orleans during the week of Mardi Gras.

    The plot of the novel can be summarized quite simply: A flying team composed of a pilot, a "jumper," or parachutist, and a mechanic, accompanied by a woman and her son, are desperately short of money and hope to win at least one of the purses at an air show. They live only on their winnings, which means that often they have no place to stay, little to eat, and no money for transportation within a city. They resemble circus performers, and some of the themes in the book are remarkably close to those of Ingmar Bergman's film *The Naked Night* (1953). Although the book is about the "romance" of flying, the hard physical conditions of the performers are kept firmly in the foreground. Onlookers, newspaper reporters, and members of the audience speculate on their motivation: Do they fly for money or for another reason? Are they "human" and "like us" (or a Holy Family)? If one supposes that they do not do it for money, he quickly learns that they are driven by material needs. At the same time, money cannot account for their motivation. The exploration of this conflict is central to the book. It throws considerable light on Faulkner's theme of "survival," explored in other novels and referred to in his Nobel Prize address; as *Pylon* reveals, this survival is never a purely materialistic necessity but is balanced against ideals and other claims, often extremely irrational. The book also develops Faulkner's concept of psychological necessity, that men and women must do what they are driven to do by their most profound inner motivations. This is explored through solid, complex characters who differ widely from one another and who come from a very broad variety of social strata.

One of the strangest, most unexpected relationships in the book gradually develops as it proceeds. The reporter who covers the air show becomes fascinated by Roger Shumann's flying team; he makes their acquaintance and tries to help them. This desire appears to be completely altruistic, with no self-interest. He becomes increasingly involved in the action, and, inadvertently, it is he who is responsible for the team's destruction. He devises a scheme that will permit them to buy a new, more powerful plane which will win the final trophy race that has the biggest purse. This, he thinks, will solve their financial problems once and for all. The reporter is partly in love with the female member of the team, LaVerne, but he is equally concerned about the welfare of the child and the team as a whole. His intention is like that of Gregers Werle in Henrik Ibsen's *The Wild Duck* (1884), the busybody who tries to do good but ends up creating only destruction—this is what George Bernard Shaw called "the quintessence of Ibsenism," and Faulkner's treatment of the theme in *Pylon* is masterful.

The powerful plane which the reporter contrives to buy has several defects; the reporter learns about them at an early stage and so does Shumann, but they persevere in their plan, caught up in the desire to win. A safety expert refuses to certify the plane, but they persuade other authorities to overrule him. It becomes increasingly clear that the plane has serious flaws—Faulkner beautifully handles the hurried, panicky attempts of the flying team to compensate for them and ignore their seriousness. During the final, tense race, the plane does not perform and comes apart in the air; the pilot is killed in a lake. At the end of the novel, the group disbands.

The Characters

The major characters in *Pylon* are complex. Indeed, there are few "flat" or simplified characters in the book, and they appear only in chance encounters. Some difficulty is caused by names—when a major character appears in the course of the narrative, Faulkner frequently fails to name him, and the reader is often given a phrase like "the boy" or "the woman." Keeping the characters straight is often as confusing as in a Russian novel, when the reader is given only a first name or patronymic—if anything, it is even more difficult with Faulkner. This difficulty has a rationale: Faulkner usually follows the point of view of a specific character very closely, and if that character does not think in terms of a name, then Faulkner does not provide that name. The reporter knows LaVerne only from a distance, so for him she is never LaVerne, only "she" or "the woman."

On the other hand, the characters are highly dramatic—Faulkner describes almost all of them with a heightened physical presence and various meaningful accompanying objects. For example, Jiggs the mechanic has the boots he is buying as the novel opens. These are his prized, most valuable possession, and they acquire enormous significance as the action proceeds. At the close of the novel, he pawns them. Jiggs is one of Faulkner's most successful creations: Poor, totally irresponsible, sly, and predatory, he is the cause of the first accident in the story—instead of pulling the valves from the motor and inspecting their stems, he gets drunk; the plane performs badly as a result, and the parachutist almost breaks his leg. In Faulkner's words, Jiggs is a "vicious halfmetamorphosis between thug and horse." He is a memorable addition to Faulkner's gallery of extremely harmful, evil characters, whom he succeeds in portraying not only from the outside but also from the inside, from their own point of view—an astonishing feat, of which few other novelists are capable.

In the course of the book, the reporter's name is given only once, in passing. As if to compensate for this, Faulkner endows him with a unique appearance. He is extremely thin, referred to as a scarecrow, a lath, a "person made of clothes and bones," "a cutglass monkeywrench or something."

> He did not speak loudly, and with no especial urgency, but he emanated the illusion still of having longsince collapsed yet being still intact in his own weightlessness like a dandelion burr moving where there is no wind. In the soft pink glow his face appeared gaunter than ever, as though following the excess of the past night, his vital spark now fed on the inner side of the actual skin itself, paring it steadily thinner and more and more transparent.

Perhaps the nature of his personality explains why he is almost never named; he becomes consumed by his reportorial function, a "fly on the wall" who comes to live vicariously in the lives of those he observes. He ceases to have any life of his own and even stops being a reporter—he is fired, and he becomes an active agent of the plot, almost a member of the flying team. Despite this peculiar, leechlike psychological mechanism, Faulkner makes clear that he has little understanding of those he is trying to help. Toward the end of the novel, the parachutist advises him, "Only take a tip from me and stick to the kind of people you are used to after this."

What distinguishes Faulkner's characters is, above all, their presentation both from within—from their own subjective point of view—and from without—from the points of view of others. This gives them a unique amplitude and depth. The point of view changes many times in the course of the novel, and the reader will not find the "unified sensibility" of which Henry James wrote—as a consequence he might occasionally be confused. On the other hand, the reader will encounter numerous characters presented in great depth and urgent, compelling life.

Themes and Meanings

Pylon is above all a study of human motivation, of the diverse mechanisms and drives that make people act as they do. These range from concrete, external circumstances to inner desires, compulsions, and obsessions, and they are all brought to bear on the specific character as he thinks, feels, and acts. *Pylon* especially investigates what might be termed the claims of "romance" or romantic glamour. They form an aura that surrounds the activity of flying, above all the competitive flying in air fairs. The principal characters in the book all feel the pull of this nongravitational force, which comes to alter and definitively change their lives. It assumes a different form depending on their specific personalities. With the opportunistic, cynical Jiggs, who counts his pennies, it is nevertheless potent; with Roger Shumann, it takes on an idealistic, aesthetic form; with LaVerne, it is associated with love; with the reporter Lazarus, it assumes the most extraordinary form of all—unbalanced, voyeuristic, totally impractical, and all-consuming.

The primary tool for exploring these complex motivations is the novel's style. With Faulkner, this is often close to the process of free association, but it is not chaotic or purposeless. On the contrary, the style always significantly advances the narrative at the same time that it renders the thought processes of the principal characters. This closeness to actual thought characterized the practice of modernists such as James Joyce and Virginia Woolf during the period between the two world wars, but since 1946, this intimacy has been abandoned by most novelists in favor of a more formal point of view located in the middle distance. In *Pylon* and other novels by Faulkner during the same period, there is an impressive breadth in the presentation of character largely lacking in the post-World War II novel: a thought-for-thought, heartbeat-for-heartbeat intimacy with characters combined with an ability to step back, assume distance and a sweeping perspective, then once again to enter the thoughts of that character or another. Faulkner excels at this combination of amplitude and intimacy.

The technique of jumping in and out of different people's thoughts can have drawbacks. The reader is sometimes lost, missing the firm hand of a considerate guide. Faulkner incorporates much of the complexity and some of the chaos of real life into his narrative; many readers do not seek these when they pick up a book. On the other hand, *Pylon* contains a living and breathing solidity and depth of meaning found in few other novels. After reading Faulkner, numerous readers will wish that other novelists were as daring as he.

Critical Context

Malcolm Cowley's effort to promote Faulkner's literary reputation after the end of World War II was largely successful. The Viking Portable selection from Faulkner's work—edited by Cowley—brought Faulkner once again to the attention of the serious American reading public, and his reputation steadily increased until his reception of the Nobel Prize. Cowley stressed Faulkner's achievement as a regional Southern writer, as "proprietor" of Yoknapatawpha County. Perhaps this was correct; at any rate, Faulkner's "mythical kingdom" seized the imaginations of American readers. *Pylon* has no place in Yoknapatawpha County, and for some that may seem reason enough to exclude it from the canon of Faulkner's finest novels. Yet that would be a mistake. It was written when Faulkner was producing other novels that are among his finest—*Light in August* and *Absalom, Absalom!* —and it has all their elan and creative complexity. It is an urban novel, just as successful as the novels set in his rural "mythical kingdom." It will probably continue to fall victim to critical simplification, yet it will remain one of his half dozen most impressive novels.

Bibliography

Blotner, Joseph. *Faulkner: A Biography*. 2 vols. New York: Random House, 1974. Once criticized for being too detailed (the two-volume edition is some two thousand pages) this biography begins before Faulkner's birth with ancestors such as William Clark Falkner, author of *The White Rose of Memphis*, and traces the writer's career from a precocious poet to America's preeminent novelist.

Brodhead, Richard H., ed. *Faulkner: New Perspectives*. Englewood Cliffs, N.J.: Prentice-Hall, 1983. One volume in the Twentieth Century Views series under the general editorship of Maynard Mack, offering nearly a dozen essays by a variety of Faulkner scholars. Among them are Irving Howe's "Faulkner and the Negroes," first published in the early 1950's, and Cleanth Brooks's "Vision of Good and Evil" from Samuel E. Balentine's *The Hidden God* (Oxford, England: Oxford University Press, 1983). Contains a select bibliography.

Cox, Leland H., ed. *William Faulkner: Biographical and Reference Guide*. Detroit, Mich.: Gale Research, 1982.

_____. *William Faulkner: Critical Collection*. Detroit, Mich.: Gale Research, 1982. These companion volumes constitute a handy reference to most of Faulkner's work. The first is a reader's guide which provides a long biographical essay, cross-referenced by many standard sources. Next come fifteen "critical introductions" to the novels and short stories, each with plot summaries and critical commentary particularly useful to the student reader. A three-page chronology of the events of Faulkner's life is attached. The second volume contains a short potpourri, with Faulkner's "Statements," a *Paris Review* interview, and an essay on Mississippi for *Holiday* magazine among them. The bulk of the book is an essay and excerpt collection with contributions by a number of critics including Olga Vickery, Michael Millgate, and Warren Beck. Includes a list of works by Faulkner including Hollywood screenplays.

Gray, Richard. *The Life of William Faulkner: A Critical Biography*. Oxford, England: Blackwell, 1994. A noted Faulkner scholar, Gray closely integrates the life and work. Part 1 suggests a method of approaching Faulkner's life; part 2 concentrates on his apprentice years; part 3 explains his discovery of Yoknapatawpha and the transformation of his region into his fiction; part 4 deals with his treatment of past and present; part 5 addresses his exploration of place; part 6 analyzes his final novels, reflecting on his creation of Yoknapatawpha. Includes family trees, chronology, notes, and a bibliography.

Vickery, Olga W. *The Novels of William Faulkner*. Baton Rouge: Louisiana State University Press, 1959. This volume, with its comprehensive treatment of the novels, has established itself as a classic, a *terminus a quo* for later criticism. The chapter on *The Sound and the Fury*, providing an analysis of the relation between theme and structure in the book, remains relevant today despite intensive study of the topic.

Volpe, Edmond L. *A Reader's Guide to William Faulkner.* New York: Noonday Press, 1964. While many books and articles have contributed to clearing up the murkiest spots in Faulkner, the beginning student or general reader will applaud this volume. In addition to analysis of structure, themes, and characters, offers critical discussion of the novels in an appendix providing "chronologies of scenes, paraphrase of scene fragments put in chronological order, and guides to scene shifts."

Williamson, Joel. *William Faulkner and Southern History.* New York: Oxford University Press, 1993. A distinguished historian divides his book into sections on Faulkner's ancestry, his biography, and his writing. Includes notes and genealogy.

John Carpenter

RABBIT ANGSTROM NOVELS

Author: John Updike (1932-   )
Type of plot: Social chronicle
Time of plot: *Rabbit, Run,* 1959; *Rabbit Redux,* 1969; *Rabbit Is Rich,* 1979-80;
  Rabbit at Rest, the late 1980's
Locale: The fictional towns of Mt. Judge and Brewer, Pennsylvania, and Florida
First published: Rabbit, Run, 1960; *Rabbit Redux,* 1971; *Rabbit Is Rich,* 1981; *Rabbit
  at Rest,* 1990

Principal characters:
  HARRY (RABBIT) ANGSTROM, a former high school basketball star
  JANICE SPRINGER ANGSTROM, his wife
  NELSON ANGSTROM, the son of Harry and Janice
  REBECCA ANGSTROM, the daughter of Harry and Janice, dead in infancy
  MARTY TOTHERO, Harry's former athletic coach
  RUTH LEONARD, Harry's mistress during 1959
  JACK ECCLES, an Episcopal priest
  FRED SPRINGER, Janice's father, a car dealer
  BESSIE SPRINGER, Janice's mother
  PEGGY GRING FOSNACHT, Janice's friend
  BILLY FOSNACHT, Peggy's son, Nelson's friend
  EARL ANGSTROM, Harry's father, a printer
  CHARLIE STAVROS, a car salesman, Janice's lover during 1969
  JILL PENDLETON, a teenage runaway who is killed in a house fire
  SKEETER, a black militant and fugitive
  MIRIAM ANGSTROM, Harry's younger sister
  ANNABELLE BYER, Ruth Leonard's daughter and possibly Harry's as
    well
  MELANIE, a college friend of Nelson's
  TERESA (PRU) LUBELL, Nelson's mistress, later his wife
  ARCHIE CAMPBELL, an Episcopal priest
  JUDY ANGSTROM, Harry's eight-year-old granddaughter
  ROY ANGSTROM, Harry's four-year-old grandson
  THELMA HARRISON, Harry's secret lover
  RON HARRISON, Thelma's husband and Harry's childhood classmate

The Novels
  With his sixth novel, *Rabbit Redux,* published in 1971, John Updike resumed the
life story of Harry "Rabbit" Angstrom, the antiheroic protagonist of his acclaimed
second novel, *Rabbit, Run.* Another decade and several more novels followed before
Updike came forth with his third record of Harry's adventures, appropriately entitled
Rabbit Is Rich. Rabbit at Rest, which appeared nearly a decade later, is the final vol-

ume of the tetralogy. The Rabbit Angstrom books provide an accurate, absorbing, and aesthetically satisfying social history of middle-class North America from the 1950's into the 1980's; taken together, the novels may well constitute Updike's finest achievement.

Born in 1933, a year later than his novelistic creator, Harry "Rabbit" Angstrom is at times an Everyman of sorts, at other times a kind of holy fool, yet even at his most disgraceful moments he appears to represent the voice of common sense. His mundane adventures, meanwhile, are consistently backlighted by contemporaneous events in political and cultural history, to which they may frequently be seen as a response. The end product of such a technique is an impressive social chronicle, brought close to the reader by the generally amiable, if not always admirable, character of Harry Angstrom himself.

When Harry first emerges on the scene, in *Rabbit, Run*, he is twenty-six years old, a veteran of Stateside service during the Korean War, married not long thereafter to Janice Springer, who happened to be carrying his child. Although demonstrably intelligent, Harry did not attend college and is thus limited in his job prospects: At the start of *Rabbit, Run*, he is employed as a demonstrator of kitchen gadgets, barely managing to support his young son and pregnant wife. His only claim to fame, already growing stale, derives from his erstwhile prowess on the high school basketball court.

Janice, daughter of a rather prosperous used car dealer, has grown lazy and apathetic, with an unfortunate fondness for strong drink. One evening, the sordidness of his domestic scene catches up with Harry and he flees, driving aimlessly about the countryside until daybreak. Unwilling to return to either home or job, he seeks refuge in the garret inhabited by Marty Tothero, his former basketball coach, who has quit his job in disgrace. It is through Tothero that Harry meets Ruth Leonard, moving soon thereafter into Ruth's apartment.

Ruth Leonard, an unemployed secretary of Harry's own age, is perhaps less a prostitute than a "kept" woman with several occasional "keepers." At Harry's urging, however, she soon reserves her attentions for Harry alone, reluctantly falling in love as she does so. To her credit, Ruth is both more affectionate and "better company" than Janice; she is also, in general, a good influence on Harry, allowing him the opportunity to sort out the tangled threads of his life.

It is while he is living with Ruth that Harry is first befriended by Jack Eccles, rector of the Episcopal church attended by Janice's parents. Although ostensibly sent by the Springers to prepare a reconciliation, Jack becomes fascinated by Harry's simple yet strong personal faith and seemingly adopts him as a separate case, unrelated to that of his estranged wife. Soon the two young men are playing golf together, and it is Eccles who finds steady work for Harry in the garden of an elderly widow. Still living with Ruth and working for Mrs. Smith, who adores him, Harry leads an idyllic life that is cut short only by the birth of his and Janice's baby, a daughter to be named Rebecca.

Reluctantly recalled by Eccles to face his true responsibilities, Harry gamely attempts to repair his relationship with Janice, doing most of the housecleaning himself. Janice, however, has learned little or nothing from their separation, and it is not long before Harry escapes again, returning to Ruth's apartment only to find that Ruth is not there. No sooner has Harry left the flat than Janice begins drinking heavily, recklessly, in an effort to console herself: Enveloped in an alcoholic haze, her reflexes dangerously impaired, she accidentally drowns baby Rebecca while attempting to give the child her bath.

Perhaps inevitably, given their respective personalities, Harry and Janice will blame each other for Rebecca's death; after all, reasons Janice, the accident would not have happened if Harry had not walked out on her. As befits the title *Rabbit, Run*, in keeping also with his athletic conditioning and background, Harry has spent much of his time running, literally as well as figuratively. Thus will he flee the scene of Rebecca's funeral, running as if for his life with Father Eccles in ineffectual pursuit. Deciding thereafter to resume his affair with Ruth, generally pleased to learn that she is pregnant with his child, Harry suddenly balks at the thought of divorce and remarriage, finding himself on the run once again, with no particular destination in sight or in mind as *Rabbit, Run* comes to an end.

Written almost completely in the narrative present tense with occasional shifts in point of view, exploiting also the "free indirect discourse" borrowed by James Joyce from Gustave Flaubert, *Rabbit, Run* is notable for its narrative technique as well as for its contribution to the tradition of social realism exemplified by the works of Sinclair Lewis and John O'Hara. In its evocation of rural Pennsylvania and its people, *Rabbit, Run* is, in fact, strongly reminiscent of O'Hara except in the area of technical innovation, a refinement which O'Hara generally eschewed. At the same time, the novel speaks eloquently of and for a younger generation both liberated and alienated by its potential freedom. A decade later, borrowing his Latinate title from the medical profession, Updike would show Harry Angstrom "led back," "recovered," even recuperated by the society that he once sought to flee.

At the start of *Rabbit Redux* the reader learns that Harry, reconciled with Janice not long after the baby's funeral, has been employed ever since as a Linotype operator in the same shop where his father still works as a printer. By 1969, however, both men's jobs are threatened by the imminent prospect of automation. Also threatened, perhaps even more seriously than before, is Harry's marriage to Janice: Employed by her father in the office of his new Toyota dealership, Janice has commenced a torrid affair with one Charlie Stavros, Springer Motors' top car salesman. No sooner has Harry confronted Janice with his suspicions than she moves out of the ranch-style tract home where they now live, ostensibly to clear her head at her parents' summer cottage but in fact to share Stavros' small apartment.

To a greater extent than in the earlier novel, current events loom large in *Rabbit Redux*; prior to Janice's flight, Harry engages Charlie Stavros, a liberal, in a heated discussion of the war in Vietnam; not long thereafter, he reflectively watches the televised landing of American astronauts on the moon. Janice's departure has created a rent in the surface of Harry's presumably well-ordered life, and before long the world rushes in from outside: Alternately fascinated and repelled, Harry finds himself playing host to two representatives of the youthful counterculture: Jill Pendleton, a runaway from an affluent Connecticut family, and the black man known only as Skeeter, a fugitive from justice, possibly the son or brother of one of Harry's coworkers at the print shop. Thirteen-year-old Nelson Angstrom, housed with his father for the unspecified duration of his mother's defection, soon develops a hopeless crush on the eighteen-year-old Jill, even as Jill divides her physical favors between Harry and Skeeter under Nelson's watchful eyes. Skeeter, meanwhile, is determined to raise Harry's middle-American, conservative consciousness with liberal doses of illegal drugs and underground political philosophy, conducting responsive readings from the works of Eldridge Cleaver and others.

Predictably, the cohabitation of Harry and Nelson with a black militant and a white female "hippie" begins to provoke gossip, and worse; on one occasion, Harry is ambiguously threatened by two of his neighbors on his way home from the bus stop. Still, he is reluctant to take action, being somewhat mesmerized by Skeeter, half in love with Jill, and more than a little afraid of them both. Peggy Fosnacht, a longtime friend of Janice and the mother of Nelson's best friend, beckons to Harry from his "own" world, suggesting the desirability of an affair now that both have separated from their spouses. Yielding at last to Peggy's blandishments, Harry is in her apartment when his house burns to the ground with Jill Pendleton still inside, Skeeter having escaped at the last minute to hide in the woods nearby. Later found hiding in the backseat of Harry's car, Skeeter persuades Harry of his innocence and successfully hitches a ride toward freedom. Although no arrests are ever made in the arson and murder, Harry's suspicion naturally falls on the neighbors who had threatened him.

The memory of Jill Pendleton, like that of baby Rebecca, will continue to haunt the Angstroms as a family. Young Nelson, in particular, will carry his grief and resentment well into adulthood, inwardly and at times outwardly accusing his father of allowing Jill to die. In time, Janice and Harry will come back together; Charlie Stavros, it seems, feels consigned to bachelorhood by the same chronic heart ailment that exempted him from military service, free also to enjoy brief "flings" with such people as Harry's sister Miriam, who has flown east from her life on the fringes of the show business and gaming world to pay her respects to the terminally ill Mrs. Angstrom, senior.

Narrated, like its predecessor, in the present tense, with frequent use of free indirect discourse, *Rabbit Redux* continues Harry's saga as if without interruption. Perhaps even more significantly, it provides a most informative and thoughtful chronicle of the turbulent late 1960's, brought fully to life by the credible if outrageous portrayals of Skeeter and Jill. Writing in the affectless third person, the author manages also, before the Watergate case, to express his own heavily ironic views of the Nixon presidency.

In *Rabbit Is Rich*, Harry Angstrom has at last arrived in the bourgeoisie to which he has more or less aspired, thanks mainly to his co-ownership, with Janice and her mother, of the Toyota dealership inherited from her late father. Laid off from his job setting Linotype at the end of *Rabbit Redux*, Harry was hired not long thereafter by Fred Springer as a salesman and potential successor, working without friction in close proximity to Charlie Stavros, who has since become his friend. Unable to rebuild their own house after the fire, Harry and Janice are still living with Mrs. Springer but are planning to buy a house of their own, which they can now easily afford.

Now that he has "arrived," with respectable standing in the community and a regular golf foursome, Harry at forty-six finds himself increasingly concerned with the idea of himself as a father. Nelson at twenty-three is something of a disappointment, unsure of the future, keeping company with one woman while another is carrying his child. Almost in desperation, Harry fixes his attentions upon a ripe young blonde glimpsed by chance at the Toyota dealership, imagining her to be his daughter by Ruth Leonard. This obsession will occupy Harry throughout most of *Rabbit Is Rich*, alternating with his anxieties over Nelson's uncertain future and tangled interpersonal relationships. Harry's relationship with Nelson, always somewhat problematic, has remained seriously flawed since Jill Pendleton's death; his relationship with Janice, meanwhile, has become more stable than ever before, frankly rooted in mutual economic self-interest; she and Harry are now partners in most possible senses of the term.

Throughout *Rabbit Is Rich*, as in *Rabbit Redux*, current events figure prominently in the action: The characters freely discuss President Carter, Afghanistan, and the Iran hostage crisis; Harry, taking advantage of recent changes in United States fiscal policy, grows richer still through shrewd short-term investments in gold and silver coins even as he anticipates possible negative economic influences on the Toyota import trade. Fittingly, the Toyota car itself serves as both the subject and the "vehicle" of some of Updike's most telling observations; the various models and their prospective buyers are described in considerable detail as American tastes turn toward smaller, more fuel-efficient cars. So total is Harry's absorption in his job that the firm's best-known slogans begin to creep into his speech and even into his unspoken monologues.

Nelson Angstrom, an intermittent student at Kent State University some years after the infamous National Guard incident, finds himself torn between his ambitions and his origins; although moderately successful as a student, befriended by the intellectually inclined Melanie, Nelson nevertheless chooses his mistress and consort from the university's secretarial pool, feeling less threatened by his "own kind" of people. Teresa Lubell, known ironically as "Pru" since childhood for her apparent prudery, is a year or two Nelson's senior, generally likable yet hardly better suited to Nelson than Janice once was to Harry. Both Harry and Janice, however, believe that Pru and Nelson should have a proper church wedding before their child is born; Nelson, unwilling to resume his studies, attempts to find himself both a job and a "place" at Springer Motors, the better to support his family.

The tension between Nelson and Harry, hitherto perceived mainly on Nelson's side, erupts into open warfare when Harry consistently blocks Nelson's entry into the firm, against the strong support of Janice and her mother, his co-proprietors. Nelson, hoping to impress his father, talks his mother and grandmother into letting him develop, at Springer Motors, an ancillary trade in antique cars; Harry, feeling outmaneuvered, so frustrates Nelson with his opposition that Nelson rams one of his newly acquired old cars with another, thus ruining them both. In the end neither side wins; although Nelson has correctly perceived a market for such cars, the argument with Harry has killed his enthusiasm. After a brief stint at selling Toyotas, failing to meet his father's expectations, Nelson will return to Kent State, leaving Pru behind to bear their baby under the protection of his parents and grandmother. Harry and Janice, meanwhile, have finally bought a house of their own over Mrs. Springer's objections, with enough money left over from Harry's precious-metal speculations to afford a brief winter trip to the Caribbean in the company of Harry's golf companions and their wives.

Not long after the Caribbean trip, highlighted by "discreet" mate swapping, Pru Lubell Angstrom is delivered of a healthy baby daughter. Harry, his paternal instincts aroused once again, sets forth in search of the elusive blonde whom he believes to be his child. A brief encounter with Ruth, recounted in *Rabbit Redux*, has helped to encourage his suspicions; his subsequent encounter, toward the end of *Rabbit Is Rich*, repeats the acrimonious tone of the previous meeting, with Harry's questions left unanswered. In all likelihood, Annabelle Byer is indeed Harry's child, but Ruth Leonard Byer, by now a farm widow with two sons in addition to "Annie," will give Harry no such satisfaction; as a woman wronged, she will even misrepresent her daughter's age in one final effort to rid her life of Harry Angstrom. As *Rabbit Is Rich* draws to a close, Harry sits in his Barcalounger with his infant granddaughter in his lap, pondering in his fashion the mysteries of life and death.

Rabbit Is Rich is perhaps more indebted to Sinclair Lewis than either of the previous novels in the sequence. In a sense, Rabbit has at last become Babbitt, thanks to forces somewhat beyond his control. Trained at an early age toward athletic success, Harry, with the onset of middle age, has at last found employment suited to his competitive skills, albeit with the help of the Springers, from whom he has frequently estranged himself. With all his failures plainly visible behind him, his political outlook tempered by contact with the counterculture, grown even more cautious before the threat of global economic crisis, Harry nevertheless perseveres in his pursuit of "American" values, intent on "conserving" whatever might remain of their validity. Like George Babbitt, he is frequently at odds with his wife and offspring, yet for all his disillusionments he retains a generally positive outlook that will probably sustain him well into, and possibly through, his retirement.

Rabbit at Rest begins in 1988 on the Gulf Coast of Florida, where Harry, now semiretired from running the Toyota dealership in Brewer, Pennsylvania, and his wife Janice spend six months every year. They await the arrival of their son Nelson and his family. Harry, once a high-school basketball hero, is overweight and unable to resist eating cholesterol-filled junk food. He now has a bad heart. His son's visit culminates with the fifty-five-year-old Harry being hospitalized following a heart attack, brought on by his attempt to rescue his granddaughter during a boating accident. Back in Brewer, Harry undergoes angioplasty to clear his coronary arteries, refusing a needed bypass operation. He is attended at the hospital by a young nurse who proves to be the daughter of his former mistress. The thought that the nurse may be his daughter intrigues him, but he chooses not to pursue it.

Harry's physical concerns intensify his sense of mortality. In addition, his and his wife's peace and prosperity are threatened by their discovery that Nelson, who has been managing the family Toyota franchise, has been embezzling from the business to support a cocaine habit. Although Nelson eventually agrees to enter an addiction-treatment program and Harry returns from Florida to straighten things out, the corporation withdraws its franchise. Its Japanese representative trenchantly censures the American people for lack of discipline, Nelson for his immaturity, and Harry for inept parenting. A corollary to this outcome is that the protagonist constantly finds himself at odds with both his wife and his son, who take defensive positions on the matter of Nelson's perfidy and find ways to blame Harry for it. Nelson refuses responsibility for what he has done to the family business. Janice, unwisely ignoring evidence of her son's shiftiness, lets him remain in charge of the dealership until it is too late. Ensuing financial constraints pressure Harry and his wife to share a house with their son and his family. Harry's family unconsciously prepares itself to survive him, his wife and son making decisions about the family business that leave him out. Janice enrolls in real estate courses and emerges as energetically businesslike. Harry admires this but notices that she occasionally talks about him in the past tense.

Throughout the story, Harry is seen as a receptor of cultural and historical changes and events. References abound to the television sitcoms Harry watches and the news events he observes through broadcast media. Impressed by the limitless information offered by the media, he muses on news of China, ozone depletion, Panamanian leader Manuel Noriega, and the beginning of the fall of Communism; he becomes somewhat obsessed with such death-dealing events as the Lockerbie air disaster and the demise of television personalities. Thoughts of mortality pervade Harry's thinking. While still recuperating from surgery, Harry has a premonition of death while visiting an adoring former lover, Thelma Harrison, who is dying of lupus. As is true for other women with whom he has been involved, he is incapable of feeling deep affection for Thelma. He is later accurately accused of this when encountered by her husband as she lies close to death in a hospital.

In the penultimate portion of the novel, a depressed and demoralized Harry finds himself left alone one evening with Pru, his equally depressed daughter-in-law. Harry characteristically obeys his instincts, and the two end up in bed. When Janice finds out and angrily demands that her husband confront the family, he flees to his Florida condominium. His reaction is surprise at his wife's anger rather than shame. His family does not pursue him, and he maintains a lonely existence, eventually suffering a terminal stroke while playing basketball with a boy whom he does not know. Lying in a Florida hospital, unable to communicate with his family when they arrive, Harry dies at the age of fifty-six, never having taken control of his life.

The Characters

Owing something to the schlemiel of the Jewish tradition as well as to the stereotype of the American boy athlete, Harry "Rabbit" Angstrom remains, throughout his questionable adventures, one of the more credible and memorable main characters in recent American letters.

Although confronted with failure, death, and destruction, in part as a result of his own weaknesses, Harry Angstrom retains throughout his life the deep if inarticulate religious faith that evokes the interest of Father Eccles in the chronicle's first volume. Moderate to abstemious in his approach to liquor and tobacco, owing perhaps to his early indoctrination as an athlete, Harry is nevertheless doubly obsessed with sex and with religion from adolescence onward, his sexual fantasies often merging with the solid bedrock of his unquestioning belief to produce a peculiar, honest obstinacy. Harry can rarely look at a woman without disrobing her in his mind's eye (or in fact), yet he endures his tribulations with the patience and prescience of a modern Job, as unquestioning of his sufferings as he is of his belief in an underlying principle of order.

To Updike's credit, the character of Harry Angstrom remains consistent throughout the sequence, developing slowly but plausibly as Harry passes from his twenties into his fifties. From volume to volume, the author presents Harry from an angle of compassionate detachment, his restrained irony suggesting that Harry is to be viewed as representative rather than exemplary: Harry may learn from his mistakes, but he never seems to learn quite enough. He remains oddly insensitive to the needs of those around him, even as his experiences should have taught him otherwise.

Among the greater, no doubt intentional, mysteries surrounding Harry Angstrom is his continued attachment to Janice. Although described in physical detail, further revealed through her speech and actions, Janice remains a shadowy figure, more of an enigma to the reader than she apparently is to Harry. At the end of *Rabbit, Run*, Jack Eccles's wife suggests to her husband that perhaps the Angstroms would be better off divorced; her suggestion, although it goes unheeded, continues to reverberate through succeeding volumes of the sequence. Janice, to be sure, is at least the partial cause of Harry's major problems; self-centered and shallow, she never appears to accept her responsibilities toward Harry, nor does she appear deserving of his continued allegiance and support. Apart from a certain physical attraction, intermittently short-circuited by Janice herself, there seems little enough reason for Harry not to leave her. In *Rabbit Is Rich*, however, the union is at last "explained" by economic self-interest, as Janice and Harry are shown as co-conspirators against the competition of other auto dealers.

Of the two "other women" in Harry's life, Ruth Leonard is perhaps the more memorable, although it is Jill Pendleton whose early death will cast the stronger shadow. Ruth, although no older than Harry, serves him as a kind of mother figure, strong and commonsensical, with few illusions. The waiflike Jill at first appears to be a stereotypical "flower child," on the run from her comfortable bourgeois surroundings. With Harry, however, she seems about to emerge from stereotype when her life is cut short by the house fire.

Similarly, the angry young militant Skeeter, Jill's fellow "houseguest" in *Rabbit Redux*, gradually emerges from stereotype to stand as one of Updike's more masterful and memorable creations. Restless, intelligent, possessed of manic vital energy, Skeeter reaches into Harry's consciousness at a level achieved by few other characters in the sequence: In thus affecting Harry, he also affects the reader, giving tangible form and shape to the prospect of world revolution.

Like John O'Hara before him, Updike derives no small part of his total effect from the skillful evocation of rural Pennsylvania and its ethnic types, particularly those of German extraction. Janice's parents and even Harry's, despite the Scandinavian surname, provide strong local color with their attitudes and accents. Peggy Gring Fosnacht, a former schoolmate of Harry who later becomes Janice's friend and would like to be Harry's mistress, is likewise a recognizable regional type, as is Charlie Stavros, the Greek-American car salesman whom Janice takes as her lover. Throughout the sequence, Updike's portrayal of such characters is generally compassionate and free of condescension, aimed toward authenticity rather than toward satire.

Indeed, given the tone and scope of the Rabbit Angstrom novels, the satirical tone is surprisingly restrained throughout, with few characters presented in broad caricature. A notable exception, however, is Updike's portrayal of the two Episcopal clergymen who appear in the story. Both, in different ways and for different reasons, turn out to be remarkably ineffective in their chosen mission: Jack Eccles, for all his earnestness, has clearly lost the support of his wife, Lucy, who somewhat reluctantly finds herself attracted to the errant Harry Angstrom. After the death of little Rebecca, Lucy will go so far as to blame her husband for his mismanagement of the situation. Jack's eventual successor, Archie Campbell, called in to officiate at Nelson's wedding, is drawn even closer to caricature, an apparent homosexual given to self-parody in speech, gestures, and attire. Implicitly, both portraits tend to highlight the authenticity of Harry's understated, even touching, religious faith, suggesting that the Almighty might indeed be better served by the laity than by the clergy.

Themes and Meanings

Taken together, the Rabbit Angstrom novels provide, at the most literal level, a highly accurate and entertaining record of United States history during the years of Harry Angstrom's life. It is perhaps no accident that Harry was born during the same month that saw Franklin D. Roosevelt inaugurated as president of the United States. Harry's childhood and young manhood are closely linked to political events of the time; as he ages, such events begin to take on greater significance, suggesting that Harry is, at least in part, the product of historical forces that he himself perceives only barely, if at all. Although Harry's politics are conservative, it is clear from the outset that the author's are not; the ensuing counterpoint sharpens Updike's social observation to a keen edge, leaving for future generations of readers an unforgettable record of American society in transition.

Like O'Hara before him, Updike is also a keen observer of sexual mores, not excluding sexual activity and practice, described in full detail. By 1960, however, the American reading public was in general more receptive to such description, sparing Updike's work the expressions of shock and outrage that had greeted O'Hara's novels a decade or so earlier. In the case of Harry Angstrom, the prevalence of sexual activity is amply prepared for and justified by character; given Harry's limitations, sex is both an understandable preoccupation and a natural, even logical form of personal expression.

Harry's childlike religious faith, closely related at times to his sexual preoccupation, is deeply embedded in the substructure of all three novels. Updike is careful never to present Harry as a saint, nor to suggest that he is somehow "better" than other mortals: Harry's faith is simply another of his personal characteristics, along with his height and hair color; it does not prevent him from acting stupidly, nor does it afford him any special insight into human character. At the very least, however, it allows him to endure such shocks as the deaths of baby Rebecca and Jill Pendleton, and possibly even to prevail.

Critical Context

With the publication of *Rabbit Is Rich* in 1981, Harry Angstrom emerged at last as Updike's most enduring and memorable fictional creation. Updike's novels exhibit an enormous range, but the success of the third Rabbit novel, consistently on pitch, suggested to some critics that he is at his best when practicing the domestic realism that has also distinguished his finest short stories.

After the death of O'Hara in 1970, Updike remained perhaps the only committed chronicler of small-town America, notable like O'Hara for his short stories as well as for his novels. With Updike, however, the social chronicle gained an added dimension absent from the works of O'Hara, as from those of Sinclair Lewis before him. Updike, an accomplished poet and essayist as well, is a more conscious stylist than either of his predecessors, applying to the social chronicle the technique and polish of elevated literary art. The Rabbit Angstrom novels, in particular, are as notable for the way in which they are told as for the story which they tell.

Bibliography
Boswell, Marshall. "The Black Jesus: Racism and Redemption in John Updike's *Rabbit Redux.*" *Contemporary Literature* 39 (Spring, 1998): 99-133. Boswell explores the ramifications of race in Updike's *Rabbit Redux*. He argues that, in spite of the ambiguity of Updike's portrayal, the novel does make a significant contribution to the continuing discussion about race in America.

DeBellis, Jack. "'The Aweful Power': John Updike's Use of Kubrick's *2001: A Space Odyssey* in *Rabbit Redux.*" *Literature and Film Quarterly* 21 (July, 1993): 209-217. DeBellis argues that Updike often incorporates allusions in his novels that refer or comment upon specific traits in his characters. In the case of *Rabbit Redux*, Updike relates the quest theme in the novel to the developing personality traits of Janice and Harry.

Schiff, James A. *John Updike Revisited.* New York: Twayne, 1998. Schiff endeavors to understand Updike's entire body of work, putting individual works in context for the reader. Schiff provides commentary on works that have largely been ignored by the public, as well as books that have received little critical attention. Includes a critical analysis of the Rabbit Angstrom novels.

Updike, John, and James Plath, ed. *Conversations with John Updike.* Jackson: University Press of Mississippi, 1994. A collection of interviews given by Updike between 1959 and 1993. A revealing portrait of Updike's background and personality; his views on life, sex, politics, and religion; and his evolution as a writer.

David B. Parsell

RAGTIME

Author: E. L. Doctorow (1931-   )
Type of plot: Historical fiction
Time of plot: The early twentieth century, from 1906 to approximately 1915
Locale: New York, Massachusetts, Philadelphia, Egypt, Mexico, Alaska, and Germany
First published: 1975

> *Principal characters:*
> LITTLE BOY, the narrator
> FATHER, a manufacturer of fireworks and flags, an amateur explorer, and the narrator's father
> MOTHER, the narrator's mother
> MOTHER'S YOUNGER BROTHER, an inventor of fireworks, bombs, and grenades
> TATEH (BARON ASHKENAZY), a pioneer filmmaker
> THE LITTLE GIRL, Tateh's daughter
> SARAH, the mother of an illegitimate baby and a housemaid
> COALHOUSE WALKER, JR., Sarah's lover and the father of her child, a ragtime pianist and murderer

The Novel

Ragtime chronicles the lives of three families: a white Anglo-Saxon Protestant (WASP) family (composed of the narrator when he is a young boy, Mother, Father, Mother's Younger Brother, and Grandfather); a black family (Sarah, Coalhouse Walker, Jr., and their illegitimate infant); and an immigrant family (Tateh, Mameh, and The Little Girl). At the beginning of the novel these families' existences are entirely segregated from one another, but by the story's end the three families have become one in a uniquely American type of ethnic heterogeneity.

It is significant that the story begins from an exclusively WASP perspective, told in retrospect by the Little Boy grown to manhood. This perspective, the reader is meant to understand, was America's in the early years of the twentieth century, when Teddy Roosevelt was president and when "Everyone wore white in summer." It is an ideal (and idealized) period, when there "was a lot of sexual fainting. There were no Negroes. There were no immigrants." In such an America, everyone was presumed to be patriotic, for "patriotism was a reliable sentiment in the early 1900's." Father is the model patriot as a maker of flags, buntings, and fireworks; his family is supposed to be a model American family. This, at least, is the status quo when Father, an amateur explorer, leaves with Robert Peary on his third (and ultimately successful) expedition to discover the North Pole. It is 1906, and Father will take part in the actual discovery in 1909. While Father is away, however, his WASP family undergoes a surprising change, only the first of several Americanizing changes he and his family will experience. Mother is the catalyst for this first change.

Mother, a stereotypically Victorian creature with whom Father has always had to make appointments to make love, finds an abandoned black infant half-buried but still alive in her flower garden, then takes the child and its young mother, Sarah (after she is found by the police), into her home as her responsibility. Not only does she take on this responsibility, but also she assumes all the executive responsibilities of Father's business, so that upon his return he discovers that she can "speak crisply of such matters as unit cost, inventory and advertising," and she has expanded the company's sales into California and Oregon. Not the least of the changes that Mother has undergone concerns her reading: She now reads feminist and socialist literature, for example. Father, because he fornicated with Eskimo women while in the Arctic, assumes that the changes in his wife and home are God's "punishments." Another such punishment is that some of his employees have become union members.

Father's home and business are also changed, through Mother's Younger Brother, who lives in the home and works in the business. Having fallen obsessively in love with Evelyn Nesbit (the wife of Harry K. Thaw and lover of Stanford White until Thaw assassinates him), Mother's Younger Brother succeeds in wooing Evelyn for a short time, and as he is doing so he meets and becomes a follower of Emma Goldman, the political radical and revolutionary unionizer. It is through Mother's Younger Brother, in fact, that Father's family is initially (albeit peripherally) connected to the immigrant family of Tateh, Mameh, and The Young Girl—and it is through both Mother and her brother that the WASP family is infiltrated by Emma Goldman: Mother is reading one of Goldman's pamphlets when Father returns from his expedition, his employees are unionizing, and Mother's Younger Brother has already become a political radical. (He will ultimately become a revolutionary who dies in Mexico while fighting for Emiliano Zapata.)

While the life of the WASP family is complicated by Mother's discovery and harboring of the black infant and Sarah, the second story line of the novel is revealed. The third member of this black family is Sarah's former lover, the father of her child, Coalhouse Walker, Jr., a ragtime pianist. Several months after Father's return from the Arctic, Walker drives up to the family's house in a shiny new Model T Ford car; he asks to see Sarah but, by her request, is refused the visit. This happens on a Sunday. On several Sundays thereafter, Walker visits the home, plays the piano for the family, and gradually breaks down Sarah's resistance; they become engaged to be married. Walker becomes a victim of violent racism, however, and after futilely seeking retributive justice from the law—and after Sarah is killed when attempting to approach the vice president of the United States to beg him to help her fiance receive justice—Walker seeks vengeance on his own terms and kills several of the men who victimized him. While he is being hunted, Walker attracts a few young black followers who become (unlike their leader, who is concerned only with retaliation for the injustice done to him personally) fierce revolutionaries fighting for the rights of all blacks. Significantly, one of Walker's armed "soldiers" is Mother's Younger Brother, filled with the self-consuming desire to fight for the downtrodden, a desire fueled by his association with Goldman and expressed through his creation of grenades and bombs.

He transforms Father's patriotic fireworks into weapons for a different kind of patriotism—revolution. Ultimately, Walker is executed and Mother's Younger Brother escapes to Mexico; Sarah and Walker's infant (christened Coalhouse Walker III) becomes the adopted child of Father and Mother.

While the black family's story is directly linked to that of the WASP family from the moment that Mother discovers the infant in her garden, the immigrant family's story develops separately from that of the other two families throughout most of *Ragtime*. Like those immigrants whom Doctorow's narrator describes as setting "great store by the American flag," Tateh, Mameh, and The Little Girl come to America to realize the American dream of comfort, prosperity, and freedom from repression. Instead they find abject poverty in New York. Mameh and The Little Girl sew pants, for seventy cents a dozen, every day, from the time they get up to the time they go to bed, and Tateh sells his paper silhouettes on the streets. Their labor proves insufficient for their survival, their rent becomes delinquent, Mameh reluctantly sells her body for money, and Tateh—banishing his wife from the family because he views her as a whore—sets out with The Little Girl to find a secure home and an escape "from the fate of the working class." They move from New York to Massachusetts to Philadelphia, and it is in the last-named city that Tateh sells his invention ("movie books") and signs a contract for future productions of his creations.

When Father, Mother, and the Little Boy meet Tateh and The Little Girl, it is in Atlantic City, where both families are vacationing (just days before Coalhouse Walker is killed). Tateh has by this time changed his name to Baron Ashkenazy, and he has become a very wealthy entrepreneur in the nascent motion picture business. By the time of the two families' meeting, furthermore, Mother has become disillusioned and bored with Father and their marriage, and while she keeps her attraction to Ashkenazy hidden, the reader is made aware of it. Thus it comes as no surprise when, after Father is killed on the Lusitania in 1915, Mother marries Ashkenazy and they move to California. Together, then, they create the "new" American family: Jewish father and daughter, WASP mother and son, and black son. Moreover, it is his interracial family that gives Ashkenazy "an idea for a film" about "a society of ragmuffins, like all of us, a gang, getting into trouble and getting out again." The film will be *Our Gang*, as uniquely American as Doctorow's novel itself.

The Characters

While Doctorow's characters are usually memorable, they are also frequently unbelievable. Derived as they seem to be from a preconceived idea about both what America is and how the author wants to portray it, the characters often seem to be primarily embodiments of various positions in a dialectic. Indeed, Doctorow—called an ideologue by some critics—is a Shavian novelist, developing his fiction the way George Bernard Shaw developed his dramas: Thesis versus antithesis equals synthesis.

Father's exclusively WASP view of America is the ethnocentric and theocentric thesis that Doctorow gives his reader in the first few pages of *Ragtime*. In the Shavian, dialectical approach to fictionalizing, the thesis is presented as a straw man of sorts, inevitably broken down or subsumed by its dialectical opposite, the antithesis. Thus, even though Father remains a character in the story until near the end, his usefulness for the underpinning dialectical tension is exhausted much earlier in the story, and in direct proportion to the increased ascendency of his antithesis. In *Ragtime*, however, the antithesis is two-pronged, for it consists of both Coalhouse Walker's family and Tateh's family, and, significantly, parts of both are combined permanently with Father's family after he has been killed. In short, with Father's complete removal from the story, the dialectical synthesis is realized.

Coalhouse Walker provides an excellent example of how an initially complex and engaging character may be (subject as he is to his creator's intellectual and artistic determinism) reduced to little more than a static puppet with limited purpose. Although it might be argued that Doctorow is attempting to portray mimetically the kinds of limitations that have been traditionally imposed upon blacks by America, such an argument is undercut by Walker's demeanor and his own high self-esteem. For example, he annoys Father because it seems that he "didn't know he was a Negro. . . . Walker didn't act or talk like a colored man." Indeed, Walker refuses to accept the social role assigned to him by an essentially WASP-dominated society, and his sense of his own dignity precludes his expression of any type of deference expected of him because of his skin color. When several white thugs mentally abuse him, and then go several steps further by destroying his new automobile, Walker's hunger for justice—unfed by America's pro-white legal system—becomes an unassuageable passion for vengeance. Significantly, it is not because Sarah is killed that Walker decides to (and does) kill several people; it is, rather, because he wants his automobile restored to its original condition and returned to him. Hence, while Doctorow draws Walker as a dignified individual and very talented pianist early in the story, he eventually reduces him to a materialistic and monomaniacal madman, willing to sacrifice any and all lives (including his own) for the gleaming cleanness of a new machine.

Yet to say only this is unfair to Doctorow and those characters he succeeds in drawing deeply and completely. Mother and Tateh are two of the most successfully rendered of these characters. While Mother is initially portrayed as a flat character, frigidly Victorian and devoid of any genuinely authentic personality traits, she undergoes a remarkable transformation after the humanizing experience of discovering the abandoned baby in her garden. She becomes thereafter a new woman, a prototypical feminist, as she begins to read intellectual literature and grows to be quite comfortable with her sexuality by the time Father returns from the Arctic. Indeed, he finds her "not as vigorously modest as she'd been. . . . She came to bed with her hair unbraided." Even so, Mother's initial flatness of character may itself seem, to some readers, a rather obvious technique employed by Doctorow so that any change in her character will be artistically easy to accomplish, and, moreover, her later roundness and depth will stand out as remarkable when compared to her earlier stasis.

Tateh is a different matter. Initially proud of being a member of the working class, Tateh suffers immeasurable hardships, the worst of which is his wife's betrayal of him when she reluctantly sells her body for rent money. The situation is more complex than Tateh's denunciation of Mameh would lead one to believe, but his essentially two-valued orientation to the world (as well as his male ego) precludes any forgiveness of her. Nevertheless, Tateh's consequent obsession over saving his daughter from poverty-derived corruption is both poignantly believable and admirable. Likewise, after being beaten and almost losing his daughter to strangers, when Tateh defiantly lifts his head, abandons what he has come to view as an unworkable, essentially socialistic ideology, and then embraces capitalism, his transformation is lifelike and complex: "Tateh began to conceive of his life as separate from the fate of the working class. I hate machines, he said to his daughter." (Yet, his artistic creations depend upon "machines" for mass-marketing, for their success and his.) Nevertheless, though he becomes a "Count" nominally, his working-class origins are reaffirmed by the heterogeneous family he comes to call his own.

Themes and Meanings

The principal theme of *Ragtime* is summed up in Doctorow's description of novelist Theodore Dreiser, who, "suffering terribly from the bad reviews and negligible sales of his first book, *Sister Carrie*, took to sitting on a wooden chair in the middle of [his] room. One day he decided his chair was facing in the wrong direction." He turns the chair several times to the right "to align it properly," but each time he stops and tries to sit in the chair, "it still felt peculiar. . . . Eventually he made a complete circle and still could not find the proper alignment for the chair. . . . Through the night Dreiser turned his chair in circles seeking the proper alignment." Doctorow makes it clear in *Ragtime*, through his portrayal of both fictional characters and actual historical personages, interwoven throughout the story, that America is a country shaped physically and psychologically by people searching obsessively for "the proper alignment," which might better be thought of as a sure and satisfactory sense of place and belonging in the world and the universe. Besides Dreiser, two other actual historical figures whom Doctorow uses to illustrate his theme further are Robert Peary and John Pierpont Morgan.

While Dreiser's futile search for the proper alignment is enacted in a rented room where he finds himself in a nadir of self-doubt and depression, Peary's "lifetime of effort" is to find the exact center of the top of the world; yet, although the boundaries of Peary's search are incomparably wider than Dreiser's in his room, Doctorow describes the Arctic explorer's ultimate predicament as exactly the same as the writer's, as far as a proper alignment is concerned. Having arrived in the general area where he believes the North Pole to be, Peary struggles to find the exact spot of the axis of rotation. Lying on his stomach, he calculates his position but is not satisfied; he walks farther along the floe and takes another sighting, but still he is not satisfied: "All day long Peary shuffled back and forth over the ice, a mile one way, two miles another, and made his observations. No one observation satisfied him. . . . He couldn't find the exact place to say this spot, here, is the North Pole. Nevertheless there was no question that they were there." Doctorow makes it clear that there is, in fact, some "question," but the negation of such by Peary exemplifies the extent to which the human ego and need for identity can supersede scientific exactness. Indeed, scientific exactitude itself is called into question in this instance when the narrator notes: "On this watery planet the sliding sea refused to be fixed."

Whereas Dreiser's central focus, expressed through naturalistic fiction, was on the urban American society and the individual's place therein, and whereas Peary's was on his being in a central, geographical position on the earth's globe, Morgan's questing focus is on his place in the eternal universe. Believing that "there are universal patterns of order and repetition that give meaning to the activity of this planet," Morgan (a financier and symbol of monopolistic capitalism) believes that he is the reincarnation of a great Pharoah and the incarnation of "secret wisdom," which he views as an "eternal beneficent force" available only to a select and superior few. He travels to the Great Pyramid of Giza and decides to spend one night in the "heart" of the monument (he wants "to feel in advance the eternal energies he would exemplify when he died and rose . . . to be born again," and he hopes to learn "the disposition" of his soul and physical vitality in the universal patterns). Unfortunately, Morgan's quest for a sure sense of his place in the universe is futile, for during his nocturnal vigil in the pyramid he is bitten by bedbugs and resorts to pacing the great center chamber: "He paced from west to east, from the north to the south, though he didn't know which was which."

With Dreiser, Peary, and Morgan (paradigms of superior achievements in the realms of art, natural science, and economics, respectively), Doctorow draws a bleak—albeit witty—portrait of the human quest for a definite sense of place and purpose in the universe, a quest that he views as absurd and futile as long as the goal of the quest is sought in the material world rather than within the searching individual.

Critical Context

Unquestionably Doctorow's most popular novel, made into a film in 1981 and an award-winning Broadway musical in the late 1990's, *Ragtime* is one more expression of its author's satiric attempt to re-create American history and thereby create imaginative truth in place of dry, historical facts. Indeed, his fiction is deeply embedded in history, and most of his novels have dealt with a significant time in America's past: *Welcome to Hard Times* (1960) portrays the settling of the West; *The Book of Daniel* (1971) exposes the American heritage of political radicalism and repression, specifically as it is manifested in the postwar era; *Ragtime* chronicles the metamorphosis of American life at the beginning of the twentieth century; *Loon Lake* (1980) describes the traumatic repercussions suffered by Americans as a result of the Great Depression; and *World's Fair* re-creates the 1930's from another angle of vision.

As might be expected, all of Doctorow's fiction is political insofar as he portrays time and again the dichotomy that exists between how America is supposed to be ideally and the way it is actually. Yet the conflict between these two Americas is never resolved in his fiction; instead, in Doctorow's novels America is like the floe-hidden sea on which Peary searches for the North Pole in *Ragtime*: It is in perpetual flux and resists being "fixed." At one point in *The Book of Daniel*, the narrator observes: "Of one thing we are sure. Everything is elusive. God is elusive. Revolutionary morality is elusive. Justice is elusive. Human character." Doctorow makes it quite clear in *Ragtime*, as in his other novels, that America—as it is defined in the Constitution—is itself elusive.

Bibliography
Fowler, Douglas. *Understanding E. L. Doctorow.* Columbia: University of South Carolina Press, 1992. Provides criticism and interpretation of Doctorow's works.
Garrison, David. "Ovid's *Metamorphoses* in E. L. Doctorow's *Ragtime.*" *Classical and Modern Literature: A Quarterly* 17 (Winter, 1997): 103-115. Garrison asserts that classical myths from Ovid are elaborated in *Ragtime*. These allusions to Ovid create an ironic tone and exhibit a deep interest in transformation, thus *Ragtime* continues a tradition that began with Ovid.
Harter, Carol C., and James R. Thompson. *E. L. Doctorow.* Boston: Twayne, 1990. A study of Doctorow's major fiction up to *World's Fair*. Contains a chronology, a chapter on his biography, separate chapters on the novels, notes and references, and a selected bibliography. A succinct introductory study.
Levine, Paul. *E. L. Doctorow.* New York: Methuen, 1985. The first full-length study of the novelist's career. Levine provides sound and often insightful readings of individual novels as well as substantial discussions of the recurring themes in the fiction: politics, the nature of fiction and history, and Doctorow's critique of the American Dream. A useful bibliography and a discussion of film adaptations of Doctorow's work make this a comprehensive study.
Persell, Michelle. "The Jews, *Ragtime* and the Politics of Science." *Literature and Psychology* 42 (Fall, 1996): 1-14. A discussion of *Ragtime* as an allegory related to Francois Lyotard's notion of "the jews" as a term for the unrepresentable. Persell analyzes the assimilation of the character Tateh who suppresses his Jewishness.
Williams, John. *Fiction as False Document: The Reception of E. L. Doctorow in the Postmodern Age.* Columbia, S.C.: Camden House, 1992. A survey of Doctorow's works with a focus on the author as a postmodern cultural critic. Williams presents a chapter-length discussion of *Ragtime* as a historical novel.

David A. Carpenter

REBELLION IN THE BACKLANDS

Author: Euclides da Cunha (1866-1909)
Type of plot: Factual historical chronicle
Time of plot: The 1870's through the 1890's, especially October, 1896, to October, 1897
Locale: The backlands (*os sertões*) of Northeast Brazil, centered in Bahia state, especially in and around the town of Canudos
First published: Os sertões, 1902 (English translation, 1944)

    Principal characters:
        ANTONIO VICENTE MENDES MACIEL, "Antonio Conselheiro," a fanatic religious leader of the backlands rebellion
        PAJEHÚ, a guerrilla leader of the *sertanejos*, rustic, tough, mixed-race inhabitants of the backlands
        LIEUTENANT MANUEL DA SILVA PIRES FERREIRA, the leader of the government's doomed first expedition
        MAJOR FEBRONIO DE BRITO, the leader of the government's doomed second expedition
        COLONEL ANTONIO MOREIRA CESAR, the leader of the government's doomed third expedition
        GENERAL ARTHUR OSCAR DE ANDRADE GUIMARÃES, the leader of the government's fourth expedition
        GENERAL CLAUDIO DO AMARAL SAVAGET, the leader of the second column of the fourth expedition
        MARSHAL CARLOS MACHADO DE BITTENCOURT, the war minister and eventual commander of the fourth expedition

The Novel

    Rebellion in the Backlands is not fiction but rather a factual account of an actual historical event. The event—a rebellion led by a charismatic religious fanatic against the federal government of Brazil—might have sunk into obscurity but for Cunha's account, which does not merely report the event but also defines and interprets its significance. As a result, *Rebellion in the Backlands* has been called Brazil's national epic, and its influence on Brazilian fiction—indeed, South American fiction—has been substantial. The work itself, with its plot buildup, might be said to anticipate the so-called nonfiction novel of later decades.

    Cunha does not, however, begin with plot but with extensive essays on the land and the people of the backlands region. Taking up approximately one third of the book and covering geography, geology, rainfall, flora and fauna, race, ethnology, psychology, and other subjects, these two long essays are burdened by outdated nineteenth century theories of environmental influence and race. Cunha draws a daunting picture of the hot, rugged, semidesert *sertão*, periodically stricken by killing droughts, and speculates that the *sertanejo*'s personality has been formed by this harsh environment and by his mixed racial heritage (white, black, and Indian). Whereas the admixture of "superior" and "inferior" racial stocks (as Cunha expresses it) has resulted in universal "degeneration" along the Brazilian seaboard, the *sertanejo*, through isolation in his primitive backlands environment, has become "a retrograde, not a degenerate, type." He is physically robust but morally backward. The *sertanejo*'s atavistic tendencies are superbly represented by his undying devotion to the religious fanatic Antonio Conselheiro, himself a spiritualized version of the backlands mentality. In the *sertanejo*'s simple view, "Anthony the Counselor" is a backlands saint.

These long introductory essays serve to romanticize the subject matter, to set the stage for the narrative of the rebellion. The introductions make clear that the underlying causes of the conflict are cultural differences between the isolated backlands and the developed seaboard. These cultural differences first cause religious friction between the established Catholic Church and Antonio Conselheiro. Later, the Counselor begins preaching against the recently established Brazilian Republic (proclaimed in 1889), whose new taxes and new laws regarding civil marriage and the like offend him. The Counselor's idea of proper government is a vague theocracy, ruled by the law of God rather than civil law. He and his followers label the republic an Antichrist, call its laws "the law of the hound," and rip down its tax notices.

In 1893, a contingent of thirty Bahian policemen comes after the Counselor for preaching insurrection. They catch up with him in Massete, where his band routs them in a shoot-out. Another contingent of eighty soldiers turns back when the Counselor fades into the forbidding backlands. The die now cast, Antonio Conselheiro and his followers withdraw to distant, inaccessible Canudos, where they establish their theocracy and military stronghold. Actually, it is a fairly inadequate theocracy, since the motley backlands population rallying to Canudos includes not only thousands of the religiously devout but also hordes of bandits, who raid the surrounding countryside. Despite such depredations and the Counselor's growing power, the government leaves Canudos alone until October, 1896, when a trivial incident—a dispute between the Counselor and the Joazeiro magistrate over a load of lumber—precipitates the military phase of the rebellion.

With the Counselor's forces threatening to attack Joazeiro, the town's magistrate wires for help from the Bahian governor, who dispatches one hundred troops under Lieutenant Manuel da Silva Pires Ferreira to put down the nuisance. This ridiculous expedition arrives in Joazeiro, sets out for Canudos, and, after marching for days through the backlands heat, encounters perhaps thousands of the Counselor's *jagunços* at Uauá. The encounter is fierce and swift, and the surviving troops escape only because the *jagunços* do not pursue.

The government immediately begins organizing a second expedition, involving more federal troops and artillery. After some organizational delays, the second expedition of 560 men, led by Major Febronio de Brito, sets out for Canudos from Monte Santo. Again, there are days of marching through the torrid heat, this time with the *jagunços*, from the cover of the roadside *caatinga* (tangled scrub forest), sniping and making running attacks on the advancing column. The expedition's provisions give out just as, somewhat demoralized and depleted, it arrives in the vicinity of Canudos. Outside Canudos it runs into an ambush and, the following morning, a full-scale enemy attack. Forced to retreat, to the jeers of the surrounding *jagunços*, the expedition has to fight its way back along the same roads by which it fought its way in. A herd of wild goats frightened into its path proves to be a handy source of food for the men, but of troops arriving back in Monte Santo, not a single one is able-bodied.

Sterner government measures to quell rebels are called for, as well as a forceful leader. The man of the moment is Colonel Antonio Moreira Cesar, a ruthless hero of the Republican wars, whose fame is guaranteed to strike fear into the hearts of the *jagunços*. He is called up from the South to head the third expedition, consisting of thirteen hundred men with artillery.

Colonel Moreira Cesar's aggressive tactics live up to his reputation. From Monte Santo to Canudos, he leads a series of long forced marches through the backlands heat; as a result, his troops arrive quickly and relatively intact, but exhausted. The colonel decides to storm Canudos immediately, sending columns of his troops charging across the dried riverbed into town and expecting to rout the quivering *jagunços*. The results, however, are not as encouraging as expected: The troops who survive the enemy fire can be seen spreading out and disappearing down the narrow alleyways and into the wood-and-mud huts. As the attacking troops continue to be absorbed, Colonel Moreira Cesar decides to lead an inspiring cavalry charge. He himself is shot down, however, and the command falls to timid Colonel Tamarindo. Amid the mounting confusion and faltering attack, Colonel Tamarindo consults with his fellow officers, who decide on a retreat the next day. The planned retreat becomes a panic as the *jagunços* turn and pursue the fleeing troops, who abandon their equipment and wounded along the road. The *jagunços* line the roadsides with soldiers' heads and hang the decapitated corpse of Colonel Tamarindo from a bush to dry and blow in the wind.

Stunned by the defeat, the whole nation panics, with rumors flying of a Monarchist conspiracy behind the backlands revolt. The Republic calls for full mobilization of its military resources, which prove to be embarrassingly limited, but within three months a fourth expedition, commanded by General Arthur Oscar de Andrade Guimarães, is organized. The expedition divides into two columns: The first column, consisting of 1,933 men under General Arthur Oscar, leaves from Monte Santo, while a second column, of 2,350 men under General Claudio do Amaral Savaget, departs from Geremoabo. The second column must fight its way to Canudos, but it arrives in time to rescue the first column, pinned down on the town's outskirts. After the columns link up, a state of siege begins, though sometimes it is difficult to tell who is besieging whom. Since the army has a foothold only on one side of Canudos, the town has easy access to supplies, while the army has trouble getting its supplies through. Meanwhile, the army's casualties are horrendous.

Seeing the supply problem, Marshal Carlos Machado de Bittencourt, the war minister, steps in at this point and takes charge of the situation. He buys one thousand mules, sets up regular supply trains, and sends in troop reinforcements. Saved by mules, the army begins asserting itself: Through various forays and attacks, it extends its line further into and around Canudos, eventually surrounding the city. After that, Canudos is doomed, though the *jagunços* continue to resist strongly and to inflict heavy casualties. The army's artillery bombards the city, starting extensive fires, but somehow the huts absorb the cannonballs and shrapnel. When the army tightens its circle, it must stop the bombardments to avoid endangering its own troops. The center of Canudos resistance must then be taken by close fighting, including hand-to-hand combat. The army tries dynamite bombs briefly, but their effects on the civilian population are so heartrending that, even in this vicious war, they are discontinued. Only one truce is called, to allow some two hundred women, children, and old men to surrender. The remaining defenders of Canudos die to the last man, conveniently falling back into a mass grave that had earlier been dug.

The Characters

The historical personages of *Rebellion in the Backlands* are not developed or viewed from inside as are characters in a novel. Cunha often gives only their names, and even then he shows an aristocratic bias by naming only officers or leaders: The troops and common folk remain anonymous. The most prominent leaders, however, are accorded elaborate analytical introductions.

Cunha devotes his most complete analysis to Antonio Conselheiro, whom he views as a perfect embodiment of the backlands mentality. Coming from a powerful family previously involved in a bloody feud with a rival family, Antonio Maciel seems born to the pattern of violence endemic to the lawless backlands. Yet the crucial event of his life is a personal blow: When he is a young man, his wife deserts him for a policeman, which seems to leave Antonio Maciel permanently deranged. He begins wandering the backlands roads, eventually adopting the life and appearance (flowing beard, blue tunic, and staff) of an early Christian ascetic. Impressionable and superstitious, the backlands population soon accepts him as Antonio Conselheiro, whose confused message is heard as the wisdom of God. The power which this following gives him makes the Counselor a walking time bomb whose fuse is only shortened by religious and civil persecutions. Primarily important as the rebellion's instigator, the Counselor gradually fades into the background, dying during Canudos' last days either from dysentery or from deliberate starvation.

Among the army's commanders, only Colonel Moreira Cesar and Marshal Bittencourt get full-scale introductions. The heroic Colonel Moreira Cesar is notable for his incongruous physical appearance (reminiscent of a squat, froglike Napoleon) and for his epileptic seizures, a few of which interrupt the forced marches to Canudos. Cunha suggests that the progressive disease is eroding the colonel's mental faculties, which might help account for his overly zealous tactics. Contrasting with Colonel Moreira Cesar is Marshal Bittencourt, a plodding bureaucrat whose dullness superbly equips him to manage the logistics of mule trains, supplies, and reinforcements. Also contrasting with Colonel Moreira Cesar is his understudy, Colonel

Tamarindo, who stands out despite not receiving a full introduction: Nearing sixty and anticipating a peaceful retirement, he instead loses his head and is hung out to dry.

A number of unnamed *sertanejos* are also memorable, mainly for their toughness—a young boy already hardened in violence, a dried-up old grandmother looking after her wounded grandchild, an old man still fighting even though too weak to lift his gun, the set of dirt-encrusted prisoners. These individual portraits contribute to the collective characterization of the *sertanejos* as a crafty, hardy, and durable mixed breed, like the mules who save the army. In contrast, the military gives an impression of mass incompetence.

Themes and Meanings

Rebellion in the Backlands should be required reading for all military students, since it clearly points out the dangers to a cumbersome army, with outmoded tactics and long supply lines, of fighting a guerrilla war on the guerrillas' home turf. The *sertanejos* utilize classic guerrilla procedures, including local intelligence networks, hit-and-run maneuvers, enticement into ambushes, recycling of captured equipment, and psychological demoralization. Most of all, the *sertanejos* are expert at using their terrain against the army, striking after the troops have marched into exhaustion or cul-de-sacs. Finally, the *sertanejos* illustrate the determination of guerrillas fighting for a fanatical cause or merely their homes.

Notwithstanding Cunha's interest in military lessons, Rebellion in the Backlands is ultimately an antimilitaristic work. Besides showing the military to disadvantage, Cunha was condemning his country for using military power against its own citizens, poor people living in a neglected region which might be termed the Appalachia of Brazil. His condemnation may seem unfair under the circumstances, but Cunha believed that integrating the *sertanejos* into the national culture is a matter of time and education, not military force. Furthermore, Cunha's admiration of the *sertanejos* suggests that such integration does not simply mean conformity of the "backward" *sertanejos* to the "civilized" national culture. How civilized, asks Cunha, is a culture which must prevail through superior brutality? This paradox continues to plague not only Brazil but also the superpowers and "civilization" generally.

Critical Context

Rebellion in the Backlands is Brazil's own *Iliad*, with soldiers and *sertanejos* replacing Greeks and Trojans. A monumental work of the early Brazilian Republic, Rebellion in the Backlands contributed to the rediscovery of Brazil's colorful regions, particularly the Northeast, and to the creation of the *sertanejo* myth. Cunha thereby helped lay the groundwork for the modern flowering of the Brazilian novel, dominated by *Nordestino* writers. Cunha's influence can be seen, for example, in such novels as Jorge Amado's *Terras do sem fim* (1943; *The Violent Land*, 1945) and *Gabriela, cravo e canela* (1958; *Gabriela, Clove and Cinnamon*, 1962), with Gabriela as a modern embodiment of the *sertanejo* myth.

Indeed, the influence of *Rebellion in the Backlands* does not stop at Brazil's borders. It inspired, for example, a fictional retelling of the Canudos story, *La guerra del fin del mundo* (1981; *The War of the End of the World*, 1984), by Peruvian novelist Mario Vargas Llosa. More generally, Cunha and other nonfiction writers, particularly sociologists, have helped to define the subject matter of Latin American fiction and have influenced its tendency to incorporate sociology, local color, and other factual material. The bizarre nature of some Latin American fact (especially political fact), as depicted by Cunha and others, has also influenced fictional interest, by novelists such as Argentina's Julio Cortázar and Colombia's Gabriel García Márquez, in the interplay of illusion and reality, fact and fantasy.

Bibliography
Amory, Frederic. "Historical Source and Biographical Context in the Interpretation of Euclides da Cunha's *Os Sertões.*" *Journal of Latin American Studies* 28 (October, 1996): 667-685. Examines Cunha's Europeanism derived from his academic experience, as well as his training as a civil engineer in a military school. His nativism can be traced to his emotional attachment to his country, and both Europeanism and nativism form a big part of Cunha's novel.
Beebee, Thomas O. "Talking Maps: Region and Revolution in Juan Vincent Benet and Euclides da Cunha." *Comparative Literature* 47 (Summer, 1995): 193-314. Beebee discusses the use of landscape in Benet and Cunha's novels. He examines the similarities in the structure of the novels, compares the representation of conflicts between center and region, and comments on the treatment of the reader as traveler.
Cravens, Gwyneth. "Past Present." Review of *Rebellion in the Backlands*, by Euclides da Cunha. *The Nation* 255 (December 7, 1992): 706-710. Presents a detailed analysis of the plot and characterization in *Rebellion in the Backlands*. Offers insight into how Cunha's ethnic background influences the story, as well as how his development of the war theme presaged the form war would take.
Economist "Brazil's Backland's Classic." 342 (March 1, 1997): 83-84. Discusses the reasons for renewed interest in Cunha's novel and delves into the parallels between the horrendous situations described in the novel and contemporary events.
Epstein, Jack. "Centennial of a War Stirs a Nation." *Christian Science Monitor* 89 (October 2, 1997): 216-225. Examines how Cunha's novel portrays the War of Canudos, which ended in October of 1897, and details the events leading up to the final clash. Epstein also explores the impact of the book on the changing views of Brazilians concerning the massacre.

Harold Branam

THE RECOGNITIONS

Author: William Gaddis (1922-1998)
Type of plot: Social morality
Time of plot: From about 1910 to shortly after World War II
Locale: New York City, Paris, Spain, and Rome
First published: 1955

Principal characters:
WYATT GWYON, the protagonist, an artist, forger, and adventurer
ESME, a poet who seeks the truth
STANLEY, a composer of organ masses
BASIL VALENTINE, an art critic in a counterfeiting ring with Gwyon
AUNT MAY, Gwyon's aunt, a devout Calvinist, whose "face wore the firm look of election"
THE REVEREND GWYON, Wyatt's father, who is the town minister but who secretly worships the sun

The Novel

Most of the characters inhabiting William Gaddis's novel *The Recognitions* pretend to be intellectuals in order to attain fame and money. They do not seek the universe's principles, God's laws, like the novel's few true intellectuals. These few, because they struggle to recognize the universe's rules and to obey them, live moral lives. The impostors, on the other hand, do not.

Wyatt Gwyon is the novel's main character and, because he seeks fame, its main dissembler. The book follows his journey from pretense to truth, illuminating the way to discover morality.

The novel begins with Wyatt's childhood. His mother has died, so his father, the Reverend Gwyon, and his live-in relative Aunt May rear him. The two adults battle each other over whose philosophy Wyatt will follow. Gwyon tries to teach his son to think and learn. He lures him with mythology, tales of his travels, and the excitement of discovery. May tries to deaden the boy's mind with blind, unquestioning faith in God. She berates him for being one of Adam's descendants and therefore a sinner who will go to Hell unless he believes in Jesus.

May fears creativity more than anything else because man imitates God when he creates. He tries to become God, she reasons. Therefore, when Wyatt, still a child, shows her his first picture, that of a robin, she asks: "Don't you love our Lord Jesus, after all?" He says that he does. "Then why do you try to take His place? Our Lord is the true creator, and only sinful people try to emulate Him." She goes on to tell him that "to sin is to falsify something in the divine order, and that is what Lucifer did. . . . He tried to become original. . . . And he won his own domain. . . . Is that what you want? Is that what you want? Is that what you want?" From then on, Wyatt "made drawings in secret . . . more convinced as those years passed, and his talent blossomed . . . that he was damned." He buries the paintings in the yard.

Wyatt feels such great guilt for creating as a child that as an adult he ends up painting only reproductions. He becomes good at copying, and because he wants fame and money, he starts forging paintings of fifteenth century artists. Recktall Brown, a rich collector, claims that he finds the paintings in old houses he buys; Basil Valentine, a renowned art critic, first disputes, then concedes their authenticity, allowing Brown to sell them for large amounts of money, which the three men split.

The counterfeiting ring dissolves, however, when Brown dies and Wyatt tries to kill Valentine. The critic reveals to Wyatt that the fifteenth century works and, therefore, Wyatt's copies have too much extraneous detail cluttering them up. He accuses the artist of concentrating on detailed, limited work rather than trying to find "the origins of design," the order of the universe. The criticism negates all that Wyatt has done, making him murderously angry.

He flees to Spain and changes his name to Stephen. There he realizes that Valentine was right. One must not limit oneself to details if one wants to find an orderly universe, for such a universe applies its principles to all things equally. That is why it is ordered, because it has right and wrong. To find rules that apply to all things one must try to study all things; but since that is impossible, one must study a great many things, in order to recognize the rules common to everything.

Artists try to reveal principles in their works, an act that takes great creativity and imagination; for, because one person cannot know everything, he must theorize and struggle to find the rules that God made. Then he imitates them. Wyatt fears to "emulate" God because May's lesson that God punishes those who create has never left him. He has simply buried his creativity, as he buried his original paintings. His bringing the fear to light and overcoming it allows him to start seeking the eternal principles and living a moral life.

The Characters

Wyatt, of all the pretenders, changes to become a truth seeker. Most of the other characters loiter at the right bars, attend fashionable parties, and go sightseeing at the correct places. They gossip, drink, develop their images, and, whenever they can, because they have nothing better to do, antagonize and distract the moral characters. Hannah tells Anselm to "shut up," "go home," and "take a nap" when he and Stanley discuss religion. Don Bildow asks Stanley for methyltestosterone ("I'm with this girl, see") and later "the Italian word for contraceptive" when Stanley frantically pursues Esme.

Three other characters besides Wyatt seek the truth in the novel: Esme, the poet; Stanley, the composer; and Valentine, the art critic. They warrant the reader's attention because they discover truth.

Gaddis has created a fascinating character in the beautiful Esme. She has the self-discipline to make herself look beyond details to find the eternal principles. Her use of the third-person singular when talking about herself illustrates this asceticism. The use of the third person allows her to think of herself as she would another person, with the distance necessary to ignore petty needs and selfish desires. These needs only get in the way of her broad study, for they are details such as the ones Wyatt has painted for so long.

Using the third person, Esme says beautiful things. When Stanley gets her pregnant, she asks him, "Will you marry her . . . ? For he put it there and did not take it away as he promised, as he always had done before, as he promised." When the "damned black androgyne," the epithet that she gives Father Martin, holds up the cross to exorcise her, she says: "Take him away, he's hurting her." When she gets the sore on her lip which later becomes infected and kills her, she explains that "something bit her perhaps."

Unlike Esme, Stanley does not believe that man, by himself, can find the truth. He thinks that God works through prayer and ritual to make man forget the limited and look for the infinite. His efforts to convert others to Catholicism show his belief in the power of faith. Since he composes a piece of music good enough "to offend the creator of perfection by emulating his grand design," he justifies his belief.

Characters in the novel often ask the question, "Should we understand in order to believe or . . . believe in order to understand?" Gaddis never gives an explicit answer. Since both Stanley and Esme find truth, however, perhaps both methods are valid; a character's temperament determines which alternative is right for him.

Valentine, though a Jesuit priest, never says whether he thinks a person must have faith to find truth or truth to find faith; but one way or another, the art critic does find the eternal principles. His trenchant comments to Wyatt prove that. His ability to discover truth makes him an intriguing character because he lacks genius, unlike Wyatt, Esme, and Stanley. Gaddis, through Valentine, shows that average people can also look beyond details and recognize truth; they simply cannot express it as beautifully as artists can.

Themes and Meanings

Gaddis paints a Zoroastrian world in his novel, one in which good—represented by the natural, honest, alive, loving, moral truth seekers—battles evil—represented by the unnatural, pretentious, deathlike, selfish, immoral fame seekers. Evil seems to conquer good, since the truly wicked survive and even prosper, while most of the people who are wavering toward the good and many of the good themselves die. Death ultimately takes Esme, Stanley, the Reverend Gwyon, and Valentine, leaving only Wyatt to continue the struggle.

Since the evil are the victors, why should people choose the good? The answer to this question is the novel's theme. People should live morally because God exists and has made an orderly universe. He ultimately rewards those who follow His principles and punishes those who do not. Yet He deceives "good people by keeping the path to paradise littered with filth." He makes living a good life difficult by hiding His principles and not seeming to reward His followers who discover them. In this way God makes certain that only the truly good reach Heaven.

Critical Context

The *Recognitions* first appeared in print in 1955. Very few critics gave favorable reviews because the reader must stumble through 956 pages of obscure analogies, unfinished conversations and sentences, events not explicitly described, interspersed foreign languages, and characters who talk at one another in enigmatic language. Gaddis does give obscure explanations of glossed-over events and supplies some omitted details as the story progresses, so that a reader who uses his imagination and creativity to fill in the blanks can work through the story slowly. Gaddis litters the path so that only those willing to take great effort will finish.

Few people have wanted to struggle enough to uncover the novel's message until recently. The book went out of print in the late 1950's. In 1962, Meridian published it in paperback, and in 1970 another paperback edition came out. More and more people have read it and praised it, so that now numerous critical articles have been devoted to it. Some reviewers even compare Gaddis to James Joyce and T. S. Eliot.

The novel sufficiently rewards the reader who perseveres. The conversations amuse; the analogies, beautiful poetry, and poetic language provoke thought; the mention of arcana fascinates. Finally, in deciding how to live, everyone should know the argument advocating a moral life, even if the argument is ultimately rejected.

Bibliography
Comnes, Gregory. *The Ethics of Indeterminacy in the Novels of William Gaddis.* Gainesville: University Press of Florida, 1994. Comnes explores Gaddis's view on ethics and moral imperatives and notes that Gaddis "provides readers with a chance to consider what it means to have values without absolutes . . ." An excellent study that offers readers an illuminating perspective on the philosophy undergirding Gaddis's work.

Gaddis, William. "A Carnival of Disorderly Conduct." Interview by Laurel Graeber. *The New York Times Book Review,* January 9, 1994, p. 22. Presents insight into Gaddis's style and themes. Gaddis tells why he is not interested in becoming a prolific author. He also describes his approach to writing, which emphasizes dialogue over narration.

Knight, Christopher. *Hints and Guesses: William Gaddis and the Longing for an Enlarged Culture.* Madison: University of Wisconsin Press, 1998. The first scholarly work to discuss all four of Gaddis's novels, Knight's book focuses on Gaddis's significance as a social critic and satirist. Knight highlights Gaddis's major concerns, including Flemish painting, forgery, corporate America, Third World politics, and the U.S. legal system.

Moore, Steven. *A Reader's Guide to William Gaddis's "The Recognitions."* Lincoln: University of Nebraska Press, 1995. In this revised edition of his 1982 work, Moore provides synopses of each chapter of Gaddis's novel, as well as detailed annotations. A useful resource for the study of the novel.

Wolfe, Peter. *A Vision of His Own: The Mind and Art of William Gaddis.* Madison, N.J.: Fairleigh Dickinson University Press, 1997. Offers an in-depth study of major themes and characters in Gaddis's fiction, including *The Recognitions.* An indispensable study for general readers and scholars alike.

Patrick Wright

THE RECTOR OF JUSTIN

Author: Louis Auchincloss (1917-   )
Type of plot: Social chronicle
Time of plot: Primarily the first half of the twentieth century
Locale: Primarily New York City and New England
First published: 1964

>   *Principal characters:*
>   FRANCIS (FRANK) PRESCOTT, founder and headmaster (rector) of Justin
>   Martyr Academy
>   BRIAN ASPINWALL, a young teacher, Frank's would-be biographer
>   HARRIET PRESCOTT, Frank's wife
>   CORDELIA PRESCOTT TURNBULL, the youngest daughter of Harriet and
>   Frank
>   HORACE HAVISTOCK, Frank's friend since childhood
>   DAVID GRISCAM, a Wall Street lawyer and longtime trustee of Justin
>   Martyr Academy
>   ELIZA DEAN, a former fiancée of Frank
>   CHARLEY STRONG, Cordelia's deceased lover
>   JULES GRISCAM, David's son, a suicide

The Novel

Outwardly traditional in form, consisting of an assemblage of journal entries, letters, and memoirs, *The Rector of Justin* goes beyond tradition in the skillful characterization afforded each of the several narrators whose testimony combines to produce
the novel. The principal narrator of *The Rector of Justin* is Brian Aspinwall, a somewhat old-maidish graduate student who has joined the faculty of Justin Martyr Academy during the eightieth year of the fabled old headmaster's life. From keeping a journal about his life at the school, including his encounters with Dr. Frank Prescott and
his ailing wife who soon dies, Aspinwall goes on to project a Prescott biography, interviewing many of the old gentleman's family and friends; in several cases, the inter-
viewees have already written memoirs of their own, which are incorporated within the
body of the novel.

Born in 1860 and orphaned at an early age, the Boston-bred Prescott is himself the
product of a New England private-school education. From his earliest youth onward,
however, he has cherished a dream of the perfect boarding school—unlike the school
he himself attended and more on the order of such "competition" as Groton and St.
Mark's. With his friend Horace Havistock, with whom he seeks to share the dream,
Prescott spends three years at Oxford University, ostensibly to study the British public
school model. Upon his return to the United States, he briefly forsakes his dream for a
promising career with the New York Central railroad and is about to marry the vivacious young Californian Eliza Dean when he is suddenly recalled to his earlier voca-

tion in a kind of vision. Eliza, at first willing to join in his changed plans, allows Havistock to persuade her that she is not "cut out" to be a headmaster's wife; in exchange, however, she exacts a promise from Havistock that he will not teach in Prescott's eventual model school; both promises are kept, as neither Havistock nor Eliza sees fit to interfere with Frank's calling.

Leaving the railroad, Prescott enrolls in Harvard Divinity School, if only to acquire the credential needed by such a would-be founder of a church-related school; he is otherwise little interested in theology or in the Episcopalian priesthood. While at Harvard, he meets and marries Harriet, the intellectually derived New Englander with whom he will share nearly sixty years of his life. Thereafter, the facts of Prescott's life become inextricably interwoven with those of the school, which he establishes and develops into prosperity through sheer willpower.

As Aspinwall sifts through the various layers of Prescott's existence, he becomes discomfittingly aware that Justin Martyr, for all its founder's protestations, is little different from any other boys' preparatory school, particularly in the matter of elitism and snobbery; yet Prescott, even in his dotage, continues to cherish the illusion that Justin is somehow far more democratic than the competition, lamenting the philistinism of those "old boys" who, ironically, continue to provide the school with most of its financial support. So great is the force of Prescott's personality, meanwhile, that his associates would sooner lie to him than risk shattering a dream that provides inspiration even to them.

Against the background of World War II in Europe and eventual American involvement, Aspinwall, medically unfit for military service, continues his effort to interpret Frank Prescott's life and career even as he struggles with his own possible vocation toward the Episcopalian priesthood. The documents, both written and verbal, that would provide the material for his biography are often contradictory and baffling; at the time of Prescott's death in 1946, Aspinwall has joined the priesthood and returned to Justin following his studies; the projected biography, however, will in all likelihood remain unfinished, its open questions unresolved.

The Characters
Lacking a plot, save for the events of Frank Prescott's life and career, *The Rector of Justin* derives most of its considerable force through the delineation of its characters, often in their own voices. Notably absent from the list of narrators is Prescott himself, whose implied intent to speak through his actions provides the novel's heavily ironic substructure.

As the various observers among his intimates make clear, Francis Prescott possesses both the talent and the force of character to have succeeded in a number of professions. In *A Writer's Capital, Life, Law and Letters* (1974), Auchincloss readily identifies the model for Prescott as Judge Learned Hand (1872-1956), with whom he was personally acquainted. The reasons for Prescott's particular vocation, barring divine revelation, remain open to question; in any event, the vocation was sufficiently strong that he cut short a promising career in business and allowed his fiancée to abandon him. The irony is that the "unique" institution of secondary education for which Prescott apparently sacrificed so much turns out to be little different from others of the same type, owing to the simple fact that democracy can neither be taught nor fostered in an institution with high tuition and selective admissions policies. To Aspinwall's implied indignation, Prescott states that he has always admitted scholarship students, yet he concedes in the next breath that the school's only Catholics are the sons of Justin alumni who happened to marry women of that faith and that all of its ethnic Jews are in fact professing Christians. The blindness of such a stance, or of his guiding principles, appears never to have occurred to him.

Predictably, such single-mindedness as Prescott's has left frequent casualties in its wake, as Aspinwall will soon discover. Among the major casualties, apart from his former fiancée, Eliza Dean, are his youngest daughter, ironically named Cordelia, and her deceased lover Charley Strong.

Cordelia Prescott Turnbull, although perhaps a rebel by temperament, has good reason to resent a childhood in which her father's family perpetually yielded first place to his students. Her disastrous first marriage was an obvious gesture of revolt, her choice of husband a mild-mannered nonentity whose main virtues, for Cordelia, lay in his Roman Catholic faith and his public-school education—both poles apart from her father's values. A Bohemian by nature, Cordelia in her middle forties has progressed from being an indifferent if talented artist to being a highly knowledgeable critic; still, she will never forgive her father for his treatment of Charley Strong, the terminally wounded World War I veteran with whom she shared a brief idyll in Paris following the collapse of her first marriage. Charley, unique among her various consorts, was a Justin alumnus, and during the last months of his brief, doomed life, her father's psychic hold upon Charley so greatly exceeded her own that Charley's lifework, a novel of some promise, was burned on the day of his funeral, thanks to tacit collusion with Frank Prescott. Cordelia's second husband, although not a Justin graduate, soon estranged himself from her by becoming one of the school's more generous and enthusiastic benefactors. At forty-five, she remains both restless and resentful, even attempting to seduce the callow and most unwilling Aspinwall.

David Griscam, an early alumnus of the school who has become one of its strongest supporters, is a hard-nosed Wall Street attorney whose lifelong devotion to Prescott and his cause often places him in the unenviable position of mediator between Prescott's dream and the harsher realities of human nature. More than once, his chosen position causes him to perjure himself in Prescott's presence. Among Prescott's more notable failures, moreover, is Griscam's own son Jules, who died a suicide in the 1920's after an abortive attempt to destroy Prescott, in part because of Prescott's influence upon his father.

Brian Aspinwall, Auchincloss's choice of principal narrator, is, like Miss Gussie Millinder in *The House of Five Talents* (1960), an oddly neutered narrator whose asexuality makes him a privileged observer. Although not a homosexual, Aspinwall has been ailing for most of his life and voluntarily remains on the sidelines, so to speak, the better to observe the effects of full sexuality in others. In later years,

Auchincloss would still employ such narrators with considerable effect: in *The House of the Prophet* (1980), similar in structure to the present novel, the principal narrator is a writer rendered impotent for life by a severe diabetic crisis sustained in early adolescence. Aspinwall, meanwhile, is not without interest as a character in his own right; of all Prescott's intimates, he is perhaps unique in his breadth of knowledge, in his curiosity, and in his instinctive, if seldom articulated, awareness of the ironies that lurk just beneath the surface of Prescott's well-publicized life. To the end, however, he will lack the courage of his convictions, and his biography of Prescott will remain unfinished for want of simple, evident answers to the many questions raised.

Themes and Meanings

Louis Auchincloss, himself a Wall Street attorney and a product of Groton, among the most eminent of American preparatory schools, has often used such schools in his fiction to help delineate the background formation of his characters. Never before or since, however, has he so successfully presented the implicit irony, or even absurdity, of the existence in the United States of an educational alternative frankly based on the elitist British public school yet ostensibly dedicated to the ideals of democracy. Through the character, actions, and career of Frank Prescott, Auchincloss shows both the benefits and the dangers of such a hybrid; the dangers are perhaps most evident to Prescott himself who, perceiving the true nature of his accomplishment at the end of his life, honestly believes that he has failed in his appointed task.

Through his skillful use of multiple narrators and viewpoints, Auchincloss in *The Rector of Justin* also underscores the elusive nature of human truth, necessarily subjective as well as relative, and the inevitable moral blindness implicit in any and all human endeavor. Frank Prescott's ideal of democracy, which he supposes to be doubly grounded in Holy Scripture and the United States Constitution, proves considerably more ephemeral than he might have imagined, given the simple fact that both documents lend themselves to a multiplicity of readings. In the end, Prescott no doubt stands convicted of failure, not because he failed to meet his goals but rather because he failed to sustain the human relationships that he sacrificed in favor of his elusive dream.

Critical Context

The Rector of Justin was Auchincloss's first novel to reach high critical and popular acclaim; by most accounts, it still rates as his finest accomplishment, rivaled only by its immediate successor, *The Embezzler* (1966). In his two preceding novels, *The House of Five Talents* and *Portrait in Brownstone* (1962), Auchincloss had begun to develop the technique of limited-view-point, first-person narration as an instrument of social satire, a device that he would use to considerable profit in *The Embezzler* as well. *The Rector of Justin*, however, may well represent the high point of the form, providing as it does the many-sided portrait of an unwittingly complex individual whose own voice is rarely heard, and then only in conversation.

Following the death of John O'Hara in 1970, Auchincloss stood alone as an accomplished American novelist of manners, but the genre thereafter appeared to fall out of favor, kept viable mainly by Auchincloss himself at the approximate rate of one novel per year. In retrospect, his finest period is that of the early to middle 1960's, with *The Rector of Justin* securing his reputation as a major American novelist.

Bibliography
Auchincloss, Louis. Interview by George Plimpton. *The Paris Review* 35 (Fall, 1994): 73-94. A fascinating interview. Auchincloss talks about the writing process. He reveals that his work as a lawyer has helped him to develop his characters and that his characters are not wholly fictional. He also speaks about his early works, which were rejected, as well as his ideas about the teaching of writing.
Depietro, Thomas. "A Republican Soul." *World and I* 10 (March, 1995): 304-311. Chronicles Auchincloss's life and work. Discusses his thoughts on the social and moral decline of his own class, as well as the factors that influenced Auchincloss's popularity. Briefly reviews Gelderman's biography and offers a brief analysis of *The Rector of Justin*.
Gelderman, Carol W. *Louis Auchincloss: A Writer's Life*. New York: Crown, 1993. A compelling look at not only Auchincloss's life but the elite society that fostered him and was the subject of his novels. Includes a discussion of both *The Rector of Justin* and *The Embezzler.*
Parsell, David B. *Louis Auchincloss.* Boston: Twayne, 1988. An excellent critical overview of Auchincloss's works. Themes are clearly delineated from novel to novel, which helps the reader to grasp the unity of Auchincloss's work. Helpful bibliographies and an index are also included.
Tuttleton, James W. "Louis Auchincloss at Eighty." *New Criterion* 16 (October, 1997): 32-36. Although Tuttleton focuses mainly on *The Atonement and Other Short Stories*, he does discuss themes that are common to all of Auchincloss's novels, including the death of WASP society and how the prep-school Christian moral vision shapes the young for life. A good source of background information.

David B. Parsell

THE RED PONY

Author: John Steinbeck (1902-1968)
Type of plot: Story cycle
Time of plot: About 1910
Locale: Salinas Valley, California
First published: 1937, enlarged 1945

Principal characters:
JODY TIFLIN, a boy about eleven years old
CARL TIFLIN, his father, a rancher
BILLY BUCK, a middle-aged ranch hand working for the Tiflins
MRS. TIFLIN, Jody's mother
GRANDFATHER, Mrs. Tiflin's father and a former wagon-train leader
GITANO, an elderly Chicano laborer

The Novel

These stories present a young boy's entrance into maturity through his encounters with life's harsh realities. Death, disappointment, and the world's stubborn refusal to conform to human ideals break down Jody's childlike certitudes. Yet, though Jody at times is callous or bitter because of these experiences, he ultimately realizes that life holds both disappointment and promise and that acceptance of life with endurance and sympathy is the way of maturity.

In the first story, "The Gift," Mr. Tiflin presents Jody with a red pony which Jody names after the Gabilan Mountains near his home. The pony quickly becomes his chief joy and responsibility, and under Billy Buck's guidance, he prepares Gabilan to be ridden. As the horse is nearing the completion of his training, however, he is caught out in the rain on a day Billy had promised Jody it would not rain. Gabilan catches cold and, despite Billy Buck's constant attention, dies. As Jody watches buzzards descend on Gabilan's body, he kills one of them out of frustration.

Jody's next encounter with the harsh realities of nature occurs in "The Great Mountains," when an old Chicano named Gitano walks onto the Tiflin ranch on his way to the western mountains where he was born and asks to stay at the Tiflins' until it is time for him to die. Mr. Tiflin refuses to grant his request, and Gitano rides off the next morning on an old horse called Easter, but not before Jody sees that Gitano is carrying an old and beautiful rapier, passed down in his family for generations.

"The Promise" and "The Leader of the People" repeat the patterns of the first and second stories, respectively. In "The Promise," Jody receives another colt but only after the colt's mother, Nellie, is killed by Billy when she is having trouble delivering him. Jody's pleasure in his horse is soured by Billy's killing of Nellie. Another old man, Jody's grandfather, visits the Tiflin ranch in "The Leader of the People." Though Jody is eager to hear his grandfather's repetitive stories of his experiences as a wagon-train leader, the old man tells Jody that the value of his work lay not in being leader but in being a part of "westering" the general movement of people into new lands and experiences. He also confides to the boy his belief that the new generation represented by Mr. Tiflin has lost the westering spirit. As *The Red Pony* closes, Jody makes a lemonade for his grandfather to console him, indicating that he has matured enough to care for others.

The Red Pony's plot belongs to the *Bildungsroman* tradition, in which a young person, in this case Jody Tiflin, is initiated into the mysteries of life. Each of the individual stories is part of his education. The loss of Gabilan in "The Gift" reveals to Jody nature's cruelty and man's inability to predict nature accurately. In "The Great Mountains," Jody sees in Gitano both a symbol of human decay and the enduring power of human ideals, since he carries the ancient sword passed down through the generations. In "The Promise," Jody observes the wonder and pain of the reproductive cycle when he sees Nellie and a stud horse copulate violently and assists at the birth of Nellie's colt. Finally, Jody's grandfather teaches him man's special destiny of westering, and Jody's act of kindness shows that he has some perception of this spirit.

The Characters

Jody Tiflin is the main character of the story, and because its main theme is his education, he is largely a passive figure observing events rather than directing them. In the first stories, Jody is described as a "little boy" who is slightly punier than his playmates. His life is regulated almost entirely by his stern father and doting mother, and he readily acquiesces in this, since he cannot imagine anything different. The pony Gabilan is his first real responsibility and a sign that he is leaving childhood, but the pony's death embitters him. This loss of innocence is a fallen state in which he kills or annoys helpless animals, fears but no longer respects adult authority, and regards maturity as the ability to swear.

Yet Jody's disappointments also cause him to speculate on the world outside his own meager experience. When he sees Gitano's sword, he realizes that he must tell no one about it, because to do so would destroy the sword's peculiar truth; thus, Jody makes an important moral decision. In his grandfather, Jody sees that one whom he has idolized has also been disappointed by life and learns the value of sympathy. In his last action, making a lemonade, he becomes a mature and active character, who sees life without glorifying illusions.

Jody's grandfather and Gitano have a similar function in *The Red Pony*: as representations of human frailty and transcendence. Both are very old men, yet they maintain strength and dignity because they carry on a tradition: Gitano, with his ancestral sword; Grandfather, with stories of his wagon-train days. These traditions exemplify man's destiny to move into unknown areas of existence. They are embodiments of westering, whether it is the movement of the conquistadors or the American pioneers. Steinbeck also grounds these figures in physical detail, so that each is a vivid and individual character in his own right. The treatment of both men indicates that the westering spirit has died down in later generations. Jody's parents regard them with mingled pity and scorn. Neither man can fully express himself to them. The taciturn Gitano speaks only in simple, repetitious terms, while Grandfather constantly retells the same stories. Only to Jody do they reveal their true nature, and in his respect for them lies the hope that their spirit will live on.

The Tiflins might be seen as evidence of Grandfather's claim that the younger generation has lost its spirit, but Steinbeck more sensitively portrays them as conventional people who, within their narrow range, function well. Carl Tiflin is an authoritarian father who nevertheless wishes to see his son become a man by giving him the responsibilities of owning a horse. Mrs. Tiflin is a kind and intelligent parent who recognizes that her son is maturing. Yet neither can fully understand the larger world outside their ranch. Carl dislikes both Gitano and Grandfather, while Mrs. Tiflin is sympathetic but does not see their real merits. The Tiflins are good people who do not possess the imagination to respond fully to the natural world.

Billy Buck, however, does have this imagination, and he voices the book's central lesson—that no one knows what the future will bring. The son of a mule packer, Billy is a horse expert, but even he is fallible, as in the episode with Gabilan. Thus, knowing his weaknesses, he can be sympathetic to Jody and respectful to Gitano and Grandfather in a way that Mr. Tiflin, who despises weakness, cannot. Because of this, Billy functions as Jody's friend and teacher, instructing him not only in horsemanship but also in the ways of nature. Billy is Steinbeck's example of a mature human being in *The Red Pony.*

Themes and Meanings

The principal theme of *The Red Pony* is the exploration of man's complex relationship with nature, as presented through Jody's education. For Steinbeck, all nature, including man, is bound together. *The Red Pony* is filled with descriptions of natural phenomena—weather, animals, and plants—reflecting and directing events in the story, as when the rainy season gives Jody an omen of doom and, later, exposure to the rain fatally sickens Gabilan, or when Grandfather compares Jody's planned mouse hunt to the slaughter of the American Indians, showing how human mistreatment of the natural world parallels man's mistreatment of his fellowmen. The unity of nature does not, however, preclude its harshness: The deaths of Gabilan and Nellie, the approaching death of Gitano, and Grandfather's sense of failure show how nature ignores human desires. The titles "The Gift" and "The Promise" are ironic, for these stories reveal that nature makes no gifts and keeps no promises. Nor can even the wisest character in the stories, Billy Buck, alter this situation. Steinbeck is here in the naturalist tradition, which sees the world as indifferent to human notions of right and wrong.

Yet naturalism is only one side of Steinbeck's vision. He also belongs to the Emersonian transcendentalist tradition, which sees nature as mysterious but nevertheless as a bounteous wellspring of hope. Death thus becomes an opportunity for new life, as when the dead body of Gabilan provides food for vultures or Nellie's death allows her colt to be born. All life is seen as interdependent, as are human and animal life, for example, on the ranch. Billy is an expert horseman because he respects horses and is sensitive to their needs. The Tiflins teach Jody that it is wrong to hurt innocent animals. Grandfather recalls how he had to keep hungry pioneers from eating their team oxen. In each of these instances, natural and human life are seen as connected. This vision finds its highest expression in the idea of westering, in which the trek across the wilderness forges the pioneers into a single organism, an organism which embodies the human spirit. Westering also exhibits the violent side of nature in the slaughter of the American Indians, but it is the one way in which dreams can be fulfilled, for it is an educational process for the race, enabling it to attain full maturity just as the events of *The Red Pony* cause Jody to mature. Those characters who display the greatest wisdom, Gitano, Billy, and Grandfather, have all been involved in westering. They can accept personal failure and transcend it, the lesson which Steinbeck has Jody learn in the course of the story cycle.

Steinbeck's symbolism and imagery reflect this union of man and nature. The mysterious mountains to the west of the ranch symbolize the inscrutability of nature, since no one except Gitano knows what lies beyond them. The mountains also represent the connectedness of life and death, since Gitano was born in the mountains and returns there to die. Significantly, he rides toward them on the horse Easter, suggesting a link with the Christian cycle of death and resurrection. Two other symbols are the water tub—which is constantly filled with water from a pipe so that it overflows and creates a permanent spot of green grass around itself—and the ugly black cypress tree near which pigs are slaughtered. These are analogues of the Garden of Eden and the Tree of Knowledge and represent the life-giving and destructive sides of nature, respectively. Jody regards the tub and the cypress as antithetical, but in Steinbeck's vision they are both part of the natural order.

Critical Context

The Red Pony is regarded by critics as one of Steinbeck's finest fictions. With a sure hand he integrates realistic detail of life in Monterey County, which he knew so well, with mystical speculations. The theme of the interconnected quality of all life is developed in greater depth and scope in *The Grapes of Wrath* (1939), but in *The Red Pony* the reader has an excellent introduction to Steinbeck's distinctive combination of naturalism and transcendentalism. The education of Jody Tiflin in this book has been compared with Ernest Hemingway's Nick Adams stories.

Bibliography

French, Warren. *John Steinbeck's Fiction Revisited*. New York: Twayne, 1994. Thoroughly revises French's two other books in this Twayne series. Chapters on Steinbeck's becoming a novelist, his relationship to modernism, his short fiction, his wartime fiction, and his final fiction. Includes chronology, notes, and annotated bibliography.
Hughes, R. S. *John Steinbeck: A Study of the Short Fiction*. Boston: Twayne, 1989. Divided into three sections: Steinbeck's short stories, the author's letters exploring

his craft, and four critical commentaries. A good study of some of his lesser known works which includes a chronology, a lengthy bibliography, and an index.

Lisca, Peter. *The Wide World of John Steinbeck*. New York: Gordian Press, 1958. An indispensable guide to Steinbeck's work, published in 1958 and then updated with an "Afterword" examining the writer's last novel *The Winter of Our Discontent* (1961). Admired and imitated, Lisca's work set the standard for future Steinbeck studies.

McCarthy, Paul. *John Steinbeck*. New York: Frederick Ungar, 1980. A short biographical approach to Steinbeck's work that examines each novel against the forces that shaped his life. Includes a useful chronology, notes, a bibliography, and an index.

Anthony Bernardo

THE RESURRECTION

Author: John Gardner (1933-1982)
Type of plot: Metaphysical
Time of plot: The early 1960's
Locale: San Francisco, California, and western New York State
First published: 1966

> *Principal characters:*
> JAMES CHANDLER, an associate professor of philosophy at the
>   University of California at Berkeley
> MARIA CHANDLER, his wife, a caring and practical woman
> KAREN CHANDLER, their oldest daughter, age eight, already a thinker
> SUSAN CHANDLER, their middle daughter, age six, a game player
> ANNE CHANDLER, their youngest daughter, age two, who looks
>   remarkably like James
> ROSE CHANDLER, James's mother, puzzled by her late husband and
>   already mourning her son
> AUNT EMMA STALEY, a painter, now senile
> AUNT BETSY STALEY, a pianist and cultural leader of Batavia
> AUNT MAUD STALEY, a singer, now deaf
> VIOLA STALEY, the niece of the three Staley sisters, bitter and nearly
>   insane
> JOHN HORNE, a lawyer, librarian, and lay philosopher

The Novel

   The specific gravity of *The Resurrection* is very great. James Chandler, a metaphysician living in a time of analysis, feels that he was born out of time. Because of his interests, however perverse for this age, and because he is dying from leukemia, he might be forgiven for being concerned about important questions that, as a philosopher, he is prepared to discuss at an elevated level. Since James Chandler is a philosopher who comes from the mind of a novelist, he also might be forgiven for having an interest in aesthetics, though of course it is the novel itself that is Gardner's aesthetic response to very heavy questions.

   Immediately after the diagnosis of his illness, Chandler decides to return to Batavia in western New York, the town in and near which he (and the author) grew up. He, his wife, and their daughters stay there with his mother, still alive though failing; his father, an undereducated man of intelligence who spent much of his time trying to perfect a perpetual-motion machine, has died. Also still alive are the Staley sisters, whom Chandler soon visits, all mediocrities but important in the town in their day: One was a painter, though she now is senile; one still gives piano lessons; and one, now deaf, was a singer. Their vestigial status says much about the culture of Batavia. Their niece, Viola, takes care of them and their house and, ill-used by them and by life, is bitter. She becomes much less so as she comes to love James Chandler, a pipe-smoking, fair-haired, owl-faced man with glasses, who—glasses excepted—resembles Gardner.

The sisters in their varying artistic ways are trying to order life, to make it conform to some rules. So are some students at a local institution for the blind, watched in fascination by the Chandler girls, as they try to play baseball. Of course, once the ball stops rolling, the players have no way to find it except by groping—a nice trope for the metaphysician the girls' father is. The girls themselves do something similar by playing a game that they have invented, the rules of which they occasionally violate. Meanwhile, Chandler dreams of a wizened old woman with a face like a monkey and a mouth full of blood—in his weakened state of mind, she often is not far away from him. The mind, he decides, cannot handle the idea of personal death and thus comes up with such images.

Marie, his wife, is a caring and practical soul who takes care of her family and tries to care for her husband, whom she loves. She is always in the background, but she shares few concerns with James, who has decided in his last days to "seize existence by the scrotum." On returning from a visit to the Staleys, he falls and is rescued, bleeding, by Viola. From then on, her concern for him grows.

When Marie visits her husband in the hospital, she meets John Horne, an attorney who never practiced as such, but rather gave himself to being a law librarian, a scholar, and a lay philosopher. He is grotesque, misshapen, probably dying, and something of a mental patient. Mainly, however, he exists as a *deus ex machina* to ask the same sorts of questions Chandler does, though he comes up with a different answer—nihilism—than does the associate professor.

Like Chandler, however, he cannot be "cured" by logical positivism (a doctrine that assumes that any question is invalid if it cannot be analyzed by the senses; thus "God" and "afterlife," for example, are non-questions) from asking metaphysical questions. Horne confesses that he is in despair. He does get off some good lines—"Art is the self-sacrifice of a man incapable of sacrificing himself in real life"—a line that fits Chandler fairly well too. He repeatedly reminds himself that he has not involved himself fairly with his wife, his daughters, or, lately, Viola, and now he avoids Horne. Chandler begins his last work, "Notes Toward an Aesthetic Theory."

A country man tells the senior Mrs. Chandler that "Everything in the world was made to go to waste" and that "the only difference between people and trees is trees don't fret about it." Chandler, dying, has his mother drive him to Viola, where, bleeding and able only to crawl, he grasps her foot in expiation. His wife and children, meanwhile, are at Betsy Staley's last-ever recital, where the pianist bursts into no melody at all, "a monstrous retribution of sound, the mindless roar of things in motion, on the meddlesome mind of man." The audience stares at their feet "as if deeply impressed."

The Characters

James Chandler, who is dead at the beginning of the book, is a philosopher mainly concerned with metaphysics and aesthetics. Since the prologue opens with four women visiting his grave (his mother, his widow, his oldest daughter, and Viola Staley), one feels he was justified in asking questions about ultimate reality—indeed, from chapter 1, he has known he was dying. He is a man who loves, but he feels continually that he does not give people their due, especially those closest to him. His thoughts about various issues in his life's work intersperse the book, as do new thoughts raised by his immediate situation and by his visit to his old town, his former piano teacher, his father's workshop, and John Horne. Like John Gardner in appearance, Chandler also resembles him in his mystical tendencies and his interest in issues that logical positivists would say are nonsense.

Maria Chandler is an intelligent woman uninterested in her husband's work. She worries what meals will be nutritious for him in his last days and wonders where she will rear their daughters after his death. She is the sort who makes the living of a decent life possible for the James Chandlers of the world.

Karen, Susan, and Anne Chandler are too young to do much more than be girls, though Karen already is showing signs of becoming serious-minded. She asks Viola if there is a God, and she notices much, including how people play various games, in some of which she leads her sisters. Anne is owl-faced like her father, and he worries that she may be like him in other ways.

Rose Chandler, James's mother, is an ordinary woman who has lived her life in and near Batavia. She has put up with a husband whose shop always just made it; James's father was himself a tinkerer, though with things rather than ideas, so there was precedent for their son.

The Staley sisters all are old maids now watched after by their brother's daughter, but they once were the artistic center of the old Batavia. Although the singing teacher is now deaf and the painting sister is demented, the pianist sister still gives lessons, and the preparations for her annual recital resonate through the book. Its occurrence serves as the novel's conclusion.

Viola Staley, a young woman stuck with taking care of her aunts, is bitter about her lot, but she is capable of growth and change after she finds in James Chandler someone to love, though he is long in realizing the importance of her gift. Through her association with the Chandler family, she reverses a dementia and reclusiveness that seemed at first inevitable.

John Horne is grotesque in every sense. His face is distorted by disease, and his mind is concerned with questions normally encountered only in college courses in philosophy. He serves to show that Chandler is not alone in his questionings. Also, he empties out the bucket of ideas that Gardner wants emptied, without having Chandler do it; such a role would overload the character of the professional philosopher. Horne will talk to anyone who will listen, or pretend to; through him, it all gets said.

Themes and Meanings

John Gardner was a mystic, three-quarters Welsh and proud of the skepticism that Welsh people have always had of the more literal-minded English. Chandler, a philosopher, can raise all the transcendental questions the author wants to, offering no final enlightenment about such matters, except insofar as Chandler is himself resurrected at the end of the book: Just before he dies, he makes loving contact with another person for perhaps the first time when he grasps the naked foot of the waiting Viola. She had only a short time before she told him of her love, and he had suggested they have a cup of coffee; crushed, she had run away. Yet her love for him has resurrected her, too, from a life that was apparently spiraling downward, certainly into depression and perhaps into madness.

John Horne is a brilliant man who, like Chandler, is ill, but who in counterpoint comes up only with nihilism as a response. He is unable to break from the life of the mind to enter meaningfully into the life of the world; even his work had been as a librarian of law rather than as a practicing attorney.

Because Gardner writes *The Resurrection* mainly from the third-person-limited perspective but tells the story from multiple points of view, readers see that most people are not really aware of what they themselves need, of how they are perceived. Nor, the book shows, do people often communicate—enter communion—with anyone else, or with themselves.

Critical Context

The Resurrection was John Gardner's first novel. While the book was received more favorably than most first novels, Gardner's later works did better in that regard, and it was not until after the author's death that a critical reassessment of his work began. *The Resurrection* is now viewed as the novel in which Gardner sets forth his concern for the primacy of art, especially as a way of bringing apparent order out of apparent chaos. This is the "moral" task Gardner set for himself, a task he wished others also would follow.

Gardner's comparatively short career—he was killed in a motorcycle accident before he was fifty—was extremely prolific. He published widely in long and short fiction, wrote the libretto for an opera, did children's stories, and was a prominent critic, especially of medieval subjects.

Bibliography

Butts, Leonard. *The Novels of John Gardner: Making Life Art as a Moral Process.* Baton Rouge: Louisiana State University Press, 1988. Butts draws his argument from Gardner himself, specifically *On Moral Fiction* (that art is a moral process) and discusses the ten novels in pairs, focusing on the main characters as either artists or artist figures who to varying degrees succeed or fail in transforming themselves into Gardner's "true artist." As Butts defines it, moral fiction is not didactic but instead a matter of aesthetic wholeness.

Chavkin, Allan, ed. *Conversations with John Gardner.* Jackson: University Press of Mississippi, 1990. Reprints nineteen of the most important interviews (the majority from the crucial *On Moral Fiction* period) and adds one never before published interview. Chavkin's introduction, which focuses on Gardner as he appears in these and his other numerous interviews, is especially noteworthy. The chronology updates the one in Howell (below).

Cowart, David. *Arches and Light: The Fiction of John Gardner.* Carbondale: Southern Illinois University Press, 1983. Discusses the published novels through *Mickelsson's Ghosts*, the two story collections, and the tales for children. As good as Cowart's intelligent and certainly readable chapters are, they suffer (as does so much Gardner criticism) insofar as they are concerned with validating Gardner's position on moral fiction as a valid alternative to existential despair.

Henderson, Jeff. *John Gardner: A Study of the Short Fiction.* Boston: Twayne, 1990. Part 1 concentrates on Gardner's short fiction, including his stories for children; part 2 contains excerpts from essays and letters in which Gardner defines his role as a writer; part 3 provides excerpts from important Gardner critics. Includes chronology and bibliography.

_____, ed. *Thor's Hammer: Essays on John Gardner.* Conway: University of Central Arkansas Press, 1985. Presents fifteen original essays of varying quality, including three on *Grendel*. The most important are John M. Howell's biographical essay, Robert A. Morace's on Gardner and his reviewers, Gregory Morris's discussion of Gardner and "plagiarism," Samuel Coale's on dreams, Leonard Butts's on *Mickelsson's Ghosts*, and Charles Johnson's "A Phenomenology of *On Moral Fiction*."

Howell, John M. *John Gardner: A Bibliographical Profile.* Carbondale: Southern Illinois University Press, 1980. Howell's detailed chronology and enumerative listing of works by Gardner (down to separate editions, printings, issues, and translations), as well as the afterword written by Gardner, make this an indispensable work for any Gardner student.

McWilliams, Dean. *John Gardner.* Boston: Twayne, 1990. McWilliams includes little biographical material, does not try to be at all comprehensive, yet has an interesting and certainly original thesis: that Gardner's fiction may be more fruitfully approached via Mikhail Bakhtin's theory of dialogism than via *On Moral Fiction*. Unfortunately, the chapters (on the novels and *Jason and Medeia*) tend to be rather introductory in approach and only rarely dialogical in focus.

Morace, Robert A. *John Gardner: An Annotated Secondary Bibliography.* New York: Garland, 1984. An especially thorough annotated listing of all known items (reviews, articles, significant mentions) about Gardner through 1983. The annotations of speeches and interviews are especially full (a particularly useful fact given the number of interviews and speeches the loquacious as well as prolific Gardner gave). A concluding section updates Howell's *John Gardner: A Bibliographical Profile.*

Morace, Robert A., and Kathryn VanSpanckeren, eds. *John Gardner: Critical Perspectives.* Carbondale: Southern Illinois University Press, 1982. This first critical book on Gardner's work covers the full range of his literary endeavors, from his dissertation-novel "The Old Men" through his then most recent fictions, "Vlemk, The Box Painter" and *Freddy's Book*, with separate essays on his "epic poem" *Ja-*

son and Medeia; The King's Indian: Stories and Tales; his children's stories; libretti; pastoral novels; use of sources, parody, and embedding; and theory of moral fiction. The volume concludes with Gardner's afterword.

Morris, Gregory L. *A World of Order and Light: The Fiction of John Gardner.* Athens: University of Georgia Press, 1984. Like Butts and Cowart, Morris works well within the moral fiction framework which Gardner himself established. Unlike Cowart, however, Morris emphasizes moral art as a process by which order is discovered rather than (as Cowart contends) made. More specifically the novels (including Gardner's dissertation novel "The Old Men") and two collections of short fiction are discussed in terms of Gardner's "luminous vision" and "magical landscapes."

J. H. Bowden

RESUSCITATION OF A HANGED MAN

Author: Denis Johnson (1949-   )
Type of plot: Psychological realism
Time of plot: 1980-1981
Locale: Cape Cod, Massachusetts
First published: 1991

> *Principal characters:*
>> LEONARD ENGLISH, the protagonist, a man suffering from spiritual crisis
>> LEANNA SOUSA, his bisexual lover
>> RAY SANDS, the former police detective who hires Leonard
>> PHIL, a local taxi driver whose occasional gossip fuels Leonard's paranoia
>> GERALD TWINBROOK, the missing artist Leonard is hired to find
>> BERRYMAN, the reporter Sands fires

The Novel

Resuscitation of a Hanged Man is a story about the search for faith and redemption in a chaotic and uncertain world. The book is divided into four sections, and Leonard English's quest for redemption follows some of the conventions of a detective story. The first section covers Leonard's arrival in Provincetown, on Cape Cod, at the end of 1980; the second covers most of the next year, during which time Ray Sands dies from a heart attack and Leonard becomes increasingly obsessed with the case of a missing artist named Gerald Twinbrook. In the third section of the book, "May-June," Leonard finds Twinbrook but fails to find the absolution he is seeking. Twinbrook died when he hanged himself, but without faith he cannot be reborn. In "Last Days," the final section of the book, Leonard finds salvation in jail, having tried to redeem himself in a failed attempt to assassinate the local bishop. In his punishment—imprisonment—he finds the order and certainty he has been seeking.

Leonard arrives in Provincetown, a popular summer resort, during the off season. His arrival is hardly propitious: He wrecks his car and has to be driven into town in a taxi. He has come to work at two part-time jobs, one as a radio announcer and the other as a private investigator. His boss, Ray Sands, a former police detective, runs both the radio station and a private-detective agency in town. Leonard is not only here for the jobs; he is running from his failed suicide attempt and a crisis in faith.

His first day in Provincetown reveals a town full of transvestites and homosexuals. Already, Leonard's shaky sense of self is challenged. He makes an unsuccessful confession at the local church, where he also meets Leanna Sousa, with whom he falls in love instantly. Leanna, however, is a lesbian and appears to be uninterested in Leonard.

Leonard's first assignment is to follow Marla Baker, who turns out to be Leanna's lover. Overcome with guilt and disgust at his own corruption, Leonard puts an end to the investigation by writing an anonymous note to Marla, letting her know that she is being followed. Shortly after that, Marla leaves town, and Leonard becomes involved with Leanna.

Through a reporter at the radio station, whom Ray Sands fires, Leonard hears about a paramilitary group called the Truth Infantry. After Sands dies, Leonard learns that he was the head of the Truth Infantry. Shortly after Sands's death, Leonard is inexplicably kidnapped and brutally beaten. Resuming his search for Gerald Twinbrook, he finds Twinbrook's notes on the 1870 resuscitation of a hanged man by two doctors. The man was a criminal, but reading the accounts of his resuscitation, Leonard wonders if he was really the victim.

Looking for meaning in unrelated events, he starts to see connections between the Truth Infantry, his kidnapping, Ray Sands, and Gerald Twinbrook. Leonard begins to believe that God is trying to get a message to him and that if Leonard can act on the "inner rebop," if he "can follow every impulse as if it started from God," perhaps he will be healed. Within this framework, he understands that nothing is a coincidence: Everything that happens is part of God's plan for him.

By the "May-June" section of the book, the beginning of the tourist season, Leonard is becoming more and more paranoid. He can no longer deal with Leanna, who has taken up with Marla again yet wants to continue seeing him. Leonard traces Twinbrook to Franconia, New Hampshire, the headquarters of the Truth Infantry. Trekking up to their campsite, Leonard finds Twinbrook hanging from a tree. He has succeeded where Leonard failed. From this moment on, Leonard crosses the thin line between spiritual fervor and insanity.

Leonard returns to Provincetown, dresses in Leanna's clothes, and goes to church to seek absolution one more time. Calling himself "May-June," he tells the priest that he is in disguise. By now, Leonard's assumptions—about his sexuality and his religion, about death and life—have been stripped from him. In one of the novel's more bizarre and hallucinatory scenes, replete with crucifixion imagery, Leonard makes his way to the water; in a final act of redemption, he shoots at the local bishop, but he misses.

The Characters

Leonard is characterized by his actions and thoughts. The story is told in the third person from his point of view. From the beginning, the reader understands Leonard as a desperate man, one who is searching for something he probably will not find. Although Leonard is not a saint—he is drunk when he arrives in Provincetown and wrecks his car—he is a spiritual innocent. He has lost his faith, yet he still believes that he can redeem himself and find forgiveness for his actions. Like Dorothy in the film *The Wizard of Oz* (1939), he has come from Kansas to a place seeking what he cannot find in himself; as in Oz, everything that is mundane and normal for Provincetown takes on a sinister meaning for Leonard. Leonard's greatest weakness and strength, as pointed out by a reader of auras, is his ability to empathize with others. His ability becomes a problem only when he starts to empathize with imaginary situations.

Leanna Sousa, one of Leonard's objects of redemption, is a local woman descended from Portuguese immigrants who settled the area. She runs a hotel, and while she initially tells Leonard that she is a lesbian, once Marla leaves town, she is quick to sleep with Leonard. As presented, this switch is not very convincing; Leanna is reduced to another element of Leonard's confusion. Leanna's bisexuality and the apparent ease with which she accommodates both Leonard and Marla in her life are unexplained; Leonard is unable to pin her down. The scenes between them best illustrate her elusiveness and the strangeness of their relationship.

Ray Sands, a former police detective, is seen by Leonard as two bosses—one at home, from where he runs his detective agency, and another at WPRD, the radio station. He seems to find nothing morally questionable about the spying he has Leonard doing, yet it is difficult for Leonard to judge him, especially after seeing the mild way he treats his unpredictable, possibly senile wife Grace. They have been married for forty-two years, and Sands knows how to "love without hope." Around the radio station, however, Sands behaves with the stupidity of "the boss," irrationally firing a reporter for no reason Leonard can see. Again, Sands is not what he appears to be; after his death, Leonard discovers three false passports in his desk and comes to believe that he was the head of the Truth Infantry.

Gerald Twinbrook is dead, but as a character, he functions as another paradox in Leonard's life. Like Leanna, Twinbrook is an object of redemption; if Leonard can find him, perhaps he will be able to make meaning of his own life. His obsession with death and resuscitation gives the novel its title and core; through his notes, Leonard finds a kindred soul, one who talks to him in his paranoid imagination, giving him the guidance for which he longs.

Themes and Meanings

There are many themes explored in the novel, most connected by biblical and religious references. Johnson's main point, around which all of Leonard's actions and discoveries evolve, is to question the purpose of life. For Leonard, the quest for personal redemption brings him to Provincetown and dictates much of what he does in the book. He cannot die until he has justified his life, found some meaning in his actions, and redeemed himself in the eyes of God. As a Catholic whose faith has failed him, however, he is searching for absolutes in a world, Provincetown, where everything is inverted. Men might be men, or they might be women dressed as men; the woman he falls in love with is a lesbian; Ray Sands, a former policeman and keeper of justice, is the head of a paramilitary organization and has three false passports in his desk; even the priest from whom Leonard seeks absolution is gay.

From Leonard's point of view, the town is both absurd and corrupt. Simple, mundane elements are magnified; he looks for significance where there is none, searching for meaning in external events that mirror his inner confusion. One of Leonard's first actions on arriving in Provincetown is to go to Mass and seek absolution, but he finds himself unable to make a "committed" confession. He falls instantly in love with Leanna, whom he meets at church. She is "strictly P-town," yet Leonard pursues her. Perhaps he can redeem her, sexually, and in so doing redeem himself. His obsessive search for Twinbrook also shows how important redemption is to Leonard.

The issue of death, as part of life, is also important. The title for the novel comes from Leonard's investigation of Twinbrook. Twinbrook was obsessed with an experiment by two doctors in the nineteenth century who attempted to resuscitate a hanged man using electricity. Although the man is brought back to life—his heart beats, he breathes, and he responds to light—he cannot speak. He is alive, but he has not been reborn. A man who cannot speak or hear has no faith and therefore has no life. In this, Johnson questions the restoration of life to the dead and whether such a life is worth living. Leonard cannot articulate his reasons for committing suicide. He did die when he hanged himself, but he has not been reborn, because his assumptions about himself and his church have failed him.

Leonard experiences death on many levels—emotional death, moral death (when he finds himself spying on Leanna and her lover as part of an investigation), the death of his identity, and the death of his assumptions about the world. Johnson shows the thin line between religious fervor and insanity, and how a religious framework can be used to give meaning to seemingly random events. It is a dangerous impulse that can be used to justify the actions of saints and mass murderers alike, as Leonard shows in the end.

The metaphors and imagery in the novel reflect these concerns. Johnson relies on references to the Bible, Christ, and martyrs such as Simone Weil to develop Leonard's obsession. As Leonard comes to see himself as a Christ figure toward the end of the book, images of crucifixion and light come into play. The last section of the book, entitled "The Last Days," further echoes the last days of Christ, describing Leonard's final sense of redemption as he finds comfort and peace in the ordered life of the prison.

Critical Context

Resuscitation of a Hanged Man is Johnson's fourth novel and continues his exploration into the spiritual lives of characters living on the edge of mainstream America. Johnson's four collections of poetry and previous novels have focused on misfits, people who cannot speak for themselves or articulate their experiences of life.

Johnson began his career as a poet, receiving recognition at an early age. When he was nineteen, his first collection, *The Man Among the Seals* (1969), attracted substantial critical attention, and his third collection, *The Incognito Lounge and Other Poems* (1982), was a National Poetry series selection. Yet Johnson always wanted to be a novelist, and in 1983 his first novel, *Angels*, was published. *Resuscitation of a Hanged Man* firmly established Johnson as a serious contemporary writer remarkable for the complexity and depth of the material he tackles in his work. In 1992, he published a collection of short stories, *Jesus' Son*.

Johnson uses bizarre, freakish characters and incidents as more than trendy window dressing in his fiction. Through them, he explores the chaos and corruption of a modern society lacking a spiritual core. Johnson's skill lies in making characters such as Leanna and Leonard's crazed kidnappers transcend the absurd and sometimes incredible aspects of the novel.

Critics have remarked on Johnson's fascination with such grotesque characters, suggesting that it is perhaps gratuitous, serving no function in his work. Yet Johnson believes that his concerns about redemption, punishment, death, and rebirth are best explored with depictions of people who are not ordinary but who live on the edge, their lives unstable and transient.

Interestingly, Johnson himself did not have a religious upbringing. In fact, his childhood was marked by a distinct absence of any kind of discussion of spirituality. His sense of God as an "audience"—a "future agency" looking down on humanity, with understanding and forgiveness—grew over time, in relation to his writing. Johnson has said that the only thing worth trying "is to try to reconcile the ways of God to man." *Resuscitation of a Hanged Man* reflects Johnson's understanding of death, rebirth, heaven, and hell on this plane, rather than in some distant hereafter.

Over the years, Johnson's work has appeared in popular magazines such as *The New Yorker*, the *Atlantic*, and *Esquire*, and his popularity as a writer continues to grow. Johnson rarely grants interviews, preferring to let his work speak for itself.

Bibliography
Elie, Paul. "The Shape of Distant Things." *Commonweal* 118 (September 13, 1991): 522-523. Elie sees the novel as a provocative yet odd "work of religious art." He talks about the paradoxes in the story, the "double-edge of sanctity and insanity." The focus of the review is Johnson's skill as a novelist who refuses to distance himself from his characters.
Hull, Lynda, and David Wojahn. "The Kind of Light I'm Seeing: An Interview with Denis Johnson." *Ironwood* 13 (Spring, 1985): 31-44. A rare interview with Johnson, who discusses his development as a writer and talks about the religious themes in his poetry and fiction. Although the interview is dated, much of what he says is relevant to his more recent work.
Krist, Gary. "Cape Hell." *The New Republic* 204 (June 3, 1991): 41-42. Krist briefly analyzes the themes of Johnson's previous work, arguing that Johnson's concern with how the religious impulse "operates in . . . a context of spiritual catastrophe" is a recurrent theme in his work. Krist concludes that the novel "raises large doubts about the possibility of faith in any world like our own."
Miles, Jack. "Resuscitation of a Hanged Man." *The Atlantic* 271 (June, 1993): 121-125. Offers a brief review of Johnson's novel within the context of the body of his work, including his short stories. Praises Johnson's book as "his most perfectly realized work."

Geeta Kothari

RICH IN LOVE

Author: Josephine Humphreys (1945-   )
Type of plot: Bildungsroman
Time of plot: The early 1980's
Locale: Mt. Pleasant, South Carolina
First published: 1987

   Principal characters:
        LUCILLE ODOM, the narrator
        WARREN ODOM, her father, a businessman
        HELEN ODOM, her mother, a woman who is bored with her life
        RAE ODOM, her older sister, who is pregnant
        BILLY McQUEEN, Rae's new husband, a doctoral candidate
        RHODA POOLE, an African American friend of the family
        VERA OXENDINE, a hair stylist

The Novel

   Rich in Love is the account of a six-month period when the seemingly predictable lives of the Odom family are changed forever. The novel is divided into thirteen chapters. The first-person narrator is Lucille Odom, who was a seventeen-year-old high school senior when these events took place. Throughout the book, Lucille stresses her opposition to any alteration in the family. Her opposition to change may well be one reason that she does not bother to take her examinations so that she can graduate from high school. However, in the last two pages of the novel, which serve as an epilogue, it is evident that during the two years that have passed since that difficult time, Lucille has come to realize that change is not only inevitable but also often best for all concerned, including Lucille herself.

   The book begins on May 10, when Lucille arrives home to find that her mother, Helen Odom, has left home. In a note to her husband, Warren, Helen says that she intends to start a new life. Although she promises to telephone, Helen leaves no clue as to where she has gone. Warren immediately starts to look for his missing wife, a difficult task, since she is unconventional enough to have gone almost anywhere. Lucille is as anxious as her father to find Helen; like him, Lucille is convinced that if they could just bring her back home, everything would return to normal. Nevertheless, they cannot find her. In fact, Helen remains absent throughout four-fifths of the novel. Although she finally allows first Rae and then Lucille to come and see her, Helen does not go back home until the family is threatened with tragedy, and even then it is not to stay.

   As soon as their mother vanishes, Lucille contacts her older sister Rae, who is working in Washington, D.C., and demands that she return to Mt. Pleasant at once. However, Rae seems to have problems of her own, and she will not agree to come before the sixth of June. When she does arrive, what she meant becomes only too clear.

She has just been married to Billy McQueen, who is finishing his doctoral dissertation in history but at present has no source of income or job prospects. The reason for their precipitous decision is also evident: Rae is pregnant. At first, Rae and Billy seem to be passionately in love with each other. However, as the months go by, Rae falls into a deep depression and becomes less and less interested both in baby and in her husband. She begins talking about giving the baby up for adoption, and eventually she tells Billy that after the child is born, she wants him to leave. Now the house contains two men who have been rejected by their wives.

By this time, however, Warren has found someone to console him. Even though he keeps searching for Helen, he is spending time with Vera Oxendine, the woman who cuts his hair. When Lucille finds Vera in the bedroom dressed in some of Helen's more glamorous nightwear, she realizes that if her mother does not return soon, the family may never get back to what Lucille defines as normal—in other words, to life as it used to be.

Billy, too, is unhappy. He seems to have lost his wife and baby, and he is living with strangers in a place that, as a Yankee, he finds incomprehensible. In Lucille, he finds someone who will listen to him, sympathize with him, and go with him on excursions. Although she has always found Billy attractive, Lucille has no idea that their comfortable friendship will ever develop into anything more. She would not betray Rae; moreover, she is still trying to figure out how he feels about her boyfriend, Wayne Frobiness. Wayne is a good person, intelligent and compassionate, and he is devoted to Lucille. However, she does not find their sexual encounters particularly exciting. In her erotic dreams, Billy starts to appear in Wayne's place. After returning from trick-or-treating on Halloween, Lucille and Billy are overwhelmed by their desire for each other, and they have sex in the back yard. Billy immediately declares that he will never let Lucille go, but she makes no commitment. When they go into the house, the two discover that Rae has given birth without realizing what was happening to her. The baby is still alive, but Rae is in danger of bleeding to death.

Phoebe's birth, which is the climax of the novel, is also the catalyst that forces all these complicated relationships to be sorted out. The near-tragedy brings Helen home, but only to help with the baby. The Odom marriage is over. After Rae is well enough to come home, Helen moves out again, taking Lillian with her, and Warren marries Vera. However, Billy and Rae re-establish their relationship. Wayne goes off to college, and Lillian, now nineteen, is last seen talking to Phoebe about whether or not she will ever get married.

The Characters

Josephine Humphreys excels at developing convincing, well-rounded characters. In *Rich in Love*, her narrative method enables her to reveal character in several ways. Lucille reports the past history of everyone she knows, as well as their present conduct. Sometimes, as with her mother's desertion, the present does not seem consistent with the past, when her mother seemed devoted to her family. However, when Helen unburdens herself to Lucille, it becomes clear that she was never as happy with her life as she appeared to be. Therefore, though her leaving home indicates that she has changed enough to have made a decision about her life, her family's earlier assessment of her was never very accurate. It is also clear that Lucille erred even in her initial description of her mother when she typed her as a woman dominated by her imagination. Helen proves to be much more than merely someone with a curious mind, belatedly searching for her own identity. She also has a heart. When she learns that Rae is having problems, Helen sends for her, and when the baby is born, Helen comes out of hiding to help. Lucille's misreading of her mother is most evident in the fact that, having been told by Rae that she was meant to be aborted, Lucille has never felt that her mother really loved her. Seeing how overjoyed Helen is to see much of Lucille in Phoebe, Lucille realizes that her mother has always adored her.

It is true that the characters in *Rich in Love* do change, even during the brief period when readers see them in action. Rae is first a young woman overcome by love, then one overwhelmed by pregnancy, and finally a contented adult. However, though Lucille may be surprised by Rae's descent into depression, her comments on Rae's beauty and popularity suggest that such a reaction is almost inevitable, just as her statements about Rae's strength of character make her recovery quite believable.

To a marked degree, then, seeming changes in the characters are merely new expressions of their real identities. Warren's taking up with a new love may shock Lucille, but after all, he is a practical man who tries to forget about his wife's defection by nailing shingles onto the roof. Billy's vowing eternal love to Lucille after their encounter is in keeping with his getting Rae pregnant so that she will marry him; he is a decent man who cannot separate sex from respectability. Readers are not even surprised by the fact that Lucille ends up alone. At this point in her life, she is much too busy reflecting on all that is around her to surrender her detachment for some lesser state.

Themes and Meanings

Even though it is set in an area rich in history, *Rich in Love* focuses on private life. Lucille may be a conservative, but her interest is not in political life or even in the community. Rather, she simply wants to keep her family unchanged. Of course, that is impossible; even if her parents had not broken up, age would have altered them, and with all their lives before them, both Rae and Lucille herself are bound to find themselves changing in ways they cannot now imagine.

The author does not attempt to minimize the fear of change, which indeed afflicts most human beings at one time or another. Instead, she presents a remedy. When Billy remarks that Lucille begins most of her sentences with "I love" and that she therefore must be filled with love, Lucille realizes that he has indeed defined her. Lucille knows that one does not have to be in love with a particular person in order to love life. Actually, what she sees that momentous summer and fall of the misery that can result from passionate love leads Lucille to doubt that it is really worth the pain. Lucille transcends the fear of change by realizing that she is truly "rich" in her ability to love. Salt air and moonlight, the old house she did not want to leave and the new house where she now lives, her family as it now is and the memories of what it used to be: By embracing them all, Lucille finds that she is truly "rich."

Critical Context

With her first novel, *Dreams of Sleep* (1984), Josephine Humphreys established a place for herself in contemporary southern fiction. While her focus was on private life, the backdrop of that book and of the two novels that followed it was the Charleston, South Carolina, area, which until recently seemed immune to change. Although one cannot blame changing society for all the problems Humphreys's characters face, certainly such trends as the disintegration of the family influence their attitudes and their decisions. Neither *Dreams of Sleep* nor *Rich in Love* would have developed in the same way if divorce were not an acceptable option. However, it is not social upheaval but natural disaster that sets the stage for *The Fireman's Fair* (1991). In it, the survivors of Hurricane Hugo attempt to restore order, both in their community and in their own lives.

Humphreys's next project involved helping a black woman with an interesting story find a way to write it down and get it published. *Gal: A True Life* (1994), by the pseudonymous Ruthie Bolton, was both a critical and financial success.

In her work with Bolton, Humphreys demonstrated the generosity of spirit which is so evident in her novels. While she is highly praised for her craftsmanship and for her masterful evocation of the South Carolina setting, Humphreys is perhaps most respected because while admitting that contemporary life is not easy, she insists that order can come out of chaos and that apprehensions about change can be overcome by the power of love.

Bibliography
Humphreys, Josephine. "Continuity and Separation: An Interview with Josephine Humphreys." Interview by Rosemary M. Magee. *The Southern Review* 27, no. 4 (Autumn, 1991): 792-802. Focuses on the author's sense of purpose and on her approach to her craft.

_____. "My Invisible Self." In *A World Unsuspected: Portraits of Southern Childhood*, edited by Alex Harris. Chapel Hill: University of North Carolina Press, 1987. A reminiscence revealing the author's early realization that one's identity is always a mysterious matter.

Jackson, Shelley M. "Josephine Humphreys and the Politics of Postmodern Desire." *Mississippi Quarterly: The Journal of Southern Culture* 47, no. 2 (Spring, 1994): 287-300. Argues that the subject of *Rich in Love* is the development of relationships between women, independent of their involvement with men.

Millichap, Joseph. "Josephine Humphreys." In *Contemporary Fiction Writers of the South: A Bio-Bibliographical Sourcebook*, edited by Joseph M. Flora and Robert Bain. Westport, Conn.: Greenwood Press, 1993. An excellent introduction to the author and her work. Includes sections on biography, themes, and critical reception, as well as a bibliography.

Vinh, Alphonse. "Talking with Josephine Humphreys." *The Southern Quarterly* 32, No. 4 (Summer, 1994): 131-140. Discusses such themes in the novels as obsession with tradition and the fear of change.

Walker, Elinor Ann. "Josephine Humphreys's *Rich in Love:* Redefining Southern Fiction." *The Southern Quarterly* 47, no. 2 (Spring, 1994): 287-300. Insists that by stressing personal history while admitting the perceiver's fallibility, writers such as Humphreys are creating a new kind of southern fiction.

Rosemary M. Canfield Reisman

RIDERS OF THE PURPLE SAGE

Author: Zane Grey (1872-1939)
Type of plot: Western
Time of plot: 1871
Locale: Southern Utah
First published: 1912

> *Principal characters:*
> JANE WITHERSTEEN, a young Mormon heiress
> JIM LASSITER, a gunman engaged in an eighteen-year search for his sister
> BERNE VENTERS, a non-Mormon befriended by Jane Withersteen
> ELDER TULL, a Mormon leader, one of the principal villains
> BISHOP DYER, another Mormon, suspected by Lassiter of having led his sister astray
> OLDRING, the leader of an outlaw band
> BESS, Oldring's "masked rider" until she is unmasked by Berne Venters

The Novel

Riders of the Purple Sage begins in Cottonwoods, a little Utah border settlement where life is made possible by Amber Spring, belonging to Jane Withersteen. Although her father has left her a fortune and she owns most of Cottonwoods, her fellow Mormons, led by the evil Bishop Dyer and Elder Tull, try to dominate her. They especially dislike her friendship with Berne Venters, a young rider who does not share their faith. When they attempt to whip Venters and drive him out of Utah, Jim Lassiter, a Texas gunfighter, intervenes.

For years, Lassiter has been searching for his sister, Millie Erne, spirited away from her husband by Mormons. He now learns she is dead and vows to wreak vengeance upon the Mormon who ruined her life. Jane has taken in a non-Mormon orphan girl named Fay Larkin. She has continued her friendship with Venters and is romantically drawn to Lassiter. Elder Tull—who wants to make Jane one of his wives—Bishop Dyer, and their accomplices attempt to break Jane's spirit by stampeding her cattle and intimidating her riders. She hires Lassiter to ride for her but attempts to discourage his use of violence.

A gang of rustlers, under the leadership of the outlaw Oldring, is operating in the area. One member of Oldring's band never appears without disguise and is known only as the "masked rider." On the range, Venters comes upon Oldring and his rustlers, one of whom is the masked rider. Oldring escapes beneath a canyon wall, but Venters shoots two of his companions, killing one rustler and wounding the masked rider. He discovers to his amazement that the masked rider is a girl named Bess. He nurses her for several weeks, during which time he falls in love with her. Later, the young lovers discover a hidden valley, which Venters names Surprise Valley. The entrance is guarded by a great balancing rock, probably put there by some ancient peoples. Venters and Bess settle down in their paradise like a chaste Adam and Eve. Venters assures himself that, despite the years Bess has spent with Oldring and his men, she is innocent of both criminal and sexual wrongdoing.

From time to time, Venters must leave the valley to get supplies. On one such occasion, Lassiter trails him and learns the location of Surprise Valley. Eventually, Venters rides into Cottonwoods; confronting Oldring in a bar, he invites the rustler outside, where he shoots him to death in the street. Lassiter is also contemplating violence, for he has decided that Bishop Dyer is the man who seduced Millie Erne away from her husband. In an attempt to stay his hand, Jane reveals that it was her own father who despoiled Millie, that it was he for whom she was taken. Lassiter is undeterred. He will use his six-guns to free Jane from the "invisible hand" of Mormonism. The conflict between Jane's loyalty to her religion and her growing attraction to Lassiter now reaches a climactic point.

Lassiter methodically executes Dyer, torturing him with superficial wounds before administering the *coup de grâce*. Now Lassiter must flee Cottonwoods. Jane makes her choice: She will break with her old Mormon life and flee alongside the Texas gunfighter, taking little Fay Larkin with her. A Mormon posse, led by Elder Tull, is soon in hot pursuit. The fugitives head for Surprise Valley and meet Venters and Bess, who are just leaving for Venter's old home town of Quincy, Illinois. Here, Bess's story is finally told by Lassiter, who learned it during an earlier conversation with the outlaw Oldring. Bess is, in truth, Elizabeth Erne, daughter of Millie. Bishop Dyer took her from her mother at the age of three and gave her to Oldring, the purpose of this act being to obliterate her family roots. Dyer anticipated that she would be reared as an outlaw. Oldring, however, soon came to think of himself as the girl's father and brought her up honest and pure, despite the fact that she rode with his gang of rustlers. Jane is so moved by this story that she gives the young couple Night and Black Star, her two favorite horses. Venters and Bess flee from Utah astride these fastest racers on the sage.

Lassiter, Jane, and Fay Larkin slip through the entrance to Surprise Valley with the Mormon posse nipping at their heels. The only way to escape is to roll the balancing rock. If Lassiter rolls the rock, however, the pursuers will be permanently sealed inside Surprise Valley. Jane makes her choice; she urges Lassiter to heave the rock into place (this will crush the pursuing Tull), and he does so.

The Characters

Riders of the Purple Sage, Grey's most popular novel, develops the character types he would use for another twenty-seven years. The reading public responded so well to these characters and their stories that Grey became one of America's best-selling authors.

Jane Withersteen is the frontier woman—strong and independent but tolerant of others, courageous but vulnerable to the assaults of evil men, dependable but adaptable. The central conflict in the novel is hers, the conflict between her commitment to her religion and her commitment to the man she loves. Lassiter is the typical Grey hero, an uncomplicated man of the West. He has no internal conflict. He has no doubts as to what the solution to his problem should be. He will find the man who stole his sister away into Mormon slavery and kill him. He has an additional and higher motivation for gunning down Bishop Dyer—the bishop's and Elder Tull's mistreatment of Jane—but his violent resolution would have been the same had he never met Jane.

Venters and Bess are the novel's *ingénues*. In this young non-Mormon's loyalty to Jane Withersteen and his defiance of the Mormon majority (he is referred to throughout the text as a "Gentile"), he represents the struggle of the individual against tyranny. Bess is one of several Grey females who romantically, and implausibly, disguise themselves as male riders. The lack of coarseness in her nature, her purity even while living in the midst of an outlaw gang, is romantic in the extreme. Grey accounts for her growing up to be a "good girl," despite all of her role models being cutthroats and thieves, through yet another romantic convention. Oldring takes his role as foster father seriously and protects the girl from the wickedness of his men, even locking her in on those occasions when he must be away from camp. The outlaw with a good heart, a rough sense of honor, or simply tender feelings for the female sex is a recurrent character type in Grey's fiction.

The villains, Elder Tull and Bishop Dyer, represent authority. Grey often portrays authority in a negative light, even when it is not corrupt. His idealized Westerner strives to be free of all artificial constraints, and this idea is elaborated in many lengthy scenes picturing man or woman alone on the majestic plains or mountains. In *Riders of the Purple Sage*, authority is corrupt. In addition to committing what would be crimes if there were a civil law to judge them, Tull and Dyer are religious fanatics and hypocrites. Grey portrays the Mormon community as a tyrannical theocracy and Tull and Dyer as the "invisible hand," the evil priests who manipulate the malice against Jane Withersteen and her Gentile friends. In fact, the novel is, from beginning to end, virulently anti-Mormon. In 1912, that aspect of the novel was not especially controversial.

Themes and Meanings

The landscape of the West—the plains, valleys, deserts, mountains, canyons—and its effect upon the people who inhabit it provide one of the themes in any Zane Grey Western. *Riders of the Purple Sage* is one of seven Grey novels set in Utah. The purple sage of the title covers a wild upland waste where several breakneck rides occur during the course of the novel. Grey's descriptions of the natural features of the Western terrain are frequent, lengthy, and vivid. Even critics who fault his plotting, characterization, and occasional clumsiness of style agree that his descriptions of the West are masterful.

A second recurrent theme is the blindness of organized religion to the complexity, and occasional ambiguity, of moral choices. Grey does not limit his negative portrayal of religious groups to the Mormons. He is understandably more oblique in his criticism of other Christian communities, since much of his middle-American audience would belong to these very communities. Yet it is sectarian narrowmindedness that sends the protagonist of *The Rainbow Trail* (1915), the sequel to *Riders of the Purple Sage*, out west at the beginning of that novel. Reverend John Shefford leaves Quincy, Illinois, after breaking with his congregation. In *The Vanishing American* (1925), Grey did offend some religious groups by portraying the head missionary on an Indian reservation as a criminal who hides behind the Bible (which he calls the "Old Book"). Grey also writes of the absurdity of the idea that the Indians could be converted to Christianity in a short time. A major theme in *Riders of the Purple Sage* is that when the heart is in conflict with religious dogma, one should follow the heart.

Critical Context

In 1907, Grey, still an easterner, accompanied Charles Jesse "Buffalo" Jones on an Arizona hunting trip. The trip was a seminal experience for Grey, in the long term imbuing him with a lifelong wonder at the majesty of the American West and, more immediately, furnishing the material for several books—*The Last of the Plainsmen* (1908), *The Heritage of the Desert* (1910), *Roping Lions in the Grand Canyon* (1924), and *Riders of the Purple Sage*. As Mormons guided Jones and Grey across rivers and through desert and mountain terrain, the writer developed an unfavorable opinion of them. He hinted at his disapproval of Mormonism in *The Heritage of the Desert* and made it explicit in *Riders of the Purple Sage*. However, the grandeur of the West, the chivalry of the Western hero, and the strength of the Western heroine are the elements that have made *Riders of the Purple Sage* the most popular and most favorably reviewed of Grey's many books.

Grey and Owen Wister, the author of *The Virginian* (1902), virtually created the Western novel, which, in turn, spawned the motion-picture Western. Between 1918 and the end of the twentieth century, Grey's novels and short stories were adapted as feature films, serials, or made-for-television movies approximately 115 times. In addition, a weekly television series, *Dick Powell's Zane Grey Theater*, which ran from October, 1956, to September, 1962, used material only loosely connected or wholly unconnected to Grey's writings. It is probable that more of Grey's work has been adapted for the screen than that of any other American author. *Riders of the Purple Sage* alone was filmed five times—in 1918, 1925, 1931, 1941, and 1996. In the first four productions, the gunman Lassiter was portrayed by stars of the genre: in turn, William Farnum, Tom Mix, George O'Brien, and George Montgomery. In evaluating the 1941 production, a critic suggested that the story was creaking with age and had little life left in it. However, in 1996, Ed Harris and Amy Madigan produced and co-starred in a television adaptation—quite faithful to the romantic tone of the novel—that was a popular and critical success, thus reaffirming the appeal of this quintessential Western romance.

Bibliography
Farley, G. M. *Zane Grey: A Documented Portrait*. Tuscaloosa, Ala.: Portals Press, 1986. A meticulous study of Grey's career, listing everything he ever wrote and every movie adapted from his works.

Hardy, Phil. *The Film Encyclopedia: The Western*. New York: Morrow, 1983. One volume in a nine-volume series. Contains cast and production information as well as critical evaluations and synopses for hundreds of Western films from the sound era, including the 1931 and 1941 versions of *Riders of the Purple Sage*.

Jackson, Carlton. *Zane Grey*. Rev. ed. Boston: Twayne, 1989. A biographical-critical entry in Twayne's United States Authors Series. Contains a chronology and a selected bibliography.

Scott, Kenneth W. *Zane Grey, Born to the West: A Reference Guide*. Boston: G. K. Hall, 1979. A thoroughly annotated bibliography containing a biographical-critical introduction and chapters on "The Fiction of Zane Grey," "Zane Grey on Film," and "Writings About Zane Grey" from 1904 through 1977.

Zane Grey: The Man and His Works. New York: Harper, 1928. A valuable compilation of articles by and about Grey, brought out by his longtime publisher at the height of his popularity.

Patrick Adcock

THE RISE OF DAVID LEVINSKY

Author: Abraham Cahan (1860-1951)
Type of plot: Social realism
Time of plot: 1865-1915
Locale: Czarist Russia and New York City
First published: 1917

> *Principal characters:*
> DAVID LEVINSKY, a successful clothing manufacturer
> MATILDA MINSKER, who helps David go to America
> MAX MARGOLIS, a peddler who befriends David
> DORA, Max's wife, with whom David falls in love
> MEYER NODELMAN, who helps David start his business
> FANNY KAPLAN, to whom David becomes engaged
> ABRAHAM TEVKIN, a Hebrew poet and real-estate broker
> ANNA TEVKIN, his daughter, who rejects David as a suitor

The Novel

In 1913, in response to a request from the popular *McClure's* magazine for articles describing the success of East European immigrants in the U.S. garment trade, Abraham Cahan, editor of the *Jewish Daily Forward* and also a successful English-language novelist, wrote several short stories instead. Subsequently published as a novel, these pieces of fiction permitted Cahan to explore problematic aspects of the process of Americanization, produce vignettes of immigrant Jewish life, and describe the development of a major American industry.

The Rise of David Levinsky purports to be a memoir written thirty years after young David Levinsky arrived in the United States in 1885 with four cents in his pocket. Now the owner of a leading cloak-and-suit factory, he has accumulated more than two million dollars, but he is not a happy man. The novel is divided into fourteen books, each of which consists of several chapters.

The first four books, approximately one-sixth of the total pages, deal with Levinsky's life in Russia. Orphaned at the age of three, he grew up desperately poor in the small Russian town of Antomir. Encouraged by his mother, he entered a Yeshiva as a scholarship student at the age of thirteen and studied the Talmud for the next seven years. One Easter, on the way home from the synagogue, David was beaten by a group of young boys. His mother, rushing out to confront his attackers, was killed by a Gentile mob. David lost his enthusiasm for study and, aided by Matilda Minsker, a secular-minded young woman who was attracted to him, decided to join the Jewish exodus from Russia to America.

Books 5, 6, and 7 describe Levinsky's early years in New York City. Finding his way to the Lower East Side, he attempts to sleep in a synagogue, as he had in Antomir, but he discovers this is forbidden in America. He is befriended by a pious old Jew who buys Levinsky some American-style clothes, finds him a room, and gives him a few dollars. David tries to support himself as a peddler but is unsuccessful, even though Max Margolis, another peddler, teaches him the tricks of the trade. David's lifestyle erodes his religious habits, and he finally shaves his beard. Studying English in a public evening school arouses David's ambition to attend City College. He learns to operate a sewing machine and saves most of his wages, planning to attend school full time.

The next three books describe Levinsky's business success, interweaving commercial details with a description of his unsuccessful love affair. He becomes a boarder in Max Margolis's apartment, where he falls in love with Max's wife Dora. David slowly wins Dora's affections, but when he succeeds in consummating the affair, she insists that he leave immediately and never return. Angry over an insult by his employer, Levinsky decides to entice the firm's outstanding designer to join him in a business venture. Meyer Nodelman, a successful manufacturer whom David had tutored in English, provides help and useful advice on how to get started. Though beginning in a fit of spite, David soon feels a sense of adventure. The few dollars he had saved for college are quickly used up, and David abandons all thought of continuing formal education. Trying to dress and act like a genteel American, Levinsky imitates the buyers of his merchandise, but he always feels inferior to his American-born customers.

The final four books describe Levinsky's continuing business success along with his failure as a human being. He survives the Depression of 1893, expanding his factory in the prosperous years that follow. Meyer Nodelman and his wife introduce Levinsky to a variety of unmarried young women, but none appeals to him. When attractive Matilda Minsker arrives in New York to raise money for Russian revolutionaries, Levinsky approaches her only to find that she is repulsed by his expensive fur coat and bourgeois bearing. Seeking to start a family, David becomes engaged to Fanny Kaplan, daughter of a well-off Orthodox Jew whose lifestyle David admires. Yet David does not love her. During a brief stay at a Catskill resort hotel, he meets the vivacious Anna Tevkin and falls in love with her, only to find that she does not return his affections. David pursues her by becoming a friend of Anna's father, praising his Hebrew poetry and investing in real estate with him. This wins David regular access to the Tevkin household, where the children vigorously debate Zionism and socialism, but Anna still spurns his love. Although proud that he helped build one of the great industries of the United States and can now live in a luxurious hotel suite, Levinsky laments that he is a lonely, unhappy man, without a family and cut off from his roots.

The Characters

With the exception of David Levinsky, who is drawn with much personal insight, the other characters in the novel remain stock figures. Although given distinctive individual characteristics, their function is to illustrate various common aspects of the Jewish experience in Russia and the United States. David's mother sacrifices everything to help her son become a renowned Talmud scholar. Matilda is the typical young, secular Russian Jewish intellectual, sexually liberated and full of revolutionary fervor. Dora Margolis, easily the most sympathetic character in the novel, holds her family together, although she is unhappily married to a crude husband and regretfully watches her young daughter's command of English and adaptation to the American environment far exceed her own. The Kaplan family, an Orthodox household transplanted to the New World, reminds David of his heritage and leads him to become engaged to Fanny, although he does not love her. Abraham Tevkin abandons the Hebrew poetry that made him famous in Europe, becoming a real-estate salesman in America.

In contrast, Levinsky is drawn with considerably more nuance and complexity. Cahan, who was a leading Jewish socialist, does not make his capitalist protagonist wholly attractive. Levinsky's egotism, his chauvinism, and his driving materialism are presented realistically, but Cahan also describes Levinsky's pain and frustration as an inexperienced immigrant, unsure of the customs and mores of his new environment. Early in his business career, Levinsky invites a customer to lunch at a luxury restaurant, but he has to ask his guest how to read the menu and how to use the elaborate array of glasses, knives, and forks placed before him. Even as a wealthy man at the end of the novel, he still remains intimidated by supercilious waiters, thinking they are sneering at him. In his business and social contacts with Gentiles and American-born Jews, Levinsky always feels inferior, uncertain whether his gestures and his language fulfill the standard of genteel behavior he tries to emulate.

Levinsky is sexually attracted to women he cannot have and contemptuous of women he can have. The married women he desires are unwilling to accept his attentions even when they are unhappy in their marriages. The single women he approaches find him intellectually and socially unattractive. Girls who are introduced to him as prospective marriage partners seem primarily after his money. For sex he turns to prostitutes, even though he despises their way of life.

Many of the problems Levinsky faces in America stem from the conflict between the values he learned as a child and his American experiences; this discord causes him great inner tension and pain. Levinsky revels in the material comfort that his wealth provides, yet he believes that he would be happier had he entered an intellectual profession and made less money. "My past and my present do not comport well," he laments in the closing words of the novel. "David, the poor lad swinging over a Talmud volume at the Preacher's Synagogue, seems to have more in common with my inner identity than David Levinsky, the well-known cloak-manufacturer."

Themes and Meanings

Cahan uses the life of David Levinsky to explore three interrelated themes. From the opening paragraph, in which Levinsky asserts that although he is a millionaire he is not a happy man, Cahan examines the ambiguous meaning of success and the personal and psychological cost of achieving material gains. Success distances Levinsky from his friends—the companions who came to America with him and those who helped him during his early and difficult years in the New World. His great wealth overawes them, making them uncomfortable in his presence. In turn, Levinsky can never be certain whether people associate with him out of friendship or because they hope to get some of his money. His business success is accomplished through methods that are unethical when they are not illegal, in violation of the values he learned as a child. Appealing to the Social Darwinist creed of "survival of the fittest" to justify his actions, Levinsky is too insecure psychologically to be certain he is, in fact, truly one of "the fittest."

A second major theme is the development of the American ready-to-wear clothing industry and the surprisingly rapid rise to prominence within that industry of recent Russian Jewish immigrants. Levinsky's success illustrates how this occurred, but the contradictions between his methods and his inherited values make the meaning of success ambiguous.

The third theme, the process of adaptation to American life by Russian Jewish immigrants of Levinsky's generation, takes up large segments of the novel. Levinsky experiences the teeming Lower East Side, with its peddlers and markets, its storefront synagogues of recent immigrants, their poverty-stricken homes, and their vigorous intellectual life. As he rises in wealth, Levinsky describes the overfurnished homes of the wealthy, their religious compromises, and the lavish resort hotels that also serve as marriage marts. The novel contains a social history of Jewish immigrants in the years before World War I, as they adapt to a new American reality.

Critical Context

In fulfilling the commission from *McClure's*, Cahan used his fictional manufacturer to show how, in the late 1880's and early 1890's, Russian Jews replaced German Jews at the head of the cloak-and-suit trade. Levinsky, always short of cash during his early years, learned to use unethical subterfuges to postpone payment of his bills. He could undercut major firms on prices because the Orthodox East European Jewish tailors he hired were willing to work longer hours for lower wages in return for not having to work on Saturday. Concentrating his clothing line on a few successful designs, frequently illegally copied from those of established manufacturers, Levinsky achieved an economy of operation that permitted him to sell stylish goods at low prices, a process that made fashionable clothes readily available to the majority of American women.

Critics have favorably compared the social realism of Cahan's works with that of Stephen Crane and Theodore Dreiser. When he turned his *McClure's* short stories into a longer work, with far greater depth of characterization and scope of social observation, Cahan created the first major novel portraying the Jewish experience in America. In effect, he also created a new literary genre within which there have been many followers. Such acclaimed writers as Bernard Malamud, Philip Roth, and Saul Bellow have continued to explore themes first articulated by Cahan.

Bibliography

Chametzky, Jules. *From the Ghetto: The Fiction of Abraham Cahan*. Amherst: University of Massachusetts Press, 1977. This critical study of Cahan's fiction in Yiddish and English devotes a chapter to *David Levinsky*, calling it a masterpiece of immigration literature.

Girgus, Sam B. *The New Covenant: Jewish Writers and the American Idea.* Chapel Hill: University of North Carolina Press, 1984. Analyzes *David Levinsky* as a study of the negative aspects of the American Dream that encourage conformity, materialism, and dehumanization.

Howe, Irving. *World of Our Fathers.* New York: Harcourt Brace Jovanovich, 1976. An outstanding sociocultural history of the East European Jewish migration to America during the years 1880-1924, containing many references to Cahan.

Marovitz, Sanford E. *Abraham Cahan.* New York: Twayne, 1996. A biography of Cahan stressing his English-language fiction. Chapter 6 provides a perceptive analysis of *David Levinsky.*

Sanders, Ronald. *The Downtown Jews: Portraits of an Immigrant Generation.* New York: Harper & Row, 1969. Sanders organizes a description of the social, cultural, and political life of the Lower East Side around a biography of Cahan.

Milton Berman

A RIVER RUNS THROUGH IT

Author: Norman Maclean (1902-1990)
Type of plot: Family
Time of plot: 1937
Locale: Western Montana
First published: 1976

> *Principal characters:*
>> MACLEAN, the respectable eldest son, an experienced Forest Service
>> crew chief, narrator of the family story
>> PAUL, Maclean's hard-living younger brother, a newspaper reporter,
>> gambler, and expert fly fisherman
>> MACLEAN'S FATHER, initially a Scotch Presbyterian minister, retired at
>> the end of the story

The Novel

A River Runs Through It compresses the events of several summers into one, the summer Norman Maclean's brother Paul dies. In establishing background, Maclean explains the importance of fly fishing as the main activity through which the males of the family related to one another. Fishing also provided spiritual education. By describing their fishing trips and related events during the summer of 1937, a much older Maclean seeks to understand the tragedy of his brother's death, to pay homage to him, and to show appreciation for his father's love and wisdom.

A River Runs Through It is written in first-person limited narration. Maclean the narrator is the protagonist, his character derived from the author's memories and reflections. He tells the story chronologically, often referring to characters in terms of their familial roles, as "my father," "my brother," "my mother-in-law." In addition to the three male Maclean characters, there are two female Macleans: the mother, wife of the minister, and Jessie, Maclean's wife. Jessie's family provides two other significant characters, her brother, Neal, and her mother, Florence.

The story reads as if it were a highly stylized personal essay. As an introduction to the family members and their culture, Maclean begins, "In our family, there was no clear line between religion and fly fishing." Even though these are minister's children, they receive nearly equal instruction in spiritual concerns and in fly fishing. Paul's fishing ability early transcends the ordinary, causing Maclean to feel great respect for his younger brother. As men, Maclean and Paul are both successful in their own ways. Maclean has done well in school and in the Forest Service. Paul is a newspaper reporter who does not allow work to interfere with his fishing.

As the events of the summer begin, Maclean asks Paul, as a favor, to go fishing with him and his brother-in-law Neal. Paul agrees out of respect for Maclean's mother-in-law, who has requested the expedition. Neal is a newly returned Montana native whom Paul accuses of having become a lowly bait fisherman. As boys, the brothers had taken it for granted that Jesus would have been a fly fisherman. Before enduring

Neal's company, Paul persuades Maclean to slip away for a day on their own special river, the Big Blackfoot.

Once they begin fishing, Maclean describes Paul as almost miraculous in his fishing ability, so amazing that a woman gazes at him raptly while her husband keeps repeating "Jesus." That evening, Paul becomes so drunk and disorderly that he is jailed along with his Indian girlfriend; when Maclean goes to the jail to get them, the desk sergeant warns that Paul's excessive drinking is chronic and that his gambling is out of control. Thus we see Paul travel from a state of grace to a drunken failure in one brief interval, a pattern he continues until his death.

The fishing trip with Neal and Old Rawhide, a prostitute he brings along, follows in the same vein with some comic relief. Maclean and Paul experience the purity of fishing. Neal and the woman forget to bring a fishing pole, steal beer to go with their whiskey, become drunk, and fall asleep in the sun totally naked. The two are badly sunburned. Maclean and Paul must get rid of Old Rawhide and return Neal to the women of his family as quickly as possible. Maclean's wife and her mother become angry with Maclean for not keeping Neal out of trouble. Maclean is forgiven by the women, but they remain upset, and he decides to go fishing again, this time with Paul and their father. This is the Maclean men's last fishing trip together. Soon after, Paul is beaten to death, presumably because of the gambling debts.

The Characters

Maclean's characters are drawn from his family, in terms of the significance their lives. Initially, Maclean's father instills in his sons a sense of wonder and the conviction that God is to be found in nature and in the four-count rhythm used in fly fishing. While this strict father cannot overcome Paul's defiance of his biblical teaching, he cannot ignore Paul's beauty either.

The problem is that while Paul achieves grace and beauty in fishing, he is unable to attain peace and acceptance in his personal life. In addition to his drinking and gambling, he prefers exciting relationships with women to long-term ones. The narrator's uneasiness over Paul's prodigal yet forceful character forms the conflict at the heart of the tale. His own tough but integrated character is revealed as he struggles to fish successfully and to keep peace with his relatives. Family communication is carried out in the typical Scottish manner, cryptic and often unfinished, leaving Maclean troubled.

Paul's character is complex and taciturn. On fishing trips, he tells personal anecdotes. In one such story, Paul is so raptly watching a jackrabbit in his headlights that he misses a turn and smashes his car. He claims to have been lonely and to have found company in the jackrabbit, but Maclean suspects that the accident may have resulted from alcohol. Maclean does not know if he is supposed to be amused or concerned, but, as with subsequent problems, he proves unable to be his "brother's keeper." Paul refuses even to acknowledge offers of help. After the debacle with Neal, Paul does show his love for Maclean by suggesting another fishing trip and by including their father, who had already retired his fishing gear.

After Paul's death, their father suggests that by making up a story and the people to go with it, Maclean will be able to understand the events of his life and why they happened. The father goes on to explain that the people we love and should know are the very people who "elude us." By telling the story, Maclean creates an elegy, not only to Paul but also to his father's power as a believer who loves his sons deeply.

Maclean's mother, wife, and sister-in-law are portrayed as strong Scottish women who defend family honor and who also act as peacemakers when needed. These women are caregivers. Maclean's mother shows near-adoration of Paul despite his failings. Yet the women are not expected to fish or even to know much about fishing and so are not central to the story, although their love and approval are clearly important to Maclean.

Themes and Meanings

Much of the power of *A River Runs Through It* derives from its unusual perspective that the Protestant Christian beliefs of the Maclean family present no conflict with nature. Maclean describes a seamless unity between his family and the environment in which they live. There is no reference to human dominion over the earth, nor is there a threatening wilderness. The characters experience emotional confusion and pain as a result of human interaction. The natural world in Montana is a sacred place, making Neal and Old Rawhide's behavior especially mortifying. Montana's ruggedness requires the chosen people, Maclean and his family, to be tough but moral in their own way.

When fishing, the brothers enter a "world apart," one in which there are further worlds to experience. On one trip, Maclean explains how he is able to forget the tumult in his life, item by item, until he achieves oneness with the river. To further animate this theme, methods of fishing, the equipment used, and actual fishing activities are described in detail throughout the novel. Casting is always done in four-part rhythm, the trajectory beginning between two and ten o'clock. Instead of a fishing "pole," fly fishing is done with a "rod" made of split bamboo with silk thread wrappings. In a scene where Paul's artistry in shadow casting merges him with the supernatural world, the water creates a halo around him. Such detailed accounts of fishing, written with religious imagery, reveal the possibility of grace and beauty to otherwise fallen humans. Fishing in a new hole creates a "fresh start in life" reminiscent of baptism.

Just as fishing cleanses the spirit, writing is a way of landing the most significant catch, a meaningful life. Near the end of the novel, Maclean and his father discuss the opening of the first verse of the Gospel of John, "In the beginning was the Word. . . ." At issue is whether the Word came before the rocks in the river or if the rocks and the river somehow created the Word. They argue about what Paul would say, but he is busy catching the last fish they will ever see him catch. Although he has grace and beauty, he lacks the moral connections to society and God that would save him.

The ending of *A River Runs Through It* is poetic but enigmatic, the pronouns "it" and "their" having unclear antecedents. After Paul and the father are long dead, Maclean still fishes the Big Blackfoot River, where, "Eventually, all things merge into one, and a river runs through it." The river was cut by a "great flood" and runs over "rocks from the basement of time." He concludes that under the rocks are words that are "theirs," as he ends, "haunted by waters."

Critical Context

Norman Maclean began writing *A River Runs Through It*, his first novel, after he retired from a highly respected career as a teacher at the University of Chicago, where he was a noted Aristotelian critic. He received honors for excellence in undergraduate teaching three times. His knowledge of literature, his humanity as a teacher, and his critical expertise gave him the background to write about his life in Montana. The imagery of Maclean's prose style and the subject matter of *A River Runs Through It* did not attract commercial publishers, however. The University of Chicago Press took on the book, the first fiction it had ever published, out of respect for Maclean's university career.

The novel was an immediate critical success and went through printing after printing as word of its quality spread. It became a serious contender for the Pulitzer Prize. Critics compared the novel to Ernest Hemingway's "Big Two-Hearted River" and *The Sun Also Rises* (1926) and to Henry David Thoreau's *A Week on the Concord and Merrimack Rivers* (1849). Maclean's novel attracted many film offers, none of which suited Maclean, who wanted artistic control to a degree unknown in the movie industry. Finally Robert Redford, a respected advocate of Western literature and film, persuaded Maclean to let him direct the film version, but Maclean died before the film was finished. It was released in 1992 and received three Academy Award nominations, winning an award for best cinematography. *A River Runs Through It* is a modern classic, bringing increased recognition to the deep regard that Western American people feel for the land and its resources.

Bibliography

Foote, Timothy. "A New Film About Fly Fishing—And Much, Much More." *Smithsonian* 23, no. 6 (September, 1992): 120. Effectively tells of the novel's unique origination, history, and transition to film.

Ford, James E. "When 'Life . . . Becomes Literature': The Neo-Aristotelian Poetics of Norman Maclean's *A River Runs Through It*. *Studies in Short Fiction* 30, no. 4 (Fall, 1993): 525. For readers who want to understand how Maclean's background as a critic shapes his fiction.

MacFarland, Ron. *Norman Maclean*. Western Writers Series, No. 107. Boise, Idaho: Boise State University Press, 1993. Brief, authoritative introduction to Maclean as a Western writer.

MacFarland, Ron, and Hugh Nichols, eds. *Norman Maclean*. Lewiston, Idaho: Confluence Press, 1988. A chronology and collection of Maclean's speeches and essays, two interviews, and criticism. Includes major essays in critical analysis and commentary by Wallace Stegner, Glen A. Love, and Wendell Berry.

Margaret A. Dodson

THE ROBBER BRIDE

Author: Margaret Atwood (1939-   )
Type of plot: Social
Time of plot: The late twentieth century
Locale: Toronto, Canada
First published: 1993

　　Principal characters:
　　　　TONY, a professor with a yen for war who almost loses her husband to
　　　　　　Zenia
　　　　CHARIS, a mystic flower-child who loses her lover to Zenia
　　　　ROZ, a wealthy financier who loses her husband to Zenia
　　　　ZENIA, a female villian who devours other women's men

The Novel

　　The Robber Bride, Margaret Atwood's eighth novel, opens at the trendy Toronto restaurant Toxique, where middle-aged friends Tony, Charis, and Rox have their monthly lunch. Although they come from different backgrounds and their personalities are much at odds, they share a common denominator: All have lost a lover or spouse to the nefarious, ravishing she-devil Zenia. Friends since their 1960's days at Toronto University, over the last thirty years they have helped each other in turn survive Zenia's poisonous onslaughts. Although Zenia is dead—they attended her cremation in order to be sure—they continue their supportive meetings. To their great consternation, however, an even more dazzling, resurrected Zenia walks right by them in the restaurant.

　　Most of the novel recounts the women's ordeals after the sinister Zenia enters their lives, steals their men, and shatters their worlds. The first narrative deals with Tony, a professor of military history, who has managed to salvage her placid musicologist husband from the evil Zenia's talons. At college, Tony falls deeply in love with Zenia's roommate, West. Although Zenia demonstrates friendship to Tony, she is really after her notes, papers, and ultimately, her inheritance.

　　The second story revolves around the quirky but loveable Charis. Charis's life rotates around Billy, an American draft-dodger who manipulates Charis to conceal him on her island hideaway, until Zenia pays an uninvited visit. She plays on Charis's good nature, begging her to care for her while she battles cancer—from which she does not suffer. Charis moves her into her home, nurses her, and financially supports her as well as Billy, only to find herself one day pregnant and deserted by both Billy and Zenia.

　　The third story chronicles Roz, a rich girl who marries Mitch, a charming philanderer. Roz finds some comfort in the fact that Mitch loves her best—that is, until he too falls under the Zenia's spell. Earlier, after Zenia had played on her sympathies, Roz had given the unemployed Zenia a job managing one of her magazines. Zenia pays back Roz by seducing her husband, who becomes so enraptured with her that he commits suicide when Zenia ultimately spurns him. Atwood delves deeply into each woman's life to demonstrate the paramount role their early years played in their psychic development and the choices they make as adults. Charis's fastidious daughter August and Roz's hilarious teenage twins and troubled son Larry are also introduced, as well as Roz's gay, poetry-quoting secretary Royce.

The last quarter of the novel returns to the present, with Tony, Charis and Roz attending a dinner meeting at the Toxique restaurant. Now they realize that Zenia had earlier faked her own funeral. Unbeknownst to the others, each had earlier confronted Zenia at her hotel. Tony, desperate to make sure Zenia does not woo back her husband, stalks Zenia with a gun but fails to use it. Charis, despondent over her chances of ever finding her stolen lover Billy, experiences a psychotic episode. Roz, intent on protecting her son from Zenia's depravity, falls victim to Zenia's threats and timidly leaves. All undergo catharsis, however, when they realize that they did not surrender to their base instincts, their raw hatred and rage (although this is not clear in the case of Charis) and did not kill Zenia, their nemesis. After each woman explains her various run-ins with Zenia, Charis experiences a psychic premonition; she is sure Zenia is dead, this time for real. The three friends rush to Zenia's hotel, where they find Zenia in Ophelia-like fashion, head down in a fountain. The police investigation reveals that Zenia, in keeping with her shrouded past, may have been a spy or a drug-dealer or may even have committed suicide, since she had a terminal illness. After Zenia's death, Tony finds greater love in her marriage, Charis reconciles with her daughter August, and Roz's troubled son Larry reveals his homosexuality and his relationship with Royce to a more loving mother. Zenia's past remains a mystery.

The Characters

Three of the primary characters of Margaret Atwood's novel grow as individuals throughout, but the central character, Zenia, remains a trope, forever the evil villainess. With the exception of Roz's son Larry and Tony's husband West, the male characters show no signs of growth. In this sense, Atwood demonstrates a talent for character development while keeping within her thematic framework.

Tony, a mass of contradictions, captures the reader's interest immediately. Physically diminutive, she is a mental giant, an expert in siege techniques of the Middle Ages. A nurturer, homebody, and flower collector, she specializes in the study of war—the bloodier the battles the better. Abandoned by her philandering war-bride mother, she is reared by an indifferent, abusive, alcoholic father (who in time commits suicide) and learns at an early age to fend for herself. Tony's penchant for reversing words is merely her way of taking on a compensatory identity. She approaches her relationship with her weak and dependent husband West with almost servile appreciation, taking on the role of his protector but feeling all the while incompetent in Zenia's shadow.

Charis, the psychic, herb-growing earth-mother, floats through life thinking well of everyone and diffusing any oppressive thoughts that might put her in touch with her

justified rage. It is not until Charis's background is revealed that readers behold her
actions as psychological defense mechanisms. She was originally known as Karen;
her unknown father met and abandoned her mother during the war. After her severely
abusive mother is institutionalized, the youngster has to suffer the sexual assaults of
an uncle. Survival necessitates the repression of Karen and the emergence of Charis,
who looks at the world through rose-colored lenses. In her showdown with Zenia, Karen emerges, and by the novel's end, both identities merge into a whole woman.

Roz, the business tycoon with the heart of gold, eats to stifle her feelings of unworthiness. Her charming Jewish father does not return from World War II to her strict
Catholic mother until Roz is about seven years old. Up until this point, she attends
Catholic school and helps her mother clean their rooming house. Shortly after her father returns, however, the family is catapulted into a mansion. In time, it becomes
clear that her father's wealth is based on paintings stolen from the Nazis during the
war. Although Roz excels in the family business, her hormones betray her into marrying Mitch, who is much more in love with her money. Throughout the novel, Roz is
torn between love and lust, Catholicism and Judaism, repression and aggression. The
root cause of this split is an inner sense of unworthiness, and she looks to others to val-
idate her existence. After surviving her husband's suicide and her debacle with Zenia,
she rebounds.

Zenia, a present-day Lady MacBeth, is every female villian. She spans time and
continents, surviving even death. Although her face could launch a thousand ships,
her insides are putrid. While the reader may at times feel admiration for Zenia's boldness, there can never be any sympathy. She slithers her way into other women's lives,
robs them of their men, and leaves. At the end of the novel, Zenia gets her comeup-
pance when she goes hurtling off a balcony. A question remains, though: Would the
others ever have developed and grown had this vampire not invaded their lives?

Themes and Meanings

The structure of this tragicomedy suggests an onion that the reader must peel layer
by layer to get at the central meaning. Atwood reverses the Brothers Grimm's "The
Robber Bridegroom." While the fairy tale chronicles the exploits of a sinister bridegroom who destroys young women merely for pleasure, Zenia the bewitching robber
bride relishes other women's men; especially delicious are men belonging to her
friends. *The Robber Bride* examines the incongruity of woman as villain by presenting three engrossing, nice, and well-behaved women. They are reminiscent in some
ways of William Shakespeare's passive, docile, and mad Ophelia, who ends up dead,
face down in a river, after having tormented herself in her efforts to please the
weak-willed Hamlet. Nice women finish last, Atwood would maintain. Tony, Charis,
and Roz provide nurturance, comfort, financial support, sex—anything it takes to
please their men—even if it means putting their own needs and desires aside. It is only
when the villian Zenia enters the scene that they can come to view their own lives of
self-deception, become less agreeable, change, and grow as individuals. They must do
battle with Zenia to break free of her control.

Battle strategy and war provide a framework for the novel. Atwood examines not only the war between the sexes but also women's war against one another. In addition, she posits the idea that military war affects not only the men who actually fight but also the women who stand and wait, and she deftly illustrates war's long-range intergenerational effects. Tony, Charis, and Roz's fathers all fought in World War II.

In addition, the novel continues the theme of dual-identity characters found throughout Atwood's novels, particularly *Alias Grace* (1988). In *The Robber Bride*, all three child protagonists split into two discernable frames of mind in an effort to cope with their dysfunctional worlds. This deception, however, often leads them to re-live familial history. Atwood uses a textual echoing device to achieve her purpose: Although the characters are very different, they have lived strikingly similar lives. To a great extent, they also emulate or echo their mothers' lives. In this way, Atwood weaves in her concern with Canadian identity, particularly the sameness of Canadian women's lives. Also apparent is the author's theme of the self-deception of middle-class women and the idea that women cannot be trusted. On the other hand, Atwood suggests another feminist theme, that there is strength in numbers: When women trust one another, they contribute to one another's lives and grow.

Critical Context

Margaret Atwood, perhaps the foremost figure in Canadian literature, is an astute critic of Canadian culture. In addition to developing her complex feminist themes, *The Robber Bride* demonstrates a deep concern with Canadian identity, particularly the constricted similarities of Canadian women's lives. The novel provides absorbing and insightful glimpses into the female individual and female relationships and asks several questions: Can women reach the same powerful heights that men do without breaking society's rules? Do nice girls finish last? The methodologies of feminism and psychoanalysis are used throughout to confront Atwood's ongoing concerns with domestic and sexual violence, self-image, and gender and power politics.

Bibliography

Atwood, Margaret. *Selected Poems II: Poems Selected and New, 1976-1986*. New York: Houghton Mifflin, 1987. Contains Atwood's poem "The Robber Bridegroom," which was influential in the creation of *The Robber Bride*.

Bronson, J. Brooks. *Brutal Choreographies, Oppositional Strategies, and Narrative Design in the Novels of Margaret Atwood*. Boston: University of Massachusetts Press, 1997. A scholarly but approachable work that draws heavily on feminist and psychoanalytic theory to examine the ongoing themes in Atwood's novels.

Cooke, Nathalie. *Margaret Atwood: A Biography*. Downsview, Ontario: ECW Press, 1998. Although some critics have questioned its content, this is the first comprehensive biography of Atwood, and it does provide insight into her novels.

Mycak, Sonia. *In Search of the Split Subject: Psychoanalysis, Phenomenology, and the Novels of Margaret Atwood*. Downsview, Ontario: ECW Press, 1997. A scholarly but accessible critique and analysis of the dual identities adopted by many Atwood characters.

Wilson, Sharon Rose. *Margaret Atwood's Fairy-Tale Sexual Politics*. Oxford: University Press of Mississippi, 1993. Considers Atwood's thematic use of fairy tales and their gender implications.

M. Casey Diana

THE ROBBER BRIDEGROOM

Author: Eudora Welty (1909-   )
Type of plot: Satiric folk/fairy tale
Time of plot: Pioneer days
Locale: Along the Natchez Trace in Mississippi
First published: 1942

> *Principal characters:*
> JAMIE LOCKHART, the robber bridegroom, a gentleman and the leader of
>   a band of bandits
> CLEMENT MUSGROVE, a kindly, innocent planter
> ROSAMOND MUSGROVE, his beautiful young daughter
> SALOME, Rosamond's jealous and possessive stepmother
> MIKE FINK, the legendary river boatman of American folklore
> GOAT, a foolish, interfering creature, the "familiar" of Salome
> BIG HARP and
> LITTLE HARP, bandit brothers
> THE INDIANS, anonymous and mysterious, but important presences

The Novel

This deceptively simple novel is both a bit of American folklore which depicts the rough-and-tumble life of the frontier and a satiric fairy tale which draws from and parodies the tales of the Brothers Grimm. As is typical of fairy tales, the story is highly plotted. It begins when Clement Musgrove, an innocent planter, meets Jamie Lockhart, a bandit, and Mike Fink, the famous folklore figure, at an inn. When Jamie saves Clement from being murdered and robbed by Fink, Clement tells Jamie of his past, when his first wife and his two sons were captured, tortured, and killed by the Indians. Only his daughter Rosamond remains, and he has remarried an ugly woman named Salome, whom the Indians did not kill because they were afraid of her. The relationship between Rosamond and Salome—the beautiful young girl and the evil stepmother—is right out of "Cinderella" and "Snow White": "If Rosamond was as beautiful as the day, Salome was as ugly as the night." Salome harasses Rosamond, who in turn fights this by creating her own fantasy world; even though she means only to tell the truth, lies fall out of her mouth like "diamonds and pearls."

The witch-like Salome has, as witches often do, her familiar, a foolish young man who, because of his habit of butting his way out the door when his mother locks him in, is named Goat. Salome hires Goat to follow Rosamond and to "finish her off" if he finds the chance. The plot begins in earnest when Jamie Lockhart, dressed as a robber rather than as a gentleman, complete with berry juice stains on his face as a disguise, encounters Rosamond in the woods and robs her of all her clothes, making her go home "naked as a jaybird." When Clement hears of this, he goes to get Jamie to avenge his daughter's honor. In the meantime, Jamie once more carries Rosamond off into the forest and robs her "of that which he had left her the day before"—that is, her virginity. When Clement brings Jamie to his home, Rosamond is so begrimed, in typical Cinderella fashion, that he does not recognize her. Moreover, since he is now the gentleman, with no berry juice on his face, he is not recognized by her. Salome, however, who sees traces of the berry juice, knows everything.

Rosamond tries to find out where Jamie lives, for after he has dishonored her, she feels pity for him. She finds the house of the bandit gang and, like Snow White at the house of the seven dwarfs, sets about cleaning it up. While being kept captive at the bandit hideout, she begs Jamie to wash the berry juice off his face so that she can know who he is. As in the classical Cupid and Psyche story, however, Jamie insists on keeping his other identity a secret.

Being so preoccupied with Rosamond, Jamie neglects Clement's request to find the violator of his daughter, until once again he takes it up and runs into Big Harp and Little Harp. Big Harp is only a decapitated head, having lost his body to an executioner's ax; Little Harp, who knows Jamie the bandit to be also Jamie the gentleman, uses this knowledge to blackmail Jamie and to move into his home. Rosamond returns to her father, telling him of her robber bridegroom, and Salome gives Rosamond a recipe to remove berry stains so that she might know his true identity. Little Harp tells the bandits that he is entitled to the bandit chief's woman, but they get him an Indian girl instead, whom he then brutally rapes and murders. Rosamond catches Jamie asleep, removes the berry stains, and discovers that he is only Jamie Lockhart; at the same time, he knows her to be Clement Musgrove's silly daughter. Because of Rosamond's distrust, Jamie runs away.

In a rapid series of events, Rosamond follows Jamie, Salome goes to the woods to try to find him to cut off his head, and Clement searches for his daughter and Jamie. All are captured by the Indians who seek to avenge the murder of the Indian girl. Goat frees them one by one, and Jamie and Little Harp fight until Little Harp is killed. Salome dies in an unsuccessful attempt to make the sun stand still by her dancing. Rosamond wanders through the woods until she arrives in New Orleans, meets Jamie Lockhart again, and they get married. In the spring, Clement Musgrove goes to New Orleans and finds them where they have everything they could want in the world. Thus, the story ends in typical "They lived happily ever after" fairy-tale fashion.

The Characters

All the characters in the story, with perhaps the exception of Clement Musgrove, are one-dimensional figures drawn from American folklore and the fairy tales of the Brothers Grimm. What makes Clement more complex is his awareness of the changing nature of the frontier and his knowledge of the essential duality of life—both central themes in the story. Clement tells Jamie earlier in the novel that the Indians know their time has come; "they are sure of the future growing smaller always, and that lets them be infinitely gay and cruel." When he discovers that Jamie is both the gentleman he met and the bandit who raped his daughter, he says that all things are double: "All things are divided in half—night and day, the soul and body, and sorrow and joy and youth and age. . . ." Thus, Clement is the central figure, both innocent in the ways of the world and wise in the meaning of that which he discovers.

Jamie, the robber bridegroom, is the central embodiment of the novel's duality; he is both the handsome prince who comes to claim the beautiful daughter, as well as the stereotypical outlaw of the old frontier. Rosamond is the beautiful princess who at first rebuffs and then accepts her captor and violator; she is the fanciful and resilient adolescent heroine of countless fairy tales. Salome, the evil stepmother, not only is jealous of Rosamond's beauty but also is an embodiment of the grasping materialism that gradually destroys the freedom of the frontier, for she continually insists that Clement increase his land holdings and build an empire in the wilderness. The minor characters—Mike Fink, Goat, and the Harp brothers—are the stock figures of folklore and fairy tale. They are both functions of the plot, serving to further the complications of the action, and embodiments of the violence and grotesque humor inherent in folk traditions.

Themes and Meanings

This novel seems so childlike and simple that one is tempted to think it carries no theme at all, but that it is rather merely an extremely well-done satire of fairy tale conventions. Welty herself once said that the story came from "a lifetime of fairy-tale reading." Nevertheless, there are two underlying themes in the work—a cultural one concerning the nature of the inevitably changing American frontier and a psychological one typical of all great fairy tales.

On one level, the story is about the gradual loss of American frontier life; Clement, goaded by his possessive and greedy wife, is a reluctant embodiment of the taming of the wildness of the frontier by the civilizing effect of landowning. The Indians, mysterious and mostly unseen presences in the story, represent both the violence and the innocence of the wilderness; as Clement understands, they know that their time is limited. The central duality of Jamie, who is both a gentleman and a robber, suggests the transition point of the wilderness that the novel attempts to capture, for it takes place at a time in American history which hovers between the freedom of lawlessness and the restraint of civilized society.

Because the story also makes use of fairy-tale conventions as well as those of American folklore, it is not only the innocence, violence, and youth of the country that is depicted but also these same characteristics of the individual, for these are aspects upon which the fairy-tale genre particularly focuses. Thus the youth of America and the youth of the individual are paralleled in the story. Just as this duality dominates the overall story, the tone and the characters of the story also exhibit a duality, for the tale is one of innocence and of violence at the same time. Moreover, just as the characters are caught between their dual selves as well as between the past and the present, so also is the reader caught between fantasy and reality. As is typical of the youth of the nation and the youth of every individual, the two realms of fantasy and reality blend together in such a way that one can never be too sure what realm one inhabits. As Clement says about the duality, "This should keep us from taking liberties with the outside world, and acting too quickly to finish things off." Thus, the story's most basic theme has to do with the elusive nature of reality itself, which is chimerical and ever-changing.

Critical Context

Eudora Welty is better known for her short stories than for her novels, and in this, her first novel, one can appreciate her familiarity with the folktale and fairy-tale conventions that contribute to her own work and to the short-story form in general. When *The Robber Bridegroom* first appeared, many critics admired it for its clever satire and for its pure and sustained and ironic style, but few saw it to be a serious work of fiction with an important theme. Several reviewers thought that it was a tour de force of technique likely to be appreciated by admirers of Welty's short fiction, but to be of little interest to the general reader. Later, however, critics took the story more seriously, exploring its sources in folklore and works of American humor and probing its cultural and metaphysical themes.

Most of Welty's works, both novels and stories, are mythic and fantastic to some degree, although perhaps none is so deeply imbued with fairy-tale conventions as is *The Robber Bridegroom*. Welty is more concerned with what she has called "the season of dreams" than she is with the world of external reality. Thus, her stories are seldom realistic, although she invariably sets them in recognizable places and inhabits them with characters who, although often grotesque, possess human qualities that are easily recognizable.

Welty's best-known stories, many of which are anthologized in short-story textbooks, are from *A Curtain of Green* (1941), *The Wide Net and Other Stories* (1943), and *The Golden Apples* (1949). All are characterized by her fascination with myth and legend and her blending of the characters and events of archetypal stories with ordinary people of the American South. Eudora Welty is, without doubt, one of the greatest American short-story writers in the twentieth century, and *The Robber Bridegroom*, drawing on her intimate familiarity with folklore, myth, and fairy tale, is a compendium of the sources of her art.

Bibliography

Champion, Laurie, ed. *The Critical Response to Eudora Welty's Fiction*. Westport, Conn.: Greenwood Press, 1994. In her introduction, Champion presents an overview of the criticism on Welty's fiction. Four separate essays by different scholars are devoted to various aspects of *The Robber Bridegroom*. Includes a helpful bibliography of works for further reading.

Gretlund, Jan N. *Eudora Welty's Aesthetics of Place*. Newark: University of Delaware Press, 1994. A comprehensive overview of Welty's work focusing on the vivid sense of setting and place that Welty brings to her novels. Includes two interviews with Welty.

Horn, Miriam. "Imagining Others' Lives." *US News and World Report* 114 (February 15, 1993): 78-79. Profiles Welty, who has spent most of her literary career revealing mythic dimensions in the most ordinary of lives. Explores Welty's genteel southern background and briefly examines some of her works, including *The Robber Bridegroom*.

Kreyling, Michael. *Author and Agent: Eudora Welty and Diarmuid Russell*. New York: Farrar, Straus, and Giroux, 1991. Emphasizing their correspondence, this book explores the relationship between Welty and her agent Russell. Kreyling examines Welty's development as a writer, as well as the encouragement and devotion of Russell to her work. Many of her novels are discussed.

Waldron, Ann. *Eudora: A Writer's Life*. New York: Doubleday, 1998. An unauthorized biography, as well as the first to be written, about Welty that presents new material about her personal life and career. Although Waldron does not present in-depth analysis of Welty's works, this book sheds light on her background and writings.

Charles E. May

THE ROCK CRIED OUT

Author: Ellen Douglas (Josephine Haxton; 1921-   )
Type of plot: Realism
Time of plot: The 1960's and the 1970's
Locale: Homochitto County, Mississippi
First published: 1979

> *Principal characters:*
> ALAN MCLAURIN, the protagonist, a young white man returning home
>   to Mississippi after spending time in the North
> MIRIAM WEST, Alan's Northern girlfriend who is visiting him in
>   Mississippi
> PHOEBE CHIPMAN, Alan's cousin who was killed in an automobile
>   accident when they were teenagers and who was the only true love
>   of Alan's life
> DALLAS BOYKIN, a friend of Alan from childhood who has remained in
>   Mississippi working as a laborer and who resents Alan's not having
>   fought in Vietnam
> SAM DANIELS, a black man and a good friend of Alan; he oversees the
>   family's country place
> LEILA MCLAURIN, Alan's free-spirited aunt; she has had an affair with
>   Sam

The Novel

Ellen Douglas tells the story of the emergence of a new South. She also tells about a local Mississippi boy who comes home to discover that new South and to discover the truth about the past. The novel opens with Alan McLaurin making his way back home to Mississippi after having spent a number of years in the Northeast. Hitchhiking, he is picked up by a carload of blacks. Marveling at the changes, he explains that he has been away from Homochitto County, Mississippi, for a number of years, but that now he is home to settle down on his family's land in the country. Having quit his job in a sugar refinery and separated from his live-in girlfriend, Miriam West, Alan has left Boston to "live on the land" and write poetry. A conscientious objector who did not serve in the Vietnam War, Alan had left home to go to school in the North. He had left behind a South in racial and social turmoil and now has returned home to discover what is left of the land that he abandoned.

The discovery process provides a framework for the novel's action. Told as a recollection by Alan, the writer, several years after the events in the novel have taken place, the novel moves as a first-person account from the narrator's present back to the events in the novel and even back to the 1960's. The novel is also a discovery process for the reader, for not until the book's end do the pieces of the puzzle fit together.

After arriving at the family place, Alan becomes reacquainted with Sam Daniels, the black caretaker of the family land, and catches up on events in the community. As each character is introduced, there are flashbacks to past events that put the characters in perspective. In Sam's case, she describes him as a stubborn man, living right on the edge of danger during the turbulent 1960's. Sam has been integral to the McLaurin family for years; he has tended the family land, has had a love affair with Alan's Aunt Leila McLaurin, and has driven the car in which Alan's cousin, Phoebe Chipman, was killed. Douglas then goes on to describe Phoebe's accident. Her death haunts Alan throughout the novel and ultimately leads to his own violent action. Furthermore, his present girlfriend, Miriam, bears a striking resemblance to Phoebe. The reader learns at this point in the novel that Phoebe was killed in an accident in which Sam drove with her down a gravel road not far from home. Sam vaguely recollects rocks striking the windshield, temporarily blinding him, and making him run off the road. This one incident sends out tendrils to nearly every other event in the novel. In one sense, the entire book is about Alan's search for the true nature of this accident.

With Sam's help, Alan sets about fixing up an old house on the family place. He plans to live there alone; his parents live in the city and come out to the country only during the summers. Gradually, old friends from the past appear to help Alan with his project. Dallas Boykin, a boyhood friend, shows up one day to help with the house. The reader learns that Boykin served a tour of duty in Vietnam, returned home to settle down, and married a Fundamentalist wife. They live in a house trailer, and Dallas earns his living hauling pulpwood from the pine forests.

After several months of celibacy, Alan invites Miriam, who is in Boston, for a visit, and his liberal, artistic Aunt Leila comes to "chaperone" the couple. At a party, Alan learns from a drunken Leila about her affair with Sam. Also at the party is Lindsey Lee, a local boy turned hippie whom they had met earlier at a general store. Miriam becomes attracted to Lindsey Lee and they form a sort of trio. The three of them, Miriam, Alan, and Lindsey, set out to discover the truth about the new South by interviewing locals, including Sam's eighty-five-year-old father, Noah Daniels. Their tape recordings allow Douglas to unearth another layer of past history, but the precious truth remains elusive.

Meanwhile, Sam and Leila rekindle their romance, while Lindsey Lee and Miriam also become lovers. Tension builds among the trio as Alan, almost an outsider, tries to reconcile his relationship with Miriam. They had promised that they would not possess each other, but Alan cannot give up his claim to her sole affections.

The novel's climax comes in a twenty-five-page monologue in which a distraught Dallas drives wildly all over the county in his truck, talking nonstop on his CB radio. Thinking that he is talking to his wife, Dallas confesses to her—and also to Alan, who is listening on another radio—that he, too, once loved Phoebe. Dallas also tells the real story of her death. Phoebe's death occurred during the most violent time of the civil rights struggle. Several churches were burned down in Homochitto County, including one near the McLaurin family place. Naturally, whites—including members of the Ku Klux Klan—were trying to stop black civil rights progress in this rural Mississippi community. On the day of Phoebe's death, Sam was driving her in the car down a country road. Dallas and some of his friends (including Lindsey Lee) were watching a meeting at a black church through the scopes on their high-powered rifles. They saw Sam's car coming down the road, and for some reason, Dallas explains in his monologue, he fired. That was the shot (Sam thought it was gravel) which made him wreck the car.

Furious that Dallas had killed his beloved cousin, Alan sets out across the county to find him, finally catching the man near a small dam which is about to overflow. As Alan and Dallas fight, the escaping water knocks them down a ravine and Dallas is killed. "I knew he was dead," Alan says. "A horrible pain, unassuageable grief, seized me, worse than any kick in the balls, worse than any ice pick in my liver. I had killed him."

By the end of the novel, Douglas brings the reader full circle to the present Alan McLaurin, who talks about finally settling down to write the truth about the past and about the new South—a truth the reader experiences as *The Rock Cried Out*.

The Characters

Much of Douglas's strength lies in her characterization. She does well writing a first-person account from a male point of view and her skillfully crafted Alan McLaurin grows from a naive, idealistic youth into a cynical, worldly man. He becomes a metaphor, in some ways, for so many in his generation whose idealism was fueled by a protest against a war in which they did not believe and a struggle to correct a region's racial attitudes, which were clearly oppressive. Then his generation grew up to find a morally ambiguous world. He grows up by searching for the real story of the past and matures as he puts together some of the unpleasant aspects of that painful reality. In the final chapter, Alan McLaurin displays a certain confidence and peacefulness—much like the confidence displayed in his new South as it, too, emerges from a trial by baptism and fire.

Douglas's other characters all exhibit originality. She avoids cliched Southern characters but still represents all aspects of the South about which she writes. For example, the free-spirited Aunt Leila puts love and compassion ahead of community mores, but she is still a Southerner. She loves Sam Daniels; his being black does not matter.

Dallas Boykin represents the confused, poor Southerner. After fighting for his country in Vietnam and against racial equality in the South, he emerges at the end of the 1970's confused and quietly angry. Feeling guilty for his transgressions, he tries to make amends, yet the new South gives him little, save religion, to hang on to. His wife is the born-again, talking-in-tongues, Southern Fundamentalist who escapes the modern world by living in a religious cocoon. Dallas accepts her, but he does not really find peace in the life that she represents.

To her credit, Douglas takes the stereotypes and molds them into real human beings. Her blacks, for example, become genuine people in a racially confused South. Noah, born of a generation of shuffling old "Uncle Toms," is a witty, spry, three-dimensional character. Perhaps most interesting of all, however, is Sam. He has fought all of his life. Refusing to succumb to the white man, he almost but not quite pushes his independence too far. For example, refusing to say "sir" to white men, Sam "talks around" those kinds of references. Also, he becomes a lover to a white woman. Sam, however, does spend some time in jail for attacking the navy's satellite tracking station (SPASURSTA), which sits on a parcel of McLaurin property rented to the government. He simply got angry one day and crossed the fence with his cows to start destroying the equipment. Stoically, he accepted his punishment.

Other characters also evidence Douglas's skill. There is Lindsey Lee, the local boy turned hippie who goes around the county taping "quaint old black men and local rednecks" for a story that he is going to write for a large East Coast paper. The naïve Miriam West also fits in with the patronizing Lindsey Lee. She comes from the North with her preconceived notions about the South and naturally has an affair with Lindsey.

Themes and Meanings

The essential theme of the novel is the search for what is real in the new South. Alan McLaurin comes home to a land he does not really understand to try to piece together his life and, more specifically, to try to understand Phoebe's tragic death. To separate truth from fiction becomes Alan's mission. A poet at the novel's beginning, he seems to discard art as an organizing principle rather quickly, perhaps partially because his poetry is unsuccessful.

Douglas skillfully leads the reader along Alan's discovery process. By telling the story in the first person, Douglas must reveal to the reader little bits of truth at the same time that she allows Alan to discover them. These revelations—the truth—have a powerful effect on Alan, driving him, a registered conscientious objector, to kill at the novel's end. It is almost as if by finding out the truth about Phoebe's death, Alan also finds out the truth about himself and about the world. This point is evidenced in the novel's title, taken from an old spiritual about trying to escape: "I went to the rock to hide my face./ The rock cried out, 'No hiding place.'/ No hiding place down there."

An attachment to the land, a major theme in many Southern novels, also plays an important part in this work. Alan returns not only to his native South but also to his "old home place." There, living in a rustic old house, he observes nature and the seasons. With SPASURSTA, Douglas makes an obvious comment on the relationship between nature, the new South, and technology. When Sam finally loses all patience with the new technology's invasion of his pastoral life, he attacks the radar station. Douglas seems to be saying that what destroys nature also harms mankind.

This fenced, steel, computer-operated SPASURSTA that sits in the middle of old Mississippi pasture land becomes a symbol for the blending of the old South and the new South. The old South, with its surreptitious miscegenation, its bigotry, violence, and steadfast commitment to the old ways, haunts Alan McLaurin, blinding him to the truth. To discover the truth, he must face and conquer these ghosts while realizing, at the same time, the futility of trying to destroy the machinery of the new, progressive South. The two, Alan learns, must live in harmony.

Critical Context

Douglas's reputation has grown steadily since the publication of her first novel, *A Family's Affairs* (1962). In each succeeding novel, she has managed to transcend the banality of Faulknerian imitations to make fresh statements about the South and about the human condition.

Born in 1921, Douglas is one of a group of writers who, although influenced by the Southern Renaissance, have looked for new meanings in the Southern experience. In *The Rock Cried Out*, Douglas writes a novel for the contemporary reader. While this novel bears a likeness to her earlier work, it also shows that Douglas writes about the modern world; she is not mired in the past. The book also provides a bridge to her next work, *A Lifetime Burning* (1982), another well-received novel about contemporary times.

Bibliography

Douglas, Ellen. "Interview with Ellen Douglas: February 25, 1997." Interview by Charline R. McCord. *The Mississippi Quarterly* 51 (Spring, 1998): 291-321. A revealing interview in which Douglas examines the nature and importance of identity in America's rural South. She discusses her background growing up during the 1920s and notes that her characters embody the awareness that she gained from her experiences.

Jean Haskell Speer. "Ellen Douglas." In *Southern Women Writers: The New Generation*. Tuscaloosa: University of Alabama Press, 1990. A perceptive essay that traces Douglas's career as a writer and offers some criticism of her works. An ideal introduction to Ellen Douglas.

John Canfield

ROGER'S VERSION

Author: John Updike (1932-   )
Type of plot: Novel of ideas
Time of plot: 1984-1985
Locale: An unnamed New England city
First published: 1986

> *Principal characters:*
> ROGER LAMBERT, a divinity-school professor
> ESTHER LAMBERT, Roger's current wife
> DALE KOHLER, a graduate student in computer science
> VERNA EKELOF, Roger's niece, a single mother who lives in a housing
> project in the same city as the Lamberts
> PAULA EKELOF, Verna's illegitimate two-year-old daughter

The Novel

John Updike's long-standing interest in religious issues and his continuing fascination with human sexual behavior are combined in this novel set in New England, the landscape that admirably served an earlier American novelist, Nathaniel Hawthorne, for his investigation of similar subjects in his American classic *The Scarlet Letter* (1850). Told from the point of view of Roger Lambert, the novel presents an intriguing narrative of modern concerns with science and theology. Lambert, a divinity-school professor married for the second time and living happily in an older suburb near the university, is approached by Dale Kohler, a graduate student in computer sciences at the same institution. Dale wants Roger's support in obtaining funding for a most unusual project: He wishes to use the university's computer to prove the existence of God. After an impassioned conversation, Roger provides Dale with the information he needs to seek a grant from the theology school.

Dale has sought out Roger at the suggestion of Roger's niece, Verna Ekelof. The daughter of Roger's half-sister, Verna has fled the family home in Cleveland with her illegitimate mulatto child. Roger has had nothing to do with his niece, but at Dale's insistence, he visits her; he is immediately attracted to her sexually, and the worldly-wise Verna takes advantage of his interest to manipulate him throughout the novel.

Roger's efforts to help Verna finish her education provide him with opportunities to see her, and their family ties make it easy for him to invite her to Thanksgiving dinner. Dale receives an invitation, too, and Roger's wife Esther immediately takes a strong interest in the computer-science student. During the remaining months of winter, Dale prepares his materials to seek the grant, Roger continues to assist Verna in several ways, including financially, and—in Roger's mind, at least—Esther and Dale engage in an affair, using the third-floor studio in the Lambert home or the slovenly student apartment where Dale lives with his Korean roommate.

In February, the Grants Committee awards Dale his grant, and his search for the proof of God's existence begins in earnest. Roger imagines the graduate student seated before his computer screen, manipulating data, cross-referencing information, searching for patterns that might suggest an intelligent being at the seat of creation. Excited by the repetitions of certain combinations, Dale presses on until first a face, then a hand, emerges on the screen—then the computer overloads and shuts itself down.

While this investigation goes on, Verna's situation at home deteriorates. Lambert is called one evening in the spring to come immediately to Verna's apartment, because her daughter Paula is apparently ill. Roger discovers a clear case of child abuse; he takes charge of the situation, delivers mother and daughter to the hospital, and then tries to make excuses for Verna with the doctors and social workers. When Verna is forced to leave the girl overnight at the hospital, Roger takes her back to her apartment, and the two finally make love.

After the consummation of Roger's physical attraction to his niece, the novel moves quickly toward its conclusion. Dale decides to give up his project, claiming that it has eroded his faith; his affair with Esther seems to wane, too. Roger helps Verna come to the conclusion that it would be better for her to return to her mother in Cleveland. In the final scene, Roger and his wife have returned to what is for them a normal lifestyle; the twin crises in their lives, caused by the intrusion of the two young people who have placed unusual and competing demands on them, is apparently over. All is not as it was before Dale Kohler and Verna Ekelof entered the picture, however; Esther is pregnant, presumably with Dale's child. Roger is left to accept this permanent alteration in their lives.

The Characters

Roger Lambert is both narrator and principal subject of this novel. As narrator, he serves as the medium through which events in the story are filtered, and his unusual capacity for self-reflection allows readers significant insight into his character. It also nudges readers to adopt his opinions of other characters, however, which may be at variance with the truth. A former pastor and now divinity-school professor, he represents the attitude of many Americans toward religion: For him it has become a form of social psychology and an intellectual exercise, divorced from any of the fervor of faith that characterized believers in earlier ages. He is uncomfortable when a devout believer such as Dale Kohler accosts his complacency. Nevertheless, the author creates him with sufficient sympathy for the reader to see him as a typical Updike hero: a complex individual struggling with desires of both the spirit and the flesh.

Esther Lambert is less well developed, largely because she is seen only through the eyes of her husband. A woman possessed of courage, she is willing to brook social convention to steal Roger from his first wife (ruining his work as a pastor in the process) and then to take up with Dale to fulfill a sexual appetite that her husband cannot satisfy. Though certainly not devoid of intelligence, she serves primarily as a complement to Roger's overindulgence in intellectual pursuits.

Dale Kohler is a true believer in God; his passion for seeking the deity stands in contrast with Roger's cool, analytical approach to religious questions. The young computer-science student's idealistic—and ultimately unsuccessful—attempt to use scientific knowledge (in this case, the power of the computer) to demonstrate with certainty that God is not a figment of the human imagination is both a typical application of the scientific method and an extension of a long philosophical and theological proof for God's existence.

Verna Ekelof, like Esther, complements Roger's intellectual side in that she is almost totally sensual. A rebellious young adult who has defied parents and social custom by becoming an unwed mother through an interracial relationship, she serves as a living reminder to Roger that he has yearnings of the flesh that are as powerful as his desire to explore the ideas and idiosyncrasies of heretics who influenced the Christian church in its early centuries. She also reminds Roger that he has responsibilities to society that extend beyond the domain of the university at which he earns a comfortable living.

Though not a fully developed character, Paula Ekelof, Verna's illegitimate daughter, serves important functions in the novel. She plays a key role in the plot, since her presence drives Verna to the housing project. She is also the proximate cause of Roger's lovemaking with his niece, since Verna's abuse of Paula causes Roger to leave his home in the middle of the night to help his niece cope with her problem.

Themes and Meanings

In *Roger's Version*, John Updike develops a complex narrative interweaving several themes. Primary among them is the investigation of modern religious beliefs. It is no accident that Roger Lambert's specialty at the divinity school is the exploration of heresies. His comfortable view of God as totally Other and unknowable is challenged by Dale Kohler's curious brand of fundamental assent to the literal tenets of the Bible coupled with his conviction that God can be discovered through the use of sophisticated computer technology. The conflict is more than a simple test of wills between individuals: Kohler's approach to the proof of God's existence is an extension of the scientific community's method of discovering the nature of all reality. In exhibiting an intense dislike for Dale, and in manipulating the younger man's research efforts to discredit and discourage him, Roger is actually representing a religious community that still feels threatened by advances in science. He cannot accept the notion that science might in some way help support the tenets of theology.

The novel is also an investigation of modern domestic relations and of people's sexual needs. Roger appears on first meeting to be a happily married man; readers learn as the story progresses, however, that his earlier affair with Esther led to the breakup of his first marriage and to the loss of his position as a pastor. Nevertheless, Roger and Esther's conventional life in the quiet suburb near the university is set in contrast to that of his niece Verna, who lives as a single mother with her illegitimate mulatto daughter in a housing project populated by economically deprived African Americans. Though neither Roger nor Esther really feels comfortable with Verna, they find that they must take some responsibility for her welfare; they are the only family she has who can come to her aid when she is in need.

Additionally, each of the four main characters in the work is driven toward sexual gratification. Even though the novel is told from Roger's point of view, there is sufficient evidence that Dale, Verna, and Esther seek physical as well as intellectual satisfaction in their lives. Roger is preoccupied with sexual activity—his own and other people's. Try as he might to convince readers that he is an intellectual being, he proves by his thoughts—and later by his actions—that even a clergyman is a prisoner of his libido. The message from Updike is clear: Every person is both soul and body, and there is no escape from this inextricable linkage that makes people human.

Critical Context

Roger's Version is the middle novel in a trilogy Updike wrote as an extended commentary on Nathaniel Hawthorne's *The Scarlet Letter.* Hawthorne's story of religious intolerance and sexual repression is for Updike a profound commentary on the American character. Over a thirteen-year period, Updike wrote three novels, each focusing on these topics from the point of view of a character modeled on one of the three principal personages in Hawthorne's tale: the adulteress Hester Prynne, whose character is reprised in Sarah Worth in the novel *S.* (1988); her lover, the respected minister Arthur Dimmesdale, recast as Tom Marshfield in *A Month of Sundays* (1975); and the relentless persecutor of Hester and Dimmesdale, Roger Chillingsworth, the model for Roger Lambert in *Roger's Version.* As in almost all of his works, Updike focuses on the domestic scene, detailing the lives of everyday middle-class people struggling with their sexual desires and with a feeling of *angst* brought on by a modern world which has turned its back on God and is much the worse for having done so. The characters in this novel share many similarities with others in the Updike canon. In several ways, Roger is an intellectual version of Harry "Rabbit" Angstrom, principal character of four Updike novels which also examine people's preoccupation with their sexual desires and their anxieties about the significance of their lives.

Bibliography
Duvall, John N. "The Pleasures of Textual/Sexual Wrestling: Pornography and Heresy in *Roger's Version.*" *Modern Fiction Studies* 37 (Spring, 1991): 81-95. A poststructuralist analysis of the novel focusing on Roger's unconscious erotic relationship with Dale. Duvall points out parallels between Roger's interest in theology and pornography.
Greiner, Donald J. "Body and Soul: John Updike and *The Scarlet Letter.*" *Journal of Modern Literature* 15 (Spring, 1989): 475-495. Greiner discusses the ways Updike uses Hawthorne's *The Scarlet Letter* as the basis for his discussion of modern American mores and interests in three novels: *Roger's Version, A Month of Sundays,* and *S.*
Neary, John. *Something and Nothingness: The Fiction of John Updike and John Fowles.* Carbondale, Ill.: Southern Illinois University Press, 1992. Describes the re-

action to the novel by several early reviewers. Neary argues that Roger is not really Barthian in his views; rather, the novel presents a Gnostic portrait of the deity. Though Roger manages to crush Dale's spirit, the younger man's optimism lives on in the transformation Esther undergoes.

Newman, Judie. *John Updike*. New York: St. Martin's Press, 1988. Newman briefly summarizes the main action and shows how Updike has carefully crafted his narrative strategies to highlight his themes, theology and technology.

Schiff, James. "Updike's *Roger's Version*: Revisualizing *The Scarlet Letter.*" *South Atlantic Review* 57 (November, 1992): 59-76. Schiff compares the treatment of myth and witchcraft in New England as portrayed in Updike's novel and Nathaniel Hawthorne's *The Scarlet Letter.*

Wilson, Raymond J., III. "*Roger's Version*: Updike's Negative-Solid Model of *The Scarlet Letter.*" *Modern Fiction Studies* 35 (Summer, 1989): 241-250. Wilson discusses the many parallels between Updike's novel and Hawthorne's romance. He delineates ways *Roger's Version* is more complex than its predecessor; he also demonstrates how Updike transforms Hawthorne's tragedy into a comic vision of life.

Laurence W. Mazzeno

ROLL OF THUNDER, HEAR MY CRY

Author: Mildred D. Taylor (1943-   )
Type of plot: Historical realism
Time of plot: 1933-1934
Locale: Rural Mississippi
First published: 1976

> *Principal characters:*
> CASSIE LOGAN, the nine-year-old only daughter of a black family in
> rural Mississippi during the Depression
> STACEY LOGAN, the twelve-year-old eldest son in the Logan family
> CHRISTOPHER JOHN LOGAN, the cheerful, sensitive, and passive
> seven-year-old middle son
> CLAYTON CHESTER LOGAN, nicknamed "Little Man," a bright
> six-year-old boy
> MARY LOGAN, the mother of the four Logan children, a teacher
> DAVID LOGAN, the Logan children's father
> BIG MA, David Logan's sixty-year-old mother, who helps to care for
> the children
> T. J. AVERY, a fourteen-year-old schoolmate of Stacey
> LILLIAN JEAN SIMMS, an adolescent white girl
> KALEB and THURSTON WALLACE, white brothers who run the local
> grocery store by day and lead the Ku Klux Klan by night

The Novel

Based to a large extent on Mildred D. Taylor's experience as a child visiting relatives in Mississippi, *Roll of Thunder, Hear My Cry* depicts the many dimensions of the racism of the Deep South in the 1930's. The Logan family is a strong, close-knit black family struggling to keep their four hundred acres of land during the hard times of the Depression. Against the forces of national economic catastrophe and intense social prejudice, they fight for the survival of their nuclear family, for freedom from racially motivated attacks, and for better educations and adequate livelihoods.

In the first of twelve chapters that encompass a year in the family's life and in the community's turmoil, Cassie Logan and her brothers, in their Sunday best, take the several-mile walk to The Great Faith Elementary and Secondary School, the large segregated school where black children begin their new school year in October after the cotton picking is finished. Cassie's education in the harsh realities of the bigotry of her society begins. The open animosity of whites; the pervasive institutionalized racism in schools, commerce, and laws; and the nighttime violence of vicious vigilante gangs form the cultural context for her growth from innocence to experience. In the next few months of watching, listening, feeling, and thinking, she becomes aware for the first time of the importance that white people give to skin color, and she gradually recognizes how stifled the voices and lives of her family members truly are.

In the geography of racial hatred, rural Mississippi in the 1930's is both homeland and heartland. Terror rules the day-to-day lives of black men and women, from the small-time intimidations of the white children's schoolbus to the cold-blooded murders that go unacknowledged and unpunished. Cassie and her brothers seek what is "fair," and the innocent child's insistence on fairness grows into the adult's desire for social justice. Stacey finds some secret fairness when they ambush the schoolbus, and Cassie finds satisfaction in her carefully orchestrated but hidden revenge on Lillian Jean Simms. Public justice, however, for the Berry family, the Barnetts, or T. J. Avery cannot be achieved. Cassie learns and keeps unspeakable secrets. Nine-year-old Cassie tells her story in first-person narration; it is the story of her education in the dangerous consequences of speech and her lessons in when to keep silent.

The warm bonds of love in the Logan family, their pains and their hopes, their individual and collective strength, and their intelligence and principled behavior are particularly dramatic in a novel in which white characters are few and villainous. One black character, T. J. Avery, seems a scoundrel, but next to the heinous crimes of the white people—the Wallaces and the Simmses—T. J.'s crimes seem petty and child-like.

The new year, 1934, brings an escalation of violence in the community as David Logan, Cassie's father, is shot and his leg broken in a late-night Klan attack. The threat of danger to the Logan family has built continually, but through what seems to be a combination of cleverness and good luck they escape any more serious physical harm.

The climactic eleventh and twelfth chapters, in which T. J. is captured and beaten and is then saved from lynching by David Logan's arson, open with a preface that sounds like a traditional spiritual. The first lines are an invocation, the enigmatic phrases of the novel's title, "Roll of thunder/ hear my cry"; the last lines express determined defiance of the "Ole man" and his whip. This preface to the closing chapters connects the powers of physical nature with the eruption of personal pain into expression. The physical forces of fire and rain are connected in Cassie's mind to the unbearable onslaught of yet more violence and wronging of her race as she watches and responds to the terror of that last night of her childhood.

The Characters

Cassie Logan's innocence allows the reader to experience racial intolerance in the pure light of her naïveté and thereby to share her dawning consciousness of its violence, horror, and injustice. Expecting to gain knowledge of herself and others from books, she instead discovers "the way of things" in the physical and emotional violence of her racially dichotomous society. The reader follows her progress through a hazardous course in how to survive in a world hostile to one's very skin. Like many books for the young, this novel shows issues in black and white, but here that does not make them simpler. Cassie undergoes a rite of passage from the simplicity of family unity to the complexity of the fear and fury of racial discord. Yet the positive values instilled in her by her family live on. Her family's support and love seem to strengthen in the face of adversity. Paradoxically, with new experience and new knowledge gained, Cassie's loss is profound. Her closing words are elegiac; she weeps and laments both the injuries done T. J. and the injuries done the land.

Stacey Logan, Cassie's eldest brother, also matures in the course of this year. A moody, serious twelve-year-old, he is a typical enough young adolescent to be chagrined that his own mother is his seventh-grade teacher. He learns important lessons about loyalty, friendship, and responsibility. In his father's absence, he strives to be the head of his household. He evolves from acting according to a blind allegiance to his friends (as when he refuses to betray T. J.'s cheating at school) to reasoned accountability for his own actions, as when he confesses to his mother that he has broken his promise not to go to the Wallaces' store.

Christopher John Logan is unlike both his brothers and his sister in his passivity. Even on the night of T. J.'s beating and the fire on the Logan land, he refuses to budge from the house. He makes no waves; he sees no evil. Six-year-old Clayton Chester Logan, "Little Man," seems to have been born an adult. A compulsion for neatness in his personal grooming extends to an insistence on logic and order in the world around him. The incident of the dirty book on the first day of class not only reveals his intelligence, pride, and fierceness but also dramatizes Cassie's caring and generosity.

Mary Logan, a strong, protective mother, has worked for fourteen years as a teacher. She is horrified by the burnings of three members of the Berry family. She responds by organizing a boycott of the Wallace store, because the Wallaces seem to be behind such acts of violence. She is a positive role model for her children as a loving person, a well-educated professional, and a socially concerned member of her community willing to sacrifice for principles and the betterment of the community.

David Logan is a hardworking and gentle man forced to leave his family in order to support them. His greatest pride is the four hundred acres of "Logan land." The land holds the roots of his family and literally and figuratively nourishes their future. His children's love and admiration for him are boundless. His strength as a provider, his devotion to his family, and his cunning and courage in the face of mortal danger counter stereotypes of the irresponsible self-involved black male.

T. J. Avery, a fourteen-year-old con man and petty thief, gets into trouble when he falls for the exploitive flattery of two young white men. Although T. J. is disliked and distrusted by virtually everyone, his punishment far exceeds the weight of his crime. He is duped into helping to rob a store. His companions attack and kill Mr. Barnett, one of the owners, and then frame T. J. for the crime. After a bad beating and a narrow escape from lynching, T. J. is thrown in jail, in all likelihood to be hanged for murder. The final and greatest injustice of the novel is T. J.'s fate. Although T. J. is not guiltless, he is no murderer; the fact that he is a child and a dupe of the real murderers creates the kind of moral complexity that Cassie is coming to recognize and trying to understand.

Uncle Hammer Logan, David's brother, has fled the racism and poverty of the Deep South for the freer and more profitable streets of Chicago. Although he is hot-tempered, this Logan male also exemplifies positive qualities of caring, personal courage, and responsibility.

Themes and Meanings

The title *Roll of Thunder, Hear My Cry* symbolizes the novel's focus on the cataclysmic events which wash over the Logan family and their small rural community. Their pain, expressed in both cries of grief and cries of protest, comes from a rising consciousness of the oppression and injustice dominating their individual, family, and social existence.

Cassie's year-long transformation and her new awareness of injustice and modes of resistance prefigure the beginnings of a new society-wide consciousness and emerging resistance to oppressions. The acts of resistance to injustices by the Logan family and their neighbors foreshadow the nationwide active and vocal opposition to racial discrimination during the Civil Rights movement a few decades later.

Education is a central concern of this novel. Formal education is a travesty in Cassie's community. Authorial outrage is implicit in Little Man's rage at the condition of his book, and the cowardice and cruelty of his teacher speak for themselves. These children's education is separate but not at all equal to that of the white children a few steps away at Jefferson Davis County School, with its buses, sports field, and fluttering Confederate flag. The larger and more vital education for Cassie and her brothers takes place outside the classroom: They learn how dangerous their world is and acquire some strategies for staying alive.

The rising action of the plot builds a clear sense of threat to the well-being of the Logan family. Only in the last two chapters is the tension released in the frenzy of violence and fear at the Avery house, where all the disparate forces in the community confront one another. The sharecroppers are torn from their home and subjected to the blows of the night riders. The attack is led by the actual murderers of Mr. Barnett, now intent on destroying Avery.

The novel skillfully escapes sentimentality and predictability. Taylor's style and characterization, although accessible to young readers, are quite sophisticated. Although moral and social issues may be somewhat simplified (as they would be in a nine-year-old's perceptions), universal truths shine through. The novel's close does not sugarcoat the injustice and does not suggest that everyone will live happily ever after. With her eyes now opened, Cassie is entering a world of clear and present danger. What she has learned of racism in the classroom is on display on a large scale in her community's stores, streets, and churches. Black men can be lynched, torched, and beaten; they can be robbed of their livelihood, possessions, human rights, human dignity, and lives.

Critical Context

Roll of Thunder, Hear My Cry is the second in a series of semiautobiographical novels in which Mildred D. Taylor portrays the hardships and courage of African Americans in the South. At the time of its publication in 1976, the book was one of the few novels depicting minority experiences for young readers; it became a best-seller and is widely accepted as a classic. Taylor was only the second African American writer to be honored with the Newbery Award for the most distinguished contribution to American literature for children. In her acceptance speech in 1977, Taylor dedicated the award to her father. She attributed her inspiration to him and to memories of her childhood trips to Mississippi.

The joys and pains of these years of her life gave rise to the ambition to write a series of novels about a family in rural Mississippi. The first, *Song of the Trees*, a short, illustrated book for children, appeared in 1975. Subsequent works in the series include *Let the Circle Be Unbroken* (1981) and *Mississippi Bridge* (1990). A novel not about the Logan family, *The Friendship* (1987), is also set in the South in the 1930's; it focuses on the dynamics of a relationship between an elderly black man and a white shopkeeper. A novella, *The Gold Cadillac* (1987), recounts an Ohio family's visit to Mississippi in an expensive 1950's car and explores the hostility provoked by this symbol of affluence.

Bibliography
Dussel, Sharon L. "Profile: Mildred D. Taylor." *Language Arts* 58 (May, 1981): 599-604. The great strength of Taylor's work, Dussel notes, is its autobiographical ring of truth. Taylor is able to represent a child's painful growth from innocence to awareness, from openness to bitterness, from optimism to disillusionment.
Hannabuss, Stuart. "Beyond the Formula: Part II." *The Junior Bookshelf* 46 (October, 1982): 173-176. Hannabuss commends Taylor's work for its vivid representation of social issues central to American life—racial enmity, economic hardship, violence, educational inequities, and violations of human rights.
Huck, Charlotte S., Susan Hepler, and Janet Hickman. "Historical Fiction and Biography." In *Children's Literature in the Elementary School*. 5th ed. Orlando, Fla.: Harcourt Brace Jovanovich College Publishers, 1993. In an extensive review of types of historical fiction, Huck, Hepler, and Hickman place *Roll of Thunder, Hear My Cry* in literary context and assess the values of such fiction. Taylor's portraits of positive family experiences, they say, offset the overall grim hues of the tale's events. Brief discussion of the three others in Taylor's Logan family series is also included.
Rees, David. "The Color of Skin: Mildred Taylor." In *The Marble in the Water: Essays on Contemporary Writers of Fiction for Children and Young Adults*. Boston: Horn Book, 1980. Rees contends that several American authors for children, including Taylor, have confronted directly and honestly the fear, anger, and violence so often directed at people of color.
Scales, Pat. Review of *Roll of Thunder, Hear My Cry*, by Mildred D. Taylor. *Book Links* 4 (January, 1995): 12-15. Scales presents suggestions for teaching Taylor's novel in the classroom. She offers questions for classroom discussion, activities, and suggested readings. Although geared toward teachers, this essay will be useful to general readers who wish to dig deeper.

Sims, Rudine. *Shadow and Substance: Afro-American Experience in Contemporary Children's Fiction*. Urbana, Ill.: National Council of Teachers of English, 1982. According to Sims, *Roll of Thunder, Hear My Cry* is a distinguished example of "culturally conscious" fiction. Strong connections between generations of a family, vivid language, and pleasurable portraits of unique customs and qualities of the culture are positive influences on young African American readers. Yet the tone does not suggest optimism about the possibility of black and white people living in harmony.

Virginia Crane

RUNNER MACK

Author: Barry Beckham (1944-   )
Type of plot: Absurdism
Time of plot: A time resembling the Vietnam War era of the 1960's
Locale: An Eastern American city and Alaska
First published: 1972

Principal characters:
  HENRY ADAMS, the protagonist, a young black man
  BEATRICE MARK ADAMS, Henry's wife
  RUNNINGTON (RUNNER) MACK, a revolutionary
  "MR." PETERS, the personnel manager at Home Manufacturing
    Company
  "MR." BOYE, the supervisor at Home Manufacturing Company
  CAPTAIN NEVINS, an officer in the Alaskan War

The Novel

  Runner Mack follows Henry Adams through a period in his life during which he moves from confusion and ignorance to a hard-bought understanding. At the beginning of the book, he has brought his new wife, Beatrice, to a Northern city, where he expects to become a baseball star. As the novel proceeds, Henry is beset by all the evils that human nature and American society can devise. As one confusing incident follows another in a world which is never explained to Henry, the dreams of stardom fade and are replaced by dreams of revolution. The revolution fails, however—indeed, it never begins—and at the end of the book, Henry has increased wisdom but diminished hopes.

  The novel is divided into three segments. In the first, Henry has a single goal: to support his beloved new wife, Beatrice, while he waits for the big break that will make him a baseball star. Yet even that goal is difficult to realize in an absurd world. Beatrice is miserable in the city apartment where she and Henry live. The ceiling leaks; there is no heat; the neighbors are noisy; the Puerto Rican superintendent is apathetic. When Henry goes to the Home Manufacturing Company to apply for a job, he is hit by a huge truck. Although he gets the job, Henry is branded as a troublemaker; after overhearing a discussion which seems to threaten him, Henry leaves. Meanwhile, his baseball tryout has been unpromising, and his relationship with Beatrice is deteriorating. She is choked by polluting fumes and deafened by the noise of the city, and both she and Henry are terrified after an unexplained raid which soldiers make on their apartment.

  In the second segment of the book, the lesser worries are dwarfed by a major crisis: Henry is drafted and shipped to "the war" in Alaska, which seems to involve butchering caribou and seals in order to protect the United States. Here Henry meets the revolutionary Runner Mack, who plans to desert, bomb the White House, and take over the country. Runner Mack and Henry escape in a helicopter and begin a mysterious journey which is supposed to end in revolution and in a remade world.

In the third part of the book, Henry blindly follows Runner Mack's directives as the two travel by train and by car, periodically changing disguises, presumably toward Washington. Somehow they find themselves in Henry's old neighborhood. Leaving Runner Mack briefly, Henry visits Beatrice, only to find that she is deaf. The noise has at last conquered her. When Henry and Runner Mack go to the union hall where the revolutionaries are to meet, they find only eight people. In despair, Runner Mack hangs himself in a toilet stall, and Henry runs out into the street. As the novel ends, a truck is bearing down on him.

The Characters

The name of the protagonist of *Runner Mack* ironically recalls a classic work of American literature: *The Education of Henry Adams* (1907). Barry Beckham's Henry Adams gets his painful education in a world which contains two kinds of people: those who mouth words which they are programmed to say, like the executives at the Home Manufacturing Company and the military officer in Alaska, and those who genuinely communicate their thoughts. It is only through those who view the world with independent minds that Henry can grow in understanding. Although Henry comes to disagree with his father's philosophy of humility, he can at least follow his reasoning: that a really big man does not become angry. Sometimes Henry can talk to Beatrice, but generally he must simply hear her complaints, which do keep him in touch with the real world in which he and she must live. At the Home Manufacturing Company, no one will admit that he does not know what he is doing. Finally, Henry's supervisor, whom neither Henry nor the reader knows as other than "Mr." Boye, communicates with Henry, beginning with baseball talk and ending with the admission that he has never understood what he is doing or even what the plant is making. Later, Boye is reprimanded.

The person who most deeply reveals himself to Henry is Runner Mack, who has learned enough about the world to decide on revolution. Runner Mack can explain to Henry how hollow are many of the promises in which he has believed. Convincing Henry that the road of humility leads nowhere, Mack persuades him that revolution is the only answer. Mack, in Henry's eyes, has become a hero whom all black men should follow. When Mack can fly a helicopter without training, Henry is not even surprised. When Mack's organization provides clothing, transportation, even a picnic lunch from a limousine, Henry comes to believe that Runner Mack, who has read everything and knows everything, has the world under control. Clearly, Mack can perceive reality, for he has interpreted Henry's world and explained its falseness; clearly, he is going to change it. That confidence which Runner Mack has in himself and which Henry has in him does not break until the disaster in the union hall, when only eight people show up for the revolution. At that point, Runner Mack himself realizes that nothing changes, that everything repeats itself, and that there are no answers. No longer believing in his own heroic stature, Mack kills himself.

Henry Adams, whose thoughts lead the reader through the events of the book, has much of his father's ability to accept life. When the truck runs him down, he picks himself up and goes on to the job interview; when he is not told what his company is manufacturing, he waits patiently for a revelation. In this absurd world, Henry waits for understanding, just as he waits for a telephone call from the Stars, the team for which he hopes to play. Run down by a truck, shocked by a wired baseball, raided, drafted, and wounded, Henry is bewildered, not angry. It is only when he returns to Beatrice to find her deaf, forever cut off from him, that he vents his anger by kicking in the television screen. He has ceased to trust an absurd world whose inhabitants only pretend to understand it.

Themes and Meanings

Beckham's world is an absurd one. Superficially, the events of this world seem to be ruled by the laws of cause and effect: If one is good enough at baseball, one can become a major league player; if one works hard at one's job, one can advance in the company; if enough people are discontented with society, they will rebel and change their society. Ultimately, however, the events of the novel, viewed realistically, suggest that there is no logic in human responses or in human institutions. In this world, human beings keep themselves very busy convincing themselves and others that the world is not absurd.

As in every novel of initiation, Henry Adams moves toward understanding, and he does come to understand some truths about the nature of the world. He learns that one cannot depend on human beings: His friend on the baseball team cannot really help him, and the supposed revolutionaries will not turn up for the revolution. Yet although people's words are unreliable, they produce them with great enthusiasm and distrust anyone who questions their relation to fact, as the Home Manufacturing Company staff distrusts Henry. Furthermore, although everyone will talk, very few people will communicate. "Mr." Boye is reprimanded for talking honestly to Henry, and throughout the novel Beatrice continues in her misery to distance herself further and further from Henry and from the world of which he is a part until at last she is totally deaf. Finally, most people will not protest cruelty, whether it be in the form of a trick baseball or in the government-sanctioned butchery of innocent caribou. Indeed, there is something in man which enjoys killing—a common denominator which reduces Henry to the level of his commanding officer in Alaska.

Critical Context

As a novel of the black experience, *Runner Mack* includes the expected incidents and attitudes: the stereotypes, the denial of dignity, the assertion of authority without explanation, whether in a raid or in military orders. Beckham, however, also dramatizes the plight of modern man in an urban wasteland of filth, pollution, noise, slums, and junkyards. Henry Adams is not puzzled merely because he is black. Therefore, Henry also becomes a modern Candide, surrounded by optimistic Panglosses. Like Candide, he moves from the search for a simple good—for Henry, his Beatrice and his career in baseball—to an inquiry as to whether the search itself can be successful. Yet unlike Candide, who at least can find meaning in work, Henry is left without a goal and with one more truck bearing down upon him.

It should be mentioned that although Beckham's effective use of absurdist techniques in order to dramatize a modern urban black man's perception of his world is his most significant accomplishment in this novel, critics have also been interested in his use of baseball metaphors throughout the book. It is not surprising that Henry, the baseball player, sees life as a baseball game. Evidently, for everyone, a strikeout is inevitable.

Bibliography

Draper, James P., ed. *Black Literature Criticism*. 3 vols. Detroit: Gale Research, 1992. Includes an extensive biographical profile of Beckham and excerpts from criticism on his works.

Klotman, Phyllis R. *Another Man Gone: The Black Runner in Contemporary Afro-American Literature*. Port Washington, N.Y.: Kennikat Press, 1977. Klotman includes a chapter-length analysis of *Runner Mack*.

Pinsker, Sanford. "About Runner Mack: An Interview with Barry Beckham." *Black Images* 3 (1974): 35-41. Beckham furnishes insights into the background and composition of his novel.

Umphlett, Wiley Lee. "The Black Man as Fictional Athlete: *Runner Mack*, the Sporting Myth, and the Failure of the American Dream." *Modern Fiction Studies* 33 (Spring, 1987): 73-83. Explores Beckham's use of baseball as a metaphor for the condition of the modern urban black man.

Weixlmann, Joe. "Barry Beckham: A Bibliography." *College Language Association Journal* 25 (June, 1981): 522-528. A listing of newspaper and magazine reviews of Beckham's works as well as Beckham's own writings through 1981.

Woodward, Loretta G. "Barry Beckham." In *Contemporary African American Novelists: A Bio-Bibliographical Critical Sourcebook*, edited by Emmanuel S. Nelson. Westport, Conn.: Greenwood Press, 1999. Woodward provides a biographical and critical assessment of Beckham's works as well as a primary and secondary bibliography for further study.

Rosemary M. Canfield Reisman

SABBATH'S THEATER

Author: Philip Roth (1933-   )
Type of plot: Comic realism
Time of plot: The 1940's to the 1990's
Locale: New York, New Jersey, and New England
First published: 1995

Principal characters:

MICKEY SABBATH, the protagonist, a former puppeteer
NICKI, Sabbath's first wife, who disappears mysteriously
ROSEANNA, Sabbath's second wife, who becomes an alcoholic
DRENKA, Sabbath's Croatian American mistress
DIJKTA, Drenka's husband, the owner of a local inn
MATTHEW, Drenka's son, a police officer
MORTY, Sabbath's brother, killed in World War II
NICK COWAN, Sabbath's friend in New York
JOHNSON, a carpenter in love with Drenka
COUSIN FISH, Sabbath's one-hundred-year-old cousin
LINCOLN GELMAN, Sabbath's onetime theatrical sponsor

The Novel

Sabbath's Theater is a story about a man at the end of his rope, a man for whom life is a punishment. He is shown in the last stages of that life, when he has to decide whether he will continue to live or whether he should commit suicide. Morris (Mickey) Sabbath is a sixty-four-year-old former puppeteer and a sexual deviant consumed by lust. His life revolves around one aberrant sexual exploit after another. In the 1950's, he runs a puppet theater opposite the gates of Columbia University in New York City. He uses his fingers as puppets and as a vehicle for fondling young girls in his audience. He is caught, and an indecency charge is filed against him. Sometime soon after, his first wife Nikki disappears without a trace. Disconsolate, he leaves New York with his lover Roseanna for the quiet and simplicity of a small Massachusetts town.

Sabbath, however, is incapable of leading a simple life. Very quickly, he finds a way to complicate it. Although he secures a job directing theater at a local college, his career is cut short when he is forced to resign over a scandal with a coed. During these years in Massachusetts, Roseanna, now his wife, becomes an alcoholic. Living with Sabbath is too much for her. He destroys her sense of well-being and confidence and makes her life a hell. She becomes the target of his frustration and despair. Even when she is recovering, he goads her mercilessly.

When he finds his home life no longer appealing, Sabbath becomes involved in an adulterous affair with an exotic and powerful Croatian American woman, Drenka Balich, who with her husband owns the local inn. With Sabbath's encouragement, she develops erotic needs that know no bounds. She is not only promiscuous but also unquenchable. Sabbath encourages her to have affairs with other men and then to describe them in detail to him. Much of Sabbath's sexual pleasure comes from listening to these descriptions. However, the book takes a tragic turn when Drenka develops cancer. Her slow and painful death leaves him a desperate man capable of anything, including suicide.

The plot unfolds in a series of powerful flashbacks to various moments in his life that deal with major personal losses. The first of those is an experience from Sabbath's years as a teenager. His beloved older brother Morty enlisted during World War II, became a pilot, and was shot down and killed by the Japanese in 1944. Morty's death destroys the family. Morty's loss slowly drives his mother insane, and throughout the novel Sabbath relives that death and his mother's insanity as if both events happened yesterday. Other losses compound his sense of despair and send him reeling: the disappearance of his first wife, his loss of his career as puppeteer, the end of his career as theater director, Roseanna's alcoholism, and finally the loss of his beloved Drenka. When his best friend and former business investor, Lincoln Gelman, dies, Sabbath decides to leave Roseanna and drive to New York for the funeral. Part of his motivation for attending the funeral is to see how it is done so that he can prepare his own.

In New York, he finds refuge in the home of an old friend, Norm Cowan, whom he promptly repays by trying to seduce his wife and engaging in sex with a graduation picture of Cowan's pretty daughter. The last sections of the book describe Sabbath's futile attempt to kill himself. In a bizarre ending fitting for a bizarre book, a stranger thwarts Sabbath's final act. In a macabre series of events, he is forced to go on living. The book ends with Sabbath remarking bitterly that there is no point to killing himself because "everything I hate is here."

The Characters

Mickey Sabbath is not a new character to readers familiar with Roth's work. Perhaps the first version was Alexander Portnoy, the protagonist of Roth's 1969 *Portnoy's Complaint*. They share a colossal misogyny, self-hatred, enormous libidinous energies, world-weariness, and boredom. They lack a spiritual center that might be a guide through the turmoil of life. For them, there is no meaning in anything except self-gratification, which turns out to be an empty exercise. Sabbath's efforts to find gratification through sex know no limits. His unleashed libido is capable of the most grotesque forms of experimentation. Yet that satisfaction is only momentary and only leads him to more bizarre experimentation.

Yet Sabbath is the psychological center of this novel. All the other characters are projected as he sees them and interacts with them. Although deformed in many ways, Sabbath is capable of love, or at least remembered love. His love for his immediate family is a critical element in his psyche. He remembers a happy childhood for the family of mother, father, Morty, and himself. As the younger brother, Sabbath looked up to Morty, who in high school not only earned good grades but also was well liked, a star athlete, and president of his class. During the war, Morty decided to enlist; when the family learned that he had been shot down and killed in combat by the Japanese, they were devastated by grief. His mother began a slow decline into insanity, and his father lost interest in life. Sabbath's response, perhaps to protect his own sanity, was to develop an intense hatred of anything Japanese.

Sabbath's various love affairs with Nikki, Roseanna, and Drenka are very passionate, at least until the passion burns out, as it does with both Nikki and Roseanna. His love affair with Drenka, however, does not burn out, and his caring and tenderness for her through the final six months of her life suggest a kind of redemption. Yet that redemption is tempered by the reader's awareness that Sabbath's lovemaking required that Drenka unleash her own storm of passion and lavish it on a whole series of other men. Roth does not condemn Drenka for her adultery. Rather, she comes off as nearly an earth-mother figure. Her sexuality and good humor attain nearly mythic proportions. The fullness of her character, her joy in life, and her sexuality are reminiscent of James Joyce's Molly Bloom.

Themes and Meanings

Sabbath's involvement with Drenka gives a glimpse of the dark side of his personality, which clearly dominates the book. He is the quintessential twentieth century man for whom there is no value or meaning in the world, who is without a creed or system of beliefs, who fumbles in the dark and screams in the void. Other critics have pointed to Franz Kafka as a source for Roth, but there is a closer relationship between Roth and Samuel Beckett. Typically, Beckett's characters not only have no place to go but have also lost the ability to be mobile. They literally either cannot move or can barely move. This physical paralysis reflects their psychological paralysis and their metaphysical despair. Life for them is a void. They live suspended in time, outside history, with nothing to do but contemplate the meaninglessness of existence and the futility of living. Sabbath would feel right at home in such a setting. When at the end of *Sabbath's Theater* he dismisses suicide by remarking, "Why should I leave? Everything I hate is here," he could easily be one of Beckett's antiheroes.

There is no escaping the theme of sexual perversity that dominates the book. Sabbath is a man of prodigious sexual appetite who is totally faithless to the women he loves. His single consuming desire is to have sex with any woman who appeals to him. Consequently, he loses his two wives, one who disappears mysteriously, another who turns into an alcoholic. His sexuality leads him to perform gross sexual acts, including urinating on Drenka's grave and masturbating over the picture of the college-age daughter of his friend, Norman Cowan. Not since *Portnoy's Complaint* has Roth depicted a character so consumed with libidinous energy that he is totally out of control as a social being. The result is to make Sabbath an outsider, a pariah; it is only fair to see his masturbation as a part of his near-total absorption in himself.

What makes Sabbath less than utterly self-absorbed is the love he bears for his brother and his family, a love and sense of loss that still haunts him at the age of sixty-four. The death of Morty, which results in the destruction of the lives of the other family members, is the decisive event of this haunting story. Micky's life appears to stop with Morty's death; everything he does for the rest of his life seems destined to fail.

Critical Context

A winner of the 1995 National Book Award for fiction, *Sabbath's Theater* was published thirty-five years after Roth first won the award for his widely acclaimed 1959 first novel *Goodbye Columbus*. *Sabbath's Theater*, Roth's twenty-first book, represents something of a breakout from what critics had noted as a relatively quiet time in the author's life, a period that followed his fight with depression in 1987. During this "quiet time," Roth's father died; his death is the subject of *Patrimony* (1991). Roth also published the autobiographical *The Facts* (1988) and the novel *Deception* (1990). These books lack the verbal pyrotechnics for which Roth is famous, and many critics concluded that Roth had entered a new, more mellow phase. In *Operation Shylock* (1993), *Sabbath's Theater* (1995), *American Pastoral* (1997), and *I Married a Communist* (1998), however, Roth appears to have returned to form, pouring out verbal venom unequaled by any other writer of his generation. The themes of his earlier work—misogyny, sexual indulgence, alienation of the modern Jew, and self-hatred—are back in full force.

Critical reception of *Sabbath's Theater* was mixed. Some reviewers expressed a preference for *Operation Shylock* and *An American Pastoral*, commenting that those books tell richer stories, are less claustrophobic, and embrace more of the cultural and historical events of their time. *Sabbath's Theater*, on the other hand, tells the story of one man and his obsessive concerns, a character largely outside history. He does not read the newspapers or watch television; his great interest is lust and personal loss. Unlike *Operation Shylock* and *An American Pastoral*, therefore, *Sabbath's Theater* lacks a base in the context of history and ideas.

Bibliography

Cooper, Alan. *Philip Roth and the Jews*. Albany: State University of New York Press, 1996. An excellent book that explores the range and depth of Roth's work, including some juvenilia and lesser known works and *Sabbath's Theater*. Cooper discusses the material in the context of the political, social, and literary climate surrounding each work.

Greenberg, R. M. "Transgression in the Fiction of Philip Roth." *Twentieth Century Literature* 43, no. 4 (Winter, 1997): 487-506. Places *Sabbath's Theater* in the context of Roth's previous novels that deal with the protagonist's transgressing against society. Sabbath is an absurd hero who, like his forbears, believes in nothing.

Kelleter, F. "Portrait of the Sexist as a Dying Man: Death, Ideology, and the Erotic in Philip Roth's *Sabbath's Theater*." *Contemporary Literature* 39, no. 2 (Summer, 1998): 262-302. Kelleter discusses the major themes of the novel, which he identifies as death, eros, and ideology. An excellent in-depth article.

Shatzky, Joel, and Michael Taub. *Contemporary Jewish Novelists: A Bio-Critical Sourcebook.* Westport, Conn.: Greenwood Press, 1997. Good sourcebook for biographic and critical information on Roth, including critical information about *Sabbath's Theater.*

Wisse, Ruth R. "Sex, Love, and Death." *Commentary,* December, 1995, 61-65. Wisse notes that Sabbath is an autonomous character, unlike so many of Roth's previous heroes. She points out several relationships between Roth's work and Kafka's and concludes that Roth's work falls short of Kafka's.

Wood, James. "My Death as a Man." *The New Republic,* October 23, 1995, 33-39. Wood describes *Sabbath's Theater* as a departure from Roth's books that present the author in disguise. Sabbath is a character larger than life and a character unto himself.

Richard Damashek

SACRED FAMILIES

Author: José Donoso (1924-1996)
Type of plot: Psychological symbolism
Time of plot: The early 1970's
Locale: Barcelona, Spain
First published: Tres novelitas burguesas, 1973 (English translation, 1977)

> *Principal characters:*
>
> "Chattanooga Choo-Choo"
>> ANSELMO PRIETO, a doctor whose hobby is painting
>> MAGDALENA PRIETO, Anselmo's wife
>> SYLVIA CORDAY, a model
>> RAMON DEL SOLAR, an architect married to Sylvia
>
> "Green Atom Number Five"
>> ROBERTO FERRER, a dentist and painter, about forty years old
>> MARTA MORA, his wife
>
> "Gaspard de la Nuit"
>> MAURICIO, Sylvia Corday's sixteen-year-old son
>> SYLVIA CORDAY, a model
>> RAMON DEL SOLAR, an architect, Sylvia Corday's second husband

The Novel

Sacred Families comprises three connected novellas about the middle class. The first one, "Chattanooga Choo-Choo," revolves around two couples who have recently met. Their encounter begins as a superficial relationship that becomes more serious when Sylvia Corday, who is married to Ramon del Solar, has an affair with Anselmo Prieto, Magdalena's husband. On the night on which they consummate the affair, Anselmo notices that Sylvia does not have a face or a pair of arms. Upon her request, he provides her with a mouth using red paper. After consummating their affair, Anselmo realizes that a vital part of his male anatomy has disappeared. What follows is a sequence of events that inform the reader that the wives have been playing a game in which they have disassembled their husbands' bodily parts and are keeping them in a briefcase. The women have given special attention to that one vital male part; they keep their husbands' penises in a little velvet bag, and they interchange them frequently.

The second novella, "Green Atom Number Five," unfolds to reveal Roberto and Marta, a middle-aged couple who have purchased a brand-new apartment. The apartment represents the fulfillment of their lifelong dream. They proceed to furnish the dwelling with the finest things: as a finishing touch to the decoration of their home, they compromise in placing Roberto's oil painting, *Green Atom Number Five*, on the wall nearest the front door. After the departure of a visitor, they notice that the painting has disappeared, which puzzles them very much. In a series of circumstances, everything is taken away before their very eyes and they find themselves unable to do anything. After losing everything they become increasingly vicious toward each other, eventually ending up naked and fighting like mad dogs.

The third novella, "Gaspard de la Nuit," pivots around Mauricio, who is coming to visit his mother, Sylvia, for three months. He has been living with his father and grandmother, "Abuelis," since his parents were divorced seven years previously. Mauricio neither likes nor approves of his mother's lifestyle and does not want to become part of the society in which she lives, much to her frustration and dismay. Instead, he goes out every day and spends his time strolling the streets while whistling a Maurice Ravel piece *Gaspard de la Nuit*, and trying to find a soul mate. One day, in a forest, he meets a vagabond about his age whom he teaches to whistle the Ravel piece. He and the vagabond become closely acquainted until a fantastical sort of metamorphosis occurs: Mauricio becomes the vagabond and the latter becomes Mauricio. After that, the situation at home improves greatly, since the new Mauricio accepts all the material things with which his mother has been trying to bribe him in an attempt to keep her son at home. Mauricio's changed attitude makes everyone happy.

The Characters

"Chattanooga Choo-Choo" pits men against women. The husbands, Anselmo and Ramon, regard themselves as the ones who set the rules and dominate the battle of the sexes. That is, however, a very simplistic evaluation. In fact, the women, Sylvia and Magdalena, are the ones who control the situation, in a very efficient and subdued fashion. They pretend to be the victims but are actually the opposite. The men are depicted as business-minded personages who believe that they get what they want when they want it in their dealings with women. The truth is that whether they get something or not, the quality and quantity will depend upon the women.

"Green Atom Number Five" is a thorough study of a couple, Roberto and Marta. They are well-characterized before, during, and after the crisis that tears them apart. Roberto, a very successful odontologist, is a man who knows what he wants in life, is sure about his priorities, and dogmatic and pragmatic to the point of thinking that a change in life must start with a change of address. Now that he has moved into his own place, he thinks that everything will be under control. The only disturbance in his apparently peaceful existence in the foreseeable future is the one empty room in the apartment, where he had planned on installing a studio for painting. His fondness for painting, which has been stimulated by Marta, diminishes when she, under the impulse of an angry reaction, tells him that his painting *Green Atom Number Five* is nothing extraordinary and that her choice of the painting instead of an emerald jewel was motivated more by kindness on her part than by any real talent on her husband's part.

In this novella, as throughout *Sacred Families*, Donoso suggests that identity is unstable. Marta, Roberto's sweet and unselfish wife of many years, who has been unable to bear children, has acted as Roberto's mother as well as wife. She has never argued or protested, yet now she starts changing for the worse. Indeed, both Roberto's and Marta's behavior increasingly worsens, going from love to the most profound hatred. That modification in conduct is achieved slowly. Donoso has proceeded through episodes and incidents, the effects of which have rebounded on the characters. Other supporting characters have merely given a direction to the changes that occur in the main characters.

In the third novella, "Gaspard de la Nuit," the theme is the obsession that affects the people in the story, especially two of them, although to different degrees. This obsession can be seen in Mauricio, the protagonist, in his endless search for identity; in Sylvia, Mauricio's mother, the obsession is evidenced by her insistence on making him a part of her world. There are very few digressions, either in the novella's structure or in Mauricio's mind. Mauricio's continual search runs through the story: When he finds himself, and the metamorphosis takes place, the obsession and the story are both over.

All the characters that appear in the novellas are interrelated in some fashion. The character of Sylvia is presented in two different lights: In "Chattanooga Choo-Choo" she is a plastic, faceless mannequin, while in "Gaspard de la Nuit" she plays a very concerned, flesh-and-blood mother.

Themes and Meanings

In "Chattanooga Choo-Choo," an evident mutual exploitation between men and women is shown. Neither respects the individuality of the other: One woman is all women, one man is all men. This is represented through the mutual disassembly and convenient use of one another without regard for sentiment. To these characters, making love becomes a formula, a mechanical engagement.

The emphasis on makeup shows that people masquerade their real being—everything is changed through cosmetics. The people's behavior at parties illustrates the lack of sincerity in their relationships. Convenience and opportunism are the keys to success: People are used and then disposed of when they are no longer useful.

In "Green Atom Number Five," the apparently happily married couple find their relationship deteriorating when their well-organized material world starts to collapse. There is a sharp contrast between the couple's sweet behavior at the beginning of the story and their savage conduct at the end.

Roberto and Marta have built their happy and harmonious relationship in part on Marta's pretended admiration for her husband's painting. This has been a lie: She considers his talent mediocre. Roberto goes from unconditional devotion to Marta's generosity and love to thinking of her as a selfish woman, doubting her intentions and even her honesty after her disclosure. The nightmarish way in which the objects disappear parallels the increasing deterioration in the couple's relationship.

The theme in "Gaspard de la Nuit" is the obsession of the protagonist, Mauricio, with finding his identity. The obsession is displayed in his continuous whistling, which he uses as an instrument to penetrate other people's intimacy as he tries to find the right person to help him fulfill his search. He whistles on his daily strolls through the streets, which last many hours. While he walks, he also looks at people, attempting to find the long-awaited double who will either implement him or replace him.

He shows his displeasure with the type of life he has been compelled to live with his father and grandmother, and he does not like his mother's way of living either. Yet he refuses his mother's offers of a stereo, a motorcycle, and a tour through Europe. He wants to be left alone to continue his search. His obsession stops when he finds his double and becomes a docile youngster ready to comply with his mother's desires.

The role that nature plays in Mauricio's transformation is important. The Vallvi-drera Forest, where Mauricio meets the other boy, is a peaceful place that provides the right setting for Mauricio's music; on the other hand, it can be equated with paradise, where life starts easy but also can turn into the beginning of a life of hardship. When Mauricio leaves the forest, he has already become another person with responsibilities that frame him in a completely different fashion.

Critical Context

Since writing *Coronación* (1957; *Coronation*, 1965), *Esta domingo* (1966; *This Sunday*, 1967), and *El obsceno pájaro de la noche* (1970; *The Obscene Bird of Night*, 1973), among other works, José Donoso has been writing about middle-class people and their fruitless existence. He has depicted this social class as decadent, and as a victim of its conventionality, its blind submission to rules, and its absolute acceptance of whatever is in fashion. *Sacred Families* is no exception: The three novellas revolve around the bourgeoisie and its most negative characteristics. In each case, below the surface action lies the impossibility for the characters to be themselves: Regardless of the fight that some of the characters may put up, they will finally bend to the rules and become part of the society.

Bibliography
Finnegan, Pamela May. *The Tension of Paradox: José Donoso's "The Obscene Bird of Night" as Spiritual Exercises*. Athens: Ohio University Press, 1992. Finnegan examines the novel as an expression of man's estrangement from the world. The novel's two alter egos, Humberto/Mudito, perceive and receive stimuli, yet they regard the world differently, even though they are interdependent. In a series of chapters, Finnegan follows Donoso's intricate treatment of this idea, showing how the world composes and discomposes itself. A difficult but rewarding study for advanced students. Includes a bibliography.

McMurray, George R. *Authorizing Fictions: José Donoso's "Casa De Campo."* London: Tamesis Books, 1992. Chapters on Donoso's handling of voice and time, his narrative strategies (re-presenting characters), and his use of interior duplication and distortion. Includes a bibliography.

_____. *José Donoso*. Boston: Twayne, 1979. An excellent introductory study, with chapters on Donoso's biography, his short stories, *The Obscene Bird of Night*, and *Sacred Families*. Includes chronology, detailed notes, and annotated bibliography.

Magnarelli, Sharon. *Understanding José Donoso*. Columbia: University of South Carolina Press, 1993. See especially chapter 1: "How to Read José Donoso." Subsequent chapters cover his short stories and major novels. Includes a bibliography.

Mandri, Flora. *José Donoso's House of Fiction: A Dramatic Construction of Time and Place*. Detroit, Mich.: Wayne State University Press, 1995. Chapters on all of Donoso's major fiction, exploring his treatment of history and of place. Includes detailed notes and extensive bibliography.

Rebeca Torres-Rivera

SAINT JACK

Author: Paul Theroux (1941-   )
Type of plot: Social morality
Time of plot: 1953-1971
Locale: Singapore, at an unnamed American college
First published: 1973

> *Principal characters:*
> JACK FLOWERS, the protagonist, a water clerk and pimp
> WILLIAM LEIGH, a British accountant from Hong Kong
> EDWIN (EDDIE) SHUCK, a United States government official
> CHOP HING KHENG FATT, the ship chandler and Jack's employer

The Novel

Saint Jack centers on the efforts of Jack Flowers, a middle-aged American expatriate in Singapore, to achieve a success that he believes is almost within his grasp. Jack is an eternal optimist who considers being poor "the promise of success." Jack is ostensibly employed as a water clerk for Hing, a ship chandler, but he uses the contacts he makes through his work for Hing, who pays him little, to conduct his real business: He is a pimp who obtains customers for his "girls" from among sailors, tourists, and the lonely inhabitants of his "tedious little island."

The first section of the novel focuses on Jack's having to escort William Leigh, a British accountant from Hong Kong, who has come to Singapore to work on Hing's books. Leigh is a stuffy dullard who ignores Jack's suggestions about how he could be spending his time. When Leigh realizes that he is a hustler and smugly asks, "How do you stand it?" Jack is upset. He sees pimping as a means to an end, realizes that it is degrading, but tries to carry it out as much as possible within a code of conduct. The ambiguous nature of morality is central to all the actions and themes of *Saint Jack*. The unease which Leigh causes Jack is increased when the accountant suddenly dies of a heart attack, awakening Jack to a sense of his own mortality.

The novel returns, by means of a flashback, to Jack's arrival in Singapore fourteen years earlier, when he "enjoyed a rare kind of happiness, like the accidental discovery of renewal." This sense of or attempt at renewal becomes a pattern in Jack's life. There are then flashbacks to the cause of his exile. At thirty-five, Jack goes to college on the GI Bill and tries to write a novel. When he is charged with possessing drugs without a prescription and procuring drugs for a minor, he flees the United States and becomes a seaman. He intends never to return to America, accepting his exile as final, almost as inevitable.

Prior to his encounter with Leigh, Jack has two opportunities to achieve the big success of which he dreams. He establishes Dunroamin, his own house of prostitution, but is kidnapped by one of the secret societies which control vice in Singapore. The thugs tattoo Chinese obscenities on his arms and burn down his house. Later, he has the tattooed Chinese characters converted into flowers—a symbol of his philosophy of making the best of awkward situations, his never giving in to his frequent bad luck.

His second limited success comes when Eddie Shuck, a shady operator working for the American government, puts Jack in charge of a brothel for servicemen on five-day leaves from Vietnam. (The dubious morality of this enterprise is meant to parallel that of the war in Vietnam.) Jack's good fortune ends abruptly when the army closes the operation, which officially has never existed.

After Leigh's death, Jack experiences a sense of desperation and asks Shuck for help. Shuck involves him in blackmailing Andrew Maddox, a corrupt general, but Jack backs out at the last minute when he realizes that Shuck's corruption is as great as Maddox's, that Shuck is trying to entrap the general in the same way that circumstances have entrapped Jack. The simplicity and shallowness of Shuck's view of the world finally disgusts Jack too much—Jack attains a level of ironic sainthood by refusing to be part of it all.

The Characters

The only major character in the novel is Jack Flowers. Born in 1918 as John Fiori, the second child of Italian immigrants in the North End of Boston, he is a combination of innocence and experience, control and chaos, with similarities to Joseph Conrad's Lord Jim, Jake Barnes in Ernest Hemingway's *The Sun Also Rises* (1926), Saul Bellow's Augie March, Yossarian in Joseph Heller's *Catch-22* (1961), and Mark Twain's Huckleberry Finn. The novel's first-person narrator, he is a complex, multifaceted protagonist who evolves over the course of the action; as he explains at the beginning, "being slow to disclose my nature is characteristic of me." With red hair—what is left of it—big belly, and tattoos, he is "the ultimate barbarian" to some, especially those, such as Eddie Shuck, who accept his surface as the real Jack: "I resented comparisons, I hated the fellers who said, 'Flowers, you're as bad as me!' They looked at me and saw a pimp, a pornocrat, an unassertive rascal marooned on a tropical island, but having the time of his life: a character."

Jack is both searching for and denying his identity. He says that his assumed name is "an approximation and a mask"; he always hides behind one mask or another. Around Yardley, Frogget, Yates, Smale, and Coony, the English expatriates who frequent the Bandung bar and are the closest that Jack comes to having friends, he tries "to give the impression of a cheerful rascal, someone gently ignorant; I claimed I had no education and said 'If you say so' or 'That's really interesting' to anything remotely intelligent." They all despise Leigh, but when he dies, Jack becomes "the grieving person they wanted me to be."

Jack sees Leigh as his double, and the Englishman's death seems to be a warning about actions and expectations, denying Jack the luxury of not questioning his life: "I could not say . . . that I had arrived anywhere. I was pausing . . . and there was no good reason for any of my movements except the truthful excuse that at the time of acting I saw no other choice." The unease that Jack feels in the face of Leigh's criticism of his life, of Leigh's pathetic death, causes him to write this book, finally to confront the meaning and direction of his life: "Fiction seemed to give me the second chances life denied me."

The other characters are merely reflectors of aspects of Jack's nature. Hing so devotes himself to his work that he has no other life, loses what individuality he ever had. The Bandung Englishmen retreat into their camaraderie, their drinking, their memories of the United Kingdom, their hopes of returning, to try to drown out the hideous silence of their lonely exile. Eddie Shuck is as much a pimp as Jack, manipulating people from behind the scenes, justifying it all because his side will always be the right one.

Themes and Meanings

Through the character of Jack Flowers, *Saint Jack* satirizes certain aspects of the American Dream. Jack longs for "success, comfort, renown," hustles to keep the possibility of the dream alive, but essentially hopes that it will come about suddenly, dramatically, through no direct effort of his own. Someone somewhere will spot some special something in Jack and bestow great wealth and privilege upon him. The irony is that the American Dream is supposed to be the reward for hard work and initiative, and Jack does work hard for long hours. He prides himself on the quality of his pimping, on his charging much less for his prostitutes than he could actually get. He is an honest, industrious man, but where does it get him? He merely survives.

Jack wishes that he could be even more than a president, more than a king: He wants to be a saint. His work on the streets, in the bars, is not hustling but "conscientious shepherding": "It wasn't the money that drove me; I can't call it holy charity, but it was as close to a Christian act as that sort of friendly commerce could be, keeping those already astray happy and from harm, within caution's limits." Jack does not fool himself about the value of the service he provides; he is certain of its necessity. His "unselfish" dedication to his customers protects them from greedy cabbies, secret societies, transvestites, sadists, venereal disease. Jack's world is hardly pure, but it lacks the evasions and self-justifications of that of Eddie Shuck: "I took blame, I risked damnation, I didn't cheat: *A Useful Man*, my tombstone motto would go." He looks after others in the way that he wishes someone would look after him; he is the kind of beneficient angel whom he has long been hoping will visit him.

Theroux and his protagonist recognize the moral ambiguity of a society cluttered by war, pornography, and corruption, but they also realize the individual's responsibility not to make this society any worse than it need be. Such an individual in such a less-than-perfect world can be a kind of saint.

Critical Context

From *Fong and the Indians* (1968) to *The Mosquito Coast* (1982), Theroux has examined the cultures of Third World countries and the interactions of outsiders, usually Americans, with them. Singapore is a most appropriate setting for a Theroux novel: "In such a small place, an island with no natives, everyone a visitor, the foreigner made himself a resident by emphasizing his foreignness." Jack Flowers is a chameleon who can fit himself into any environment; he is proud of the Chinese and Malay touches in his brothel, especially since so much of Singapore has fallen prey to fast food and other Western influences. Other Theroux visitors to the Third World fail to adapt and sometimes die in the attempt.

Jack, however, like so many characters in contemporary American fiction, would be something of an outsider wherever he found himself. He is a picaro, a rogue, a con man, but he is not a comic figure, is not alienated. He is believably complicated, a closet puritan with admittedly old-fashioned attitudes about sex despite his offers to supply "anything" for his customers. His innocence, combined with his self-knowledge and lack of self-pity, makes him a remarkable achievement, almost a Dickensian character with an awareness of Sigmund Freud, a Graham Greene character who will never burn out. Much of Theroux's subsequent fiction and nonfiction has displayed an impatience with human imperfections bordering on misanthropy, but *Saint Jack* is full of unsentimental compassion for the fallibility of man. Jack sees himself as "a person of small virtue; virtue wasn't salvation, but knowing that might be."

Bibliography

Coale, Samuel. *Paul Theroux*. Boston: Twayne, 1987. A comprehensive examination of Theroux's work, which includes in-depth analyses of his novels. Ideal for general or scholarly study, this volume includes a helpful bibliography and index.

Wheeler, Edward T. "What the Imagination Knows: Paul Theroux's Search for the Second Self." *Commonweal* 121 (May 20, 1994): 18-22. Regarded as one of the most prolific contemporary Catholic authors, Theroux stresses the importance of imagination in the human search for meaning. Wheeler explores these "pilgrimages of imagination" in several of Theroux's novels, including *Saint Jack*. He declares that the novel is a "wry and unsentimental look at fifties Catholic boyhood" and praises the book for its evocative images of a time now past.

Michael Adams

SALLY HEMINGS

Author: Barbara Chase-Riboud (1939-   )
Type of plot: Historical realism
Time of plot: 1759-1835
Locale: Paris, France; Virginia
First published: 1979

>   *Principal characters:*
>   SALLY HEMINGS, a beautiful, white-skinned woman born into slavery
>   who is mistress to Thomas Jefferson
>   THOMAS JEFFERSON, the third president of the United States and author
>   of the Declaration of Independence
>   NATHAN LANGDON, a lawyer and census taker in Virginia, who
>   befriends Sally Hemings after Jefferson's death
>   AARON BURR, a politician and enemy to Jefferson
>   JAMES and DOLLEY MADISON, the fourth president and First Lady,
>   friends of Jefferson and abolitionists
>   JOHN TRUMBILL, an artist who paints portraits of important historical
>   figures
>   ELIZABETH HEMINGS, Sally's mother, housekeeper and boss of
>   Monticello
>   GEORGE WYTHE, Jefferson's former schoolteacher and sometime
>   mentor
>   JOHN and ABIGAIL ADAMS, the second president and First Lady, friends
>   to Jefferson who supervise Sally during her stay in France
>   MADISON and ESTON HEMINGS, sons of Sally and Jefferson
>   JAMES HEMINGS, Sally's brother

The Novel

Since Thomas Jefferson's lifetime, it has been accepted by many historians, though never officially proven, that the third president had for a mistress a slave who bore him several children. Barbara Chase-Riboud takes this matter as fact in writing the novel *Sally Hemings.*

The work is based in great part on facts that are substantiated by documentation and historical records. Essentially, however, the novel itself is fiction; dialogue, characterization, and plot are all creations of the novelist, who takes great license with what is known and established about Jefferson and his relationship with Sally Hemings.

The book is divided into seven chapters according to place and time; however, the arrangement is not chronological. Most of the story is told by the novelist herself, writing in the third-person-omniscient point of view. In a few of the chapters, though, Sally Hemings tells her own story from the first-person point of view.

The book begins in 1830 in Albemarle County, Virginia, after Jefferson's death. Monticello has been sold, and Sally Hemings is living as a freed slave (and white woman) with her two sons on a small farm near the president's old plantation. A census taker visits to get the facts of her existence for public record. Infatuated first with Sally's story and then with Sally herself, young Nathan Langdon becomes intrigued with her beauty (even though Sally is now an old woman and Nathan is much younger) and history, and they become friends. Nathan's curiosity about slavery, Jefferson's two families, and race relations provide the author with a way to engage and entice the reader into concern for Sally's circumstances. Sally's two sons, Madison and Eston, are naturally suspicious of the white man and his motives, but they are unable to prevent the friendship.

The novel then switches in time and location to Paris, France, in 1787. Here, young Sally and her brother James, functioning as servants, travel with the Jefferson family when Jefferson is serving as ambassador to France. Under French law, the two slaves are free and cannot be held against their will or forced to return to the United States, where they will once again be legal slaves. Jefferson himself seduces the two into returning, more or less by making promises to free them. This promise is not kept to James Hemings for another several years; Sally is freed only at Jefferson's death many years later. Be that as it may, the chief interest of this chapter is the relation between Jefferson and Sally, for it is in Paris where he first seduces the beautiful fifteen-year-old girl, falls in love with her, and makes her his lifelong mistress.

In the next section of the novel, Chase-Riboud again focuses on the United States. It is now 1833, and Nathan Langdon is trying to find all the information he can about the Jefferson and Hemings families. He interviews the artist John Trumbill, who knows the facts but will not tell them, thinking that the facts would only besmirch the name of the great Jefferson. Like all other major characters in the novel, white or black, and including Sally herself, no one is willing to tell the story directly. All remain silent, not only about Jefferson and Sally, but also about the institution of slavery itself and the way in which Jefferson's two families (the white one and the black one) lived together, loved one another, and otherwise conducted their affairs and familial relations.

The middle section of the novel records these family histories from 1795 to 1809. The author explores the ways in which two sets of children, one white and one black, could live together given the social hypocrisy and the legal implications of the various blood relationships. Similarly, slave life is depicted, and certain historical characters are introduced by the novelist in order to give differing points of view about what is going on at Monticello. Jefferson is described at length. Always, the most important matter is his love for Sally, which is returned. Sally bears children to Jefferson and suckles the offspring of her white sisters. One by one, her own children leave (some with their father's knowledge and blessing, some without) for the north and freedom, where they must thereafter live as whites and can have no contact with their parents.

In the last chapter of the novel, Chase-Riboud makes clear that her main purpose is an indictment of slavery and the people who perpetuated the institution, even would-be do-gooders such as Jefferson himself. As Jefferson became older, his finances deteriorated, and he was forced to sell off slaves to keep Monticello his own.

With his death, the demise is complete: The plantation is sold, as are most of the remaining slaves, even though many of them are family members and blood relations to Jefferson. The cruelty of the actions here, all going back to Jefferson himself, do not succeed to balance, in Sally's life, her love for him or his love for her. She remains a victim of the economic system, but most of all a victim of Jefferson himself.

The Characters

Sally Hemings is the centerpiece of the novel in every way. It is she who commands the story, telling much of it. Victimized by slavery, Jefferson, love, and herself, Sally does not so much grow and mature as she becomes older; rather, she merely endures changes in her circumstances. Always, Sally is seen making choices: The novel opens with her deciding whether to talk to Nathan Langdon; in her youth, she must decide if she will remain in France and be free or return to Virginia and slavery; through the years, she repeatedly elects to stay with Jefferson and to love him; as Jefferson's death approaches, she must decide to what extent she can and will help her children escape slavery; finally, after Jefferson's death, she remains illegally in Virginia in order to live on a small farm near Monticello. The character is described by the author almost throughout; however, in three or four instances she does speak for herself in small subchapters given to her first-person point of view.

Thomas Jefferson is always depicted externally, as are most of the characters in the novel. Readers see him in action and hear him speak but seldom know what is occurring in his mind. The novelist, to her credit, does not attempt to debunk myths surrounding the historical Jefferson; his greatness is left intact, though readers will doubtless be disturbed by the omnipresent fact that Jefferson continued to own slaves and to live his life within the confines of slavery as an institution. His greatness and role in history are not undermined, but much of his hypocrisy is exposed. Chase-Riboud has assured this by prefacing the chapters with actual historical writings, documents, and letters, most of which are directly from Jefferson himself.

Nathan Langdon grows and learns more than any other character in the work. A Southerner himself, he fully understands the functions and techniques of slavery, but he is unable to understand how Thomas Jefferson could have had such a relationship with Sally Hemings. Langdon plays something of a proxy for the reader, for his questions to the various characters would likely be the reader's own questions. Inevitably, what he learns is that Jefferson is a hypocrite; he also learns that Sally acted out of love to cause her own destruction.

Madison and Eston Hemings, as the only surviving sons of Sally and Jefferson, live in a world where they are legally black but otherwise white. Fixed forever in this messy state of affairs, their circumstances serve to expose the evils and corruption of the society itself. Their primary action in the novel is to object to their mother's new friend, Langdon. They do not trust him, because he is white. Sally, too, comes to distrust him, though for differing reasons.

Aaron Burr is one of the most memorable characters in the novel. Again, Chase-Riboud's description does not significantly vary from the traditional picture of the historical man. As an enemy to Jefferson, he acts to expose him for his miscegenation at home. A political creature who has few morals, Burr is never silenced except by old age.

John Trumbill appears throughout the narrative in significant episodes. As the sensitive artist who has painted Sally Hemings and Thomas Jefferson as well as other important historical figures of the time, Trumbill knows what is going on in the personal lives of these people. According to propriety, he must remain silent and does so. Chase-Riboud makes important not so much what Trumbill says but what he remains silent about.

Sally's mother, Elizabeth Hemings, has in many ways lived the same life as Sally. With white skin, education, and manners, Elizabeth knows very well the trap into which her daughter is falling with her love for Jefferson; too, the mother knows and forewarns Sally that nothing good can come from it, that Sally will pay with her life. Elizabeth serves to prove to the reader, and Sally herself, that mistakes are passed from one generation to the next.

Themes and Meanings

First and foremost, the novel is the imagined story of Sally Hemings. The bare historical facts of her life remain intact; nevertheless, most of the story is a creation of fiction. The skeletal events of the novel are well established by historical documents and common knowledge. The excitement, intrigue, and suspense, however, are created by Chase-Riboud.

The dominant theme is simply the story of the forbidden and illegal love of Sally Hemings and Thomas Jefferson. The novelist explores the possibilities for love against all such obstacles and shows that it is real, something that both lovers give themselves to. At the same time, the story is an exploration of slavery. Chase-Riboud's intentions are not to expose the evils of slavery—this had been done, of course, a century earlier with such works as *Uncle Tom's Cabin, Or, Life Among the Lowly* (1852)—but to explore the conscience of the slaveholders. Chase-Riboud tries to show how the two races (literally of one blood) could live and survive together in one house, in one society, and in one Union. How could Jefferson have two families, one white and one black, and be at peace with himself, given the flagrant differences between the ways he treated them publicly and privately?

Intricacies of the legal system that permitted slavery are also attacked. The census taker wishes not only to know the facts of the Jefferson-Hemings lifelong love but also to understand how Jefferson could love Sally, her children, and other family members and yet treat them as he did. Moreover, after Jefferson's death, the society permits Sally to remain in Virginia as a free woman, even though it is illegal.

Critical Context

Sally Hemings is Barbara Chase-Riboud's first novel. First published in 1979, it is a statement about a fact of history: Thomas Jefferson's forty-year love relation with one of his slaves. Inescapably, the novel is important because of messages that have importance for contemporary race relations in the United States. Of first concern here is not the fact that a founding father had a black mistress, but that he loved her and kept her in servitude. The social meaning is clear: Those who control power cannot continue to want brotherhood privately but not publicly.

Sally Hemings indicates the maturity of the black novel in American literature. Published at a distance of some ten years after the Civil Rights movement of the 1960's, it makes clear that equality remains a goal—an ideal—for which the nation should work. Chase-Riboud's thrust is not to expose the evils of slavery but to relate a matter that explains something in the national character. This movement toward equality and human rights is depicted in a historical setting so as to emphasize that such social changes have not yet been realized.

Bibliography

Brooks, Valerie. Review of *Sally Hemings*, by Barbara Chase-Riboud. *New Republic* 181 (July 7, 1979): 38. Brooks emphasizes the historical elements of the novel and briefly questions the belief that Hemings was actually Jefferson's mistress. She retells the basic events of the plot, finding other matters to be accurate. This favorable review of the novel serves as a brief outline of its contents.

Crandall, Norma Rand. "*Sally Hemings*." *America* 141 (November 3, 1979): 267. Unlike other reviewers, Crandall finds the novel to be primarily about Jefferson himself, rather than about Sally Hemings. Crandall focuses on Jefferson as statesman and politician, as he is depicted in the work. She also emphasizes his role as father to two families, one black and one white; similarly, she de-emphasizes his role as slaveholder.

Levin, Martin. "*Sally Hemings*." *The New York Times Book Review*, October 28, 1979, p. 14. Explains some of the blood ties of Jefferson's two families, the white one and the black one. Levin finds the narrative itself weak and uneventful; he sees problems in Chase-Riboud's telling of events and judges the novel to be too impressionistic.

Peterson, V. R. "Word Star Barbara Chase-Riboud Rewriting History." *Essence* 25 (December, 1994): 56. Brief profile of Chase-Riboud. Records public reaction to her critically acclaimed novel *Sally Hemings*, reporting that it was attacked by American historians who denied Hemings's liaison with Thomas Jefferson.

Rushdy, Ashraf H. A. "'I Write in Tongues': The Supplement of Voice in Barbara Chase-Riboud's *Sally Hemings*." *Contemporary Literature* (Spring, 1994): 100-136. Rushdy argues that the importance of oral sources in African American historical fiction can be understood through Jacques Derrida's concept of supplement. He explores the way Hemings compares her personal history with the way history is conceived by Jefferson's associates. The relationship between the two histories is discussed.

Carl Singleton

THE SALT EATERS

Author: Toni Cade Bambara (1939-1995)
Type of plot: Expressionism
Time of plot: 1978
Locale: Claybourne, Georgia
First published: 1980

> *Principal characters:*
> VELMA HENRY, a black activist in her late thirties whose life has nearly ended in suicide
> MINNIE RANSOM, an ancient faith healer who may be able to restore Velma's mental health
> OLD WIFE, a querulous spirit whose folk wisdom and Christian belief guide Minnie
> FRED HOLT, an unhappy bus driver whose only friend has been killed
> OBIE (JAMES LEE HENRY), Velma's husband
> DOC SERGE, the director of the Southwest Infirmary, a man with a checkered past
> M'DEAR SOPHIE HEYWOOD, Velma's godmother and a potent force for good in her life

The Novel

The Salt Eaters tells the story of Velma Henry, a bone-weary, despairing black woman whose marriage is on the skids and who has begun to falter seriously as she attempts to juggle a commitment to social activism, a career, and life as a wife and mother. In addition to being the story of Velma, the novel tells a larger story of African Americans in the late twentieth century as they come to grips with themselves, their country, and the world.

The central action of *The Salt Eaters* occurs in the short space of time it takes for the "fabulous healer," Minnie Ransom of Claybourne, Georgia, to "bring through" her patient Velma, who that same day has attempted to take her own life. From three o'clock in the afternoon of an early spring day until the novel ambiguously concludes less than a half hour later, the two women sit facing each other on stools in the Southwest Infirmary, a century old black-founded hospital where modern medicine is practiced side by side with traditional healing arts handed down from slave and Indian times.

Velma has slashed her wrists and crawled headfirst into a gas stove. Now, the veteran political worker, civil rights activist, and computer consultant sits quietly in a hospital robe as the ancient crone—abetted by Old Wife, her familiar, her guiding spirit—attempts to unravel the twisted psyche of the younger woman. Both are legends in the black community, Minnie for her supernatural powers and Velma for her organizational ability and aggressive self-confidence, now reduced to depression and confusion.

Those familiar only with her better-known short stories such as "Gorilla, My Love" and "Raymond's Run" will find Toni Cade Bambara's first and only novel very different. In its narration and style, the novel is indebted to such earlier authors as James Joyce and William Faulkner. Like Joyce's *Ulysses* (1922), *The Salt Eaters* is concerned with the events of a single day; like that novel and Faulkner's *The Sound and the Fury* (1929), Bambara's book makes use of stream-of-consciousness narration, jumps in place and time, and free associations. Because the narration plunges backward and forward in time, jumps about in the presentation of events, and frequently alternates perspectives, even the persistent reader may often encounter difficulties.

Velma occupies a central position inside the hospital; she is perched uneasily on a stool undergoing therapy and surrounded by a local prayer group of twelve elderly people known as The Master's Mind and by a number of curious hospital personnel. From there, the untraditional plot radiates out into the street, the surrounding neighborhood, and often to a bus approaching the city limits of Claybourne carrying among its passengers an interracial group of women led by Velma's sister. While Velma is being treated by Minnie, numerous people wander in, out of, and by the infirmary. Julius Meadows, a light-skinned physician, steals out of the room to walk the streets. Fred Holt, who has parked his bus, peers in at the curious ritual going on inside. Velma herself has a restless mind that leads her back to her childhood, to her husband Obie, and to her current lover Jamahl, a self-styled guru whom she cruelly but accurately dismisses as just "a jive nigger."

Little by little, the reader comes to see that the Black Power movement of earlier years has become a fragmented host of antagonistic parties, each making its impetuous demands on Velma. Her activities have taken a grievous toll on her marriage, so that she comes to reflect within herself the shattered state of her people, radicalized into factions that defy reconciliation.

Outside the hospital, the divided black community is preparing to celebrate a rite of spring, an ambiguous Mardi Gras-like festival that appears both boisterously merry and ominous. Though a carnival atmosphere exists in the streets, it is constantly undercut by allusions to the "Hoo Doo Man," by disconcerting encounters with transvestites, and by the recurring reminder that weapons stolen from an armory may be stashed at the Academy of the Seven Arts, Obie's community self-help center. The center, which conducts adult-education classes and has a well-equipped gym, is sponsoring a midnight parade that could easily turn into an armed uprising.

The academy, like the festival and like the strange storm that suddenly sweeps the streets with wind and rain, resists an entirely satisfactory interpretation. The outcome of Velma's treatment as the book comes to a close suggests that the first stage of healing has been reached, however, and that auspicious sign may well comment equally on the hope for the values of the community now in disarray.

The Characters

Velma is a take-charge woman, ever ready to adopt a new radical cause and careless of whom she offends. Committed to a number of civil rights projects, she has only recently become aware of environmental issues and seen an interrelatedness where previously she discerned none. She is convinced that Claybourne's largest employer, Transchemical, drives workers to early deaths and that its pollution is part of a global conspiracy of the privileged to enrich themselves through exploitation of the wretched of the earth, largely people of color. Just before her attempted suicide, she has been questioned about the destruction of Transchemical's computer records. Her disturbed state of mind makes her sketchy thoughts, including flashbacks to the recent past as well as to her childhood, often difficult to grasp, while her friends' recollections of her range from impatient and envious to unqualifiedly admiring. In perhaps Minnie Ransom's most difficult case, Velma is fighting for her life.

Minnie Ransom and Old Wife ought not to be considered separately but rather as a team. This old woman and her spirit mentor resemble a married couple whose impatience with each other cloaks deep affection. Although Minnie, a consummate herbalist, combines a variety of techniques in her healing, she relies mostly on commonsensical counseling combined with generous doses of love. Nothing about the low-key performance in the pleasant room suggests the bizarre. That these women, who probably represent body and soul—though which is which is often hard to say—are miracle workers is attested by a pregnant teenager, Nadeen, who sees the slashes on Velma's wrist vanish.

Fred Holt, an aging black Everyman, has no direct connection to Velma. He merely drives her sister's Third World sorority, The Seven Sisters, to Claybourne, where he is scheduled to pick up a charter group for extra money. Yet he represents the sort of man Velma must understand and even love if she is to love and help her people. Fred longs for his dead friend Porter, the only other African American at his company, although he could not mention his white wife to him and did not even see the man outside work. When Fred deliberately swerves to run over a raccoon, he is trying to kill the "coon" in himself, his alienated black identity.

Obie, a barely developed yet important figure in the novel, is the last to know that his wife is in the hospital—just as she was the last to know that he is "sleeping around." Who is to blame for the present state of their marriage is impossible to determine, but his claim that she has abandoned him and their twelve-year-old son makes a certain amount of sense, though Velma airily dismisses it. The masseur at the academy, where Obie once ruled unchallenged, tells the now-ineffectual cuckold that his body is a mass of knots.

M'Dear Sophie Heywood, the "auntie" with chiffon roses in her hat, has mythic dimensions that lift her from being merely Velma's godmother to something approaching a fairy godmother. She is to Velma what Old Wife is to Minnie, a guide through life, interpreting the omens that Velma fails to read. Sophie runs a celebrated rooming-house where Dr. Meadows is currently staying, and she never hesitates to mount the barricades in the cause of racial justice.

Doc Serge, half confidence man, half saint, directs the infirmary, managing somehow to meet its bills and payrolls. His title is purely honorary; he has done many things in his day, even pimping. A flashy, street-smart survivor, he commands respect for his convictions and strength of character from people who know that the line between the criminal and ethical is not as clear to those on the fringe as it may be for others.

Themes and Meanings

The Salt Eaters poses questions: What has happened to the wonderful promise of the 1960's for African Americans, and can the movement of those days be brought back on course?

Although the novel was published in 1980, it was written in the late 1970's and depicts a time when the protagonist suffers not only a crisis in confidence and faith but also a midlife crisis. The seemingly gratuitous references to Velma's menstruation are evidence that Velma is as concerned about lost youth as the lost promise of her cause. Many will ignore this aspect of the novel, though it in no way diminishes the larger theme of lost direction in the Civil Rights movement or the book's pervasive feminist concerns.

Velma and Obie were once glittering role models in the early years of the Black Power movement. Now, as forty looms, Velma has turned to a man she does not love, afraid, too, that she has lost the affection of her son, Lil James.

If *The Salt Eaters* proclaims that a woman can meet menopause and disappointment in relationships when offered support from those who love her, may not a similar answer apply to the fragmented cause of racial equality? Such a solution is offered in the novel's somewhat diffuse treatment of The Seven Sisters, women of color who unite amid their acknowledged diversity, presenting a solid front against oppression of all kinds, including militarism, environmental pollution, and the nuclear threat.

As a feminist, Bambara was often impatient with men—white men of authority in some places, but black men as well. In bitter pages, she describes the "boymen," a parasitical breed who live off women while avoiding all responsibility. They haunt the periphery of the black matriarchy, fathering children, pleading for money from their women, and wasting their lives in a haze of alcohol, drugs, and empty daydreams. More despicable yet are the "boymen's" successful brothers, vain self-serving peacocks who use the black community to boost their egos and establish their own importance. They too exploit women as foot soldiers in their political and civil rights campaigns, assigning them tedious jobs of organization and logistics while reserving for themselves glamorous roles of leadership and oratory. Often they reject their faithful female sisters, whom they treat as servants, for more alluring, less committed female companionship, even of another color.

Critical Context

Reviews greeting *The Salt Eaters* remarked on the book's difficulty. Even the title remains a bit murky, though "salt eaters" appear to be those with whom things are shared, such as traditional basic foods of bread and salt. Salt is also seen in the novel as an antidote to wounds, as a stancher of blood, and as a necessary ingredient to a salutory body chemistry.

Such opacity, however, is not the rare exception in Bambara's novel. Varied points of view, narrative interruptions, a multiplicity of characters frequently overwhelm the reader. Yet if *The Salt Eaters* is confusing, repetitious in its assertions, and strained in some of its dialogue, this unforgiving novel is still a tour de force, a mosaic of brightly colored tiles wherein elements of myth, folklore, local color, psychology, and impassioned exposition come together. A woman's odyssey offering a searching look into the African American psyche, *The Salt Eaters* influenced many of the prominent African American women writers of the 1980's.

Bibliography

Alwes, Derek. "The Burden of Liberty: Choice in Toni Morrison's *Jazz* and Toni Cade Bambara's *The Salt Eaters.*" *African American Review* 30 (September, 1996): 353-367. Alwes argues that the distinctive visions in both Morrison's and Bambara's novels constitute alternate sociopolitical paradigms of the African American community. She discusses the generational isolation of the characters, freedom to choose love, and social constraints on personal relationships.

Burks, Ruth Elizabeth. "From Baptism to Resurrection: Toni Cade Bambara and the Incongruity of Language." In *Black Women Writers (1950-1980)*, edited by Mari Evans. Garden City, N.Y.: Anchor Press/Doubleday, 1984. Burks shows that often "the language of the mind has usurped the language of action" in the novel, or that thoughts and imaginings of characters are presented as more real than actuality. Thus, Fred Holt does not actually drive his bus into the swamp, but only believes he has—a scene that has puzzled readers.

Byerman, Keith E. *Fingering the Jagged Grain*. Athens: University of Georgia Press, 1985. A helpful summary of the novel. Makes the point that "simply reversing the direction of oppressions" serves to perpetuate oppression and observes that harmony of life and mind is to be found within the unifying principles represented by Minnie's folk arts.

Collins, Janelle. "Generating Power: Fission, Fusion, and Post-modern Politics in Bambara's *The Salt Eaters.*" *MELUS* 21 (Summer, 1996): 35-49. Collins examines nuclear power as a dominant metaphor in *The Salt Eaters*. She discusses ecological and ethical concerns relating to nuclear energy, the nationalist and feminist positions of the author, and the ineptness and arrogance of the nuclear industry.

Kelley, Margot Anne. "'Damballah Is the First Law of Thermodynamics': Modes of Access to Toni Cade Bambara's *The Salt Eaters.*" *African American Review* 27 (Fall, 1993): 479-493. Kelley discusses problems in studying Bambara's work, her narrative techniques, and the attempts of the novel to direct readers' attention to personal and political wholeness. Presents an extensive character analysis.

Stanford, Ann F. "He Speaks for Whom?: Inscription and Reinscription of Women in *Invisible Man* and *The Salt Eaters.*" *MELUS* 18 (Summer, 1993): 17-31. Focusing on Ralph Ellison's and Bambara's novels, Stanford discusses the issue of gender erasure, the consequences of double invisibility and silencing, patterns of imagery and thematic similarities, the role of memory, the use of language, and textual corrections and record-correcting.

James E. Devlin

SAPPHIRA AND THE SLAVE GIRL

Author: Willa Cather (1873-1947)
Type of plot: Historical realism
Time of plot: From 1856 to c. 1881
Locale: Southwestern Virginia
First published: 1940

Principal characters:

SAPPHIRA COLBERT, a slave owner and the invalid mistress of Mill
    House in Back Creek, Virginia
HENRY COLBERT, Sapphira's husband, a miller
NANCY, a slave girl in the Colberts' household
RACHEL BLAKE, the Colberts' daughter, a widow who holds abolitionist
    views
MARTIN COLBERT, Henry's nephew, a notorious rake

The Novel

The novel opens on a dinner quarrel. Sapphira Colbert has announced to her husband, Henry, her intention of selling a slave girl, Nancy, to neighbors. Henry refuses to countersign the necessary documents, although the slaves belong legally to Sapphira. "We don't sell our slaves!" is Henry's blunt reply. Sapphira, portrayed as a particularly strong-minded woman, begins to devise other means to rid herself of Nancy, who has lost favor (and an easy job as light maid) because of a perceived favoritism paid to the lovely girl by Sapphira's husband, a favoritism that Sapphira feels (wrongly) is sexual. Her determination to sell Nancy does not sit well with her daughter, Rachel Blake.

Determined to have her way, Sapphira comes up with a plan to force Henry to agree to let Nancy go. Inviting Henry's lecherous nephew, Martin Colbert, to come stay with them, Sapphira hopes to compromise Nancy's morals, a situation that would make Nancy's continued place at the Colberts' unthinkable, according to the slaveholding ethos. When Martin arrives, it looks as though the ploy will work. Sapphira is charmed by the younger man's flatteries and bonhomie. The hardworking Henry, however, is not, and he questions Sapphira when Martin's stay becomes obviously prolonged.

Meanwhile, Nancy has indeed caught Martin's eye, but she knows of no way to deflect his—a white man's—flirtatious suggestions. His persistence and boldness begin to terrify the girl, so Sapphira, feigning concern, arranges for her to sleep in the hallway outside Sapphira's bedchamber (and within easy reach of Martin). One day, Martin finds her while she is picking fruit. Although she attempts to climb the tree, Martin sees her and pulls her down, causing Nancy to scream and alerting nearby field hands who take note, but keep working. Nancy has, by this time, begun to be talked about around the slave quarters.

Rachel Blake, who has opposed her mother's slave owning, devises a plan of her own when it becomes clear that Nancy is being terrorized because of Sapphira's vindictiveness. With the help of local Quakers, who have connections with the Underground Railroad, and with the tacit approval of Henry, she convinces Nancy of the necessity for escape. At first Nancy resists the suggestion, but Martin's pursuit of her forces her to realize that escape is her only solution. At length, Nancy flees to Canada. Meanwhile, Rachel, who has been banned from Sapphira's house, loses a daughter, Betty, to diphtheria, and the two women are finally reconciled through mutual grief.

An epilogue, "Nancy's Return," takes place twenty-five years later. Nancy's return to Virginia is witnessed through the eyes of a child who is identified as Cather. Although Nancy has grown into an agreeable, handsome woman, there is a poignancy to her character that comes from exile. That this is perceived through a child's eyes—as much of this dream has been seen through Nancy's—concludes the novel on a note of unexpected continuity.

The Characters

Certainly the most striking character in the novel is Sapphira Colbert. Cather presents Sapphira as "entirely self-centered" and stubborn, feeling that she has a right to do with her slaves as she pleases. She is also, unfortunately, capable of vindictiveness and cruelty. Her determination to rid herself of Nancy sends profound reverberations throughout the household and the larger social environment. At the same time, Sapphira is also capable of isolated acts of magnanimity, as in her tender solicitousness toward Tansy Dave, a youth deranged after an unhappy love affair.

By contrast, Henry Colbert is a gentle soul troubled by the immorality of slavery, against which he can find no explicit condemnation in the Bible, which he reads feverishly each night. He is genuinely fond of Nancy but does little to protect her from Martin's designs. His assistance in Nancy's escape takes the form of a feeble gesture: He leaves some money for her in an overcoat. Tellingly, he keeps his bed at the mill and ventures forth to meet Sapphira only at mealtime.

Nancy's affection for Henry Colbert is entirely innocent, and yet the punishments to which she is submitted begin to make even her fellow slaves cast a doubtful look at her. As Nancy believes (at first) that she is unable to escape, her fear of Mrs. Colbert—and later of Martin Colbert—reaches the level of hysteria, giving her plight a nightmarish quality. Despite the degree and nature of her victimization, her decision to escape is not an easy one to make. After all, her entire world is circumscribed by the Colbert household.

Meanwhile, Rachel Blake has long been at odds with her mother over the issue of slavery. The feeling of resentment is compounded with the fact that she feels she has also been a disappointment to her mother. Because of this resentment, it is Rachel who arranges for Nancy's escape. A widow, Rachel herself once felt rescued by Michael Blake, who "dropped from the clouds . . . to deliver her from the loneliness." Nancy's troubles reinforce the memory of that deliverance and help motivate Rachel to act.

Martin Colbert, a suave, former military man, entertains the Colbert household with his tales of derring-do and exotic places. His surface sophistication and mild flirtations amuse Sapphira but quickly leave Henry at a loss for anything to say. Martin's chief characteristic, however, is his unappeasable lechery. As intended, he quickly spots the demure and pretty Nancy and resolves on a course of relentless pursuit with a view to making her one of his conquests.

Themes and Meanings

Sapphira and the Slave Girl is a novel about the evils of private ownership, in this case, the ultimate crime of owning other human beings. Individual ownership and the right of the owner to do with his property exactly as he saw fit, regardless of how low his tastes and motivation might be, were forms of anarchy that Cather saw as inimical to ordered, civilized life—the basis of peaceful human existence.

Although the Civil War plays no part in the novel, the sundering of relationships that were to take place within a decade are prefigured in the Colbert family, which is broken by the fact of slavery itself. The desire to possess and control determines both character and plot. Sapphira's determination to sell Nancy brings her husband's opposition. Faced with a dilemma, she hatches a wicked plan of sexual harassment to force the issue. Martin's obsessive desire to possess Nancy results in the desperate and dangerous plan to escape. The very fact of slavery produces rifts that can only be healed over time. In the reader's last glimpse of Sapphira and Henry, Sapphira remarks forgivingly: "We would all do better if we had our lives to live over again."

Yet the spirit of reconciliation is more metaphorical than real. Nancy's return in the epilogue, after Sapphira and Henry are long dead, has a dreamlike aura around it. One suspects that Sapphira and Henry have survived in the child's mother and father. The narrator's mother dominates the household just as Sapphira did, and the father, like the passive Henry, is not present when Nancy returns.

Moreover, part of the drama of this novel derives from the fact that Sapphira and Henry do not let their differences show explicitly (except in the opening scene). Bitter feelings are hidden by manners and an atmosphere of domestic tranquillity. Nancy's dilemma is thus set in relief against these mores, which provide the Colberts a defense which the slave girl cannot possess.

Critical Context

Cather's last novel brings the author's career full circle by dealing with her Virginia origins. While most of her work concerns life in the West, *Sapphira and the Slave Girl* deploys characters based on her earliest memories of family life to dramatize her lifelong opposition to the increasing materialism of American life. The epilogue suggests that the story of Sapphira and the slave girl, Nancy, may well represent Cather's own fundamental psychological drama, that of the well-meaning but ineffectual father, the domineering mother, and the orphaned protagonist. Be that as it may, the work is Cather's final statement in the novel form concerning the question of what America will finally become and her hope that the tide would finally turn against the forces of materialism—as represented by the abuses of private ownership. This novel of slavery and division argues in an elemental way against that tide and its attendant mentality with an authority that comes only with long experience.

Bibliography

Bloom, Edward A., and Lillian D. Bloom. *Willa Cather's Gift of Sympathy.* Carbondale: Southern Illinois University Press, 1962. Considered a classic on criticism of Cather's works. The Blooms look at this author's gift of sympathy and skillfully relate it to her thematic interests and technical proficiency. Deals with not only Cather's fiction but also her poetry and essays, which in themselves form an important commentary on her ideas.

Bloom, Harold, ed. *Modern Critical Views: Willa Cather.* New York: Chelsea House, 1985. Bloom says of this volume that it gathers "the best literary criticism on Cather over the last half-century." The criticism selected emphasizes Cather's novels *Sapphira and the Slave Girl*, *My Ántonia*, *Death Comes for the Archbishop*, and *A Lost Lady*. The volume concludes with a study by Marilyn Arnold on what are considered Cather's two finest short stories, "A Wagner Matinee" and "Paul's Case." Contains a chronology and a bibliography. A must for serious Cather scholars.

Fryer, Judith. *Felicitous Space: The Imaginative Structures of Edith Wharton and Willa Cather.* Chapel Hill: University of North Carolina Press, 1986. Although there are many full-length studies on Cather's writing, this volume is particularly noteworthy for its examination of Cather using current feminist thinking. Fryer explores Cather's fiction in terms of the "interconnectedness between space and the female imagination" and cites her as a transformer of social and cultural structures. A thorough and interesting study, recommended for its contribution to women's studies in literature. Includes extensive notes.

Gerber, Philip. *Willa Cather: Revised Edition.* New York: Twayne, 1995. Incorporates discussion of new materials and criticism that have appeared since 1975 edition. Rather than calling Cather a "disconnected" writer, as have some critics, Gerber takes the view in this study that there is unity in her writing. Gerber demonstrates the development of her artistry from one novel to the next. Includes a chronology and a selected bibliography.

Meyering, Sheryl. *A Reader's Guide to the Short Stories of Willa Cather.* New York: G. K. Hall, 1994. Chapters on each short story, discussing publication history, the circumstances of composition, biographical details, significant literary and cultural sources, connections to Cather's novels, and an overview of how each story has been interpreted.

Murphy, John. *Critical Essays on Willa Cather.* Boston: G. K. Hall, 1984. A compilation of criticism on Cather's work, including general essays from a variety of contributors as well as reviews and literary criticism of specific titles. The introduction emphasizes her creativity, and the volume concludes with reviews of her last four books. Most useful for its breadth of criticism on Cather. Contains a selected bibliography.

Shaw, Patrick W. *Willa Cather and the Art of Conflict: Re-visioning Her Creative Imagination*. Troy, N.Y.: Whitston, 1992. Separate chapters on all of Cather's major novels. Reexamines Cather's fiction in terms of her conflicts over her lesbian sexuality. The introduction provides a helpful overview of Cather criticism on the topic.

David Rigsbee

SARAH PHILLIPS

Author: Andrea Lee (1953-   )
Type of plot: Bildungsroman
Time of plot: The 1960's to the 1970's
Locale: Philadelphia
First published: 1984

> *Principal characters:*
> SARAH PHILLIPS, an African American minister's daughter who
> matures from a young child to an adult woman in the course of the
> novel
> HENRI, Sarah's French boyfriend during her college years
> THE REVEREND JAMES FORREST PHILLIPS, Sarah's father, the pastor of
> the New African Baptist Church in Philadelphia
> GRACE RENFREW PHILLIPS, Sarah's mother
> MATTHEW, Sarah's elder brother
> LYN YANCY, Sarah's best friend in fourth grade
> LILY, EMMA, and MAY, aunts of Sarah
> GRETCHEN MANNING, Sarah's best friend in seventh grade
> MARTHA GREENFIELD, Matthew's white college girlfriend
> MRS. JELLER, an old convalescent taken care of by Sarah's mother
> CURRY DANIELS, a male friend of Sarah at Harvard

The Novel

  Sarah Phillips presents the experiences of an African American woman growing up in a middle-class environment. It covers the period from the early 1960's until the mid-1970's. The setting and themes of the book are similar to those of the author's own life.

  Sarah Phillips is divided into twelve episodes. Each of these are a complete story in themselves but also develop the overall narrative. The story is told by a first-person narrator. It is recounted in the form of an autobiographical reminiscence.

  The book begins with the narrator and protagonist, Sarah Phillips, living in France during a year abroad as a college student. Sarah is having an enjoyable time, reflecting with amusement on the French myths about America that come to the surface during her conversations with French people. When her French boyfriend, Henri, makes an insensitive racial joke, however, Sarah's sense of serenity and fun is shattered. She begins to realize that although she had previously thought that Europeans did not possess American racial stereotypes, these stereotypes are difficult for her to escape. Sarah is reminded anew of her racial background and identity. She begins to reflect back on her childhood days.

  Sarah had been born the daughter of a prominent African American minister. Sarah is reared in a middle-class residential section of Philadelphia. At the age of ten, she sits on a summer Sunday in a pew of the New African Baptist Church, where her father preaches. The world of the church, where Sarah is surrounded by her extended family, seems all-encompassing to the young girl. The long hours of prayer and singing begin to bore Sarah, however, and she idly fantasizes about playing outdoors in a treehouse. Sarah feels both protected and stifled by the rich atmosphere of the church.

Despite his profession, the Reverend Phillips does not maintain a strict religious grip on the household. Sarah and her older brother Matthew grow up in a loose and relaxed spiritual atmosphere. Even so, Sarah feels that she cannot live up to her father's expectations of her as a good Christian. She is made particularly nervous by the rite of baptism. When her Aunt Bessie urges her to volunteer to be baptized, Sarah refuses. Sarah expects her parents to be angry, but their reaction is surprisingly mild. Her father's reluctance to punish Sarah makes an impression on her and becomes a major ingredient of her bond to her father. By not imposing his own expectation on her character, the Reverend Phillips permits Sarah to become her own woman.

On the surface, Sarah's childhood appears unexciting, but even the most ordinary people and places offer unexpected possibilities. Sarah's mother, who appears sedate and domestic, always exudes an air of the thrilling and the forbidden despite her prudish exterior. With her best friend, Lyn, Sarah is enthralled by tales of gypsies stealing children, and she is quite disappointed when the gypsies never come to perform their dark task.

Sarah's father is active in the Civil Rights movement. As the push for racial equality becomes more intense in the mid-1960's, Sarah's private life is increasingly affected by social changes. Sarah wants to attend a march in Washington led by Martin Luther King, Jr., but her father does not permit her. She watches the march on television with her family, feeling that she is missing out on taking part in a historic event.

When Sarah reaches the seventh grade, she enters an elite boarding school for girls in Pennsylvania. In the outside world, civil unrest rages, and the racial turmoil of the nation mounts, but Sarah's world at the school is placid and tranquil. With her best friend, Gretchen, who is white, she explores areas of the school grounds forbidden to them by authorities. On one of these expeditions, the girls stumble upon the sparse and dingy living quarters of the school's African American maids. Sarah is reminded that she leads a much more privileged life than most other African Americans.

Racial issues enter Sarah's life in a different way when Matthew brings home a white girlfriend, Martha Greenfield, during his first year at college. Sarah's parents treat Martha in a hostile way. They are used to a segregated world and are not ready to accept interracial dating. Sarah gains new insight into the predicament of African Americans as well as into the dynamics of her own family.

Sarah goes away to summer camp, where her life is dominated by a teenage gang called the Thunderbirds. As a good student from a prosperous family, she naturally feels different from this gang, but she is also attracted by their defiance of social regulations. At the end of camp, she is accepted in a way by the Thunderbirds, although she will always be different from them.

While Sarah is shopping for clothes with her mother, Mrs. Phillips takes her to visit Mrs. Jeller, an old convalescent who had been a parishioner at the Reverend Phillips's church. Mrs. Jeller tells a story about how, as a young girl, she had been forced by her pregnancy into a loveless early marriage. This had occurred long ago in a impoverished section of Kentucky, and the baby had died when it was only a year and a half old. Sarah feels that her comfortable middle-class identity is further questioned by this tale.

Sarah goes to Harvard University. There she meets Curry Daniels, a dynamic young photographer. Curry convinces Sarah to let him take photographs of her in the nude, but they never have a romantic relationship. In a way, Sarah is disappointed in this. Sarah's college years are filled with social and personal accomplishment, yet there remains an unsatisfying aftertaste about the entire experience.

Sarah is still at Harvard when her mother calls to tell her that the Reverend Phillips has had a stroke. Sarah rushes home, at once horrified by the news and feeling that it possesses a strangely unreal quality. Sarah returns to the scene of her nurturing childhood, this time not celebrating life but commemorating death. Seeing her former life through adult eyes, she comes to a new understanding of herself that enables her to accept her father's passing. Feeling she has at last begun to know herself, Sarah sets out back to Harvard. She has no idea what her ultimate destination is, but she feels that her individual journey has finally begun.

The Characters

Sarah Phillips, the heroine and narrator of the book, guides the reader on a tour of the various stages of her life. The other characters in the book function as auxiliary figures who fill in the outlines of Sarah's progress through the first two decades of her life.

Intelligent, sensitive, and observant, Sarah nevertheless doubts herself and her own capacity to come to terms with her experience. Sarah is grateful to her parents for their loving attention, but she never feels herself a part of their world. Attracted by the romantic appeal of the gypsies and the Thunderbirds, she is too straitlaced to stray far outside the middle-class contours established by her parents. At first oblivious to her racial identity, Sarah determines to come to grips with the contradictions of being a middle-class, educated African American.

The Reverend Phillips, Sarah's father, is a figure of great wisdom and power. Yet he uses his authority not to discipline Sarah and her brother but rather to make them feel protected and loved. Sarah feels somewhat distant from her father, whom she reveres but does not fully know. Reverend Phillips, however, clearly is the dominant figure in his daughter's life.

Sarah's mother, Grace Renfrew Phillips, is more elusive. Beneath her placid, bourgeois exterior lurks a far more exciting and illicit world of adventure and intrigue. Sarah's mother seems more traditional and self-effacing than her intelligent, ambitious daughter. Sarah, though, gets much of her questing spirit, her desire to encounter new realms other than the one into which she is placed by birth, from Mrs. Phillips.

Matthew, Sarah's brother, provides a male perspective on many of her childhood experiences. Sarah's aunts, Lily, Emma, and May, help to compose the comfortable church setting of Sarah's youth. They also point up traditional, socially endorsed behavior patterns of African American women from which Sarah sharply departs. Mrs. Jeller, an aging convalescent, indicates the vast differences between Sarah's well-off status in life and those of older African American women.

Sarah's friends, Lyn Yancy, Gretchen Manning, and Curry Daniels, are introduced in order to underscore certain stages in Sarah's development. They call attention to the ever-present factor of race in all of her personal relationships. Sarah's French boyfriend, Henri, initiates the narrative of the book through his racial insult.

In general, the characters other than Sarah are in the book to illustrate specific aspects of the novel's themes. They do not grow or develop. Sarah, on the other hand, progresses from child to adult as the novel proceeds.

Themes and Meanings

The novel's primary theme is the tension of growing up both African American and middle-class. Rebelling against the conventional stereotype of African Americans as constrained within a cycle of bleak poverty and crime, Lee presents a stable, loving, and prosperous family. Sarah defies traditional images of African American women by her assertiveness and intelligence. Sarah is not one of life's victims; she is a member of what the African American thinker W. E. B. DuBois termed the "Talented Tenth" of African Americans.

Yet Sarah is also made constantly aware of the other ninety percent, those African Americans who do not get to go to prestigious boarding schools and colleges. Sarah realizes that her privileged life is possible only because of the struggles of the Civil Rights movement, largely accomplished by men and women of her father's generation. Sarah also realizes that for many African Americans who still have to endure poverty and discrimination, these struggles have yet to bear fruit.

The novel's focus is not, though, exclusively social. Sarah goes through private experiences common to the maturation process of any young woman. She loves her parents but feels that they do not understand her. She has close friendships but feels that there are many aspects of her character that her friends can simply never get to know. The novel is animated throughout by the tension between Sarah as an individual and Sarah as a type, a representative of the new generation of prosperous, educated African Americans that came to maturity in the 1970's.

Critical Context

It is interesting that the novel's title is the name of an individual person. This was a common practice in the nineteenth century, as evidenced by such books as Charles Dickens's *David Copperfield* (1850) and Leo Tolstoy's *Anna Karenina* (1877), but it has been far less common in the twentieth century. Lee's novel, like its nineteenth century counterparts, chronicles the tension between public and private experience. *Sarah Phillips* has an affirmative faith in the capacity of an individual to prevail against worldly obstacles. One of the novel's principal accomplishments is its skilled interweaving of personal and social realms. To some extent, Sarah is free to determine her fate, but the pressures of society and race are never minimized.

Andrea Lee first came to prominence with the publication of *Russian Journal* in 1981. That book, written in lapidary prose, was a candid account of Lee's personal experiences while visiting the Soviet Union during the "era of stagnation" presided over by Communist Party leader Leonid Brezhnev. Full of observant and idiosyncratic reportage, *Russian Journal* garnered praise from across the American critical spectrum. This feat was especially impressive in light of the fact that Lee was only twenty-eight at the time the book was published. After *Russian Journal*, Lee's readers eagerly awaited a novel from her. Their expectations were satisfied with the publication of *Sarah Phillips* in 1984.

Bibliography

Gibson, Donald. Review of *Sarah Phillips*, by Andrea Lee. *African American Review* 29 (Spring, 1995): 164-165. Generally favorable review that notes that the value of the book stems from its complexity, especially regarding the intersections of race, class, and color. Gibson praises the book as "a novel to be reckoned with."

Hogue, Lawrence. "The Limits of Modernity: Andrea Lee's *Sarah Phillips*." *MELUS* 19 (Winter, 1994): 75-90. Hogue views Sarah Phillips as an alienated person who attempts to escape the values of her past and overcome black bourgeoisie values.

Kapp, Isa. "The First Time Around." *The New Leader* 67 (December 10, 1984): 5. Discusses the insecurity felt by the title character and her dissatisfaction with the conflicts induced by her class privilege.

Murrell, Elizabeth J. Review of *Sarah Phillips*, by Andrea Lee. *Freedomways* 25 (Summer, 1985): 119. Examines the novel's African American consciousness and its contribution to awareness of racial issues.

Obolensky, Laura. "Scenes from a Girlhood." *The New Republic* 91 (November 19, 1984): 41-42. Discusses the potential for elitism in Sarah's self-portrait. A principal concern is Sarah's relationship with her father.

Shreve, Susan Richards. "Unsentimental Journey." *The New York Times Book Review* 89 (November 18, 1984): 13. Praises Lee's personal honesty and luminous style. Emphasizes the skill with which even minor characters are drawn.

Taylor, Linda. Review of *Sarah Phillips*, by Andrea Lee. *The Times Literary Supplement*, April 5, 1985, p. 376. Examines the novel's meditations on African American issues from a British perspective. Addresses particularly the question of style in the work.

Nicholas Birns

SAVE ME THE WALTZ

Author: Zelda Fitzgerald (1900-1948)
Type of plot: Autobiographical romance
Time of plot: The 1920's
Locale: Alabama, New York, France, and Italy
First published: 1932

> *Principal characters:*
>> ALABAMA BEGGS, the youngest and wildest of the Beggs daughters, but a thoroughbred
>> DAVID KNIGHT, Alabama's artist husband
>> BONNIE KNIGHT, the daughter of Alabama and David
>> JUDGE AUSTIN BEGGS, Alabama's father, a living fortress of security
>> "MISS MILLIE" BEGGS, Alabama's mother, whose "fixation of loyalty . . . achieved in her life a saintlike harmony"
>> DIXIE BEGGS, the oldest daughter of Judge and Mrs. Beggs, who moved to New York and married an Alabama man "up there"
>> JOAN BEGGS, the middle daughter, who "was so orderly she made little difference"
>> JACQUES CHEVRE-FEUILLE, a French aviator
>> MADAME, a Russian ballet mistress

The Novel

Save Me the Waltz, according to its author, derives its title from a Victor record catalog, and it suggests the romantic glitter of the life which F. Scott Fitzgerald and Zelda Sayre Fitzgerald lived and which Scott's novels have so indelibly written into American literary and cultural history.

Divided into four chapters, each of which is further divided into three parts, the novel is a chronological narrative of four periods in the lives of Alabama and David Knight, names that are but thin disguises for their real-life counterparts. The four chapters loosely follow four distinct phases of the author's life up to the death of her father: her childhood filled with romantic dreams of escape from the increasingly stifling family; her exciting escape via marriage to a painter and their early life together in Connecticut, New York, France, and Switzerland; the increasing emptiness of that life; and a final escape into ballet training, concluding with the return to Alabama for her father's final illness.

These four phases conclude with a party given by the Knights in Alabama, at which once more David is the idol of the evening and once more Alabama and David are envied for their exciting and glamorous lives. The talk at the party, for Alabama, "pelted her consciousness like the sound of hoofs on a pavement," an effect evocative of the remoteness and boredom in lines from T. S. Eliot's "The Love Song of J. Alfred Prufrock": "In the room women come and go/ Talking of Michelangelo."

The tragic events of Zelda's reverse fairy tale remained to be played out in real life in the devastating effects that she and her husband had on each other: his alcoholism, her many bouts with insanity, and finally, in 1948, her death in a fire at a mental institution. To the end, neither seemed to understand the other. Nicole Diver in *Tender Is the Night* (1934) and David Knight in *Save Me the Waltz* are graphic demonstrations of the masculine and feminine defenses, respectively, that each built against the other.

The Characters

The novel begins with a description of Judge Austin Beggs as a living fortress who provides his family with security. Equally strong is his "detached tenderness," his bulwark against the disappointments of life, the most important of which is the loss of an only son in infancy. His anger and outraged sense of decency take over from time to time when additional disappointments invade his concentration on the "origins of the Napoleonic code" and on his attempts to provide financially for his family of three socially frivolous daughters. His handling of situations is direct, as when he "brusquely grabbed the receiver" of the telephone "with the cruel concision of a taxidermist's hands at work" to ask a beau never to attempt to see Dixie, his eldest daughter, again.

"Miss Millie" Beggs, Alabama's mother, on the other hand, possesses a "wide and lawless generosity," "nourished from many years of living faced with the irrefutable logic of the Judge's fine mind." Because her sense of reality was never very strong, she could not "reconcile that cruelty of the man with what she knew was a just and noble character. She was never again able to form a judgment of people, shifting her actualities to conform to their inconsistencies till by a fixation of loyalty she achieved in her life a saintlike harmony." Her strategy in life consists of avoiding or preventing difficult situations, so that when Alabama tells her that she does not want to go to school any longer and her mother can react only with a faintly hostile surprise, Alabama merely switches the subject to save her mother the difficulty of listening to an explanation that she cannot comprehend. Millie's major battles are fought over dresses remade for one daughter from an older sister's clothes.

Alabama's older sisters, Joan and Dixie, the belles of Montgomery society and the envy of their younger sister during her childhood, eventually settle into conventional patterns of life in New York and Connecticut. Alabama finds the social whirl exciting at first and then suffocating; her pattern for life is established early, when her first escape arrives one day in the person of a handsome military officer from the north, David Knight. He is, indeed, the knight come to release his princess, as he refers to her in his letters. He even expresses a wish to keep her in his ivory tower for his "private delectation." What Alabama realizes much later is that despite all the initial excitement of the escape, the disillusioning sense of entrapment eventually sets in. She leaves her father's fortress for the ivory tower of her husband's success and popularity as a painter. The need to create her own destiny and identity always lurks beneath the fairy-tale surface of her life. Her affair with a handsome French flyer and the constant adoration of her husband by women and by their daughter, Bonnie, only serve to intensify the emptiness of her glamorous, Bohemian existence.

In desperation, Alabama, at an age at which most ballet dancers have matured, begins achingly long days of lessons with a Russian ballet mistress. She spends less and less time with husband and daughter as her obsession with the ballet consumes her totally. This latest escape is aborted when she undergoes foot surgery in Naples, where she has been dancing in her first professional role. Shortly thereafter, she returns to the emptiness of a life without a purpose.

When she, David, and Bonnie return to Alabama on the occasion of her father's death, she is aware of the pattern that their lives have taken. David continues to be a successful artist; she finds her old feelings of uselessness returning. He is still the idol of guests at a party they give, and their glamorous lives still draw the envy of local society. At that party it is the forms and shapes of things that hold Alabama captive as "the talk pelted her consciousness." Scolded by David for not being the proper hostess, Alabama responds that her premature dumping of the ashtrays is expressive of herself, that she simply lumps "everything in a great heap which I have labelled 'the past,' and having thus emptied this deep reservoir that was once myself, I am ready to continue."

In real life, Alabama (Zelda) went on to compete with David (Fitzgerald) in his own chosen art form (writing). In *Save Me the Waltz*, the next escape has not yet taken shape.

Except for one major event in the novel, that of Alabama's professional ballet engagement in Naples—Zelda never danced professionally—the real life of the Fitzgeralds is only thinly disguised. Like Alabama, Zelda was twenty-two years of age when she met the man who was to become her husband. The Southern childhood of Alabama is Zelda's own. Millie Beggs, as Nancy Milford points out in her biography of Zelda, is given a name that combines the names of Zelda's and Fitzgerald's mothers, Minnie and Mollie, respectively. Like Millie Beggs, Zelda's mother provided the quiet and harmony necessary to Judge Sayre and the attention to the practical needs of their daughters. Zelda's older sister Rosalind wrote society columns for the local newspaper, as does Alabama's older sister Dixie. Zelda and Fitzgerald's daughter Scottie and their Japanese servant Tanaka are the Bonnie and Tanka of the novel. Events in the Knights' odyssey from Montgomery to the New York area, the Riviera, Paris, and Switzerland—then back to Alabama—follow closely those of the Fitzgeralds. Especially significant are the portraits of Zelda's father and of her husband. Judge Sayre symbolized both security and inaccessibility, and her husband, as surrogate father, became both. The contradictory impulses of authority on the one hand and freedom on the other are the poles between which the pendulum of her life swung and between which Zelda could find no stable point.

A major difference between Zelda's self-portrait and that which her husband paints of her as Nicole Diver in *Tender Is the Night* is one of the most intriguing revelations of the novel. Nicole is an irrationally jealous wife whose unpredictable tantrums create marriage problems. Alabama Beggs, on the other hand, although jealous of the attention her idolized husband receives, is in her own words an empty, deep reservoir that she tries desperately to fill. It is from these irreconcilable views that the two companion novels draw their central characters.

Themes and Meanings

It is inevitable that the major theme of the novel is seen as an intense attempt on the part of the wife of one of America's most famous novelists to reorder and shape her own destiny by writing about her attempt to do so. The novel was written during the early stages of a series of mental breakdowns that became the pattern in the remaining years of Zelda's life. It was written also during the time that her husband was working on his own novel, *Tender Is the Night*, in which the two leading roles of Alabama and David Knight are depicted (from a masculine point of view) in the characters of Nicole and Dick Diver.

Although traditional prerogatives of a male society had been broken down by some gains in women's rights during the early years of the twentieth century, it remained for those freedoms to become a reality for most women. Zelda wrote magazine articles on the subject during the 1920's and attempted to achieve that reality for herself. For ten years or so, between her marriage and her schizophrenic attacks, she worked toward this goal, ironically realizing it eventually, not in her ballet dancing, but in the same artistic medium as that of her husband: writing a novel that, although not the aesthetic equal of her husband's work, is an important book in its own right. From the vantage point of more than fifty years after the novel's publication, the novel thus has for its major theme the identity crisis of a woman for whom the ideal of the American Dream seems only to turn to ashes, like those cigarette ashes that Alabama impolitely dumps before all of her guests have left the party.

It is no mere literary convention that Zelda begins and ends the novel with events at the center of which is her father. Like Judge Beggs, her own father—Judge Sayre—represented a fortresslike security that merely changed form in the ivory tower that her husband seemed to her. Both father and husband were, as in the case of Alabama Beggs, ultimately inaccessible. The fictive account of Zelda, however, allowed for the heroine's realization of some personal success in an actual ballet performance in Naples. In this respect, the writing of the novel had some therapeutic, even if temporary, effect on the real-life dancer who never had this opportunity. The fragility of a romantic upbringing and events such as the foot injury conspired to abort Alabama's attempt to shape her own life and to realize fully the newly won feminist freedoms.

Critical Context

Save Me the Waltz makes fascinating reading for a student of literary history in several ways. First, there is the matter of the novel's being read by one of the most famous twentieth century editors, Maxwell Perkins, who liked it well enough to give it serious consideration. Fitzgerald, however, also read the novel and made many changes, against the wishes of Zelda, although she eventually agreed to them. He had been working on his own novel about their marriage, *Tender Is the Night*, at the time, and had his way regarding matters he wished deleted or changed in the original manuscript of *Save Me the Waltz*. Together, Harry Dan Piper states, "these two chronicles of the same marriage seen from the wife's and the husband's points of view, form one of the most unusual pairs of novels in recent literary history."

In a later edition (1960), the novel includes a preface by Harry T. Moore, a note on the text by Matthew J. Bruccoli, a set of emendations, and "an exact type transcript of the typescript opening of Chapter 2 in the form originally set in galleys."

Scholars and critics have shown interest in the novel primarily because of the prominent position occupied by F. Scott Fitzgerald in American literary history. Consequently, critical concern has focused on autobiographical insights rather than on the aesthetic merits of *Save Me the Waltz*. Most critics, however, have mentioned the turgid prose and overblown metaphors in parts of the novel, especially at the outset. One in particular has been noted: "Incubated in the mystic pungence of Negro mammies, the family hatched into girls. From the personification of an extra penny, a street-car ride to whitewashed picnic grounds . . . the Judge became, with their matured perceptions a retributory organ, an inexorable fate. . . . Youth and age: a hydraulic funicular, and age, having less of the waters of conviction in its carriage. . . ." Yet as the action of the novel develops, the self-consciousness of the writing settles down, as in the description of Alabama's sick father: "The noble completeness of the life withering on the bed before her moved her to promise herself many promises." In the final paragraph of the novel, the linguistic awkwardnesses disappear, as Alabama and David sit in the "pleasant gloom of the late afternoon," and amid "the silver glasses, the silver tray, the traces of many perfumes," they watch "the twilight flow through the calm living room that they were leaving like the clear cold current of a trout stream."

Beyond the interest that important scholars have taken in the novel, beyond its autobiographical value, and in spite of its embarrassingly self-conscious language, Zelda's fictive autobiography slowly catches even the discriminating reader in a rhythmic involvement in the feminist imagination and feminine psychology that have a fascination all their own.

Bibliography

Davis, Simone W. "'The Burden of Reflecting': Effort and Desire in Zelda Fitzgerald's *Save Me the Waltz*." *Modern Language Quarterly* 56 (September, 1995): 327-351. Davis examines the novel's exploration of dilemmas confronted by women in the 1920's. Feminine identity is examined in a culture where it is the "work" of leisured women to add meaning to someone or something.

Lanahan, Eleanor A. *Zelda, An Illustrated Life: The Private World of Zelda Fitzgerald*. New York: Harry N. Abrams, 1996. An illustrated book of Fitzgerald's own drawings, paintings and private photographs. A fascinating glimpse into Fitzgerald's creative expression.

Milford, Nancy. *Zelda: A Biography*. New York: Harper & Row, 1970. A well-written and thoroughly researched account of Fitzgerald's life.

Nanney, Lisa. "Zelda Fitzgerald's *Save Me the Waltz* as Southern Novel and *Kuntslerroman*." In *The Female Tradition in Southern Literature*, edited by Carol S. Manning. Urbana: University of Illinois Press, 1993. An interesting discussion.

Payne, Michelle. "5′4″ × 2″: Zelda Fitzgerald, Anorexia Nervosa, and *Save Me the*

Waltz." Bucknell Review 39 (1995): 39-56. A discussion of the work and its relation to eating disorder.

Wood, Mary E. "A Wizard Cultivator: Zelda Fitzgerald's *Save Me the Waltz* as Asylum Autobiography." *Tulsa Studies in Women's Literature* 11 (Fall, 1992): 247-264. Wood asserts that *Save Me the Waltz* should be considered asylum autobiography though there is no explicit mention by Fitzgerald of her mental illness.

Susan Rusinko

SEA GLASS

Author: Laurence Yep (1948-   )
Type of plot: Bildungsroman
Time of plot: The early 1970's
Locale: Concepcion, California
First published: 1979

> *Principal characters:*
>> CRAIG CHIN, an overweight Chinese American of middle-school age
>> CALVIN CRAIG, Craig's father, a storekeeper who wants his son to excel in sports
>> JEANNIE CRAIG, Craig's compassionate and loving mother
>> KENYON, a female classmate of Craig
>> UNCLE QUAIL, Craig's great-uncle, a Chinese American who remembers the old days
>> STANLEY, Craig's cousin who excels in sports
>> SHEILA, Craig's cousin and classmate
>> UNCLE TIM and AUNTIE FAYE, the parents of Stanley and Sheila
>> RALPH BRADLEY, a friend and classmate of Craig

The Novel

Set in the Chinatown of Concepcion, California, in the early 1970's, *Sea Glass* is the story of a second-generation Chinese American boy who is struggling to find his identity as a Chinese, as an American, and—most important—as a person. Pressing against young and overweight Craig Chin are two seemingly overwhelming problems: His father expects him to excel in sports in order to achieve acceptance as an American, and, when the novel opens, Craig is undergoing troubles as the new boy at school. His family has just moved to Concepcion from San Francisco.

The novel is organized into ten chapters of approximately equal length and importance. Each is divided into shorter subchapters to give the work something of an episodic effect and substance. The work has only one narrator, young Craig Chin himself; thus the point of view is entirely that of the adolescent boy as he struggles with his problems and new surroundings. The setting of the novel, in its entirety, is Concepcion, California.

The book opens with Craig trying unsuccessfully to play football with some new acquaintances upon his arrival in the new town. Craig's father stands on the sidelines to shout instructions to Craig and the other players. Because Calvin Craig had been successful in high school as an athlete, he believes his son can achieve acceptance in American society only by becoming a sports hero at school. Craig is fat and uninterested in football or any other such activity; however, he cannot make his father accept these facts.

In the next chapter, Craig's father has changed the game from football to basketball, where the same pattern occurs again. Craig cannot play basketball well, no matter how hard he tries; he succeeds only at humiliating himself and his father, who relentlessly claims that enough practice and hard work will make Craig a star player. He claims this even when it is clear to everyone that it cannot possibly be the case.

In the middle sections of the novel, two other main characters are introduced and become central to the action. Craig's job at the family store is to deliver groceries to older people in the community, one of whom is Calvin's great-uncle, Uncle Quail. This older Chinese gentleman, who never trusts the "white demons," lives alone in a small cottage near a cove on the ocean. Through his regular Saturday visits, Craig and Uncle Quail become friends who enjoy swimming together in the ocean in their own secret place. At the same time Craig is befriending Uncle Quail, he strikes up an acquaintance with a classmate named Kenyon, the daughter of two extremely liberal parents. The father is a poet and the mother a political activist. Kenyon and Craig recognize in each other kindred spirits because of their differences from the other children at Dana Middle School: Craig is different because of his Chinese ethnicity; Kenyon is different because of her parents' liberal lifestyles.

Because of his relationships with Kenyon and Uncle Quail, Craig's life seems to be getting better. At least he has friends and companions whom he enjoys. Kenyon, however, elicits from Craig the promise to ask Uncle Quail's permission for her to swim in the cove. Uncle Quail is horrified; he does not want any white people on his property and is offended that Craig would even ask. Yet he gives in to Craig's pleadings that Kenyon is "different," and a date is set. Kenyon is unable to keep the appointment, and through a series of misspoken statements, Craig alienates himself from both Uncle Quail and Kenyon. In the middle of these events, Craig loses his ability to maintain feelings of respect for his father in the Chinese fashion, and he violates the social order by screaming at his father the truth—that he is no good at sports, does not like them, and does not want ever to play or pretend to play them again.

Thus Craig has only his mother left for affection and friendship. She counsels him simply to wait patiently for the father, the uncle, and the friend to reconcile. Eventually, Uncle Quail thaws toward Craig, whereupon he visits Craig's father and, as the elder Chinese gentleman of the community, tells him to let Craig pursue his own interests and activities. Kenyon, too, softens and reestablishes her friendship with the young man. The novel concludes with Uncle Quail, Craig, and Kenyon taking a swim in the secret cove and diving for abalone. Instead, they find "sea glass," broken pieces of glass that have been smoothed and shaped by many years in the sea. It is clearly a happy ending, as Craig Chin is now at peace with those around him and with himself.

The Characters

Craig Chin, the first-person narrator of the story, tells of events that are important to him as he finds identity and peace. This occurs on several levels, but the most important of these is his relationship with his father. Both father and son love each other in an unquestioned, unconditional way, yet problems occur because of the father's insistence that Craig become a sports star. At the same time, Craig experiences severe difficulties because of his birth and ethnicity. On the one hand, he is Chinese by looks and blood; on the other, his way of thinking, his central culture, and his own goals in life are distinctly American. Readers learn of these difficulties and their resolutions through the revelations of the main character's thoughts and actions.

Calvin Craig, Craig's father, is the most loving and helpful and understanding of all fathers except for one matter: He is unable to accept that his son will never be any kind of successful athlete. His attitude is revealed primarily through his actions. Always on the sidelines encouraging and advising his son in football and basketball, he fails to realize the torment he is working upon the person in the world whom he loves most. For Calvin himself, sports had been the ticket to acceptance in American life.

Uncle Quail is the stereotypical "last generation" from the Old Country. In one section of the story, Uncle Quail tells of the experiences of his own father's generation as they built the United States' railroads and performed other such tasks. Then he explains the discrimination against them that occurred once the rails had been laid. He survives as a "Chinaman" gentleman, one who clings to the old ways of life and will not trust the "white demons" again. This works to Craig's benefit when Uncle Quail visits Craig's father and plays the part of family sage, essentially instructing the father to leave the boy alone to pursue his own interests.

Kenyon is the female foil and counterpart to Craig. She has problems similar to those experienced by Craig, and both come to realize that these are not because of Craig's Chinese heritage. Both are outsiders to the society of middle-school children because they do not conform to some unspoken, unknown mold and code of behavior. Kenyon's character and relation with her own parents give Craig the example and strength to stand up to his father and finally to speak the truth: that he will never be an athlete no matter how long or hard he tries.

Craig's mother, Jeannie Craig, is in some ways a stereotypical gentle, caring mother figure. She listens, encourages, and directs, and she works to keep peace between father and son as well as to help Craig develop as a young man who is pointed in the right direction in life.

Stanley and Sheila, Craig's first cousins on his mother's side, are examples of Chinese Americans who have seemingly made the transformation to being mainstream Americans without difficulty. Stanley is something of the son Calvin wishes he had had, because Stanley does very well in sports. Sheila, because of her quickness and sense of humor, is similarly accepted by the American-born white children at school. In fact, Sheila is so much accepted that she feels free to ridicule Craig for his ethnicity, although both children are entirely of Chinese descent.

Uncle Tim and Auntie Faye similarly appear in contrast to Craig's own parents. Evidently, they live as Chinese Americans without problem or difficulty, fitting well into the society at large because they do not push their children to overachieve for the sake of social acceptance.

Ralph Bradley is the only new friend other than Kenyon that Craig makes in Concepcion. Ralph represents in many ways that which is best of white Americans in terms of racial tolerance and acceptance of others. Ralph immediately understands why Craig's father pushes him on the sports field, and he does all he can to help Craig succeed in sports.

Themes and Meanings

Sea Glass is at once an ethnic novel and a novel of initiation. Craig Chin must grow up and find his place in the society around him—and he must do so as a Chinese, as an American, and as a Chinese American. The events·of the book unfold so as to assure his success on all counts. Ironically, the only major obstacle to this attainment is his father, the person who would help him most because he truly loves him. To the credit of the author, Craig's problems are never really derived from the youth's Chinese ancestry (as the father would seemingly have it) or from the American society at large (as Uncle Quail would have it). Rather, the problems are primarily at home in the heart of the father who would dictate that his son become a sports hero whatever the cost.

Such thinking is not localized with Craig Chin's parents. The attempt to relive within the lives of children that which was not achieved by the parents is common to human nature. Sadly, Craig must become the worst of an American (that is, a disrespectful youth who would scream at his father and throw something of a tantrum) in order to make this point to his father.

The chief literary device used by the novelist is that of metaphor. Yep takes the commonplace knowledge that "life is a game" and shows human tensions and conflicts to be a series of ongoing "plays"—here, ones which are off the field. The real games in the story are the ones between father and son, between Uncle Quail and Craig, between Kenyon and Craig.

The overriding metaphor and symbol of the novel are indicated by the title. Life is like an ocean, and people as individuals are like broken pieces of glass. Persons can, in time, be shaped by the forces of nature and society into something smooth and beautiful—something like "sea glass."

Critical Context

Sea Glass was Laurence Yep's fourth novel to be published in the 1970's, and all dealt with problems of Chinese American childhood. These novels reveal a particular maturity and sophistication in that they do not simplistically blame white Americans for all the problems experienced by Chinese immigrants. Yep recognizes that the mainstream society may all too often be responsible for problems of racism and discrimination, but he argues that meaningful resolution of such difficulties finally lies within the selves of his characters.

Yep, himself a native-born American, is a product of the American 1960's. His sensitivity to the social turmoil and upheavals occurring during his own life are present in his work, if not through description of event then at least in attitude and perspective. Yep's books have won several awards. *Child of the Owl* (1977) won the *Boston Globe-Horn* Fiction Award; *Dragonwings* (1975) won recognition as the American Library Association Notable Children's Book in 1975 and the Newbery Honor Book in 1976. He has continued to write novels, expanding his domain from ethnic fiction to works of mystery and suspense.

Bibliography

Burns, Mary M. "*Sea Glass*." *The Horn Book Magazine* 55 (October, 1979): 542. The reviewer focuses mostly on conflicts between children and parents but also emphasizes the clash between American and Chinese cultures in the United States. There is some discussion of Yep's narrative techniques, style, and structure in the novel.

Burnson, Patrick. "In the Studio with Laurence Yep." *Publishers Weekly* 241 (May 16, 1994): 25-26. Although Burnson's article does not mention *Sea Glass*, it offers an interesting overview of Yep's life and career.

Dinchak, Marla. "Recommended Laurence Yep." *English Journal* 71 (March, 1982): 81-82. Dinchak provides a thorough discussion of *Sea Glass* as well as three other novels by Yep: *Sweetwater* (1973), *Dragonwings*, and *Child of the Owl*. She makes valid comparisons among the teenage protagonist-narrators of the four works. In so doing, she takes up matters of adolescent conflicts, rebellion against parents, and communicating with others.

Fritz, Jean. "*Sea Glass*." *The New York Times Book Review*, January 20, 1980, p. 30. Fritz's review focuses mostly upon the problems of Chinese Americans proving themselves as Americans. She explains Yep's purposes in retelling the story of a father-son conflict, finding the resolution of the plot to be less important than the characters themselves.

Johnson-Feelings, Dianne. *Presenting Laurence Yep*. New York: Twayne, 1995. Provides biographical information about this Chinese American award-winning author and presents critical essays of his works for young adults. A good overall source for comparing and contrasting Yep's works.

Kao, Donald. "*Sea Glass*." *Interracial Books for Children Review* 11, no. 6 (1980): 16. Kao discusses the concept of achievement and success as it is understood by young Americans and as revealed in *Sea Glass*. He sets forth the idea that Craig is a "star" about things in life that are truly important and make sense. He identifies real-life problems and barriers as issues in the novel and discusses how "outsiders" to mainstream society deal with them.

Lenhart, Maria. "Finding the Courage to Be Oneself." *The Christian Science Monitor*, October 15, 1979, p. B11. This discussion is primarily concerned with the development of the main characters in the novel. The critic explains the faded dreams of the past (Craig's father) in the light of his own goals and expectations in life. She also discusses the dialogue of the first-person narrator, finding it credible.

Sutherland, Zena. "*Sea Glass*." *Bulletin for the Center for Children's Books* 33 (February, 1980): 124. Sutherland gives perhaps the best discussion of *Sea Glass* as literature. She takes up the matter of the metaphor and symbol of "sea glass" itself, explaining how it relates to Craig. She also comments about changes within the main character.

Carl Singleton

THE SECOND COMING

Author: Walker Percy (1916-1990)
Type of plot: Philosophical comedy
Time of plot: The late 1970's
Locale: The affluent rural community of Linwood in North Carolina, especially the golf course and its adjacent wild countryside
First published: 1980

Principal characters:

> WILL BARRETT, the protagonist, a middle-aged, prosperous lawyer who is recently widowed
>
> ALLISON (ALLIE) HUGER, a young woman who escapes from a mental hospital
>
> LESLIE BARRETT, Will's grown daughter, a fiercely religious, fundamentalist Christian
>
> LEWIS PECKHAM, the golf pro, one of the few unbelievers in this religious community, who appreciates classical music and good books
>
> THE ELDER BARRETT, Will's father, who committed suicide when Will was twelve years old and may have tried to kill his son as well in a hunting "accident"
>
> EWELL MCBEE, a small-town businessman and longtime bully who poaches deer on Barrett's land
>
> JACK CURL, a complaisant chaplain of the nursing home built by Will's late wife's money
>
> KATHERINE (KITTY) VAUGHT HUGER, Allie's mother, an old girlfriend of Will

The Novel

The Second Coming is a seriocomic tale in which a wealthy, middle-aged man who is contemplating suicide and a young woman who has recently escaped from a mental hospital save each other from depression and psychosis and win their freedom from conniving relatives. It is not the usual kind of love story, in which the primary conflict is some obstacle in a romantic pursuit. Each is engrossed in a very private struggle with the crippling emotions peculiar to his or her own past. Their encounter is a happy accident—or perhaps the grace of God extended to two social misfits who cannot make it alone.

Will Barrett seems to have everything: money, social position, friends, early retirement, and a good golf game. In abstract, metaphysical terms, his main adversary is the meaninglessness of his life, even though he and his late wife had been much involved in "good works." The more immediate antagonist, however, is his skeptical father, who shot himself when Will was a boy and intimated that someday his son would follow his example. Much of Will's mental life is spent recapturing in minute detail the reality of his relationship to his father and his legacy of death. Therefore, much of the action, though comical in itself and infused with satiric observations about American, especially Southern, society, still has a somber undertone of self-analysis.

Allison Huger's problem is also psychological, though its sources in the past are not so clear. While Will suffers from obsessive memories, Allie struggles from extreme withdrawal and forgetfulness, the latter exacerbated by repeated electroshock treatments. She manages, nevertheless, to escape the sanatorium and take possession of an abandoned greenhouse, which she inherited from an aunt. Her intention is to prove that she can survive in the world without the help of the psychiatrist and the parents who committed her to the mental hospital.

Will becomes a part of Allie's life when he literally falls into her greenhouse potting shed. He embarks on an insane religious quest, trying to determine once and for all if God exists. Will, like his father, is an unbeliever, but he is surrounded by religious fanatics. He decides to hide away in a local cave and starve until God gives him a sign of his presence. If God does so, he will emerge and repudiate his father's cynicism and atheism. If God is silent, he will starve to death and thus fulfill the destiny he inherited from his father.

As usual, God does not oblige with a sign—unless the excruciating toothache that Will develops is a gift of the Almighty. The pain and nausea drive all metaphysical speculations from his mind and set him blundering for the exit. He stumbles, drops his flashlight, loses his way, and falls into an unexplored shaft that plunges him headfirst through tangled vines straight into Allie's greenhouse, where he knocks himself out on the cement floor. The former owner had used the constant temperature of cave air to moderate the climate of the greenhouse. Thus Will, who could not be a born-again Christian like his daughter, is ironically born again from the mountain and nursed back to health by a young woman who has been judged incompetent to conduct her own life.

Will and Allie ultimately outwit the doctors and the assorted relatives and self-seeking friends who try to gain control over their lives and, not incidentally, their financial assets. When Will determines to marry Allie, he rises in the night, retrieves his father's German Luger and the shotgun with which he killed himself, and throws them into the gorge. Thus, he repudiates his father's cynicism and resolves to give life another chance.

Moreover, he and Allie plan to rescue several other lost souls they know: an old gardener, two physically handicapped but knowledgeable builders, and a former bookkeeper who needs emotional support. Will met the first three in the retirement home in which his daughter had tried to place him for safekeeping when he was diagnosed as having a rare form of epilepsy. The last is a woman friend of Allie, a patient in the mental hospital. Taking off the shelf these still valuable persons discarded by society, they hope to develop Allie's neglected property, beginning with her cave-air-ventilated greenhouse. The story suggests a vision somewhat analogous to the ending of Voltaire's *Candide* (1759), wherein a group of wounded people pool their efforts to compensate for individual limitations in order to "cultivate their garden" in an absurd world.

The Characters

   The Second Coming has a large cast of distinctive characters who are cleverly delineated, though not in great depth. This is partly because they are seen through the ironic consciousness of Will Barrett. He is unusually perceptive about fakery or seeming inconsistencies in human behavior, including his own. It bothers him, for example, that his daughter Leslie, so insistent about the joy of her personal relationship to Jesus, is continually frowning. He asks the chaplain Jack Curl point-blank if he believes that God exists and perceives in Jack's confusion and double-talk the paucity of his religious knowledge. He intuits the meaning of Allie's poetic and nonidiomatic speech, recognizing that she tries to express the truth of experience. Most of his acquaintances speak in jargon and trite phrases which have no precise meaning.

   Yet Will's experience of other people may be colored by the peculiar sickness of his soul. Certain characters seem to represent facets of Will's own personality, his shadow selves, so to speak, whom he must exorcise in order to be sane. The most conspicuous of these, without doubt, is his father, whose preference for death has infected his very soul. There are others, however, such as his friend Lewis Peckham, who seems to represent the intellectual, or perhaps pseudointellectual, as ruined "natural man." Lewis turns for meaning to classical music and great books, yet he seems curiously empty of any conviction. A more comic shadow self is Ewell McBee, a vulgar bully out of Will's past who seems to represent his more bestial nature.

   Will's character remains something of a mystery to himself, to other people, and to the reader, an enigmatic combination of genial tolerance and inner coldness, at once curiously wise and hopelessly naïve, suspecting the worst, yet yearning for the best that human imagination can devise.

Themes and Meanings

   This ironic story of mental and emotional regeneration from the edge of insanity has psychological, philosophical, and religious overtones. It is full of ambiguous symbols, yet they are never obtrusive. Even Will's symbolic death and rebirth, covered with the slime of cave clay, has a concreteness of detail that gives it a comic plausibility. Similarly, Allie's ingenious recovery of a huge, nineteenth century cookstove from an old burned-out house on her property is perfectly natural, yet almost a miracle. The stove had fallen through the floor into the basement and thus was saved from destruction in a fire long ago. She takes it apart piece by piece, cleaning each part as she goes, lifts the heavy pieces with block and tackle, moves them on creepers borrowed from an auto store, and reassembles the huge wood and coal stove in her greenhouse to provide heat in the winter. The stove is almost brand new, waiting to be reclaimed from the rubbish of the past. It, too, becomes a symbol of regeneration, and the two marginally sane people fall in love in the genial warmth of its presence.

One of the implications of this story, even though it seems to satirize religious believers, is that there is a saving kernel of truth in the Christian message. Will ironically combines some of the qualities of an absurd, blundering Christ and a modern Job, harried by a disembodied devil-father until he demands an audience with the Lord. Will complains that there are only two classes of people: those who believe anything, indiscriminately but frivolously, and those like his father who believe nothing. He questions both extremes.

Will is surrounded by Episcopalian do-gooders, born-again Baptists, Scientologists, Jehovah's Witnesses, ardent astrologers, married Catholic priests of a reformed church, true believers of every stripe who are all, nevertheless, devoted to the hedonistic pursuit of pleasure, sometimes feebly disguised as good works. The peak of achievement for the American, upper-middle-class male of whatever persuasion seems to be playing golf. Both the psychological and religious quests of *The Second Coming* might be expressed as escaping the golf course, which features prominently in the novel's fictional geography. Playing golf is not intrinsically evil; it simply seems inadequate as the be-all and the end-all of human existence. As the golf pro, Lewis Peckham admits, "You and I know that golf is not enough."

The golf pro, one of the few unbelievers in the community, claims that he and Will are alike because they are both once-born in a society of twice-born and must make their way without "Amazing Grace." Will is appalled, however, at the aridity of Peckham's unbelief. Nevertheless, Lewis is the person who shows Will the secret back entrance to the cave in the tangled patch of wilderness that borders the golf course. To switch from a religious to a psychological metaphor, Peckham acts, all unknowingly, like the Jungian Shadow who points the way to the subconscious and a new understanding of the self. Thus, while unobtrusive on the realistic level (caves are a common feature of Southern geography), the cave is rich in traditional symbolic associations of womb, tomb, subconscious mind, eternal return to the source of being, and so on.

Percy is not playing with signs and symbols as mere literary decoration, but as an integral part of the philosophic meaning of the novel. The story demonstrates man's propensity as a symbol-making creature to interpret or perhaps to distort objective reality in order to create a subjective meaning. The world is not actually solipsistic but it is continually colored by institutionalized preconceptions or private need. Human beings need to choose their symbols wisely.

Will and Allie are not only acting out elaborate psychodramas but also trying desperately to see and understand the real world. The way men choose to symbolize the world and reflect that reconstructed reality in language defines the nature of society and the relative happiness or meaninglessness of human life. If the world began with God's Word, human society begins with man's word, the language he uses to describe it, which is all too often frivolous and misleading.

Critical Context

Percy has always been concerned in his fiction with the mental and spiritual health of persons in a society that sends confusing, distorted signals about reality. In Percy's *Love in the Ruins* (1971), science and psychology received the brunt of his satire, while in this novel the excesses of Southern religiosity are more prominent, but both novels have an underlying theme of the quest for sanity, truth, and spiritual renewal.

Percy himself is familiar with the intellectual situation of having a foot in the camps of both science and religion. He is a converted Catholic and identifies himself as a Christian novelist. He is also educated as a physician, specifically as a pathologist. Thus, his criticism of institutional biases is, to some extent, from the inside.

The Second Coming demonstrates Percy's interest in semiotics, the study of signs, and probably in phenomenology. Allie's difficulty with speech seems to have something to do with the attempt to express phenomenological reality. This effort to speak truth might theoretically, at least, be aided by a loss of memory for familiar ways of evading truth with borrowed, trite interpretations. Percy has been very interested in existential thought, especially the work of Søren Kierkegaard, with his insistence on the nonrational leap of faith.

Like other Southern writers, Percy often treats the South as a microcosm of American experience. The South was the last region of the country to undergo modernization and industrialization, and the process was accordingly accelerated; thus, one finds jammed together in the South both archaic prejudices and up-to-the-minute amoral commercialism, a combination which, from the viewpoint of a satirist, may offer the worst of two worlds. Nevertheless, it is still a place where the religious quest can be seriously pursued.

Bibliography

Allen, William Rodney. *Walker Percy: A Southern Wayfarer.* Jackson: University Press of Mississippi, 1986. Allen reads Percy as a distinctly American, particularly Southern writer, claiming that the formative event in Percy's life was his father's suicide, not his reading of existentialist writers or conversion to Roman Catholicism. Allen's readings of individual novels emphasize the presence of weak fathers and rejection of the Southern stoic heritage on the part of Percy's protagonists.

Coles, Robert. *Walker Percy: An American Search.* Boston: Little, Brown, 1978. An early but always intelligent and certainly sensitive reading of Percy's essays and novels by a leading psychiatrist whose main contention is that Percy's work speaks directly to modern humanity. In Coles's words, Percy "has balanced a contemporary Christian existentialism with the pragmatism and empiricism of an American physician."

Desmond, John F. *At the Crossroads: Ethical and Religious Themes in the Writings of Walker Percy.* Troy, N.Y.: Whitston, 1997. Chapters on Percy and T. S. Eliot; on Percy's treatment of suicide; on Percy and Flannery O'Connor; on his treatment of myth, history, and religion; and his philosophical debt to pragmatism and Charles

Sanders Peirce. A useful, accessible introduction to Percy's background in theology and philosophy.

Hardy, John Edward. *The Fiction of Walker Percy.* Urbana: University of Illinois Press, 1987. The originality of this book, comprising an introduction and six chapters (one for each of the novels, including *The Thanatos Syndrome*), derives from Hardy's choosing to read the novels in terms of internal formal matters rather than (as is usually the case) Percy's essays, existentialism, Catholicism, or Southern background. Hardy sees Percy as a novelist, not a prophet.

Lawson, Lewis A. *Following Percy: Essays on Walker Percy's Work.* Troy, N.Y.: Whitston, 1988. Collects essays originally published between 1969 and 1984 by one of Percy's most dedicated, prolific, and knowledgeable commentators. Discussions of *The Moviegoer* and *Lancelot* predominate.

Percy, Walker. *Conversations with Walker Percy,* edited by Lewis A. Lawson, and Victor A. Kramer. Jackson: University Press of Mississippi, 1985. This indispensable volume collects all the most important interviews with Percy, including one (with the editors) previously unpublished. The volume is especially important for biographical background, influences, discussion of writing habits, and the author's comments on individual works through *Lost in the Cosmos.*

Quinlan, Kieran. *Walker Percy: The Last Catholic Novelist.* Baton Rouge: Louisiana State University Press, 1996. Chapters on Percy as novelist and philosopher, existentialist, explorer of modern science. Recommended for the advanced student who has already read Desmond. Includes notes and bibliography.

Tharpe, Jac. *Walker Percy: Art and Ethics.* Jackson: University Press of Mississippi, 1980. Ten essays by diverse hands, plus a bibliography. The essays focus on settings, existential sources, Martin Heidegger, Percy's theory of language, the semiotician Charles Sanders Peirce, Percy's politics, and *Lancelot* (in terms of his essays, Roman Catholicism, medieval sources, and semiotics).

_____, ed. *Walker Percy.* Boston: Twayne, 1983. Reading Percy as a Roman Catholic novelist concerned chiefly with eschatological matters, Tharpe divides his study into ten chapters: "Biography, Background, and Influences," "Theory of Art," "Christendom," "Techniques," one chapter on each of the five novels through *The Second Coming,* and conclusion. The annotated secondary bibliography is especially good.

Katherine Snipes

A SEPARATE PEACE

Author: John Knowles (1926-   )
Type of plot: Psychological naturalism
Time of plot: Summer and fall, 1942, and 1957
Locale: The Devon School, a boys' prep school in New Hampshire, and Boston
First published: 1960

> *Principal characters:*
>> GENE FORRESTER, a Southern sixteen-year-old student at the Devon
>> School
>> PHINEAS (FINNY), Gene's best friend and rival at the Devon School
>> BRINKER HADLEY, a conservative student leader at the Devon School
>> ELWIN LEPELLIER (LEPER), an eccentric, romantic Devon student

The Novel

The entire story of *A Separate Peace* is narrated by the main character, Gene Forrester. Every action in the novel is presented through his eyes, as Forrester looks back upon the summer and fall of 1942 from the perspective of 1957. Gene Forrester, therefore, is a thirty-one-year-old man looking back at the year 1942, when he was sixteen years old at the Devon School.

Gene Forrester has come to Devon from the South, although Knowles never specifically identifies Forrester's home state. At Devon, Forrester is exposed to a distinctly New England environment as personified by three characters at the school: Brinker Hadley, Elwin "Leper" Lepellier, and Phineas (called "Finny," with no last name given). There is not much action in *A Separate Peace*, as the novel primarily explores the highly complex psychological bond that is established between Forrester and Finny. Whereas Forrester is an exemplary student, Finny is indifferent to his classroom activities and does not envy Forrester's superiority in his studies. Finny is, however, a superior athlete, and Forrester is clearly envious of, yet attracted to, his friend's physical prowess.

The first four chapters of *A Separate Peace* are perhaps the most important in the novel. While he is drawn to Finny, especially as Finny possesses a carefree attitude toward everything around him, Forrester feels compelled to compete with his friend: Finny wins the Galbraith Football Trophy and the Contact Sports Award, so Forrester aims at becoming the head of his class on graduation day, winning the Ne Plus Ultra Scholastic Achievement Citation. Vying with Finny in this way, and in many others, Forrester is still not content. He wishes to be Finny's athletic equal, which leads him to abandon his studies (the day before a critical examination) for an unexcused trip to the beach. This kind of competition also takes Forrester up into a tree, out of which he jumps into a river, at Finny's dare.

The tree is at the center of the novel's action. At the end of chapter 4, while Finny is preparing for his own jump into the river, Forrester deliberately jostles the limb on which Finny is standing (in an earlier part of the novel, Forrester slipped on this same limb and almost fell; he was saved, however, by Finny). Finny falls and severely breaks his leg; his athletic career is over, and while he convalesces at home, Forrester tries to account for his actions. At one point during the summer he visits Finny's home and tries to tell Finny that he made him fall on purpose, but Finny refuses to believe that Forrester intentionally harmed him.

When school resumes at Devon, Finny is still recuperating, so Forrester must find other allegiances at the school; at the same time, a new development begins to dominate the atmosphere of Devon: Enlistments are beginning for World War II. All the boys are eager to enlist; all do enlist before the novel ends, but Forrester is last because, on the day he intends to join, Phineas returns to the Devon School. Thinking that Finny needs him for an effective recovery, Forrester temporarily abandons his enlistment plans. This allows Knowles to introduce two key episodes. First, the eccentric Lepellier sneaks out of Devon to enlist immediately for the war; quickly, however, he suffers an emotional breakdown in boot camp and is discharged in a state of shock. This is the first indication that the reality awaiting the Devon School boys is not an attractive one. A second and more important event occurs when Brinker Hadley initiates a mock trial of Forrester, to enquire if Forrester maliciously caused Finny's accident. Although Hadley is not truly serious, Finny reacts violently to the episode: He runs away from the trial, falls a second time, and, again, breaks his leg. This injury leads to a second confrontation between Forrester and Finny, in which Finny admits that he knows Forrester deliberately caused his fall. During the second operation, Finny dies.

At the novel's end, something also dies inside Gene Forrester; some evil or uncontrollable part of his nature disappears with Finny's death. Forrester finds that he is finally at peace with himself (thus the novel's title), but he is not a happy individual. As he describes it, his life after the war is a monotonous routine.

The Characters

Gene Forrester is a character whose worst enemy is himself. Although he is a capable athlete and an excellent student, Forrester is unable to prevent the dark side of his inner self from perverting and distorting his enjoyment of the world and the people around him. As Forrester admits to himself in chapter 7, he always finds something bad in the things around him; or, if he does not find it, he invents it. This proclivity, clearly the product of a subconscious force, results in paranoia. At one point in the novel, Forrester entertains the absurd idea that Finny is deliberately trying to destroy his scholastic success (even though Finny is obviously unconcerned). Forrester's personal insecurity is such that it drives him toward somehow getting even with Finny, which he eventually does by causing Finny's fall from the tree. Even though Finny's accident and subsequent death liberate Forrester from his dark interior impulses, something vital inside him also dies.

Finny may symbolize the kind of person Forrester wishes he could be; Finny is an almost complete opposite of Forrester, a natural athlete and a complete individualist, interested in immediate and innocuous personal pleasures. Against the confining background of the Devon School strictures, Finny constructs his own world out of his imagination: It is Finny who invents new games to play; it is Finny's idea to jump from the tree into the river. Whereas Forrester is all calculation, Finny is all spontaneity. Like Forrester, Finny represents an extreme. Forrester's eccentricity is built on his inability to cope with his dark subconscious mind; Finny's way of dealing with the world is geared toward completely ignoring unpleasant realities of any kind. At the end of *A Separate Peace*, Finny is forced to confront a world he cannot physically dominate or imaginatively reshape. Thus, he flees from Hadley's trial of Forrester, refusing to deal with Hadley's emphasis on facts; similarly, he refuses (for as long as possible) to acknowledge Forrester's deliberate injury to him. Dealing with such realities seems to break Finny's will at the novel's end, which may be one reason that he dies during his second operation.

The other characters in the novel are simple foils to Forrester and Finny, although both Brinker Hadley and Leper Lepellier represent two other ways of coping with oneself and the external world. Hadley is a walking personification of a conservative, law-abiding mentality. He monitors the order at Devon School and always does things logically: For example, when the Devon term is over, he will enlist because that is the correct path of action. For a time, during Finny's absence, Forrester aligns himself with Hadley's way of acting. Significantly, however, when Finny reappears at Devon, Forrester immediately gravitates toward his old friend and all the complex things that Finny represents to him.

Leper Lepellier is an even less influential character, whose dominating personal characteristic is a romantic form of eccentricity. A passive creature, Leper derives his pleasures through such pursuits as snail collecting, sketching outdoor scenes, or awakening in the place where the sun first shines on the continental United States. At Devon, Leper's urge is to become a part of the quiet, natural world around him. Then, when the war fervor changes the nature of the outside world, Leper is the first to enlist. He pays a significant price for his impulsive brand of romanticism; at boot camp, he suffers a nervous breakdown from which he does not fully recover in the novel. Still, it is Leper who forces the boys at Devon to acknowledge the harsh realities awaiting them outside the walls of the Devon School.

Themes and Meanings

At its most meaningful level, *A Separate Peace* presents a thoughtfully executed psychological study of its main character, Gene Forrester. Forrester's sense of himself is an extremely dark and critical one, provoking feelings of insecurity particularly when he is in the company of Finny. Knowles explores the dual directions these feelings take: On one level, Forrester desires to get even (to outperform) Finny, he therefore resents Finny's superior athletic skills. On another level, Forrester also wishes to be like Finny, to share his carefree, selfless attitudes and actions. In fact, Forrester clearly is most happy when he is at peace with Finny. At the end, however, Forrester's dark side wins this psychological conflict; the final "peace" that is established between the two occurs after Forrester causes Finny's fall, from which Finny never recovers. This action, in a psychological sense, eliminates Finny as Forrester's rival and allows Forrester to feel less anxious about himself.

Yet less anxious does not mean good. At the conclusion of *A Separate Peace*—when Finny finally asks Forrester why he caused the fall—Forrester replies that he did not do it out of any personal hatred of Finny. Instead, Forrester is fighting himself—out of blindness and ignorance, as he himself admits—and Finny ultimately understands, before he dies, how he has been victimized by Forrester's own psychological conflict. Essentially, then, Finny is simply an object (albeit a very important object) playing a part in Forrester's personal battles. The finishing touch to Knowles's psychological study occurs with Finny's burial, when Forrester cannot cry because he has the feeling that part of himself is being buried with his friend. Thus, when Forrester eventually enlists and goes off to World War II, he does so without any genuine animosity. He has symbolically killed the enemy inside himself, and so he has no further need to find another person to symbolize his dark interior self.

Knowles's exploration of how people are controlled by psychological forces which they do not understand far surpasses the war theme that is worked into *A Separate Peace*. This theme involves Forrester's attempt to find a way to cope with World War II, a different kind of reality that awaits the Devon School boys after their school year. Different ways of dealing with the exterior world are offered by Finny (who ignores it, for as long as he can), Hadley (who approaches everything logically and reasonably), and Leper (whose romanticism fails to prepare him for the violence of enlistment and military service).

Once Forrester's psychological battle with himself is over—it ends with Finny's death—these themes are quickly dropped in *A Separate Peace*. Readers do not find out what happens to the secondary characters, nor does Knowles reveal what Forrester did during his military service. Forrester reveals that he did not do any fighting during the war, but that is all he has to say about it, and Knowles does not provide any information on Forrester's life after the war, either. The basic theme of *A Separate Peace* concerns Forrester's reconciliation with himself—the peace he establishes "separate" from the war—but the price he pays is a severe one since Forrester is far from being a happy or fulfilled individual at the novel's end. The other themes of the novel—involving the other main characters and also the basic contrast between Forrester (as a Southerner) and Finny (as a typical Bostonian)—simply vanish at the novel's end.

Critical Context

A Separate Peace is acknowledged to be, by far, the best piece of writing produced by John Knowles. In 1960 it won the first William Faulkner Award for a writer's first novel, as well as the 1960 Rosenthal Award of the National Institute of the Arts. By 1976, *A Separate Peace* had sold more than four million copies, and it continues to be one of the most widely read postwar American novels, particularly popular with teenage readers. *A Separate Peace* illustrates Knowles's ability to penetrate and explore the workings of the interior mind with the skillful precision and objectivity necessary for a successful study of human psychology.

Bibliography

Bell, Hallman B. *A Separate Peace*. Boston: Twayne, 1990. A collection of critical essays that give an excellent overall view of Knowles's novel. Includes a useful bibliography.

Flum, Hanoch, and Harriet Porton. "Relational Processes and Identity Formation in Adolescence: The Example of *A Separate Peace*." *Genetic, Social, and General Monographs* 121 (November, 1995): 369-390. The authors view the process of identity formation through the lens of the story of an adolescent boy's experiences during World War II at a boarding school in New Hampshire. Using the events of the book as examples of the necessary connections that are essential to the process of development, the authors explore male adolescent growth.

Christopher J. Forbes

SETTING FREE THE BEARS

Author: John Irving (1942-   )
Type of plot: Comic realism
Time of plot: Spring and summer of 1967, with flashbacks to the years 1938-1955
Locale: Primarily Austria (especially Vienna) and Yugoslavia
First published: 1969

> *Principal characters:*
> HANNES GRAFF, a failed university student
> SIEGFRIED (SIGGY) JAVOTNIK, a university dropout, motorcycle
>   salesman, and adventurer
> HILKE MARTER, Siggy's mother
> GALLEN, a country girl and Hannes's girlfriend
> ZAHN GLANZ, Hilke's boyfriend before the war
> GRANDFATHER MARTER, Hilke's father
> ERNST WATZEK-TRUMMER, a chicken farmer and an Austrian patriot
> VRATNO JAVOTNIK, an apolitical Yugoslav survivor and Siggy's father
> GOTTLOB WUT, a German soldier, head of a motorcycle unit in
>   Yugoslavia

The Novel

   Setting Free the Bears is divided into three parts. The first, titled "Siggy," is narrated in the first person by Hannes Graff, one of the principals in the book. The second part contains Siggy's notebook, with entries alternating between his "Zoo Watches," in which he spies on the guards and animals at the Heitzinger Zoo outside Vienna preparatory to freeing the animals, and his "Pre-History," in which is recounted the personal history of Siggy against a background of World War II, particularly during the Anschluss and with the partisans in the mountains of Yugoslavia. The third section, again narrated by Hannes Graff, relates the zoo break which Hannes stages with the help of his girlfriend, Gallen, in order to fulfill the fantasy of his now dead companion, Siggy.

   The narrative begins when Graff, who has recently failed an important university examination, meets a strange young man whom he has been watching in the Rathaus Park. Together they purchase a seven-hundred-cubic-centimeter, vintage Royal Enfield motorcycle to take to Italy, where they plan to enjoy the spring. After a stop at the Heitzinger Zoo, where Siggy explains that he plans to free the animals, the two heroes ride into the Austrian countryside, declaring that they will live off the land. They pick up Gallen, a young country girl who is on her way to work for her aunt, who owns an inn. Hannes burns his legs on the exhaust pipes of the motorcycle, and the two young men lay over at the hotel owned by Gallen's aunt. Siggy assaults the local milkman, whom he sees beating his draft horse, and is pursued by the police as he flees back to Vienna to prepare for the zoo escapade. A few days later, he returns to rescue Hannes from Gallen and her aunt but dies while trying to elude the local police when he slides under a truck loaded with beehives and is stung to death.

Hannes discovers Siggy's diary, and the second section of the narrative is made up of entries from it. Alternating between Siggy's notes on the guards at the zoo, especially O. Schrutt, and the tales of his ancestry, the notebook passages fill in the details of Siggy's past and explore some of the horrors of World War II as it was experienced by Siggy's mother, Hilke Marter, and her family and her boyfriend, as they witness the humiliation of the German Anschluss of Austria during the early spring of 1938. The family flees Vienna for the relative safety of Kaprun, near Kitzbuhel, in the Alps, in the taxi of Hilke's boyfriend, Zahn Glanz, who has turned from his studies at the University of Vienna to demonstrate against the Nazi takeover of his homeland. Zahn disappears while smuggling an anti-Hitler newspaper editor out of the country and is never heard from again. The narrative, Pre-History II, switches to Siggy's father, Vratno Javotnik, and his role, or nonrole, amid the brutal internecine fighting among the various partisan bands in the mountains of Yugoslavia during the war.

Vratno Javotnik is politically uncommitted and wants only to survive the hostilities, but he finds himself unavoidably allied with an Ustashi terrorist group, and he is assigned to kill a German officer, Gottlob Wut, the leader of a motorcycle unit. The reasons for killing Wut are extremely vague but have something to do with Wut having been suspected of tampering with the motorcycle of the Italian entry in the Grand Prix of 1930, thereby winning pots of money for himself and for those who knew of the sabotage. Javotnik likes Wut and prolongs his life, only to have Wut killed in the urinal of a nightclub by a rival political group. Vratno escapes from the nightmare of Yugoslavia on Wut's 1933 Grand Prix racing motorcycle, arriving in Vienna in 1945, at the time of the Soviet liberation of the city, where he meets Hilke, and, after it is discovered that she is pregnant by him, the two marry. Siggy's father dies at the hands of some former Yugoslav soldiers while celebrating the death of Stalin in 1953. Hilke abandons her family in 1956, shortly after they move back to Kaprun, and the section closes with the death of Hilke's father, Grandfather Marter.

The concluding section of the novel details the zoo break and its tragic aftermath. Hannes talks Gallen into helping him carry out Siggy's fantasy of freeing the animals, but the results are disastrous, with most of the beasts being captured immediately after their release. The novel concludes, however, on a hopeful and enigmatic note. Hannes retreats to the country to talk over the failure of the gesture of freeing the creatures with Ernst Watzek-Trummer, and there, alone in the woods, he sees the two "Rare Spectacled Bears" wandering together down a forest road and recognizes that his effort has not been totally wasted. His vision in the woods provides him with a sense of accomplishment and self-knowledge, suggesting that his journey has not been in vain and that the lessons of history will help him to understand his own mortality and what life has in store for him.

The Characters

Setting Free the Bears is peopled by an eccentric collection of historical and fictional characters. The background of history is manipulated and controlled by actual figures such as Kurt von Schuschnigg, Chancellor of Austria, who replaces the previous head of state when he is assassinated by Nazi sympathizers. While Hitler, Hermann Goring, and the Austrian Nazi Artur von Seyss-Inquart plan the Anschluss, Ernst Watzek-Trummer, a chicken farmer who lives on the outskirts of Vienna, dons a homemade suit of pie plates covered with feathers in order to protest the coming of the German troops by appearing as the Habsburg eagle in downtown Vienna. Gottlub Wut, leader of the scout outfit, Motorcycle Unit Balkan 4, helps Siggy's father escape from the clutches of the Slivnica family: Dabrinka, the fair; Julka and Baba, the sulky and the squat; Bijelo, the eldest; Gavro and Lutvo, the idiot twins; and Todor, the leader. The names and characters are as loony as the events which make up the adventures which beset Siggy's father as he wanders his way north out of Yugoslavia toward his meeting with Siggy's mother in Vienna.

In the midst of this collection of hapless and often crazy people, the novel focuses on Hannes Graff, a conventional but historyless university dropout who is fascinated and finally seduced by the antics of Siegfried (Siggy) Javotnik, who supplies through his journal the central portion of the narrative and who plans the zoo break which Hannes eventually carries out after Siggy's death. It is Siggy who is preoccupied by history, both his own and the history that has formed the world into which he was born. His journal entries become the most engaging portion of the book and present the reader with the characters that are most memorable both for their eccentricities and their thoughts. In comparison to the Pre-History sections, the protagonists Siggy and Hannes seem to be pale, one-dimensional figures. In fact, it could be easily demonstrated that the most engaging character of the book is Vratno Javotnik, whose adventures during the war provide an instructive point of comparison with the adventures of his son and Hannes.

The rest of the novel is rounded out by the Marter family, Grandfather and Grandmother, Hilke, and Ernst, who joins them as an adjunct member of their household when they leave Vienna during the Nazi takeover. All the characters become living, or, more often, dead witnesses to the irrationality and whims of history as one by one they disappear or meet unexpected, often violent, deaths at the hands of those who haunt them from the past. They carry forward their own delusions about themselves, about their personal myths, and about history, which keeps surprising them with its randomness and cruelty.

Themes and Meanings

The heart of the novel concerns the quest for freedom which is pursued by the characters, both major and minor, as they struggle to escape the trap of history and their sense of helplessness in the face of historical necessity. The two main historical events of the novel reflect this lack of control. The Anschluss demonstrates the impotence of the remnants of the Austro-Hungarian world, with its historical preeminence, in the face of the modern and superior force of the Nazi military machine. Equally powerless are the citizens of the various Serbo-Croatian regions of modern-day Yugoslavia, who also collapse in the face of the political and military chaos wreaked by the contending forces of Fascism and Communism as the Germans and Soviets and their local minions battle for control of the Balkans. In the midst of this repression, murder, and corruption, ordinary people try to get on with their lives, rearing families, occupying meaningful jobs, striving for personal dignity, struggling to be free from the shackles of the past. The extended metaphor of freeing the zoo animals forms the controlling image of the book in spite of its obvious impracticality. That Hannes Graff feels called upon to carry out the zoo break to its conclusion by actually setting the bears free, becomes an acknowledgment of the impossibility of his idealism and a gesture of Graff's indebtedness to his friend for his tutelage. Still, however misdirected Siggy's intentions may have been, the presence of the two spectacled bears at the end of the book provides a final vision for Hannes to take with him on his further travels.

Critical Context

Setting Free the Bears was well received for a first novel, garnering complimentary reviews in such publications as *The New York Times Book Review* and *Saturday Review*. The flaws in the novel detected by those early reviews, however, have not really diminished with the passing of time. The novel is still criticized for being a little short on characterization, especially that of the two main protagonists, Siggy and Hannes, and the critics still complain about the division of the novel into three uneven parts. What has happened as John Irving's reputation has grown with his subsequent novels is that the themes and figures of his first book now can be seen in the context of his subsequent fiction, which clarifies some of the material thought confusing on first reading. Seen from this perspective, it is apparent that even with the book's faults, it is the work of a major talent. The distinctive narrative voice and the humor and inventiveness which have characterized Irving's later novels are all present, if in embryonic form, in this first work. The world of Hannes Graff contains the beginnings of the world of T. S. Garp, whose adventures have brought his creator sufficient recognition to be considered a literary force in postwar American fiction.

Bibliography

Campbell, Josie. *John Irving: A Critical Companion.* Westport, Conn.: Greenwood Press, 1998. Offers a brief biography of Irving's life, as well as an overview of his fiction. Devotes an entire chapter to *Setting Free the Bears*, which includes discussion of plot and character development, thematic issues, and a new critical approach to the novel.

Irving, John. Interview by Suzanne Herel. *Mother Jones* 22 (May-June, 1997): 64-66. Irving discusses his views on religion, censorship, literature, abortion, and wrestling. His thoughts on these topics illuminate the tone and philosophy of his writings.

Reilly, Edward C. *Understanding John Irving.* Columbia: University of South Carolina Press, 1991. Chapter 8 gives a thorough analysis of Irving's characterization and symbolism and a brief summary of critical reviews.

Rickard, John. "Wrestling with the Text." *Meanjin* 56 (1997). Rickard presents an incisive analysis of Irving's autobiography, *The Imaginary Girlfriend*. Although Rickard does not address any of Irving's novels in depth, his review of Irving's memoir provides valuable insight into Irving's creative process.

Charles L. P. Silet

SETTLERS OF THE MARSH

Author: Frederick Philip Grove (Felix Paul Greve, 1879-1948)
Type of plot: Historical realism
Time of plot: The early decades of the twentieth century
Locale: The Big Grassy Marsh District in northern Manitoba, near Lake Manitoba
First published: 1925

> *Principal characters:*
> NIELS LINDSTEDT, a shy young settler in pursuit of a dream
> ELLEN AMUNDSEN, the elusive centerpiece of Niels's dream
> CLARA VOGEL, the lusty destroyer of Niels's dream
> LARS NELSON, Niels's friend and fellow settler
> MRS. LUND, the feisty wife of a failed settler
> BOBBY, the adopted son of the Lunds, Niels's hired hand

The Novel

Settlers of the Marsh is the story of a young Swedish immigrant who becomes a successful farmer in the Canadian West, is rejected by the woman of his dreams, and unwittingly marries the nearby town's prostitute. The novel's pattern includes five main motifs: anticipation and preparation, rejection, degeneration, expiation, and re-generation.

Niels comes to the New World on a quest: He will work hard to build a farm that will personify his dream, namely a piece of land, a house of his own with a wife to love, and children all around. For some time, he does not know who that woman will be, until he comes to know Ellen Amundsen. His love for her and for his dream energizes him to work harder than anyone to cultivate his land and to build the biggest and worthiest house in the region, but Ellen fails to respond with a show of romantic interest. It seems that Niels has nourished an impossible dream. He throws himself into his labor with even more intensity, but now as an escape. His life is regulated only by the seasons.

Gradually, however, Ellen's aloofness softens, and a friendship of sorts develops between them. Niels, of course, needs and hopes for more. One fateful day, she tells Niels the painful reason why the relationship can never go beyond friendship. Ellen has made a vow to her dying mother that "no man was ever to have power over me." She did so in response to her mother's confession that her husband had treated her like an animal. He had forced her to leave small children behind in Sweden, had forced himself on her even when she was sick, had blamed her when she became pregnant, and had manipulated her to find ways of miscarrying. The third miscarriage also ended the mother's own wretched life. The abuse had embittered her mother, and her tale so repulsed Ellen that she promised she would never marry. She wants and needs Niels as a friend, even a brother, but he cannot be her husband.

Niels's dream is now shattered. He leaves Ellen, not to return, because he cannot be merely her friend. He resolves that he will shun social relationships and marry himself to the land, but he discovers that it is difficult to ignore his sexual desires. One day, all too naïvely, he succumbs to the artful wiles of the town's "merry widow," Clara Vogel, who has had her eye on him for many years. His moral rectitude dictates that he marry her at once, but it soon becomes obvious to both that this marriage was not made in heaven. Clara's masklike makeup, trivial knick-knacks, and showy finery represent her counterfeit values, which now invade Niels's home and dreams. When Clara discovers that Niels does not love her but that his principles make him unable to divorce her, she sets out to destroy his life. Strife, discontent, and hate separate them. Niels moves out to live in a little shack with Bobby, his hired hand. When eventually he discovers what everyone else has always known, namely that he has in fact married the district whore and that Clara has turned his house of dreams into a brothel by entertaining midnight visitors, his moral universe disintegrates; in a fitful rage, he kills her. The noble quester has become a murderer.

It is a crime that cannot go unpunished, but public sympathy is on Niels's side. He is sentenced to ten years in jail, but aided by the influence of a kindly warden, he is paroled after only six for his exemplary behavior. Now forty, he returns to his farm and, in one of the most effective scenes in the novel, discovers that Bobby, Mrs. Lund, and even Ellen have maintained the place well in his long absence. Niels burns all the reminders of Clara's onetime presence and then sets out to make his peace with Ellen, asking her forgiveness for turning away from her. However, in his long absence, Ellen too has come to a new realization: She also needs more than friendship; she too wants a home and children. In a serene but moving final scene, Niels's dream becomes a shared dream, the vision between them joining them for a future together.

The Characters

Because Grove is strongly theme-oriented, his characters tend to function more as types than as individuals. At its best, a type can rise to the level of individualization; at its worst, it descends to stereotype.

Niels Lindstedt comes close to engaging the reader's sympathetic identification, mainly because Grove endeavors to present him as an archetype. Niels has the incorruptible dream of Everyman, from Homer's Odysseus to Steinbeck's Lennie and Fitzgerald's Gatsby: The dream of a place called Home where one is anchored, secure, content, at peace, and loved.

All the main characters are connected to that dream to a greater or lesser degree. To Niels, Ellen is the embodiment of his vision and thus functions as symbol of his ideal. Her very aloofness attracts him initially and intensifies his pursuit of the "impossible dream." Yet Ellen, though remaining the ideal, explodes the dream as impossible. Grove uses Clara Vogel as Ellen's opposite: not the embodiment but the destroyer of the dream. She too functions as symbol and remains mostly on the level of the stereotypical wanton who needs sex to fill an emotional void. In contrast to Ellen's unadorned but genuine femininity and humanity, Clara's lavish makeup and aggressive carnality serve death in Grove's design, for underneath her mask is the face of a corpse. That is what she soon becomes, fit punishment for destroying the dream. Though she is a pathetic figure, her use as type is underscored by the fact that no one mourns her murder; she is simply cleared from the stage.

Figuring less prominently but still significantly in the dream motif is Lars Nelson, a fellow Swedish immigrant and settler and Niels's friend. Lars pops in and out of the plot as an occasional comparison and contrast to Niels. Lars is not the visionary that Niels is. He is merely ambitious and thus lacks depth. He marries the first girl that happens to be available and pursues material success as an end in itself. There is a hint that he coarsens as he grows more affluent. In contrast, Niels by the end of the novel has become more refined and reflective even as his riches have multiplied.

Mrs. Lund contrasts to Ellen's mother. Her feisty, assertive nature has survived an irresponsible husband, hardship, and financial failure. She has retained her humanity, and in the end she functions as Niels's substitute mother who takes care of his place while he is incarcerated. Gratefully, Niels bestows on her an acre of his land and a fully furnished house.

Bobby, the hired hand, who has been almost like a son to Niels, the son he had always wanted but never had, is also rewarded. He and his growing family join the homestead, and they receive their own piece of land and a share of the profits. When Ellen finally reneges on her vow, Niels's dream will be realized after all: He will be home, at peace and surrounded by love.

Themes and Meanings

Settlers of the Marsh intends to impress on the reader the purity of the human dream for perfection and the inevitable tragedy such a dream entails. Niels towers above all the others in his single-minded pursuit not of material things but of satisfying his soul. All of his physical strength and emotional longings are spent in the service of that goal. Yet Grove shows that such idealistic visionaries necessarily suffer in a flawed world where cruel circumstance and twisted human nature can turn dreams into nightmares and hope into despair.

The novel follows an archetypal pattern of theme and meaning: The hero sets out to possess his dream; the dream is thwarted but retained; the dream is denied, the hero defeated; the dream is fatally defiled and mocked, the hero enraged; the hero, dehumanized (he kills both the guilty and the innocent, his wife and his horse), must do penance; the hero returns to human community, ready to accept a compromised dream.

Clearly, Grove injects an aura of doom into his story. A movement toward tragedy is foreshadowed in the gathering storms of nature. Yet the structural pattern moves beyond tragedy toward comedy. Significantly, the novel begins with the onset of winter and ends with the renewal of spring. It begins with the vision of youth. At its close, eighteen years later, the dream has been subjected to the trials of hell, but it is still intact, now as a shared vision between two mature adults whose youth has long fled, who have suffered much, but who, renewed, will come home together.

Critical Context

Grove lived and taught among recent immigrants in the Big Grassy Marsh country for a few years. The experience occasioned several books, including nature sketches and novels. Grove, however, was not really interested in documenting pioneer life. It was his passion, rather, to hold high in the new country the ideals at the heart of a Judeo-Christian and Roman/Greek tradition, ideals that would stave off the encroaching materialism of the United States. Influenced by Ralph Waldo Emerson and Henry David Thoreau, among others, Grove focuses on the basic question of life's purpose and meaning in nearly all of his writing. In his fictionalized autobiographical novel *In Search of Myself* (1946), the young hero searches for the eternal values of truth, justice, and goodness. In *The Yoke of Life* (1930), the radical response to material limitations is to transcend them toward a spiritual reality. In *Fruits of the Earth* (1933), the protagonist is mocked at the height of his material success by its hollowness. *The Master of the Mill* (1944) warns that a dream fastened to material gain turns into a monster that diminishes and destroys the dreamer. Only the striving after the unattainable, Grove insists in *In Search of Myself*, is a worthy human quest.

    Settlers of the Marsh was intended as part of a trilogy, but publishers persuaded Grove to condense the three parts into one. Though critically acclaimed, it ran into censorship problems over Ellen's frank discussion of parental sex, which at the time precluded it from becoming a popular success. Yet it poignantly dramatizes the worthiness of the dream that expresses the longings of the human heart and spirit, and the heartbreak that so often accompanies the effort to possess the dream. At Grove's death, Northrop Frye, the renowned Canadian literary critic, observed that he was the most serious of prose writers and may well be one of the most important.

Bibliography

Gammel, Irene. *Sexualizing Power in Naturalism: Theodore Dreiser and Frederick Philip Grove*. Calgary: University of Calgary Press, 1994. An analysis of the family as an imprisoning institution in Grove's fiction, with an especially helpful commentary on Ellen as feminist.

Nause, John, ed. *The Grove Symposium*. Ottawa: University of Ottawa Press, 1974. Includes a useful essay on women in Grove's novels.

Spettigue, D. O. *FPG: The European Years*. Ottawa: Oberon, 1973. Adds important information about Grove's first thirty-some years in Germany.

_____. *Frederick Philip Grove*. Toronto: Copp Clark, 1969. A comprehensive study of Grove's life and works, with a particular emphasis on debunking Grove's account of his early years.

Stobie, M. R. *Frederick Philip Grove*. New York: Twayne, 1973. An aptly critical assessment of Grove's weaknesses and strengths as person and as writer.

Sutherland, Donald. *Essays in Comparative Quebec/Canadian Literature*. Toronto: Macmillan of Canada, 1977. Includes a provocative chapter on Grove's humanism and naturalism.

Henry J. Baron

THE SEVEN MADMEN

Author: Roberto Arlt (1900-1942)
Type of plot: Magical Realism
Time of plot: The 1920's
Locale: Buenos Aires and its suburbs
First published: Los siete locos, 1929 (English translation, 1984)

> *Principal characters:*
> REMO ERDOSAIN, the protagonist, a white-collar worker and would-be
>   great inventor
> ELSA, his estranged wife
> GREGORIO BARSUT, Elsa's cousin, tied to Erdosain by hatred and
>   mutual need
> THE PHARMACIST ERGUETA, another friend-enemy of Erdosain, a
>   pharmacist and apocalyptic maniac
> HIPOLITA, a prostitute, married to Ergueta and befriended by Erdosain
> THE ASTROLOGER, a charismatic leader who recruits unstable misfits
>   with his grandiose notions

The Novel

The Seven Madmen chronicles the disaffiliation of Remo Erdosain from normal, middle-class life and his increasing involvement with the mysterious conspiracy of The Astrologer. During a period of only a few months, Erdosain moves from being an accounting clerk with a pretty, respectable wife to being the colleague of various denizens of the underworld, occultists, and political fanatics. The novel closes with Erdosain among these dangerous companions, under the charismatic sway of The Astrologer, and working on an invention that, if successful, would be fatally toxic to the population of Buenos Aires. A footnote promises that the outcome of these unpromising circumstances will appear in a sequel, *Los lanzallamas* (the flamethrowers), which in fact was published in 1931.

While Erdosain is becoming more deeply enmeshed in The Astrologer's schemes, the reader of *The Seven Madmen* is finding it increasingly difficult to distinguish the realistic from the magical and fantastic elements in the novel. He is unclear whether The Astrologer is a Socialist revolutionary, a Fascist, or the leader of a religious revival. His followers, with the exception of the earnest protagonist, often seem not to believe in the worth of The Astrologer's project. They hint that no serious revolution is being planned and that the conspirators are merely distracting themselves from boredom with the shared fiction of a grand undertaking. It is this mix of realistic descriptions and plot elements with bizarrely imaginative ones that has won for *The Seven Madmen* its fame as an important early example of Magical Realism.

The Characters

Remo Erdosain is considered one of the most memorable incarnations of alienated modern man in all Latin American literature. Within the first pages of the novel, he demonstrates his disaffection from society and its norms. Caught embezzling from his firm, Erdosain is brought to the manager's office and required to explain his motives and purposes in taking the money. He admits that he stole for no reason and dispersed the money in a gratuitous way.

The loss of his job coincides with the flight of his wife, Elsa, who has lost patience with Erdosain's inexplicable lack of interest in career progress and the establishment of a regular home life. These two breaks with the middle-class world set Erdosain adrift. Subsequently, he only associates with individuals whose livelihood and personal lives follow an eccentric or disturbed path.

The protagonist's need for strange companions allows Arlt to create dialogues and monologues full of exotic, mysterious talk. Among the most notable are the prophetic harangues of The Pharmacist Ergueta. Drawing equally on his deranged reading of Scripture and his knowledge of Buenos Aires lowlife, Ergueta uses a jumbled apocalyptic jargon that horrifies but fascinates his listeners. Gregorio Barsut also has the power to compel the attention even of disgusted listeners. Obsessively afraid of going mad, Barsut retells his dreams and neurotic symptoms for hours on end. Hipolita, whom Ergueta marries while on a manic spree, continually switches her persona and manner of talking in her desperate eagerness to please. Other eccentric, fascinating talkers include The Gold Seeker, who mesmerizes Erdosain with tales of adventure; Haffner (The Melancholy Ruffian), who builds elaborate theories to justify his unsavory existence; and Bromberg (The Man Who Saw the Midwife), another unhinged mystic.

All the characters mentioned, except the well-bred Elsa, fall in with The Astrologer. This character has as his announced goal to provide modern humankind, alienated from traditional sources of spiritual orientation, with a renewed sense of purpose. To achieve this end, he is willing to resort to demagogy, deceit, and "mind games." The Astrologer often hints that he is indifferent to the viability or outcome of his conspiracy, so long as those involved can escape the pervasive meaninglessness of modern existence.

Themes and Meanings

The Seven Madmen is an existential novel, a novel full of myth and magic; at the same time, it includes realistic descriptions of social circumstances. Indeed, the fact that no reader can say definitively what the novel is "about" is what gives it its lasting appeal. New meanings and themes continue to surface as new readers come to the work.

One of the work's most unmistakable statements is that modern man, without the guidance provided by religion and tradition, is an unstable creature, easily swept up in totalitarian movements, mass manias, and occultism. Yet the character who upholds traditional values, Elsa, is not very appealing. Indeed, the only figures mentioned as leading spiritually meaningful lives belong to earlier eras. The novel's comment on twentieth century life is a sour one, for its characters experience a fullness of meaning only when they are engaged in dangerous and self-deluded enterprises or lost in vivid fantasies.

Another strong theme is the power of imagination. The novel contains numerous tributes to earlier times in which human beings were transformed by a transcendent vision—for example, the days of chivalry. Even in the impoverished modern era, individual characters have brief moments when they rise above the banality of their circumstances through inspired eloquence.

Even though *The Seven Madmen* often leaves the reader unsure as to the reality of the events of the plot, it is a realistic work in two important ways. First, it accurately describes the Buenos Aires of the late 1920's, with special attention to the precarious situation of the lower-middle class in the overheated, poorly balanced economy of the times. Second, it shows, through fiction, some of the forces behind the 1930 military takeover. Indeed, the resemblance to real-world events is so strong that Arlt needed to add a note to post-1930 editions pointing out that he wrote the novel before the military coup and had been unaware of the gathering conspiracy.

Critical Context

Both as an early example of Magical Realism and as a literary achievement in its own right, *The Seven Madmen* is held in high esteem. It is the most widely discussed work by Roberto Arlt, generally deemed a great original figure in Latin American writing. Though Arlt produced three other novels, two volumes of short stories, many journalistic pieces, and several plays, none is quite as successful at fusing realism, existential preoccupations, and wild imagination as *The Seven Madmen*.

Arlt was a newspaper writer whose style was often rough, though he also was capable of lyric prose. The varieties of language and style in *The Seven Madmen* have irritated some readers and fascinated others. Yet even Arlt's greatest admirers concede that his writing is of very uneven quality; some passages of *The Seven Madmen* are simply too histrionic, "purple," or sentimental.

Any reader of the Latin American New Novel, especially those of the magical vein worked by such authors as Gabriel García Márquez (of Colombia) and Julio Cortázar (of Argentina—an avowed follower of Arlt), should turn to Arlt's novel to understand the beginning stages in the development of this highly original form.

Indicative of Arlt's role in the development of Latin American literature is the changing degree of recognition accorded his work. During the 1920's and 1930's, Arlt won considerable attention as an unusual and flamboyant figure on the Buenos Aires literary scene, but his work was not always considered to be of lasting significance. For example, although *The Seven Madmen* won for Arlt the Municipal Prize in the category of novels published in its year in Buenos Aires, it also had many detractors who deemed the novel to be too rough in language and irregular in its construction.

After Arlt's death many of his titles went out of print for considerable lengths of time. An interest in Arlt and his work was considered a sign of literary Bohemianism and of a taste for the perversely experimental. No doubt, Arlt's declining reputation can be attributed in great measure to the rise of realistic fiction during the 1940's and 1950's. The prominence of existential themes in Argentine fiction of the 1950's contributed to some revival of interest in Arlt, but his wildly imaginative fiction has a very limited resemblance to the sober exposition favored by 1950's-style existential novelists.

It was in the late 1960's that Arlt's reputation began to rise dramatically. The upsurge of interest in Arlt, and especially in *The Seven Madmen*, is directly attributable to the widespread success of the Latin American New Novel of the 1960's and 1970's. This movement was characterized by a mingling of realistic and fantastic or magical constituents, by an inclusion of rougher language (and indeed by a thoroughgoing willingness on the part of writers to transgress the constraints of decorum), and by puzzling narrative arrangements. The traits of the New Novel were, in effect, those of Arlt's novel; it is not surprising that many writers of the new form, such as Cortázar, expressed a debt to this neglected forebear. Readers had been schooled in the abilities needed to appreciate Arlt's work. The New Novel taught its readership to piece together plots from fragmented bits of information, to accept unexplained elements in the narrative, and to grant the novel license to use diverse registers of language and a variety of styles. These readers were prepared to understand Arlt's irregular novelistic practices, and the cult figure now assumed the status of a much read and much cited staple of Argentine (and Latin American) literature. Since then, the availability of Arlt's writings has been consistently good; several of his plays have been restaged; and *The Seven Madmen* has been filmed, translated into various languages, lampooned, discussed, and generally given a prominent place in Argentine literary culture. Ahead of its era and slow to be accepted, this is a work whose time has come at last.

Bibliography

Gray, Paul. "The Seven Madmen." *Time* 124 (August 27, 1984): 58. A review and plot synopsis of Arlt's novel. Gray notes that Arlt disregarded the rules of grammar and the sensibilities of critics.

Hayes, Aden W. "Roberto Arlt." In *Latin American Writers*, edited by Carlos A. Solé and Maria I. Abreau. Vol 2. New York: Charles Scribner's Sons, 1989. An essay on the life and career of Arlt. Includes analysis of his works and a bibliography.

Lindstrom, Naomi, ed. "Focus on Roberto Arlt." *Center for Inter-American Relations Review* 31 (1982): 26-41. An overview of Arlt's life and career.

Semilla, Marían. "Roberto Arlt." In *Spanish American Authors: The Twentieth Century*, edited by Angel Flores. New York: H. W. Wilson, 1992. Profiles Arlt and includes an extensive bibliography of works by and about the author.

Naomi Lindstrom

SHANE

Author: Jack Schaefer (1907-1991)
Type of plot: Western
Time of plot: 1889
Locale: The Wyoming territory
First published: 1949

>   *Principal characters:*
>   SHANE, a mysterious, former gunman
>   JOE STARRETT, a homesteader
>   MARIAN STARRETT, his wife
>   ROBERT MCPHERSON (BOB) STARRETT, their son
>   LUKE FLETCHER, a crooked cattle baron
>   CHRIS, a Fletcher ranch hand
>   STARK WILSON, Fletcher's hired gunman
>   ERNIE WRIGHT, an irritable farmer

The Novel

Shane has sixteen chapters falling into three five-chapter parts and an epilogue. In chapter 1, Shane rides into a Wyoming valley and meets the Starretts. In chapter 6, Chris is introduced. In chapter 11, Stark Wilson enters.

Bob Starrett, the narrator, observes Shane riding one summer afternoon into the valley where the Starretts have a farm and small herd of cattle near a town dominated by Luke Fletcher and his rowdy ranch hands. Shane courteously asks for water but is persuaded by Joe Starrett, Bob's husky father, to share supper prepared by Marian, Joe's hospitable wife, and remain overnight. Next day, when a peddler delivers a cultivator and seeks to overcharge Joe, Shane quotes the correct price and coldly faces down the irate peddler. Joe and Shane then have an epic battle with the stump of an enormous tree. Watching fascinated, Marian lets her apple pie burn. Accepting Joe's job offer, Shane performs many chores with fierce, smooth energy but remains apart. One day when Bob is playing with a broken pistol, Shane demonstrates his skill with his own revolver; he defines a gun as only a tool, good or bad like its owner.

Luke Fletcher returns from Washington, D.C., having wangled an Indian reservation beef contract. He spreads the word that he now requires the whole range and plans to buy the land or scare the farmers off it. Worried neighbors meet at Joe's house for his advice. Shane takes a broken forklift to town for repair, and he is insulted at the saloon by Chris, a nice but reckless Fletcher hand. Shane quietly buys some soda pop for Bob and walks away. Fletcher's men rile the farmers so much that Shane feels impelled to seek out Chris and offer him some pop. Chris misses this chance to make amends but instead attacks Shane, who deftly breaks his arm. Beseeched to remain, Shane praises Marian and assures her of the Starretts' safety. Autumn comes, and one Saturday in town while Bob's teacher is talking with his parents, Shane is attacked by four of Fletcher's men. He almost outmatches them, flooring two, but he is held by a third and pummeled by a fourth. Joe rushes in, hurls one attacker away, and watches as Shane demolishes the other. Joe senses that Marian is aware of Shane's alluring invincibility but will stand by her husband.

Fletcher imports Stark Wilson, a flashy professional killer. Acting on Fletcher's information, Wilson locates Ernie Wright, an irascible farmer, and insults him. When Wright clumsily draws a gun, Wilson easily shoots him down. Shane is disgusted that the neighbors did not instantly inform him of Wilson's arrival, since he might have prevented this "legal" murder. The other farmers grow terrified.

As Shane predicts, Fletcher and Wilson next turn on Joe, whom Fletcher offers to make his foreman and gives until evening to answer. Wilson drawls out an off-color remark about Marian. Shane steps between Wilson and Joe to prevent the latter's certain death. Shane also knows that if Joe goes into town to reject Fletcher's offer, Wilson will kill him. Shane knocks Joe unconscious, assures Marian that what he is doing is not for her alone but also for her family, packs for his departure, and dresses for battle. Telling Bob to love his valley and to grow straight and clean, he rides into town, finds Wilson in the saloon, and tells him his killing days are over. The two exchange fast gunplay, Wilson dies, and Shane sustains an abdominal wound. When Fletcher tries to shoot him from the saloon balcony, Shane whirls and kills him too. Shane rides into the night, gone forever. Learning the outcome, Joe welcomes Chris, mending and wiser now, as his new hired hand. Bob agrees with his mother: Shane will always be a precious part of their lives.

The Characters

Jack Schaefer's presentation of characters is complicated by the fact that Bob as narrator must be solely relied on to recall the events. As a child, he is puzzled by much of the adult action and frankly says so; as an adult, he can make a few comments, some analytical, others poetic. Like Mark Twain's Tom Sawyer, Bob is of indeterminant age. He goes to school, plays with a gun, tussles with a chum, but finds comfort once in his mother's lap.

Not much above average height, Shane is lean and sinewy, quick as a leopard, and often silent, like a predator. When asked his name, he replies, "Call me Shane." This echoes "Call me Ishmael," the famous first line of Herman Melville's *Moby Dick, Or, The Whale* (1851). When Shane does speak, his listeners usually take note. Shane both rejects ignorant, cowardly action and shrugs it off by suggesting a fatalism in human events. Bob sees this paladin in epic proportions. Bob loves and respects Joe, whom he always addresses as "Father," but Shane looms larger than life in his eyes—able, confident, honest, unselfish, and alternately gentle and terrifying. At first, Bob barely comprehends his hero's career, that of a former gunman eager to shed his reputation by drifting northwest, but partly understands his looking into the distance as though into a shadowy past. Shane helps Bob, lecturing him, buying him a knife, and giving him soda pop. In action, he fulfills the boy's dream of the adventurous hero; he has eldritch weaponry and a horse of Homeric proportions.

Marian is the nonpareil Starrett. Her husband is burly; he uproots the stump with Shane's help, and he is valued as a community leader. Yet he almost gets himself killed when Wilson goads him, and he can be stopped from fatal recklessness only by Shane. Joe says Marian is worth dying for, but when he thinks Shane has been killed, he wants to move to Montana. It is Marian who says that such a move would dishonor Shane's memory. Joe never sees Shane as a sexual rival, and it would have been unseemly for Schaefer to present him thus, given the mindset of Bob, Schaefer's narrator. Yet Shane clearly adores Marian, once even stroking her hair, and but for her being married would undoubtedly wish to remain, as planted on the Starretts' land as the corral posts that he embeds there and that symbolize the Starretts' rootedness. His past, however, dooms Shane to keep moving, like countless other restless heroes of Western fiction.

Fletcher, with contacts in the East, and Wilson, up from violent Kansas, are complementary villains. Fletcher, once handsome but now a bit soft, is the mind behind his hirelings' physical action. He orders his men to taunt the farmers, sets Chris on Shane, and brings in Wilson, the doomed arm of Fletcher's will. Wilson is almost a cardboard villain—"stark" like his first name, which Bob calls funny. Tall, broad-shouldered, and arrogant, he is inevitably mustachioed and swaggering, and he carries two pistols. Earlier, Shane has told Bob that one weapon is sufficient if a man knows how to use it, that a second revolver is merely for show.

Chris, ennobled by Shane's power, redeems himself by bringing Bob a cherry soda, honestly calls himself a poor replacement for Shane, and promises to work loyally for Joe. This proves the accuracy of Shane's sorrowful prediction: that time will cure Chris's one dangerous trait, youth.

Ernie Wright is memorably characterized. When Shane asks Joe to identify the farmer most likely to be prodded into opposing Wilson, Ernie is instantly named. Shane tries to save him but is too late. Ernie is unfortunately so ashamed of the rumor that his mother was an Indian that he curses Wilson for saying so and is killed. Schaefer singles out Ernie from most of the other farmers early and thus prepares the reader to regard him as a likely victim. Schaefer also depicts Ernie as foolish but brave in facing certain death from the smiling gunman.

Themes and Meanings

Shane is concerned with the decline of the cattle business in and around Wyoming, with its violence, and with its being replaced by settlers and their families, then by towns and schools. Fletcher's personal ineffectuality is indicated by his having to bring in Wilson, symbolic of the lawless and fading past, to try to drive the farmers off "his" land. This ruthless cattle baron cannot finally win against well-led settlers.

Related to the inevitability of Western settlement is the theme of the solitary hero's unalterable fate. Shane, though the means of Fletcher's ruin, is himself an expendable anachronism. On his own from his teenage years, he is now a reformed gunman with a past he cannot shed. Bob, he says, has a chance he never had to grow straight and clean through the dirty years of adolescence. Shane must play the cards dealt him, and

Shane, like much Western fiction, is loaded with card imagery. The typical cowboy knows that life combines chance and skill, like a poker game. In another image, Shane says he cannot break the mold in which circumstances cast him.

In the course of the narrative, each character develops helpful self-knowledge. If he remains in the region, Shane knows, he will inhibit its sociopolitical progress, given his rigidities; he thus hints to Bob that his ultimate gift is to leave. Joe recognizes and accepts his limitations when measured against his epic savior. Marian quickly sheds her infatuation with Shane. Soon after altering her hat to conform to the new fashion Shane describes, she casts it aside. Bob learns to temper his worship and later puts all events in proper perspective.

Critical Context

Jack Schaefer had a versatile career before writing *Shane*, his first novel. Born in Cleveland, he majored in English literature at Oberlin College and attended Columbia University, but he soon regarded graduate work as arid. He became a reporter, an editor, and a Connecticut reformatory administrator. He published a three-part serial entitled *Rider from Nowhere* in *Argosy* in 1946 and revised it as *Shane*. It has enjoyed more than seventy editions and has been translated into more than thirty languages. The 1953 movie *Shane*, scripted by A. B. Guthrie, Jr., the author of *The Big Sky* (1947), and starring Alan Ladd as Shane and Jack Palance as Wilson, popularized the story. In 1977, the Western Writers of America voted *Shane* the third-best Western ever written, after Owen Wister's *The Virginian* (1902) and Walter Van Tilberg Clark's *The Ox-Bow Incident* (1940); in 1985, the group acclaimed *Shane* as number one.

Schaefer followed *Shane* with two novels and two collections of short stories. In 1955, he settled in New Mexico. His later works demonstrate both versatility and a steady desire to reconcile his love of individualism with the need for humankind to band together in tolerance, resistance to techological "progress," and love of nature.

Bibliography

Bold, Christine. *Selling the Wild West: Popular Western Fiction, 1860 to 1960.* Indianapolis: Indiana University Press, 1987. Compares *Shane* critically to other popular Westerns.

Haslam, Gerald. *Jack Schaefer.* Boise, Idaho: Boise State University Press, 1975. An introductory survey of Schaefer's major works.

Robinson, Forrest G. *Having It Both Ways: Self-Subversion in Western Popular Classics.* Albuquerque: University of New Mexico Press, 1993. Regards *Shane* as unconsciously revealing the dangers of Western "male hegemony."

Work, James C., ed. *Shane: The Critical Edition.* Lincoln: University of Nebraska, 1984. Includes critical essays, some discussing *Shane* as an allegory of good versus evil, the hero as mythic figure, and the novel's considerable didacticism.

Robert L. Gale

THE SHARPEST SIGHT

Author: Louis Owens (1948-   )
Type of plot: Detective and mystery
Time of plot: The early 1970's
Locale: California and Mississippi
First published: 1992

> *Principal characters:*
> RAMON MUNDO MORALES, a deputy sheriff
> GLORIA MORALES, his wife
> ATTIS MCCURTAIN, a Vietnam veteran, part Choctaw and Cherokee,
>   part Irish
> COLE MCCURTAIN, his brother
> HOEY MCCURTAIN, their father, part Irish, part Choctaw
> LUTHER, an aged Mississippi swamp dweller, Hoey McCurtain's
>   Choctaw uncle
> ONATIMA, his friend, sometimes called Old Lady Blue Wood
> JESSARD DEAL, a tavern owner, also a Vietnam veteran
> LEE SCOTT, an FBI agent
> DAN NEMI, a rancher, the wealthiest landowner in the county
> DIANA NEMI, his daughter

The Novel

Although the plot of *The Sharpest Sight* involves a double murder mystery, the novel is far more than a whodunit, as it concerns several people of mixed ancestry who have to discover and come to terms with their identity, acknowledge their American Indian heritage, its values and meaning, and the position of Indians in a predominantly white society. The novel also deals with the trauma of the Vietnam War on its walking wounded.

The narrative opens with Mundo Morales, deputy sheriff of Amarga, California, driving his rounds on a night when it is raining so hard that the ordinarily dry Salinas River is flooding. Mundo thinks he sees a panther in his headlights, but when he gets out to investigate, he catches a glimpse of a dead body being tossed in the churning waters. It is his best friend, Attis McCurtain. They had grown up together, played basketball together, and gone to Vietnam together. While Mundo made a shaky adjustment back to American life, however, Attis cracked up, stabbed his girlfriend, Jenna Nemi, to death, and was institutionalized in the local hospital for the criminally insane. No one except Mundo, Attis's father and brother, and the murderer now believe that Attis is dead; everyone else with an interest in him insists that he escaped from the asylum and is on the run. Mundo cannot find the body, but he is sure that whoever cut the fence wires and helped Attis to escape did so in order to kill him. The likeliest suspect is Dan Nemi, the father of the murdered daughter. So thinks Hoey McCurtain,

Attis's father, who in turn is gunning for Dan to avenge his son's murder. Mundo therefore has to solve one murder while preventing another.

The authorities have vested interests in killing the case, however, and want Mundo to shut down his investigation altogether. Since Attis was a veteran and escaped from a veterans' hospital, the Federal Bureau of Investigation (FBI) enters the scene in the person of Lee Scott, a singularly obnoxious agent who boasts of being a Vietnam veteran who had no trouble adjusting to civilian life. The FBI and government seek to prevent any embarrassing negative publicity about Attis as a psychological casualty of the war, which is still going on. The sheriff wants to protect Dan Nemi, the wealthiest and most powerful man in the county, and threatens to discharge Mundo and send him back to his former job as janitor, the best work he could find after coming home from Vietnam. If Mundo is to pursue the case, he must do so on his own time.

Just as the Salinas River runs deep underground when it is dry on the surface, there are mysteries beyond the murder mystery, for Hoey McCurtain's Uncle Luther, an ancient Choctaw who lives in a swamp by the Yazoo River in Mississippi, has second sight that lets him know not only what has happened two thousand miles away but also what may happen in the future. Furthermore, Luther has a visitor in his cabin, the ghost of the murdered Attis, who cannot rest until his body has been found and given proper burial. In California, Mundo also receives occasional visits from the ghost of his grandfather. With these supernatural visitations, the novel moves from a Tony Hillerman-style murder mystery involving Indian heritage and part-Indian police into the realm of Magic Realism, as the living have dialogues with the dead and dream visions may be more real than waking sight.

Attis's younger brother, Cole, must visit that realm, both to discover his own identity and to enable his brother's spirit to rest. Cole has received a draft notice, but after his brother's experience, he resists going to Vietnam. His father sends him to Mississippi, both to find refuge in the swamp and to learn from Uncle Luther. Luther, in turn, learns from his college-educated friend Onatima, a venerable Choctaw whom he calls Lady Blue Wood, who blends traditional wisdom with that of great literature.

The title comes from a passage by the eighteenth century Puritan theologian Jonathan Edwards: "The arrows of death fly unseen at noon-day; the sharpest sight can't discern them." Despite his best efforts, Mundo never really proves who murdered Attis; probably it was not Dan Nemi. For a while, it looks as if it might be Dan's oversexed daughter Diana, who seduces Cole, tries to seduce Mundo, and boasts of having made love to Attis in the bed of Attis's lover, her murdered sister. Perhaps it is the psychopathic tavern owner Jessard Deal, another of the walking wounded from Vietnam, who periodically goes berserk and attacks his customers. The novel ends in an explosion of violence that leaves the question of Attis's murder moot. As the FBI agent says, it no longer matters who killed Attis any more than it does who killed the soldiers in body bags in Vietnam. Cole, however, succeeds in finding the body and taking it back to Mississippi so that his brother's bones can rest with his ancestors and his ghost can be released.

The Characters

Though much of the story is told from the perspective of Mundo Morales, he does not dominate it, for the narrative shifts back and forth among him, Cole McCurtain, and Uncle Luther; one chapter is even told from the point of view of the corpse. A veteran of Vietnam, Mundo has a shaky position as a deputy sheriff; his boss threatens to throw him back to being a janitor if he persists in asserting himself instead of being a docile subordinate. Despite opposition from all the authorities, he continues his investigation with intelligence and tenacity. Mundo's Mexican ancestors once owned all the land in the Salinas Valley; now most of it belongs to Dan Nemi, the chief suspect in the murder. Yet Mundo does not feel sorry for himself; he has a good marriage and self-respect, and he comes to appreciate the part-Indian ancestry that he shares with the McCurtains.

Hoey McCurtain's Irish father would not let him speak the language of his Choctaw mother and labeled him "white" on his birth certificate, but Hoey has chosen to consider himself an Indian and to direct his son Cole back to his roots. Cole could pass for white yet has not only a Choctaw grandmother but also a Cherokee mother; it is by learning the lessons of the Choctaw shamans that he finds himself and allays his murdered brother's troubled spirit. Diana Nemi, the white teenage princess, is addicted to having sex with Indians as a substitute for finding her own identity. The ghost of Mundo's grandfather calls her a witch, a "bruja." Hoey's Uncle Luther and his friend Onatima express most of the wisdom (as well as the humor) of the novel as they explore with Cole the significance of Indian values and the nature of the evil running amok in a world out of balance. Jessard Deal, the enormous, violent, poetry-quoting tavern owner, alludes to Jonathan Edwards, believes in innate depravity, and manifests it in his own actions.

Themes and Meanings

The Sharpest Sight champions the heritage of Native Americans and condemns their exploitation by a society that drafts them into the military and sends them to a senseless war in Vietnam, from which no one escapes without at least psychological trauma. There, Indians are given the most dangerous assignments, put "on point" because they supposedly have innate tracking skills. The government wants to hide Attis's tragedy, the way it has been hiding Indians on reservations "so they won't embarrass rich white folks by looking poor and hungry." Vietnam becomes a symbol of a world "screwy, cockeyed," of the circles broken, the balance destroyed. While soldiers die in Southeast Asia, students are shot at Berkeley and Kent State. Though Uncle Luther is trying to learn more about his people's history and in turn relate it to Cole, he concludes that there may be no difference between a warrior and a murderer; instead, he says, "We just kill each other over and over, forever." Just as ghosts visit him and Mundo, the ghosts of the dead haunt the jungles of Vietnam. Luther says the healing Indian medicine must go beyond the swamps, must go through the entire world, because "the whole world's out of whack and people like us Indians is the onliest ones that knows how to fix it." Such people will heal the world by respecting every part of it, treating it with care, not raping it as the whites have done. To do this, to live in balance, one must learn the stories of one's people. To prevent a blood feud from spreading, Luther sends Cole back to California to find his brother's body once Cole has learned what he needs to know.

There are many searches in the novel—for Attis's body, for his murderer, for vengeance, for identity, for insight, and for roots. Owens writes with sharp, precise imagery, dramatic dialogue, poetic description, and a vivid sense of place to produce a novel that is far more than a genre mystery.

Critical Context

The Sharpest Sight is volume 1 in the University of Oklahoma's American Indian Literature and Critical Studies Series, which also includes Louis Owens's *Other Destinies: Understanding the American Indian Novel* (1992). Owens, a professor of literature at the University of California at Santa Cruz, is a specialist on the work of John Steinbeck and coauthor with Tom Colonnese of *American Indian Novelists: An Annotated Critical Bibliography* (1985). *The Sharpest Sight*, his first novel, reflects his own mixed Choctaw, Cherokee, and Irish ancestry. In it, he combines ingredients from Tony Hillerman, John Steinbeck, William Faulkner, and the Magic Realism of Latin American novelists to come up with a work that is strikingly original.

The Indian protagonists and their cultural background resemble those of Hillerman, but with Choctaws and Cherokees rather than Navajos. The California episodes take place in Steinbeck country and show how the Chumash Indians had their lands stolen by Mexican settlers, who in turn were dispossessed by aggressive white invaders. In the Southeast, the five civilized tribes had their land stolen and were sent west on death marches in the 1830's. The Mississippi episodes not only take place in Faulkner country but also have Uncle Luther allude to Ikkemotube, or Doom, the Indian chief who features in a number of Faulkner's fictions.

Onatima brings Luther books of literature so that he will turn from Westerns to the stories that count, the ones that change the world. At the moment, she is reading Thomas Pynchon. She is worried that white people, with no homes, no roots, and no concern for the earth, make heroes of immature people who perpetrate senseless violence. Among the more amusing as well as enlightening parts of the novel are Luther's Choctaw explications of *Moby Dick: Or, the Whale* (1851) and *The Adventures of Huckleberry Finn* (1884). The Choctaws also have their own stories to give words to the spiritual dangers in the world. Yet literature is not enough, for Jessard Deal throws out allusions to poetry while committing atrocities. Attis believed that "we have to accept responsibility for our lives, for everything within us and around us." Tragically, Vietnam derailed him from doing this.

Bibliography

Cunningham, Lisa. Review of *Other Destinies*, by Louis Owens. *American Studies International* 36 (February, 1998): 93-94. A critical work by Owens that discusses the works by a variety of Native American authors. Although this work does not cover Owens's fiction, it provides valuable insight into the role of American Indian fiction in the American canon.

Gish, Robert F. "*The Sharpest Sight*, a Novel." *The American Indian Quarterly* 17 (Summer, 1993): 433-444. Discusses how Owens mixes realism and Magical Realism, as well as the Western and mystery genres, to create a novel that mirrors Native American experience.

Jakowski, H. Review of *The Sharpest Sight*, by Louis Owens. *Choice* 29 (June, 1992): 1546. Though he calls the landscape a "palpable character" in the narrative, Jakowski misplaces the Mississippi sequences in Arkansas. He praises Owens's "lyrical prose" and calls the novel "a graceful literary production" that he compares to the poetry of Wallace Stevens, William Carlos Williams, and Hart Crane.

Mitten, Lisa A. Review of *The Sharpest Sight*, by Louis Owens. *Library Journal* 117 (January, 1992): 176. Mitten calls the narrative a voyage to discover the self and the false divisions between this world and the spirit world. She praises Owens's work as "a fine inaugural novel" for the beginning of the Oklahoma series on the American Indian.

Paulson, Gary. "Noonday Arrows of Death." *Los Angeles Times Book Review*, June 21, 1992, 12. Paulson, a novelist himself, praises Owens's novel as a mystery but shows how it extends the genre into a serious, even philosophical work that investigates "the relationship of Anglo literature to Native America." Yet he consistently confuses the Choctaw Indians of the novel with the Chickasaws.

Seaman, Donna. Review of *The Sharpest Sight*, by Louis Owens. *Booklist* 88 (February 15, 1992): 1089. In its study of the destruction of the Indian nations and the evil of Vietnam, Seaman finds Owens's novel "a wise and poetic tale set to the seductively enigmatic music of magic and dreams."

Vizenor, Gerald. "Authored Animals: Creature Tropes in Native American Fiction." *Social Research* 62 (Fall, 1995): 661-683. Vizenor explores the ways in which animals are used as tropes in American Indian fiction. He asserts that the animals portrayed in Native American fiction are rarely literal representations, but function metaphorically. Works discussed include Owens's *Bone Game* and *The Sharpest Sight*.

Robert E. Morsberger

THE SHAWL

Author: Cynthia Ozick (1928-   )
Type of work: Novella and short story
First published: 1989

> *Principal characters:*
> ROSA LUBLIN, a survivor of a Nazi internment camp
> MAGDA, her infant daughter
> STELLA, her niece
> SIMON PERSKY, an elderly man interested in Rosa

The Novel

The Shawl is the book publication of Cynthia Ozick's metaphorically complex and morally profound short story about the horrors of the Holocaust combined with her longer follow-up novella about the personal reverberations of that horror some thirty years later.

"The Shawl" is a breathtaking story. In seven short, poetically terrifying pages, Cynthia Ozick compresses the unspeakable horrors of the Holocaust into a story that is as close to perfection as a story can be. The plot is thin to the point of nonexistence—a young Jewish mother loses her infant child to the barbarism of the Nazis. The characters are not so much real as they are highly compressed embodiments of tortured terror. It is therefore neither event nor persons that make this story so powerful, although history agrees that the cultural event described is the most shameful in modern life, and the characters in the story suffer more pain in a moment than most human beings will in a lifetime. Rather, as is typical of great works of art, it is the voice and language of the speaker that make this miniature narrative the powerful story that it is. Therefore, it is not possible to summarize its events without also referring to the words used to describe them.

The style of "The Shawl" is a combination of short, unembellished descriptive and narrative sentences and nightmarish metaphors of human ugliness and transcendent beauty. The story opens with a march through a winter landscape toward a Nazi concentration camp. There are only three characters: Rosa, a young Jewish mother, her fifteen-month-old daughter Magda, and her fourteen-year-old niece Stella. The Nazi soldiers are monstrous mechanical abstractions that inflict pain and death rather than real human presences. Rosa is described as a "walking cradle" as she hides the baby between her breasts under her clothes. She feels in a trance, like a "floating angel." While Magda is like a squirrel in her nest, Stella, her knees like tumors on sticks, is jealous of her cozy safety.

Ozick uses language to humanize and dehumanize her characters simultaneously. The face of the child is round, a "pocket mirror of a face"; one small tooth sticks up from Magda's bottom gum like an "elfin tombstone." The duct crevice of Rosa's empty breast is like a "dead volcano, blind eye, chill hole." For lack of physical nourishment, the child sucks on the shawl that gives the story its title—a shawl that Ozick calls magical, for it has nourished the child for three days and nights. Because Magda occupies herself with the shawl, never uttering a sound, she has so far been spared. On the horrifying day described in the story, however, Magda scurries into the prison yard crying loudly for her mother, for Stella has taken her shawl away from her. Although Rosa runs quickly to retrieve the shawl to quiet the baby, she is too late. When she returns to the yard, she sees Magda being carried over the head of a guard and thrown into the electrified fence of the camp: "She looked like a butterfly touching a silver vine." The story ends with Rosa stuffing Magda's shawl into her mouth to stifle her own screams so she will not also be killed.

The story is so powerful that the reader can hardly bear it, which is Ozick's point: Rosa, like the millions of others caught in the horror of the Holocaust, can hardly bear it. Yet bear it she must, and "Rosa," the second story in the collection, recounts how Rosa has borne it. This story is quite different from the first. It is less poetic, less compact, and more discursive; it is more focused on character and consciousness than on visceral and poetic impact. Thirty or forty years after the event of "The Shawl," Rosa is living in Miami, Florida. Just before the story begins, she has gone "mad" and destroyed her junk store in New York. She is now a middle-aged woman staying in a hotel that caters to the elderly. Her niece, Stella, who still lives in New York, sends her money.

The events of the story focus on a few days of Rosa's life in which the following events occur: She meets an elderly man, Simon Persky, who is interested in her and wants to get to know her better; she receives a request from a sociologist, Dr. James Tree, who wants to interview her as part of a study he is doing on Holocaust survivors; and she receives the "magical" shawl that she has requested that Stella send to her. Rosa meets Persky, whose wife is in a mental hospital, in a laundromat, where he often goes to meet women. When Persky asks her, "You ain't got a life?" she replies "Thieves took it." When Rosa goes home and discovers that she is missing a pair of her underpants from the laundry, she thinks that she has been the victim of another thief, believing that Persky has stolen them. While she is considering this violation of her privacy and person, she receives a more pointed invasion—a letter from Dr. Tree, who wants to treat her as a subject of study; he is developing a theory about survivors of the Holocaust.

Rosa's search for her lost underpants takes her on a journey into the heart of darkness of the Miami night. Accidentally wandering onto the private beach of one of the large Miami hotels—an ironic image of a Nazi concentration camp, but an enclosure that now harbors the analytical Dr. Tree—she cannot escape the barbed-wire compound that encloses her until she is thrown out by the manager. When she returns to her hotel room to find Persky waiting for her, and to find that her underpants have simply gotten mixed up with the rest of her laundry, she begins to accept Persky's interest and to make connections to the world outside. She gets her telephone reconnected, and she allows Persky to visit her. The story ends with the lines: "Magda was not there. Shy, she ran from Persky. Magda was away." This does not mean that Rosa is finally free of her obsession, but it does suggest that she has begun to allow real people to replace the magical shawl of her memory.

The Characters

The only real character in these two stories is Rosa, for it is her conflict and her loss that is the focus of the first, and it is her isolation and her anguished efforts to "reconnect" that constitute the longer story that bears her name. In "The Shawl," the infant Magda is little more than the moon-faced creature of Rosa's womb that she hides between her dried-up breasts. In the second, Magda is the child of her fantasy, who she imagines is now a professor of Greek philosophy at Columbia University, and to whom she writes letters that she never mails. In "The Shawl," Stella is an unfortunate fourteen-year-old child who clings to life; even if she decides that she must sacrifice the infant Magda, her situation is so extreme that she cannot be blamed. In "Rosa," where the reader only meets Stella in letters and a telephone call, she serves as a reminder of the truth of the past to a Rosa who does not want to remember. Stella chastises Rosa for wanting to hold on to the past, as she wants to hold onto the talismanic shawl.

Because Rosa must bear so much, both as the symbolic Jewish mother of all those lost in the Holocaust in the first story and as one still stunned and entrapped in the past in the second story, she is more complex than any of the other characters, who exist primarily to reflect her complexity. Her efforts to protect her child and to survive, her inarticulate helplessness even to rage or grieve at the death of her child, her confused entrapment in the memories of the past, and her valiant effort to survive on her own terms without becoming the victim of those she fears will violate her further make her the powerful center of both of these stories.

The most significant aspect of Rosa's character is a stylistic one, for in the novella that bears her name she is not only a distracted and disoriented aging woman who is often irrational and neurotic, but she is also, when she writes to her imaginary daughter Magda, a sensitive and articulate spokeswoman of all that the Holocaust stole from its victims. Indeed, those parts of the story in which readers are privileged to read Rosa's letters to Magda, in which she invents fictions to retrieve her past, are the most powerful parts of the story.

Themes and Meanings

It is difficult to articulate any single thematic meaning for "The Shawl." Like Shirley Jackson's famous story, "The Lottery," with its mixture of myth and reality and its shocking climax, Ozick's story has an immediate visceral impact; moreover, it is structured with such consummate skill that it impresses one as a stylistic *tour de force*. When the story won first prize in the 1981 annual *O. Henry Prize Stories*, editor William Abrahams said in the introduction to that collection that "The Shawl" is one of those stories where one believes that the author has been inspired—has received the story and written it in a single go, without even pausing for the manipulations of craft. In reality, what makes the story so memorable is precisely that it is so well crafted it has the force of a breathtaking work of art.

What Ozick has achieved so brilliantly in the story is to capture the horrors of the Holocaust in one unforgettable symbolic scene and horrifying image. Writers have long known that to try to reflect the persecution of the Jews under Adolf Hitler by realistically depicting its magnitude is futile. The very immensity of the tragedy numbs the mind and freezes the feelings. Ozick uses the power of language to capture the horror in its quintessential reality. Even though in reality the death of a single child represents only one inconsequential event in the midst of the murder of millions, in Ozick's story all the accumulated sorrow and horror of that unbelievable historical tragedy is expressed by Rosa's stuffing the shawl into her mouth to prevent her own screams.

The meaning of the longer story "Rosa" is easier to discuss, for it contains more exposition and more direct emphasis on the themes of violation, exploitation, memory, and the human attempts to hold on to the past and yet to escape it. "Rosa" is quite emphatic about the very power that makes "The Shawl" difficult to discuss—the power of language. When Rosa writes to the nonexistent Magda, the pen unlocks her tongue, for she is immersed in language. Writing for her is the power to "make a history, to tell, to explain. To retrieve, to reprieve! To lie!" By giving Rosa's writing her own highly articulate voice, Ozick is able to present the writer as a maker of parables, one who tells fictions that have more truth value than the accounts of history: The stories the writer tells are concrete, specific, and powered by emotion and desire rather than by facts, figures, or abstract ideas.

Critical Context

Cynthia Ozick is a Jewish writer in the tradition of Bernard Malamud, for her stories, like many of his, are a special blend of lyricism and realism; they create a world that is socially immediate and recognizable while also being mythically mysterious and distant. She is also a Jewish writer in the tradition of Saul Bellow, for her fiction, like much of his, is powered by an underlying political and cultural vision. Ozick is a skilled novelist and poet as well as a powerful essayist on Judaism, art, feminism, and other subjects both contemporary and eternal. It is probably her short stories, however, that most significantly reflect her genius. When "Rosa" won first prize in the O. Henry competition three years after "The Shawl" did, William Abrahams said he would not hesitate to name her one of the three greatest living American writers of short fiction. "The Shawl" is one of those magical stories that so capture the imagination they become instant classics. Already, the story has been widely anthologized in college-level short story anthologies, where—with its eerie and unreal imagery, its distanced and transcendent point of view, and its horrifying climactic event—it will continue to shock and astonish readers for many years to come.

Bibliography

Alkana, Joseph. "'Do We Not Know the Meaning of Aesthetic Gratification?': Cynthia Ozick's *The Shawl*, *The Akedah*, and the Ethics of Holocaust Literary Aesthetics." *Modern Fiction Studies* 43 (Winter, 1997): 963-990. Discusses Ozick's use of the midrashic approach in *The Shawl* to emphasize the irreconcilable cultural and historical tensions that resulted from the Holocaust. Combining fiction and parable, Ozick's novel preserves personal, social, and historical experiences to create a recounting of the Holocaust.

Cohen, Sarah Blacher. *Cynthia Ozick's Comic Art: From Levity to Liturgy.* Bloomington: University of Indiana Press, 1994. Offers an overview of Ozick's use of comedy in her short fiction. Chapters focus on single or multiple works, including *The Shawl.* Includes a selected bibliography of other critical works.

Lowin, Joseph. *Cynthia Ozick.* Boston: Twayne, 1988. A good overall introduction to Ozick's thought and art. Places her within the Jewish American literary tradition and discusses "The Shawl" within the context of her other short fiction. Includes an annotated bibliography of additional criticism on Ozick.

_____. "Cynthia Ozick, Rewriting Herself: The Road from 'The Shawl' to 'Rosa.'" In *Since Flannery O'Connor: Essays on the Contemporary American Short Story*, edited by Loren Logsdon and Charles W. Mayer. Macomb: Western Illinois University, 1987. Lowin argues that, like the French symbolists, Ozick paints not the thing itself but its effect. Discusses how each of the three major characters uses the shawl as a life preserver. Describes "Rosa" as being within the tradition of Ozick's earlier midrashic writing such as "The Pagan Rabbi."

Powers, Peter Kerry. "Disruptive Memories: Cynthia Ozick, Assimilation, and the Invented Past." *MELUS* 20 (Fall, 1995): 79-97. Although this essay does not focus on *The Shawl*, it does present a revealing view of Ozick's thoughts on the threat of cultural incorporation in literature. Ozick points out that Jewish American writers have generally achieved success by avoiding that which is historically Jewish in favor of the short-lived idea of Jewish racial group identity.

Scrafford, Barbara. "Nature's Silent Scream: A Commentary on Cynthia Ozick's 'The Shawl.'" *Critique* 31 (Fall, 1989): 11-15. Claims that the short sentences of "The Shawl" and its concise syntax tell the story with a minimum of rhetoric. Argues that it derives most of its power from its ironic contrast between a barbarous place, where lives end, and motherhood, where life begins. The story is a skeleton itself, says Scrafford, for it is almost pure form, pure shape.

Charles E. May

THE SHINING

Author: Stephen King (1947-   )
Type of plot: Fantasy horror
Time of plot: The 1970's
Locale: Sidewinder, Colorado
First published: 1977

> *Principal characters:*
> JACK TORRANCE, a former professor and a freelance writer
> WENDY TORRANCE, Jack's wife and the mother of their one child
> DANNY TORRANCE, their five-year-old, psychic son

The Novel

In order to provide for his family, Jack Torrance, a former college professor and writer, becomes a caretaker at a resort hotel in the mountains of Colorado. Torrance's life is a shambles: Following the example of his violent father, he abuses his wife, Wendy, and his five-year-old son Danny, and he has become an alcoholic. When he is fired from his job at Stovington University, Torrance finds the only job that he can, at the Overlook Hotel, which is closed for the winter. Torrance's job is to maintain the furnaces and to repair any broken items. He is relieved that it is so easy because for the past year he has been planning to write a play.

Once the family gets to the hotel, the horror slowly begins. The cook, Dick Hallorann, who is about to leave for the season, shows Wendy and Danny around the kitchen. As he does so, he is able to communicate with the child telepathically. Recognizing a fellow psychic, Hallorann admits his own powers to the child and tells Danny to call him if he is in need.

Early in the season, as Torrance is checking the roof for broken shingles, he finds a wasps' nest. Remembering that he once had an empty wasps' nest as a boy, he thinks that Danny might like it in his room. After smoking out the insects, Torrance hangs the nest in his son's room. That evening when Danny is asleep, he is stung by the "dead" wasps. This is the first of many unexplained incidents involving Danny and his father.

One day while working in the garden, Torrance sees the topiary animals moving menacingly toward him. He begins to think that his imagination is playing tricks on him, but he is still able to resist taking a drink as he fights the bizarre appearances and happenings in the deserted rooms.

Over the course of the winter, Jack begins to recognize danger in the hotel, but he cannot bear to leave it because of his pride. He is determined to hold on to this job. The hotel, haunted by the sins of the many evil humans who have lived within it, becomes a malevolent character as it recognizes Jack's weakness for alcohol and uses drink to seduce him.

The hotel provides him with gin; the formerly empty bottles in the bar are suddenly filled with drink. Somehow, the hotel knows that Jack will not be able to resist its evil when he is drunk, that he will lose his reason and fulfill the hotel's evil purposes.

Meanwhile, Jack's wife and son have their own problems. Wendy, her marriage on the rocks because of Jack's violence, fears that Jack will hurt Danny as his own father hurt Jack. Her anxieties are well-founded, for Jack has already broken Danny's arm in a fit of anger, and Wendy lives in fear that Jack's temper will be provoked, and that he will be unable to stop himself from destroying her and the child.

Danny's psychic power, his "shining," allows him to recognize the evil in the hotel: The hotel seizes him and holds him in its power with its dark secrets. The child sees in the empty rooms the figures of the evil people who have died there. The boy is almost strangled by the body of a woman who committed suicide many years before, while in another room he sees blood on the walls where a gangster was shot.

At the horrifying climax of the novel, Jack, having become totally possessed by the malevolent forces in the hotel, tries to kill his wife and child with a mallet; he fails and kills himself instead when his son forces him to resist the hotel by calling up within Jack the remaining shreds of fatherly love. Wendy and Danny, both wounded, barely manage to escape before the hotel burns, its furnace exploding in the same way that its evil has already exploded.

The Characters

Jack Torrance, a brilliant but uncelebrated writer, must deal with the underlying emotional problems caused by his violent childhood. He uses drinking to escape from his problems but in doing so creates still more problems for himself. Alcohol makes him lose his job, reinforces his feelings of inadequacy, and causes his already hot temper to grow even worse: On one occasion he breaks the arm of his son Danny while punishing him for spilling beer on his papers. Torrance is a pitiful figure, the weakest in the family, and he is the most clearly drawn. He is a study in the collapse of a human being.

Wendy Torrance is drawn, like many of King's women, as a traditional wife and mother. Wendy has some psychological problems of her own: She is always unconsciously competing with her mother, who resented Wendy for the death of a younger sister, and who has derided her choice of Jack as a husband, and criticized the way she is rearing Danny. Wendy tries to be patient and understanding, but she has little pity or forgiveness for Jack, forever reminding him of his failures. She does not trust her husband to be alone with Danny and competes with him for Danny's affection. In this family tug-of-war, it seems that Wendy has won, but Danny has not stopped loving his father even though Wendy almost has.

Danny Torrance is a very likable little boy, barely five years old, yet startlingly mature for his age. He has strong psychic powers, a "shining," that he cannot yet control. At first the power is either a mere bother or a pleasant diversion, but soon Danny's abilities grow too powerful for him to handle. The hotel, with its evil atmosphere, wants to corrupt Danny and use his power. It seeks to add him to the ghosts which haunt its halls.

Themes and Meanings

The primary theme of this novel, one popular with writers of horror, is that evil or pain remains even when its object is long dead. The ghost of Jack's abusive father, the monsters in the haunted hotel, Jack's nightmares about abusing Danny, and the voices from a party that took place in 1927, all blend into a mélange of evil surrounding the isolated family.

The haunted hotel shows how the unconfessed sins of humanity build up and remain, finally detonating a deadly explosion. The evil in the hotel mirrors the darkness in Jack's soul as he wrestles with the twin devils of drink and despair. The novel reminds the reader how much pain and stress a human mind can stand before it finally gives in to the horror and collapses upon itself.

King's dialogue supplies a tone that darkens the story even during its lighter moments—and there are light moments, such as the scene in which Jack, Wendy, and Danny are sledding, happy and contented, in the snow surrounding the hotel. Yet even here the sadness and sorrow return: Jack sees once again the menacing figures of the animal topiaries in the garden coming for him.

King's strength lies in his ability to create tension and atmosphere. Many of his descriptions are nearly Poe-like in their evocation of horror in the darkened halls. His dialogue is realistic, and the tortured thoughts of the evil-haunted Torrance, the silent cries for help from Danny, and the voices of the long-dead revelers blend into a fine buildup of suspense.

Critical Context

The Shining was Stephen King's third novel. His first, *Carrie* (1974), became an immediate best-seller. His later books, from *'Salem's Lot* (1975) to *The Girl Who Loved Tom Gordon* (1999), have been consistent best-sellers.

His work is important because of its understanding of the depths of human misery. His stories and novels show human problems in an austere light. He shows no mercy for human faults, and he is not above endowing his characters with many vices when he deems them necessary to move a plot along.

King has also admittedly no shame about the lengths to which he will go to produce an effect. In *Danse Macabre* (1981), in which he reflects on the horror genre and on the evolution of his own work, he says that he recognizes terror to be the finest emotion. He tries to terrify the reader; if he cannot terrify, he will attempt to horrify, and if he cannot horrify, he will "go for the gross-out, I'm not proud."

Bibliography

Beahm, George. *Stephen King: America's Best-Loved Bogeyman*. Kansas City, Mo.: Andrews and McMeel, 1998. Beahm provides an intriguing glimpse into Stephen King's life as a celebrity and publishing phenomenon. An excellent resource that helps readers gain deeper insight into King's works.

Bloom, Harold. *Stephen King*. Philadelphia: Chelsea House, 1998. A collection of critical essays that address various aspects of King's work. Useful for gaining a comprehensive overview of King's canon.

Hohne, Karen A. "The Power of the Spoken Word in the Works of Stephen King." *Journal of Popular Culture* 28 (Fall, 1994): 93-103. A defense of King's work against the "snobbery of scholars who look down upon the rustic tradition of popular language." Hohne gives a solid overview of King's work and calls for academia to recognize "its potential to mobilize mass support."

Magistrale, Tony. *The Dark Descent: Essays Defining Stephen King's Horrorscape.* New York: Greenwood Press, 1992. A collection of essays that explore King's works in depth. Includes "Complex, Archetype, and Primal Fear: King's Use of Fairy Tales in *The Shining*," by Ronald T. Curran. Also features a helpful bibliography for further reading.

Russell, Sharon. *Stephen King: A Critical Companion.* Westport, Conn.: Greenwood Press, 1996. Offers a brief biography of King, as well as an overall view of his fiction. Entire chapters are devoted to each of his major novels, including one on *The Shining*. Discussion includes plot and character development, thematic issues, and a new critical approach to the novel.

Julia M. Meyers

THE SHIPPING NEWS

Author: E. Annie Proulx (1935-   )
Type of plot: Magical Realism
Time of plot: The 1980's and the 1990's
Locale: Newfoundland, Canada
First published: 1993

> *Principal characters:*
>> QUOYLE, the ungainly, unlucky protagonist, who finally finds himself
>> by returning to his maritime roots
>> AGNIS HAMM, a yacht upholsterer who is Quoyle's aunt
>> WAVEY PROWSE, the Newfoundland widow with whom Quoyle
>> unexpectedly falls in love

The Novel

The Shipping News consists of thirty-nine chapters, the majority of which begin with epigrams and illustrations taken from Clifford W. Ashley's 1944 how-to book *The Ashley Book of Knots*. *The Shipping News* concerns the adventures of Quoyle, a thirty-six-year-old "third-rate newspaperman" from Mockingburg, New York, whose life is a steady stream of failures until he and his small family pick up stakes and move to their ancestral home in Newfoundland. *The Ashley Book of Knots* helps to tie together their improbable, comic—and sometimes even Gothic—adventures by providing a framework for the book and a subtle commentary on its action.

Quoyle's voyage towards happiness is set in motion by the death by suicide of his parents, whose farewell message to him is cut off by his answering machine. Then his estranged wife, Petal Bear, is killed in a car crash. Although Petal had borne Quoyle two children, Bunny and Sunshine, she had also been flagrantly unfaithful to him, and after her death, Quoyle is obliged to call in the police to retrieve his daughters from a pornographer to whom Petal had sold them. To cap off his catalog of woes, Quoyle is fired from his job covering the municipal beat at *The Mockingburg Record*.

Quoyle's father's sister, his Aunt Agnis Hamm, then intervenes, offering him the chance to begin a new life by moving to their ancestral homestead on Quoyle's Point, near Killick-Claw, Newfoundland. The house, which has stood empty for forty-four years, is still standing—but only because it is lashed with cables to iron rings set in the rocky outcropping that is Quoyle's Point.

On the way out to the Point, Quoyle is beset by "the familiar feeling that things were going wrong." Yet once he and his family actually arrive, it does seem possible to come to terms with the past and make a fresh start. Aunt Agnis, it seems, is a self-sufficient, rather well-heeled yacht upholsterer whose determination and pocketbook permit the refurbishment of the old house. Quoyle also finds—much to his amazement—that he fits right in with the eccentric staff of the local newspaper where he has been hired to cover the shipping news.

The paper, *The Gammy Bird*, is named for a sociable eider duck with a habit of gathering in large squawking colonies that gave rise to the term "gamming." In the days of sailing ships, when two vessels met on the open seas, they often drew up close to one another so that their crews could exchange news by shouting at one another. This practice came to be known as gamming, and now it is Quoyle's job, in his new maritime location, to report the all-important shipping news, to "gam"—and also to cover car wrecks.

Quoyle finds, somehow, that his new job suits him. For one thing, he is surrounded by individuals whose peculiarities more than match his own. *The Gammy Bird* is owned by a lobster fisherman named Jack Buggit, a man who punctuates his speech with the expression "cockadoodle," which he employs like an oath. The paper is managed by the perennially irritated Tert Card and staffed by Billy Pretty, an old fisherman who writes the paper's homemaker's column, and B. Beaufield Nutbeem, a British expatriate whose gossip column seems to focus mostly on local sex scandals. *The Gammy Bird* itself is a tissue of lies, its pages filled with fake advertisements and trumped-up stories: Jack Buggit's instructions to Quoyle are that he run a front-page photo of a car wreck every week, whether or not a wreck occurs. Still, Quoyle grows into his job, lending the kind of attention to reporting the shipping news that causes other journalists to take notice of him. Having returned to his ancestral home, he begins to find a kind of peace and dignity that life had always before denied him.

Agnis Hamm, too, gains a measure of peace in returning home. She had last seen Quoyle's Point almost fifty years earlier, when she was fifteen years old. Just as Quoyle's return was occasioned by the deaths of his parents and his partner, death has freed his aunt to revisit her roots. She comes back to Newfoundland carrying the ashes of her brother, Quoyle's father, and accompanied by an old dog she has named after her deceased lover, a woman named Warren. Agnis also carries within her a deep hurt she does not share with her nephew: that her brother raped her when she was a girl. One of her first acts upon landing at Quoyle's Point is to empty the dead man's ashes into the outdoor privy that she and her newfound family will be using every day. Eventually, Quoyle will learn his aunt's secret from a crazy old cousin, Nolan Quoyle—his only other remaining relative—who haunts the Point, leaving hexes made of knotted twine on the thresholds of the rooms in Quoyle's home.

Quoyle is forced to institutionalize the mad old man; not long afterward, the old house Nolan has hexed is swept away in an especially fierce storm. The Quoyles are released at last to begin a totally new life in their Newfoundland. While Agnis sets up an upholstery business with a new partner, Quoyle finds true love with Wavey Prowse, a long-legged widow. Toward the end of the novel, Proulx underscores the possibility of resurrection and rebirth in this magical place by having the drowned Jack Buggit come sputteringly back to life at his own wake.

The Characters

The world of *The Shipping News* is peopled by eccentrics. One need only look at their names to see that most are embodiments of comic traits: Tert Card, B. Beaufield

Nutbeem, Jack Buggit. Even those characters for whom Quoyle (and Proulx) has great affection—Agnis Hamm, Wavey Prowse—bear oddball names. Some names are meant to reflect the colorful Newfoundland dialect, but others—such as Petal Bear, and even Bunny and Sunshine, Quoyle's bewitched little girls—are clearly intended to be ironic monikers for natives of a place called Mockingburg.

Quoyle himself is an outsider from birth; he is described as odd in appearance, and the narrator remarks that "his earliest sense of self was as a distant figure: there in the foreground was his family; here, at the limit of the far view, was he. Until he was fourteen he cherished the idea that he had been given to the wrong family. . . ."

When, however, he finds his way back to the land of his forebears, a land filled with others as conspicuously idiosyncratic as he, Quoyle is able to find his rightful place in society, to find respect and even love. The object of his affection is a perfect match for him. Abused by her now-dead husband, mother to a retarded son, Wavey, like Quoyle, is one of "the kind who stood with forced smiles watching other people dance, spin on barstools, throw bowling balls." In a place where drowned men rise from the dead, it is possible, in the end, for two such people to discover that "love sometimes occurs without pain or misery."

Themes and Meanings

The Shipping News is a work about another world. In one sense, that world is the richly regional, vanishing world of Newfoundland. In another sense, it is Never-Never Land, a place of magic spells carried in knotted cords and prescient dreams. Proulx, herself a native New Englander with Canadian roots, knows much about small-town life, which she explores with a surfeit of telling detail. Before becoming a fiction writer, she spent nineteen years working as a freelance journalist who supported herself by writing primarily for outdoor magazines, and that experience shows in her work. She writes with surpassing beauty about the land and seascape of Newfoundland and observes the minute particulars of a seal hunt with a practiced eye.

The specificity of such description is set off against the narrative shorthand employed by most of the characters, even the narrator: "The motel's neon sign, TICKLE MOTEL, BAR & RESTAURANT, flickered as he steered into the parking lot, weaving past parked trucks and cars, long distance rigs, busted-spring swampers, 4WD pickups, snowplows, snowmobiles." Such lists often serve to set the scene and, like the diagrams and epigraphs from *The Ashley Book of Knots*, serve to tie the book together in a way that is less than explicit, that says much by saying little. The interstices between the words, in effect, create a space where the two worlds of the novel meet, where the large, lumbering Quoyle becomes Everyman and Killick-Claw a kind of magical kingdom.

Critical Context

The Shipping News was E. Annie Proulx's second novel, and it seemed to come out of nowhere to win all the major awards that the literary community could shower on it, including the National Book Award and the Pulitzer Prize in fiction. Her first novel,

Postcards, was published in 1991, when she was fifty-six years old. Throughout the preceding decades, Proulx had earned a living writing nonfiction on a wide array of subjects, meanwhile garnering rejections for short stories that contained too much detail, too many characters.

In *The Shipping News*, Proulx seemed to strike a pleasing balance between a simple plot and an excess of information. Although her next novel, *Accordion Crimes* (1996), was also a best-seller, it failed to garner the same level of critical approval. In her third novel, Proulx seemed unable to tame her desire for detail, using a multitude of unrelated characters and narratives, and the book's unifying device, a small accordion, seemed too slight to bear the weight of significance Proulx gave it. *The Ashley Book of Knots* performs an analogous role in *The Shipping News*, but its exact purpose is unstated, its presence a grace note.

The Shipping News has been called a novel of small-town life, a romance, and a Gothic narrative. It manages to be all these things and more, and it does so by leaving much of its meaning ambiguous. Quoyle is an unheroic hero, an unlikely but compelling protagonist. Readers want him to end well, and it seems that he does. Proulx, though, leaves it to readers to endorse her tentative conclusion that "it may be that love sometimes occurs without pain or misery."

Bibliography
DeMont, John. Review of *The Shipping News*, by E. Annie Proulx. *Maclean's* 107 (April 25, 1994): 57. Emphasizes Proulx's connections to and understanding of Canadian maritime life.
Kaveney, Roz. Review of *The Shipping News*, by E. Annie Proulx. *New Statesman* 6, no. 281 (December 3, 1993): 39. Notes Proulx's light touch and her use of the techniques of fantasy.
Klinkenborg, Verlyn. Review of *The Shipping News*, by E. Annie Proulx. *The New Republic* 210 (May 30, 1994): 35-38. Although the reviewer finds fault with the novel, she acknowledges Proulx's descriptive prowess.
Skow, John. "The Arts & Media Books: True (as in Proulx) Grit Wins." *Time*, November 29, 1993, 83. A brief review of Proulx's biography and an overview of her career.

Lisa Paddock

THE SHIPYARD

Author: Juan Carlos Onetti (1909-1994)
Type of plot: Existential allegory
Time of plot: The late 1950's
Locale: The fictional city of Santa Maria and its hinterland, modeled after the River
   Plate basin towns of Argentina and Uruguay
First published: El astillero, 1961 (English translation, 1968)

   Principal characters:
      E. LARSEN (JUNTACADAVERES, a name which means "corpse-
         collector"), the protagonist, a former pimp in declining middle age
      DON JEREMIAS PETRUS, the aged owner of the idle shipyard
      ANGELICA INES PETRUS, the idiot daughter of Don Jeremias, who is
         courted by Larsen
      A. GALVEZ, the nominal administrative manager of the shipyard, who
         is bent on revenge against Petrus
      GALVEZ'S WIFE, who is unkempt and pregnant, and whose given name
         appears to be Maria; she is also courted by Larsen
      KUNZ, the nominal technical manager of the shipyard
      DR. DIAZ GREY, a Santa Maria physician

The Novel

   The narrative focus of *The Shipyard* provides a closely detailed, agonizing, but simultaneously ironic inside view of Larsen's doomed attempt to make a comeback and
acquire respectability in the Santa Maria area, from which he was exiled five years
earlier for his connection with a brothel there. Having returned to Santa Maria for a
day at the beginning of the novel, Larsen goes upriver to Puerto Astillero and obtains
the meaningless post of general manager of an idle shipyard. Its decayed plant is presided over remotely by its owner Jeremias Petrus. The only employees on hand are the
administrators Galvez and Kunz, who do not receive their salaries and perform no
work except occasional clandestine sales (for their own survival) of the rusted parts
that remain from the days when Jeremias Petrus, Ltd., was a bustling enterprise.

   Larsen throws himself into a senseless routine at the several degraded locales
which provide the grotesque setting and the recurring chapter titles of the novel: Santa
Maria, the shipyard, the summerhouse, the house, and the shack. At the shipyard, he
pores over yellowing contracts and faded blueprints from times past and continually
tells himself that a good managerial hand is all that is needed to set the phantom enterprise in motion again. Each afternoon, he visits the summerhouse of the Petrus estate
in a comically decorous ritual of courtship with Petrus's feebleminded daughter, Angelica Ines. From the grounds, Larsen gazes at the Petrus house, which he hopes to inherit and occupy, "to devote the rest of his life to revenge without consequences, to

sensuality without vigor, to a heedless, narcissistic power"—aspirations which reflect the severe limits of Juan Carlos Onetti's fictional world.

With no salary, Larsen soon finds it necessary to take his meals in the shack occupied by the sardonic Galvez and his wife, a Faulknerian stoic female, whom Larsen also courts. Larsen slips back into Santa Maria in an attempt to save Petrus from imprisonment for an old forgery, and despite the vague danger of apprehension and new expulsion, he cannot resist looking up former acquaintances such as Dr. Diaz Grey, whose conversation fills Larsen with memories of his Santa Maria past. The river—reminiscent of the tributaries of the actual River Plate—also functions as an important symbolic setting, most notably when a defeated (or, in the alternate ending provided, a still somewhat game) Larsen takes his last, presumably fatal trip north on the ferryboat, away from the Santa Maria country.

The Characters

The Shipyard belongs to that large group of contemporary novels which express loss of self. Onetti, however, is less radical than some of his contemporaries—a Samuel Beckett, for example—in his creation of depersonalized characters. The denizens of *The Shipyard* may have only an initial for a first name, but their selfhood acquires enough unity to make nearly round characters of them. Onetti sustains character and situation even as the text is expressing, directly or indirectly, that the characters are not persons, have no real identity.

Larsen is the antihero of both *The Shipyard* and Onetti's 1964 novel, *Juntacadaveres*. (Only in this later novel were the events preceding the action of *The Shipyard* and the nickname "Corpse-collector" fully explained: Larsen, then manager of Santa Maria's first and only brothel, put together a collection of metaphorically dead female bodies.) The intense third-person account of Larsen's thought process in *The Shipyard* reveals the stubborn deliberateness and absurd logic that rule his self-defeating outward actions. With his low-life swagger, carrying his concealed pistol, Larsen walks through interpersonal roles that are models of deception and self-deception. Long experience in the lower depths should perhaps have left him thoroughly cynical before the action of *The Shipyard* begins. Like most Onettian protagonists, he does have a good dose of cynicism, but he is also a kind of degraded artist, even an oblique projection of the author. In the most hopeless circumstances, he resorts to his imagination in order to project a better world. Despite the many ironies that undermine conventional characterization, real sympathy is generated for Juntacadaveres Larsen, whose nickname identifies him as a vestigial exemplary sufferer, a post-Christian Jesus Christ.

The other male characters may all be read as doubles of Larsen, variations on his existential dilemma. Petrus, too, engages in deception, fostering in himself and others the chimerical project of resuscitating the shipyard. He plays an empty role, the capitalist with no capital, the man of affairs with no affairs to manage. Petrus is a caricature of the ruthless entrepreneur, and his surname marks him as a kind of pope—a Saint Peter—in the cult of self-betterment and prosperity to which Larsen adheres.

Galvez, the more vocal and sarcastic of the cynical pair formed by himself and
Kunz, harbors deep resentment against Petrus and against his own condition. Like
Larsen, Galvez is acutely aware of the abiding inauthenticity of the life he leads, but
he responds differently. Larsen plays at the game of capitalist faith. Galvez's only
hope is in the forged bond, the evidence against Petrus, with which he sleeps every
night. After finally making his denunciation, he has played his part, and he drowns
himself in the river.

Dr. Diaz Grey, a key character of Onetti's novel *La vida breve* (1950; *A Brief Life*,
1976), which began the cycle of Santa Maria novels, appears in one chapter of *The
Shipyard* as yet another double of Larsen. Diaz Grey's dreary nightly routine as a
bachelor is broken by the visit of the former brothel-keeper. The point of view in this
scene is that of Diaz Grey, and the doctor's reflections on Larsen provide perspective
on the former pimp's paradoxical, degraded form of heroism:

> This man who lived for the last thirty years on the filthy money which filthy women were
> glad to give him . . . this man of unknown origins, hard and brave, who had one kind of
> faith and now has another, who was not born to die but to succeed, to impose himself, who
> at this very moment imagines that life is a territory infinite in time and space, in which it is
> necessary to advance and gain advantages.

Larsen realizes at one point that Angelica Ines Petrus and Senora Galvez are "only
one woman, they come to the same thing." Both the privileged mental defective who
lives in the big house and the impoverished, loveless woman in the shack are typical
Onettian females, condemned to represent the inexorable misfortune that is the basis
of existence in the Santa Maria country. Angelica Ines would be Larsen's access to
Petrus's fortune and respectability if Petrus had either and if there were any real possibility of a relationship with a woman whose virtual inability to articulate sentences
brings her close to the status of an infant. She is an extreme figure of the madness of
Larsen's entire world. Galvez's wife has few qualities other than endurance and her
physical being, which Larsen continually imagines washed, combed, and clothed in
other than the man's shoes and man's overcoat uncomfortably fastened with a pin over
her pregnant belly. The Galvez woman sees through the desultory hypocrisy of their
relationship.

Themes and Meanings

Larsen and all the characters, in reflection of and in relation to him, face an existential void: Their lives lack purpose, and they are reduced to doing what Larsen in meditation refers to as "one thing and another and another, all alien, without worrying
about whether they turned out well or badly." The need to maintain narrative impetus
does generate some tension between the characters' faith in the future and the sense
that there is no future, but the essential tone is a lucid pessimism, the atmosphere one
of disintegration and death-in-life. The shipyard acts as the central metaphor of these
themes right up to Larsen's final departure from Puerto Astillero, when, "deaf to the
din of the boat, his eager ear could still make out the whisper of moss growing among

the piles of bricks and that of rust devouring metal." Throughout, the human body is visualized in decay; interaction among the characters, as pure theater devoid of the vitality of real life. Galvez's suicide in this context has seemed like an attainment of authenticity.

Positive values in the Onettian world exist mainly as absence or nostalgia. This world lacks true community, sense of purpose, and any conventional religious sense of a power that would confer higher meaning of life. Some remote nostalgia for religion can be felt in the abundant (albeit degraded and ironic) Christian allegory of the novel, which appears not only in the names of characters but also in their functions. Larsen, the debased Christ figure, nurtures the ambition of acceding to Petrus's house, "the empty form of a paradise he had coveted and had been promised; the gates of a city he longed to enter." Petrus is not a divinity, but he holds the keys to the coveted kingdom. Angelica Ines is linked to the Petrus faith not only by her name but also by her characteristic backward-leaning gait, compared with that of someone carrying a figure in a religious procession. Galvez's wife seems to be named Maria, and Larsen realizes the significance of her name when the calendar tells him it is the feast of the Immaculate Conception. This significance is noted as such but not explained in the narration; Onetti's allegory differs from the medieval variety in that it does not serve to confirm but ironically serves to mark the absence of an effective communal faith.

Another allegorical level of the novel can be found in the Freudian depths of its presentation of women from Larsen's male point of view. The visualizations of the Galvez woman and even of Angelica Ines stress their maternal aspects. Larsen's alienation may ultimately be generic, traceable to expulsion from the womb. Passing by the shack as he is about to leave on his last journey, he spies Maria Galvez in labor. One may predict that her child is about to be initiated into the trauma of life outside the mother.

The Shipyard is dedicated to Onetti's friend and political patron Luis Batlle Berres, who was the last leader of the long-reigning liberal Colorado Party before its historic defeat in the 1958 elections, a defeat attributed to the financial ruin experienced by Uruguay in the 1950's and in the decades that followed. Some critics have chosen to read the dedication as a satiric statement, seeing in the story of Petrus's bankrupt shipyard an allegory of the decline of the Uruguayan welfare state built by the Colorados in the approximately fifty years preceding the publication of *The Shipyard*. Certainly the novel's tone of disillusionment fits the public mood of Uruguay since the mid-1950's, a mood in which alienation has not needed to be metaphysical in nature.

Critical Context

In 1963, Onetti deservedly won the William Faulkner Certificate of Merit for *El astillero*. The novel is an innovative transmutation of the themes and techniques of Faulkner, the Uruguayan author's most influential literary model. Onetti's Santa Maria country is a fictional locale suggested by but not simply copied from Faulkner's Yoknapatawpha County. The religious allegory of *The Shipyard* is Hispano-Catholic in content, but it has technical precedents in Faulkner novels such as *Light in August*

(1932). The multiple point of view of *The Shipyard* also can be traced to Faulkner. Criticism has not always pointed out the differences between Onetti and Faulkner, but *The Shipyard* displays some, such as the greater measure of pessimism present in Onetti, and the Uruguayan writer's more pointed reflexive dimension. The distinctive Onettian narrative voice repeatedly comments on the progress of its narration, which itself seems tainted by the arbitrariness and insubstantiality of the lives being told:

> Now, in the incomplete reconstruction of that night, as part of the whim of giving it histor-
> ical importance or meaning, as part of the inoffensive game of cutting short a winter eve-
> ning, manipulating, combining and playing tricks with all those things which interest no
> one and which are not indispensable, there comes the testimony of the bartender of the
> Plaza.

Onetti is the best of the River Plate writers who quite independently of the French developed an existential fiction in the 1940's and 1950's. He is one of the earliest and most redoubtable craftsmen of the Latin American New Narrative, and for all its reminiscence of Faulkner, the Santa Maria saga was itself highly influential long before the 1980's, when Onetti's life work was awarded Spain's Cervantes Prize and Uruguay's National Literature Prize. With Santa Maria, Onetti stimulated the equally ambitious projects of younger writers such as Gabriel García Márquez and Mario Vargas Llosa. No novel of the saga is as intense as *The Shipyard*, or more successful in maintaining Onetti's ambiguous play between disintegration and imaginative attempts to prevail against it, between the somber theme of mortality and the comic treatment of it.

Bibliography
Adams, Michael I. *Three Authors of Alienation: Bombal, Onetti, Carpentier.* Austin: University of Texas Press, 1975. Adams presents a sociopsychological critical interpretation of three Latin American authors whose works share similar themes. Includes a chapter focusing on Onetti's view of spiritual disillusionment as inevitable in the urban setting.
Ainsa, Fernando. "Juan Carlos Onetti (1909-1994): An Existential Allegory of Contemporary Man." *World Literature Today* 68 (Summer, 1994): 501-504. A tribute to and biographic profile of Onetti as well as an analysis and evaluation of his work.
Jones, Yvonne P. *The Formal Expression of Meaning in Juan Carlos Onetti's Narrative Art.* Cuernavaca, Mexico: Centro Intercultural de Documentación, 1971. An overview of Onetti's narrative technique, use of language and voice. Includes a bibliography.
Kadir, Djelal. *Juan Carlos Onetti.* Boston: Twayne, 1977. Kadir provides a critical and interpretive study of Onetti with a close reading of his major works, a solid bibliography, and complete notes and references.
Lewis, Bart L. "Realizing the Textual Space: Metonymic Metafiction in Juan Carlos Onetti." *Hispanic Review* 64 (Autumn, 1996): 491-506. Lewis compares Onetti's style to Boris Pasternak. Lewis asserts that through his works, Onetti reveals that

there are many openings to be filled in the fictional scheme because fictional characters live in a web of words.

Murray, Jack. *The Landscapes of Alienation: Ideological Subversion in Kafka, Celine, and Onetti*. Stanford, Calif.: Stanford University Press, 1991. Includes a chapter on Onetti that explores *The Shipyard* and the psychological games the characters in the novel play on each other. Murray examines the ways in which the shipyard represents the state of the Uruguayan nation.

_____. "Onetti's *El Astillero* as an Ideological Novel." *Symposium* 40 (Summer, 1986): 117-129. Examines the ideological perspective of *The Shipyard*.

Verani, Hugo J. "Juan Carlos Onetti." In *Latin American Writers*, edited by Carlos A. Solé and Maria I. Abreau. Vol 3. New York: Charles Scribner's Sons, 1989. An essay on the life and career of Onetti. Includes analysis of his works and a bibliography.

John F. Deredita

SHOELESS JOE

Author: W. P. Kinsella (1935-   )
Type of plot: Sports
Time of plot: The 1970's
Locale: Iowa, Boston, and Chisholm, Minnesota
First published: 1982

Principal characters:

> RAY KINSELLA, a baseball enthusiast who builds a ballfield on his Iowa
> farm
> ANNIE KINSELLA, his wife
> KARIN KINSELLA, his young daughter
> MARK, Annie's brother, a land developer who wants Ray to sell him the
> farm
> SHOELESS JOE JACKSON, a player banned from baseball after the World
> Series scandal of 1919
> J. D. SALINGER, a well-known writer of the 1940's and 1950's
> ARCHIBALD "MOONLIGHT" GRAHAM, a ballplayer who became a
> small-town doctor
> JOHNNY KINSELLA, Ray's father

The Novel

Shoeless Joe is a baseball story with a large admixture of fantasy. "Shoeless" was the nickname of Joe Jackson, a player on the infamous Chicago White Sox team of 1919 that lost the World Series in the biggest scandal in the history of professional baseball. Eight players, including Jackson, admitted to taking bribes from gamblers who paid them to lose the series. They were suspended for life from organized baseball.

Sixty years later, an Iowa farmer named Ray Kinsella, while sitting on his front porch, hears a baseball announcer's voice that tells him to "build it" and "he will come." What is "it," and who will come? Ray had grown up hearing baseball stories from his father, including how Joe Jackson was punished unfairly because he tried to give back the bribe he had taken and had played his best to win, leading both teams in hitting. Ray instinctively senses how to interpret the mysterious message: He is to build a baseball field, and then the legendary Jackson will come to play on it. He pursues this wild dream by plowing up some of his farm, seeding it with grass, laying out the infield and outfield, and putting up bleachers for spectators. Then he waits, and waits some more, and hopes. Eventually, the incarnation of Jackson as a young man in a baseball uniform appears on the field, soon to be joined by the other players from the 1919 White Sox team. Ray, his wife, and daughter sit in the bleachers to watch the games and eat hot dogs. Outsiders who are unbelievers, like his brother-in-law Mark, only see an empty field without any players and think that Ray may be going crazy.

A second adventure begins for Ray when he hears the voice again: "Ease his pain." How should he interpret this mysterious message? Again his instinct tells him what to do: he is to locate J. D. Salinger, a well-known author of the 1950's, and take him to a big-league baseball game. Salinger had gained fame with the book *Catcher in the Rye* and other stories but had published nothing new for twenty years, apparently suffering from the pain of writer's block. Ray had read a memorable baseball story by Salinger and hoped to "ease his pain," namely to bring back his enthusiasm for writing, by taking him to a ballgame. This far-fetched mixture of fact and fiction is just barely plausible because of the love for baseball shared by the two men.

Ray finds Salinger living as a recluse in rural Vermont and virtually has to kidnap him to go to a Red Sox baseball game in Boston. At the game, the scoreboard suddenly displays a message seen only by the two men. It shows the major-league record of a player named Archibald "Moonlight" Graham, who had played in only one major-league game back in 1905, for one inning, without ever coming up to bat, making no outs or errors. (This information can be verified in the 1990 edition of the Macmillan *Baseball Encyclopedia*.) Graham must have had the shortest major-league career of all time, and one suspects that there is a story behind it. In any case, Salinger and Ray make a trip to Chisholm, Minnesota, where Graham had died in 1955.

Upon arriving in Chisholm, the two men try to find out as much as they can about Archibald Graham. After his disappointing one inning in the majors, he had gone to medical school and become a small-town doctor. Old newspaper articles and interviews with senior citizens who knew Graham provide a portrait of a beloved town benefactor. One foggy evening, Ray goes for a walk and meets a reincarnation of Dr. Graham, who shares baseball anecdotes with him. The fantasy continues on the next day when Salinger and Ray pick up a youthful hitchhiker named Archibald Graham, whose goal is to become a professional ballplayer.

Ray invites Salinger and young Graham to his home in Iowa to see the ballfield he has built on his farm. Meanwhile, Ray's brother-in-law has been trying to foreclose on the mortgage to get the farm for himself. Several loose ends of the story now are neatly tied up by the author: Graham gets his wish to play ball with Jackson and his reincarnated teammates; tourists come to watch the games, buying admission tickets that save the farm; Salinger is invited to accompany the ballplayers as they disappear into the cornfield behind left field; and Ray's father, who had died in 1962, makes an appearance in which some tensions between father and son that had not been resolved during his lifetime are finally put to rest.

The Characters

The central character in *Shoeless Joe* is Ray Kinsella, the Iowa farmer who builds a baseball field on his land. Like Don Quixote, Ray envisions an impossible dream and then works to make it into reality for himself and those who believe in him. He responds to a voice that no one else has heard. He embarks on a quest to bring back to life the players who had been banished from baseball sixty years earlier.

Annie Kinsella, Ray's wife, supports her husband's quest without reservation. Although building the baseball field takes time and land away from farming, she accepts her husband's need to carry out his crazy scheme. She sits in the bleachers beside Ray and sees the reincarnation of the players just as he does. Karin Kinsella, their young daughter, is another enthusiastic believer who watches the games with her parents, never doubting the reality of what she sees.

J. D. Salinger was a talented author who abruptly stopped writing in the 1960's. Ray barges in on Salinger and insists on taking him to a baseball game. After some resistance, he becomes a willing companion for Ray. Together, they try to track down Moonlight Graham who had briefly played ball many years ago. Becoming involved in Ray's quest to find out what happened to Graham renews Salinger's spirit. Eventually, he accompanies Ray to his Iowa farm where he too becomes a believer in the magical reincarnation of Shoeless Joe and his teamates.

Annie's brother Mark is a scheming businessman whose goal is to make money by buying farmland and reselling it to a corporation. Ray's farm is significant to him only for its economic value. He cannot see the ballplayers that Ray and his family are watching. Mark sees only an empty field with good land going to waste. He is blind to the idea of a family living out a dream on their own land. Eventually, Mark learns that a dream can become reality when crowds of baseball fans arrive at the farm, providing the income needed for mortgage payments.

Archibald "Moonlight" Graham was a baseball player who had only one opportunity to play in a major-league game. Although he loved the game, he did not want to go back to the minor leagues, so he changed careers and became a doctor. In the novel, Graham is reincarnated twice, first as a young man who gets another chance to play on the magical Iowa farm field. Then, in a sudden twist of the plot, he has to assume his true role as an elderly doctor in an emergency to save Ray's daughter Karin from choking.

Themes and Meanings

"Shoeless Joe Comes to Iowa" was published first as a self-contained short story about the 1919 Chicago baseball team brought back to life. Having been banished from the game in their lifetime, the players received a second chance through the magic of reincarnation. The author was encouraged to expand his idea into a full-length book. What resulted was a collection of five stories about people with frustrated life goals, loosely tied together by their love of baseball. Shoeless Joe, J. D. Salinger, Moonlight Graham, and Ray Kinsella's father were all real persons who are summoned back to live again, to try again. The concept of reincarnation has appeal because it is optimistic about the future. It suggests that a person who does something wrong, or fails to do something right, will have a chance to do better in a later lifetime. Using the sport of baseball as an analogy, there will be another game tomorrow, or next season, to overcome the memory of a defeat.

The hero of *Shoeless Joe* has the same last name as the author, which suggests an autobiographical connection. In the novel, Ray had a strained relation with his father that was never resolved while the father was still alive. Perhaps it is Ray's lingering pain over this relationship that brings his father back to life so that the son can play ball with him on the magic baseball field and finally put his mind at ease. It is part of the human condition that everyone has feelings of regret; *Shoeless Joe* is an appealing book in part because it provides a light-hearted, magical solution for such "if only" speculation.

Critical Context

William Kinsella's career as a published author started when he was already in his forties, after a variety of other occupations. He wrote more than fifty short stories that were rejected by various editors. His first success was a book of stories about Indian life on and off a reservation. *Shoeless Joe* was his first novel, for which he received the Houghton Mifflin Literary Fellowship Award in 1982. National acclaim came to the author in 1989 when the book was made into the movie *Field of Dreams*, starring Kevin Costner, which received three Academy Award nominations.

Kinsella is a prolific writer. He has published more than two hundred short stories in various magazines. Based on his success with *Shoeless Joe*, he has written several other novels that combine baseball with imaginative fantasy. Critics have given generous praise to Kinsella's fiction. For example, one reviewer in *The New York Times Book Review* commented that Kinsella "defines a world in which magic and reality combine to make us laugh and think about the perceptions that we take for granted." He has also become a sought-after speaker at creative writing workshops. In an interview addressed to young writers, he said, "Fiction writing . . . consists of ability, imagination, passion and stamina. . . . I know it is a cliché but though inspiration is nice, ninety-eight percent of writing is accomplished by perspiration."

Bibliography

Cheuse, Alan. "An Outsider's Homage to Baseball Lore." Review of *Shoeless Joe*, by W. P. Kinsella. *Los Angeles Times Book Review*, May 23, 1982. A very favorable review. Cheuse comments that the novel, despite its bizarre plot, leads the reader into "a world of compelling whimsy" and nostalgia for the great American pastime.

Kinsella, William P. Interview by Robert Dahlin. *Publishers Weekly* 221 (April 16, 1982): 6-7. An interesting interview with biographical information about the author, William P. Kinsella. With reference to *Shoeless Joe*, he said that he wanted to write "a book for imaginative readers, an affirmative statement about life."

_____. *The Iowa Baseball Confederacy*. Boston: Houghton Mifflin, 1986. This novel is a fantasy on a much bigger scale than *Shoeless Joe*, featuring time travel, magic, and a ballgame that lasts more than two thousand innings.

Hans G. Graetzer

SHOSHA

Author: Isaac Bashevis Singer (1904-1991)
Type of plot: Historical realism
Time of plot: 1914-1952
Locale: Warsaw, Poland, and Tel Aviv, Israel
First published: Neshome Ekspeditsyes, serially in 1974 (English translation, 1978)

Principal characters:

AARON GREIDINGER, the narrator, a writer
MORRIS FEITELZOHN, a writer and Greidinger's mentor
DORA STOLNITZ, an idealistic Communist, one of Aaron's mistresses
CELIA CHENTSHINER, another of Aaron's mistresses, an intellectual
HAIML CHENTSHINER, Celia's husband
BETTY SLONIM, a Russian-born Jewish actress, another of Aaron's
    mistresses
SAM DREIMAN, Betty Slonim's rich American patron and lover
TEKLA, the maid at Greidinger's apartment house, another of Aaron's
    mistresses
SHOSHA SCHUI DIENER, Aaron's childhood playmate, whom he later
    marries

The Novel

The year is 1914. Aaron Greidinger, the seven-year-old son of a rabbi, lives in an apartment at number ten Krochmalna Street in Warsaw. Across the hall live Bashele and Zelig Schuldiener and their nine-year-old daughter, Shosha. Although Aaron is a prodigy of learning and Shosha is intellectually backward, he finds her attractive, and the Schuldieners' apartment, as lavishly furnished as his own is sparse, becomes his second home.

This youthful idyll soon ends when the Schuldieners move to number seven Krochmalna Street, two blocks away. Under constant scrutiny because he is the rabbi's son, Aaron no longer can visit Shosha. Other difficulties follow. World War I brings poverty and hunger, so that by 1917 the Greidingers are forced to move to Old Stykov in Galacia, where Aaron's father and then his brother Moishe serve as rabbi.

While his family clings to traditional Judaism, Aaron does not. Impressed with the Haskalah, the Enlightenment, that comes to Poland with the war, he returns to Warsaw to earn his living as a writer. Here he begins an affair with Dora Stolnitz, a member of the Communist Party who regards the Soviet Union as the Promised Land. At the Writers' Club he encounters the eccentric philosopher Morris Feitelzohn, author of *Spiritual Hormones*. At once lecherous, mystical, religious, and skeptical, he becomes Aaron's spiritual and intellectual guide.

Morris also helps Aaron monetarily. Though he is himself always in need of five zlotys, he introduces Aaron to Betty Slonim and Sam Dreiman, who have come to Poland in search of a play. Betty is a minor actress, but Sam wants to make her a star. To achieve this end, he is prepared to rent a theater in Warsaw and commission a play. He chooses Aaron as his dramatist when he learns that Aaron already has written the first act of a play about a nineteenth century woman who becomes a Hasidic rabbi. For his efforts, Aaron receives regular and generous advances. Aaron's dramaturgical abilities are not great, though, and he suffers further from the assistance of Betty, Sam, and other members of the proposed cast. The result is an unproducible piece that fails in rehearsal.

Aaron's association with Betty Slonim leads to more than a botched play, though. When he is not writing—which seems to be most of the time—he often serves as Betty's lover and tour guide. On one of their excursions, Aaron takes her to see his old street, which he has not visited in twenty years. There he finds Shosha; she has hardly changed, remaining essentially a child both mentally and physically. Inexplicably, he falls in love with her, and after the failure of his play, he moves in with Shosha and her mother, severing his ties with his former associates and with the members of the Writers' Club.

With Sam Dreiman's blessing, Betty offers to marry Aaron and take him to the safety of America. Although he realizes that to stay in Poland is to invite death at the hands of the Nazis, he rejects her offer. Instead, he resolves to marry Shosha and remain in Warsaw.

Again war comes, and again Aaron's life changes. He flees Warsaw with Shosha, but she is too frail to survive the ordeal; two days out of the capital, she dies. Dora Stolnitz vanishes, and Betty commits suicide. Aaron reaches America through the Orient and becomes a successful writer, but he remains haunted by his past.

The Characters

Aaron Greidinger is a portrait of Isaac Bashevis Singer as a young man. Both are red-haired vegetarians who grew up on Krochmalna Street. Both are the sons of rabbis but have abandoned traditional Judaism for the secular world. Both are writers, and both write about dybbuks, demons, and false Messiahs. Both are puzzled by the mysteries of the universe; both are irresistibly attractive to and attracted by women.

Shosha is not, however, absolute autobiography. Whereas Singer's first-known literary effort (in 1925) won a prize, Aaron must struggle many years before success comes to him. Aaron also remains in Poland longer than did Singer, who left in the early 1930's and thus did not face the rising tide of anti-Semitism in the country. Nor did Singer ever return to live on Krochmalna Street once he had left. Through Aaron, then, he seems to imagine what his life might have been like had he chosen another course.

While Aaron bears certain similarities to Singer, Shosha does not at all resemble his first wife. This woman (Shosha) who remains a child does not seem likely to interest Aaron, who is involved in affairs with four other women when he meets her again after two decades. Perhaps, though, her innocence fascinates him; perhaps, too, in marrying her, he seeks to reunite himself with a past that he has rejected intellectually but emotionally has never abandoned. Throughout his adulthood, he has dreamed of Shosha, suggesting that while his rational life is rooted in modernism, his irrational side that expresses itself only in dreams remains bound to tradition.

One may thus regard Shosha as an allegorical representation of the old Jewish ways. Her very name is a variation of Shoshana, the rose, hinting at the biblical Rose of Jacob that is the Jewish people. Her death in the flight from Warsaw reflects the demise of European Judaism with its centuries of culture and tradition. Like this way of life, she cannot survive when severed from her roots on Krochmalna Street. (One must recall that in the 1930's, Warsaw, with its 300,000 Jews, was the epicenter of Jewish literature and philosophy.)

The other women in *Shosha* also represent aspects of life before World War II. Dora is the self-deluded idealist. Even after she hears of the arrests and murders of foreigners who have come to the Soviet Union, she refuses to believe the reports. She maintains that those who have been imprisoned, tortured, and killed by Joseph Stalin deserve their fate, that those who are innocent have nothing to fear.

Celia Chentshiner, an atheist, worships the intellect. Brilliant but bored, she represents European secular culture. She, too, dies in Warsaw as World War II destroys the world with which she has identified herself. Betty, meanwhile, is the artist, devoted to beauty rather than to intelligence, and Tekla is the peasant, neither brilliant nor artistic. She is, however, dependable, doing her work effectively, stolidly, tied to the ways of the country and the rhythms of nature even when she lives in the city.

Themes and Meanings

Shosha is Singer's *Paradise Lost*, an attempt to justify the ways of God to man. It is *Paradise Lost* written from the perspective of one who has seen two world wars and the Holocaust and who lives in the shadow of nuclear Armageddon. "If God is wisdom, how can there be foolishness? And if God is life, how can there be death?" asks Haiml Chentshiner. Shosha wonders why flies bite and why horses cannot live to be a hundred. "What can one do? How is one to live?" Dora asks. Singer's reply is less confident than John Milton's. In the final scene of the book, Haiml poses questions to Aaron as they sit in a small dark room. Haiml's second wife opens the door and asks these symbols of wondering humanity why they sit without light. Haiml replies, "We're waiting for an answer."

If an answer exists, it has not yet been given. Meanwhile, what remains for man to do? For one thing, he must remember. "Let us say that a fly has fallen into a spiderweb and the spider has sucked her dry. This is a fact of the universe and such a fact cannot be forgotten," Haiml states. Aaron writes about Jewish history: the false Messiahs of the seventeenth and eighteenth centuries, the Maiden of Lublin of the nineteenth century. Writing for him is an act of memory. *Shosha*, too, is such an act. By summoning the sounds, smells, tastes, and sights of a vanished Warsaw, Singer preserves that vanished world. Shosha and Celia are dead, the Warsaw ghetto is no more, but through literature one can again experience the past. As Alexander Pope wrote, "The groves of Eden, vanished now so long,/ Live in description and still are green in song." So, too, the streets and people of another era remain alive in the pages of fiction.

One cannot, must not, forget the past, but one must live in the present. On the eve of World War II, Aaron observes that in the opera houses one sees the same old comedies and tragedies, as though destruction were not imminent. In the store windows, one finds the same jewelry and furniture. The women still wear the latest fashions, and the men still ogle them approvingly. Even as Aaron contemplates the absurdity of the charade, he smells coffee and fresh rolls, and he, too, yields to his present appetite. He realizes that "every one of us will die with the same passions he lived with." For life must go on. Celia dies, but Haiml remarries. Aaron's life in Poland ends, but he creates a new one in America.

For the suffering in this life there is no explanation. From suffering, however, one does learn. Aaron becomes a vegetarian after watching the atrocities in a slaughterhouse. Haiml learns that insects and mice are also God's creatures. In Nazi-ruled Warsaw, Morris Feitelzohn finally discovers the philosophical insights that have eluded him for so long. The false Messiah Jacob Frank had urged Jews to sin, and Feitelzohn claims that in a sense Frank was correct: One should oppose the will of God to achieve salvation. "If He wanted evil, we had to aspire to the opposite. If He wanted wars, inquisitions, crucifixions, Hitlers, we must want righteousness, Hasidism, our own version of grace."

Critical Context

A few months after *Shosha* appeared, Singer was awarded the Nobel Prize for Literature. Just as the Nobel Prize is a fitting tribute to a lifetime of letters, so *Shosha* is an epitome of that life. Like all of Singer's other work, it is superficially a simple narrative. Yet it articulates all the themes that inform Singer's writing. Here is the mysticism of dybbuks and demons, which Shosha sees in her dreams. Here is the closed world of Hasidic Jewry confronting the infinite secular universe. Here are the passions of the flesh and the metaphysical yearnings of the soul. Here is the search for the meaning of suffering and life, and here is the lack of an answer.

Though Singer has left the world of Polish Hasidism behind him, he carries it with him, too. In the yeshiva, the best student is not the one with the right answers but the one with the right questions. For *Shosha*, Singer deserves to go to the head of the class.

Bibliography

Biletzky, Israel Ch. *God, Jew, Satan in the Works of Isaac Bashevis Singer.* Lanham, Md.: University Press of America, 1995. This critical work examines Singer's novels in light of his major themes, including the oppositions between reality and unreality, belief and doubt, past and present, and order and chaos.
Farrell, Grace, ed. *Critical Essays on Isaac Bashevis Singer.* New York: G. K. Hall, 1996. This collection of critical essays from a variety of prominent scholars presents wide ranging views on Singer's work. The essays focus on specific novels as well as general themes that run throughout the body of Singer's work, including his

treatment of religious belief, his portrayal of women, and his views on male homo-sexuality. Includes a helpful bibliography and index.

Hadda, Janet. *Isaac Bashevis Singer: A Life*. New York: Oxford University Press, 1997. Hadda takes a detailed look at the cultural and familial influences that shaped Singer's life and work. Written from a psychoanalytic perspective, this portrait examines the impact his parents and siblings had on him, and candidly describes his flaws as well as his charm.

Telushkin, Dvorah. *Master of Dreams: A Memoir of Isaac Bashevis Singer*. New York: Morrow, 1997. A poignant view of Singer's life and work. Drawing from her own diaries tracing both the literary and personal association she shared with Singer, Telushkin's memoir reveals a troubled but brilliant man who is fighting against the physical breakdown that comes with old age. Offers an illuminating perspective on the background of some of Singer's most popular works.

Zamir, Israel. *Journey to My Father: Isaac Bashevis Singer*. New York: Arcade, 1995. Although this book is a memoir and does not offer any critical understanding of Singer's novels, it addresses Singer's belief in ghosts and demons, his curiosity, and love of the Yiddish language, all of which figured prominently in Singer's work.

Joseph Rosenblum

SHOW BOAT

Author: Edna Ferber (1885-1968)
Type of plot: Local color
Time of plot: The 1880's to the 1920's
Locale: The Mississippi River and Chicago
First published: 1926

> *Principal characters:*
> MAGNOLIA HAWKS RAVENAL, the protagonist
> CAPTAIN ANDY HAWKS, Magnolia's father, the original owner of the
> Cotton Blossom Show Boat
> PARTHENIA ANN HAWKS, Magnolia's stern mother, who disapproves of
> the showboat
> GAYLORD RAVENAL, a weak gambling addict, Magnolia's husband
> KIM RAVENAL, Magnolia and Gaylord's daughter, a successful
> Broadway actress
> JULIE DOZIER, a biracial riverboat actress turned prostitute

The Novel

 Show Boat re-creates the little-known phenomenon of life on a turn-of-the-century showboat as it brings theatrical entertainment to backwoods Midwestern river towns from Ohio and Illinois to New Orleans. The rivers themselves, the Mississippi especially, become live participants in the stories of the people who travel them—the actors, the steamboat operators, the cooks, the African American dock workers. The popularity of this particular development of American theater is told through three generations of hardworking middle-class people, centering on the love, marriage, and eventual desertion of Magnolia Hawks Ravenal by her gambler husband.

 As the lively daughter of Captain Andy Hawks, the child Magnolia experiences the rich and varied life both on shore and within the traveling troupe of actors on board her father's Cotton Blossom Floating Palace Theatre showboat, despite her mother Parthenia's puritanical objections. When the ingenue Elly deserts her adoring husband to follow another man, Magnolia becomes the leading lady in the melodramas. When southern laws against miscegenation force the biracial Julie and her white husband to leave the showboat, the impecunious gambler Gaylord Ravenal joins the troupe in New Orleans as the leading man in the plays. He soon captures Magnolia's heart, both on stage and off, despite careful chaperoning by Parthenia and tolerant acceptance by Captain Andy. Escaping Parthenia's suspicious eye, the lovers slip away to be married on shore.

 When Captain Andy dies trying to save his beloved showboat, Ravenal comes in full conflict with Parthenia and forces Magnolia to chose between him and the showboat. Reluctant to leave the river life she loves, Magnolia follows Ravenal to Chicago to participate in his precarious life as a professional faro gambler. Their existence in

Chicago seesaws between opulence and poverty, causing Magnolia to place their young daughter Kim in the stability of a convent school. Although Ravenal tries to protect his wife from the tawdry aspects of the Chicago scene, Magnolia feels her moral values compromised by the corruption and decadence of the turn-of-the-century Chicago reformers, politicians, and underworld characters. Although she enjoys the cultural challenge and big-city excitement of Chicago, the instability of Ravenal's fortunes make Magnolia long for the relative simplicity of the river life.

The conflict comes to a crisis when Magnolia's mother announces her visit to Chicago during a time when Ravenal's fortunes are at low ebb. Ashamed of their impoverished state, Ravenal borrows money to gamble. Still unwilling to admit any possible fault in her marriage, Magnolia denies the truth of her husband's failing fortunes until she discovers that he has borrowed money from a brothel-owner. Forcing herself to return the money without her husband's knowledge, Magnolia finds that her actress friend Julie has become a prostitute; ironically, when Magnolia seeks employment in a variety-hall restaurant, she discovers that her best talent is in singing the melancholy riverboat spirituals from her childhood. That same evening, she discovers that her husband has abandoned her and their child for the golden opportunities of California, where he eventually dies without further contact.

Although Ravenal leaves them with the remainder of his gambling winnings, Magnolia is forced to carve a career for herself in American theater rather than return to her mother's bitter dominance. When Parthenia dies and leaves her the showboat, Magnolia forsakes the variety hall and vaudeville stage to return to the happy life of her riverboat childhood, assured that her daughter has a successful life as a legitimate actress in the new mode.

The Characters

When Magnolia's father purchases the Cotton Blossom, the child leaves the rigid world of her rigidly critical mother Parthenia to plunge wholeheartedly into the glamourous world of a theatrical troupe traveling down the rivers of America toward New Orleans. The life along the American rivers provides a social, geographical, and multicultural education for her, as her life shifts from that of a shy child to an ingenue to the wife of the wastrel gambler Gaylord Ravenal. She follows him to the gambling world of Chicago and, when he deserts her and their child, makes a name for herself as an actress, only to return to the river to manage the showboat after her mother's death.

Gaylord Ravenal, a smooth-talking southern charmer, has a fatal weakness for faro, an improvident taste for the good life, and a deep passion for his wife. However, outside his gambling element, he is ineffective and improvident. Too ashamed to find other work when his fortunes fail, he leaves Magnolia to build a life for herself and their daughter. He dies without contacting them further.

Captain Andy Hawks, a shrewd man, loves his nomadic showboat life so much that he dies trying to save the Cotton Blossom from grounding. He is Magnolia's ideal father because he introduces her to tolerance and humor.

Parthenia Ann Hawks, a displaced New England schoolteacher, provides contrast and conflict for the easygoing life on the riverboat. Although she considers life on the riverboat sinful, she amasses a fortune from the revenues as owner and operator. Her rigid view of life forces Magnolia to choose Ravenal over the riverboat; her letters to her daughter show an unchanging I-told-you-so attitude.

Kim Ravenal, daughter of Magnolia and Gaylord, is a prototype of the actress schooled in modern techniques of the legitimate theater rather than in the melodramatic or vaudeville dramas her parents performed. Her marriage is coolly modern, lacking the passion of her mother and father. She loves her mother but does not understand her passion for the showboat life.

Julie Dozier, a biracial actress passing as white, serves to demonstrate racial inequality at a time when miscegenation was illegal in some states.

Themes and Meanings

All Ferber's works carry social history along with social criticism, centering on middle-class values of midwestern Americans under the pressure of social and economic change. *Show Boat*, for example, gives a panoramic view of three women confronting the rivers of change in American society. Parthenia and Captain Andy instill the virtues of hard work and loyalty in their daughter, who, in turn, encourages her own daughter Kim to be the best actress she can be. Since theater itself is based on illusion and deception, Ferber's characters are romanticized, escapist, and overly sentimental, even to the point of melodrama. When Magnolia meets the love of her life in Ravenal, she follows her father's tolerant and romantic nature and blinds herself to his faults. However, when she understands the true nature of their relationship, she calls on her mother's strength to survive.

Ferber's importance is twofold: She preserves a lost view of American life and theater that might be easily forgotten, and she also presents the problems of the working class beset by economic change. Just as the Mississippi shifts its sandbars, so also do Ravenal's and Magnolia's fortunes ebb and wane; as the Mississippi continues to flow toward the sea, so also does the love and passion between the main characters continue to grow until Ravenal leaves. This passion is mirrored in the heightened sense of excitement that the live performances on the showboat bring to the farmers and farmhands in the small river towns, a moment of sparkle in their dull lives. It romanticizes a part of American culture never before highlighted and illuminates the development from showboat to variety hall to vaudeville to legitimate theater.

The actors themselves are a predictable mélange of literary stereotypes—Magnolia, the beautiful and sensitive heroine; Ravenal, the dashingly handsome lover and rogue; Frank, the villain unrequitedly in love with Magnolia; Elly, the flighty blonde ingenue; Julie, the smoky-voiced seductress. On the showboat itself the same types appear in Parthenia's rabid morality, Captain Andy's Gallic tolerance, the cooks' laid-back personalities, and the tugboat men's drinking.

Eternally optimistic and ebullient, the showboat life represents a positive feminine balance to Huckelberry Finn's masculine journey from innocence through the world of experience into a higher innocence. Magnolia succumbs to the river's spell to regain her innocence, just as America, Ferber suggests, should return to its roots to maintain its innocence.

Although revivals of the 1920's musical *Show Boat* have caused protest by ethnic groups, the issue of race is a relatively minor one in the novel. Ferber's Captain Andy treats the African American characters as worthy employees with a dignity of their own, even to the point of envying them. It is the outside world that stigmatizes and degrades them.

Critical Context

Ferber began her career in journalism and turned to fiction only after she had a nervous breakdown. Her first efforts were short stories published in magazines, especially the popular Emma McChesney stories of a widowed traveling saleswoman. The success of a woman competing in a man's world encouraged her to see the modern woman as necessary to the working class as characterized by various areas of America.

Her continued interest in theater led to collaboration with playwright George S. Kaufman. Prompted by a theatrical colleague's casual reference to showboats, Ferber researched the American phenomenon of riverboats by residing on the James Adams Floating Palace for two months in Cincinnati. Her subsequent view made the Mississippi itself a major character for its strength and adaptability. Jerome Kern and Oscar Hammerstein adapted this concept into an African American work song praising the Mississippi, "Ol' Man River." To modern audiences, revivals of the musical may seem to underscore racial stereotyping. Kern and Hammerstein turned the novel *Show Boat* into the first musical comedy with social significance, with the songs arising from the story rather than serving as mere showcases for individual talent. In the novel, the social reality of a post-Civil War attitude toward African Americans is presented sympathetically and with no condescension; Captain Andy's understanding and acceptance of his employees is especially notable. Ferber won a Pulitzer Prize for *So Big* (1924), and her subsequent works follow similar themes of investigating relatively little-known regions of America. These tales are told through the story of a sympathetic female character who becomes the symbol for the entire area, much like the traditional epic hero often stands for a country's values.

Bibliography

Dickinson, Rogers. *Edna Ferber.* Garden City, N.Y.: Doubleday, Page, 1925. Early and laudatory minibiography, with literary criticism and some valuable quotes from Ferber's articles and autobiography.

Fennell, Tom. "Roll On, Big River: A Lavish Show Boat Christens a New Theatre." *Maclean's* 106, no. 44 (November 1, 1993): 72. Evaluation of the content and intent of the 1993 musical production, particularly with regard to racial issues.

Gilbert, Julie Goldsmith. *Ferber: A Biography.* New York: Doubleday, 1978. Helpful biography that centers on the last years of Ferber's life. Written by her niece.

Kanfer, Stefan. "The Boat That Changed Broadway." *The New Leader* 77, no. 10 (Oc-

tober 10, 1977): 22. A critical review of the musical version of the novel as a Broadway piece, from Kerns and Hammerstein's original to Hal Prince's production.

Kronenberger, Louis. "*Show Boat* Is High Romance." Review of *Show Boat*, by Edna
Ferber. *The New York Times Book Review*, August 22, 1926, p. 5. An interesting
early review of the novel.

Anne K. Kaler

THE SHROUDED WOMAN

Author: María Luisa Bombal (1910-1980)
Type of plot: Feminist surrealism
Time of plot: The first half of the twentieth century
Locale: The southern part of Chile and the fantastic realm of Death
First published: La amortajada, 1938 (English translation, 1948)

> *Principal characters:*
> ANA MARÍA, the protagonist, a typical housewife of the Latin American
> upper social strata
> RICARDO, her lover when both he and Ana María were adolescents
> ANTONIO, her husband
> FERNANDO, an older man who courts her in the later years of her life

The Novel

   In *The Shrouded Woman* María Luisa Bombal skillfully juxtaposes the unknown and supernatural realm of Death with concrete reality. At the beginning of the novel, Ana María lies dead and is surrounded by those who once had a relationship with her. Although she is dead, Ana María can still hear and see those who are mourning her. Simultaneously, while she lies in her casket, the protagonist is led into the past as she recalls events significant to her life, and she enters the supernatural space of Death inhabited by mysterious voices, uncanny landscapes, and strange insects and flowers. The juxtaposition of Life and Death is created in the novel through the cinematic technique of a montage presented in counterpoint. Such a montage captures the coexistence of elements of reality traditionally conceived as separate entities: The past binds to the present, both merging into a single instant; consciousness survives beyond death; and the concrete objective reality fuses with the mysterious zone of Death. Besides the basic omniscient narrator, there are several other narrators who give their own testimony on Ana María, in this way adding conflicting views and interpretations to the story of her life. Thus, Ana María becomes a multifaceted character: a passionate lover, a selfish woman, a naïve girl, a strict mother, and an intuitive human being with mystical doubts about God. In the same manner that the shrouded woman acquires a new understanding of her life through the fragmented memories of the past, the reader adds these different perspectives about Ana María to realize finally that a human being is what he thinks of himself as well as the different images he projects on others. The protagonist's journey into Death is the ultimate act of Life, not only because she now comprehends the real meaning of her existence but also because Death has allowed her to annul the worries of everyday life, penetrating thereby into the mysteries of people and nature. Ironically, then, the burial of Ana María at the end of the novel becomes a symbol of what true Life should be: the profound and wise experiences of the Self as part of a wider cosmic order.

The Characters

Ana María is a prototype of the Latin American women in the 1930's who did not have an active participation in economics or politics. Therefore, in the restrictive role of wife and mother, the protagonist searches for love as the only means to achieve a goal in life. Her relations with Ricardo, Antonio, and Fernando reveal three crucial stages in her life: sexual initiation, the passive acceptance of social conventions symbolized by marriage, and erotic sublimation in unconsummated adultery. Significantly, these three stages mark the progressive degradation of those instinctive and primordial elements in feminine character being slowly eroded by societal conformism.

The love experiences with Ricardo are tinged with sensuality nurtured by sensations equated with nature. Ricardo's adolescent body is compared to the vitality of the wild forest and the indomitable strength of a stallion. His caresses are described as a dark and wild carnation. Ana María ignores social regulations that demand virginity and gives in to instincts deeply rooted in nature. Thus, when she becomes pregnant, she feels completely identified with budding trees, the graceful flight of doves, and the sounds surrounding her. She is, in fact, intimately united to Matter. Ricardo's abandonment and the accidental abortion destroy this natural and harmonious relationship with nature. She encloses herself in her room and passively accepts Antonio's marriage proposal.

Married life is described as empty and unfulfilling. In spite of her frustration, Ana María feigns happiness, keeping up with appearances, although she is conscious of the unfair situation regarding men and women. This view of society is made explicit in the following statement: "While women have men as the pivot of their life, men succeed in directing their passion to politics or work. But the fate of women seems to be to turn over and over in their heart some love sorrow while sitting in a neatly ordered house, facing an unfinished tapestry."

As the years go by, Ana María withdraws into herself, becoming narrow and petty. She encourages Fernando to court her, a selfish act that gratifies her vanity, but she never allows him to kiss her—thus protecting herself from moral transgression in committing real adultery. Her relationship with Fernando is marked by selfishness and cruelty; moreover, although she is not in love with him, it is significant that her life is still dependent on a relation with a man. Fernando's visits become a *raison d'etre* for the protagonist, and even on her deathbed she anxiously waits for him.

Ana María's trajectory must be defined in terms of this existential subordination to men, characterized in the novel as symbols of power; in this sense, the lover motif is highly significant: domination and physical strength in Ricardo, pride and power in Antonio, selfishness and rationality in Fernando. These primary characteristics of the male, as perceived from a female perspective, are, in fact, the qualities usually attributed to men in Latin American society, according to recent sociological studies on sex roles.

Ana María represents a tragic view of women and their place in society. As though screened in by a shroud, the protagonist ends up alienated because she is forced into a passive acceptance of the status quo. Ironically, the solution to this dilemma lies not in changing her historical role but rather in the supernatural realm of Death. It is only when she is dead that she is able to unveil the intrinsic nature of those she knew in life. Moreover, death allows her to penetrate the secrets of nature: the intensity of night, the sounds of rain, the beauty of tree bark.

Themes and Meanings

As a true exponent of the avant-garde movement, *The Shrouded Woman* expresses a preoccupation with those mysterious aspects of reality that lie beyond the limits of scientific and rational parameters. Shortly after the publication of the novel, María Luisa Bombal said: "I think people have willingly ignored that we live on the surface of the unknown. We have organized a logical system on a well of mystery. We have chosen to ignore what is primordial to Life: Death." Therefore, the literary representation of Death is not only a supernatural locale of the novel but also an important theme that enlightens the conception of Life. Death is seen as a process of immersion in the primordial cosmos. The archetypal motif of the journey into death is presented in counterpoint to other experiences in the realm of the living. Only in death does Ana María comprehend the tragic and profound significance of her life and that of others. Thus, Death is a spiritual experience that leads not only to the hidden meaning of life but also to an integration with the cosmic forces that are the origins of Life. A mysterious voice invites Ana María to abandon her coffin and explore a magical zone that belongs to the unknown. Light and darkness, Life and Death emerge in the supernatural gardens underground, as in the primordial stage of biblical Genesis. The dead protagonist descends into the origins of the Universe, going down into the earth where she encounters flowers of bone and marvelously intact human skeletons with their knees drawn up as if once again inside the womb. After she is buried, she feels an infinity of roots spreading from her body into the earth like an expanding cobweb through which the constant throbbing of the universe rises. Immersed in the ancient flow of Life and Death, she now feels new islands emerge, far-off mountains of sand tumble down to give rise to other forms of life in a cyclic movement of death and regeneration. Her dead body disintegrating in the earth becomes a new source of life in the cosmic cycle where matter never dies but only assumes a new form.

The Shrouded Woman is also a denunciation of Latin American women's predicament in the twentieth century. The theme of love as the sole gratification for women is conceived in the novel as a spiritual search, which is achieved in society only through a subordinate relation regulated by men. Moreover, María Luisa Bombal, in a view very similar to that of the French feminist Simone de Beauvoir, states that women's total dependence on love deprives them of the right to mold their lives in a truly independent way. Ana María is a prisoner of love, and, very symbolically, she realizes at a later stage in her life that her concept of love has been a deception created by a culture where women are supposed to be sentimental and passive. Therefore, the message of the novel implicitly makes a distinction between love as a spiritual and innate drive in human beings and love as a social activity that reinforces the primary roles of men and women in a patriarchal society. At the end of the novel, after Ana María has returned to the ancestral realm of the earth, she recapitulates her life in a highly symbolic statement—she believes that while she was alive she lived the life of a dead person, restricted by her society, which only allowed her to attain the goal of marriage, without ever having the opportunity to overcome subordination.

Critical Context

When María Luisa Bombal published *La última niebla* in 1934 (*The Final Mist,* 1982), she was immediately acclaimed by critics as one of the most outstanding writers in Latin America. Radically departing from the realist mode in vogue, she constructed this first short novel on the ambiguous juxtaposition of dreams and reality experienced by a female protagonist who escapes her tragic social predicament through alienation. The publication of *La amortajada* in 1938 reaffirmed her position as an innovative writer, and, in 1942, her second book was awarded the National Prize as the best novel in Chile. In 1948, the English version, *The Shrouded Woman*, was published in the United States, and it was subsequently printed in Sweden, Germany, Great Britain, and Japan. The Spanish version of *The Shrouded Woman* has had eleven different editions, and, even today, it is a best-seller in Latin America.

Although literary criticism of Latin American literature has always undergone changes and revisions, *The Shrouded Woman* has remained one of the most significant Latin American novels ever published. Its impeccable technical elaboration and the presentation of a reality where the concrete and the marvelous coexist have made this novel a landmark of surrealistic accomplishment in Latin America. It is also a remarkable expression of women as second-class citizens with no right to change society. Its protagonist has been excluded from an active participation in history. It is precisely this marginal status that has caused a basic alienation, rendered through daydreaming, erotic fantasies, and an immersion in the primordial realm of the cosmic. As recent feminist studies have demonstrated, Bombal's images of women not only denounce feminine subordination but also represent the innate essence of women as deeply rooted in nature. While according to her worldview men regulate natural forces to produce civilization, women as individuals of an intuitive nature grasp the mysterious irradiations of the universe in search of ancestral harmony. Power, violence, and civilization are, for the author, the basic expressions of the masculine, which, as opposed to the erotic and ancestral feminine, become irreconcilable forces doomed to noncommunication and sterility. Ana María in *The Shrouded Woman* as well as the other women presented in María Luisa Bombal's works are subjected to the dominant male order, and the defeat of the female is the real source of their tragic destiny. While in *The Shrouded Woman* the only exit is death, in *The Final Mist* it is death in life conceived as a shrouded and oppressive mist that symbolizes social regulations imposed on women. If on the surface this appears to be a highly pessimistic view of women, subsequent works written by Latin American women have consistently coincided with María Luisa Bombal's lucid testimony, which is presented through an artistic elaboration that is considered exceptional.

Bibliography

Adams, Michael I. *Three Authors of Alienation: Bombal, Onetti, Carpentier.* Austin: University of Texas Press, 1975. Adams presents a sociopsychological critical interpretation of three Latin American authors whose works share similar themes.

Alegría, Fernando. "María Luisa Bombal." In *Latin American Writers*, edited by Carlos A. Solé and Maria I. Abreau. Vol 3. New York: Charles Scribner's Sons, 1989. An essay on the life and career of Bombal. Includes analysis of her works and a bibliography.

Guerra-Cunningham, Lucía. "Mariá Luisa Bombal." In *Spanish American Authors: The Twentieth Century*, edited by Angel Flores. New York: H. W. Wilson, 1992. Profiles Bombal and includes an extensive bibliography of works by and about the author.

Mujica, Barbara. "The Shrouded Woman." *Americas* 48 (January/February, 1996): 61-62. A review of Bombal's novels. Mujica sees Bombal as a precursor of the Magical Realists and part of a literary elite that sought to integrate fantastic elements and social criticism into her work. A brief analysis and synopsis of *The Final Mist* and *The Shrouded Woman* are included.

Ryan, Bryan, ed. *Hispanic Writers: A Selection of Sketches from "Contemporary Authors."* Detroit: Gale Research, 1991. Entry on Bombal gives an overview of her life, writing, and critical reaction to her work.

Lucia Guerra Cunningham

62: A MODEL KIT

Author: Julio Cortázar (1914-1984)
Type of plot: The novel as play
Time of plot: Uncertain; possibly the 1950's or the 1960's
Locale: Paris, London, Vienna, Arcueil, and an imaginary city
First published: 62: Modelo para armar, 1968 (English translation, 1972)

Principal characters:
>JUAN, an Argentine translator
>HÉLENÈ, a young French anesthetist
>MARRAST, a French sculptor
>NICOLE, a French illustrator and the mistress of Marrast
>TELL, a Danish woman, Juan's travel companion
>CALAC, an Argentine writer and critic
>POLANCO, another Argentine, the inseparable friend of Calac
>CELIA, a young French teenager who is pampered by the group
>AUSTIN, a young English lutenist
>FEUILLE MORTE, a female character whose only words are "Bisbis"
>THE PAREDROS, an impersonal entity

The Novel

The novel begins on the twenty-fourth of December in Paris. As Juan spends Christmas Eve alone in a gloomy restaurant, he examines the relationship between thought, word, and action and he questions the value of reasoning itself. The deceiving nature of memory is then explored in passages which change swiftly and without warning from a first- to a second- and third-person narrator. Glimpses of specific details of what is going to happen, or has already happened, are introduced mostly through Juan's thoughts. In the midst of a labyrinthine beginning, which will set the tone of the text, some explanation is provided as to what constitutes the city and the paredros, key elements in the book.

For a great part of the novel, the friends are scattered in different European cities. In London, Marrast, Nicole, Calac, and Polanco amuse themselves at the expense of the British and their sense of decorum. Yet if a museum and the streets of London offer the possibilities of freedom and games, inside their room of the Gresham Hotel Marrast and Nicole live their last days together. Nicole is in love with Juan, and Marrast becomes the frustrated witness of her melancholy. Their exasperating state of mind is portrayed carefully by the use of dialogue, inner reflections, or letters.

At the same time, Juan is translating for an international conference in Vienna, accompanied by Tell. Tell, the crazy Dane, as Juan calls her, makes him forget the treachery of language, and her sense of humor relieves him from the pain of his unrequited love for Hélenè. In their pursuit of play, they decide to follow the steps of Frau Marta—a gray, repulsive old lady—whom they have watched develop a bizarre friendship with a young English female tourist. Tell and Juan couple their wish of adventure with the historical background of a legend and become detectives in a modern story of vampirism.

In Paris, the attention is focused on Hélenè, an anesthetist, and the teenage Celia. The same day that Celia runs away from home, Hélenè has lost a young man—who reminds her of Juan—at the operating table. The anesthetist invites Celia to her apartment; the prose switches back and forth between Celia's surprisingly mature and thoughtful analysis of Hélenè and Hélenè's memories and her actual displacement to the streets of the imaginary city. In the city she searches for a certain hotel and for a certain room where she is to deliver a package. Dialogue and interior monologue cut into each other constantly, and any attempt to establish a rational continuity is doubly frustrated by the tale of Juan and Tell in Vienna, which alternates with the episode in Paris. That night, Hélenè seduces Celia in a scene which is presented both in a lyric and a violent fashion. The broken doll in the morning, and Celia's horrified scream at its sight, stress the dark and mysterious aspect of the plot.

Shortly before the final gathering of the group, the various tensions produced by desire and adventure and play come to their conclusion. Nicole attempts suicide; Celia falls in love with Austin, the young English lutenist adopted in fun by Calac and Polanco in London, and Hélenè and Juan finally confront each other and see themselves reliving the myth of Diana and Acteon. Nearing the end of the novel, all of the friends, including Feuille Morte and Osvaldo, a pet snail, converge in France. The occasion is the unveiling of the statue of Vercingetorix, sculpted by Marrast and commissioned by the city of Arcueil. The sculpture turns out to be quite scandalous, for it appears that the hero of Gaulle has its backside pointing heavenward. On their return to Paris, Hélenè and Juan keep repeating the same words, their language and themselves unable to advance anywhere except toward the city, the imaginary city which has haunted them from the start. It is in the room of a hotel where Hélenè had a date, where she was to make a delivery, that Juan finds her, Austin's dagger in her chest, her body crushing the package, which contains a doll. As the train approaches Paris, Calac, Tell, and Polanco wait anxiously at the gate for Feuille Morte, who appears to have been forgotten. Feuille Morte, delighted at being rescued, ends the book with a joyful "Bisbis bisbis." Echoes of the initial fragments of the book come to mind as in déjà vu. To find out if all the parts of the model kit are really there, at this point in the novel, the reader is unavoidably tempted to return with Juan to a gloomy Parisian restaurant on Christmas Eve.

The Characters

It is in section 62 of Cortázar's *Rayuela* (1963; *Hopscotch*, 1966) that the basic components of *62: A Model Kit* are to be found. Morelli, a character in *Hopscotch*, is working on a book in which the actors "would appear unhealthy or complete idiots." He adds that "any standard behavior (including the most unusual, its deluxe category) would be inexplicable by means of current instrumental psychology." In the introduction to *62: A Model Kit*, Cortázar warns the reader about the various transgressions in the novel at the level of the characters or the plot. The former, it is true, behave in a very bizarre manner: They are childlike, unpredictable, or caught in a web of thought that laboriously seeks for answers which are never given. They have no complete names, they have no background or history other than the one that involves them in the zone, their common territory. Cortázar has thus stripped from his characters the traits which traditionally enhance development in a realistic manner.

In certain cases, it is possible to establish a few associations. Juan, for example, who works (perhaps) for the United Nations, brings to mind Cortázar himself. Some characters in *Hopscotch* find their parallels in this novel. Juan's main intellectual ruminations are similar to Oliveira's; Hélenè, the loner of the group, in her serious and ordered life mirrors Pola; Tell, innocent and unreflective, reminds one of La Maga. Calac and Polanco, like so many of Cortázar's literary figures, are both Argentine writers displaced in Paris, and they depict intensely the aspect of life valued by the author. They are also the most eminent speakers of an invented language shared by the group—to the dismay of good citizens around them—that echoes the giglico speech of *Hopscotch*.

Following the usual manner in which characters are presented, it is also possible, for example, to see Nicole and Tell as opposites. For Nicole, living has been reduced to perpetual introspection and a sense of passive bondage; for Tell, on the other hand, life is seen as action and freedom of movement. Marrast is tortured, torn between a free intellectual, artistic unconventionality and the traps that his love for Nicole sets for him. Couples do not fare well in Cortázar's novels. Love is described as a possessive, closed universe that curtails erotic freedom and play. Thus, Celia and Austin, in the mutual discovery of their bodies, depict the beauty of the erotic side of human desire; in their narrow and private world, by contrast, they become merely ordinary.

Any in-depth analysis of the characters of *62: A Model Kit* will be frustrated by the author's designs to de-psychologize the classic individuality given to characterization. Consequently, the language and the tools to study the protagonists in a traditional way will always fall short and outside the realm of the novel itself. The very essence of the ego's subconscious is devalued by the fact that the group dreams in common. The paredros, an impersonal entity who at any given time can speak for any character without ever being identified, stresses further the notion of the decentered subject.

Themes and Meanings

Cortázar's writings are marked by an effect of discontinuity and fragmentation which is attained through various literary means. In *Hopscotch*, the sequential modality of chapters is broken by altering the continuity of their numbers. In *Libro de Manuel* (1973; *A Manual for Manuel*, 1978), the typical page is distorted by the inclusion of journalistic passages and by other devices. *62: A Model Kit* is no exception to the experiment that seeks to break away from the established institution of the novel. Cortázar, through Morelli's above mentioned book, proposed that some of the main elements of this genre need to be revised or discarded in order to provide space for the "final mutation" of man. This new man, writer and reader, yearns to dislodge himself or herself from old, worn forms, such as realism, psychology, reason, feeling, and pragmatism. Cortázar willfully deviates from the "true-to-life" feature that is expected to produce an identificatory reality in fiction. In this case, the transgression is done at the level of the genre itself. The characters, however, constitute a group whose rebellious stand reaches beyond the limits of the book to criticize some aspects of Western culture and society.

The group, for example, takes precedence over the concept of the individual. Play and eroticism, two important areas in the novel, require more than one person in order to take place. The voice of the paredros decenters the discourse of any given subject, and since he or she could be a number of characters, it affirms the group at the expense of the individual figure. The doll, like the anthropological mana, is a gift (perverse, transgressive in this case) which binds Juan, Tell, Celia, and Hélenè; by extension, it binds all of the friends, except Feuille Morte. The imaginary city, known to all of them, but where meetings never occur, is enveloped by an aura of darkness and death. There one is alone. It is in the city, also, where the characters cease to laugh and play. Cortázar, throughout the novel, attacks the idea of the serious in a dionysian, joyous vein, and he stresses the importance of the game. Monsieur Perteuil, patriotic and hardworking, exemplifies all the virtues of the middle class but turns out to be blatantly ridiculous.

Critical Context

No doubt there is the temptation to see the incoherent plot and erratic behavior of the characters as a theme of the existentialist absurd. Cortázar, nevertheless, had refuted in *Hopscotch* the existentialist project, and in the dialogues between Marrast and Nicole, he refutes it once more. It is no longer a matter of capitalizing on an established theme, which after all tends to bind man to an irreversible existing condition in the world. The cut piece of the postcard from Bari, Italy, shows rather clearly the author's intentions: "upside down and cut out, on a different stairway, from a different step," the little segment detaches itself from reality to become an object of pure beauty. Cortázar, therefore, tries to do away with the terminology by which man and life have been made so far explainable in pragmatic, realistic notions. He alters the order of the pieces and disrupts the expected pattern of novel (and life) to find out whether a puzzle with new shapes and perspectives can be achieved.

Bibliography

Alazraki, Jaime, and Ivar Ivask, eds. *The Final Island: The Fiction of Julio Cortázar.* Norman: University of Oklahoma Press, 1978. Perhaps the finest collection of criticism on Cortázar, a representative sampling of his best critics covering all the important aspects of his fictional output.

Boldy, Steven. *The Novels of Julio Cortázar.* Cambridge, England: Cambridge University Press, 1980. The introduction provides a helpful biographical sketch linked to the major developments in Cortázar's writing. Boldy concentrates on four

Cortázar novels: *The Winners*, *Hopscotch*, *62: A Model Kit*, and *A Manual for Manuel*. Includes notes, bibliography, and index.

Guibert, Rita. *Seven Voices: Seven Latin American Writers Talk to Rita Guibert*. New York: Knopf, 1973. Includes an important interview with Cortázar, who discusses both his politics (his strenuous objection to U.S. interference in Latin America) and many of his fictional works.

Harss, Luis, and Barabara Dohmann. *Into the Mainstream: Conversations with Latin-American Writers*. New York: Harper & Row, 1967. Includes an English translation of an important interview in Spanish.

Hernandez del Castillo, Ana. *Keats, Poe, and the Shaping of Cortázar's Mythopoesis*. Amsterdam: J. Benjamin, 1981. This is a part of the Purdue University Monographs in Romance Languages, volume 8. Cortázar praised this study for its rigor and insight.

Peavler, Terry L. *Julio Cortázar*. Boston: Twayne, 1990. Peavler begins with an overview of Cortázar's life and career and his short stories of the fantastic, the mysterious, the psychological, and the realistic. Only one chapter is devoted exclusively to his novels. Includes chronology, notes, annotated bibliography, and index.

Stavans, Ilan. *Julio Cortázar: A Study of the Short Fiction*. New York: Twayne, 1996. See especially the chapters on the influence of Jorge Luis Borges on Cortázar's fiction, his use of the fantastic, and his reliance on popular culture. Stavans also has a section on Cortázar's role as writer and his interpretation of developments in Latin American literature. Includes chronology and bibliography.

Yovanovich, Gordana. *Julio Cortázar's Character Mosaic: Reading the Longer Fiction*. Toronto: University of Toronto Press, 1991. Three chapters focus on Cortázar's four major novels and his fluctuating presentations of character as narrators, symbols, and other figures of language. Includes notes and bibliography.

Laura Riesco Luszczynska

THE SLAVE

Author: Isaac Bashevis Singer (1904-1991)
Type of plot: Historical fiction
Time of plot: The middle and late 1600's
Locale: Poland and Palestine
First published: Der Knekht, 1961 (English translation, 1962)

> *Principal characters:*
> JACOB, the protagonist, a devout and scholarly Jew
> WANDA BZIK, Jacob's non-Jewish mistress, later his wife
> JAN BZIK, Wanda's peasant father and Jacob's master
> DZIOBAK, the village's Catholic priest
> ADAM PILITZKY, a pessimistic Polish nobleman who owns the village
> of Pilitz
> THERESA PILITZKY, his wife
> GERSHON, Pilitzky's Jewish overseer, Jacob's rival

The Novel

In the Chmielnicki massacres (1648-1649), the Cossacks kill Jacob's wife and children. He survives by fleeing his native Josefov, but his fate is little better than his family's: Captured by brigands, he is sold as a slave to Jan Bzik.

Wanda, Jan Bzik's daughter, falls in love with Jacob. When he tends the cattle in the mountains during the summer, she brings him special foods from the village. When he is sick, she cares for him; when he is bitten by a snake, she saves his life. Because he remains an Orthodox Jew, Jacob will not work on the Sabbath—thus, Wanda performs his chores for him. She wants Jacob to marry her or, if he will not marry, to live with her.

For a long time Jacob resists. Wanda is not Jewish, so he cannot marry her, and without marriage he refuses to sleep with her. Finally, though, his love and lust overcome his scruples. Further, despite Polish law, which makes the conversion of a Gentile a capital offense for both the convert and the Jew who has caused the conversion, Wanda embraces Judaism.

Jacob's life with Wanda ends abruptly when Jews from Josefov ransom Jacob from slavery. Back in his native village he teaches Hebrew, serves as beadle in the study house, and restores damaged sacred texts. The Jewish community wants him to remarry and finds a rich widow for him. One night, shortly before the marriage is to occur, he dreams that Wanda is pregnant with his child; the next morning he sets off to find her.

Reunited, Jacob and Wanda go to a new village, Pilitz. Wanda assumes the name of Sarah, the first Jewish convert. To prevent the community from discovering her lack of Yiddish and her peasant accent, she feigns dumbness. When Adam Pilitzky, in a drunken fit, threatens her husband, though, Wanda/Sarah breaks her silence to plead for his life. Instead of destroying their scheme, her action benefits them. Pilitzky believes that he has witnessed the miracle he has longed for; convinced that Jacob and Wanda are holy people, he appoints Jacob as his overseer in place of the dishonest Gershon.

In labor, Wanda speaks again, revealing her entire history. The Jewish community, which had never accepted Sarah, rejoices at the exposure of the "miracle" and excommunicates Jacob for seeking to convert her. They reject the conversion and her marriage, declaring her son, Benjamin, to be illegitimate. After her death in childbirth, the Jews refuse her burial in holy ground. Jacob's son is taken from him, and he is arrested by Pilitzky.

On his way to certain death, Jacob escapes once more. He returns to Pilitz for his son, and together they flee to Palestine. Twenty years later, he comes back to Pilitz to reclaim the bones of his wife, so that he may bury them in Palestine, but no one can find her unmarked grave. Jacob suddenly sickens and dies; preparing to bury him, the gravedigger finds Wanda's corpse, still preserved. Taking this discovery as an omen, the elders agree to bury Jacob next to her and finally accept her not only as a Jew but as a saint.

The Characters

Although *The Slave* is filled with villagers and peasants, only two characters, Jacob and Wanda, are fully developed. Physically, Jacob does not look quite Jewish: He is tall and blue-eyed. He speaks a better Polish than his Jewish compatriots in Pilitz, and while they cringe before their Gentile overlord, Jacob stands up to him. Jacob is ashamed of his co-religionists' failure to resist the Cossacks; when soldiers attempt to carry him off, he fights and defeats them.

Jacob is different, not because he is less Jewish but rather because he is more. Jacob, whose biblical namesake was a successful wrestler, admires the ancient Jewish heroes, whom he takes as his model. His beliefs, too, are firmly rooted in the Bible. Alone in the mountains, he begins to engrave the commandments on a large rock, just as Moses had. He keeps a calendar and, like the Jews in the days of the Temple, watches the phases of the moon so that he may observe all the holidays at their proper time. To avoid violating the Sabbath, he gathers extra food for himself and his cattle during the week, just as the Jews in the desert collected extra manna on Friday because none fell on the Sabbath.

Observing the rituals is important to Jacob, but even more important is respect for his fellowman. Following Amos, he is just, merciful, humble. Unlike his predecessor, also supposedly a religious Jew, he does not abuse Pilitzky's trust, nor does he foment factionalism in the community. During his last visit to Pilitz, he chooses to sleep in the poorhouse rather than in more comfortable lodgings.

It is in the spirit of biblical Judaism that Jacob converts Wanda, for he knows that before Christian law forbade the practice, Judaism was a proselytizing religion. Yet Wanda is no ordinary Christian any more than Jacob is a typical Jew—she senses that she has a Jewish soul that has mistakenly been born into a Gentile body. She rejects numerous eligible Christian husbands, and her behavior differs so markedly from that of her mother, sister, and the other villagers that they dub her "the Lady." Her love for Jacob is equaled by her passion for learning and decency in a world of ignorance and nastiness.

Like Leah, Rachel, and Ruth, she leaves her family to follow the God of Jacob. Her devotion allows her the right to rebuke the Jews who have rejected her and earns for her a saintly reputation after her death.

The other characters in the book are not as well developed; they are types rather than individuals. Adam Pilitzky is a decadent, despondent nobleman, autocratic yet weak, domineering yet henpecked. He is too hesitant even to carry out evil intentions, such as killing Gershon or banishing the Jews from his village. In his despair and dissolute nature, he represents the decaying aristocracy that left Poland a prey to her neighbors. Dziobak is an anti-Semitic, ineffectual priest. If he were to spend as much time and energy teaching his parishioners the Gospel of Christ as he does inciting them to hate the one Jew in their midst, he might overcome some of the paganism that is the real religion of the peasants.

Gershon, a Jewish leader in Pilitz, differs little from Dziobak—there are hypocrites in all religions. He observes the minutest of rituals but cheats his employer. Like Dziobak, too, he plots against Jacob, even after Jacob saves his life.

Themes and Meanings

For Singer, history is not linear but cyclical; the past is never lost. Toward the end of the novel, as Jacob, impoverished, flees with his son across the Vistula, he thinks about his patriarchal namesake:

> His name was Jacob also; he too had lost a beloved wife, the daughter of an idolater, among strangers; Sarah too was buried by the way and had left him a son. Like the Biblical Jacob, he was crossing the river, bearing only a staff, pursued by another Esau. . . . Perhaps four thousand years would again pass; somewhere, at another river, another Jacob would walk mourning another Rachel. Or who knew, perhaps it was always the same Jacob and the same Rachel.

The forests have not changed since Creation. The peasants seem to predate that event, vestiges of worlds that God made and destroyed before He created Earth. Even the Chmielnicki massacre, though a discrete historical episode, is part of a recurring cycle of persecution. The line of history curves back on itself.

Nothing changes, not even the Jews. Jacob thinks of the first chapter of Isaiah, in which the prophet rejects prayer and sacrifice unaccompanied by human kindness. Like those Jews in Isaiah's time, the Jews of Pilitz observe the easy commandments; they eat kosher food and go to the synagogue. While they discharge their duties to God, however, they ignore their responsibilities to their fellowman. The poor are not cared for properly. Beile Peshe will not assist Wanda in childbirth. The burial society steals Jacob's money.

If the Jews have wandered from the biblical ideal, the Christians have strayed even farther. Jacob notes the distance between Jew and Christian when he visits Pilitzky's castle, where "the very air . . . smelled of violence, idolatry, and concupiscence." The Jews of Pilitz are not vegetarians (Jacob is), but they do not wantonly destroy animals, either. Though they gossip, they do not murder or launch pogroms. Given the choice between victim and victimizer, Singer chooses the former.

Singer also offers another sort of choice, that between types of slavery. On one level, the novel's title refers to Jacob as Jan Bzik's slave. Jacob realizes, though, that "man cannot be entirely free. . . . Man goes in harness, every desire is a strand of the rope that yokes him." Pilitzky owns a village, but he is a slave to his wife, who in turn is such a slave to lust that she hangs herself when one of her lovers abandons her. Waclaw the ferryman believes that he is free, for he lives alone and owns nothing. He has paid a high price for that liberty, though: He refuses to marry and cuts himself off from all ties of family and friendship. If life, if society, is to continue, "somebody must plow and reap. Children must be raised."

Everyone, then, is a slave. Jacob chooses to be God's slave. His master, Bzik, the peasants, Pilitzky, Gershon are slaves, too, slaves to their greed, passions, or fears. Jacob frees himself by surrendering himself to God, while the others, casting off God's yoke, only make tighter chains for themselves.

Singer thus offers choices, for he believes in free will. The world is a motley web: "Next to the poorhouse, in garbage and excrement, grew grass and wildflowers—white blooms, yellow blooms, feathery seed puffs, hairlike green fringes." One may focus on ugliness or on beauty. Jacob tells the well-meaning Reb Leibush Mayer, "One should look for the good in people, not the bad." Like the Bible it so often echoes, *The Slave* offers its readers a choice between spiritual life and death and urges them to choose the former.

Critical Context

Singer has said that writing can rely on words or action; he has always sought to portray deeds. *The Slave* is faithful to this intention, for it is full of adventure and suspense. Will the peasants kill Jacob? Will he and Wanda be reunited? Will the Jews of Pilitz learn Wanda's secret identity? Singer never forgets that one reads a novel first of all for the story.

The Slave also offers many passages of great lyricism: Singer is a master of words as well as of action. When Jacob looks at the night sky, he sees that "the stars looked like letters of the alphabet, vowel points, notes of music." He likens the snow to "fleece and the dust of diamonds." Singer evokes the life of the peasantry and the benighted spirit of seventeenth century Poland.

Beneath this brilliant surface lies a profound metaphysic. Here is the eternal battle between good and evil, the sacred and the diabolical, fate, foreknowledge, and free will. Though he writes from a modernist perspective, Singer nevertheless worries about the salvation of his characters' souls, for he believes in souls, salvation, and damnation. Perhaps even more significant, he makes his reader worry about this issue also. For Singer, God is alive, ruling the world wisely if not mercifully. In later works,

Singer steps back a bit from such optimism, but in *The Slave* he expresses a belief in the triumph of virtue and of man's capacity for redemption. Like the biblical story that the novel retells, narrative serves philosophical and religious ends.

Bibliography
Biletzky, Israel Ch. *God, Jew, Satan in the Works of Isaac Bashevis Singer.* Lanham, Md.: University Press of America, 1995. This critical work examines Singer's novels in light of his major themes, including the oppositions between reality and unreality, belief and doubt, past and present, and order and chaos.
Farrell, Grace, ed. *Critical Essays on Isaac Bashevis Singer.* New York: G. K. Hall, 1996. This collection of critical essays from a variety of prominent scholars presents wide-ranging views on Singer's work. The essays focus on specific novels as well as general themes that run throughout the body of Singer's work, including his treatment of religious belief, his portrayal of women, and his views on male homosexuality. Includes a helpful bibliography and index.
Hadda, Janet. *Isaac Bashevis Singer: A Life.* New York: Oxford University Press, 1997. Hadda takes a detailed look at the cultural and familial influences that shaped Singer's life and work. Written from a psychoanalytic perspective, this portrait examines the impact his parents and siblings had on him, and candidly describes his flaws as well as his charm.
Telushkin, Dvorah. *Master of Dreams: A Memoir of Isaac Bashevis Singer.* New York: Morrow, 1997. A poignant view of Singer's life and work. Drawing from her own diaries tracing both the literary and personal association she shared with Singer, Telushkin's memoir reveals a troubled but brilliant man who is fighting against the physical breakdown that comes with old age. Offers an illuminating perspective on the background of some of Singer's most popular works.
Zamir, Israel. *Journey to My Father: Isaac Bashevis Singer.* New York: Arcade, 1995. Although this book is a memoir and does not offer any critical understanding of Singer's novels, it addresses Singer's belief in ghosts and demons, his curiosity, and love of the Yiddish language, all of which figure prominently in Singer's work.

Joseph Rosenblum

SMALL CHANGES

Author: Marge Piercy (1936-   )
Type of plot: Social criticism
Time of plot: The late 1960's through the early 1970's
Locale: Primarily Boston, but also New York City, Syracuse, Cleveland, and rural
  New Hampshire
First published: 1973

> *Principal characters:*
> BETH WALKER, a young woman who runs away from her oppressive
>   marriage in search of independence and self-awareness
> MIRIAM BERG, an intelligent and sensual woman balancing her need for
>   love with her career as a computer scientist
> PHIL, Miriam's lover and friend, who is a junkie and an aspiring poet
> JACKSON, a lover of Miriam and a friend and roommate of Phil
> NEIL STONE, Miriam's boss, whom she eventually marries
> WANDA ROSARIO, the leader of a women's theater group who becomes
>   Beth's friend and lover

The Novel

The novel's ironic title, *Small Changes*, indicates the nature of the action—small but often significant change taking place in the lives of most of the major characters. Although Piercy provides commentary on almost all the social and political concerns of the 1960's and the 1970's, she parallels the development of the two protagonists, Beth and Miriam, with the similarly erratic and often painful progress of the women's movement.

The novel opens with the marriage of Beth Phail, a shy and seemingly conventional girl, to her high school sweetheart, Jim Walker. What society perceives as a beginning seems a dead end to Beth, so she runs away to find a more independent life in Boston. Although she must take unskilled and unsatisfying jobs, she slowly gains self-confidence and expands her network of friends. One of these friends is Miriam Berg, who eventually gets Beth a job as a keypunch operator at the computer corporation, Logical Systems Development, Inc., where Miriam works as a member of the technical staff.

Piercy then takes the reader back to another beginning in "The Book of Miriam," which recounts Miriam's unhappy childhood in Flatbush, Brooklyn, where she grew up feeling unloved and ugly. At college, however, she loses weight and gains her health. Her new sensuality is revealed and refined by a young poet named Phil, who is delighted to find her a virgin and "sexually, a tabula rasa." Miriam's connection to Phil as her lover, mentor, and best friend lasts throughout the novel. Phil's friend and roommate, Jackson (both men are referred to by only one name), also becomes involved with Miriam, and at one point, the three of them live together in a fascinating but turbulent relationship.

The lives of Beth and Miriam touch and diverge often in the next few years. The third section of the novel, "Both in Turn," sees Beth set back when her husband attempts to force her to return to the marriage she loathed. She runs away again and, after drifting for a while, returns to Boston and the women's commune she has founded there. A divorce is arranged, and she immerses herself in the growing women's movement. Having become briefly involved in a lesbian relationship before her return to Boston, she is confused about her "sexual identity" and remains celibate until she meets Wanda Rosario, the inspirational leader of a women's theater group.

Miriam, meanwhile, has left Phil and Jackson in order to concentrate on her career. At Logical Systems Development, Inc., she meets Neil Stone, a serious, quiet man who is also her immediate supervisor. She marries him, satisfied that finally she has found the love and security for which she has yearned without compromising herself as a professional. Gradually, however, Miriam sees that as a woman, she is not welcome in her technical field; also, she begins to have serious moral reservations about the military applications of her work. Soon she succumbs to her husband's pressure to have a baby, rationalizing that she can complete her doctoral dissertation while she is on maternity leave. Although she does eventually get her degree, the pressures of child rearing, her husband's increasing demands, and her stagnating career take their toll. By the end of the novel, she has lost much of her vigor and intensity. Ironically, just as she resolves to do it all better, a new character is introduced, the other woman. Miriam's husband is preparing to leave her for a woman more willing to please.

The Characters

Miriam Berg and Beth Walker share the protagonist's role in the novel. Piercy painstakingly characterizes both women, allotting each a section in which enough of each woman's adolescence is chronicled to allow the reader to find cause and effect in her family life and class background relative to her adult personality. Piercy's approach to characterizing Beth and Miriam is to derive them from their fictional but representative childhood environment (family life in the United States of the 1950's and the 1960's), which automatically creates conflict, since that environment was essentially hostile to women. The two women's parents share the conventional assumptions about female children, victimizing their daughters by their neglect of the individual in the girl.

Piercy endows both the young Beth and the young Miriam with considerable intellect and insight, which enable them to perceive the repression in their upbringing. Nevertheless, both women undergo a slow and painful process before they even begin to realize the extent of the psychic damage that has been done to them—and, by extension, to most women.

With Beth, Piercy illustrates active progress toward liberation. Beth's development as a character is symbolic of many women's enlightenment and of their slow but

steady growth toward self-love and love of women (not necessarily in lesbian relationships only but also through appreciation of the qualities and strengths of women
in general). Beth leans toward androgyny throughout much of the novel, allowing
Piercy to emphasize the existence of that option, and Beth's eventual connection with
Wanda Rosario in a lesbian relationship evolves from the respect and affection earned
by Wanda long before a sexual relationship develops between the two.

In contrast, Miriam's progress toward self-love and liberation is impeded by her
ongoing relationship with Phil and her even more destructive love for Jackson, Phil's
ascetic and bitter friend. Phil's self-destructiveness combines with Jackson's demands ("she felt as if he demanded all of her, then took only a piece and went away,
that he shut the door leaving her outside still vainly offering herself"), forcing her to
be lover, mother, playmate, and friend to them in order to fulfill their bottomless appetite for her. They sap her of any energy that she might otherwise have turned outward
toward her career or inward for herself. When Miriam does free herself of Phil and
Jackson, her career and her relationships with women flower. She returns to health
and energy only to direct it and drain it once more in the service of love for a man, her
husband, Neil Stone. Miriam, formerly full of intense energy and sensual force,
stalls, drained by the quest for the love that she was taught to believe only a man could
give her.

The characterization in *Small Changes* follows another important principle, the rip-
ple effect. All the characters in the novel represent a network, or web, in which even
the smallest tremor is felt and reacted to by its many constituents. (Piercy chose to title
her 1982 collection of poetry *Circles on the Water: Selected Poems*.) All the characters in *Small Changes* are affected by the changes experienced by Miriam and Beth.
Even the most recalcitrant male, Jackson, ends up pondering the advantages of allowing a self-realized woman into his life. This approach to character and conflict is not
unusual, but when a network of individuals is caught up in profound social change,
such as the women's movement, the predictable personal influence of one character
upon another becomes a means of political activism. It is this combination of the personal and political that distinguishes Piercy's fiction.

Themes and Meanings

Although character development and theme are always closely related, in *Small
Changes* they are intertwined to an unusual degree. Every change and response of a
character is both a contribution to that character's growth and a support for the integration of the personal and political—a central theme of the novel. Piercy's choice of
setting for *Small Changes* also provides a natural vehicle for this theme. The 1960's
and 1970's were a time of social upheaval in America, and the novel illustrates the
personal and political interrelationships of most of the issues that troubled the con-
sciences of the youth of the time: the Vietnam War, the women's movement, academia
versus activism, research versus military applications, alternative life-styles, ecology,
natural foods, drug use, and so on. As the title suggests, the societal impact of some
changes is not necessarily in proportion to the way in which society measures or val-

ues change. When one person refuses to accept an oppressive sex role, she or he has made a measurable contribution to the movement, even if that change is seen as "small" (insignificant) by other members of the society.

Of all the elements of change working on the characters, it is the women's movement which must be considered the central issue of the novel, not because it is inherently more important than war protest or ecology but because, without it, half the population of potential activists would be limited in the extent to which they could commit themselves to any cause. One of many examples of this is Wanda Rosario, who, before meeting Beth Walker, was a significant force in various antiestablishment protests until she married another activist; then she became Joe's wife first and catalyst for social change only in her spare time—her most notable contribution to the revolution being the care of Joe's house and children. In Marge Piercy's view, this is an irony which should arouse anger.

With Beth as disciple, then apostle, of the movement, and Miriam as the precious soul in jeopardy, Piercy has created and taken advantage of many opportunities to raise and argue the issues. The fundamental concerns of equality and respect are often shrouded in their small, but accurate, representations—who cooks, who cleans, who wears the pants in the family. Nevertheless, the struggle, the pain that both Miriam and Beth endure is indicative of how deeply ingrained are assumptions about sex roles. It is repression that is culturally, socially, psychically, spiritually, and physically reinforced in all but the most rarified of environments (specifically Beth's communes in New Hampshire, where, she feels, it is almost possible to forget about the repression that in the rest of the world is "common as Social Security numbers and fillings"). Although the men of the 1960's and the 1970's did not create this repressive order, they are, in the eyes of feminists such as Beth, responsible for perpetuating it. Miriam is less certain of this viewpoint, but ironically her fate confirms the validity of Beth's radical stance.

The alternatives available to women by the end of the novel seem limited by the examples set by the protagonists: a housewife in danger of losing her husband's love or a radical lesbian turned criminal and fugitive in order to live with her lover and her two children as a family. Yet Piercy has not intended these examples to be the only choices; Miriam and Beth represent extremes. They are forced to pay the price that an oppressive society exacts for fighting the status quo or, in Miriam's case, accepting it so miserably. There are several alternatives forming the background to the struggles of Miriam and Beth. They are not all ideal either, but Dorine, a formerly self-hating and servile woman who has found her self-respect in a career and a reasonable lover in a reformed Phil, offers contrived hope for the future of heterosexual relations, and Beth and Wanda's efforts to hold their family together are optimistic and admirable in spite of the circumstances.

While the polemics of feminism rage in the forefront of the novel, the relationships, or, as Piercy calls them throughout the book, the connections between the characters, remain the source of change and therefore of power. As the personal and political merge, active resistance to whatever or whoever is oppressive can take place. Even

Miriam, who is at her weakest and most vulnerable point as the novel closes, feels the strength of "the connections she had somehow preserved through attrition":

> Out of such connections she could weave no security, no protection against her worst fears. But of such connections were wrought an end to the slow relentless dying back she had known and the slow undramatic refounding, single thought by small decision by petty act, of a life: her life.

Critical Context

Small Changes was Marge Piercy's third novel. Her second, *Dance the Eagle to Sleep* (1970), received critical praise as an especially lean and energetic account of political activism. *Small Changes* was termed disappointing by some critics of the time who did not appreciate Piercy's shift from fast-paced revolution to the small, incremental changes of Beth and Miriam. Feminists and the so-called progressive publications, however, hailed the novel as a breakthrough. It chronicles and applauds the changes taking place in women's roles in the 1970's, something that the less radical *The Women's Room* (1977), by Marilyn French, would do again with popular success several years later.

In writing *Small Changes*, Piercy drew on previous feminist literature, notably Virginia Woolf's *A Room of One's Own* (1929), reemphasizing the basic needs of women, such as independence and self-fulfillment, and the solidarity of the movement. Indeed, *Small Changes* is in many senses a classic of the second wave of feminism, and feminist criticism has cited it for its pioneering efforts in the areas of female character development and the inspired interweaving of that which is felt with that which must be done if sexual inequities are ever to be overcome.

Small Changes also develops many of the themes to which Piercy has returned and which she has refined in later novels, such as *Vida* (1980) and *Braided Lives* (1982), and in much of her poetry. Few writers can convey the despair invoked in the modern woman by the "dead ends and broken connections" forced on her by a repressive society as realistically as Piercy does. She has perfected the shock of recognition, so that, while a reader might be able intellectually to disregard or evade the political and social issues which Piercy raises, she or he is compelled to confront such issues on a personal level. For Piercy, who believes that the personal and the political are one and the same, that is a victory.

Bibliography
Piercy, Marge. "A Harsh Day's Light: An Interview with Marge Piercy." Interview by John Rodden. *Kenyon Review* 20 (Spring, 1998): 132-143. Piercy discusses her insistence on the role of politics in poetry, her relationship with other female relatives, and her attempt to write science-fiction novels. Offers interesting insight into her life and work.
_____. "Marge Piercy: A Class Act." Interview by Dawn Gifford. *Off Our Backs* 24 (June, 1994): 14-16. Piercy offers her assessment of the problems faced

by the feminist movement in the United States, stating that she believes that the situation has improved between 1993 and 1994. She discusses works by other authors that most influenced her writing, including those of James Joyce and Simone de Beauvoir.

Shands, Kerstin W. *The Repair of the World: The Novels of Marge Piercy.* Westport, Conn.: Greenwood Press, 1994. Provides biographical information as well as criticism and interpretation of Piercy's novels. Includes bibliographical references and an index. A valuable resource offering a solid overview of Piercy's works.

Blair M. Hancock

THE SMALL ROOM

Author: May Sarton (1912-1995)
Type of plot: Realism
Time of plot: The 1950's
Locale: A New England women's college
First published: 1961

> *Principal characters:*
> LUCY WINTER, a new instructor at Appleton College
> CARRYL COPE, a brilliant medieval history professor
> HARRIET (HALLIE) SUMMERSON, the head of the English department
> JENNIFER FINCH, a professor of mathematics
> OLIVE HUNT, a wealthy trustee
> JANE SEAMAN, a student at Appleton

The Novel

Set on the campus of Appleton College, a small, prestigious New England women's college where scholarship is emphasized, the action of *The Small Room* takes place in one semester. The primary focus is on the faculty, although necessarily a few students play important roles. The tale is told from the point of view of Lucy Winter, a twenty-seven-year-old woman whose broken engagement to a medical student marks a major turning point in her life. Academically well qualified with a doctorate from Harvard, Lucy, not really committed to teaching, is a new appointee to the faculty. Although in the center of activity on a college campus, Lucy feels lonely from time to time.

In the narrative, Lucy relates some of her classroom experiences. She believes that the relationship between professor and student should develop only around course work; for this reason, she refuses to listen to Pippa Brentwood's tales of her recently deceased father. Lucy also sits in on a class taught by Harriet Summerson (Hallie) and is impressed by Hallie's masterful handling of the learning situation. As an educator, Lucy is also a learner.

Lucy is also a learner as she becomes more familiar with Carryl Cope, whose friend Olive Hunt is one of the college trustees. Olive is vehemently opposed to the appointment of a resident psychiatrist to the faculty. Cope, too, appears to be against it, but Lucy suspects that Cope is being influenced by Hunt.

Lucy spends an evening reading compositions written about the *Iliad*. Somewhat depressed because the compositions are bland papers worthy of only mediocre grades, Lucy, to relax before falling asleep, decides to read from *Appleton Essays*, a recent publication that Cope has given her. Her choice of reading material, however, serves only to arouse her, because she is certain that, while preparing to teach the *Iliad*, she has read one of the essays from the Appleton collection in an obscure periodical in the library. On the following day, Lucy locates the source for the essay, which has been plagiarized by a promising Appleton senior, Jane Seaman. She is aware that Appleton policy dictates that plagiarism is cause for dismissal from the college. Wishing that she had not uncovered so flagrant a violation, Lucy goes to Hallie with the evidence, thus setting in motion a process that cannot be stopped. Lucy and Hallie raise difficult questions: What will happen to Jane Seaman? What made her commit this act? And what effect will its revelation have on Carryl Cope, Jane's mentor?

Cope, learning of Jane's deed and assuming some responsibility for her protégée, prevents the involvement of the college judicial bodies. Because the students know what has happened, however, and because Jane is not contrite before them, they are irate. Pippa Brentwood confronts Lucy, and Lucy attempts to show Pippa that Professor Cope believes herself to be responsible, and that Jane's mixed-up family situation and her inability to adjust to college pressures make the easy disposition of the case impossible. Lucy really shows Pippa the heartlessness of automatic judgments based on inflexible moral standards.

The person who suffers in this case is Carryl Cope. She is the one who has had to accept the blame for the sin of omission—not giving her heart to Jane when Jane needed her. Also, the Jane Seaman case is being used by the faculty as a basis for needing a resident psychiatrist, thus leading Olive Hunt to change her will—and forcing Cope to break with her. The price of excellence is enormous; so, too, are the responsibilities of the dedicated professor.

The Characters

Lucy Winter, who becomes involved with campus people and events, has no loyalties and no preconceived likes and dislikes. She also has no philosophy of education, probably because she had not planned to teach and has no prior experience. The fact of Lucy's broken engagement suggests her capacity to love, to give of herself to others. She is respected by many on campus as a confidante, a tower of strength, and a voice of integrity. Lucy's loneliness without her former fiancé does not establish marriage as an ideal; Lucy is simply an individual whose plans had included marriage.

On the other hand, Carryl Cope, the medieval history professor who is recognized as an authority in her field, discreetly has her love affair with Olive Hunt, a wealthy trustee. Cope truly believes that the college is devoted to the pursuit of excellence, and she erroneously thinks that Jane Seaman shares this passion for excellence for its own sake. Although Cope misreads Jane, Cope herself does not waver in her position. She is a professor and a scholar. If Hunt proceeds to withdraw her bequest of millions of dollars and her allegiance to Appleton, she will have to part with Cope, who, although voting against the hiring of a psychiatrist, will remain loyal to her profession and to Appleton. Until the Seaman affair materializes, the diminutive Cope appears to be a giant. She finally admits to Jennifer Finch, a professor of mathematics, that she has been afraid to give love to Jane, for whom love was a basic need. Here, then, is Cope's failure.

Hallie Summerson, head of the English department is an example of the sagacious professor who can lead the students to think and to comprehend. She makes no attempt to impose learning on her classes; instead, she gently inspires and leads the students toward discovery. Hallie is an uncomplicated individual who is able to maintain her own integrity; she expects others to do likewise.

Another professor whose opinions matter is Jennifer Finch. She has a keen, logical mind; she is able to reduce complicated matters to the basic components. Her appearance is unassuming, but she has the respect of her fellow faculty members. She herself, however, defers to her autocratic mother, to whose outrageous demands she regularly submits.

Olive Hunt has had power over Carryl Cope. Hunt introduced Cope to Europe and the pleasures of travel which Cope combines with study. Hunt, growing old, believes that she no longer has much influence over Cope, and she attempts to control Appleton and Cope by threatening to change her will. Hunt recognizes that she is being contrary and stubborn, but she believes that she cannot change her nature.

Themes and Meanings

Sarton, in *The Small Room*, examines the role of the professor in a small New England college. Just what are the duties and responsibilities of the professor? What kind of commitment is necessary? What does this commitment demand of the individual? What is the price of excellence?

Emotions, too, are important. Sarton maintains that emotions show feeling which is an integral part of being alive and effective and happy. The loneliness of the professional woman is understandable, and the loneliness of women professors at Appleton is evident, primarily in Lucy Winter. The others seem to find fulfillment in their work and their interactions with colleagues.

The need for love and concern is not only a need of faculty; it is also a basic need of the student. Cope's seeming indifference to Jane's quiet pleas and Lucy's attempt to ignore Pippa's obvious expressions of need for attention, or love, serve to emphasize that faculty should be concerned about the whole person—not merely the academic needs of the student. That these students are mature individuals becomes clear when the plagiarism case is given to the student council for action. Sarton points out that students, too, can act with wisdom and understanding.

Teaching in a women's college is, according to Cope, a special kind of challenge. She also believes that those individuals who have roots in their work also have roots in life. What happens in the many small rooms at Appleton is relevant to life. In this sense, Appleton is a microcosm of the world.

Critical Context

The early novels of May Sarton were set in Europe or the British Isles, with her second novel being set in Belgium, the land of her birth. These novels reflect her interest in the impact of the Old World on the New. Some of the themes which Sarton continues to develop in her writing are apparent in these early books. How love, suffering, marriage, and family affect the individual are critical points for study in her fiction.

Beginning with *Faithful Are the Wounds* (1955), Sarton turned increasingly to New

England as a setting for her fiction. This academic novel centers on Edward Cavan, a professor of American literature who commits suicide. (Cavan was based in part on the distinguished scholar and Harvard professor F. O. Matthiessen, who committed suicide in 1950.) Loneliness and the cost of repressed emotion are important themes developed in this work, and they are important in *The Small Room* as well, the second book in which Sarton makes use of the academic world.

Frequently Sarton uses intelligent professional women as central characters in her fiction. In *The Small Room*, the main characters are women whose struggles in the academic world are treated with dignity and understanding. Of this book, Virgilia Petersen says, "a more eloquent appraisal of teaching it would be hard to find." Sarton, who did not attend college, draws upon her experiences teaching in such institutions as Harvard and Wellesley, where she had the opportunity to observe campus politics and to question the price of excellence.

The lesbian affair in *The Small Room* is very muted and delicately presented. Later works by Sarton, including *The Magnificent Spinster* (1985), are more forthright in this respect, although they remain restrained in comparison to many novels of the 1970's and 1980's. Conflict in marriage, which is a minor theme in *The Small Room*, is developed into a destructive force to the thinking and/or the professional woman in *Crucial Conversations* (1975) and *Anger* (1982): Sarton frequently suggests that marriage can stifle the growth of the individual.

Indeed, most of the basic themes of Sarton's work can be found in *The Small Room*, making it a seminal work. Some ideas are fully explored in this novel while others are only suggested. Sarton's novels, like those of Willa Cather, are simple on the surface, but actually quite complex. The intensity with which Sarton's characters react to events and to one another is also a distinguishing feature of her poetry, another genre in which she has published extensively.

Bibliography
Bloin, L. P. *May Sarton: A Bibliography*. Metuchen, N.J.: Scarecrow Press, 1978. In two parts, the first listing Sarton's poetry, novels, nonfiction, essays, and articles. The second part lists secondary sources, including book reviews. A conscientious compilation of sources that is most useful to the Sarton scholar. The author acknowledges Sarton's assistance in putting together this work.
Curley, Dorothy N., Maurice Kramer, and Elaine F. Kramer, eds. *Modern American Literature*. 4 vols. 4th ed. New York: Ungar, 1969-1976. A collection of reviews and criticisms of Sarton's poems and novels, the latest entry being 1967. Includes criticism on *Mrs. Stevens Hears the Mermaids Singing*, considered an important book and which the author says was most difficult to write. The supplement has reviews on Sarton's *Collected Poems*.
Evans, Elizabeth. *May Sarton*. Rev. ed. Boston: Twayne, 1989. In this volume in Twayne's United States Authors series, Evans upholds Sarton as a writer who speaks for women, insisting they claim their own identity; hence, her increasing popularity among feminists. An interesting addition to this somewhat standard crit-

icism is an appendix of letters of Sarton's to her editor while writing *Mrs. Stevens Hears the Mermaids Singing*. Selected bibliography.

Grumbach, Doris. "The Long Solitude of May Sarton." *The New Republic* 170 (June 8, 1974): 31-32. Grumbach draws together Sarton's philosophy, in particular the serenity of her writing in the face of her declared "traumas." Noting that critics have often ignored Sarton, Grumbach says: "Hers has been a durable fire . . . her small room seems to make most male critics uncomfortable." An article well worth reading.

Peters, Margot. *May Sarton: A Biography*. New York: Knopf, 1997. The first full-length biographical treatment of this most autobiographical of writers. After her death in 1995, there was an upsurge of interest in Sarton, and this book certainly contributes to her legacy. Peters herself is fair in her assessment of Sarton: clear about why this woman inspired such a devoted following among readers and equally straightforward about her uncertainty concerning the literary value of much of Sarton's work.

Sibley, Agnes. *May Sarton*. New York: Twayne, 1972. Obviously a must for criticism on Sarton, because there is so little of book-length size written about her—despite her prodigious output. This study discusses Sarton's poems, from *Encounter in April* in 1937 to *A Durable Fire*, published in 1972. Sibley has grouped novels under two themes that she considers relevant to Sarton: "detachment" for the early novels and "communion" for the later ones.

Virginia A. Duck

SO FAR FROM GOD

Author: Ana Castillo (1953-   )
Type of plot: Impressionistic realism
Time of plot: The 1970's to the 1990's
Locale: Tome, a small town in New Mexico
First published: 1993

> *Principal characters:*
>> SOFIA, a family matriarch who struggles to rear her four extraordinary
>> daughters alone
>> ESPERANZA, Sofia's eldest daughter, a former campus radical turned
>> successful television journalist
>> CARIDAD, the second and most beautiful daughter, a hospital orderly
>> whose failed marriage leads her into a self-destructive lifestyle
>> FE, the third daughter, whose preoccupation with appearances and
>> securing the good life leads her to reject her family
>> LA LOCA, Sofia's youngest daughter, gifted with supernatural abilities
>> following her resurrection at age three
>> DOMINGO, Sofia's wayward husband, a compulsive gambler whose
>> inability to change dooms his marriage
>> THE NARRATOR, one of Sofia's *compadres* or *comadres*, an opinionated
>> storyteller who narrates, judges, and interprets the events in the
>> novel

The Novel

Medieval Christian mythology transformed the story of Sofia, the Greek goddess of wisdom, into the inspirational story of a heroic mother and her martyred daughters. *So Far from God* is Ana Castillo's modern reinterpretation of the lives and struggles of Sofia and her four daughters, Esperanza, Caridad, Fe, and La Loca. Set in contemporary New Mexico, the novel chronicles how this family, its neighbors, and their community confront and essentially prevail over the obstacles of racism, poverty, exploitation, environmental pollution, and war. The novel, covering two decades in the family's lives, unfolds through a series of flashbacks woven into the central narrative. Blending ironic humor with scathing social commentary, the novel is told from the perspective of a highly opinionated, omniscient third-person narrator.

Beginning with a flashback to the mysterious death and equally mysterious resurrection—*El Milagro*—of La Loca at age three, the narrative quickly shatters any boundaries between the real and the unreal, the natural and the supernatural. La Loca's miraculous resurrection and ascension to a church rooftop elevates the child to the status of folk saint. Left with an aversion to people, La Loca withdraws from the world and devotes her life to prayer and to the spiritual care of her family.

From this flashback, the novel moves into the more recent past as the narrator details the stories of Sofia and her daughters. Like their mother, Sofia's three older daughters have painful, failed relationships. While at college, Esperanza, a college activist, lived with her activist boyfriend, Ruben, who upon graduation elected to trade his Chicano cosmic consciousness for a *gabacha* (a white woman) with a Corvette. The most sensible of Sofia's children, Esperanza turns her failed relationship into the catalyst for an advanced degree and a successful journalistic career. Esperanza's younger sister Caridad also experiences problems in her marriage to her unfaithful high-school sweetheart, Memo. Rather than use that failure, the self-destructive Caridad resorts to alcohol and nightly anonymous sex to deal with the rejection.

Unlike her two older sisters, who seem doomed to failed relationships, Fe, the third daughter, appears fine until she receives a letter breaking off her engagement. Unable to cope with this loss, Fe suffers a nervous breakdown, and only a miracle eventually restores her. Before that miracle, Sofia, Esperanza, and La Loca have to deal with yet another crisis—the vicious attack, horrible mutilation, and near death of Caridad. The simultaneous miraculous restoration of Caridad and cure of Fe trigger a series of changes in the family. Following the incident, Domingo, the girls' wayward father, reappears and tentatively resumes his life with Sofia; Esperanza accepts a dangerous assignment to cover the Persian Gulf War; Caridad—now gifted with foresight and prophecy—moves out and apprentices herself to doña Felicia, an eccentric *curandera*, or witch woman; Fe also moves out and resumes her job at the bank. La Loca remains at home and prays.

While covering the war, Esperanza and her news crew disappear and are presumed captured in Saudi Arabia. Her unknown fate becomes the focal point for both her family and the media community until La Loca informs her mother that Esperanza has been killed. Without the attendant news coverage, Caridad also undergoes a profound, life-changing encounter: Accompanying doña Felicia on her yearly pilgrimage to Chimayo, Caridad falls in love with Esmeralda, a mysterious woman. Unsure how to deal with the effect of Esmeralda and with her renewed emotions, Caridad also disappears. The fate of Sofia's missing daughters is partially resolved when Caridad is discovered exiled in the desert. For a time following her return, Caridad is regarded as a local folk saint. Although severely tested by the fates that have befallen her daughters, Sofia, who continues to believe in the power of faith and in the principles of social change advocated by her war-hero daughter, decides to run for mayor of Tome. Protected from the world in the cocoon of her mother's *rancheria*, La Loca continues to pray.

Fe appears close to achieving her quest for the American Dream in her marriage to her cousin Casimiro. The epitome of middle-class consumer utopia—complete with a three-bedroom, two-car-garage tract home and new sedan—deteriorates into a horrid nightmare. In order to afford the amenities of the good life, Fe quits her dead-end job at the bank and takes a job with a mysterious chemical company; the result is her slow, excruciating death from toxic poisoning. While her sisters have been victims of misguided social policies, Caridad becomes the victim of the misguided obsession of one man, Francisco el Penitente. Viewing Caridad as his God-chosen mate, Francisco begins to stalk her. Completely unbalanced after he uncovers Caridad's friendship with Esmeralda, Francisco abducts and rapes Esmeralda. When he continues to stalk them, the women commit suicide by leaping from a cliff.

The final tragedy which Sofia must face is the death of her youngest daughter, La Loca, from acquired immune deficiency syndrome (AIDS). Facing death as she had lived, with courage and acceptance, La Loca, once again elevated to the status of saint, becomes the patron of her community. Rather than end tragically, the novel returns to the themes of survival, endurance, and heroic triumph in Sofia's founding of M.O.M.A.S., an eccentric organization for the mothers of martyrs and saints.

The Characters

Esperanza, the least developed of the main characters, is presented in the role of surrogate caregiver and stabilizing influence in the family. Representative of many modern women who recognize the difficulty of maintaining both a career and a meaningful relationship, Esperanza is a successful journalist struggling to reconcile her personal needs, her political beliefs, and her professional responsibilities. The most politically active of the daughters, Esperanza functions as the novel's social conscience. Her death while covering the Persian Gulf War transforms her into a heroic symbol of outrage at death without dignity. Esperanza is both a martyr to and a symbol of the consequences of the United States' misguided foreign policies.

Presented as the passive victim of an unfaithful husband, Caridad resorts to nightly drinking and anonymous sex to deal with her failed marriage. Her mutilation, restoration, and exile are all simply preludes to her ultimate discovery that "falling in love . . . now that was something else altogether." Caridad comes to embody the redeeming power of love as she voluntarily sacrifices herself for another. The principal thematic elements—the blurring of the lines between the mythic and the everyday, and the transforming power of heroism and love—come together in the final, simultaneously selfless and self-affirming act of Caridad and Esmeralda.

Initially the least sympathetic of the four daughters, Fe is also the most unlikely heroine. Superficial, distant, and immature, Fe is anxious to get out of Tome and to get away from her family. She is eager to disassociate herself from Chicano culture and to align herself with the dominant culture's values and beliefs. The hardships that Fe must face function as rites of passage that help her evolve beyond this psychological immaturity to the courage of self-responsibility and assurance. In the process of facing her own mortality, Fe develops into an assertive, independent, compassionate woman. Like Esperanza, Fe is also a martyr and a symbol; her death is a warning against the effects of racist environmental policies.

Woven into the narrative is the story of the miraculous life of Sofia's youngest daughter. Perceived by others as retarded, mentally ill, or soulless, La Loca is the spiritual center of her family and later the patron saint of her community. Defined by the tragedies and triumphs of her family, La Loca lives without fear, fully aware of the choices she has made in life. From La Loca, the reader sees that life is to be lived with courage and wisdom, with dignity and joy, with an appreciation of its mystery.

Throughout the novel, Sofia endures and triumphs over tragedy. Sofia's heroism is seen in her repeated efforts to understand; rather than fall victim to despair, she reaches into the depths of her spirit and her faith to prevail over the obstacles that confront her. Sofia represents the heroic qualities of *hispano* women—strong, courageous, resilient women who not only survive adversity but who also prevail, endure, and pass their strength and determination on to their children and communities.

Domingo, of the Clark Gable mustache and piercing eyes, is at once the love of Sofia's life and the source of her greatest heartache. Initially the family, the community, and the reader believe that Domingo abandoned Sofia and the girls. Only later, when, after his unexplained return, he gambles away the land and the house, does Sofia "remember" that she had thrown him out.

Themes and Meanings

So Far from God, a complex, multidimensional novel, blends elements of New Mexican mythology, Pueblo stories, and European Catholicism with home remedies, recipes, and Castillo's bitingly sardonic humor to tell the story of a remarkable family. The subtext of the novel examines the brutal poverty and discrimination faced by hispanic and indigenous peoples in the Southwest.

The novel is a probing critique of the racism, sexism, and materialism of American society in general and of social institutions such as the government, the church, and large corporations in particular. Woven into the narrative is a pointed examination of such contemporary issues as political oppression, economic exploitation, and environmental pollution. One of the novel's main thematic focuses is environmental racism and the lack of protection afforded to minorities and the poor by the policies and agencies intended to safeguard them. The powerfully poetic chapter 15 juxtaposes brutal sociopolitical realities with the deep religious feelings of people making a Way of the Cross procession, presenting a catalog of social and environmental ills: minority families living below the poverty level, growing unemployment, deaths from toxic poisoning, radioactive dumping on reservations, birth defects and cancers linked to uranium contamination. The critique is not limited to sociopolitical issues, for the narrative also examines the problems of socially defined sex roles, sexuality, and women's struggle for self-respect. Throughout the novel, women strive to define themselves outside restrictive, socially acceptable roles: Esperanza struggles to succeed in a typically male-dominated profession; Caridad struggles to reconcile her feelings for Esmeralda with her internalized expectations; Sofia struggles to keep her family together and her faith intact in the face of repeated challenges and tragedies.

The novel is also about interpersonal and family relationships; about loyalty, honesty, compassion, and love as the basis for successful relationships. A compulsive gambler who cannot control his addiction, Domingo nevertheless loves Sofia and his daughters; a victim of *susto* (shock) who cannot commit to a relationship, Tom clearly loves Fe; a nearly textbook-perfect *machista* (male chauvinist) who refuses to admit his feeling and vulnerabilities, Ruben finally realizes that he truly loves Esperanza. Although the men love the women, their relationships fail because they lack mutual respect, loyalty, and compassion. Yet, it is these very qualities that form the basis of the women's relationships with one another. Even Fe, who is originally estranged from her family, grows to appreciate the importance of compassion and acceptance.

Castillo's novel is also a powerful study of personal heroism, of honor, courage, and determination. *So Far from God* is a remarkable celebration of survival with dignity and joy. The power of the novel lies in the women's ability not only to survive adversity but also to triumph over it. In the midst of death and tragedy, Castillo affirms life and the human will that sustains it. Refusing to give into despair, the women discover that within themselves they have the power and the vision—both spiritual and political—of the saints they love.

Critical Context

So Far from God is Ana Castillo's third novel. The book's favorable reception by critics and public alike secured her place among the writers at the forefront of the wave of Chicana fiction that came to mainstream consciousness in the late 1980's and 1990's. The novel's publication marked the author's move from small presses to larger publishing houses.

In the novel, Castillo successfully continues the experimentation with literary techniques that characterized her previous novels, *The Mixquiahuala Letters* (1986), which received the American Book Award in 1987, and *Sapogonia* (1990). In *So Far from God*, Castillo uses a distinctive participating narrator, flashbacks, introspective asides, and digressions from the central narrative to create a rich, complex, mythic tale.

Internationally recognized as a poet, novelist, essayist, and translator, Castillo started as a "protest poet" and continues to explore the issues—racism, sexism, oppression, inequality—to which she first gave voice in her poems. In *So Far from God*, she also continues to explore the feminist themes that have been recognized as central not only to her other two novels but to her poetry and nonfiction as well.

Bibliography

Castillo, Ana. "A Conversation with Ana Castillo." Interview by Elsa Saeta. *Texas College English* 26 (Fall, 1993): 1-6. In this interview, Castillo discusses her development as a writer, her literary influences, and her philosophical perspectives. Helps to place Castillo's work in context by providing insights into the personal, philosophical, and political concerns that define her work.

_____. "Massacre of the Dreamers—Reflections on Mexican-Indian Women in the U.S.: Five Hundred Years After the Conquest." In *Critical Fictions: The Politics of Imaginative Writing*, edited by Philomena Mariani. Seattle: Bay Press, 1991. In this critical essay, Castillo discusses some of the theoretical perspectives that influence her work. Castillo defines her poetics and examines Chicana writers' relationship to their culture, their language, and their history.

_____. A MELUS Interview: Ana Castillo, by Elsa Saeta. *MELUS* 22 (Fall, 1997): 133-149. In this extended conversation, Castillo discusses her writings, particularly the feminist perspective of her novels, and provides information about her career. The interviewer calls her "one of the most articulate, powerful voices in contemporary Chicana literature."

Delgadillo, Theresa. "Forms of Chicana Feminist Resistance: Hybrid Spirituality in Ana Castillo's *So Far from God.*" *Modern Fiction Studies* 44 (Winter, 1998): 888-889. Explores Castillo's characterization of Chicanas as a group of passive people who become victims of oppression and a patriarchal church, and their eventual emergence from subjugation.

Kingsolver, Barbara. "Desert Heat." *Los Angeles Times Book Review*, May 16, 1993, pp. 1, 9. Kingsolver's review suggests that the novel could be "the offspring of a union between *One Hundred Years of Solitude* and *General Hospital*: a sassy, magical, melodramatic . . . delightful novel." Kingsolver discusses the novel's strengths specifically: the characters and their development, the narrative voice, and Castillo's venture into North American Magical Realism.

Lanza, Carmela D. "Hearing the Voices: Women and Home and Ana Castillo's *So Far from God.*" *MELUS* 23 (Spring, 1998): 65-79. Lanza'e essay compares Castillo's book to Louisa May Alcott's *Little Women*, identifying *So Far from God* as a "postmodern inversion" of Alcott's novel. Both novels deal with the relationships between four sisters, but Castillo's book is "infused with political resistance" where women of color have an opportunity to grow spiritually and politically.

Walter, Roland. "The Cultural Politics of Dislocation and Relocation in the Novels of Ana Castillo." *MELUS* 23 (Spring, 1998): 81-97. Walter addresses the politics of dislocation and relocation as a "key aspect of interacting social and cultural practices and ideological discourses" in Castillo's novels.

Elsa Saeta

A SOLDIER OF THE GREAT WAR

Author: Mark Helprin (1947-   )
Type of plot: Bildungsroman
Time of plot: 1899-1964
Locale: Primarily Italy
First published: 1991

Principal characters:
> ALLESANDRO GIULIANI, a professor of aesthetics
> NICOLO SAMBUCCA, a young factory worker
> SIGNORE GIULIANI, Allesandro's father, an attorney
> LUCIANA GIULIANI, Allesandro's sister
> RAFI FOA, a friend of Allesandro, Luciana's fiancé
> GUARIGLIA, a harness-maker
> ORFEO QUATTA, a copier in Signore Giuliani's office who later works
>   in the defense ministry
> ARIANE, Allesandro's wife, a nurse

The Novel

Mark Helprin's *A Soldier of the Great War* relates, through a long flashback, the early manhood of Allesandro Giuliani, particularly his life during World War I. Told in the third person, the narrative begins in 1964. Allesandro is journeying by streetcar from Rome to visit his granddaughter's family. A young factory worker, Nicolo Sambucca, futilely chases the car in an attempt to board. Allesandro demands that it be stopped. Refused reentry by the driver, Allesandro decides that he and Nicolo will walk the seventy kilometers to their respective destinations. They have little in common. Allesandro, from an old and successful Roman family—his father was an attorney—is a professor of aesthetics. Nicolo, a helper in a factory, is young, naïve, and uneducated. During their walk, Allesandro relates the crucial events of his life, centering on the years of World War I.

Life is idyllic for Allesandro before the war, centering on his family and their home in Rome. One evening, he hears singing in the garden of the French Academy. Entering, he sees three young girls. The youngest, at sixteen, and the most beautiful, is Ariane. He also saves the life of a fellow university student, Rafi Foa, who had been harassed because he is a Jew. Afterward, Allesandro introduces him to his passion for mountain climbing.

In the autumn of 1914, while millions of men are marching to war and death, Allesandro travels to Munich to view Raphael's portrait of Bindo Altoviti, a painting that had survived time; Allesandro comments that "he knew from Bindo Altoviti's brave and insolent expression that he was going to stay alive forever." There Allesandro first hears the thundering cannons of war. To avoid the carnage of the infantry, Allesandro joins the navy; instead of escaping the front, however, he is assigned as a river guard in the mountains he knows so well.

It is there that he meets Guariglia, a Roman harness-maker. Although unsympathetic to the war aims of his country—or any political or economic ideology—Allesandro becomes an excellent soldier. Later, he and Guariglia are transferred to Sicily to search for deserters. In the interim, Allesandro visits Venice, where he sees Giorgione's *La Tempesta*, a painting of a woman, a baby, a male figure that Allesandro believes to be a soldier, and an approaching storm. Paradoxically, while taking the captured deserters back to trial and execution, Allesandro and Guariglia desert. Allesandro returns to Rome, where his father is dying.

Hoping to get the medicine that might save his father, Allesandro turns to Orfeo Quatta, a copier of documents in Signore Giuliani's office before the war who is presently working in the defense ministry. Orfeo, who believes that the secret to the universe is the "blessed sap," initially seems merely madly eccentric. Then, however, he confides that he is directing the Italian war effort through his documents and that he has often reversed the orders of his superiors. It was he who had assigned Allesandro to the front lines, supposedly to protect him. Orfeo has become a demented *deus ex machina* to millions. He provides the medicine, but it does not help. Allesandro is arrested and sent to a military prison for eventual execution. At the last moment, he is reprieved thanks to Orfeo's intervention. He tries to give his life for Guariglia's because of the latter's children, but he is clubbed into unconsciousness.

Returning to battle, Allesandro is injured. He is cared for by a nurse who turns out to be Ariane, the girl from prewar days, and they fall in love. Ariane becomes pregnant, but as a recovered Allesandro marches again to war, an Austrian plane destroys the hospital. Back in the mountains, Allesandro retrieves Rafi's body from a cliff in the face of enemy fire and is captured. A prisoner in Vienna at the end of the war, Allesandro flees to Munich to kill the pilot who bombed Ariane's hospital, but he changes his mind because of the pilot's young child. There, he again sees Raphael's painting of Bindo Altoviti, taking consolation from the portrait that nothing is ever lost: All can be remembered, even Ariane.

After the war, with his father dead and his sister having emigrated, Allesandro becomes a gardener. Again he visits Venice to see *La Tempesta*, which he believes should have been the story of his life—a woman and child waiting for a soldier returning from war. The guard mentions that a woman with a baby had recently cried when she viewed the painting. Hoping it could be Ariane, Allesandro finally discovers his son sailing a toy boat in Rome.

The narrative returns to 1964, to the old Allesandro and the young Nicolo. Allesandro relates his life with Ariane, who had since died, and their son, who had been killed in World War II. At the end of their long walk, Allesandro feels death approaching. Dismissing Nicolo, he descends into a valley, recollecting again his life and art.

The Characters

Allesandro Giuliani dominates the novel, since it is his life he relates to Nicolo. Although a professor of aesthetics, Allesandro is not a typical academic. He rejects the traditional critical approach, claiming that critics "parse by intellect alone works that are great solely because of the spirit." Drawn to art, Raphael's portrait of Bindo Altoviti and Giorgione's *La Tempesta* help illuminate his life. So, too, does nature—the seas, skies, and mountains. As a counterpoint, war also has its lures; as in everything else, Allesandro excels on the battlefield. Opposed to the twentieth century "isms" of communism, fascism, and nationalism, Allesandro's polestars are love and beauty.

The rest of the characters revolve around Allesandro, satellites to his world. Signore Giuliani, his father, is the great influence on Allesandro's life—his mother is almost absent from Allesandro's story—but he is a shadowy and somewhat symbolic figure who represents family, love, and stability in a universe torn by war. Luciana, Allesandro's sister, also remains a secondary figure; she too is an undeveloped character, of greater importance to Allesandro than to the reader.

Even Ariane remains obscure. When they meet in the hospital, she literally sits in the shadows, remaining nameless. She becomes the great love of Allesandro's life, and he seeks her in both art and life until he finds her. Yet the reader is left with little knowledge of Ariane except through Allesandro's own words and feelings, which illumine him but not her.

Nicolo, young, innocent, and uneducated, is an antithesis to Allesandro. Allesandro treats Nicolo as a professor might approach a student: imparting knowledge and wisdom and hoping that the lesson will have effect. In turn, Nicolo validates Allesandro's life, not only because he listens to the story but also because he will live into the future. Nicolo, because of his youth and innocence, is still malleable, and nothing is lost that can be remembered.

Guariglia is also Allesandro's antithesis. Guariglia is unattractive and uneducated; he works with his hands, not his head. Yet the furnace of war unites them in the same manner as the later walk unites Allesandro and Nicolo. Beauty is more than appearance, and Guariglia is sanctified by his love for his family.

Other than Allesandro, the most notable character is also the most fantastic: Orfeo Quatta. A repulsive dwarf who could populate the pages of Charles Dickens, Orfeo is mad. Convinced of the reality of the "blessed sap" and fearing that the advent of the typewriter will lead to civilization's demise, Orfeo at first seems a harmless eccentric. In the insanity of war, however, Orfeo's dementia takes a sinister turn; his is the perverse hand on the levers of power. Orfeo wants Allesandro to live—he transfers Allesandro to the front instead of allowing him to drown on a naval ship, and he aborts Allesandro's execution—but his megalomania and irrationality are a paradigm of the war itself. In the end, however, even he is a minor figure. It is Allesandro who is at the center of the novel's universe.

Themes and Meanings

"'I was born to be a soldier,' Allesandro said, 'but love pulled me back.'" For Allesandro, love and beauty are the essences of life, and one of the most obvious themes in Helprin's novel is its contrast of the beauty of art and nature and the love of family and friends with the evil, madness, and anarchy of war. Yet these polarities are also inseparable. Love comes with carnage and death: Ariane and Allesandro find each other in the darkness of a military hospital, and as he is about to be executed as a deserter, Guariglia's last words are "God keep my children." Allesandro's interpretation of Giorgione's *La Tempesta* conjoins the soldier, storm, woman, and child as a unity. On the night before he is to be executed, Allesandro, looking out his prison window, is overcome with the starlight, and his heart rises in response. After he leaves Nicolo, Allesandro's last sight is of a flight of swallows, "the unification of risk and hope," slaughtered in mid-flight by a hunter.

Love and beauty are not merely transcendent, they are redemptive. In prison in Vienna at the war's end, Allesandro is confronted by several socialists and anarchists who ask him if he believes in God. He replies that he does, since both nature and art affirm God's reality, but he denies that God's existence can be proved by reason; thus, he explains, he never followed the formalities of organized religion. He expects no afterlife, but he says that "I love God nonetheless, with every atom of my being, and will love Him until I fall into black oblivion." Still, Bindo Altoviti's portrait suggests that art can be eternal, and Allesandro's plaintive and hopeful last words are addressed to God: "I beg of you only one thing. Let me join the ones I love. Carry me to them, unite me with them, let me see them, let me touch them."

Allesandro's life consists of many journeys: from Rome with Nicolo at the end of the novel and his life, from the Edenic days of peace to the mayhem of war, from innocent youth to experienced old age, from the life of the many to the inevitable death of all, from this life to whatever might await after death. *A Soldier of the Great War* is thus a *Bildungsroman*, as Allesandro and his world receive a bloody education in the eternal necessity of morals and values in a twentieth century society seemingly dedicated to their eradication.

Helprin asks the great questions about goodness, beauty, and love in a world of madness and chaos. Allesandro can be compared with Voltaire's Candide: Allesandro's is not the best of all possible worlds, and after the war is over, he accepts employment cultivating his own family's former garden. Like Voltaire, Helprin can be ironic and satirical with many of his characters and their actions, but there is also a profound seriousness in his commitment to the realities of love and beauty. There are risks for a writer taking this path, but Helprin's brilliant use of language allows his themes to soar above the level of cliché and banality.

Critical Context

A Soldier of the Great War was Mark Helprin's third novel, following *Refiner's Fire* (1977) and *Winter's Tale* (1983). He has also published many short stories and has written for children. Many years in the writing, *A Soldier of the Great War* is the most ambitious of Helprin's works. A serious author who has attained best-seller status, he claims that he is basically a teller of tales who eschews the modernist literary concerns of introspection and alienation in his characters.

Helprin's first novel, *Refiner's Fire*, also uses the flashback technique, recounting the picaresque adventures of a widely traveled Israeli soldier who has been mortally injured in the Yom Kippur War of 1973. *Winter's Tale*, Helprin's second novel, is a surrealistic fantasy that relates the lives and adventures of a number of characters, including a horse who flies, in an idealized New York City. Popular with readers, the book received mixed reviews from critics. Helprin's father, to whom Helprin was very close and who died in 1984, suggested that he make his next work more realistic. As Helprin has noted, in contrast to the previous novel, there is "nothing that violates the laws of physics" in *A Soldier of the Great War*. It too became a best-seller.

All Helprin's novels have in common the struggle against mortality. In *Refiner's Fire*, Marshall Pearl, although apparently dying, exhibits the will to live as he rises from his bed. The same battle and victory is true of many of the characters in *Winter's Tale*. Although many characters physically die in *A Soldier of the Great War*, the spiritual, through art, beauty, and love, can and will endure. At times out of step with much of modern literature, Helprin's works are life-affirming, humanistic tales of heroic adventures.

Bibliography
Eder, Richard. "Radiance Is in the Details." *Los Angeles Times Book Review*, May 5, 1991, p. 2. Praises the novel for its magical radiance, which "claps together comedy and sudden beauty . . . as a gateway not to skepticism but to wonder." Argues that the battle scenes are less successful, however, for they are merely realistic and have been done before.
Edwards, Thomas R. "Adventurers." *The New York Review of Books* 38 (August 15, 1991): 43-44. Suggests that Helprin's novel may be part of a new literary trend, reacting against certain current expectations in art and life. States that the work exhibits a disillusionment with secular explanations but at times becomes portentous and abstract.
Keneally, Thomas. "Of War and Memory." *The New York Times Book Review*, May 5, 1991, p. 1. Keneally admires Helprin for asking the big questions and notes that the author's answers are sometimes banal but often illuminating. Keneally suggests that Anton Chekhov would have hated Helprin's work, but he points out that Chekhov disliked Fyodor Dostoevski's concern with God's mysteries.
Linville, James. "The Art of Fiction." *The Paris Review* 35 (Spring, 1993): 160-199. A revealing interview that examines Helprin's obsession with privacy, his reactions to criticisms of his work, the influence his military career has had on his writing, and his desire to convey beauty through his work.
Solotaroff, Ted. "A Soldier's Tale." *The Nation* 252 (June 10, 1991): 776-781. Noting that the tension in the novel is between the glory of war and its horror, Solotaroff finds Helprin's account more lyrical than dramatic. For Helprin to be a great novelist, Solotaroff argues, he must become less facile.
Steinberg, Sybil. "A Soldier of the Great War." *Publishers Weekly* 238 (March 8, 1991): 68. A brief but complimentary review that praises Helprin's ability to "create vivid settings; magnificent landscapes teeming with activity and colored by ex-

tremes of weather, illuminated with the clarity of a classical painting."
Wade, Alan. "The Exquisite Lightness of Helprin." *The New Leader* 74 (August 12,
    1991): 19-20. Calling the work a marvelous fairy tale for adults, Wade claims that
    Helprin is the "most gifted American novelist of his generation." His gift, Wade
    says, is in creating great adventures, not complex characters or literary realism.

Eugene Larson

SOLDIERS' PAY

Author: William Faulkner (1897-1962)
Type of plot: Impressionistic realism
Time of plot: April and May, 1919
Locale: Charlestown, Georgia
First published: 1926

>*Principal characters:*
>>DONALD MAHON, the central character, a young, wounded, and dying
>>flyer, engaged to Cecily Saunders
>>JULIAN LOWE, a young air cadet whose desire for martial glory is
>>frustrated by the Armistice
>>JOE GILLIGAN, age thirty-two, a demobilized soldier who becomes
>>Donald Mahon's guardian
>>MARGARET POWERS, the novel's moral center, a young war widow who
>>nurses and later marries Donald Mahon
>>JOSEPH MAHON, the Rector, Donald's father, an Episcopalian priest
>>who has lost his faith in God but who clings to the illusion of his
>>son's recovery
>>JANUARIUS JONES, a fat, satyrlike, slightly androgynous Latin teacher,
>>who pursues the principal females
>>CECILY SAUNDERS, nymphlike, self-centered, and flirtatious; she is
>>engaged to Donald, the war hero, but elopes with George Farr
>>GEORGE FARR, a young man whose jealous love for Cecily is a constant
>>agony
>>EMMY, the housekeeper at the rectory, Donald's former lover, finally
>>bedded by Jones

The Novel

A work of literary modernism influenced by T. S. Eliot's *The Waste Land* (1922),
William Faulkner's first novel, *Soldiers' Pay*, brings "the lost generation" to Faulkner's native ground. In describing the impact upon a small Southern town of the return
and slow death of an aviator horribly wounded in World War I, the novel re-creates the
mood of disillusionment, deflation, and spiritual malaise which was prevalent in postwar American society and art. Eliotic despair is substantially countered, however, by
Faulkner's insistence, often in rich, poetic prose, on natural cycles of renewal, on the
essential decency, strength, and humanity of the principal characters, and on the faith
and integrity of the blacks who have remained impervious to white society's spiritual
alienation.

The novel opens with an ironic epigraph taken from an "Old Play (about 19-?)," a
fragment of dialogue about shaving between Achilles and Mercury cast as sergeant
and cadet. The scene is a graphic undercutting of the heroic mood and an effective in-

troduction to Joe Gilligan and Julian Lowe, a demobilized soldier and a young air cadet, respectively, whose opportunity for martial glory has been "cruelly" thwarted by fate: The Armistice had been declared before they could reach the Western Front. On a train heading south from Buffalo, they give vent to their frustration in drunkenness, dramatizing their essential isolation while casting themselves as "lost foreigners" in a "foreign land."

Into this histrionic scene enters Donald Mahon, a young pilot with a ghastly scar across his brow. He is a symbol of the physical and psychic wounds inflicted by the war, while serving as a focal point of the characters who project onto him their unrealized aspirations. For Lowe, Mahon is the epitome of glamour and heroism, a dying pilot whose wings suggest both angelic martyrdom and, unconsciously, sexual achievement. "Had I been old enough or lucky enough, this might have been me," Lowe thinks jealously. Yet the novel soon moves beyond Lowe's adolescent romanticism (and, appropriately, he disappears after chapter 1, persuaded by Margaret Powers to return home—he reappears only through his semiliterate love letters to her) in order to explore the real costs of war, suffered by the soldiers and noncombatants alike.

If Mahon represents the wounded, dead, and dying soldiers, Margaret Powers, whom Gilligan and Lowe meet on the train, represents the women who become widows before their time. Margaret's husband, Dick, whom she had married on an impulse, was killed in France before he could receive from her a letter saying that she did not love him. Entangled in a web of unresolved emotions, she sees in Mahon the image of her dead husband and thus an opportunity to expiate her guilt through a process of association and substitution: She attempts to "undo" her rejection of Dick by caring for, and eventually marrying, Mahon.

Joe and Margaret are intimately linked by their compassion for Mahon, and they decide to bring him home to Mahon's father in Charlestown. Their principal mission will be to prepare Mahon's father for both Mahon's "resurrection" (he had been reported as dead) and coming death, and to mediate between Mahon and his fiancée, Cecily, who will be repelled by Mahon's scar and who will refuse, finally, to marry him.

By a technique of counterpoint and flashback, the next section of the novel introduces the world of Charlestown before the arrival of Mahon, Margaret, and Joe Gilligan, a world insulated until now from the stark realities of war, but one clearly affected by the postwar mood of spiritual enervation. Here Januarius Jones and the Rector, Donald's father, walk within a jaded pastoral landscape, discoursing languidly about God and man. The garden in which they walk emerges as a symbol of the Rector's retreat into an artificial landscape of imagination and illusion.

The goatlike Jones finds this talk wearisome, however, and he is soon diverted, and then obsessed, by Emmy, the housekeeper, and Cecily Saunders. Lustful and antagonistic, Jones spends his time in pursuit of these not-quite-elusive nymphs, the one homely and faintly wild, the other slim, graceful, and artificial. He chases not so much to capture them (and in this sense, he resembles the lover in John Keats's urn) but for the imminent promise of conquest continually deferred. These are the young people the war left behind, their slightly malevolent play symptomatic of their essential isolation.

When Donald arrives upon this scene, he becomes the vacant yet powerful center about which the other characters revolve. He has no memory and soon goes blind, and is therefore more fully reflective of the projections of others. Though scarred, blind, and dying, he is for Cecily the returned war hero to whom she is glamorously engaged; to the Rector, he is the dead son miraculously resurrected; to Margaret, he is an incarnation of Dick, her dead husband; to Emmy, he is the faunlike boy with whom she roamed the moonlit hills and made love, in the prewar days of innocence.

Opposed to Mahon's static condition of death-in-life is the desperate and futile activity around him. Jones continues his mad chasing, while Cecily escapes abruptly her furious vacillation by eloping with George Farr, leaving Margaret Powers with the realization that Mahon may die unwed. Margaret asks Emmy whether she would marry Mahon, but Emmy refuses impulsively, waiting painfully, and in vain, to be asked again. Then, in an act of compassion less for Mahon than for his father, Margaret marries Mahon herself, symbolically repeating her original marriage, and becoming twice a widow at twenty-four.

Mahon dies following a brilliant and vivid scene in which he suddenly recovers his memory of the moment he was shot down. His past and present now connected, he regains his vision, recognizes his father for a moment, and dies with the explanation, "That's how it happened." His death brings the disintegration of the group orbiting around him, the most significant and painful breach being that between Margaret and Joe. The novel closes with Joe and the Rector walking through the countryside at dusk, listening to the singing of blacks at a church service and feeling dust in their shoes.

The Characters

Soldiers' Pay reveals clearly the nature of Faulkner's mastery of characterization, the genius with which he conjures in the reader's mind vivid and convincing characters. His technique combines luminous detail with understatement: A few significant strokes are often sufficient to bring a character to life. This method invites the reader to become a cocreator of the character, allowing him to project himself into the narrative and to supply with his own imagination the missing details.

In addition, Faulkner brings the reader into the narrative by involving him in the points of view of the characters themselves: A character is seen primarily as others in the narrative see him. For example, Donald Mahon is not described from an objective, omniscient point of view when he first appears in the novel. Rather, the reader sees him as Julian Lowe first does: "He saw a belt and wings, he rose and met a young face with a dreadful scar across his brow." Similarly, when Jones sees a photograph of Mahon as a boy, the narrative lets the reader in on his perspective: "The boy was about eighteen and coatless: beneath unruly hair, Jones saw a thin face with a delicate pointed chin and wild, soft eyes." The subjective, impressionistic manner in which characters are rendered is also clearly demonstrated by Lowe's description of Margaret Powers: He remarks on "her pallid distinction, her black hair, the red scar of her mouth, her slim dark dress," a description which becomes even more quintessential a few pages later, where she is imagined as "tall and red and white and black, beautiful."

The narrator does not restrict himself exclusively to the points of view of the characters, however, and reserves the freedom to add levels of description and symbolism which the characters themselves do not provide. The narrator, for example, compares Margaret Powers to an Aubrey Beardsley drawing, acknowledging that neither Lowe nor Gilligan could have made that connection. More typically, the narrator will compare his characters to animals, nymphs, trees, and flowers in an effort to enrich their symbolic texture. The Rector, for example, is once described as a "laurelled Jove," whose "great laugh boomed like bells in the sunlight, sent the sparrows like gusty leaves whirling." In his garden, the Rector is a kind of wood-god, whose arm lies "heavy and solid as an oak branch across Jones' shoulder." Jones himself is explicitly compared to goats and satyrs: "Jones' eyes were clear and yellow, obscene and old in sin as a goat's"; while Cecily is often compared to trees: "A poplar, vain and pliant, trying attitude after attitude, gesture after gesture. . . . She bent sweetly as a young tree." As always, Faulkner's technique is designed to render the felt moment of experience, the perceiving subject's momentary impression: Jones's "yellow eyes washed over her warm and clear as urine." Cecily's "voice was rough, like a tangle of golden wires."

Faulkner is a master at rendering his characters' exteriors; nevertheless, *Soldiers' Pay* also reveals his growing technical mastery of psychological realism, his ability to individuate his characters from within. Each character is associated with a recurrent stylistic pattern, a verbal motif that is meant to express his most intimate desires, his most secret pains. Beneath the surface of the Rector's embattled, pathetic optimism, for example, runs the poignant, silent refrain, "This was Donald, my son. He is dead." Margaret Powers laments her dead husband and expresses her strained ambivalence with the recurrent phrase, "No, no, good-bye, dear dead Dick, ugly dead Dick." George Farr's memory of Cecily's naked body becomes an obsessive image, rendered as "her body, like a little silver water sweetly dividing." With such verbal motifs, Faulkner effectively reveals the dynamic of his characters' inner lives.

Themes and Meanings

Soldiers' Pay portrays a world forever changed by the war, a world in which sustaining illusions have been shattered and old certainties dissolved. As in Eliot's *The Waste Land*, the April of *Soldiers' Pay* is a cruel month, a season of false renewal (the hollow Easter "resurrection" of Donald Mahon), unfulfilled desire (the breach between Margaret and Gilligan), and displaced sexuality (personified in Januarius Jones). Faulkner's principal theme, however, is not the complete absence of meaning and the continual presence of despair, a fashionable theme of the 1920's, but rather "the human heart in conflict with itself" (in Faulkner's famous Nobel Prize formulation), the necessity of each individual's struggle to create meaning in the absence of transcendental values. Though God may be dead, the eternal human verities of compassion, courage, pity, endurance, and sacrifice remain.

Faulkner's concern for the individual's struggle is reflected in the novel's structure: At the center is Donald Mahon, and the novel unfolds according to a series of personal responses to him. The characteristic movement of each response is toward disillusionment. Though painful and enervating, disillusionment is a necessary prelude to a full and mature acceptance of self, nature, and society.

Moreover, the novel moves beyond despair in its richly comic and nonrealistic elements, in the festivity and symbolic resonances of its language, and in its final reference to an enduring black community, united in its faith in God. Though they feel the dust in their shoes, Gilligan and the Rector are fully responsive to the black congregation's singing, to their expression of "all the longing of mankind for a Oneness with Something, somewhere," and the novel makes it clear that they will endure.

Critical Context

With his first novel, *Soldiers' Pay*, written in New Orleans in 1925 under the encouragement of Sherwood Anderson, William Faulkner emerged from a diverse apprenticeship in poetry, graphic arts, and the writing of prose sketches and stories, to begin one of the world's great novel-writing careers. The work of the young novelist, *Soldiers' Pay* has been charged with containing overwritten passages, inadequate structural principles, and strained dialogue. Nevertheless, the novel is a major document of Faulkner's developing genius, and in its own right a well-crafted, often brilliantly written work of literary art.

Moreover, in its themes, techniques, characters, and structural principles, *Soldiers' Pay* prefigures many of the masterpieces to follow. As a central though "absent" structural principle, for example, Donald Mahon hints at the treatment of Caddie Compson in *The Sound and the Fury* (1929) and Addie Bundren in *As I Lay Dying* (1930); as inarticulate victim, he suggests also Benjy Compson of *The Sound and the Fury* and Ike Snopes of *The Hamlet* (1940). Cecily Saunders and Margaret Powers are prototypes of Temple Drake of both *Sanctuary* (1931) and *Requiem for a Nun* (1951), while the Rector Joseph Mahon prefigures in many respects Gail Hightower of *Light in August* (1932). In its concern for war and aviation, *Soldiers' Pay* contains narrative elements to be more fully developed in *Sartoris* (1929), *Pylon* (1935), and *A Fable* (1954).

With *Soldiers' Pay*, Faulkner established himself as one of the most gifted and promising young writers in America. As the British novelist and critic Arnold Bennett wrote on June 26, 1930:

> Faulkner is the coming man. He has inexhaustible invention, powerful imagination, a wondrous gift of characterization, a finished skill in dialogue; and he writes, generally, like an angel. None of the arrived American stars can surpass him in style when he is at his best.

Bibliography

Blotner, Joseph. *Faulkner: A Biography.* 2 vols. New York: Random House, 1974. Once criticized for being too detailed (the two-volume edition is some two thousand pages) this biography begins before Faulkner's birth with ancestors such as William Clark Falkner, author of *The White Rose of Memphis*, and traces the writer's career from a precocious poet to America's preeminent novelist.

Brodhead, Richard H., ed. *Faulkner: New Perspectives.* Englewood Cliffs, N.J.: Prentice-Hall, 1983. One volume in the Twentieth Century Views series under the general editorship of Maynard Mack, offering nearly a dozen essays by a variety of Faulkner scholars. Among them are Irving Howe's "Faulkner and the Negroes," first published in the early 1950's, and Cleanth Brooks's "Vision of Good and Evil" from Samuel E. Balentine's *The Hidden God* (Oxford, England: Oxford University Press, 1983). Contains a select bibliography.

Cox, Leland H., ed. *William Faulkner: Biographical and Reference Guide.* Detroit, Mich.: Gale Research, 1982.

_____. *William Faulkner: Critical Collection.* Detroit, Mich.: Gale Research, 1982. These companion volumes constitute a handy reference to most of Faulkner's work. The first is a reader's guide which provides a long biographical essay, cross-referenced by many standard sources. Next come fifteen "critical introductions" to the novels and short stories, each with plot summaries and critical commentary particularly useful to the student reader. A three-page chronology of the events of Faulkner's life is attached. The second volume contains a short potpourri, with Faulkner's "Statements," a *Paris Review* interview, and an essay on Mississippi for *Holiday* magazine among them. The bulk of the book is an essay and excerpt collection with contributions by a number of critics including Olga Vickery, Michael Millgate, and Warren Beck. Includes a list of works by Faulkner including Hollywood screenplays.

Gray, Richard. *The Life of William Faulkner: A Critical Biography.* Oxford, England: Blackwell, 1994. A noted Faulkner scholar, Gray closely integrates the life and work. Part 1 suggests a method of approaching Faulkner's life; part 2 concentrates on his apprentice years; part 3 explains his discovery of Yoknapatawpha and the transformation of his region into his fiction; part 4 deals with his treatment of past and present; part 5 addresses his exploration of place; part 6 analyzes his final novels, reflecting on his creation of Yoknapatawpha. Includes family trees, chronology, notes, and a bibliography.

Vickery, Olga W. *The Novels of William Faulkner.* Baton Rouge: Louisiana State University Press, 1959. This volume, with its comprehensive treatment of the novels, has established itself as a classic, a *terminus a quo* for later citicism. The chapter on *The Sound and the Fury*, providing an analysis of the relation between theme and structure in the book, remains relevant today despite intensive study of the topic.

Volpe, Edmond L. *A Reader's Guide to William Faulkner.* New York: Noonday Press, 1964. While many books and articles have contributed to clearing up the murkiest spots in Faulkner, the beginning student or general reader will applaud this volume.

In addition to analysis of structure, themes, and characters, offers critical discussion of the novels in an appendix providing "chronologies of scenes, paraphrase of scene fragments put in chronological order, and guides to scene shifts."

Williamson, Joel. *William Faulkner and Southern History.* New York: Oxford University Press, 1993. A distinguished historian divides his book into sections on Faulkner's ancestry, his biography, and his writing. Includes notes and genealogy.

Michael Zeitlin

SOLOMON GURSKY WAS HERE

Author: Mordecai Richler (1931-   )
Type of plot: Family chronicle
Time of plot: The 1840's to the 1990's
Locale: Northern Canada and Montreal
First published: 1989

>*Principal characters:*
>>SOLOMON GURSKY, the leader of the family liquor business, who escapes from the conflicted world of his family
>>MOSES BERGER, a failed writer and alcoholic who tries to fulfill a lifelong ambition to tell Solomon's real story
>>BERNARD GURSKY, the greedy and duplicitous brother of Solomon Gursky
>>MORRIE GURSKY, the weak younger brother of Solomon and Bernard
>>HENRY GURSKY, the son of Solomon who moves to the north and is closely involved in his Judaic faith

The Novel

Solomon Gursky Was Here spans two centuries as it traces an extraordinary Jewish family from its shady founder, Ephraim Gursky, to its huge success in the liquor business. The novel also provides a biographer of the family, Moses Berger, who searches for the legendary and lost Solomon Gursky.

The book begins with the arrival of Ephraim Gursky in Canada as the only survivor of the ill-fated Lord Franklin expedition of 1846 in search of the Northwest Passage. Ephraim is portrayed as a trickster who dupes the Native Canadians by announcing that he has come to save them. His story is gradually revealed later in the novel; his history includes time in jail in London, transportation to Australia, and a period as the head of a religious cult.

The central part of the family story involves Ephraim's grandsons. They rise from running a dry-goods store to become hotelkeepers when Solomon Gursky wins a hotel and a considerable amount of money in a poker game. Hotel-keeping is profitable for the family, but they find their true niche as bootleggers under the leadership of Solomon. Finally, the family becomes owners of one of the largest corporations in Canada, the Gursky liquor empire. At first, Solomon is the dominant character in the family. However, Bernard betrays him when a trial for bootlegging and bribery endangers the family. At this time, Solomon mysteriously dies in a plane crash. There is some question, however, about whether he is really dead.

In this broken family history, Ephraim's grandsons have many conflicts. Solomon Gursky is clearly favored over the other two. He is taken on an initiatory voyage to the far north, where he acquires some of the trickster spirit of his grandfather. Bernard is full of sharp practice as he leads the company from its bootlegging beginnings to success as a wealthy corporation. The younger brother, Morrie, is dominated by Bernard and submissive.

Another submissive character is L. B. Berger, who begins as a radical socialist poet in the 1930's. He sells his poetic voice to "Mr. Bernard" Gursky, and he produces birthday poems for someone who represents the capitalist class he and his friends have struggled against. His son, Moses, is disgusted with his father's betrayal of his principles for money and turns his attention to the children of Solomon Gursky to spite his father and "Mr. Bernard." His ambition is to write a book on the Gursky family, especially on the true story of Solomon, who may be still alive. However, Moses is incapacitated by his Oedipal struggle with his father; he becomes an alcoholic who has not succeeded in anything. A surrogate father, represented by the search for Solomon, may restore his creative and intellectual powers.

Moses is a Rhodes Scholar, and he is invited to catalog the Arctic material of a mysterious Englishman, Sir Hyman Kaplansky. After a series of revealing incidents, Moses discovers that Solomon Gursky and Sir Hyman Kaplansky are the same man; however, the object of his search disappears. Moses discovers later evidence that reveals that Solomon had been helping Jews in Berlin during World War II and later had helped free hostages at Entebbe.

Moses discovers the mysterious Solomon Gursky again when a financier named Corvu buys shares of the Gursky company. He does this to prevent Bernard's son, Lionel, from taking over the company and displacing Solomon's children, Henry and Lucy. The novel ends with Solomon Gursky going to the far north of Canada with Moses still pursuing him. Solomon leaves signs of his presence to Moses, but he is always a step ahead of Moses—and everybody else. Solomon Gursky remains an elusive, even mythical, presence at the end of the novel; when there is trouble for the Jews, he appears and provides the needed help. He can never be captured by Moses or anyone else but will remain a living mythic figure who appears when he is needed.

The Characters

The two major characters are Solomon Gursky and Moses Berger, although many other prominent characters have a significant role in this family chronicle. Solomon is an intriguing and elusive character. He dominates his brothers without really trying. When Morrie becomes proud of his ability as a cabinetmaker, Solomon borrows his tools to make a far superior cabinet as a gift for a lady. In addition, he is not interested in the accumulation of money that drives Bernard. He is interested in relationships with beautiful and intelligent women and causes such as Israel and the fate of the Jews.

Moses Berger is a fascinating character in his failures and his ambitions. He is an alcoholic primarily because of the problem with his father, and he never overcomes that difficulty. He does have a sympathy and affection for those who, like him, are out of the mainstream. He lives in a house in the north of Canada and has a close relationship with the down-and-out characters in the local bar and with the aloof Henry Gursky. He is a man seeking redemption for his failures and his past through his search for Solomon Gursky.

Bernard Gursky is a hilarious character, with his naked greed and his pretensions to a high position in Canadian and American society. The name he acquires, "Mr. Bernard," suggests something of these pretensions. He is ever alert to increase his fame and stature while diminishing everyone near him. Morrie is unable to find a place for himself under the shadow of his oppressive younger brother. Richler takes savage pleasure in portraying this monster, especially in the annual birthday parties that are dedicated to the homage of "Mr. Bernard."

Themes and Meanings

The most important theme of the book is fathers and sons. Moses Berger has a strong conflict with his father, L. B. Berger. First, there is the betrayal of the socialist cause for the comforts that Bernard Gursky and his wealth can provide. Moses is embarrassed to have to go to the Gursky mansion and see his father debase himself; in addition, both Moses and his father are treated as second-class citizens in the Gurky mansion. Moses is ashamed to discover that L. B. cannot use the Gursky toilet.

There is also a creative conflict between Moses and L. B. Berger. L. B. has never been able to get a poem accepted by *The New Yorker*; when Moses manages to have a short story accepted by that prestigious magazine, L. B. intercepts the notice from *The New Yorker* and replies in Moses's name that he refuses to be published in such a magazine. When Moses discovers this later, he is an alcoholic and even more deeply estranged from his devious father. In Solomon Gursky, he is clearly looking for a surrogate father who can free him from alcoholism and unlock his creative abilities.

There is also a father-son conflict between Henry Gursky, the son of Solomon, and his son, Isaac. Henry lives in the far north with the Eskimos, as far removed from the Gursky empire and its conflicts as he can get, while Isaac wants to be in the big city and live like the rich Gurskys. When he accompanies his father on a trip to the north, the plane crashes; Isaac survives by eating his dead father. The young cannibal then heads for New York to get involved in a takeover attempt by Lionel Gursky, the son of "Mr. Bernard." Isaac goes against all of the values of his father and reverts to the earlier predatory generation of "Mr. Bernard."

There are also sibling rivalries in this family cycle. Bernard dominates his younger brother Morrie and manages to exclude him from decisions concerning the liquor corporation. He cannot dominate Solomon, but he does betray him by conniving with the state so that he might be convicted of bootlegging and bribery. He does this to get power, which Solomon would never cede him, and to marry Libby, who will not marry him unless he has control of the company.

There is a continual contrast in the book between those characters who love money and power and those who abjure it. Bernard Gursky, his son Lionel, and Isaac Gursky are the primary seekers for wealth in the novel. Bernard has betrayed his brother, Solomon, at a crucial point in the family's fortunes, and Isaac has eaten his father to survive in the northern wastes of Canada. In contrast, Moses Berger, Solomon Gursky, and his son Henry refuse to be controlled by wealth; they define their lives in terms of causes, personal relationships, or spirituality. Bernard is finally displaced at the end of the novel, but there is only a tentative victory by those who reject the burdens of wealth.

Critical Context

The novel may be a *roman à clef* in which the Gursky family represents the Bronfman family, a Canadian dynasty that owns the Seagrams corporation. The Bronfman's disputed early history and later triumph provides one way to read the novel.

The novel is also of interest in its manipulation of narrative time. It begins in the middle of the nineteenth century and moves back and forth in time to give a full portrait of the Gursky family. This unusual narrative structure is used to reveal the checkered history of the family's founder, Ephraim, and to create a mythic presence in the characterization of Solomon. He is never seen in a linear narrative, but his presence cuts through a large period of history.

The novel also shows a development in the fiction of Mordecai Richler. It does have the Jewish characters of Montreal of the earlier novels as well as the humor. However, this novel has a scope and historical sweep that is new in Richler's oeuvre. The family saga that spreads over a century and a half contrasts to the concentration of the other novels.

Finally, the family conflicts of the novel will be of interest to many young readers, who may be drawn to the father-son conflicts that seem to define nearly all of this family's history. The book presents some very oppressive fathers and some blighted sons. However, the novel does seem to point to a displacement of these fathers as a younger generation comes to power.

Bibliography
Cohen, Sarah Blacher, ed. *Jewish Wry: Essays on Jewish Humor.* Bloomington: Indiana University Press, 1987. The essay on Richler in this collection calls attention to one of the most important elements of Richler's style, humor.

McNaught, Kenneth. "Mordecai Richler Was Here." *Journal of Canadian Studies* 26, no. 4 (Winter, 1992). A discussion of Richler's critical view of Canada and its embodiment in his recent novels.

Richler, Mordecai. *Home Sweet Home: My Canadian Album.* New York: Alfred A. Knopf, 1984. An amusing collection of essays that show Richler's critical view of Canadian culture.

Sheps, David, ed. *Mordecai Richler.* Toronto: Ryerson Press, 1971. A discussion of Richler's early novels, themes, and style.

Todd, Richard. "Narrative Trickery and Performative Historiography: Fictional Representation of National Identity in Graham Swift, Peter Carey, and Mordecai Richler." In *Magical Realism: Theory, History, and Community,* edited by Wendy B. Faris and Lois Parkinson Zamora. Durham, N.C.: Duke University Press, 1995. An interesting discussion of Richler's use of postmodern techniques.

James Sullivan

SOLSTICE

Author: Joyce Carol Oates (1938-   )
Type of plot: Psychological realism
Time of plot: The 1980's
Locale: Rural Pennsylvania
First published: 1985

>   *Principal characters:*
>   MONICA JENSEN, a recently divorced schoolteacher trying to come to
>   terms with her former life
>   SHEILA TRASK, a successful and eccentric artist, the widow of a famous
>   artist

The Novel

Solstice is divided into four parts, with Emily Dickinson's poem "After great pain a formal feeling comes" serving as an epigraph to the novel. It is the story of two women seeking balance in their lives.

The novel is written in a third-person limited voice. The reader is allowed to know Monica Jensen's thoughts and feelings but can only guess at Sheila Trask's, as Monica does. The story begins with Monica's move to Glenkill, Pennsylvania, to teach at an all-boys private school, Glenkill Academy. She rents an old farmhouse that is next to Sheila Trask's estate, which is called Edgemont. Although the two women meet briefly at a party, they do not really speak until Sheila makes an unannounced visit by horseback to Monica's new home.

Sheila quickly takes over Monica's life and becomes her main social outlet. Monica works long hours at the academy and is often required to work late into the evening at home. However, she always manages to find time for Sheila. They meet weekly for dinner, and gradually, Monica finds herself spending most of her free time with Sheila, in Sheila's studio or on jaunts that Sheila suggests.

Eventually, Sheila convinces Monica to accompany her on her weekly pub-crawling escapades. For these adventures, both Monica and Sheila assume other identities. Sheila becomes "Sherrill Ann," and Monica becomes "Mary Beth." Sheila/Sherrill Ann is always the leader of these forays into the rural nightlife; she is careful to maintain control of any situation the women encounter and to make a hasty exit if the men in the bars get too aggressive.

The women always say that they are divorced with children and that they must get home right away because their babysitters have strict rules. Monica/Mary Beth is shy in the bars and must be coerced into dancing with the men, but Sheila/Sherrill Ann is flirtatious and sexy. She easily draws the attention of men, and she enjoys their attention. However, she avoids anything more than semiserious flirtation. When Sheila/Sherrill Ann's behavior raises the anger of a man who insists that Sheila/Sherrill Ann had told him she was interested in him, the scene erupts into a car chase from which the women narrowly escape. After this episode, they end their adventures as Sherrill Ann and Mary Beth without discussing the matter, but apparently by mutual consent.

Throughout the novel, Sheila Trask is working on a series of paintings, entitled *Ariadne's Thread*, for a show she is supposed to give. Although she is sometimes thrilled about her successes with the paintings, more often she is depressed by her inability to convey her meaning. She abuses drugs and alcohol, and she subsequently abuses Monica, verbally and emotionally.

Meanwhile, Monica is attempting to adjust to her new life. She attends dinner parties and dates a lawyer named Keith Renwick, who is attractive and polite. Monica considers him a nice date but cannot sustain an interest in a serious relationship with him.

Monica travels home to Indiana over the Christmas holiday. She expects this trip to be warm and relaxing; however, the vacation turns out to be disappointing. Her family notices that she is looking tired, and she faces some memories while at home. These memories are not unpleasant, but they serve to remind her that she has not really managed to become her own person.

When Monica returns from her week off, she jumps determinedly into her life in Glenkill. She becomes more active in the academy and the community, and she begins exercising and reading.

Sheila does not telephone her, and Monica does not telephone Sheila. However, Monica's curiosity eventually gets the best of her, and she calls the studio where Sheila's show is to be. The gallery informs her that Sheila has left the country. Later, in a casual conversation with an acquaintance, Monica learns that Sheila has left for Morocco and may not return until the following fall.

To fill the time of Sheila's absence, Monica goes on dating Keith, and also becomes even more engaged in the activities she began upon her return from Indiana. She also works on her house, painting and cleaning, and buying furniture to fill the rooms.

Eventually, though, Sheila returns, and she and Monica quickly fall into their old pattern. Sheila begins working once again on *Ariadne's Thread*, and Monica gradually ceases the activities she had taken up while Sheila was gone.

Sheila gets sick. She does not eat, and she abuses drugs heavily. She refuses to allow Monica or anyone else to help her, and Monica sees her sickness as a reproach to her for neglecting Sheila. Eventually, Monica also gets sick, but no one is aware of her sickness. She begins to neglect her work in order to take care of Sheila, to visit her at the studio, and to keep her accounts in order.

As Monica continues to get sicker over the weeks, she is scolded at the academy for allowing one of the boys to read a poem stating his homosexual urges, and she is raped by a man whom she meets at a party thrown by Sheila. Shortly afterward, Monica gets seriously ill and does not recover. She gets progressively sicker until the novel's end, when Sheila finally discovers her and whisks her away to the hospital, berating her for not asking for help.

The Characters

Solstice is really a novel about its two main characters. It is a study of a co-dependent relationship and how each party deals with the relationship. Sheila Trask is an abuser of drugs and alcohol and also an abuser of Monica Jensen. Sheila indulges in violent mood swings and remains private and secretive throughout the novel, but she insists on Monica's consistent cheeriness and willingness to share her thoughts and feelings. Because Sheila is so secretive, the reader never really learns what her true feelings are for Monica. However, she manipulates Monica by appearing to be interested in her. She also manipulates Monica by her constant talk of suicide and of the "mirror-ghoul" that stares back at her from the mirror, reminding her of her own mortality. At times, it seems that without Monica, Sheila would kill herself or become violently ill from refusing to take care of herself, but eventually, the reader discovers that the exact opposite is true. Sheila is in control, and it is Monica who is unable to take care of herself.

Although Monica never openly acknowledges the fact, it is clear that Sheila takes more of an interest in her than her husband (or any man) ever did, and that interest is what Monica craves; she vehemently desires to be liked. She thinks of herself as a "golden girl" and frequently recalls her younger days in high school and college, when she was a cheerleader and sorority girl who was very popular. She basks in Sheila's interest in her, although she can never quite figure out why Sheila is interested; she is not an intellectual, and her life is fairly mundane. Monica fears that Sheila will suddenly discover these facts and will no longer like her.

Indeed, it seems that Monica defines herself by Sheila's interest. It is only when Sheila goes away to Africa that Monica seeks out activities on her own; even then, these activities are determined by what she thinks others view as appropriate activities. She does things to be interesting rather than because she is interested in them. In fact, she finds the activities exhausting, but she continues with them until Sheila returns and once again provides a definition for Monica. For Monica, the mirror-ghoul is not her own mortality but the shallowness of her life. Deep down, she knows that she does not define herself, yet she is never able to face this fact and determine her own identity. Instead, she becomes violently ill, and she is saved only by Sheila's curiosity.

Themes and Meanings

Solstice explores the fear of death and the fear of living alone, and it explores the question of who determines one's identity. Monica moves from an abusive relationship with her husband—who caused the scar that she often fingers on her chin as well as quite a few emotional scars—into another abusive relationship with Sheila Trask in an effort to find an identity and a meaning for her life.

Solstice also confronts the questions of suicide and of what it really means to take control of one's death, and thus one's life. Sheila seems to understand the meaning of control, and she speaks openly of suicide as a viable option when she becomes "fed up" with living. In this way, she copes with her frustrations as an artist, reminding herself that she does not need to continue to live if she chooses not to. Suicide for Sheila seems to be an excuse to go on living; it gives her a chance to see what will happen, knowing that there is outlet if she does not like the outcome.

Monica, however, sees suicide as an escape. She often worries that Sheila will kill herself, and toward the end of the novel, she contemplates suicide as an escape from her illness. Although she is unable to commit the act, she constantly reflects on her razor blades and focuses on them as a means of ending her misery.

Keith Renwick, on the other hand, sees suicide as a selfish act, meant to punish those who are left behind. Although Keith is only a minor character, Keith puts the idea of suicide into perspective. He tells Monica that she should get away from anyone whom she knows who is contemplating suicide. He suggests that considering suicide shows an inability to focus on anything but oneself and thus is a sign of an unhealthy individual. Monica does not reflect on this conversation, but it is interesting to note that she does not seriously consider suicide until she is utterly alone and incredibly ill.

Critical Context

Joyce Carol Oates is a prolific writer, and *Solstice* is her sixteenth novel. Joanne Creighton, in *Joyce Carol Oates* (1992), describes Oates's style as "postmodern romantic." This term accurately captures both the disjointedness of Oates's novels and the focus on the self and feelings, which is especially evident in *Solstice*. This novel explores the opposite sides of the self, the "mirror-ghouls," and presents two opposite women who essentially complete each other.

Oates's earlier works explore the difficulty of creating an identity for oneself in the context of the American Dream, which focuses on materialism and financial success, as well as on the difficulty of defining oneself as a woman in a world where men define everything. *Solstice* seems to be the next step, in that it is both essentially void of any male principal characters and that both of the female characters are financially secure and living materially independent lives. As such, they face the next identity crisis: "What am I, now that I am alone and successful?"

In many of her novels, Oates explores sexuality and violence, often combining the two into acts of molestation or violent sex. However, in *Solstice*, sex is carefully avoided except for one short rape scene that almost seems to be a dream. The two women carefully avoid touching each other and also keep themselves separate from the men they date. It is clear, though, that there is an erotic tension between the two women, and each definitely has jealous tendencies when the other spends time away from the friendship. This tension serves to question whether female sexuality has strict borders, defined by sexual acts, or whether there are levels of sexuality and sexual relationships not defined by physicality.

Although Oates does not fit easily into any circle of writers, her work has made a definite impression on the American literary scene. She pushes the boundaries of the novel, using it to explore psychological and metaphysical questions and daring others to do the same. She is important specifically because she is outside the borders of traditional literature.

Bibliography

Bloom, Harold, ed. *Joyce Carol Oates*. New York: Chelsea House, 1987. Critical essays on Oates's work.

Creighton, Joanne V. *Joyce Carol Oates: Novels of the Middle Years*. New York: Twayne, 1992. A thorough analysis of Oates's fifteen novels written between 1977 and 1990, including *Solstice*.

Daly, Brenda. *Lavish Self-Divisions: The Novels of Joyce Carol Oates*. Jackson: University Press of Mississippi, 1996. A critical look at the female characters of Oates's novels.

Johnson, Greg. *Invisible Writer: A Biography of Joyce Carol Oates*. New York: Dutton, 1998. A thorough biography, including a series of pictures provided by Oates.

Oates, Joyce Carol, comp. *First Person Singular: Writers on Their Craft*. New York: Persea Books, 1983. A compilation of essays by twentieth century writers on writing, including an essay by Oates herself.

Amy Beth Shollenberger

SOMETHING HAPPENED

Author: Joseph Heller (1923-1999)
Type of plot: Psychological melodrama
Time of plot: The late 1960's or early 1970's
Locale: New York City and a Connecticut suburb
First published: 1974

> *Principal characters:*
> ROBERT (BOB) SLOCUM, the protagonist, a middle-level executive with
>   a large company
> HIS WIFE, a housewife who drinks throughout the day
> HIS DAUGHTER, an unhappy fifteen-year-old
> HIS SON, an unhappy nine-year-old
> DEREK, his brain-damaged third child

The Novel

Bob Slocum is a character who uses dreams and memories, which make up a substantial portion of the novel, as part of his ongoing struggle to determine the key event, the "something" that "happened" to him, to cause him to be the man he is. Very early in the book, he thinks, "Something did happen to me somewhere that robbed me of confidence and left me with a fear of discovery and change and a positive dread of everything unknown that may occur. I dislike anything unexpected." Because life is unpredictable and the unexpected happens daily, Slocum has come to dislike his life, but because death and change are also unpredictable and unexpected, even those alternatives provide no hopeful option for him.

Bob Slocum is a character suffering what pop psychologists would call a midlife crisis. The outer circumstances of his life change very little during the first three-fourths of the novel, but within his mind he contemplates changes in almost every area. He considers divorce. He contemplates how a proposed promotion might affect his life. He tries to face the necessity of institutionalizing his retarded child. Through dreams and memory, he even tries to re-create the happy and sad experiences of his growing-up years in search of a security that he feels he once had but which is now missing. He becomes particularly obsessed with the memory of a girl he knew when he was seventeen and working part-time for an insurance company. After many years of knowing that the girl, Virginia Markowitz, committed suicide while he was in the army, Slocum still clings to the hope represented by their innocent and unconsummated passion for each other.

Slocum's exploration of his life is, in part, a struggle to establish a valid point of view from which to make the decisions he faces. At one point he asks himself, "Where is a frame of reference now for any of us that extends even the distance to the horizon, only eighteen miles away?" Although Slocum understands other people fairly well, he cannot translate that understanding and perception into actions or relationships. He remains trapped within his own mind, which he imagines oozing excess matter and ready to explode.

The relationship between Slocum and his wife is neither happy nor unhappy. He says that he has always wanted a divorce, even before he met his wife and married her. Yet he has not. He is regularly unfaithful with both whores and women he meets at work and at parties, but it is his wife who is his most satisfying sexual partner. He must sometimes use her as a fantasy figure in order to be fully aroused with others. He is terrified by the possibility that she might be unfaithful to him. Finally, her main failure seems to be her inability to make Slocum feel the same absolute and total security he remembers from very early childhood. He is somewhat annoyed by her drinking habits, but only when they cause her to embarrass him at parties or to be too assertive in the home. Their relationship is essentially unchanged over the course of the novel.

Slocum resents his daughter's sullen, aggressive personality and her sexual maturity, from which she refuses to shield him by dressing in ways to obscure it. He feels compelled to best her in arguments and battles of wit, even as he realizes that besting one's fifteen-year-old child is no real victory. He feels enormous rage and anger at the thought that some male might seduce her, and he wants to protect her from her own unhappiness and all the world's dangers. Yet he also wants to be her superior; thus, he fails to develop any relationship beyond the hostility that he initially sets out to comprehend and control.

It is the nine-year-old son whom he calls his "boy" that Slocum says he loves more than anything in the world. The most positive actions in the novel are made in the boy's behalf. Slocum intervenes to spare his son the macho wrath of a physical education instructor. He tries to persuade the boy not to give away his money, pennies and nickels mostly, but takes secret pride in his spontaneous and generous nature. Perhaps the most terrible alienation Slocum feels, in a novel entirely about his alienation, is the feeling of isolation from this boy, who suddenly takes to spending all his hours at home behind a closed bedroom door, exactly like his surly sister. The novel's climax, which comes very late, occurs when the boy is injured by a runaway vehicle in a shopping plaza. Slocum, anxious to help him, holds the child so tightly to his chest in an effort to comfort him that the boy dies of asphyxiation.

The third child, Derek, is never actually present in the novel's action, but his offstage presence is overwhelming. For both Slocum and his wife, Derek's birth seems to be a turning point, the place where life's hopes and possibilities are irrevocably diminished. Although both know that they must eventually send the child away, they cannot, even by the novel's end, bring themselves to do so.

Woven through what is essentially a static story about upper-middle-class family life are scenes at the vaguely defined company where Slocum works. His promotion, at the expense of a man who trusted and confided in him, coincides with his son's death, making the climax of these secondary plots part of the larger family story. For Slocum, the world of the office is as disillusioning and frustrating as is the world of the family. When the romantic notions of his recollected youth collide with the hardened cynicism of his middle age, his emotions lead him to conclude that his personal inadequacies are the cause of his failures: "I am guilty. . . . I am numb with shame. I feel so helpless and uncertain."

The Characters

Bob Slocum reveals himself and all the other characters in the novel through his own tormented consciousness, a tricky decision on Heller's part because Slocum is essentially unlikable, especially with regard to his perceptions of others. Thus, the novel is filled with characters in whom the reader can find little to admire.

Despite his apparent distaste for the flux of human experience, Slocum is an acute and perceptive observer of those around him, even when he tries to ignore their presence, as he does with Derek, his wife, his daughter, his coworkers, his lovers, and almost everyone whom he encounters at some point in his relationships with them. These observations give the reader an understanding of the book's other characters—an understanding, however, that is obviously limited and erroneous, the product of what Slocum himself recognizes as a flawed perspective.

Slocum is an insecure and frightened man, perhaps on the verge of a breakdown but ironically also on the verge of his greatest professional success. The reader comes to know of the deep-seated nature of his irrational fears and emotions through Slocum's own thought process. He analyzes his dreams, his memories, and his past and present experiences in a frank, sometimes brutally honest way. His ego appears to be all-absorbing and all-consuming. Even when his speculation and self-analysis lead him almost to acknowledge that other characters might deserve his (and the reader's) sympathy and compassion, he cannot, ultimately, stay outside his own overwhelming need long enough to give the others what he knows they deserve: "Whenever I feel sorry for someone, I find that I also feel sorry for myself."

The minute detail that characterizes Slocum's observations of all the other characters in the novel suggests that he is, in addition to his other qualities, sensitive in a way that his behavior belies. He knows from the merest body stance, the subtlest facial expression, how his wife and his children, except Derek, feel, and he knows that Derek cannot feel. One of the many ironies of his character, however, is his inability to turn sensitive observation into equally sensitive behavior, a failure which makes his existence more tortured than it would be were he not so acutely aware of others around him. At times, Slocum longs for the insensible world he believes his idiot son to inhabit, for without feeling, there is no pain.

Because Slocum is a first-person narrator, and because he chooses not to reveal the names of three of the members of his family, preferring instead to identify them in terms of their relationship to him, the reader can assume that they are being revealed only as they relate to him. The reader never sees his wife or his daughter engaged in any activity outside the home. Slocum does narrate several incidents that involve his older son, the one of whom he is particularly fond, in a way that generates sympathy and compassion for the boy. In one scene, the child is being harassed by playground bullies while Slocum watches from a distance. The reader sees that the boy is passive and afraid, qualities that mesh precisely with his father's sense of his character. Yet these more objective scenes do not really increase the reader's trust in Slocum as a narrator and a judge of character because this is the one character of whom he is entirely fond.

All three of the unnamed family members are afraid of Slocum—they frequently accuse him of "yelling," behavior which he sees as emphasizing his point. Yet all three are apparently desperate to receive his attention and affection. The total inability to love or acknowledge Derek, coupled with the overwhelming guilt he feels about this inability, seems only a more extreme version of the way Slocum feels about the entire family, and perhaps about all others. The reader is left only with a very strong sense of what sort of people Slocum perceives his family to be; there is no way to know what kind of people they really are.

In many ways, the minor characters are more fully realized in traditional terms than are the members of Slocum's family, in part because these minor characters do not so currently and directly impinge upon his consciousness. With characters such as Virginia Markowitz and even his mother, Slocum seems better able to hold simultaneous visions of what he wanted them to be and what he now, with disappointment and cynicism, perceives them to be. Thus, the innocent voluptuousness of Virginia's body is not destroyed by his older, wiser sense of her psychological problems. The mother whose last words stick in his mind as a complete dismissal of his worth is also the woman who provided the only real security and love he has ever felt, the woman who sent out for ice cream on hot summer nights. With his own present family, Slocum is apparently incapable of such dualities.

The men and women with whom he now works and the women with whom he has affairs are much more stereotypical than the novel's other characters. The men at his office tend to be named for colors: Green, Black, Brown, and White, one indication of their being types. All of them seem to be unhappy and competitive, modern-day Babbitts, relentlessly and sometimes ruthlessly pursuing things they no longer want for reasons they themselves could neither state nor respect, if they paused for reflection. It is their apparent lack of self-analysis that separates them from Slocum. Some of his coworkers, such as Andy Kagle, turn to Slocum, asking him to analyze their lives, but Slocum does so only as it pleases him at the moment. No one can ever trust his motives or his answers—it is Andy Kagle's job that he gets at the novel's end.

Themes and Meanings

Because *Something Happened* is a novel so little concerned with plot and character in the traditional sense, theme becomes particularly important. Heller clearly intended to demonstrate the vast emptiness of modern life among the neatly constructed suburbs of the upper-middle class. He also wanted to establish, however, that those who most embody that emptiness, men such as Bob Slocum, did not desire such a world. Near the end of the novel Slocum states quite directly what he does want from life:

> I wish I were part of a large family circle and enjoyed it. I would like to fit in. I wish I believed in God. I liked shelled walnuts and raisins at home when I was a child and cracked the walnuts and mixed them all up with the raisins in a dish before I began eating. My mother sent out for ice cream often in the spring and summer. In the fall we had good charlotte russes. I would spin tops. I remember the faces of the street cleaners.

Clearly he longs for traditional values, a world of love, trust, and simple pleasures. Yet, caught up in a world too complex and too alienating for such simplicity and security, he becomes both disillusioned and compulsively needful and insatiable. Finally, his intense desire to love his son in the way he himself wants to be loved destroys the son, an ironic climax, all the more stark and chilling for its apparently insignificant impact on the daily life of Slocum and his surviving family.

The death of the son, the one remaining object of pure and simple love, serves two important functions thematically. First, because his one last hope of having the kind of love he longs for disappears, Slocum appears to be freed to enter even more wholeheartedly into the empty, spiritless world of his career. Ironically and more significantly, the son's dying before his alienation from his father reaches the fixed and hopeless state that marks Slocum's relationships with his wife and his daughter allows the duality of romantic hope and cynical despair that characterizes Slocum's other memories to become part of his thinking about the family. The boy dies before Slocum's hatred for him can destroy the love he feels.

Apparently the something that happened to Bob Slocum is growing up, and, thus, this novel becomes one in a long American tradition of stories about the terrible cost of the collision between naïve romanticism and harsh reality.

Critical Context

Something Happened, Heller's second novel, was published thirteen years after *Catch-22* (1961), his most famous novel and the one on which his reputation most securely rests. In *Catch-22*, the military and war are the objects of Heller's satire. The worldview in *Something Happened* is not so different from that in the earlier novel, but the shift from the military setting to a domestic and corporate world somehow seems to remove the playfulness and comedy from the vision. Perhaps the reason that the situation in *Something Happened* produces less comic satire than is found in *Catch-22* is that military service can never be permanent in the same way that family life and a chosen career can.

In *Good as Gold* (1979), Heller turned his satire to the political world, and some of the comic flair evident in *Catch-22* returned. His fourth novel, *God Knows* (1984), looks at the religious world with the same basic vision that pervades the previous work. Heller also wrote a play, *We Bombed in New Haven* (1967). *Something Happened* remains the darkest and bleakest of his books, as well as the longest and most labored.

Bibliography

Craig, David M. *Tilting at Mortality: Narrative Strategies in Joseph Heller's Fiction.* Detroit, Mich.: Wayne State University Press, 1997. Craig analyzes the form and structure of Heller's novels and includes a discussion on *Something Happened.*

DelFattore, Joan. "The Dark Stranger in Heller's *Something Happened.*" In *Critical Essays on Joseph Heller,* edited by James Nagel. Boston: G. K. Hall, 1984. DelFattore explores Heller's treatment of the stranger in *Something Happened.*

Heller, Joseph. "An Interview with Joseph Heller." Interview by Charlie Reilly. *Contemporary Literature* 39 (Winter, 1998): 507-508. Heller discusses several of his books including *Something Happened.* The interviewer also comments on the detached voice of the first-person narrator of the novel.

Keegan, Brenda M. *Joseph Heller: A Reference Guide.* Boston: G. K. Hall, 1978. A comprehensive bibliography of criticism on Heller and his works.

Mellard, James M. "*Something Happened*: The Imaginary, the Symbolic, and the Discourse of the Family." In *Critical Essays on Joseph Heller,* edited by James Nagel. Boston: G. K. Hall, 1984. Mellard details the narrative structure, symbolism and applies psychoanalytic approaches to the novel.

Merrill, Robert. *Joseph Heller.* Boston: Twayne, 1987. Merrill provides a critical and interpretive study of Heller, with a close reading of his major works, a solid bibliography, and complete notes and references.

Seed, David. *The Fiction of Joseph Heller: Against the Grain.* New York: St. Martin's Press, 1989. An extensive critical and interpretive study of Heller's novels. Useful for an overview of Heller's works.

Jane F. Hill

SOMETHING TO BE DESIRED

Author: Thomas McGuane (1939-   )
Type of plot: Psychological realism
Time of plot: 1958 to the 1980's
Locale: Deadrock, Montana
First published: 1984

> *Principal characters:*
> LUCIEN TAYLOR, an immature young man who has left his wife, his child, and his government job to come to the aid of a former lover who has shot her husband
> EMILY, Lucien's strong-willed and hard-hearted former lover who has killed her abusive husband and is fleeing the police
> SUZANNE, Lucien's strong-willed and tender-hearted former wife, who divorced him when he abandoned her and whose trust and respect he must work to regain
> DEE THOMPSON, Lucien's unhappily married lover in Deadrock
> WICK TOMPKINS, Emily's lawyer, who befriends Lucien
> W. T. AUSTINBERRY, Emily's hired hand, whom she seduces and kills

The Novel

When Lucien Taylor in Thomas McGuane's *Something to Be Desired* abruptly leaves his wife, child, and job to aid a former lover who has shot her abusive husband, his motives are not purely altruistic. He is restless and still finds Emily attractive. Eventually, he realizes that he desires neither adventure nor Emily but the love of his family; as he sets out to reclaim it, he acquires self-knowledge and a sense that his life finally has a "center" that makes it rewarding.

Something to Be Desired is divided into twenty chapters. Filled with Lucien's memories, the third-person narrative is so closely focused on Lucien that it has the immediacy of a first-person tale.

In the first chapter, Lucien and his irresponsible father are entering the final, disastrous phase of their relationship. Long absent, the father has suddenly reappeared to take his son on an "adventure" camping trip. The boy and his father have been lost for two days. Before Lucien locates their campsite, they stumble upon and bathe in a hot spring.

Filled with self-pity, the father ends the trip abruptly. Lucien sees him pick up a prostitute along the way; the boy also watches him brutally strike his bitter and vengeful former wife before he leaves for good after a last drunken quarrel.

After years of living with his alcoholic and abusive mother, Lucien goes away to college, where he meets the other two women who will influence his life. Although he is obsessed with Emily's beauty and passion, she leaves him to marry the other man with whom she has been having an affair. Lucien then meets and marries the beautiful

Suzanne, who is as principled, generous, and stabilizing as Emily is unprincipled, selfish, and unsettling.

Common sense tells Lucien that Suzanne is Emily's superior. Nevertheless, he is troubled by a "lack of high romance in his life." When they learn that Emily has shot her husband, he abandons his family and goes to Emily's ranch near the spring in Deadrock. While he admits that his behavior has begun "the process of stain" in him, Lucien also sees himself as carrying out a mission, part of which is to have Emily love him again, a feat he thinks he can accomplish by rescuing her—paying her bail. The doubts of Emily's lawyer, Wick Tompkins, about her chances and character are confirmed when Emily disappears with W. T. Austinberry, the hired hand.

Left alone with the ranch, Lucien engages in a halfhearted affair with the unhappily married Dee. He begins to recognize that he is on the road to loneliness. After spending a year in a despairing, alcohol-induced daze, he announces that he is "going to start something tremendous." Encouraged by Wick, he decides to transform the ranch and its spring into a spa. When the resort is hugely successful, Lucien calls Suzanne to tell her. Cautious but hopeful, she agrees to bring James to visit Lucien, who is "head over heels in love."

Lucien continues the process of self-discovery. He reflects on his own mortality and on the importance of tradition and continuity. He realizes that he is not interested in making even more money, and his desire to provide his son with a sense of security continues to grow.

Lucien has other trials to undergo. Although James comes around, Suzanne does not. Dee announces that she is leaving, and Emily reappears, carrying a gun. Finally unmoved by her, aware that she could destroy his life, Lucien informs Suzanne of her arrival and tells Emily that she must leave. Partly in anger, Suzanne concludes her visit; while James twists around to wave goodbye, Suzanne "keeps her eyes on the road."

The Characters

Lucien's thoughts, actions, and language indicate that he finds it difficult, if not impossible, to make and to commit himself to choices that are clearly in his best interests. This Hamlet-like indecision seems to stem from his childhood. He was attracted by what he saw as the romance of his father's life and is often driven, like his father, by sexual desires he refuses to control. Lucien (whose name suggests the devil that often seems to control him) is saved from self-destruction, ultimately, by his fine ironic sense and by his willingness to find a center to his life in the form of his son.

A lover of well-told tales, he often sees his life unrealistically, in terms of a story. In college, he is torn between two girls sketched in outlines suited to tales of the Old West; they have old-fashioned names and seem to represent vice and virtue. Even though the values and codes represented by the myths of the Old West appeal to him, he is not a storybook hero. As he rushes off to "save" Emily, he abandons his own child.

When he feels that he can go no lower, he finds that he can turn to his advantage resources that he has used successfully before: his organizational skills, his business acumen, and his "willingness to please." He is a kind of fallen angel who starts to rise again as he begins to create a new life, this time one that he invests with meaning.

Suzanne is a stabilizing influence; she remains a wonderful wife and mother throughout. Suzanne rejected all other suitors to marry Lucien. Stung by his abandonment, she forces him to fight for her, as he did not before, until she considers him a responsible adult. Suzanne manages to occupy the moral high ground without appearing "sappy," as Lucien thinks her to be at one point. Even though her unhappiness hardens her and makes her able to shock Lucien, she is still, in many ways, an idealized character.

Emily is the other woman, the bad girl whose most notable characteristics are selfishness and amorality. She represents the Wild West at its wildest. When she kills a second time, she becomes not only a villain but also a literal outcast from American society. Emily represents a dislocation of body and soul; in chasing her, Lucien sees, he is courting death.

Lucien's father appears only in the opening chapter, but his presence haunts Lucien. He and his wife are the source of Lucien's instability. Alcoholic, childish, self-pitying, and abusive, he is impulsive, ignoring the consequences of his actions and leaving loose ends everywhere. He runs from problems and lies to himself, excusing his behavior by telling Lucien that "we are all animals." Lucien, sadly, recognizes that his father's childish and underhanded approach to fighting with his wife is "wholly characteristic." He is an antifather; a worse model is hard to imagine.

Dee's behavior provides a counterpart to Lucien's. Caught in an unhappy marriage, she has no illusions when she slips into an affair with Lucien. She surprises—and impresses—him when she breaks the slender tie that connects them to begin a new and independent life for herself. Dee is given a few sharp, ironic words to say; she appears mainly in the narrator's description of their sad, squalid encounters.

Wick Tompkins, Emily's lawyer, comes to like Lucien, and the obvious affection of this wise, amusing, and basically decent man for Lucien indicates that there is hope for Lucien's future.

With the absurdly grand name of W. T. Austinberry, Emily's hired hand is not even a cowboy in name only. He is another source of disillusionment to Lucien. A far cry from the idealized figure of the Old West, he has no love for the land. He is inadequate as a lover and contemptible as a sportsman; he dumps quantities of bleach into a river when he wants to catch fish.

Themes and Meanings

The themes of *Something to Be Desired* are traditional and typical of McGuane's work: the desire to be close to and to respect nature, the search for a way to deal with contemporary society's corruption and materialism, and the desire to find stability in an unstable world while maintaining a sense of individuality in a culture that encourages sameness.

McGuane believes that "authentic" modern fiction has as its vantage point dislocation, and a sense of instability and displacement pervades the novel. From the beginning, Lucien has difficulty securing a footing on the shifting grounds of modern life. The failure of his parents' marriage seems inevitable in a society where traditional moral and ethical codes of behavior are no longer in effect. He even finds his own happy marriage unsatisfying and seems to value it only when he must run enormous risks to regain it.

The theme of dislocation and instability is also apparent in Lucien's realization that the romantic image he had of the Old West, the last outpost of new beginnings, is now insupportable. Schooled in its myths, Lucien grew up admiring a variety of rugged individualists, heroes such as Lord Nelson, Vasco da Gama, Theodore Roosevelt, and the anonymous ranchers and cowhands who created new lives for themselves in the frontier. He has always valued an Emersonian self-reliance, and he occasionally tries to adhere to certain codes of behavior (he admires Suzanne for her stubborn belief in the value of such a code).

In Deadrock, however, the discrepancy between the myths and the reality is glaringly and often comically apparent. Lucien's ranch supports "sulphur taffy" rather than cattle; his most libidinous encounters are not with prostitutes but with vacationing nannies; the villain he must confront does not challenge him to a duel but overcharges him for seamless gutters. Lucien needs to find ways he can live in this new, "tame" West.

The novel is also about the relationship between fathers and sons. Lucien's unclouded memory of his "adventure" with his father reveals nothing about his feelings; the boy seems to be holding his judgment in abeyance, as if to deny what he is seeing and feeling. It is years before he can tell himself with some revulsion that in leaving his family he is repeating the pattern set by his father. Unlike his father, Lucien wants to be a hero to his son, and when he sees a copy of a book of "true tales of the old West" by the sleeping boy's bedside, he begins to sense that he has found his home.

Critical Context

Something to Be Desired, McGuane's sixth novel and seventh book, was not as well received as his earlier novels. Critics faulted McGuane for inconsistent control of the narrative, for stylistic artificiality, for "working hard" to achieve certain effects, and for depending on familiar approaches to characterization and thematic development.

Generally, however, critics agreed that McGuane was moving in a new direction. At first, Lucien seems to be like McGuane's other protagonists. They are nonconformists seeking personal fulfillment, often through unconventional means, and their searches usually end unsatisfactorily, if not disastrously. Lucien's problems, however, do not seem to be self-imposed. Unlike the parents in McGuane's earlier novels, Lucien's mother and father are unstable emotionally and financially. In addition, Lucien's unhappiness never brings him so low that he would willingly die. His comic sense is eventually accompanied by common sense, which in this case permits him to acknowledge his need for Suzanne and James.

The most obvious characteristics of McGuane's novels—the machismo exhibited by his protagonists, their yearning for adventure and romance, the impossibility of their finding an appropriately glamorous vehicle for succeeding in that search, the spare, tough dialogue, the particular beauty of the passages dealing with natural settings, the eruptions of violence, and the concern with place, especially Key West and Deadrock—all of these have caused McGuane to be labeled a follower of Ernest Hemingway and William Faulkner. Also apparent, however, are the effects of McGuane's early interest in the romance and adventure found in the works of W. H. Hudson and Ernest Thompson Seton, and of his study and enjoyment of the "serious" comedy of Aristophanes, Lazarillo de Tormes, Miguel de Cervantes, Mark Twain, and Evelyn Waugh. This greater comic exuberance, the softening of the protagonist, and Lucien's belief that "anything was possible once the center had been restored" indicate why McGuane has called *Something to Be Desired* a "positive" novel.

McGuane's skill at using dialogue to reveal character is apparent in the numerous screenplays with Western themes that he wrote during and after a stay in Hollywood. He is one of a number of new writers, such as David Long and Rick Bass, who are reshaping the New West as a landscape for other writers and new readers to explore. He is also a literary critic and the author of numerous essays on hunting and fishing.

Bibliography
Ingram, David. "Thomas McGuane: Nature, Environmentalism, and the American West." *Journal of American Studies* 29 (December, 1995): 423-469. Ingram examines McGuane's focus on the old mythologies of the frontier in the ecology and politics of the modern American West. Ingram concludes that McGuane's position of these issues is complicated and unclear, alternating between the liberal, radical, and conservative.
McCaffery, Larry, and Sinda Gregory. "The Art of Fiction LXXXIX: Thomas McGuane." *The Paris Review* 27 (Fall, 1985): 35-71. Illuminating and immensely readable, this focuses on McGuane's style, themes, and comic vision. The authors find in *Something to Be Desired* less "rambunctiousness," more control over language, and more complex and subtle techniques of characterization than appear in the earlier novels.
McClintock, James. "'Unextended Selves' and 'Unformed Visions': Roman Catholicism in Thomas McGuane's Novels." *Renascence: Essays on Values in Literature* 49 (Winter, 1997): 139-152. McClintock examines the Roman Catholic themes in McGuane's works. McClintock asserts that although McGuane's works are not Catholic in an orthodox sense, he often investigates Catholic themes, topics, and use of language that specifically refers to Catholic matters.
Morris, Gregory. "How Ambivalence Won the West: Thomas McGuane and the Fiction of the New West." *Critique: Studies in Contemporary Fiction* 32 (Spring, 1991): 180-189. Excellent discussion of McGuane's use of the "New West." Argues that while both the language and the action of the novel illuminate Lucien's attraction to the landscape and to the myths of the Old West, his efforts to find a place for himself in the New West require him to deny acceptance of the old.

Neville, Jill. "Getting Away from It All." *The Times Literary Supplement*, May 17, 1985, p. 573. An interesting discussion that focuses not on the disappearance of the Old West but on Lucien's "odyssey," as he moves from being the son who refuses to put away childish things to the man who ceases being self-destructive and yearns for "health, emotional stability, and Nature."

Roper, Robert. "Lucien Alone in Deadrock." *The New York Times Book Review*, December 16, 1984, p. 11. Asserts that *Something to Be Desired* is McGuane's best book. Roper comments that McGuane's comic gifts and lively style are well suited to conveying Lucien's struggle to understand himself, to accept his "softer qualities" as he matures.

Wallace, Jon. *The Politics of Style*. Durango, Colo.: Hollowbrook, 1992. Argues that McGuane finds language "an end in itself." Although McGuane's characters' words and thoughts often seem incoherent or meaningless, Wallace claims, the mixed codes in his language reflect their fragmented sense of being and their attempts to bring themselves into being in a world without style or unity. Includes a useful bibliography.

C. L. Brooke

SOMETHING WICKED THIS WAY COMES

Author: Ray Bradbury (1920-   )
Type of plot: Fantasy
Time of plot: The early 1930's
Locale: Green Town, Illinois
First published: 1962

> *Principal characters:*
>> WILL HALLOWAY, an open, innocent young boy nearing the age of fourteen
>> JIM NIGHTSHADE, his best friend, a dark enigmatic boy, also approaching fourteen
>> CHARLES HALLOWAY, Will's father, a middle-aged janitor in the town library
>> J. C. COOGER and
>> G. M. DARK, the owners of a traveling carnival and buyers of human souls
>> MISS FOLEY, a schoolteacher who desperately wants to recapture her youth

The Novel

Something Wicked This Way Comes is a story of good versus evil, with love and laughter overcoming fear and illusion, somewhat in the manner of a medieval morality play. Yet Bradbury puts life into this ancient literary tradition to produce an entertaining and interesting work that falls just short of being a fantasy masterpiece. The setting is Green Town, Illinois, an idyllic Midwestern small town which is also the locale of his partly autobiographical *Dandelion Wine* (1957).

The prologue contains the enigmatic sentence, "One year Halloween came on October 24, three hours after midnight." The subject of time and its distortion by evil forces becomes a crucial element in the novel. The sentence refers to the arrival of Cooger and Dark's Pandemonium Shadow Show in Green Town. The show is heralded by Tom Fury, a mysterious lightning-rod peddler, who appears to the protagonists Will Halloway and Jim Nightshade and sells Jim a lightning rod in anticipation of an approaching storm. It is significant that Fury sells the rod to Jim, a dark-haired, intent boy born one minute after midnight on October 31, in contrast with his best friend and next-door neighbor, Will, a blond, good-natured boy born one minute before midnight on October 30. While Will participates joyously in uncomplicated, boyish activities, Jim has a desire for strange, often forbidden experiences, a desire which attracts him to the Cooger and Dark carnival and nearly causes his damnation.

The traveling show creates no suspicions in the minds of Green Town's adults, but the active imaginations of Will and Jim are immediately aroused when a carnival, something usually associated with summer, appears so late in the year, in a train of outdated design and with a calliope playing bizarrely altered church music. An atmosphere of menace seems to hang over the apparently festive carnival. Miss Foley, the boys' seventh-grade teacher, becomes lost in the Mirror Maze, which tantalizes her with reflections of herself in youth. Later, the two friends see Mr. Cooger enter the carousel and, as the carousel turns backward, become younger and younger until he is an eight-year-old boy, whereupon he masquerades as Miss Foley's nephew Robert. Will fears that Miss Foley is in danger, but Jim sees in the magic carousel a way of rapidly entering the adult world. When Cooger enters the ride a second time to age forward, Will jams the controls and Cooger is transformed into a wizened old man. This draws the wrath of the show down on the two boys, who must flee both from the carnival people and from the police, becoming isolated within their own town.

The boys turn to Will's father, Charles Halloway, a middle-aged man who married late in life. Mr. Halloway learns that the Cooger and Dark show has traveled around the country for at least eighty years, always arriving someplace in October. It is apparently an immortal band of freaks who live off of the sufferings of others, whom they tempt with forbidden enjoyments, using people's own desires to destroy them. Mr. Halloway discovers that love and laughter are the only defense against the carnival, and he uses these weapons to destroy it before Jim can be artificially aged into a replacement for Mr. Cooger. The novel ends with the ordered world still intact and both Will and Jim aged, not through perverted magic, but through the natural maturing process.

The Characters

As is appropriate, given Bradbury's intentions, the protagonists, Will Halloway and Jim Nightshade, are essentially allegorical figures rather than realistic, fully developed characters. In the novel, they function as Bradbury's picture of boyhood split in two, portraying the dual nature of boys, innocence and mischief, nostalgia and the passionate desire to gain the status of an adult. The story's events take place just before their fourteenth year, so they are in a time between carefree childhood and adolescence, which brings the beginnings of responsibility. The carnival is their first direct contact with the malevolent yet attractive outer world. Will, content to remain a child, is repulsed by the Shadow Show. His danger is that he will be paralyzed by fear, as at one point he is paralyzed by a fortune-teller's magic, yet Will does acquire the courage to strike back at the freaks in order to save Jim, indicating that he is growing up. By contrast, Jim is eager to enter the adult world by any means and nearly joins the carnival to accomplish this. Jim's interest in life's dark side is not in itself evil, but it could easily lead to perversity. By the novel's end, his restless spirit has been chastened by his contact with Cooger and Dark, and he is ready to develop at a natural pace.

Cooger and Dark, the carnival's proprietors, are living embodiments of evil. Dark, with his tattoo-covered body, is obviously taken from Bradbury's *The Illustrated Man* (1951), while Cooger and his carousel transformations had previously appeared in "The Dark Ferris" (1948). They and their followers are the "autumn people," according to Mr. Halloway, those who fear the approach of winter and death so much that they enter an immortal half-existence and stay outside the cycle of life. To maintain this state, they must periodically feed on human souls, their victims eventually becoming members of the carnival. They prey upon human fears and vanities, especially those connected with time, such as the fear of growing old or the desire to grow up rapidly, so that their victims come willingly. Halloway suggests that everyone is at times an autumn person, and this revelation is the center of the carnival's horror.

Charles Halloway is the most fully realized figure in the book and one of Bradbury's most interesting characters. Halloway, a middle-aged janitor, hardly seems to be a heroic figure, yet it is he who ultimately defeats the carnival. For years a rootless wanderer with intellectual yearnings, he settled down and had a son fairly late in life. His age weighs heavily on him: He envies the boys' vitality and believes that he is too old to be a proper father for Will. If anyone would be vulnerable to the carnival's seductions, so it seems, it would be Halloway, but in fact his painfully acquired self-knowledge and his strong love for his family allow him to see through Cooger and Dark's show. Like Will and Jim, Halloway is in an in-between time, with vigorous adulthood on one side and old age on the other. He uses wisdom and compassion, the weapons of age, against the carnival, yet he also discovers that he possesses a vitality which he thought he had lost. Halloway is a hero, but he is a human, fallible one, who feels temptation and can overcome it. Hence, he is a more engaging hero for his fallibility.

Miss Foley, an example of the pathetic victims of the freaks, is "a little woman lost somewhere in her gray fifties." She is a friendly, affectionate woman, but, being a spinster, she has no close familial ties. Even her nephew Robert is, in reality, the transformed Mr. Cooger. Fearing the onset of old age and death, she welcomes the carnival's offer of restored youth, even going so far as to betray Will and Jim to the police and to Mr. Dark to prevent them from interfering. When her wish is granted, she finds that as an adult woman in a little girl's body she is isolated from natural life, as she had already isolated herself morally. The only place for her is with the physically and spiritually deformed inhabitants of the Cooger and Dark show.

Themes and Meanings

The novel centers on time and its meaning for human life. Dates, seasons, ages, and hours of the day all contribute to the novel's effect, and its central conflict is one between two views of time. The first sees time as an eternally recurring cycle of birth, death, and rebirth. This view is represented in the novel by Green Town, which, as the name suggests, lives in tune with the seasons. In Green Town, time is accepted, and its changes are ritualized by holidays, birthdays, and religious worship. The second view, that held by the autumn people, sees time as the agent of senseless destruction. The carnival exists in an eternal October, where there is no death and, therefore, no rebirth. Mr. Halloway, acting as Bradbury's spokesman, explains that man is the only animal that is conscious of time and mortality; hence, he can transcend simple egoism by devoting himself to others who will live on after him. The carnival people recoil from the consciousness of time and go back to a bestial, predatory existence. Appropriately, love and laughter are the best defenses against the autumn people, since they require an abandonment of the self. The carnival thrives on isolation and self-preoccupation; significantly, the characters who prove most vulnerable to the traveling show are the spinster Miss Foley and the fatherless Jim Nightshade.

Bradbury places his themes into the framework of a Gothic tale to provide an embodiment for his abstract speculations. The disruption and restoration of order in an almost pastoral community, the use of simple characters whose names and appearance mirror their spiritual states, and the employment of supernatural terror and occult wisdom (symbolized by the library where Halloway works) are all standard elements of the Gothic tradition. In addition, Bradbury uses some of the more modern developments of suspense-writing such as the innocent or even festive situation which conceals evil or the isolation of the protagonists from society by their consciousness of this evil, so that they must evade pursuit not only by the evil forces but also by society itself. Bradbury understands both the ancient fear of demonic external forces and the modern fear of alienation and combines them to heighten the novel's terror.

Critical Context

Aside from *Fahrenheit 451* (1953), *Something Wicked This Way Comes* (which appeared in a film version in 1983) is Bradbury's only full-length novel of the fantastic. Critical reaction has been mixed on the work. While the premise of the story is compelling, some critics have suggested that Bradbury's highly metaphorical, lyric prose style, often one of his greatest strengths, slows the pace of narrative; at times, the imagery seems to overcome the novel entirely.

The novel does present many of Bradbury's favorite subjects in one work. An interest in children and their special insights, a nostalgic portrayal of the Midwestern small town, a fascination for the grotesque and its attractions, and a conviction of the value of literature, especially fantastic literature—all play a large part in Bradbury's work. There are also several specific links to Bradbury's other writings in this novel. As previously noted, Mr. Cooger, the Illustrated Man, and Green Town had appeared in earlier stories. In addition, the Pandemonium Shadow Show might have been suggested by the short-story collection *Dark Carnival* (1947), and the autumn people are first mentioned in *The October Country* (1955). This wealth of cross-references and recurring themes makes the novel a good introduction to Bradbury's fictional world as well as entertaining reading in its own right.

Bibliography

Greenberg, Martin Harry, and Joseph D. Olander. *Ray Bradbury.* New York: Taplinger, 1980. An insightful collection of critical essays that addresses various aspects of Bradbury's writing, including his use of the frontier myth. Features a helpful index and bibliography.

Mogen, David. *Ray Bradbury.* Boston: Twayne, 1986. An excellent collection of critical essays on Bradbury's novels, including *Something Wicked This Way Comes.* Includes a selected bibliography and index.

Nolan, William. *The Ray Bradbury Companion*. Detroit: Gale Research, 1975. A classic reference that includes critical essays, a brief biography, a comprehensive bibliography, and facsimiles of Bradbury's unpublished and uncollected works on all media. Features an introduction by Bradbury.

Touponce, William F. *Ray Bradbury and the Poetics of Reverie: Fantasy, Science Fiction, and the Reader.* Ann Arbor, Mich.: UMI Press, 1984. Written from a reader-response critical perspective, Touponce's study offers keen insight into Bradbury's works. Includes a bibliography and index.

Anthony Bernardo

SOMETIMES A GREAT NOTION

Author: Ken Kesey (1935-   )
Type of plot: Realism
Time of plot: 1961
Locale: Southwest Oregon coast
First published: 1964

>   *Principal characters:*
>   HANK STAMPER, the protagonist, thirty-six years old
>   LELAND "LEE" STANFORD STAMPER, Hank's half brother, twenty-four
>   years old
>   VIVIAN "VIV" STAMPER, Hank's wife
>   HENRY STAMPER, Hank's father, the patriarch of the family
>   JOE BEN STAMPER, Hank's cousin
>   JONATHAN DRAEGER, an agent of the national logger's union
>   FLOYD EVENWRITE, the local union's representative

The Novel

The events of *Sometimes a Great Notion* revolve around a logging strike which pits the Stamper family against the local union and, thus, against the members of the small coastal community in which the family lives. Through Kesey's dazzling manipulation of point of view, the characters of the community are portrayed in relationship to Hank Stamper, who is the leader of the clanlike family, and who functions as the traditional hero in classical terms. The strike dramatizes a fundamental clash of values: the fierce individualism inherent in this wildcat logging way of life against the need for cooperation among the various members of the community for their mutual well-being.

As the novel opens, a critical contract for the survival of the family logging business—to supply the sawmill of a national logging corporation with cut timber—has almost expired with only a small portion of the quota cut and with none of the timber delivered. The family needs every available man to work in the woods to meet the contract conditions, and since no one in the local community will work in defiance of the strike action, the family must send for Lee, Hank's younger half brother. Lee had left the area with his mother when he was a child of twelve and is now a graduate student at Yale University. The novel's action revolves around the developing relationship between Hank and Lee. Their relationship is complicated by Lee's knowledge that as a teenager, Hank had a sexual relationship with Myra—Lee's mother and Hank's stepmother—which Lee believes contributed to Myra's suicide. This Oedipal situation is transferred in the present action to Hank's wife, Viv. She becomes a focus for the tension between the two brothers as Lee, in revenge for Hank's sexual relationship with Lee's mother, attempts to seduce Viv and to confront Hank with that knowledge.

As the novel moves toward a climax, Hank is tested in all the areas which constitute his sense of self, and which define the community's concept of the hero. Physically, he must perform extraordinary feats in the daily logging operation, and he must continue to lead the other members of the family to perform similar feats. Hank's most demanding tests, however, are emotional: He must not only withstand the great social pressures of the community to conform to the conditions of the strike, but, because of his love for Lee, Hank must also attempt to bring Lee to some awareness of his own worth as a person. Hank must also be a husband to Viv, and above all, he must retain his faith in his own individual values, the most important of which is a sense of his integrity.

At the climax of the novel, Hank's father loses an arm in a logging accident and lies dying in the hospital; Joe Ben, Hank's cousin who functions emotionally as a brother to Hank, loses his life in the same accident; and Lee successfully seduces Viv. Viv, who realizes that she loves both brothers, also realizes the full nature of the conflict between them. In reaction to this awareness, and in response to her life circumstances in general, she leaves both of them to make a new life for herself. In this final test, Hank must learn a new lesson: that a certain kind of weakness—the weakness of the meek who "shall inherit the earth"—makes for a certain kind of strength.

With this newfound knowledge, Hank once again engages in action, defining himself by that action, and once again achieves heroic stature. Hank's actions provide a focus for the novel's brilliant presentation of the realistic detail of a way of life in the Pacific Northwest—with its emphasis on self-reliance, its world of outdoor work, the mystical presence of nature, its dynamics of family relationships—and the mythical elements which have developed from that way of life.

The Characters

In the history of American regional literature, Hank Stamper is perhaps the most completely rendered character native to the Pacific Northwest. He is admirable in that he possesses a great integrity to the dictates of his inner self, a self which is a sanctuary, with "a door that can never be forced, whatever the force, a last stronghold that can never be taken, whatever the attack . . . but . . . can only be surrendered. And to surrender it for any reason other than love is to surrender love." He is a self-reliant man with great confidence in his abilities, a man of tremendous animal vitality who is also sensitive to others. These traits have created a sensibility which embodies typical Western values: a preference for the natural world over the civilized and for individual over collective action; a fierce belief in self-sufficiency; a confidence in instinctive emotions rather than in rational processes. These characteristics have been portrayed in countless Western genre stories and films, and Hank himself is aware of how these values are stereotyped in popular culture. This awareness—which often surfaces in his humor—adds to his rich fictional reality for the reader.

Hank's character stands in contrast to that of Lee, who has been reared by his emotionally distraught mother, a woman who was faced with marriage to a man—Henry Stamper—who could not fulfill her emotional needs. Lee's sensibility has been formed by his painful childhood and by Eastern urban society. He is a confused young man, without a real sense of self—immediately before he receives the letter inviting him to Oregon to work in the family logging operation, he attempts suicide. In the Oregon experience, Lee discovers the courage to face life's circumstances, learning this courage from Hank's example. He also develops a sense of self, with the corresponding ability not to give up on himself when confronted with trying circumstances. Hank, in turn, learns from Lee that there are different kinds of moral strength—that in fact, the meek can often survive misfortune which undoes the strong.

The relationship between Hank and Viv is complex, one of the strongest aspects of the novel because of the emotional depth of both characters. She is a memorable character—certainly Kesey's most fully realized woman figure—who is compassionate and giving to those around her. She is not native to the region, however, and she suffers a feeling of cultural displacement, which results in an emotional emptiness—a loneliness—which she cannot overcome. This loneliness has been compounded by the loss of her unborn child. As a housewife, Viv represents the traditional role of women in this way of life, a role which does not provide the necessary emotional fulfillment to sustain her. Traditionally, women have been excluded from participation in the outdoor world of work with its tremendous demands for great physical exertion, and with its corresponding emotional fulfillment. Hank is not able to change her circumstances for her: His own circumstances, the demands of his own role, prevent him from discovering—and attempting to provide—the changes that she must have in order to sustain their relationship.

The character of Joe Ben, Hank's cousin who helps him run the family logging operation, illustrates Kesey's versatility as a novelist. Joe Ben provides much of the book's humor with his stereotypical opinions and attitudes, and yet at the same time he represents the values of the Western lifestyle. This type of humor—which is often related to the concept of self-reliance—is manifest in a number of vividly drawn characters, such as Hank's father, Henry; Indian Jenny, a local sorceress; and Floyd Evenwrite, the local union representative.

The character who stands in strongest opposition to Hank is Jonathan Draeger, the agent for the national union. Draeger represents the larger, sophisticated forces of collective society, with its emphasis on collective action and its belief in rational processes. In the climax of the novel, Draeger's view of man directly opposes Hank's actions, with the outcome of the events clearly indicating Kesey's preference for Hank's individualism.

The mythical dimensions of the novel are achieved through archetypical, nameless characters who suddenly appear in point-of-view shifts, with their dialogues of rich vernacular. It is their presence in the novel which gives an epic scope to the action, providing comment on the present events, the past history of community and families, and the nature of the culture. Usually, such views are portrayed with a humor that adds to the complexity of tone in the novel.

Themes and Meanings

Kesey has stated that his concerns in the novel were to portray "a man, a family, a town, a country, and a time"—a comment which indicates the ambitious scope of the work. His success in achieving this scope rests on his technical abilities as a novelist—in particular, on his splendid manipulation of point of view. Various first-person narrators and various third-person centers of consciousness, which brilliantly render the vernacular speech of the region, as well as an omniscient narrator whose voice varies from factually realistic to lyric, enable Kesey to create a community and its values while portraying the actions of complex characters.

The great independence of the wildcat gyppo—a logger who is paid not an hourly wage, but in direct proportion to the amount of work that he accomplishes, to the amount of logs he "rolls in" to the sawmill—is portrayed in the novel as a value which has developed from the difficult and dangerous demands of this profession, of this way of life. This value—with its roots in the traditional American heritage of self-reliance—is finally ambiguous, for the fierce individualism which it fosters often is in conflict with a competing value: the need for joint action to ensure survival for the members of the community. So on the one hand, Hank's independent actions—his refusal to participate in the strike, his attempt to fulfill the conditions of his own private contract—represent the admirable virtue of self-reliance; on the other hand, however, his actions threaten the community's well-being. Yet Hank does not wish to take advantage of his fellowman, to work to destroy the well-being of the community, nor are his efforts primarily for material rewards; rather, he is an idealist who views his actions as the only way in which he can be true to himself, the only way that he can maintain that inner sanctuary of the self.

Within the framework of these thematic concerns, Kesey celebrates the physical surroundings through Hank's response to the spiritual presence of nature. This celebration is found in scenes which portray a sudden, transcendental awareness of the physical landscape—in a sunset, for example—as well as Hank's daily work in the woods. Although on the surface level, Hank must combat the forces of nature—a miscalculation can result in immediate dismemberment or death, as it does for Hank's father, Henry—on another level such work provides the opportunity for man to achieve a kind of natural communion, so that the forces lying dormant within himself are awakened to join in a mystic manner with the larger forces in nature. Such communion imparts a fuller dimension to man's character, and this fuller dimension of character is one of the highest achievements of the novel—an achievement which gives *Sometimes a Great Notion* a high standing in modern American fiction.

Critical Context

Although Kesey's earlier novel *One Flew over the Cuckoo's Nest* (1962) has received more popular attention from the mass audience, many critics believe that *Sometimes a Great Notion* is a more accomplished novel. Its epic scope—with its presentation of a way of life for a region of the United States, the Pacific Northwest—makes it one of the most ambitious of modern American fictions. Ultimately, the novel is not confined to any region: Like all outstanding regional writers—William Faulkner, John Steinbeck, Larry McMurtry—Kesey transforms local situations and events into universal concerns.

Because of Kesey's use of a quickly shifting point of view, the novel requires a commitment on the part of the reader: As is true of many outstanding novels in modern American fiction, a first reading of *Sometimes a Great Notion* provides merely a first step in understanding the events and characters, a first step in appreciation, with subsequent readings adding to that appreciation.

Bibliography

Brown, Chip. "Ken Kesey Kisses No Ass." *Esquire* 118 (September, 1992): 158-166. Profiles Ken Kesey as a literary prankster and details his offbeat personality. Describes Kesey's image of himself as a "magician" and the art of writing as magic. Brown's profile gives many personal insights into Kesey's life and writing.

Carnes, Bruce. *Ken Kesey.* Boise: Idaho State University Press, 1974. Provides brief biographical information and critical background to Kesey's works.

Kesey, Ken. "Ken Kesey: The Art of Fiction CXXVI." Interview by Robert Faggen. *The Paris Review* 35 (Spring, 1994): 58-94. Kesey discusses his views on the role of the writer, whom he feels has the right to impose his ideas and attitudes on readers. Includes biographical information and a discussion of the Kesey novels that were made into motion pictures.

Leeds, Barry H. *Ken Kesey.* New York: Ungar, 1981. A critical interpretation of Kesey's works.

Porter, M. Gilbert. *The Art of Grit: Ken Kesey's Fiction.* Columbia: University Press of Missouri, 1982. Porter's discussion of Kesey's early work is an excellent starting point for study of Kesey.

Tanner, Stephen L. *Ken Kesey.* Boston: Twayne, 1983. Tanner provides a critical and interpretive study of Kesey, with a close reading of his major works, a solid bibliography, and complete notes and references.

Ronald Johnson

SON OF MAN

Author: Augusto Roa Bastos (1917-   )
Type of plot: Social protest
Time of plot: From 1910 to the end of the Chaco War in the mid-1930's, and the period immediately following
Locale: Itapé, Sapukai, and the site of the battle of Boquerón
First published: Hijo de hombre, 1960 (English translation, 1965)

> *Principal characters:*
>   CRISTÓBAL JARA (KIRITÓ), a Christ figure
>   MIGUEL VERA, the spectator-narrator, a Judas figure
>   GASPAR MORA, a leper, the carver of a wooden Christ figure
>   MACARIO FRANCIA, a mythical man

The Novel

Son of Man is a novel of "man crucified by his fellow man." The plot includes nine stories, or chapters, not in chronological order, each appearing at first to be independent of the others. The novel jumps from one time to another to introduce an important event or to present a character, acquiring its unity from the repetition of certain symbols and events, and from the voice of Miguel Vera, who is the protagonist-narrator in five of the stories (the odd-numbered chapters), and the omniscient spectator-narrator in the other four (the even-numbered chapters).

Miguel Vera begins by remembering his childhood in Itapé. Vera recalls the figure of Macario Francia, a blind old man, and the stories that he would tell the youngsters, particularly Gaspar Mora's story, in which Mora, Macario's nephew, leaves the village for the nearby hills after contracting leprosy. When Mora dies, an image of Christ that Mora carved is found in his house. The peasants take the image to the town, where it presides over their lives, becoming a symbol.

In the following chapter, a little town near Itapé, called Sapukai, has suffered an enormous explosion during an insurrection. In the blast, thousands of people have died. One day, Alexis Dubrovsky, a Russian doctor, suddenly appears in the Sapukai railway station. He dedicates his life to curing the peasants and takes care of a colony of lepers (a common disease in Paraguay at that time).

Miguel Vera next narrates his train journey to Asunción, where, as a young boy, he was going to enter military school. During his trip, Vera listens to the passengers' conversations, which reveal a variety of characters. Alexis Dubrovsky is among them, and Vera witnesses the moment when Alexis is thrown off the train in Sapukai—this is the moment at which the previous chapter begins.

In chapter 4 comes a description of the terrible conditions in the Paraguayan *yerbales* (plantations where cocaine, marijuana, and other drug-producing plants are grown), and Cristóbal Jara is introduced. Casiano Jara, his wife, Natí, and their newborn baby boy, Cristóbal, flee the brutality and the inhuman life that they have been forced to endure in the yerbales. At the end of Vera's narration of their odyssey, they obtain their freedom.

In the fifth chapter, Miguel Vera has been confined in Sapukai because of disciplinary problems, and there he meets Cristóbal Jara, who is also called "Kiritó" (the Guarani word for Christ). Kiritó asks Vera to be a military instructor for a rebel group, but, at the beginning of chapter 6, the rebel conspiracy has failed. All the rebels have been shot or taken to prison except Kiritó, who hides in the cemetery and escapes, disguised as a leper.

Vera, in diary form, next narrates his imprisonment and the Chaco War in which he voluntarily enlists. In the Chaco War, Kiritó has been given the mission to bring water to Vera's company, which is besieged at the front. After all kinds of adversities, Kiritó manages to arrive, but Vera takes him for a mirage and kills him.

Finally, the war has ended, and Vera has become the mayor of Itapé. Life has not changed much. The spirit of rebellion is growing again. Vera feels his solitude and puts an end to his life.

The Characters

Central to *Son of Man* is the juxtaposition of two main characters, Miguel Vera and Cristóbal Jara, or Kiritó.

Vera represents the intellectual who cannot completely become one with the oppressed, although he understands them and sympathizes with them. Vera is aware of the need for social revolution in Paraguay. Yet, because he is an introvert and a sentimentalist, he is unable to contribute to that revolution. He simply observes the tragedy of his people from the sidelines. Vera unwittingly becomes a Judas figure. He denounces his comrades, he shoots Kiritó, and at the end of the book, by becoming Itapé's mayor, he even becomes an official member of the oppressors.

Kiritó is unquestionably the "son of man," the Christ figure. Kiritó is a silent, uneducated man, the antithesis of Vera. He leads his people by the force of his character. He symbolizes the potential for the salvation of mankind by man himself. Kiritó sacrifices himself for his fellowmen, and he is fully conscious that this is his mission: "For now the only thing that mattered was to go on, always at all costs. . . . That was his destiny."

Another Christ figure in the book is Gaspar Mora, a maker of musical instruments. Mora contracts leprosy and flees his village to protect his fellowmen from infection and to suffer in solitude his slow death. Mora represents the isolation of human beings, and his leprosy is a symbol of the suffering that he accepts in the name of the people. Yet Mora does not completely die. He remains among his people by leaving behind a part of himself. He carves a Christ image that resembles him, as a reminder of his generosity.

Many other characters populate the book, individual characters, mass-characters (entire communities), and the storyteller Macario Francia. Macario is the conscience of his country. He is a "bridge" between two generations, a living myth. Through his stories, he can propagate the popular wisdom in his native language, so rich in metaphors and symbols: "Man is like a river, my sons . . . a river which is fed by other rivers, and which in turn feeds them. It is a bad river which ends up in bog."

Themes and Meanings

Son of Man is not simply a historical or a mythical novel, yet it presents Paraguayan history from Francia's regime to the Chaco War against Bolivia. The story and its structure reveal a concern for individual human beings, and at the same time, they show a clear vision of the history of the Paraguayan people.

The main theme in the novel is the desire for the social redemption of a country. These men are moved not by their reason but by their hearts. Their hearts lead some of them to take heroic actions that are symbolic for the others.

Like many writers, Roa Bastos sees the Christ figure as a powerful symbol of man's redemption by man himself. Hence, the figure of the "son of man"—Cristóbal Jara, or Gaspar Mora—appears throughout the book as an outstanding individual who reveals himself in death. His death may not reduce the people's oppression, but it supports them by reinforcing their belief in brotherhood.

The carved Christ of Itapé is one of the most important symbols of redemption, symbolizing man crucified by men, a man who must be avenged. At the same time, it is a symbol of the individual who sacrifices himself for his fellowmen.

Roa Bastos does not give answers in his book. He presents facts, and, unfortunately, these facts are repeated throughout time. The world spins like a whipping top: The more it spins, the more static it looks. Nothing changes in spite of the passing of time. "Everything is the same, it seems the time does not move over the enormous slow whipping top."

Critical Context

Son of Man won first prize in Editorial Losada's International Novel Contest in Buenos Aires in 1959 and was published in 1960. It was a great success, in spite of the dissatisfaction the author himself felt with the book. In 1960, Roa Bastos wrote the screenplay for *Son of Man*. The film received the first prize of the Argentine "Institutode Cinematografía," and it was considered the best film in the Spanish language for that year.

In his novel, Roa Bastos presents his country, his people, and his own experiences. Roa Bastos was sent to military school in the capital at the age of eight, like Miguel Vera, the narrator of the story. Roa Bastos fought in the Chaco War against Bolivia. In the early 1940's, he traveled among the yerbales, where he learned about the exploitation and the degradation of the yerbales workers. All these facts make *Son of Man* a realistic novel with a historical base transformed by the magical imagination of the author.

Roa Bastos, like other South American writers, wants to present in his novel the essence of his country—the "intrahistory," as Rodríguez-Alcalá calls it. Yet the novel is more than history. The author presents, at the same time, his vision of the world, and his vision of man: "Man has two births. One when he is born, the other when he dies. . . . He dies, but he remains alive in others, if he has dealt kindly with his neigh-bours. If he has helped others during his lifetime, when he dies, the earth may devour his body, but his memory will live on. . . ."

Bibliography
Bach, Caleb. "Augusto Roa Bastos: Outwitting Reality." *Americas* 48 (November/De-cember, 1996): 44-49. Bach profiles Roa Bastos's life and career and discusses the theme of power in his novels.

Flores, Angel, ed. "Augusto Roa Bastos." In *Spanish American Authors: The Twenti-eth Century.* New York: H. W. Wilson, 1992. Profiles Roa Bastos and includes an extensive bibliography of works by and about the author.

Foster, David W. *Augusto Roa Bastos.* Boston: Twayne, 1978. Foster provides a criti-cal and interpretive study of Roa Bastos, with a close reading of his major works, a solid bibliography, and complete notes and references.

Marcos, Juan Manuel. "Augusto Roa Bastos." In *Latin American Writers,* edited by Carlos A. Solé and Maria I. Abreau. Vol 3. New York: Charles Scribner's Sons, 1989. An essay on the life and career of Roa Bastos. Includes analysis of his works and a bibliography.

Weldt-Basson, Helene C. "Augusto Roa Bastos's Trilogy as Postmodern Practice." *Studies in Twentieth Century Literature* 22 (Summer, 1998): 335-355. A discussion of the author's trilogy on the "monotheism of power."

_____. "A Genetic Approach to Augusto Roa Bastos's *Hijo de hombre.*" *Confluencia* 11 (Fall, 1995): 134-147. A discussion of *Son of Man.*

Mercedes Jimenez Gonzalez

SON OF THE MORNING

Author: Joyce Carol Oates (1938-   )
Type of plot: Psychological realism
Time of plot: The 1940's to the 1970's
Locale: The United States
First published: 1978

>   *Principal characters:*
>   NATHANAEL VICKERY, a sensitive boy who has powerful religious
>   visions
>   OPAL VICKERY, Nathan's grandmother, a deeply religious woman
>   THADDEUS VICKERY, Nathan's grandfather, a doctor and a rational man
>   ELSA VICKERY, Nathan's teenaged mother
>   THE REVEREND MARIAN MILES BELOFF, a popular southern preacher
>   LEONIE BELOFF, the Reverend Beloff's daughter, a sexual temptress
>   WILLIAM JAPHETH SPROUL III, Nathan's most devoted disciple

The Novel

Son of the Morning consists of four parts with titles that have biblical connotations: "The Incarnation," "The Witness," "Last Things," and "The Sepulcher." The four sections trace Nathan Vickery's beginnings, his rise as a boy preacher, his fall from grace and renewed preaching career, and his final estrangement from his former self; the plot serves as a rough parallel to the life of Jesus. The title is ambiguous: Is Nathan a bright star bringing God's light to the masses, or is he the fallen Lucifer, sinning through pride?

Although most of the novel is told from a third-person point of view that represents Nathan's look back at his life, the novel begins with Nathan's first-person internal dialogue with God, which recurs throughout the novel and ends it as well. The author also uses limited third-person narrators to relate events that happened before Nathan was born and to other characters who touch upon his life.

Nathan's plea to God to speak to him as He once did opens the novel. The story then jumps back to the 1940's, before Nathan's birth. Nathan's uncle, Ashton Vickery, waits, concealed above dead chickens that he has placed in a ditch to lure a pack of wild dogs who have been terrorizing the countryside. The history of the pack of dogs is revealed, their all-consuming hunger as they race about, led by "a ragged German shepherd" whose "wisdom [was] to run half blind, his nose close to the ground." Ashton slaughters them all mercilessly with his rifle and shotgun. Not long afterward, his fifteen-year-old sister Elsa is attacked and raped by a gang of strange men as she walks home alone one evening. Her life is ruined; she is considered despoiled and a shame to her family. Even Ashton turns away from her. She is also pregnant, but has no idea who fathered her child.

When Nathan is born, Elsa finds that she cannot properly love or care for him; she even begins to abuse him. Mrs. Vickery comes upon Elsa as she lunges at Nathan's eye with a spoonful of baby food, and soon afterward, Elsa leaves the Vickery household, leaving baby Nathan in the care of his grandparents. Opal Vickery does love the baby and gives him the affection he lacked with his mother.

At the age of five, Nathan has the first of his seven visions of God. This intense experience is brought on when Opal takes Nathan to a Pentecostal prayer meeting where the minister and his followers handle venomous snakes when they feel that the spirit of God is upon them. Opal is alarmed by the intensity of the service, but Nathan goes into a trance and handles the serpents without being harmed. He is convinced of his spiritual calling and begins to preach at the local church. The power and authority of his ministry attracts a wide following, and soon Nathan is traveling to many southern Christian churches.

When he is eleven, he attracts the attention of the Reverend Marian Miles Beloff, a popular preacher, who shrewdly recruits Nathan to bring in more converts and donations. Beloff's daughter, Leonie, is attracted to the young man and teases him mercilessly. Nathan has left school early to pursue his ministry and has little experience with normal human interactions. When Leonie finally arouses him, his intense passion frightens her, and she rejects him. Feeling keenly his fall from grace, Nathan punishes himself by publicly putting out one eye during a televised Good Friday service.

His recovery is slow, but Nathan finds that when he returns to preaching, his following swells. Nathan's new ministry, the Seekers of Christ, carries him through the troubled 1960's. His visions grow increasingly intense and horrific. By now, his followers call him "The Master." In one vision, Nathan sees the pages of the Bible and even the image of Christ burn up and disappear. Nathan interprets this as meaning that Christ failed, and Nathan's God whispers that Nathan is the Second Coming, who will fulfill what Christ did not. The Seekers purchase land and establish communities throughout the United States, while Nathan grows ever more distant from his followers and his own humanity.

Japheth Sproul becomes Nathan's most devoted follower after attending one of his prayer meetings. Nathan eventually detects homosexual longings in Japheth's devotion and casts him out of the Seekers. Japheth retaliates by attempting to kill Nathan.

After this second recovery, Nathan is fully convinced that he is an immortal Christ figure. Yet soon afterward, at one of his most ambitious appearances, Nathan has his final vision, which ends his ministry. He sees what he believes is the face of God Himself: "shapeless, twisting and undulating and coiling and writhing and leaping." Horrified, Nathan feels his intimacy with God desert him.

The novel ends as Nathan, now calling himself William, wanders through his hometown, endlessly seeking to recapture his state of Grace, willing to wait as long as it takes, uninterested in doing anything else with his life.

The Characters

Oates explores the intense psychological workings of her characters, highlighting their torments and illuminating the certainties that shape their lives. Not one of her characters is flat, but some also serve as types to convey the themes of the story. Many of the characters repeat biblical verses to themselves in their attempts to understand the mysterious will of God.

Nathan is the most fully rounded character in the novel. Although his life is the focus of the novel, Oates does not make him a sympathetic character, a fact that at times makes the novel a difficult struggle. Because he begins his preaching career as a young boy, Nathan never experiences the normal phases of human life nor learns common social interactions. The joy he finds with other humans is limited to his sense of his audience as souls to be saved; he sees their bodies as merely fleshy containers to be ignored. As his ministry and influence grow, Nathan becomes more alienated from humanity, until he fails to see other people as having any objective reality.

Opal Vickery, Nathan's grandmother, provides the religious fervor that informs his life. Oates portrays Opal as an average, uneducated Christian, blindly accepting religious authority. Opal believes wholeheartedly that her grandson has been touched by God and facilitates his career as a preacher, keeping faith with him until the end.

Thaddeus Vickery, Nathan's grandfather, is appalled at the boy's predilection for religious sentiment and protests that they are failing their trust. A rational man, Thaddeus serves as a foil to the irrationality of his wife's and grandson's faith. Thaddeus finds his solace in reading the meditations of Marcus Aurelius, but he studies the New Testament to try to understand the religiosity of his wife and grandson. He finds there not a loving and accepting Christ, as he expected, but a psychopathic bully. Shortly after Dr. Vickery reaches this conclusion, he has a stroke and dies.

Elsa Vickery, Nathan's mother, an attractive girl of only average intelligence, never recovers mentally from her rape and the social ostracism that follows. She abandons the infant Nathan after abusing him and makes a new life for herself in a distant city. Even when Nathan is grown, she never feels comfortable around him.

The Reverend Marian Miles Beloff preaches a message of "simple love for God and fellow man and faith in the Scriptures." He shrewdly sees in Nathan new talent to exploit and popularizes the boy's more rigid view of Christianity. The Reverend Beloff represents the typical evangelist who enjoys full coffers and the good life that success brings while minimizing the effect his belief has on his own conduct.

Leonie Beloff serves as the fleshly distraction that nearly destroys Nathan. Engaged several times to be married, Leonie enjoys flirting and flaunts her own sexuality. She does not have the wisdom to understand Nathan's inexperience with human desire. Her ultimate rejection of Nathan sets the stage for his final denial of all human feeling and relationships.

William Japheth Sproul III is a divinity scholar from a long line of scholars who is so disturbed by Nathan's preaching that he becomes obsessed by the messenger. Japheth represents the rational man who allows himself to be caught up by the charisma of a powerful leader; he also serves as a Judas figure who betrays Nathan. Japheth believes that his attempt at murdering Nathan succeeded but that Nathan returned to life through God's power.

Themes and Meanings

Oates examines the phenomena of the charismatic evangelist and individual religious experience in depth. The narrative allows for two opposing interpretations of the life of Nathan Vickery. As an abused, sensitive child exposed to rabid religious sentiment, Nathan is ripe for the onset of visions. The physical description of his episodes suggests seizures and possible schizophrenia. Nathan in this sense is a victim of his sordid beginnings and unfortunate cultural upbringing. Encouraged in his religious fervor, untutored in normal human interactions, and revered by thousands as having special knowledge and favor, Nathan eventually believes himself to be the monster that they have created. Through all of this, he seeks most fervently his own redemption, an intimacy with the spirit of God that he has never known among his own people.

A second interpretation of Nathan's experience provokes a startling, though no less tragic, conclusion. If readers allow themselves to believe that Nathan's religious experience is valid, that he truly communes with God and seeks to follow His will, then Nathan's evolution follows a path that leads him increasingly farther from humanity. To believe in the biblical messages as fully as Nathan does causes him to retreat from personal contact; to accept the message that God is all we need drives him further away. When Nathan understands that his followers and even his fellow preachers do not share his intense understanding, his isolation grows and develops into a self-centered importance that elevates him far above the people who hunger for his message. Oates reveals the inherent destruction of the literal message of Christianity. Nathan's final vision of an all-devouring God of Chaos shakes him yet does not cure his desire be one with that greater force. A recurring theme is that of hunger, whether of the wild dogs at the beginning of the novel or the masses who flock to hear Nathan's apocalyptic message. The image of a hungry stray dog recurs twice: during Leonie's seduction of Nathan, implying his physical hunger, and at the end of the book, symbolizing his spiritual hunger.

Critical Context

Around the time *Son of the Morning* was published, another charismatic preacher led his followers to the ultimate sacrifice in Jonestown, Guyana. The Reverend Jim Jones had amassed wealth as Nathan does in the novel and also sought to lead his followers to a safe place away from the nonbelievers of the world. Since then, many charismatic leaders have emerged and led their followers to death, including David Koresh of the Branch Davidians and Marshall Applewhite of the Heaven's Gate cult. The significance of *Son of the Morning* cannot be understated in light of such occurrences. Oates provides a compelling psychological look at what can happen to a human being caught up in fervent religious belief and also shows how easily ordinary people will turn to these leaders as authority figures in their lives. Although the novel troubled reviewers in some Christian publications, its message of alienation and blind devotion are worth study.

Bibliography

Bender, Eileen Teper. *Sacred and Profane Visions*. Bloomington: Indiana University Press, 1987. Discusses *Son of the Morning*.

Friedman, Ellen G. *Joyce Carol Oates*. New York: Frederick Ungar, 1980. Extensive discussion of Oates's early work. Examines *Son of the Morning* in an epilogue.

Johnson, Greg. *Invisible Writer: A Biography of Joyce Carol Oates*. New York: Dutton, 1998. Extensive critical biography of Oates.

Wagner, Linda, ed. *Critical Essays on Joyce Carol Oates*. Boston: G. K. Hall, 1979. Contains essays on Oates's individual works, including an essay on *Son of the Morning*.

Waller, G. F. *Dreaming America: Obsession and Transcendence in the Fiction of Joyce Carol Oates*. Baton Rouge: Louisiana State University Press, 1979. Discusses Oates's early work mainly through comparison of her with D. H. Lawrence.

Watanabe, Nancy Ann. *Love Eclipsed: Joyce Carol Oates's Faustian Moral Vision*. Lanham, Md.: University Press of America, 1998. Uses rather elevated academic language to discuss the author's theory regarding Oates's work, including *Son of the Morning*.

Patricia Masserman

THE SOURCE

Author: James A. Michener (1907-1997)
Type of plot: Historical chronicle
Time of plot: The frame of the novel takes place in 1964; flashbacks cover approximately twelve thousand years of Israel's history, starting in 9831 B.C.E.
Locale: The Tell of Makor, the "source," in western Galilee
First published: 1965

Principal characters:

DR. JOHN CULLINANE, an Irish Catholic scholar and archaeologist who heads the dig at Tell Makor

JEMAIL TABARI, an Arab trained at Oxford, who assists at the dig in the role of a "scientific archeologist"

DR. ILAN ELIAV, a Jewish statesman and archaeologist who acts as the official "watchdog," or chief administrator, of the dig

DR. VERED BAR-EL, a Jewish archaeologist and Israel's "top expert in dating pottery sherds"; she is the only woman on the dig and is engaged to Dr. Eliav

PAUL J. ZODMAN, a wealthy Jew from Chicago who is financing the dig

THE FAMILY OF UR, the original ancestors of Makor, whose genealogy begins with Ur in 9831 B.C.E. and ends with Jemail Tabari in 1964 C.E.

The Novel

The principal action of *The Source* takes place on the Tell of Makor, an imaginary archaeological site undergoing excavation in 1964 under the direction of Dr. John Cullinane. This tell, or mound, which has been uninhabited for nearly seven hundred years, has a history reaching back some twelve thousand years to 9831 B.C.E. The Hebrew name "Makor" means "source," indicating the existence of a well or natural water supply nearby, while the settlement itself represents "the patiently accumulated residue of one abandoned settlement after another, each resting on the ruins of its predecessor, reaching endlessly back into history." It is to this mound that Cullinane has come to excavate the various layers (fifteen in all) of civilization that settled Makor. Three other archaeologists join him: Jemail Tabari, Dr. Ilan Eliav, and Dr. Vered Bar-El, a Muslim and two Jews respectively. Cullinane is a Catholic, and the obvious tripartite religious significance of this group should not be overlooked. The excavation is financed by Paul J. Zodman, a Jew from Chicago, whom Cullinane must keep happy if he wants to continue working at Makor for more than five years.

In the opening chapter, the three archaeologists meet at Makor to begin their work (aided by a group of local kibbutzniks). As they excavate the two main shafts, or tunnels, down through seventy-one feet of debris that comprise the tell, they discover fifteen objects from fifteen different historical levels. The objects are recorded and diagramed by Cullinane and each offers the basis for a dramatized episode of the people and events that successively built and destroyed Makor throughout its history. In this way, the true focus of the novel starts taking shape and the dig becomes a structural vehicle. Interspersed throughout the historical narratives, the novel returns to the present, giving Cullinane and his colleagues a chance to discuss various historical and philosophical questions regarding the formation of the Jewish, Christian, and Muslim religions, and their oftentimes stormy relationship in the past and present.

The greater part of the novel is devoted to the historical flashbacks that form the backdrop of the story. The present-day team discovers at the bottom level evidence of the family of Ur who helped to formulate the first organized society at Makor in 9831 B.C.E. It is here that man first learned to cultivate and harvest wheat. As a result of this discovery comes the vague realization that man is at the mercy of the rains and winds. Unclear notions of religion creep into their lives, and they erect a nameless monolith which they hope will placate nature's wrath and ensure their crops' survival. Thus man's first notion of religion springs forth, but with it comes a new fear: "the mystery of death, the triumph of evil, the terrible loneliness of being alone, the discovery that self of itself is insufficient." It is an anxiety that will haunt humankind forever.

Eight thousand years pass, and Ur's descendant, Urbaal, is the leading figure of Makor, and the nameless monolith has been christened El. The religious practices of the people are rooted in the fertility of the earth, and it is into this "corrupting" atmosphere that Joktan, leader of a nomadic tribe called the Habiru (forerunners of the Hebrews and reminiscent of Moses), and his followers enter Makor. The tribe and their one God are quickly absorbed by the lusty rituals and gods of the townspeople, yet the seeds of monotheism have been sown and begin to grow.

After a span of eight hundred years, another descendant of Ur, Uriel, and another leader of another nomadic Hebrew tribe, Zadok, meet and come into bitter conflict over their respective gods. El Shaddai (later Yahweh) orders the destruction of Makor's Canaanites for their worship of "Baal" and other "false" gods, as well as for their sexual "abominations," in which some Hebrews have taken part. This is an important episode, for in it the Hebrews are, for the first time, singled out by their God as His "chosen" people. It also demonstrates how fixed the Hebrews have become with the notion of one god for all.

Approximately four hundred years pass, and Ur's descendant, Jabaal, a Canaanite architect, is married to a Jewish woman, Kerith. Makor is now a mixture of sects, all living peacefully under the leadership of King David. It is made clear in this episode that the Canaanites are still rooted to the earth through their gods, while the Hebrews long for spiritual growth, represented by Jerusalem and Yahweh. By the year 600 B.C.E., the "stiff necked" Hebrews have known both triumph and defeat under the direction of Yahweh. Their greatest trial to date is about to occur: their exile into Babylon. Again a descendant of Ur, Jeremoth, tries to save Makor (this time from Nebuchadrezzar), but the Hebrews, under direct orders from Yahweh, offer themselves up as willing captives, clinging tenaciously to their religion.

After almost three hundred years of exile, the Hebrews find their way back to Makor and, for a time, live peacefully. Again their endurance and faith are tested, first by political laws and then by religious persecutions. For a few hundred years the Jews live in harmony with the Hellenistic culture established at Makor. Yet little by little their freedom to worship is usurped and their traditions are mocked. Greek rule, however, fades quickly, only to be replaced by a harsher rule, that of Rome. The Jews now fall under the leadership of Herod, who eventually manages to kill tens of thousands of Jews. This is the one episode in which Michener breaks his common practice of using the third-person narrator. The entire chapter is unfolded in the first-person voice of Timmon (architect and descendant of Ur). It is also the only chapter in which there is no clear portrait drawn of a Hebrew leader standing up for the right to worship Yahweh.

The Jews of the first century make up for this silence. When Makor is once again threatened with destruction, a Jewish leader, Yigal, the first Hebrew descendant of Ur, resists openly under the misguided leadership of Josephus. Through an ironic turn of events, Yigal is betrayed and murdered as Makor burns once again. By the year 350 C.E., Makor is rebuilt, and the Jews living there reach an important cornerstone in their history. The chapter is somewhat drawn out, but its significance is pivotal, for at this point in time the Talmud, the second great book of Judaism, is formulated and codified. Thus in the face of Christianity, a religion of "love and redemption," the rigidity of the Talmudic laws, although harsh at times, ensures the Jews' endurance just as firmly as monotheism did centuries earlier.

After the Christians, the Muslims are next to enter Makor. Following many persecutions of both Jews and Christians, the three groups settle peacefully for several hundred years. Then come the German knights on their holy Crusades. In their frantic search for the infidel Muslims, they slaughter Christians and Jews alike. A group of knights, led by Volkmar (who marries a descendant of Ur), builds a great castle which protects Makor until 1291 C.E., when the town is destroyed for the final time.

The Jewish spirit of Makor lives on in a nearby town called Safad. In 1500 C.E., out of the intellectual and mystical atmosphere of Safad, come two factions of Jews: the Ashkenazi, concerned with following the rigid Talmudic laws, and the Sephardi, who open up a new mystical side of Judaism found in the cabala. In this way both the practical and spiritual endurance of the Jews is once again enforced.

Safad's Jews, now under Turkish rule, live peacefully once again, while Makor, now only a mound of desert dust, is barely a memory. Then in 1948 C.E., a new generation of Jews, no longer willing to accept their ancestors' role of "enduring" yet "homeless" Jews, fights openly for the establishment of Israel. During this "war" Eliav and Bar-El first meet as dedicated enemies not only of the Arabs (of which Tabari is one), but also of the spiritual stagnation of the old rabbis.

With the successful establishment of Israel, the novel returns to the present. Yet the past still remains, for Cullinane's questions still remain: Why do the Jews make life so hard for themselves? How have they endured for so long? A third one arises: What gives them the right to claim the Holy Land as their own? The novel attempts to answer the first two questions with monotheism and Talmudic laws; the third remains unanswered.

In the closing pages Tabari finds, at last, the hidden "source," the well of Makor at which his ancestors first drank twelve thousand years before. Cullinane, immersed more than ever in the question of the Jews, is promised more funding for his dig. Eliav finally realizes his own purpose as a Jew: to live life. Yet it is Vered Bar-El and Paul Zodman who open up a new possibility for the Jew: the willingness to keep the spirit of Judaism alive without being trapped by the rigid laws of the Talmud. It is a solution met with mixed reactions.

The Characters

John Cullinane, the head archaeologist of the dig, is not only responsible for commenting upon the historical aspects of the artifacts found in the tell, but also instigates the philosophical questions that run throughout the novel. A scholar, an Irish Catholic, and most important, a man free from any preconceived prejudices (at least as free as anyone can be), Cullinane is anxious to immerse himself in the history of the Jews, and by extension the Arabs, in order to discover the "spirit" that built Makor. He is a man with both "enthusiasm and a shovel," who probes not only the earth but also the hearts of its people.

Michener is not known for his ability to create compelling characters (after all, in a novel covering twelve thousand years they are onstage for such a short time), but his characters are functional to the movement of his novels, especially *The Source*. As for Cullinane, one can see Michener himself as the prototype for the archaeologist: one who travels to a land, probes, digs (literally and figuratively), searches for information, questions, listens, and above all tries to understand. This is what Michener did while writing this novel, and this is what Cullinane does throughout the novel. He asks age-old questions to which Michener wants the answers.

As for Jemail Tabari and Ilan Eliav, they too are important for their function in the novel, rather than in any sense of character development. Each in his own way represents the "new" man of modern Islam and modern Israel. If at one time they were deadly enemies (as were their ancestors), now they are able to work side by side at the dig, with the hope that they will also work side by side in settling the strife between their two peoples. These are the two men to whom Cullinane turns time and time again with his questions. Each man, Tabari and Eliav, offers Cullinane (and the novel) a link to the past and present, as well as the possibility of understanding both.

The next two characters are also functionary, yet at first their functions are not clear. Vered Bar-El, the modern Jewish woman, seems to be at the dig merely to add a romantic triangle to the novel. Engaged to Eliav, who, it turns out, cannot marry her because of an ancient Talmudic law (any descendant of a Cohen cannot marry a divorced woman), she is also drawn to Cullinane, who wants to marry her. The triangle itself, as it is played out, is rather tedious and forced, and Bar-El is conveniently sent to America on a public relations mission. As for Paul Zodman, his role seems merely to give money to the dig, and once he makes his initial visit, he too returns to America. It is not until the final chapter, when both Bar-El and Zodman return to the dig, that their true function comes clear.

Bar-El represents the new Jewish woman: She fought in the war; she is educated; she wears no makeup; and she no longer believes in that "Mickey Mouse" nonsense handed down by the old rabbis. Zodman represents the American Jew, wealthy and free from the inflexible laws of the old rabbis, yet earnest in his desire to keep the Jewish "spirit" alive. Their marriage represents the joining of this new "spirit" and offers Michener a way in which to reconcile the old with the new and answer some of the novel's questions.

The last character to discuss is the Family of Ur as each descendant appears in his respective "level." Throughout the twelve thousand years, "Ur" has been a caveman, a Canaanite, a Greek, a Roman, a Hebrew, a German, and an Arab. In each role, he has come up against, or been a part of, the Jewish problem in Makor. At times he took sides and at other times he remained neutral; at all times he was immersed in the welfare of Makor and its survival. He (in his different guises) acts as a paradoxical double to the various Jews with whom he came into contact at Makor. For just as it was the Jews' rigidity in adhering to Yahweh and the Talmudic laws which allowed them to endure, it was Ur's ability to adapt and change that allowed him to endure.

Themes and Meanings

The overriding metaphor of the novel, which develops naturally into its main theme, is introduced in the opening chapter just after Cullinane has arrived at Tell Makor. He is walking around the tell trying to decide the crucial spot to dig his two main tunnels when he notices a grove of "incredibly old" olive trees, whose age is measured in "centuries and millennia." Yet one tree in particular, one with a rotting trunk, catches Cullinane's attention: "A veritable patriarch whose gnarled trunk was merely a shell through which one could see many directions. The tree bore only a few branches, but these were thick with maturing olives, and as the archaeologist stood inquiringly beside the stubborn relic, he was as close to the mystery of Makor as he would ever be." The ancient water well at Makor may have allowed the town to grow and flourish, but it is the olive trees (the same ones that Ur tended in 9831 B.C.E.) that endure, just as the Jews have endured. Their foundations and laws may be old and gnarled and dry, such as the old rabbis and their Talmud, but the new branches, those such as Eliav, Bar-El, and the kibbutzniks, are strong and getting stronger.

Michener sets up this tree, or theme, in the beginning of the novel and returns to both as each level is revealed. Makor is destroyed some five times, but the olive grove remains intact. Michener, as does Cullinane, returns to this tree in the closing chapter and overtly points out the link between the tree and the theme. His second theme is also represented by a physical object, or objects: the three men, Cullinane, Tabari, and Eliav (Christian, Muslim, and Jew). It is the theme of brotherhood.

The three men open the novel by coming to work at the dig. As they work, and the different levels are narrated, the attempts and failures of the various sects to settle Makor peacefully and share its walls and water are continually revealed. This theme of a brotherhood of mankind is common to Michener's novels, for it is a theme in which he truly believes. By the end of the novel, each of the three men has voiced his belief in this goal, and each goes his separate way, hoping that he can someday accomplish it.

It is not only the themes of endurance and brotherhood that hold the novel together; it is the structure of the land itself, the Tell of Makor, that gives the novel unity. With the framework of the novel (the opening and closing chapters), set in 1964, the body of the novel takes the form of the earth as its structural model. The narration starts at the bottom and oldest level of Makor and moves steadily upward and forward in time. The artifacts that the archaeologists find act as a means to introduce each particular episode, while the accompanying maps help to show the changes Makor went through (walls, buildings, size, and shape) as well as those two objects which endured: the well and the site of the first nameless monolith. As each layer reveals the past, the present is kept sharply in focus, for upon the past the future is built, and rebuilt.

Critical Context

Next to *Hawaii* (1959), *The Source* is considered Michener's greatest and most complex novel, both in scope and in theme. The concerns of the Middle East (past, present, and future) had been in Michener's mind for nearly ten years before he wrote this novel and are sometimes judged as being too optimistic given the end of the story and the trouble that has erupted since the novel's publication. Nevertheless, Michener received wide acclaim for what he attempted to do with *The Source*, and in 1967 he received the Einstein Award for his work within an organization calling itself Americans for Permanent Peace in the Middle East. His interest in this topic also prompted him to write a number of articles, and in 1974 he was awarded an honorary degree by the Yeshiva University in New York.

Michener is never afraid to put his own questions and concerns into a novel, nor is he afraid to answer those questions or offer solutions. As a world traveler, historian, journalist, essayist, and novelist, Michener shows again and again that he believes in some sort of a bond or continuity that links all of mankind throughout the ages. *The Source* offers to Michener the topic of Judaism, one of the world's most painful and joyous examples of continued religious persecution and endurance. It is a novel celebrating endurance, and in the final words, spoken by Eliav: "Life isn't meant to be easy, it's meant to be life."

Bibliography
Day, A. Grove. *James Michener.* New York: Twayne, 1964. Day provides a critical and interpretive study of Michener's earlier works, with a close reading of his major novels, a solid bibliography, and complete notes and references.
Groseclose, David A. *James A. Michener: A Bibliography.* Austin, Tex.: State House Press, 1996. An annotated bibliography of works by and about James Michener from 1923 to 1995.
Hayes, John P. *James A. Michener: A Biography.* Indianapolis, Ind.: Bobbs-Merrill, 1984. A biography spanning Michener's childhood through the 1980's. Valuable for background on influences in Michener's development as a writer.

Michener, James. *Literary Reflections: Michener on Michener, Hemingway, Capote, and Others*. Austin, Tex.: State House Press, 1993. Michener reflects on his life as a writer and on his work. He also shares his memories of his era's most influential writers. The collection of essays gives important insights into Michener's views on literature and into his evaluations of his own works.

Roberts, F. X., and C. D. Rhine, comps. *James A. Michener: A Checklist of His Works, With a Selected, Annotated Bibliography*. Westport, Conn.: Greenwood Press, 1995. A comprehensive bibliography of Michener's books, stories, and articles by and about him.

Severson, Marilyn S. *James A. Michener: A Critical Companion*. Westport, Conn.: Greenwood Press, 1996. Severson give an overview of Michener's life and examines the characteristics and themes of his fiction. His major historical novels are discussed and analyzed for plot, structure, and theme.

Shahin, Jim. "The Continuing Saga of James A. Michener." *Saturday Evening Post* 262 (March, 1990): 66-71. Shahin gives an overview of the life and career of Michener.

Deborah Charlie

THE SOUTHPAW

Author: Mark Harris (Mark Harris Finkelstein; 1922-   )
Type of plot: Comic social morality
Time of plot: 1952
Locale: New York City; other locations have been given the fictitious names of
    Perkinsville, New York; Agua Clara; and Queen City
First published: 1953

    Principal characters:
        HENRY WIGGEN, the unlettered narrator and principal character, a
           cocky left-handed pitcher who plays for the New York Mammoths
           and who grows up in the course of the novel
        POP, his father, the driver of the Perkinsville school bus and a
           semiprofessional baseball player
        AARON WEBSTER, a well-educated, eighty-year-old astronomer, Pop's
           friend and neighbor
        HOLLY WEBSTER, Aaron's niece, the girl next door, Henry's sweetheart
           and later his wife
        PATRICIA MOORS, the daughter of wealthy Lester T. Moors, Jr., the
           owner of the New York Mammoths
         "SAD SAM" YALE, a star left-handed pitcher and Henry's boyhood idol
        DUTCH SCHNELL, the team manager, whose principal aim is to win
           baseball games
        RED TRAPHAGEN, the catcher and team intellectual, who studied at
           Harvard
        PERRY SIMPSON, a black infielder, who rooms with Henry

The Novel

Much of the action in *The Southpaw* concerns the experiences of Henry Wiggen, a young left-handed pitcher, after he joins the New York Mammoths and becomes part of their fight to win the pennant in the year 1952. Henry Wiggen relates his experiences in his own language, and his viewpoint is emphasized in the novel's full title: *The Southpaw, by Henry W. Wiggen: Punctuation Freely Inserted and Greatly Improved by Mark Harris.* Born in Perkinsville, a small town in upstate New York, Henry Wiggen, like the entire town, is devoted to baseball. When he discovers that the local library has books on baseball, he works his way through a series of "How to Play Baseball" books as well as a series of adventure books about Sid Yule, a thinly disguised version of Henry's idol, the great left-handed pitcher Sam Yale. After joining the Mammoths and becoming acquainted with Sam, Henry frequently alludes to passages in *Sam Yale—Mammoth*, a book that lauds clean living and obedience to authority, supposedly written by Sam. Sam finally suggests that Henry have his father send him the book.

When Sam reads the book which he is supposed to have written, he comments to

Henry that it is "horseshit," qualifying that judgment with the observation that the book is all right for most kids because they do not "aim very high." Sam's words are filtered through Henry's grammatical constructions: "Those that aim high when they get there finds out that they should of went somewhere else." Henry pretends to agree, but Sam discounts Henry's assumed sophistication:

> It will take you 15 years to find out. You get so you do not care. It is all like a ball game with nobody watching and nobody keeping score and nobody behind you. You pitch hard and nobody really cares.

In addition to revealing that he did not write the book that Henry has been reading and rereading once a week for years, Sad Sam tells Henry that the actual author of the book is Krazy Kress, a corrupt sportswriter with a series of angles for making money out of everything from benefit dinners to tours to Korea for entertaining the troops. These revelations inspire Henry to write *The Southpaw*, in which he sets out to tell the true story of baseball.

The action of *The Southpaw* centers on Henry's gradual recognition of the emptiness of Sam Yale, the corruption of Krazy Kress, and the lack of humanity of Dutch Schnell, manager of the Mammoths. Henry's coming of age occurs when he refuses either to apologize for or to retract the statement "Leave us forget Korea," which Krazy Kress uses as the focal point for a column attacking Henry. Henry rejects the false position of entertaining the troops, who are fighting a war in which he does not believe. Patricia Moors, the wealthy owner's daughter, tries to intimidate Henry by telling him that he owes it to the "organization" to respond to the column. Henry refuses to bow to the pressure and in so doing accepts the responsibility for his individuality and asserts a personal morality.

The story of the maturation of Henry Wiggen could have become sentimental, but this ostensibly simple story of a boy's development is interlaced with arresting descriptions of baseball games. Harris succeeds in making the reader care about the fortunes of the team, the outcome of games, the success or failure of the players. During his youthful binge of reading baseball stories, Henry happens upon those of Ring Lardner and comments that the stories do not "amount to much, half his stories containing women in them and the other half less about baseball then what was going on in the hotels and trains. He never seemed to care how the games came out." In contrast, the games themselves are brilliantly described in *The Southpaw*, engaging the reader in the play-by-play. The juxtaposition of the excitement of the game with Henry's growing awareness of what goes on in "hotels and trains" turns *The Southpaw* into a triumph of comic realism. Because this baseball novel takes a profound look at social mores, it is as memorable and thought-provoking as it is amusing.

The Characters

Henry Wiggen, the narrator and central figure in *The Southpaw*, belongs to the tradition of naïve and semiliterate narrators represented most notably by Mark Twain's

Huckleberry Finn. Henry consistently uses the Arabic numerals "1" and "2" for one and two, "then" for than, "could of" for could have, and "leave" for let. He reports the conversations he has with other people in his own dialect; the characters and what they say are always filtered through Henry's perceptions and vocabulary. In *The Southpaw*, this insistent narrative frame distances the reader from the events taking place and from Henry's assessments of them. Early in the novel, Henry blithely and approvingly quotes Leo Durocher's statement that "nice guys do not win ball games," a sentiment preserved in American slang as "nice guys finish last." By the end of the novel, Henry Wiggen recognizes, although he is unable to articulate it, that being a "nice guy" may be more important than winning.

In *The Southpaw*, Harris is especially successful in creating memorable characters. Dutch Schnell, the hard-boiled manager of the Mammoths, serves as a touchstone for understanding the motivation and values of the other characters. Schnell, as Henry observes, is "a great manager" whose "first and only aim in life is winning ball games." Henry explains the kind of man Dutch is without making moral judgments:

> There is nothing Dutch will not do for the sake of the ball game. If he thinks it will help win a ball game by eating you out he will eat you out. . . . If it is money you need he will give you money. And if he has no further need for you he will sell you or trade you or simply cut you loose and forget you.

Schnell is ruthless, but he is a winner, and, as Henry astutely perceives, there is a lot of Dutch Schnell in all the Mammoths. Even Sam Yale and Red Traphagen, whatever they say, play ball not only for the money but also for the glory of winning.

Red Traphagen, the intellectual of the team, learned his Spanish at Harvard University and perfected it in the Spanish Civil War. With more than a glance at the Ernest Hemingway hero, Red talks during the playing of the national anthem, ridicules the notion that any of the fans are free, and insists that few of them are brave.

In a discussion of whether they would become ballplayers if they had it to do over again, Dutch naturally says that he would. Sad Sam Yale, the epitome of self-interested disillusionment, says that he would not. Red, however, voices the worst assessment of their motivations: "There ain't a man on this bus that could eat like he eats in any other line of work. . . . It is better than eating somebody's crap in a mine or a mill or a farm or an office. It is the gold we are after." Red's insistence upon economic motivations, his ostensible pragmatism, masks a deep cynicism. Later, Henry sarcastically thanks Red for backing him up when he challenges Dutch about playing him when ill; Red replies that Dutch will never lose and that, young and single, Henry can afford to take risks. It is not surprising that Mike Mulrooney, manager of one of the Mammoth's farm teams, warns Henry against listening to Red Traphagen and Sam Yale off the field. Sam Yale, the disillusioned star, and Red Traphagen, the cynical intellectual, have not come to terms with the Dutch Schnell in themselves, the desire for glory that even the naïve Henry recognizes and acknowledges.

Themes and Meanings

For Dutch, the epitome of softness and failure is to become a "gymnasium teacher." A gymnasium teacher does not understand that games must be won at any cost. The principal contrast to Dutch Schnell is afforded by Mike Mulrooney, the manager of Queen City in the Four-State Mountain League. Henry describes Mike Mulrooney as "one of the grandest men that ever lived," emphasizing his humanity. Unlike Dutch, Mulrooney "will not eat you out in front of all the rest," and he "will treat you all the same, no matter if you are on the way up or the way down, for he takes the attitude that if you are not the greatest ballplayer in the world still and all you are a human being." Harris, however, avoids sentimentality and keeps the portrait balanced. To maintain his humanity, Mike Mulrooney has to be willing not "to run the whole show but just live an easygoing life and not worry you ragged about setting the whole world on fire." Mark Harris unsentimentally recognizes that the Dutch Schnells win games while the Mike Mulrooneys end up in the minor leagues. To avoid compromising, Mike Mulrooney may have to be willing to retreat to his ranch in Colorado, appropriately named Last Chance.

Henry Wiggen will never be Mike Mulrooney because he desperately wants to win, to become a baseball immortal. (Henry's father can never explain to his son why he quit after two years of professional ball and spent the rest of his life driving a school bus and playing for the Perkinsville Scarlets.) Nevertheless, he is not prepared to sacrifice everything merely for the sake of success. Summing up the challenges he faces, Henry's wife Holly tells him that "the world needs all the lefthanders it can get, for it is a righthanded world"; he is "a southpaw in a starboarded atmosphere." Henry's left-handedness, like his cowardice when it comes to military training, is identified with honesty and humanity. He rejects any kind of hypocrisy: "It seemed to me that if I was too much of a coward to go and fight in the war against Korea myself I had no business going over and playing ball for them and encouraging them to be fighting it." Thus, Henry refuses to concede to the pressures—material, social, or psychological—which eat away at the other characters.

Critical Context

The Southpaw was the first of four novels by Mark Harris featuring Henry Wiggen; the others are *Bang the Drum Slowly* (1956), *A Ticket for a Seamstitch* (1957), and *It Looked Like for Ever* (1979). Of the four, the first two are by far the most highly regarded.

In *The Southpaw*, Harris transforms elements common to "baseball books" and "juvenile sports series" into a serious novel. While Harris does examine the drive to win, to achieve, within the context of professional baseball, his analysis of contemporary values and morals is fully applicable to business, entertainment, or any other profession. Dutch Schnell, Sad Sam Yale, and many other characters in *The Southpaw* are found in any walk of life.

Henry Wiggen, the narrator of *The Southpaw*, is not so typical. He is a left-handed pitcher, a left-hander in a right-handed world. Comparison with two other young heroes in American fiction is illuminating: Huckleberry Finn and Holden Caulfield, fictional characters who have become part of our culture.

Like Huck Finn, Henry is a naïve narrator. The matter of race is raised obliquely in *The Southpaw* as it is in the *The Adventures of Huckleberry Finn* (1884). It is worth noting that this book was first published in 1953, two years before the United States Supreme Court ruled that segregation in the public schools was unconstitutional. Henry's roommate, Perry Simpson, a black infielder, is not allowed to stay with the team in certain cities. Henry does not preach about race, but the reader is insistently asked to question the social mores that turn Perry, a black man, into a second-class citizen only because of his color.

Henry Wiggen, unlike Holden Caulfield, is not presented as a victim of society. Henry is finally a more admirable figure morally than Holden Caulfield, the victim and child, helpless in the face of a society for which he feels no responsibility. Indeed, from a moral perspective, Henry is much closer to Huck Finn; he is never "precious."

Because *The Southpaw* was initially classified as a "baseball book," it was slow to receive the serious and thoughtful attention it merits, but, with *Bang the Drum Slowly*, it is now widely acknowledged as a novel which transcends its genre.

Bibliography
Fimrite, Ron. "Fiction In a Diamond Setting: Mark Harris's Novels Sparkle with Hard-Edged Realism." *Sports Illustrated* 73 (October 15, 1990): 117-122. A biographical and critical profile of Mark Harris. Fimrite details the evolution of serious literature on baseball and asserts that until the publication of *The Southpaw*, baseball literature consisted of mostly "fairy tales" boy's books written by fabulists. Fimrite also notes the influence of Ring Lardner and Mark Twain on Harris's baseball books.
Harris, Mark. *Best Father Ever Invented: The Autobiography of Mark Harris*. New York: Dial Press, 1976. In his autobiography, written during the 1960's and published in 1976, Harris portrays himself as depressed over his work, categorizing *The Southpaw* as "facile realism in a facile style." It is a fascinating early self-portrait of a writer who has since come to terms with himself and his writing.
_____. *Diamond: Baseball Writings of Mark Harris*. New York: Donald I. Fine, 1995. A collection of baseball writings by Harris spanning 1946 through 1993. Provides an illuminating view into Harris's devotion to the game and the evolution of his thinking on numerous topics. Also included is Harris's screenplay of the movie version of *Bang the Drum Slowly*.
Lavers, Norman. *Mark Harris*. Boston: Twayne, 1978. Lavers provides a critical and interpretive study of Harris, with a close reading of his major works, a solid bibliography, and complete notes and references.

Jean R. Brink

SPEEDBOAT

Author: Renata Adler (1938-   )
Type of plot: Loosely structured ironic sketches
Time of plot: Wanders between the narrator's childhood years and the middle 1970's
Locale: Primarily New York City, but touches many points on the globe
First published: 1976

> *Principal characters:*
> JEN FAIN, the narrator, a newspaper reporter and sometime columnist, college teacher, foundation consultant, and congressional staff worker
> WILL,
> SAM,
> ALDO,
> VLAD,
> JOEL, and
> JIM, an assortment of male apartment mates and confidants

The Novel

Speedboat is a conglomeration of ironic incidents presented to the reader by an equally ironic first-person narrator, a newspaper reporter named Jen Fain, who sometimes radiates an acute sensitivity and at other times seems hopelessly numbed. This "notebook" on the frenetic pace and crazy logic in everyday urban (and urbane) living also examines the landscapes of urban escape—the Hamptons, the Caribbean, the Mediterranean—where the pace slackens but the logic remains flawed, and doubles as self-directed psychoanalysis. The sketches, or vignettes, that comprise the novel most often feature Jen Fain, but some relegate her to the role of bystander and others have her curiously absent; she merely relays the incident.

Many narrative conventions are ignored. Time, for example, is not handled linearly, nor are there conventional flashbacks. The book bounces back and forth haphazardly with respect to time, as well as perspective. Fain may be watching a rat cross her path on a Manhattan street "last night," and then, a page later, she may be speeding along a rural road in a car with no reference to time, then quoting the ironic remarks of people at a funeral where she plays no part, then appearing back in Manhattan on an unnamed day at 3:00 A.M., and then appearing in the present, telling the reader about her job. She returns to her childhood years, visits her college dormitory, and shoots into the near past with little regard for temporal continuity.

Speedboat is a peripatetic account of a peripatetic life, the narrator's dualistic vision toward her role in the unfolding (and unfolded) events of an unsettling autobiography. On the one hand, Jen Fain introspectively examines the loss of what she calls her "sense of the whole"; her experience comes in ragtag pieces and she feels forced to "wait for events to take a form," to fall into order, which they never do. Thus, she finds herself leading a number of partial lives, none of them ethically satisfying. On the other hand, she is a journalist, an objective recorder of pieces, whose job is to describe events, not analyze them, to distance the self, not immerse it.

Although primarily set in Manhattan during the mid-1970's, the novel's scope covers not only a large expanse of time, but also takes the reader on journalistic junkets around the globe—to Paris, Miami Beach, Zurich, Venice, Las Vegas, London, Martha's Vineyard, Kuala Lumpur, Cairo, Biafra. Throughout her travels, Fain conducts an inner war, exhibiting the eye of both a camera and a humane witness, the ear of a tape recorder and an involved listener. She displays the ironic humor and pathos she finds in circumstances, in people's words and actions, in her own words and actions—and comes up with anecdotal sketches which invariably house *Speedboat*'s glue: a system of sometimes jolting, sometimes deflating aphorisms that alternately kick off or conclude its pieces of narration.

The novel's very first paragraph introduces the reader to one of these maxims—Fain's opinion that "many of the most important things . . . are the ones learned in your sleep." Sleep, she says, is a sustained medium through which one can capture the full "rhythm," the meaning, of events. She goes on: "The city, of course, can wreck it. So much insomnia. So many rhythms collide. The salesgirl, the landlord, the guests, the bystanders, sixteen varieties of social circumstance in a day." Her dissatisfaction with the relentless unfolding of real events, so inherent in these words, is constantly tempered by Fain's own recognized part in it all, a part she finds interesting enough that she needs to explore it, to tell the reader about it.

The narrator transports the reader, and herself, through a system of first- and third-person vignettes—high-level and low-level disturbances that upset the sense of rationality, of ethical order that she seeks. An eighteen-year-old girl, suntanning herself "with great seriousness," concludes after two hours, "When you have a tan, what have you got?" On a ferryboat ride around Manhattan, a loudspeaker blares out baseball scores—with no accompanying context—to a mystified group of foreigners. Students at the University of California at Santa Cruz boycott their classes, and grapes, on the behalf of Santa Cruz's locals. The locals despise the students and buy up all the grapes. Jen Fain can only comment: "There seemed to be no understanding among anybody."

A man refuses to answer his telephone, "on principle," deciding that if he wants to talk to someone, he will do the calling. He never considers that his "principle" might be shared. When an excitement-starved housewife from Malibu eagerly accepts a ride in a tycoon's new speedboat (one reason for the book's title), she exultantly bounces with the boat's jumps—and breaks her back. Two barbers, Lewis and Florian, have worked side by side for years; while Lewis discourages conversation, Florian dances, sings, and imparts advice freely. The single piece of reaction that anyone has heard Lewis express about his "partner" is: "Someday I'm going to kill him."

These bits of ironic exposition, and hundreds like them packaged into one or two or three paragraphs, make up *Speedboat*. They are linked together in a less amalgamated than accumulated cement that suggests hodgepodge but conveys a certain consistency because the pieces are all filtered through Jen Fain's sensibility—even though she brings her sensibility into question. After all, she, unlike the people whose actions she observes, desperately needs sensible answers, normality: "Many things serve something other than their original, arguable purpose. The left lane, for example, on the highway. Some people use it because they prefer it. Some people use it because it looks like any other. Some people use it for some other reason. But the thing is, you are supposed to be driving faster if you use that lane."

The book's ending does provide a kind of resolution. Fain's search for reasoning and wholeness seems fulfilled because she finds herself pregnant, the stuff of happy endings, new beginnings, and completeness—if only she did not think of the fetus as a "hostage."

The Characters

Jen Fain is not a character the reader easily understands. Whereas she cares about the downtrodden, ill-equipped, city-scorned victims of inequity she bumps into on her daily agenda, she paradoxically does little or nothing to remedy their plight. An example comes to mind from the novel's third "chapter," in which Fain goes down to the first floor vestibule of her apartment building to retrieve her morning paper. A bum is asleep under the mailboxes, between the unlocked outer door and the locked inner door. She says, "I could have stepped over the sleeping man, picked up my *Times*, and gone upstairs to read it. Instead, I knocked absurdly from inside the door, and said, 'Wake up. You'll have to leave now.'"

In another example, Fain finds a girl in the hallway of a friend's apartment building looking "much too fast asleep" and not "entirely alive." The narrator cannot find the callousness to leave the girl's side, but she will not take any action, either; she just stares concernedly. The thought comes to Fain to check the girl's purse or call an ambulance, but her friend says, "Maybe she wouldn't want an ambulance." Fain does not check her purse for identification, deciding that, should she become involved, the police might think she had some tie to the girl.

"My own mind is a tenement," Jen Fain says. "Some elevators work. There are orange peels and muggings in the halls. Squatters and double locks on some floors, a few flowered window boxes, half-dressed bachelors cooling on the outside fire steps; plaster falls." She views herself as inconsequential: She does not possess the power to affect events. Although she is intellectually capable (she admits that), she mistrusts her viscera; part of that mistrust can be blamed on her coldly voyeuristic occupation, part on her tendency toward bewilderment.

Fain's perplexed demeanor and intellectual urbanity also contribute to her inability to perform the functions of a "normal" person. Because she spends so much of her energy thinking and rethinking circumstances, she simply cannot get things done. She has been taking flying lessons for years, the reasoning lost in time, and still dreads the thought of landing. She bought a rifle, unassembled, for protection, but unable to put it together. She thinks of the assembly as "one of those simple operations of life that seem to complicate themselves altogether out of my range."

Jen Fain comes across as someone adept at words and the thoughts that produce words (she is, after all, a writer), but inept about actions and the thoughts that produce actions. Because she sees so much confusion in daily living, she seems admirably facile and courageous amid the hostile complexities of some of the book's more exotic situations. She is equally at home walking down a muddy path in the Biafran darkness, with bullets whistling around her, walking back from a film on Fifth Avenue in Manhattan.

Fain is the only real "main" character. Male characters—Will, Sam, Aldo, Vlad, Joel, and Jim—appear and disappear, showing that this peripatetic woman treats her men no differently from other people she encounters. They are Fain's at-the-time companions who open up her experience a little more. As vehicles, they allow her to bounce off their untroubled personalities, offering "grist" for her internal exposé.

Themes and Meanings

Sleep furnishes quiet, solitude, reverie, and a shutdown of the fast-paced system of events. Renata Adler, through her narrator, adds an unexpected dimension to sleep's powers: Sleep brings rationality to thought and the ability to be. Jen Fain, as a reporter, is more representative of a machine than a person: The reader who watches the six o'clock news can see Fain's point. Unfortunately, when she steps out of her reporter's clothes and tries to reenlist in the human race, there is a residual effect. She cannot escape the transition stage. Partially, this is a defense mechanism; the workings of the world and its people have gone haywire. The rational behavior that she imagines should be out there, is lacking. Only the description of what happens makes sense, and then only because it is observed, true. Real life, so the saying goes, is stranger than fiction, and it follows that if the sense derived from recording events is not ethically satisfying, then "unreal" life—dream life—is the only road to ethical wholeness.

Urban living, with its noise and its crowds and its practicality and its pace, is Adler's symbol for the absurdity of wakefulness. Rural living's peaceful attention to family ties, natural surroundings, and spiritual logic is the stuff of dreams. Jen Fain has a hyperextended mind from viewing too much paradox, nonsense. Her "earned" sophistication is taking her on a train ride to nowhere.

Critical Context

Speedboat, Renata Adler's first novel, earned for her the Ernest Hemingway Award for best first novel of the year. Adler has been a much-praised nonfiction writer, serving as a *New Yorker* staff writer up until and through the publishing of *Speedboat*.

What makes the novel stand out is its superb attention to detail and its disciplined approach to portraying an unraveling mind. The humility of the book's narrator makes a reader enjoy Jen Fain enough so that any bafflement with structure or confusion about point of view becomes secondary and is defused. The warmth of the narrator's "desired" heart overcomes her frustrating inability to act, to take charge of herself,

and rid herself of distance. Adler works the same avenues of character that many readers have found so amusing and likable in Donald Barthelme. What sets her apart is the
sincerity and longing she brings to Jen Fain.

Bibliography
Dinnage, Rosemary. "We." *New Statesman* 94 (August 26, 1977): 280.
Korn, Eric. "Notes on Current Books." *Virginia Quarterly Review* 53 (Spring, 1977):
    64.
Thorburn, David. "Recent Novels: Realism Redux." *Yale Review* 66 (Summer, 1977):
    587-588.
Towers, Robert. "Speedboat," in *The New York Times Book Review* 82 (September 26,
    1976): 6-7.

Jack Welch

SPIDERTOWN

Author: Abraham Rodriguez, Jr. (1961-   )
Type of plot: Bildungsroman
Time of plot: The 1990's
Locale: South Bronx, New York City
First published: 1993

   Principal characters:
      MIGUEL, a teenage crack runner, the main character of the novel
      AMELIA, Firebug's girlfriend, a crack user and college student
      CRISTALENA, also called Lena, Miguel's naïve girlfriend
      SPIDER, a young crack lord
      FIREBUG, a teenage arsonist, Miguel's roommate

The Novel
   Spidertown is a *Bildungsroman* that recounts the intellectual and spiritual growth of a teenaged boy. Sixteen-year-old Miguel falls in love with Cristalena, a preacher's daughter who despises crack cocaine and the criminals who are terrorizing her neighborhood. Because he works for Spider, the local crack czar, Miguel fears that Cristalena will reject him. Consequently, he lies about his work, and his guilt and shame propel him on a journey of self-discovery and redemption.
   As the novel opens, Miguel and his roommate, Firebug, are drinking and talking in their nearly unfurnished apartment. Firebug, a professional arsonist, invites Miguel to a "wienie roast," which is a euphemism for the torching of a building. Though he agrees to escort Firebug's girlfriend, Amelia, Miguel would prefer to stay home. He no longer enjoys the commotion of the crowd, the fire engines, and the flames. His relationship with Cristalena has shown him the perversion and ugliness of his world.
   At the fire, Miguel and Amelia sit in his car and discuss his growing disenchantment with the drug culture. Amelia says that he has too much heart to be a criminal, confesses that she has fallen in love with him, and tries to explain her relationship with Firebug, who is incapable of love.
   The next day, as he makes his usual deliveries for Spider, Miguel stops several times to call Cristalena, but she is unavailable to speak with him. Angry and dejected, he starts drinking heavily and gets behind in his deliveries. His tardiness almost costs the lives of several drug dealers, who have to dodge bullets to get to his car.
   In the morning, Miguel visits Cristalena at the boutique where she works and learns the reason for her evasion. She has not yet told her parents about him, and they are very strict and watch her closely. Miguel proposes to Cristalena, and they make plans to celebrate her birthday in bed at his apartment.
   At Spider's request, Miguel delivers ten thousand dollars to a police car parked across the street from his apartment building. One of the officers sticks a pistol in his face and threatens him. After this humiliating experience, Miguel walks to his car and

discovers that the tires have been slashed by Spider's spies to prevent him from running off with the money. Enraged by Spider's lack of trust in him, Miguel resolves to quit his job at the right moment.

Starting another day of deliveries, he meets with Spider to pick up the crack. When Spider asks him to deliver more money to the police, he refuses. He does not take Spider's threats seriously because he intends to quit soon anyway. At his last stop, a group of street thugs, led by a boy named Richie, drag him from his car and beat him severely. It is Spider's way of teaching him a lesson. When he returns to his apartment, only Amelia shows sympathy for his bruises. That night, she drugs Firebug and sleeps chastely with Miguel in his bed.

In the morning, Miguel telephones Spider and informs him that he is quitting, but Spider refuses to believe him. When Miguel picks Cristalena up that night, he starts to tell her the truth about himself, but he is interrupted by Spider, who emerges from the darkness and pounds on the windshield. Miguel gets out of his car, and they argue. After Spider leaves, Miguel tries to tell Cristalena the truth about himself, but she says he is too late and runs back into her building.

Upset by Cristalena's reaction, Miguel visits Amelia; she takes him to her private apartment, where they finally have sex. Miguel still loves Cristalena, however, and resolves to win her back. Knowing that he must first straighten out his life, he goes to see his mother, Catarina, who is living with a well-to-do importer named Nelo. She agrees to let Miguel move in with them if he will submit unconditionally to their authority. He reluctantly accepts her terms. After begging for and receiving Cristalena's forgiveness, Miguel takes Cristalena to his apartment, and they have sex.

The next day, he encounters Richie, who tries to persuade him to betray Spider. Miguel refuses emphatically. When he gets back to his apartment, he discovers that Firebug is moving out. Firebug gives Miguel a gun for protection, tells him to meet Spider at a bar, and leaves. Wanting to break with Spider amicably, Miguel foolishly goes to meet him, and he is shot twice in the back during an attack on the bar.

At the hospital, Miguel is questioned by a police officer named Sanchez and visited by Amelia and Cristalena. After his release from the hospital, he moves in with his mother and Nelo. He decides to burn his car as a symbol of his independence from Spider. Amelia, Cristalena, and Miguel create a funeral pyre for the car and set it ablaze. As the three friends walk away from the fire, Sanchez drives up, and Miguel hands him a tape of Spider's life story, narrated by the drug lord himself.

The Characters

The main characters in *Spidertown* either strive to be like their fathers or struggle to be different. Firebug became an arsonist because his father revered fire, forced him to leap flames at community barbecues, and punished him by burning parts of his body. Amelia's "masculinity" is at least partly an attempt to earn her father's respect and love. She tries to be the son he always wanted. Cristalena is a victim of her father's religious fanaticism. She rebels successfully against his effort to make her "a little child of Christ," but she cannot completely liberate herself from his terrifying sermons on sin. Miguel reads voraciously because his father hated books. Spider strives to be the antithesis of his father, who plays dominoes outside the neighborhood market. Spider's ambition is a rejection of his father's mundane existence as well as a desperate quest for excitement and purpose in life.

The most corrupt characters, such as Spider and Firebug, have become insensitive to the suffering around them. Firebug contemplates Miguel's bruises with stolid curiosity. He is incapable of feeling sympathy for a friend or love for a woman. Interested only in business, Spider betrays his associates coldly, without remorse. Other characters such as Amelia and Miguel are soft because of their compassion. Though she has learned to use people, Amelia still cares. Miguel, too, has too much heart to become a hardened criminal. He shows concern for Spider's safety even after Spider has betrayed him, and he feels guilty about the harm he is doing to his neighborhood. His conscience prevents him from developing the indifference necessary to survive in Spider's world.

Amelia and Cristalena function as reflectors for Miguel, who is both adult and child. Amelia, a twenty-one-year-old college student, represents the responsible, worldly adult, perhaps symbolic of platonic or intellectual love, while sixteen-year-old Cristalena represents the child in Miguel. Cristalena even refers to herself as a child. It is significant that the three characters walk away "arm in arm in arm" at the end of the novel. Amelia also functions as Miguel's confidante and counselor, allowing him to purge his anxiety and fear. In her role as therapist, she guides him to redemption, undergoing a parallel transformation herself as she returns to college. Cristalena and Spider represent good and evil, respectively, locked in a struggle for Miguel. Cristalena's name even suggests a divine being, capable of redeeming sinners. In his rhetoric, Spider is very much like the Devil, using flattery and deception to tempt Miguel to sin.

Rodriguez creates a colorful array of minor characters who give the novel depth and focus: giddy Rosa, Cristalena's cousin, who serves as a liaison between Cristalena and Miguel; eighteen-year-old Careta, an independent pimp who peddles young flesh and marijuana but avoids crack; Catarina, Miguel's mother, who yearns for a picture-perfect family; Nelo, Catarina's middle-class boyfriend, who personifies dullness and complacency; Richie, one of Spider's henchmen, who secretly despises Spider and plots to assassinate him; and Sanchez, the police officer who befriends Miguel after the bar massacre and tries to extract information about Spider.

Themes and Meanings

The theme of deception is central to the novel's meaning. With their lies and subterfuges, the characters weave hopelessly tangled webs and often snare themselves. Cristalena deceives her parents about her clothes, boyfriends, and parties. To sustain the deception, she must expend vast amounts of energy and creativity, even enlisting the aid of her cousin and aunt, who provide alibis and a refuge for the "little child of Christ." Fearful of losing Cristalena, Miguel lies about his profession, telling her that he works for a lumber company. He goes to great lengths to conceal the truth about himself; in the end, he almost loses Cristalena because of his deceit. By pretending to be estranged from Spider, Firebug deceives Miguel, but only for a short while. Eventually, Miguel figures out the truth on his own.

Deception is Spider's modus operandi. He lures children into his operation by promising them exaggerated wealth and power. He lies repeatedly to Miguel, first about the car tires, then about the beating. When he is caught in his lie, he reacts with insouciance and moves on to another deception, supremely confident in his abilities as a machinator. He summons Miguel for a meeting and has his thugs shower the bar with bullets. The betrayal, once realized, prompts Miguel to cooperate with Sanchez, and the cost to Spider's organization is potentially great, because Miguel can provide damaging and detailed information about the drug kingpin's operation.

At one point in the novel, Amelia talks bitterly of self-deception, accusing the people in Spider's world of deluding themselves with guns, stereos, and gold chains. They act like millionaires and generals and pretend to be important, yet they live in squalor. Like rodents and insects, they scurry from one abandoned building to another, dodging sunlight. Amelia blames white people for creating the illusion of success for blacks and Latinos and for encouraging them to deceive and kill themselves. Miguel used to revel in the "fringe benefits" of his job such as money, women, and drugs. When he realizes that it is all a "sick pretend game," however, he stops playing.

Deception perverts friendships, undermines trust, and fosters paranoia. It will inevitably cause Spider's destruction. More odious still, self-deception imprisons the soul and impedes individual growth and development. The only antidote for deception, of course, is truth. Miguel cures his self-deception by holding up a mirror to himself and seeing the truth.

Rodriguez uses Charles Dickens's *Oliver Twist* (1837-1839), which is also concerned with deception, as a model for *Spidertown*. Amelia reveals that she gave Spider a copy of the novel and that he devoured it. At their first meeting, Spider questioned Miguel about the book, and Miguel demonstrated his familiarity with it by comparing Spider to the crafty Fagin, who uses children to commit crimes, and himself to the Artful Dodger. In *Spidertown*, Miguel is actually more like the young Oliver than the Artful Dodger. Both Oliver and Miguel wander the streets of a big city until they are befriended by exploitive criminals. Because he arranges the first meeting between Miguel and Spider, Firebug is like the Artful Dodger, who introduces Oliver to Fagin.

Critical Context

Spidertown is Rodriguez's first novel but not his first book. In 1992, he published *The Boy Without a Flag*, a critically acclaimed collection of short stories about Puerto Rican Americans in the South Bronx. Several of the characters in *Spidertown* have prototypes in the stories. For example, Spider is a minor character in "Birthday Boy," and Careta makes an appearance in "The Lotto." Miguel is similar in many ways to Angel in "Birthday Boy" and to the narrator of "The Boy Without a Flag." Likewise, Cristalena resembles Dalia in "The Lotto." It is obvious that Rodriguez borrowed situations and characters from his first book to create continuity between the works.

As a *Bildungsroman*, or apprenticeship novel, *Spidertown* is a descendant of such established novels as Johann Wolfgang von Goethe's *Wilhelm Meisters Lehrjahre* (1795-1796; *Wilhelm Meister's Apprenticeship*, 1824), Dickens's *David Copperfield* (1849-1850), W. Somerset Maugham's *Of Human Bondage* (1915), James Joyce's *A Portrait of the Artist as a Young Man* (1916), and Thomas Wolfe's *Look Homeward, Angel* (1929). These novels all trace the youthful development of a male protagonist, often an artist or a writer.

By having his characters discuss *Oliver Twist*, Richard Wright's *Native Son* (1940), and Ken Kesey's *One Flew over the Cuckoo's Nest* (1962), Rodriguez creates another context for his novel. These works depict the underbelly of society and constitute sophisticated protest literature, of which *Spidertown* is an example. It is interesting to note that the literary tradition represented by these works is distinctly male, though not exclusively white or American.

Finally, *Spidertown* belongs to a body of recent literature by Latino authors. As a New York Puerto Rican writer, Rodriguez has an affinity with Nicholasa Mohr and Piri Thomas, who also write about Puerto Rican Americans in the South Bronx. *Spidertown* has been compared to Thomas's *Down These Mean Streets* (1967), an autobiography of one man's struggle with drugs and crime in New York. Rodriguez's novel can also be grouped with the works of other Latino authors, such as Mexican American author Sandra Cisneros's *The House on Mango Street* (1989) and Cuban American author Oscar Hijuelos's *The Mambo Kings Play Songs of Love* (1989), which won the 1990 Pulitzer Prize in fiction.

Bibliography
De Noyelles, Amy. Review of *Spidertown*, by Abraham Rodriguez, Jr. *Hispanic* 8 (March, 1995): 80. Praises the novel for its realistic portrayal of life on the streets of an urban center. De Noyelles describes the novel as "a true-grit, no-holds barred glimpse of life among Puerto Rican drug runners in New York City's South Bronx."
Dodd, David. Review of *Spidertown*, by Abraham Rodriguez, Jr. *Library Journal* 118 (April 15, 1993): 127. Highly recommends the novel. Dodd compares Rodriguez to Richard Wright and Fyodor Dostoevski because all three writers are willing to explore the darkest crevices of society. He praises Rodriguez's authoritative voice and vision.
Ermelino, Louise. Review of *Spidertown*, by Abraham Rodriguez, Jr. *People Weekly* 40 (July 19, 1993): 27. Summarizes and evaluates the novel briefly. Ermelino criticizes the street dialogue for being repetitive but praises the repetitiveness of the plot for highlighting the tension and desperation of the characters. She accurately describes the novel as a personal look at "teenage angst" in a war zone.
Finn, Peter. "Tenement Romance." *The New York Times Book Review*, July 18, 1993, p. 16. Finn commends Rodriguez for allowing his characters to evoke pity but complains that allusions to other writers tend to intrude upon the narrative.
Rivera, Lucas. "Bronx Author Shakes Up Latino Literature." *Hispanic* 11 (April,

1998): 16. An interesting profile of Rodriguez that discusses his personal back-ground, criticisms of other Hispanic authors, and his own experiences as a writer.
Rosenthal, Lois. "Notes." *Story* 41 (Winter, 1993): 6. Rosenthal discusses her edito-rial relationship with the writer and reveals that she helped him find a publisher for his first book. She also notes that Columbia Pictures acquired the film rights to the novel.

Edward A. Malone

THE SPORTING CLUB

Author: Thomas McGuane (1939-   )
Type of plot: Regional satire
Time of plot: The late 1960's, on the occasion of the Centennial Club's centennial
   celebration
Locale: Michigan, the Northern Lower Peninsula
First published: 1969

   Principal characters:
      JAMES QUINN, the protagonist, a Michigan businessman seeking escape
         in the Club's sporting life
      VERNOR STANTON, Quinn's friend, a madcap, sadistic, practical joker
      JANEY, Stanton's chain-smoking girlfriend
      JACK OLSON, a Northern Lower Peninsula native and the Club's
         manager
      EARL OLIVE, a purveyor of live bait who replaces Olson as the Club's
         manager
      FORTESCUE,
      SCOTT, and
      SPENGLER, old-time Club members; a collector of military miniatures,
         an obsequious professor, and the Club chronicler, respectively

The Novel

   In the epigraph to *The Sporting Club*, Thomas McGuane quotes a line from Aristophanes: "Whirl is king." Indeed, in this comic tale of the destruction of "the grandest of the original sporting clubs," the whirl of absurdity reigns. The story's action takes place on the occasion of the Centennial Club's hundredth anniversary. James Quinn and Vernor Stanton, boyhood friends and rivals, join a host of other wealthy Michigan Club members for fun and games in the northern woods. Yet what promises to be a time of reunion, sport, and cameraderie turns into a bizarre nightmare of duels, dynamiting, and depravity.

   Following an official description of the Club in "Blucher's *Annals of the North* (Grand Rapids, Michigan, 1919)," the action turns to the reunion of Quinn and Stanton. Quinn, who has recently assumed the running of his father's tool-and-die business out of a piqued social conscience, arrives at Centennial Club for a much-needed vacation. The business itself is going well, but Quinn has difficulties managing his overbearing, error-prone Canadian secretary, Mary Beth Duncan. He fares no better at the Centennial Club, however, for upon his arrival he learns that Stanton, a dynamo of competitive aggression and sadistic practical jokes, is there with his "wife." Their initial meeting results in a duel, provoked by Stanton and conducted in his basement dueling range, wherein Stanton's well-aimed shot raises a welt the size of a great wasp sting over Quinn's heart. The manner and outcome of the duel illustrate the power that Stanton has over Quinn throughout the book. Against his better sense, Quinn inevitably allows himself to be drawn into Stanton's schemes. Quinn's love-hate relationship with Stanton parallels that of Stanton's "wife"—actually his girlfriend, Janey—a blonde chain-smoker of mineral-springs origins who likes Stanton's sexual prowess sufficiently to endure his habitual assaults on her ego. Quinn and Janey on occasion appear to be interested in each other (Stanton puts a stop to any serious flirting on their part with an adeptly placed shot to Quinn's throat), but neither can break free, and consequently both of them continue to orbit Stanton, charmed by his egomaniacal heroics.

The personal stories of Quinn, Stanton, and Janey converge with the Club's story in a plot, masterminded by Stanton, to oust Jack Olson, the Club's manager. A native of the region and a born sportsman, Olson embodies all the qualities that the Club members lack. Further, many of the Club's landholdings have been acquired through legal subterfuge from men such as Olson—locals who, because they lack money and political clout, are forced to sell to the socially and financially more powerful Centennial Club. Because he knows the land and its game (having poached the Club's holdings for years), Olson maintains the job as manager, but his presence rankles the gentlemen hunters who lack his expertise, and their resentment serves Stanton's machinations. Quinn, on the other hand, admires Olson and aspires to his quality of sportsmanlike conduct. On a fishing jaunt with Olson and Stanton, Quinn sticks with Olson, and the two "fish deferentially and await their occasions"—in contrast to Stanton, who tries "to beat fish out of the water." It is Stanton, however, who emerges with a catch, and this event portends for Quinn "the beginnings of something catastrophic."

Having surfaced in "Northern Gentlemen," the book's first chapter, Stanton's plan to fire Olson comes to fruition in the second, "Native Tendencies." Here, the new manager—a live-bait dealer named Earl Olive—appears. A flamboyant dresser, a raper of wildlife and women, Olive epitomizes the physically anarchic or "native tendencies" operating within the Club and undermining its rational veneer. Olive's ascension to managerial status is heralded by the mysterious shooting and gutting of a doe and young buck, an act that would have been unheard of under Olson's tutelage. Furthermore, the orgiastic shenanigans of Olive and his cohorts clarify the mounting dissension within the Centennial Club itself between Stanton and the more staid members. Quinn, maneuvering among his friendship with Stanton, his desire for Janey, his respect for Olson, and his loyalty to the more noble aspirations of the Club, becomes, in the end of this chapter, the victim of the Centennial Club's moral disintegration. Caught in a watery torrent unleashed when unknown parties dynamite the Club lake, Quinn realizes that everything he knows of the Club is gone. The only certainty left him is "the few, clear lines" that keep "himself, Stanton, Janey, everybody, precisely separated."

The final chapter, "Centennial Moon," sees the total devolution of the Club and its members and the final ascension of Stanton as its private owner—the ascension of "whirl," or the source of chaotic action within the story, as "king." Much of the action of this chapter occurs as military skirmishes between the Club members and Olive's zany group. Yet while in "Native Tendencies" the Olive camp revealed its native grossness—highlighted by the image of a beer-gutted male and a fleshy woman fornicating astride a moving Harley-Davidson—the decorous Centennial Club members now show their base underside. From their seat of operations—a large, unhygienic tent raised after the dynamiting of the Club buildings—the Centennial Club members foray into the night to carry out their centennial celebration: the unearthing of a time capsule left by their sporting ancestors. Its sole content, an aging photograph captioned "Dearest Children of the Twentieth Century, Do You Take Such Pleasure as Your Ancestors," exposes the Club's grand heritage—a vision of sexual sport flaunting "every phase of the spectrum of perversion." Its dark side brought to light, the Club explodes in a conflagration of rhetoric and rocketry as Fortescue and Spengler attempt to extol the Club's ancient virtues while Quinn, Stanton, and Olive skirmish intermittently. In the frenzy, Fortescue turns up tarred and feathered, Stanton holds everyone at bay with a machine gun, and the police arrive. Yet while the Club expires, releasing "a century of bad air," its former sportive glories are revived when Stanton purchases it for his private domain. Meeting there in the new year, Quinn and Stanton (with Janey looking on) engage in a mock duel fought with plywood-cutout guns. In the end, the three of them retire to bed, Quinn musing over the felt presence of each of them, "compromised and happy . . . like bees in cells of honey."

The Characters

James Quinn, whose arrivals at the Centennial Club open and close the book, emerges as its central character. His perceptions and adventures provide the novel's continuity. It is his change in attitude toward Stanton—from his reticence to see Stanton in the beginning to his sense of himself as Stanton's moral bedfellow in the end—that enacts the only character transformation in the story. Given the explosive energies ignited in the destruction of the Centennial Club and its pretensions, this transition seems a meager outcome. Quinn, though content with his compromise, remains separate from Stanton and, more important, from Janey, in his cell-like existence.

Vernor Stanton changes little, if at all. He is as obnoxious at the end as he is at the beginning. His demeanor toward Janey and Quinn appears somewhat restrained in the final scene—after all, the mock duel hurts no one—but this civility is countered by his crude treatment of his servants. Stanton is probably best imaged in one of his youthful escapades, which Quinn describes for Janey—a brazen contest wherein Stanton lowered his pants in a restaurant and "contrived by an imperceptible movement of his feet to present a 'Full Moon,' that is a 360-degree view." Stanton's value for Quinn, however, lies precisely in the man's perverse idiosyncrasy.

Like Quinn, Janey is victimized by Stanton and at the same time finds his outrageous energies irresistible. She is his second choice—Stanton took up with her only after being dumped by her Aunt Judy—but cannot leave him. Nor can she and Quinn imagine a way to get together. Consequently, they center their own relationship on Stanton, each telling the other his or her story in terms of when and how Stanton appeared on the scene. In the end, Janey maintains her position with Stanton—she appears as the lady of his house—but her primary function is that of cueing him in dinner conversation, and her relationship with Quinn is reduced to a "careful familial heartiness."

The passing of the Club managership from Jack Olson to Earl Olive marks a moral transition within the Club itself. Consequently, these two characters define the parameters of that transition. A native son of the region, Olson knows the land and its wildlife; he values the sport of hunting and "the hard-earned ritual that made it sane." Sport, for Olson, is a kind of stewardship "because he guaranteed the life of the country himself." In contrast, Olive not only has a police record for sex offenses but also is a moral offense to Olson's sense of life and sport. Olson, for example, thinks that fishing with bait is sacrilege; Olive, a live-bait man, gets his worms by electrifying the ground and his grasshoppers by driving a car rigged with cheesecloth netting at top speed through a field. Olive's reliance on machinery, as well as his disregard for life and its civilities, elucidate the pretensions of the Club members who want to be rid of Olson. As a kind of nouveau-genteel class, they aspire to Olson's native talents, but they lack his moral relation to sport and, as a consequence, hate him for their failure. Olive—who is hired by Olson as his own replacement—constitutes the ultimate revenge of the region upon the wealthy Centennial interlopers.

Themes and Meanings

The Sporting Club, McGuane's first novel, traces in rough outline the main themes that recur in his later novels: American society's movement away from nature toward technology, the decline of American morality, and the disillusionment and alienation of an existential protagonist who is stranded between a depraved society and the beautiful but implacable natural world. The Centennial Club can be viewed as a microcosm of the larger world that McGuane treats with irony in such later works as *Ninety-two in the Shade* (1973), *Nobody's Angel* (1982), and *Something to Be Desired* (1984).

The Sporting Club parodies a specific social class—the gentlemanly elite of the Northern Lower Peninsula who verbally espouse the ideals of tradition, sport, and moral conduct, but whose lives expose the lurid depravity at the heart of their abstract ideals. Narratively, the novel's parodic action may be seen in the two official descriptions of the Centennial Club that frame the story. The first, the entry from "Blucher's *Annals of the North*," cites the Centennial Club as the "grandest of the original sporting clubs." While steeped in tradition—"Its charter was written in 1868 while the big timber was being converted to pioneer houses on the treeless prairie of the West"—the Centennial Club is "shrouded in mystery." Of its operations and procedures Blucher knows nothing. These "operations," however, are precisely what the story uncovers.

Near the end of the book, an entry from an "International Real Estate Brokers' annual" provides a revised estimate of the Centennial Club, describing it as a "gentlemen's sporting club with a past." The advertisement mocks the Club's grand tradition, for its "past" now includes not only the obscene photograph of its founders, but also the bizarre events of the recent Centennial Club celebration. Moreover, the new description, rather than focusing on the hermetic, mystery-shrouded past, looks toward the commercial possibilities ("tempting subdivision potential in this water wonderland northwoods vacation paradise") that promise the utter decimation not only of the Club and its heritage—which is no great loss—but also of the land itself.

Appropriately, Vernor Stanton, the one individual who lives his depravity openly, ends up as the new lord and owner of the Centennial Club. In a world stripped of its rational veneer, Stanton, the embodiment of its madness, becomes king. The old virtues, carried forward in the ritual of the duel, degenerate into self-mockery as Stanton and Quinn pace off with their plywood guns, turn, and announce soberly, "Bang. Bang." Sport itself, the moral life of the Club so tenuously valued in Quinn's one serene moment of trout fishing and lost irrevocably with the firing of Olson, is thus reduced to parodic abstraction.

Critical Context

Despite *The Sporting Club*'s veneer of realistic narrative—a stylistic device evident in the "straight" descriptions of trout fishing and in the allowance for character motivation and recognizable plot—which parallels the Club's veneer of rational order and decorum, the book appears to be a contemporary antinovel. The inherent alienation born of Quinn's moral passivity (a condition that he perceives in those "few clear lines" that isolate him from his friends and from life) is reflected in the stylistic distance occasioned by an essentially authoritative narrative voice.

Thomas McGuane has been compared to Ernest Hemingway, and in his passages describing man in nature—in the forest, in the desert, on the ocean—McGuane does achieve an eloquent simplicity reminiscent of Hemingway. Yet while Hemingway's style evolves a new narrative wherein the loss of old certainties opens into a universe of creative possibilities, McGuane, in his first novel, takes the path of contemporary writers such as Joseph Heller and John Barth, who suggest that insanity is the appropriate response to a world gone mad. In effect, McGuane answers modernist nihilism with absurdist parody.

McGuane's ironic tone toward his protagonists and their universe, along with his pessimistic worldview, prevents his fiction from being easily accessible. The ambivalence created by his alternatingly bitterly humorous and tragically pessimistic tone can be puzzling—one is not sure how the author intends his characters to be perceived. Yet in such later novels as *Nobody's Angel* and *Something to Be Desired*, McGuane's antiheroes have become more sympathetic, and his themes, such as the necessity for love in human relationships and the alarming decline of a national morality in America, have emerged more clearly through his often elliptical and always ironic style.

Bibliography

Ingram, David. "Thomas McGuane: Nature, Environmentalism, and the American West." *Journal of American Studies* 29 (December, 1995): 423-469. Ingram examines McGuane's focus on the old mythologies of the frontier in the ecology and politics of the modern American West. Ingram concludes that McGuane's position of these issues is complicated and unclear, alternating between the liberal, radical, and conservative.

McCaffery, Larry, and Sinda Gregory. "The Art of Fiction LXXXIX: Thomas McGuane." *The Paris Review* 27 (Fall, 1985): 35-71. Illuminating and immensely readable, this focuses on McGuane's style, themes, and comic vision.

McClintock, James. "'Unextended Selves' and 'Unformed Visions': Roman Catholicism in Thomas McGuane's Novels." *Renascence: Essays on Values in Literature* 49 (Winter, 1997): 139-152. McClintock examines the Roman Catholic themes in McGuane's works. McClintock asserts that although McGuane's works are not Catholic in an orthodox sense, he often investigates Catholic themes, topics, and use of language that specifically refers to Catholic matters.

Morris, Gregory. "How Ambivalence Won the West: Thomas McGuane and the Fiction of the New West." *Critique: Studies in Contemporary Fiction* 32 (Spring, 1991): 180-189. Excellent discussion of McGuane's use of the "New West." Argues that while both the language and the action of the novel illuminate Lucien's attraction to the landscape and to the myths of the Old West, his efforts to find a place for himself in the New West require him to deny acceptance of the old.

Neville, Jill. "Getting Away from It All." *The Times Literary Supplement*, May 17, 1985, p. 573. An interesting discussion that focuses not on the disappearance of the Old West but on Lucien's "odyssey," as he moves from being the son who refuses to put away childish things to the man who ceases being self-destructive and yearns for "health, emotional stability, and Nature."

Wallace, Jon. *The Politics of Style*. Durango, Colo.: Hollowbrook, 1992. Argues that McGuane finds language "an end in itself." Although McGuane's characters' words and thoughts often seem incoherent or meaningless, Wallace claims, the mixed codes in his language reflect their fragmented sense of being and their attempts to bring themselves into being in a world without style or unity. Includes a useful bibliography.

S. Elaine Marshall

THE SPORTSWRITER

Author: Richard Ford (1944-   )
Type of plot: Psychological realism
Time of plot: The mid-1980's
Locale: New Jersey, New York City, Michigan, New Hampshire, Vermont, and
    Florida
First published: 1986

> *Principal characters:*
> FRANK BASCOMBE, a divorced father and a writer for a national sports
>   magazine
> X, his ex-wife, a teaching golf professional
> VICTORY (VICKI) WANDA ARCENAULT, Frank's lover, a hospital nurse
> WALTER LUCKETT, a member of the Divorced Men's Club who forces
>   his friendship on Frank
> RALPH BASCOMBE, Frank's dead son

The Novel

In this first-person narrative, thirty-eight-year-old Frank Bascombe examines the tragedies and disappointments in his life without self-pity. Fascinated equally by the vast spectacle of life and the most mundane aspects of daily existence, Frank is satisfied by the choices life offers and the decisions he has made.

A few years out of the University of Michigan, Frank publishes a well-received book of short stories, marries a beautiful woman he refers to only as "X," and settles into a typical suburban existence in Haddam, New Jersey, midway between New York City and Philadelphia. Unable to generate the inspiration and motivation to continue writing fiction, Frank abandons literature to write for a national sports magazine. This life remains placid until nine-year-old Ralph, the oldest of his three children, dies from Reye's syndrome. A few years later, his marriage breaks up, and X becomes a teaching golf professional at the local country club. The breakup is initiated by X's discovery of letters written to Frank by a lonely woman he met on one of his sportswriting trips but with whom he has not had an affair. *The Sportswriter* opens with Frank and X meeting at Ralph's grave, as they do each year on his birthday. He begins to read Theodore Roethke's "Meditation," but X says she does not like or believe the poem: "Sometimes I don't think anyone can be happy anymore." The novel is essentially about Frank's belief not in the possibility of happiness but the necessity of it.

In the house where his family once lived happily, Frank lives alone except for Bosobolo, his boarder, a seminary student from Africa, while X and his two children live across town. X has adjusted to divorce much better than Frank, who thinks he is in love with Vicki Arcenault, a nurse, while wanting his wife (and normalcy) back at the same time. Despite telling himself he does not need such solace, Frank attends meetings of the Divorced Men's Club. One of the members, the pathetic Walter Luckett, whose wife has run off to Bimini with a water-skiing instructor, tries to force his friendship on Frank, who uneasily resists any intimacy, especially after Walter confesses a recent homosexual encounter with a business acquaintance.

Frank takes Vicki with him to Detroit, where he is to interview Herb Wallagher, a paraplegic former professional football player. Frank enjoys writing inspirational stories about the courage of athletes, but Herb, given to violent mood swings because of his medication, refuses to be a source of inspiration to anyone, preferring to seethe in self-pity. Back in Haddam, he finds the persistent Walter waiting. Unable to help himself, Walter wants some gesture of understanding from the sportswriter. Too tired for sympathy, Frank is shocked when the departing Walter kisses him on the cheek.

Frank's relationship with Vicki, whom he tells himself he loves and wants to marry, is already fragile before he spends Easter with her down-to-earth father, sullen brother, and effervescent stepmother, whom she jealously resents. As the day progresses, Vicki grows increasingly annoyed with Frank. Even news of Walter's suicide does not make her view him more sympathetically, and as he leaves, she punches him in the mouth.

Frank returns to Haddam to find the police suspicious of homosexual overtones related to Walter's death. Frank gets permission to visit Walter's apartment and convinces X to accompany him. While there, he attempts to seduce his ex-wife, who is repelled by the desperate absurdity of his suggestion. Frank goes to the local commuter train station to calm himself by watching his fellow suburbanites arrive home.

Seeing a woman he mistakes for Walter's sister arriving from Ohio, he flees to Manhattan and the camaraderie of the magazine staff gathered to complete an issue devoted to the upcoming National Football League player draft. When an attractive young intern, Catherine Flaherty, praises his work, they begin an affair. Frank soon goes to Florida in search of an illegitimate daughter whom Walter mentioned in his suicide letter, only to discover she is a figment of Walter's tortured imagination. Frank finds that he likes Florida and becomes an honorary member of a family named Bascombe.

The Characters

The events of his life might make Frank lonely, sad, and angry, much like Walter and Herb, but unlike them, he has adjusted to pain and regret, becoming surprisingly contented. His major conflict is resisting the state he calls dreaminess, meaning giving in to self-pity and despair, much as he does immediately following Ralph's death. The constantly self-analytical Frank posits a simple yet unsentimental optimism in numerous ways throughout the novel: "things sometimes happen for the best. Thinking that way has given me a chance for an interesting if not particularly simple adulthood." He claims to be willing to say "yes" to almost anything life presents. One of the problems with their marriage is X's resentment of his optimism.

Although he claims not to be searching for anything, Frank clearly longs for the stability of a traditional family. His father died when he was fourteen, and his mother treated him like a nephew. He loves his house in Haddam because it symbolizes the type of family life he seeks, even if only he and Bosobolo reside in it. Owning such a house without actually needing it provides an unusual comfort. He fantasizes about becoming part of the Arcenault family, who strike him as better than he expected. He allows himself to become addicted to mail-order catalogs, attracted not only by the products but also by "those ordinary good American faces pictured there."

Frank refuses to see people as either heroes or villains, even when he is writing about athletes. He writes an article about Haddam for a local magazine, saying that he works best if he lives in a "neutral" place, and he seems neutral about life, though not disinterested or indifferent. He attempts to offset the perception of himself as passive by claiming that he is "always vitally interested in life's mysteries, which are never in too great a supply." He is open to such mysteries without seeking them out, saying that "it may simply be that at my age I'm satisfied with less and with things less complicated." A man of contradictions, Frank loves the mystery of life but lacks curiosity about others, hence his discomfort with the confessions of Walter.

Frank's essentially optimistic view of the world lacks sentimentality because it is rooted in realism. He tells Walter that the hardest part of his job "is that people expect me to make things better when I come. . . . The fact is, we can sometimes not make things worse, or we can make things worse. But we can't usually make things better for individuals." He is reconciled to living his life a stranger to others.

Frank is impatient with Walter for not recognizing the individual's need to overcome life's disappointments: "Maturity, as I conceived it, was recognizing what was bad or peculiar in life, admitting it has to stay that way, and going ahead with the best of things." Frank, of course, does not always adhere to this philosophy, continuing to mourn for Ralph and hoping to start over with X. Just before attempting to seduce X in Walter's apartment, he tells her, "You can't be too conventional. That's what'll save you." Such inconsistencies make him believably human. Frank is alert to his frailties, and he harshly criticizes himself whenever he spots any deviance from his optimistic philosophy, as when he suspects himself of the cynicism inherent in his age and rampant among sportswriters in particular. When a retired baseball player who is going blind from diabetes wants Frank to write about him, Frank realizes that he would have nothing to say: "Some life is only life, and unconjugatable, just as to some questions there are no answers." Because of Frank's insistent belief in living in the present, Ford has him narrate his story in the present tense.

The other characters are mere satellites to the protagonist. *The Sportswriter* focuses on his sensibility, and the narrator would not presume to portray them in much detail. X's edginess contrasts with Frank's optimism: "She is still an opinionated Michigan girl, who thinks about things with certainty and is disappointed when the rest of the world doesn't." Worrying about getting older is only one example of X's refusal to live only in the present. Having also been through a divorce and death in the family, Vicki, like X, wants to exert control over life rather than simply observe its pageant, and she realizes that she cannot control Frank. Just before slugging him, she says, "You're liable to say anything, and I don't like that." Walter's desperation serves primarily to make Frank's relative normality seem more unusual. Frank's desire to have sex with X in the suicide's bed suggests his awareness of his kinship with Walter.

Themes and Meanings

Although *The Sportswriter* deals with such subjects as love, marriage, divorce, and death, it is primarily an examination of attitudes toward life. Ford refuses to sneer at or reject the conventions, however banal, of middle-class American existence. Frank's life and observations imply that there is something almost heroic about learning to live within the limitations imposed by these conventions. As Lynette Arcenault, Vicki's devotedly Catholic stepmother, observes, alienation is not a workable option. Frank argues forcefully against the randomness of life, saying that "down deep we're all reaching out for a decent rewarding contact every chance we get."

Frank also has much to say about the nature of literature, sportswriting, and sports. He abandons writing fiction for complicated reasons. His need to live only in the present makes him lose his anticipation for what will happen next, a must for the creative writer. He finds the seriousness required of the fiction writer too gloomy. He resent writers who turn people into stereotypes; he finds the real world engaging and dramatic enough. Frank credits marriage with saving him from this lonely pursuit: "I needed to turn from literature back to life, where I could get somewhere." Even the death of a beloved son and a divorce do not make this point ironic.

Since it deals with describing and analyzing real people and events, sportswriting, as defined by Frank, offers a freedom from the ambiguities and enigmas of literature, the need to impose meaning. Sportswriting is more impersonal in this sense, but it provides the companionship of fellow writers, which Frank finds highly desirable even though many of his colleagues are cynics. He also comforts himself in the knowledge that more people will read his feature articles and columns than would have read his fiction. Sportswriting appeals to him "not as a real profession but more as an agreeable frame of mind." Sports themselves appeal to Frank for bringing people together and offering a distraction from the unavoidable dreariness of life. He does not romanticize sports, however, being disturbed by the lack of individuality in athletics.

The suburbs, the other major subject of *The Sportswriter*, present a similar problem for Frank. While he feels comfortable with this way of life, he never quite fits in socially, especially after his divorce sets him apart from his more settled neighbors. Frank understands the latter attitude, since he feels at ease with the uniformity of suburban existence. He admires Haddam—and New Jersey as a whole—because it is dull, because he prefers the uneventful life and the lack of forced friendships. Most important for Frank are such comforts as "stable property values, regular garbage pick-up, good drainage, ample parking." *The Sportswriter* is not about the need to impose order on chaos but rather about the potential for finding order within chaos.

Critical Context

The Sportswriter is the novel that established Ford with critics and readers after his first two novels, though well received, sold poorly. It stands out from his other novels and stories, which feature characters who are more rootless and whose experiences are more violent and melodramatic.

Because the novel deals with the mores of contemporary American suburbia, it has been compared to the fiction of John Cheever, John Updike, and Richard Yates. Frank bears similarities to Cheever's characters in particular, resembling a saner version of the protagonist of "The Swimmer." For the most part, however, Ford's milieu is more subdued than those in typical examples of this literary subgenre.

Ford's novel stands apart from mainstream American fiction of the 1980's in several ways. His presentation of a protagonist who finds refuge in the ordinary, stubbornly refusing to give in to despair, is an anomaly in an age emphasizing alienated, often nihilistic characters. Creations such as Frank are usually presented as naïve and foolish. *The Sportswriter* is also unique in portraying Frank's optimism as stemming from his strength of character rather than from religious, political, or aesthetic values.

Bibliography

Dupuy, Edward. "The Confessions of an Ex-Suicide: Relenting and Recovering in Richard Ford's *The Sportswriter.*" *Southern Literary Journal* 23 (Fall, 1990): 93-103. Analyzes Frank as a searcher for mystery in the ordinary. Shows how Frank, unlike Walter, survives by yielding to the vicissitudes of life. Explains that Frank gives up fiction by choosing reality over the power of language. Considers the influence of William Faulkner and contrasts Frank with Quentin Compson in Faulkner's *Absalom, Absalom!* (1936).

Ford, Richard. Interview by Kay Bonetti. *The Missouri Review* 10, no. 2 (1987): 71-96. Ford discusses the writing of *The Sportswriter*, explaining how Frank differs from him, why he made Frank a sportswriter, why the ex-wife is called X, and how the novel's religious elements can be misconstrued. He defends Frank's optimism as merely an openness to choices.

_____. Interview by Matthew Gilbert. *Writer* 109 (December, 1996): 9-11. Ford reveals that he thought about quitting writing when he was working on *Independence Day*. He offers his thoughts on the public perception on the write-or-die attitude of writers, reflections on winning the Pulitzer Prize, and comments about writing a novel.

Gornick, Vivian. "Tenderhearted Men: Lonesome, Sad and Blue." *The New York Times Book Review*, September 16, 1990, pp. 1, 32-35. This consideration of the way men are portrayed in works by Ford, Raymond Carver, and Andre Dubus shows how Frank is typical of Ford's lonely, confused, hurt protagonists. Analyzes Frank's relations with women. Argues that Ford is infatuated with Frank's depression.

Schroth, Raymond A. "American's Moral Landscape in the Fiction of Richard Ford." *Christian Century* 106 (March 1, 1989): 227-230. Admires *The Sportswriter* for reproducing a complex cross-section of middle-class America. Explains that the novel is about the modern American search for integrity through sports, art, religion, friendship, love, and daily obligations.

Weber, Bruce. "Richard Ford's Uncommon Characters." *The New York Times Magazine*, April 10, 1988, pp. 50, 59, 63-65. This biographical profile explains how

Ford's fiction differs from the dominant American fiction of the 1980's, which is minimalist in style, nihilistic in spirit. Argues that Ford's style is more lyrical than that of the minimalists and discusses the difficulty critics have categorizing Ford's work.

Michael Adams

A SPY IN THE HOUSE OF LOVE

Author: Anaïs Nin (1903-1977)
Type of plot: Psychological impressionism
Time of plot: The mid-twentieth century, following World War II
Locale: A large metropolitan city identified with New York City and its environs
First published: 1954

> *Principal characters:*
> SABINA, the protagonist, a woman driven by her search for self and for love
> THE "LIE DETECTOR," the externalized pursuer of Sabina, hunting down her "guilt"
> ALAN, Sabina's complaisant husband
> PHILIP, a Wagnerian tenor, briefly Sabina's lover
> JOHN, also briefly her lover
> JAY, a painter, formerly her lover but now her confidant
> MAMBO, a black political exile who is working as a drummer in Greenwich Village
> DONALD, a homosexual who is attracted to Sabina
> LILIAN and
> DJUNA, Sabina's friends

The Novel

A psychological novel, sometimes regarded as a novella because the narrative has a narrow scope and lacks structural complexity, *A Spy in the House of Love* centers on the encounters of Sabina, a woman whose three quests are for love, vocation, and self-knowledge. In a series of brief, generally unsatisfactory sexual flings, she seeks passion but not commitment. To one of her lovers she appears to be "Dona Juana," yet she perceives herself as, at best, only a fragile counterpart to the Don Juan stereotype of a compulsive womanizer. Such a man's erotic interest in the woman ends with her conquest, but Sabina lacks the male's single-minded purposefulness. She is at best a timid pursuer of men, one tormented by guilt and anguished by her failure to experience fulfillment through passion.

On one level, the plot line of Nin's novel documents female failure, at least for a woman constituted as sensitively as Sabina, to achieve the same kind of casual sexual satisfaction that some males appear to enjoy without guilt. In her doomed quest, Sabina betrays her complaisant husband, Alan, whose nature is forgiving but who generally ignores her deepest needs for assertion. In Philip, an opera singer, she enjoys a brief sexual encounter that is heightened by her lover's appreciation of music and of nature. Her next sexual encounter is with a former airplane pilot, John, who treats her with erotic delicacy but soon vanishes from her life. Jay (who resembles Nin's longtime friend Henry Miller), a Brooklyn-born artist, had once been her lover but now serves as her confidant, confessor, and critic. Mambo, a black musician, longs for Sabina but rejects her as too timorous and self-involved to accept his passion. Finally, Donald, a homosexual, rouses in her maternal but not erotic sensations. By the end of the book, Sabina's shadowy lovers having departed, she is back at home with her husband—but, more important to her self-realization, she has retained the friendship and good counsel of Djuna, a female friend who restores her nerves to a kind of repose, if not complete emotional wholeness.

On other levels, the plot lines of the novel concern Sabina's generally unsuccessful quest for vocation and her more nearly satisfactory quest for self-knowledge. An actress, Sabina suffers from stage fright and flees from the theater, preferring to practice "acting" both by wearing the theatrical disguise of a black, swirling cape, the symbol of a greater inner freedom to display her authentic uninhibited self, and by performing the role of sexual temptress for her lovers. In actuality, her cape conceals a truly frightened soul; her roles run counter to her repressed nature, so that she feels both guilt for her actions and a sense of vacuity at the core of her being. Existentially, she is empty, devoid of the capacity for unconstrained passion. Yet, if she fails in her vocation, she succeeds moderately well in understanding herself: She becomes better aware of her limitations. Far from fatal woman, temptress, and sexual tyrant, she sees herself as a fragile complex of contradictions, protected and soothed by the power of music. The *Quartets* of Ludwig van Beethoven bring her contradictory impulses into a peaceful unity.

As a frame device for the novel, a mysterious character called the "lie detector" serves in the prologue and epilogue to place Sabina's quests in a perspective less subjective than the narrator's. She imagines herself to be a "spy" in the house of love—an observer, a recorder of secrets, but never a participant; yet the "lie detector" forces her to reveal her nature, cast off her disguises and elaborate deceptions, and confess her guilt and confront her narcissism. The "lie detector," whether he is the alter ego of Sabina or an omniscient true "spy" who sees, with disinterested lucidity, into the truth of Sabina's essential nature—both interpretations are possible—spies for the reader to establish a basis of external reality in an otherwise symbolic journey into the interior of a woman who needs to discover her soul.

The Characters

Although characters in the novel, with the exception of Sabina, tend to be shadowy, having little or no separate identity apart from their relationship to her, they function variously as lovers, confidants, or composite beings symbolic of Sabina's divided personality. In musical counterpoint, each character is symbolized by a particular piece. Alan, Sabina's husband, cares deeply for her, allows her freedom to pursue her erotic adventures, but cannot dominate her will. Modeled after Nin's husband, Hugh Guiler (also known as Ian Hugo), Alan functions as Sabina's point of refuge; her reaction to him is symbolized by Claude Debussy's *Ile Joyeuse*.

Philip, Sabina's first romantic encounter, a handsome operatic tenor, is an authentic Don Juan, in contrast to her failed Dona Juana. Virile and assertive, his musical symbol is Richard Wagner's *Tristan und Isolde*. Mambo, the black musician, seems to

Sabina to be a "primitive," but he rejects her condescending attitude; his musical symbol is the drum. John, the aviator, suffers from malaria and perhaps battle shock that has driven him nearly to madness. Sabina identifies him with the moon (earlier she had been touched by Debussy's *Claire de Lune*). Donald, whose caresses lack passion, offers Sabina calm to ease her "fevers." His effect on her is the opposite of the mood evoked by Igor Fyodorovich Stravinsky's *The Firebird Suite*.

Jay, the painter-philosopher and former lover of Sabina, reminds her of "Vienna-as-it-was-before-the-war," music of Bohemian gaiety; he introduces her to an understanding of her multilayered self, represented by Marcel Duchamp's painting *Nude Descending a Staircase*. In this Cubist painting she sees herself: "Eight or ten outlines of the same woman, like many multiple exposures of a woman's personality, neatly divided into many layers, walking down the stairs in union." Finally, Djuna restores Sabina to her inner core of serenity with Beethoven's *Quartets* (probably the last *Quartets*, with their dense organization and the "great fugue"); from this music she discovers her essential harmony deriving from complexities.

Themes and Meanings

A Spy in the House of Love is Nin's fourth novel in a loosely connected series of impressionistic studies treating varieties of woman's temperament in the twentieth century Western world. The series, published from 1946 to 1961, comprises *Ladders to Fire* (1946), *Children of the Albatross* (1947), *The Four-chambered Heart* (1950), *A Spy in the House of Love* (1954), and *Seduction of the Minotaur*, (1961; expanded from *Solar Barque*, 1958). Taken as a whole, the books were intended to resemble, in complexity and semi-autobiographical reconstruction of memory, Marcel Proust's *Remembrance of Things Past* (1913-1927). In Nin's series, three women as artists predominate: Lillian, a pianist; Sabina, an actress; and Djuna, a dancer. Lillian is primary in *Ladders to Fire* and *Seduction of the Minotaur*, Djuna in *The Four-chambered Heart* and *Children of the Albatross*, Sabina in *A Spy in the House of Love*, but the three women—all fragmented types of Nin's personality—appear in the works as personifications of the multiple nature of composite womanhood.

In *A Spy in the House of Love*, Nin concentrates on several major aspects of this complex nature, chief among them woman's need for passionate arousal. Sabina is compared to a fire. When the "lie detector" first looks at her, he reacts: "Everything will burn!" Yet her fire of sexuality burns inwardly. Although she can inflame men's passion, she cannot long sustain her own arousal. Along with the theme of deficient passion, the novel treats the modern woman's need for artifice, for cunning, to conceal her true nature. Looking at a mirror, Sabina sees "a flushed, clear-eyed face, smiling, smooth, beautiful." Yet the mirror lies: "The multiple acts of composure and artifice had merely dissolved her anxieties." Her true image, contrasted to the mirror image of external composure, is one of complexity, ambivalence, and anxiety. In this image, she takes her place among other existential protagonists of the twentieth century novel: a woman defining her role in society according to her own moral standards, true to the impulses of her authentic being.

Critical Context

To her literary agent, Anaïs Nin once described *A Spy in the House of Love* as a "poetic novel," commenting sadly: "There is no place for the poetic novel anyway. . . . I am being true to a new form which will evolve out of the new relativity of psychological reality." Nin's "relativity" form—that of viewing the action of a character from multiple points of view—was not entirely original in 1954, but it certainly was in the advanced wave of fictional experimentation.

In her series she treats the psychology of composite woman from three aspects: as Lillian, whose domestic instincts are conventionally directed toward marriage and the hopes for rearing children; as Djuna, who is generally self-contained; and as Sabina, a free spirit who challenges the sexual restraints imposed by society upon women. None of these characters is "complete"; each one needs the friendship and affection of another woman to help her assert her true identity.

By dividing her characters into fragmented psychological types, each incomplete when viewed narrowly but more nearly whole when related to the pattern of a complete design, Nin's work recalls the multidimensional fiction of other major twentieth century writers. In *The Alexandria Quartet* (1957-1960), Lawrence Durrell similarly examined his characters as psychologically fragmented, requiring a "relativity principle" of space and time to determine their integrity. Also C. P. Snow, in *Strangers and Brothers* (1940-1970), a series of novels mostly centering on professors at Cambridge University, provided "overlapping" points of view for his characters. Closest to Nin's series because of its complex treatment of a woman quite unaware of her authentic nature is Joyce Cary's Sara Monday trilogy, beginning with *Herself Surprised* (1941) and concluding with *The Horse's Mouth* (1944).

Yet in theme and design, Nin's work is also significantly different from the series of fiction by Durrell, Snow, and Cary, among other mid-twentieth century writers. Nin concentrates, after all, upon a single major subject: the psychology of woman. (In Cary's trilogy, the reader's attention is divided between two major figures—Sara and Gully Jimson.) *A Spy in the House of Love*, drawing upon the transformed experiences of the author's life, upon her fantasies and aspirations as well, is uniquely confessional. To appreciate fully Nin's reconstruction of Lillian, Djuna, and Sabina into fictional types, one must read the author's diaries—the early ones as well as the later—for insight into the sources, the matrix of her art.

Bibliography

Bair, Deirdre. *Anaïs Nin: A Biography*. New York: Putnam, 1995. A massive biography by a scholar steeped in the literature of the period and author of biographies of Samuel Beckett and Simone de Beauvoir. Supplements but does not supersede Fitch's shorter but also livelier biography.

Evans, Oliver. *Anaïs Nin*. Carbondale: Southern Illinois University Press, 1968. The result of a twenty-year study of the work and life of Nin. Through extensive research, reading, and lengthy personal interviews, Evans provides new and insightful interpretations of *House of Incest*, Nin's first two diaries, and other major fiction works, but omits Nin's nonfiction works. Nin is presented as a writer in the genre of her good friend Henry Miller. Also contains detailed end notes and an index.

Fitch, Noel Riley. *Anaïs: The Erotic Life of Anaïs Nin.* Boston: Little, Brown, 1993. As the subtitle suggests, Fitch is concerned with tracing Nin's erotic relationships and close friendships with male and female writers. A biographer of Sylvia Beach and an expert on Paris, Fitch writes with verve and expertise.

Franklin, Benjamin, and Duane Schneider. *Anaïs Nin: An Introduction.* Athens: Ohio University Press, 1979. A complete study of the canon of Nin's works, encompassing all of her early fiction works (*Under a Glass Bell and Other Stories* through *Collages*) and devoted to much discussion of the first six volumes of her diary (written between 1931 and 1966). A third section briefly covers Nin's criticism and her nonfiction and presents Nin as a feminist writer. Notes to every chapter are included, as well as an excellent selected bibliography (with an annotated list of secondary sources) and an index.

Hinz, Evelyn J. *The Mirror and the Garden: Realism and Reality in the Writings of Anaïs Nin.* 2d ed. New York: Harcourt Brace Jovanovich, 1973. Envisioned as a continuing study of a living writer, viewing Nin not only as a feminist writer but also as an American one. Her understanding and presentation of the psychological novel is examined at length in the context of her major fiction works. Nin's self-examination in her first four diaries and her critical methodology are also discussed. A bibliography of works and secondary sources (including journal articles) is included with an index.

Zaller, Robert, ed. *A Casebook on Anaïs Nin.* New York: New American Library, 1974. This collection of essays is useful as a chronological study of the emergence of Nin as a feminist and novelist. Focuses on her early novels, including *House of Incest*, and moves on quickly to *Cities of the Interior* and the first and fourth volumes of her diary.

Leslie B. Mittleman

THE STAND

Author: Stephen King (1947-   )
Type of plot: Apocalyptic novel
Time of plot: June 16, 1985, to January 10, 1986
Locale: The United States, especially Boulder, Colorado, and Las Vegas, Nevada
First published: 1978

Principal characters:

> STUART REDMAN, a widower and manual worker at a Texas calculator
> factory
> FRANNIE GOLDSMITH, his second wife, a pregnant college girl from
> New England
> LARRY UNDERWOOD, a rock-and-roll star
> HAROLD LAUDER, a teenage genius, in love with Frannie
> NICK ANDROS, a deaf-mute, a leader in Boulder
> TOM CULLEN, a mentally disabled companion of Nick Andros
> MOTHER ABIGAIL, an aged and deeply religious black woman
> RANDALL FLAGG, the "walkin' dude" or the "creeping Judas," the
> figure of the anti-Christ
> LLOYD HENREID, Randall Flagg's prophet

The Novel

On an air force base in California, a highly contagious flu virus is accidentally released, but a panicked employee escapes before the base is sealed, spreading the disease across the Southwest. The "super-flu" depopulates the country in a four-week
period in July, 1985.

The only survivors are naturally immune to the disease, and within a week, each
one dreams about two opposing forces, one heralded by the aged, pious Mother Abigail, who has received messages to prepare a meal for unknown guests. The other
force is represented by the evil Randall Flagg, the infamous "walkin' dude" or the
"creeping Judas." Flagg's first convert is Lloyd Henreid, a convicted murderer starving in a jail cell in a prison of the dead. Just when Henreid seems forced to survive by
cannibalism, he is mysteriously released: At Flagg's command, Henreid bows down
and worships him. The two set out across the country.

Meanwhile in New England, Harold Lauder and Frannie Goldsmith begin to look
for a cure for the super-flu. To impress Frannie, Harold climbs on a barn roof and
leaves a sign to inform any survivors who want to know where they have gone. On
their trip, Mother Abigail calls them west in dreams, and on the way they meet Stuart
Redman. Harold immediately becomes jealous of Redman, and begins to turn toward
the dark force.

Larry Underwood, meanwhile, has also begun to go west following the signs left by
Lauder. Meanwhile, the deaf-mute Nick Andros is also called by Mother Abigail from
his home in Arkansas to her house somewhere in the Midwest. Andros meets Tom

Cullen, a mentally disabled youth, and immediately feels sympathy for him. Even though Cullen will never progress beyond the mental age of six, he shows great wisdom. When the two men meet a beautiful girl in town who tries to seduce them, Cullen convinces Andros to avoid her, for he recognizes that she is from the "dark side." Like the other survivors, the two proceed west.

When the group gathers, their numbers are swelled by more, including Glen Bateman, an aging sociologist, and his dog, Kojak. Meanwhile, supernatural events begin to happen as Mother Abigail undergoes a harrowing encounter with the dark man and his creatures—weasels who attack her from the darkness.

Soon the survivors reach Boulder, Colorado, where they find the city mysteriously free of dead bodies. Now two groups emerge, one in Boulder and the other centered around Las Vegas, headed by Randall Flagg. Flagg's dictatorship immediately begins gathering weapons and training fighter pilots. The democracy at Boulder organizes their community under Andros's direction. Stuart Redman is appointed chairman of the executive board, and decides to send spies, including Tom Cullen, west into Nevada. When Tom is hypnotized in preparation for the trip, he becomes lucid for the first time and becomes "God's Tom."

Nadine Cross, who has been spurned and abandoned by the man she loves, turns to Harold Lauder and perverts him to the dark side. Harold then plans to assassinate the Boulder leaders. In the ensuing battle, Nick Andros is killed, while Nadine Cross and Lauder escape to the dark side.

Flagg's plans deteriorate. Underwood, Redman, Henreid, and Ralph Brentner go west at God's command and witness Flagg's destruction by the wrath of God. The survivors of the climactic events then return to Boulder to revive civilization.

The Characters

Mother Abigail is Stephen King's Christ figure in this version of the Apocalypse. At 108 years of age, Mother Abigail often reflects on the meaning of her life. As a young woman, she was a guitarist and singer and inherited money and land. The land was later taken away, bit by bit, to pay her taxes. Yet in all of her troubles, Abigail has relied on the Lord to save her and support her in her time of need—as she continues to do in the course of the novel.

Randall Flagg, the anti-Christ figure, can pass for either a black or a white man. He is not clearly of one race or the other, and his evil is such that he is against all that is good, and participates in all that is evil. He participated in Ku Klux Klan burnings, carried pamphlets by Lee Harvey Oswald, and met with revolutionaries in their councils.

Larry Underwood is a rock musician who, after years of struggle and one-night stands in seedy bars, finally makes it in the music world. With more money than he ever dreamed of, he begins to give lavish parties, take drugs, and in general go downhill. Finally, realizing that the people at his parties do not care about him, he leaves Hollywood one night to drive to New York. There his mother still lives in the same little walk-up apartment in which Underwood was reared. When the super-flu strikes, Larry is one of the survivors and endures the horror of seeing New York filled with the bodies of the dead. Larry and another survivor, a woman he picks up, travel west together. Larry's irresponsibility is demonstrated after his companion dies: He leaves her body to the scavenger birds because he does not like the thought of handling her dead body.

Frannie Goldsmith, a pregnant college girl from New England, is one of King's more realistically drawn female characters. Although unmarried, Frannie decides that she will carry the child and refuses to consider abortion. Frannie's gentleness and love add some tenderness to this bleak novel. When she meets Harold Lauder, he is an overweight, clumsy teenager who has a crush on her. Because of her encouragement, Harold begins to grow and mature; though he is ultimately drawn to evil, he has known what it is to love and care for another.

Themes and Meanings

The Stand, King's fifth novel, is a contemporary version of the Apocalypse. The four horsemen of the Scriptures are all here, and the "super-flu" serves the function of plague. Like many modern writers, King chooses United States government research as the source of the epidemic which wipes out virtually everyone in the country. The super-flu is 99.4 percent fatal and is initially developed as a weapon. Ironically, the super-flu escapes when an accident in the secret research unit frees the virus. It is carried by an escaping soldier who infects an entire town before he dies in agony.

In choosing the government as the instrument of destruction, King plays on contemporary fears—fears which, growing since the Vietnam War and nourished by Watergate, are manifested in a number of contemporary novels. King himself used sinister government characters or research in *The Dead Zone* (1979) and *Firestarter* (1980).

Randall Flagg, the anti-Christ, is also a creation of contemporary fear, especially the fear that satanic power lies behind the evil that we see on television or read about in the newspapers. When confronted with the reality of Lee Harvey Oswald's assassination of President John F. Kennedy, or a gang of racists wearing sheets of their own design to frighten and torture blacks, many people can find an explanation only in the agency of some superhuman evil. Flagg is presented as a source of such evil. He walks the land, and a great darkness is with him. His action in commanding Lloyd Henreid to fall down and worship him is the first time that the viewer sees Flagg in motion. Later in Las Vegas, where he sets up his kingdom, Flagg shows more of his power as he draws the weak (such as Harold Lauder, eaten up by jealousy) to his side. At this point, he seems too strong to be defeated under any circumstances, but he is gradually weakened by his own evil emotions and his uncontrollable temper.

Critical Context

This is a difficult novel for several reasons. The first is the length: the 1978 Doubleday edition has 823 pages of minuscule print. Besides the length, the book is difficult to follow. King's style here shifts to first-person narrative as each character is introduced, and many times pages of action follow before the reader is absolutely sure that a new and different character is being discussed. Finally, the novel is difficult because it has two endings. The first comes when the forces of good and evil are finally ready for a showdown: An atomic explosion sent from the hand of God destroys Flagg, his cohorts, and some of the good people from Boulder who are coming after Flagg. The second ending comes later, after Redman, who survived the blast in Las Vegas, returns to Boulder to discover that society has begun again. There is hope, but also fear that the forces which created the original super-flu and the original atomic bomb will one day create the same nightmare all over again.

Yet despite some flaws, The Stand is an important novel. It marks King's first attempt to deal with major issues such as the atomic bomb and secrecy in governmental research. It also portrays King's considerable power to horrify; many of the scenes in which Randall Flagg shows his powers are unforgettably frightening. Finally, King shows his growing deftness with characterization in his portraits of Flagg and Stuart Redman.

Bibliography
Beahm, George. *Stephen King: America's Best-Loved Bogeyman.* Kansas City, Mo.: Andrews and McMeel, 1998. Beahm provides an intriguing glimpse into Stephen King's life as a celebrity and publishing phenomenon. An excellent resource that helps readers gain deeper insight into King's works.
Bloom, Harold. *Stephen King.* Philadelphia: Chelsea House, 1998. A collection of critical essays that address various aspects of King's work. Useful for gaining a comprehensive overview of King's canon.
Hohne, Karen A. "The Power of the Spoken Word in the Works of Stephen King." *Journal of Popular Culture* 28 (Fall, 1994): 93-103. A defense of King's work against the "snobbery of scholars who look down upon the rustic tradition of popular language." Hohne gives a solid overview of King's work and calls for academia to recognize "its potential to mobilize mass support."
Magistrale, Tony. *The Dark Descent: Essays Defining Stephen King's Horrorscape.* New York: Greenwood Press, 1992. A collection of essays that explore King's works in depth. Includes "The Three Genres of *The Stand*," by Edwin F. Casebeer. Also features a helpful bibliography for further reading.
_____. "Free Will and Sexual Choice in *The Stand*." *Extrapolation* 34 (Spring, 1993): 30-38. Magistrale argues that King's novel reflects his philosophy of today's world, specifically addressing the power of sexuality to influence the nobler as well as the baser aspects of human nature. An intriguing look at King's thoughts on the human condition.
Russell, Sharon. *Stephen King: A Critical Companion.* Westport, Conn.: Greenwood Press, 1996. Offers a brief biography of King, as well as an overall view of his fiction. Entire chapters are devoted to each of his major novels, including one on *The Stand*. Discussion includes plot and character development, thematic issues, and a new critical approach to the novel.

Julia M. Meyers

STARS IN MY POCKET LIKE GRAINS OF SAND

Author: Samuel R. Delany (1942-   )
Type of plot: Science fiction
Time of plot: Far in the future
Locale: The planets Rhyonon and Velm
First published: 1984

> *Principal characters:*
>> RAT KORGA, the sole survivor of a destroyed planet
>> MARQ DYETH, a privileged member of the dazzling egalitarian future who forms an explosive bond with Korga
>> VONDRAMACH OKK, a tyrant of worlds, military genius, priest, and poet
>> JAPRIL, a senior official of the Web

The Novel

Stars in My Pocket Like Grains of Sand involves travel between various worlds and their diverse cultures, travel of mind and heart as well as body. The novel is structured by means of a prologue with an omniscient third-person narrator, followed by a series of thirteen monologues entitled "Visible and Invisible Persons Distributed in Space." Each is written in first-person narration and includes occasional memory flashbacks. The novel concludes with an epilogue, also with first-person narration.

The prologue narrates the experiences of Rat Korga as he undergoes the simple, voluntary operation offered by the Radical Anxiety Termination (RAT) Institute. The operation liberates him from his rage while preparing him to be docile and obedient. It resembles nothing so much as a high-tech lobotomy. The stupefied Korga then passes from job to job, his employers believing him incapable of sustained thought or feeling, until he is taken away briefly by a woman who lends him a General Information (GI) headset and allows him to rapid-read a slew of great poems and literary works. Korga now has a headful of ideas that no one knows he has or even could have. On the day of his planet's destruction, the temperature rises twenty degrees in ten seconds. During the next seventeen hours, all life on the surface of the planet is destroyed.

In the monologues and epilogue, Marq Dyeth of Velm, an Industrial Diplomat of high family, learns from a paid assassin that the planet recently destroyed, Rhyonon, was surrounded by the ships of the Xlv, an alien race, just before its destruction. He also learns that there was one survivor, that GI will refuse to divulge any information on the subject, and that the assassin will kill him if he pursues the matter.

Gradually, however, he learns more. He learns from Japril of the Web (the controllers of information) that the survivor, Rat Korga, has been rescued by the Web. Dyeth, a diplomat and person of high sensibility, discovers that he is Korga's perfect erotic object.

Korga sits in a Web life-restoration tank without blinking and demands that he be given a new world. Because of his operation, Korga lacks the precise neuronal connections that would allow him access to the advanced GI programs offered by the Web. He is therefore fitted with the rings Vondramach Okk had worn to restore her mental functioning after her own bout with a similar procedure. The rings have extraordinary power.

Korga is brought to Dyeth, and the attraction between them is consummated. Dyeth suggests that they go dragon hunting the next day. The secret in hunting dragons is to hunt one whose flight is beautiful, because one becomes the dragon one shoots, enters the dragon's being, and experiences with the dragon the dragon's flight. Delany explains, "The radar bow hooks on to a pretty complete mapping of the dragon's cerebral responses and, after a lot of translation, plays it back on your own cerebral surface." That is no more than the method. The magic is in the experience. Delany captures it exquisitely in what is the virtuoso passage of the novel.

Korga's extraordinary charisma begins to take effect, and crowds flock to see him. He is the one survivor of a world lost either to Cultural Fugue—a condition universally dreaded, in which a world's inhabitants render their entire planet uninhabitable—or to a first military encounter with the Xlv.

After an extraordinary formal dinner, at which members of the Thant family manage to upset all Dyeth's attempts at diplomacy and hospitality, Korga leaves Velm, in Japril's company. The Web has decided that it is not a suitable world for him, after all, as his presence comes close to provoking Cultural Fugue. There are even larger issues: The balance between Family and Sygn is threatened, and an Xlv fleet is circling Velm. Delany opens the door to a second volume, to be entitled *The Splendour and Misery of Bodies, of Cities*. "We can't have the two of you there," Japril says toward the end of *Stars in My Pocket Like Grains of Sand*. "We can't have the two of you together yet."

The Characters

In Marq Dyeth, Delany creates an open and forthright character to contrast with the enigmatic Rat Korga. Dyeth's education, privileged background, and nurturing family life serve as a foil to the ill-educated, abandoned social misfit Rat Korga. Even physically, the two are at odds: Dyeth is short and attractive; Korga is well over seven feet tall and disfigured. Perhaps most significant, Dyeth's successful career is based on his understanding not only of his home world but also of the myriad cultures of other planets, while Korga has never understood his home world and knows virtually nothing about any other. That these opposites are still strongly attracted to each other underscores Delany's cross-cultural and cross-racial themes.

Korga's life on Rhyonon has been one of institutional and personal servitude and exploitation. Misled by the RAT Institute to believe that he would be happy after undergoing the surgical procedure, Korga loses his freedom to an institution that strips away his dignity and profits from his mistreatment. As if his economic exploitation were not bad enough, Korga is illegally purchased by a woman—on Rhyonon only institutions can legally own slaves—and experiences sexual exploitation. Required to fulfill his new owner's erotic desires, the homosexually oriented Korga is obliged to imagine his female owner to be a man in order to perform sexually. Later, she sadistically abuses him for her own sexual satisfaction. The institution of slavery depicted in these predestruction scenes on Rhyonon comment pointedly on the institution of slavery.

Rat Korga's relationship with Marq Dyeth contrasts with the social and sexual slavery on Rhyonon. Custom on Velm promotes a relaxed sexual atmosphere in which erotic encounters between humans and evelmi are culturally sanctioned. The capacity to see "the other" as erotic object is shown as a cornerstone for healthy individual relationships, fostering cross-cultural and cross-species understanding. Delany's sexually repressed Rhyonon may correspond to Earth, where gay and interracial relationships continue to face legal and social obstacles.

Themes and Meanings

Samuel Delany is interested first and foremost in spinning a fine yarn. He is a master storyteller, as he demonstrated in *Babel-17* (1966) and as he proves again in this novel. He is also a great lover of words and language, an excellent prose stylist with occasional experimental flurries.

Delany is more than this: He is also a person of minority sexual tastes and skin pigmentation in his own nation. It is perhaps his statistical "deviance"—both an unloaded, technical, and a loaded, pejorative term—from the norm that has made him a superlative anthropologist of far future, deep space, and other worlds.

To the extent that Delany has purposes other than storytelling woven into his stories—he would deny they were "themes"—those purposes commonly include arriving at an understanding of the alien, the strange, and the unusual by virtue of his sympathetic exploration of the varied thought processes, languages, customs, and sexualities of the worlds through which he leads his readers.

In *Stars in My Pocket Like Grains of Sand*, he contrasts two rival polities, each of which rules many worlds. The Family is "trying to establish the dream of a classic past on a world [the original Earth] that may never even have existed in order to achieve cultural stability, . . . with the Sygn committed to the living interaction and difference between each woman and each world from which the right stability and play may flower."

In the sentence just quoted, "woman" is the cue to another of Delany's themes, a questioning of gender roles. "In Arachnia as it is spoken on Nepiy, 'she' is the pronoun for all sentient individuals of whatever species who have achieved the legal status of 'woman.' The ancient, dimorphic form 'he' . . . has been reserved for the general sexual object of 'she' . . . regardless of the gender of the woman speaking or the gender of the woman referred to." As in Ursula Le Guin's *The Left Hand of Darkness* (1969), a shift in gender usage confronts and skews the reader's assumptions about gender identity.

The many varieties of sexuality is another of Delany's themes. With males, females, and neuters, and several very different "races," the possibilities for both variety and repression are endless. He describes sexual acts committed with "rats" such as the early Rat Korga, who will obey any command; "sex and sculpture" arcades; the sexuality of the winged evelmi, for whom taste is the predominant sense; worlds where sex between people of different heights, of whatever gender, was considered the ultimate taboo; and worlds where interracial heterosexuality is treated as a perversion. The hunting of dragons, too, may be some kind of elevated analog of sexuality. All are described with sympathetic attention and respect.

Cultural Fugue runs like a fugal theme through the book, as through a century beset by threats of nuclear or ecological world catastrophe. It is instructive that Delany treats it as an infrequent occurrence. As noted by critic Martha A. Bartter, if any issue connects this novel with today's world, it is Cultural Fugue. Delany's message is a reassuring one.

As befits a man almost Shakespearean in his love of language, and once married to the poet Marilyn Hacker, Delany returns here to his great theme of the poet. Vondramach Okk is the latest in a line of Delany's poets, running from Rydra Wong, poet captain of the ship Rimbaud in *Babel-17*, through Lobey, the alien Orpheus in *The Einstein Intersection* (1967), to The Singers of Worlds in "Time Considered as a Helix of Semiprecious Stones" in *Driftglass* (1971). Delany himself is the poet—the man ("woman") able to move between worlds, powerful by virtue of his eyes and all that they are open to perceive, by virtue of his love, by virtue of his language.

Critical Context

Stars in My Pocket Like Grains of Sand had been drafted in 1979 and expected for publication in 1981 or 1982. The novel was enthusiastically received by critics when it was published in December, 1984. The book's publication signaled a return to science fiction for Delany, who had previously published a series of fantasy novels. Delaney was recognized early as a talented writer, and two of his early novels, *Babel-17* and *The Einstein Intersection*, won Nebula Awards while Delany was still in his mid-twenties. Delany's reputation as a serious novelist continued to grow, not only in the United States and England but also on the European continent, where he won the praise of critics and fellow artists, among them Umberto Eco.

Delany has repeatedly acknowledged his interest in issues of gay, women's, and civil rights. *Stars in My Pocket Like Grains of Sand* reflects these interests and extends them into a fictive future world. Delany's investigation of institutional slavery and cross-racial barriers to communication reveals his intention to translate many of the issues of the African American experience to a future universe.

Bibliography
Bartter, Martha A. "The (Science-Fiction) Reader and the Quantum Paradigm: Problems in Delany's *Stars in My Pocket Like Grains of Sand.*" *Science-Fiction Studies* 17 (November, 1990): 325-340. Suggests that Delany's fiction, especially this novel, subjects readers to something analogous to the paradigm of Heisenberg's uncertainty principle, with certain things unknowable. Strained in many details but provocative.

Bray, Mary Kay. "To See What Condition Our Condition Is In: Trial by Language in *Stars in My Pocket Like Grains of Sand.*" *The Review of Contemporary Fiction* 16 (Fall, 1996): 153-160. Bray contends that Delany uses the Web, an organization that controls the galaxy, as a metaphor for the ways text shapes reader response in his novel. The Web selects which events will take place and directs the perception of those events by sentient beings. She shows how Delany's alteration of standard English is similar to the way the Web molds reality.

Delany, Samuel R. "Thickening the Plot." In *The Jewel-Hinged Jaw: Notes on the Language of Science Fiction*. Elizabethtown, N.Y.: Dragon Press, 1977. Delany's own account of the way in which he conceives his plots and writes his imaginatively detailed scenes. A brilliant introspection and excellent introduction to the craft for neophyte science-fiction writers.

Massé, Michelle. "'All You Have to Do Is Know What You Want': Individual Expectations in *Triton*." In *Coordinates: Placing Science Fiction and Fantasy*, edited by Eric S. Rabkin, Robert Scholes, and George E. Slusser. Carbondale: Southern Illinois University Press, 1983. Examines the role of desire in Delany's novel *Triton* (1976), which like many of Delany's novels has a strong sexual theme. *Triton* is similar to *Stars in My Pocket Like Grains of Sand* in use of technology to adapt people's thinking; in *Triton*, people can voluntarily change their sexual preferences as well as their sexuality.

Sallis, James, ed. *Ash of Stars: On the Writing of Samuel R. Delany*. Jackson: University Press of Mississippi, 1996. An interesting collection of critical essays by various scholars that address specific aspects of Delany's fiction. Features a selected bibliography, as well as two essays on *Stars in My Pocket Like Grains of Sand*, including the one by Mary Kay Bray cited above.

Charles Cameron

THE STONE ANGEL

Author: Margaret Laurence (1926-1987)
Type of plot: Character study
Time of plot: The 1930's
Locale: Manawaka, Manitoba, a fictitious prairie town
First published: 1964

> *Principal characters:*
> HAGAR SHIPLEY, a proud, crusty heroine with a lifetime of regrets
> BRAM SHIPLEY, Hagar's unconventional husband, whom she abandons
> MARVIN SHIPLEY, Hagar's compliant but unappreciated older son
> JOHN SHIPLEY, Hagar's troubled but loved younger son, whom she
>   loses

The Novel

The Stone Angel offers a portrait of a remarkable character who at age ninety confronts her mortality and is terrified, for all she can see behind her is a wasteland of personal failures. Yet her terror becomes the necessary catalyst for a change of heart and a measure of grace that marks her final days.

Hagar Shipley looms large on nearly every page. The novel works mainly through the flashback memories of a ninety-year-old matron who faces the need for a nursing home. Her case is terminal, but she is not ready to die. Too many ghosts from the past haunt her memories and preclude peace for facing the future. Those ghosts are exposed through a skillful interweaving of past and present that cumulatively render an insightful examination of a fallen angel whose overweening pride led her into self-exile.

Hagar loses her mother early in life. She never makes her peace with that death. Yet her imperious, prominent, and self-made father tolerates no weakness of any kind; thus Hagar learns to shut the valves of emotion and live a life of negation and stoicism. Strong-willed like her father, she defies him when she comes of age and chooses to marry Bram Shipley, a good-looking but, in her father's eyes, good-for-nothing widower with two children who lives on a rundown homestead that never would afford anyone a decent living. No family member attends Hagar's wedding, and Hagar's family relationship is never restored. Besides, she soon discovers that she has made a terrible mistake. Bram has no intention of being made over by a snooty young woman who has finishing-school and pedigree credentials and pretensions of a superior sophistication. Instead, Hagar finds herself dragged down by his crudeness, poverty, and hopeless future. Still, they have two sons together: Marvin, whom she hardly acknowledges as her own, and John, in whom she recognizes herself and who is the apple of her eye. Bram feels increasingly judged and rejected by Hagar; when his outrageous behavior publicly shames Hagar, she decides to leave with her younger son, John. The two move to the Pacific coast, where Hagar finds employment as a live-in housekeeper for an elderly gentleman, Mr. Oatley. John feels displaced and eventually begins to run around with a bad crowd. Predictably, the time comes when he feels pulled back to his roots, the Shipley place and Bram, to whom he feels connected more than Hagar is able to accept. When Bram falls ill, Hagar feels compelled to return. She finds the place, including Bram and John, in an advanced state of neglect. In fact, Bram is dying, and John, who has been caring for him, is beginning to look and act much like a younger version of his father. When Bram dies, John cries, but Hagar does not. She feels John slipping away from her, yet she widens the gulf when she denounces him for dating Arlene, a girl she considers below his class. When she visits again a year later, she in effect forbids John to take his girlfriend home. Shortly thereafter, John and Arlene are killed in a freak accident, and Hagar's heart turns to stone.

She returns to Vancouver and stays with Mr. Oatley till he dies. He leaves her money in his will, with which she buys her own house. When she can no longer take care of herself, Marvin and his wife Doris move in with her. She is ill and in need of constant care in a nursing home, but it is a move for which she is not prepared.

Instead, she embarks on another journey, for which she is physically unfit but spiritually most needy. She takes the bus toward the sea, to a place aptly called Shadow Point, a valley where all the shadows of death past and future need to be confronted. There, in an abandoned cannery, Hagar enters the darkness of her soul and, in a divine delirium of sorts, makes amends with her beloved John, for whose death she has always felt responsible and therefore was never able to accept and mourn. It is at that moment that Hagar experiences freedom for the first time. After this, she is able to cry, feel grief, feel gratitude, apologize, compliment, accept help, and reach out to help another. On a hospital bed, she at last is able to face her final journey. The stone angel has come alive, and with it the recognition that the heart's true need has always been simply to rejoice.

The Characters

The character of Hagar, like Herman Melville's Ahab and Jack London's Wolf Larsen, is memorably rendered larger than life. Proud as Lucifer, Hagar surveys the wasteland of her life, unbending and unregenerate until nearly the end. That wasteland includes nearly every character in the book as a victim of Hagar's pride. As Laurence imposes on Hagar the need for self-examination, each character is summoned through flashbacks and memories. Included is Jason Currie, the father whose favor she lost when she defied him. There is also Lottie Drieser, her schoolmate whom she treated as an inferior. Especially, there are the people who became her own family and should have become an intimate part of her life, yet did not. There is Bram, the man she married mostly as an act of rebellion but whose virility she loved, and yet to whom she could never give one word of approval or acceptance. There is Marvin, her first-born, docile and serving by nature, who needed her approval and acceptance desperately but for whom Hagar nurtured an undisguised scorn. There is also Marvin's wife, Doris, who is the constant recipient of Hagar's verbal abuse. Each of these characters becomes an embodied indictment of Hagar's blindness to her own destructiveness. In that parade of witnesses, none is more poignant than John, Hagar's favorite son, for whom Hagar's blindness turns out the most destructive of all. It is John's loss that carries the most stinging indictment and festers in Hagar's memory like an open wound. Ironically, it is John's death that becomes the means for Hagar's "salvation."

Laurence's choice to have Hagar carry the point of view and be the sole voice of the story allows the reader to see much more than the tough, forbidding exterior that has kept all the people in Hagar's life at a distance. Inside, Hagar is fragile, insecure, frightened by her own vulnerability and even more by the possibility that someone will discover that vulnerability. It is this dualism that renders Hagar's character at once so complex and so compelling to the reader and establishes a sympathetic identification at the deepest level.

Themes and Meanings

Laurence's own perception of the meaning of her novel evolved over the years. Initially, she thought that she had written about the nature of freedom through Hagar's struggle for her own independence and coming to terms with her own past. Later, she noted that the theme was really about survival, the human need to survive until the moment of death with some kind of dignity and sense of personal value. Much later still, Laurence observed that Hagar at the end learns what constitutes her true significance: the ability to give and receive love.

The Stone Angel is about all of these things. It surely is about the many mental and emotional barriers that can stultify the freedom to be what one deep down wishes and needs to be. Psychic and spiritual survival requires that those barriers be recognized for what they are. Only then can a person be free to relate truly to others. The essence of relationships, Hagar discovers, is the ability to communicate and love. She does just that in her waning hours, though the habit of long neglect makes the efforts both poignant and comical.

Laurence has steeped her story in biblical allusions and imagery. The most obvious is the allusion to Hagar, Abram's Egyptian maidservant whose pride forced her to flee to the wilderness and whose son Ishmael was destined to be "a wild donkey of a man." Desert images of drought abound; the dominant color is gray, and the flowers are mostly those associated with death. In this environment, Hagar turns into a "stone angel." The water imagery at the end of the book signals the turning point of Hagar's revival, recovery, and redemption. Yet the ending, though redemptive, is hardly triumphant. What prevails in the reader reflects Hagar's own state of mind: a profound sense of regret that nearly a whole lifetime had been wasted on appearances, victimizing both self and others.

Critical Context

The Stone Angel, Laurence's first prairie novel, introduced Manawaka, the fictional town in Manitoba based on the author's hometown of Neepawa. The book was a critical success from the beginning. It was followed by three others that, as a cycle, constitute a kind of epic of small-town prairie life, authentically rendered through recurrent themes and well-developed heroines who, as early feminists, search for identity.

The main characters share an internal dissonance that lies at the heart of most of Laurence's fiction. It threatens to arrest their human development and leave them with a debilitating sense of insignificance. In Hagar, it is the tension between her pugnacious personality and her fear of emotionality. In *A Jest of God* (1966), Rachel's personality is Hagar's opposite: she is too weak-willed to rage. However, like Hagar, she too is emotionally repressed, but she is able to take action once she too has confronted and exercised her emotional needs. Stacey, in *The Fire-Dwellers* (1969), is Rachel's sister, but her dissonance is a more complex one, and she is far from submissive. Strong like Hagar, Stacey does battle with a world that threatens to alienate, isolate, and dehumanize. Like Hagar and Rachel, she finds in the end a qualified peace through an enhanced understanding of self and others. *The Diviners* (1974), structurally and thematically the most complex of the cycle, brings together a number of these characters and themes. Though the protagonist is Morag, there are references to Stacey and Rachel. It is through Morag especially that Laurence recapitulates her vision and concerns as a writer. The enemies to human wholeness include pride, selfishness, emotional paralysis, fear, bigotry, and prejudice. Morag understands at the end that to be delivered from such enemies is to enter a state of grace.

Laurence, one of the most beloved of Canadian writers, has twice won the Governor-General's Award for Fiction. She became a leading figure in the Canadian renaissance of the 1960's and 1970's. Her books have been translated into many other languages and continue to be read widely, but it is *The Stone Angel* that stands as her classic contribution to world literature.

Bibliography

Coger, Greta M. R. McCormick, ed. *New Perspectives on Margaret Laurence: Poetic Narrative, Multiculturalism, and Feminism*. Westport, Conn.: Greenwood Press, 1996. Features a variety of critical approaches by national and international contributors.

King, James. *The Life of Margaret Laurence*. Toronto: Alfred A. Knopf, 1997. A candid biography that exposes the vices as well as the virtues of the subject.

Morley, Patricia. *Margaret Laurence: The Long Journey Home*. Rev. ed. Montreal: McGill-Queen's University Press, 1991. A chronological, critical survey of Laurence as one of the major novelists of the twentieth century, with a useful emphasis on her feminism and political activism.

Thomas, Clara. *The Manawaka World of Margaret Laurence*. Toronto: McClelland & Stewart, 1976. This critical and biographical study illuminates the connection between the author's place and literary works.

Henry J. Baron

THE STONE DIARIES

Author: Carol Shields (1935-   )
Type of plot: Domestic realism
Time of plot: 1905 to the 1990's
Locale: Manitoba and Ontario, in Canada; Indiana and Florida, in the United States
First published: 1993

> *Principal characters:*
>
> DAISY GOODWILL FLETT, the principal subject, wife, mother, writer, and finally Florida retiree
>
> MERCY STONE GOODWILL, Daisy's mother, who dies in childbirth
>
> CUYLER GOODWILL, Daisy's father, a romantic who learns to connect with his second wife but never with Daisy
>
> CLARENTINE FLETT, a neighbor of Mercy who rears the motherless Daisy
>
> MAGNUS FLETT, Clarentine's husband
>
> BARKER FLETT, the second husband of Daisy, restrained, reliable, suppressed
>
> ELFREDA HOYT (FRAIDY), unrestrained and loyal college friend of Daisy
>
> LABINA ANTHONY (BEANS), initially conventional college friend of Daisy

The Novel

The Stone Diaries is the story of the life of Daisy Goodwill Hoad Flett. The novel is divided into ten chapters, beginning with "Birth, 1905" and ending with "Death." A fictional biography of a Canadian American woman, the novel spans her childhood, marriages, children, work, decline, and death.

Narrated by several different voices, but most often by Daisy herself, the novel weaves a complex pattern of stories that belie the chronological layout of the book. The description of Daisy's own birth, for example, is told by Daisy in the first person. The narration begins in Tyndall, Manitoba, with Daisy's mother, Mercy Stone Goodwill, making dinner on a hot summer day; one hour later, the mother has died giving birth. Interwoven into this chapter are the courtship stories of Mercy and Cuyler, freighted with emotions that could never have been described to the child by her father and revealing a first mystery: Mercy had not hidden her pregnancy from her husband but had simply been unaware of it herself.

Daisy is cared for by her parents' neighbor, Clarentine Flett, who takes the infant child with her when she leaves her husband and goes to Winnipeg to live with her son, a college professor. The narrative in this chapter includes description of Cuyler's building the stone tower on the grave of Mercy, and letters from Barker and Clarentine Flett advance the plot. Daisy's character develops through her response to illness, a response that includes her discovery of an "absence inside herself," a discovery that she lacked "the kernel of authenticity."

Her marriage in 1927 leads to a defining moment for Daisy: her husband's fall from a window while they are on their honeymoon in France, dramatically ending their unconsummated marriage and leaving Daisy to return to her life in Indiana, where she lives with her father and socializes with friends for the next nine years. The impetus to leave her uneventful widowed life is provided by her father's passionate marriage with Maria, a lovingly demonstrative woman known to kiss the top of her husband's head.

Daisy returns to Canada and marries Barker Flett, the man with whom she has been corresponding and to whom she has referred as "Uncle Barker" since her childhood. Her middle age is marked by the births of her three children, the death of her husband, and her taking over the writing of a newspaper column on gardening, a column that gives her an identity as "Mrs. Greenthumb."

Perhaps the most intriguing chapter, "Work, 1955-1965," is written entirely in letters. The letters suggest outlines of family conflict and most poignantly the passing of romance and love. The chapter opens with Barker's will being filed and recounts a letter he had left for Daisy to open after his death, a letter confirming Barker's place in the world of the novel: one who has missed opportunities, has gone on about the business of living without savoring passionate moments. His final correspondence with Daisy expresses regret for unshared passion. The remaining letters in the chapter are less poignant but nevertheless riveting. They sketch generosities of spirit in Daisy (taking in her pregnant niece Beverly; traveling unbidden to her daughter Alice, who was in the midst of depression on the anniversary of her father's death), the outlines of her career as Mrs. Greenthumb (letters of appreciation from readers; allusions to an affair with her editor), and finally the end of her nine-year career as a columnist.

Daisy endures an intense depression after losing her column. Shields's narrative method of various voices drives this section of the novel. Each of those closely connected to Daisy speculates on the cause of her depression, including the grandson of the Jewish salesman who witnessed her birth, Abram Skutari, as a voice explaining her depression as a result of her incurable loneliness. This chapter, "Sorrow, 1965," encapsulates a theme of the book: the unknowable center of an individual. Each speculation presents a portion of Daisy, no one of which is the essential self.

Daisy's retirement years in Florida are marked by a trip to the Orkney Islands, where she visits a rest home to see her father-in-law, Magnus Flett, famous for his having been able to recite the entire 1847 novel *Jane Eyre*. The trip with her great niece Victoria is juxtaposed with the description of Cuyler's death, his reception back into nature in the yard near his final stone construction.

The Characters

The characters of Shields's novel most often are fully realized individuals but are most important in revealing facets of Daisy.

Daisy Goodwill Hoad Flett is the ultimately unknowable center of the book, a mystery who is explained, commented on, and loved by her friends and family. Shields, with a touch of Magical Realism, uses Daisy's point of view to describe her own birth as well as her parents' courtship and early married life, providing details unknowable to her. Daisy's life is colored by the sadness of her birth, a unique and orphaned memory with which Daisy feels burdened during her middle and later years. Her unknowable center is emphasized by Shields via Daisy's close relationship to her college friends Fraidy and Beans. They are great friends, but she does not tell them about her sneeze in the moment before her first husband, Harold A. Hoad, fell out of the hotel window. Daisy withholds her essential self from all those the reader expects to be closest to her.

Cuyler Goodwill is Daisy's father, a man who knew a loveless childhood but develops a passionate attachment to Mercy Stone Goodwill, Daisy's mother. Cuyler works in stone, whereas Daisy gardens and cooks. Cuyler develops the kind of love and passion his daughter misses all of her life. He is, however, like his daughter in his ability to present representations of life; his excellent speaking skills, for example, are displayed at Daisy's graduation from college.

Barker Flett is, throughout his life, a man who unfailingly does what is expected of him; but Shields enters the essential self of this character in her description of his passion for Daisy as an eleven-year-old. The fixation on such a young girl is one that Barker only minimally admits to himself; his self-consciousness about desire, sex, and passion leads him to miss a dance with Daisy "through the back door, out into the garden, down the street, over the line of the horizon," a dance described to her at a safe distance, in a posthumously opened letter.

Fraidy Hoyt represents the friends that Daisy makes over the years. Fraidy is first a college friend, and throughout her life she corresponds with, travels with, and visits with Daisy. Fraidy is the college friend who first experiments with sex and continues to enjoy different partners. She theorizes that Daisy's depression in 1965 stems from sexual repression, and she thinks of telling the one-man (so she thinks) Daisy about her own "army of fifty-four . . . a small smartly marching army with the sun shining on their beautiful heads and shoulders."

Shields provides labeled pictures of many of the characters, but notably absent is Daisy herself, again ultimately unknowable. The pictures include postcards and photographs purchased in antique shops as well as pictures of Shields's own children. The pictures raise as many questions for a reader as they answer, but especially fitting are the conventional pose of Beans Anthony and the nude sketch of Fraidy Hoyt (a sketch credited to one of Fraidy's lovers, a professor).

Themes and Meanings

Life suspended in stone is one theme of the book. Daisy as narrator often focuses on passionate attachments of those she is describing, and Daisy's life begins in her parents' lives: Cuyler Goodwill a skilled stonecutter and Mercy Stone a heavy and still woman. Cuyler believes his marriage to Mercy and his passion for her dislodged "the stone in his throat" and gave him the power of true speech. Cuyler builds a stone tower to mark Mercy's gravesite, work in which passion and stone interplay in his carving of the images for some of the stones in the tower, leaving him to feel the presence of God in his work, life within stone.

Under his final stone production, the pyramid, Cuyler places a time capsule the small contents of which include Mercy's wedding ring. He has been unable to find the right words to accompany the ring and give it to Daisy; he finds it far less troubling "to bury this treasure beneath a weight of stone—his pyramid, dense, heavy, complex, full of secrets, a sort of machine." Cuyler's treasure beneath stone is echoed when Daisy, her great-niece Victoria, and Victoria's boyfriend Lewis Roy visit God's Gate on the Orkney Islands, where the niece and Lewis Roy closely examine the outcropping rock to "find a microscopic tracing of buried life. Life turned to stone."

The final working of this theme appears as Daisy, aware of dying, returns to the stone images: "Stone is how she finally sees herself." In her death, Daisy feels herself reunited with her mother, no longer orphaned and alone, life now suspended in stone.

Shields's novel also reveals consistent missed connections and failures of understanding, perhaps best exemplified by the fairly cool relationship between Daisy and Barker. Daisy reads women's magazines and tries to follow advice offered on keeping her husband happy, advice that never addresses the ultimate loneliness of each of them: their failure to connect. The failure to understand also appears in Daisy's not recognizing her niece Beverly's need when she stops for a visit to the family. With Beverly, however, Daisy later has and takes advantage of the opportunity to make connections, offering the young woman a home in which she can bring up her child, Victoria.

Critical Context

Shields's initial recognition as a novelist was the Arthur Ellis Award for best Canadian crime novel of 1987 for *Swann: A Mystery* (1987). Awarded the Pulitzer Prize for Fiction in 1995, *The Stone Diaries* is the seventh novel by Shields, whose poetry, drama, essays, and travel writing are also recognized to be excellent. Her poetry, like much of her fiction, centers on familiar suburban experience, examining closely the effects of time within singular moments. Nor does the fact that she is a playwright surprise the reader of her novels; her scene-by-scene descriptions and believable dialogue suggest her works' adaptability to stage or film. One of her plays, *Thirteen Hands* (1993), is about women who gather to play bridge and share stories. They are the older middle-class women who so often feel invisible in a culture obsessed with accoutrements of eternal youth and flashy possession. The play, like Shields's novels, examines the ordinary caring among women.

Lest any reader decide that Shields writes "women's fiction," the critical reception of her novel after *The Stone Diaries*, *Larry's Party* (1997), should disprove such an assumption. Her male protagonist, Larry Weller, moves through his own work and relationships, putting his past into meaningful context with his quiet and suburban present. In analyses of Weller, critics cite similarities to John Updike's Rabbit Angstrom.

The Stone Diaries well fits its late twentieth century audience: a novel of the ordinary, the uneventful, and the drama in small moments. *The Stone Diaries* succeeds because it portrays felt life, with particular emphasis on sensual minutiae and ordinary pleasures, issues of love, work, and identity recurring in Shields's work. Readers gain personal insight from her studies of relationships, which are always ironically presented. Shields's writing appeals to a populace increasingly oriented to the visual and increasingly in need of connection. She shows readers truths of their own and their parents' lives.

Bibliography
Bell, Karen. "Carol Shields: All These Years Later, Still Digging." *Performing Arts and Entertainment in Canada* (Winter, 1998): 1-3. Analyzes works in the light of Shields's experience. Particular emphasis on her novels and plays.
The Carol Shields Issue. Vancouver: Growing Room Collective, 1989. An interview with the author and collected critical essays focusing on her works; the thirteenth volume in a series entitled *Room of One's Own.*
Turbide, Diane. "A Prairie Pulitzer." *Maclean's* 108, no. 18 (May 1, 1995): 76-78. Focuses on Shields's publishing history, recounting her many awards and honors. Notes the natural connection between *The Stone Diaries* and film.

Janet Taylor Palmer

STONES FOR IBARRA

Author: Harriet Doerr (1910-   )
Type of plot: Magical Realism
Time of plot: The 1960's
Locale: The fictional town of Ibarra, Mexico
First published: 1984

>   *Principal characters:*
>   SARA EVERTON, the wife of Richard Everton
>   RICHARD EVERTON, an American engineer
>   LOURDES, their Mexican housekeeper
>   REMEDIOS ACOSTA, a Mexican woman of the village
>   JUAN GÓMEZ, the local priest

The Novel

   Stones for Ibarra began as a series of short stories that share a general location in a
central Mexican town so small it does not appear on the fictional map of Mexico. The
vignettes that constitute the eighteen chapters of the novel chronicle a series of events
focused on one character of Ibarra after another, connected by the passage of time between the arrival of Richard and Sara Everton and Sara's departure six years later.
Doerr claims that only a small part of *Stones for Ibarra* is autobiographical, but the
framework of the novel recalls the Doerr family's forays to Mexico.

   In the first chapter, "The Evertons Out of Their Minds," the fictional Sara and Richard Everton go to Mexico from San Francisco, California, to reclaim the family estate
and reopen a copper mine abandoned since the Mexican Revolution of 1910. Not long
after their arrival at the unexpectedly dilapidated house, which fails to match the faded
family photos or the Evertons's dreams, Richard is diagnosed with leukemia and
given six years to live. Despite the brevity of the second chapter, "A Clear Understanding," several months pass in which the Evertons are observed by the townspeople, who find the Americans peculiar, and the dead spirits of Richard's family, who
Sara believes are present in the house. Richard hires workers for the mine. The
Evertons travel to California, returning with special plant food and medication for
Richard's illness. By the end of a year, the village natives conclude that the Americans
are *mediodesorientado*, or half-oriented, and the Evertons understand the natives just
as little. "The Life Sentence of José Reyes" tells the tale of a decent man whose life is
changed forever by two events: the two years of drought that destroy his field and the
accident he suffers at the hands of the Palacio brothers, which results in an epilepsy he
cannot afford to treat. The first loss leads José to drunken despair in the local cantina;
his drunkenness causes him to let the Palacio brothers swing him through the air to
land on the hard cobblestones of the street. The injury from his fall produces a lesion
in his brain that causes epileptic seizures. José thus kills the Palacio brothers and is
sentenced to life imprisonment.

"Kid Muñoz" is a former boxer blinded in a fight. The tale of his injury and present life weaves in and out of Sara's consciousness as she thinks that "chance is everything" and resists the thought of Richard's diagnosis: six years to live, and one year already gone.

In "The Inheritance," a village boy, Juan, inherits his grandfather's house and his cousin Pablo, the town idiot. Juan falls in love with Otilia, but Pablo is an obstacle to their relationship and marriage. When Pablo falls in a pool near the dam, Juan hesitates just a few seconds before reaching to help him. Pablo, the real "inheritance," dies, and Juan's life is changed forever

"The Red Taxi" tells the story of Chuy Santos, whose two friends, El Gallo and El Golondrino ("the Rooster" and "the Swallow"), work at the Everton mine. Together they decide to buy an aged Volkswagen and become partners in a taxi service. Unfortunately, the two friends, working in unsafe conditions after hours in order to meet the purchase deadline, die in a mine accident. Chuy mourns the loss of his friends; nevertheless, when the Evertons give him the money to buy two coffins in which to bury them, he buys the cheaper ones and uses the difference to buy the car that was the original cause of the accident.

The town priest is a frequent visitor to the Everton home, and he figures in many of the novel's vignettes of the novel. He has a train of assistant priests, who build basketball courts, are beloved of dogs, and impregnate a woman from a neighboring village. He sponsors a town picnic and solicits donations from the nonbelieving Evertons. Other vignettes relate the sad tale of brother killing brother, the use of native remedies to protect the Everton house, Sara's Spanish lessons with Madre Petra, and the visit of a Canadian geologist and his Lebanese engineer.

The final two chapters of the novel bring together many of the earlier threads of the narrative. Richard is dead; Sara is alone in the house of his family. The geologist and engineer stop to visit without realizing that Richard is dead. Lourdes still leaves folk herbs hidden in drawers to influence Sara's destiny. Chuy brings a stranger to the house in his red taxi. The latest assistant priest holds a special mass for Richard. Sara packs and leaves, hoping that more stones will be left to mark the site of the tragedy—the early death of her husband Richard.

The Characters

The characters of *Stones for Ibarra* are revealed more profoundly by the stories told and observations made about them than by anything they themselves reveal—the deep cultural divide between villagers and expatriates is exposed. Though the eighteen chapters present numerous minor and apparently idiosyncratic characters, the narrative depends primarily on four central figures.

Richard Everton is an admirable character. A deeply moral man who cares for his workers and has some comprehension of his importance to the village as the employer of many men, Richard takes his illness and impending death in stride. When his wife Sara begins to embellish her tales of the locals' lives, he intuitively understands that she hopes her storytelling can create a new and different story for her and Richard than the dark future the physician has given them.

Sara Everton is, like her husband, near forty and a secular humanist who believes in the power of the human individual rather than in any God or gods. Her beliefs are sorely tested by Richard's leukemia and her inability to create a different future by simply imagining it. Sara's attitude is in stark contrast to that of the villagers, who believe deeply in the one and only God but also in such folk remedies as herbs against maladies and a thorn to protect the house and mine.

Lourdes, the Evertons' Mexican housekeeper, and Remedios Acosta, a village woman, interact with the strange Americans and report to the village on the foreigners' curious behavior. They present and represent the Mexican perspective in contrast to the alien Evertons' perspective. The village priest, Juan Gómez, appears almost exclusively as "the *cura*" rather than as a named individual. Though he appears frequently in many contexts, just as a true village priest would, he does not develop much as a character but rather serves as a catalyst to move the narrative forward and as a foil to the Everton's atheism. At the end of the novel, Sara remains an atheist, but she has softened toward native practices, such as the placing of stones to mark the scene of a tragedy.

Themes and Meanings

Stones for Ibarra is based on an episodic structure and a Mexican setting. It is written in a thoroughly crafted prose in which each sentence is pared down and polished until only the essential remains. As a consequence, the reader seems to somehow create the text while reading it, to discover in Doerr's spare phrases the meaning and emotion the characters themselves hesitate to reveal. The novel reveals as much about the "lost" American expatriates as it does about the Mexican natives, by shifting perspectives and allowing the reader to see each group or individual through the eyes of the other. Unlike the Mexico portrayed in novels by such authors as Graham Greene, Malcolm Lowry, and D. H. Lawrence, Doerr's Mexico is a friendlier, more humane place where the Mexicans are just as perplexed about the Americans as the Americans are about the Mexicans. It is a no less tragic Mexico, but tragedy is quotidian, a normal part of life for natives and expatriates. Despite their differences, despite the clash of cultures in the conflict zone of cultural interaction, their shared sense of tragedy and search for saving grace unites Mexican and American. *Stones for Ibarra* is about the search for that saving grace amid the relentless currents of destiny, and the lessons that each culture has to teach the other.

Critical Context

Stones for Ibarra, Doerr's first novel, was published when she was seventy-three years old. The novel began as a series of short stories based in a fictional Mexican town. Doerr wrote the first three of these stories in her late sixties, when she returned as a widow of several years to finish the bachelor's degree she had begun as a young unmarried woman. These first stories earned her a literary prize in London (the *Transatlantic Review*'s Henfield Foundation Award), a place in the writer John L'Heureux's

Stanford University creative writing class, and the attention of Viking Press editors in London and the United States. At their suggestion and with L'Heureux's help, what had begun as a series of short stories was expanded, rearranged, and re-created as a novel. The novel was an immediate popular and critical success, earning a number of awards, including the American Book Award for First Work of Fiction. Critics have recognized the influences of Graham Greene, Gabriel García Márquez, and Katherine Anne Porter in Doerr's work, but Doerr herself has simply commented that without reading, writing is impossible.

Critics have commented on Doerr's spare prose, in which each word carries enormous weight, and have noted as well the sense of oral storytelling prevalent throughout the text. By presenting a positive but complex view of the relationships among American expatriates and native inhabitants, *Stones for Ibarra* is an appropriate counter to negative stereotypes perpetuated by much expatriate writing on Mexico. Doerr continues this sympathetic portrayal of both expatriates and natives in her second novel, *Consider This, Señora* (1993), and in some of the short stories published in *The Tiger in the Grass* (1995). She thus has become a major voice on modern Mexico.

Bibliography
Daley, Yvonne. "Late Bloomer." *Stanford Magazine*, November-December, 1997, 76-79. A visit with Doerr at her home when she is eighty-seven years old and working on her autobiography, which she plans to divide into three sections: her years as a housewife and mother, her years in Mexico, and her years as a writer.
Henderson, Katherine. "Harriet Doerr." *Inter/View: Talks with America's Writing Women*, edited by Mickey Pearlman and Katherine Usher Henderson. Lexington: University of Kentucky Press, 1990. An essay based on an interview with Doerr. Provides basic biographical information and briefly discusses *Stones for Ibarra*. Explains the origin of the title from Mexican Indian practice.
See, Lisa. "Harriet Doerr." *Writing for Your Life Number Two*, edited by Sybil Steinberg. New York: Publishers Weekly, 1995. Focuses on Doerr's experiences in Mexico and their relationship to *Stones for Ibarra* and *Consider This, Señora*. Also discusses the effects of her age on her writing.

Linda Ledford-Miller

THE STORYTELLER

Author: Mario Vargas Llosa (1936-   )
Type of plot: Philosophical realism
Time of plot: The 1950's to the 1980's
Locale: Lima, Peru; the Peruvian Amazon; and Florence, Italy
First published: El hablador, 1987 (English translation, 1989)

> *Principal characters:*
> THE NARRATOR, a Peruvian novelist and former television host
> SAÚL ZURATAS, a Jewish-Peruvian student, a long-lost friend of the
>   narrator
> THE STORYTELLER, a Machiguengan man who travels the Amazonian
>   jungles telling stories
> TASURINCHI, the Machiguengan creator, whose name also denotes each
>   particular man in the tribe

The Novel

The Storyteller is an intriguing, often disturbing exploration of the Machiguengas, a real, indigenous, nomadic tribe in the Peruvian Amazon, and of the encroachment of modern life and values into their environment and culture. Mario Vargas Llosa frames this exploration as a quest for information about both the tribe and a Jewish student from Lima who may have been absorbed into it.

The narrator resembles Vargas Llosa himself. Like the author, he is a Peruvian novelist who vacations in Florence, Italy, and who once hosted a Peruvian television magazine. Although the narrator is never explicitly identified as Vargas Llosa, such identification is neither denied nor contradicted. Within the fictional world, many factual particulars of the novel suggest that it is written in the author's own voice.

At the beginning of the novel, the narrator, on vacation in Florence and immersed in a reading of the works of Dante, wanders into a photographic exhibit on the Machiguengas, an indigenous people of eastern Peru. The tribe has long fascinated him and once played a central role in an ongoing debate he had with a friend at the university, Saúl Zuratas. In one of the photos, the narrator sees a native storyteller who strongly resembles Saúl. This prompts an account by the narrator of the two students' friendship.

Saúl was an intense young Jewish man with an enormous purplish birthmark that covered half his face and earned him the nickname La Mascarita, or Mask-face. He was deeply concerned about the survival of indigenous peoples in Peru and had strong criticism for those who sought to evangelize, assimilate, or "culturally advance" such peoples under the guise of scientific, anthropological, and linguistic research. Saúl turned down a lucrative scholarship to study in France, choosing instead to remain with his aging father and continue his studies in Peru.

The narrator and Saúl shared discussions on many issues, including the Machiguengan people. The narrator found Saúl's views too strident. The narrator went to study in Europe; although he tried to maintain contact, he never heard from Saúl again. Upon returning to Peru, the narrator learned that Saúl and his ailing father supposedly had moved to Israel.

The account of the students' relationship is rendered in a speculative, impressionistic fashion. Few scenes or conversations are presented in detail; all is filtered through memory and, to a degree, emotion. Plot and action are outpaced by a wealth of information and meditation on the Machiguengas, Peruvian politics, and modern life.

Interwoven into the account of Saúl Zuratas are chapters written in the voice of the Machiguengan *hablador,* or traditional storyteller. In these chapters, Vargas Llosa employs a language that is at once naïve and wise, suiting Machiguengan lore, beliefs, and rituals. The storyteller describes Kientibakori, the spirit of evil; Kashiri, the sometimes benevolent; the seripigari, or wise men; the Viracochas, or dangerous outsiders; and Tasurinchi, the Machiguengan creator whose name is also used to refer to any Machiguengan man.

The storyteller chapters relate story after story of Tasurinchi after Tasurinchi: their family relationships, their lifestyles, and the lessons they have learned from the environment and animals that surround them. Some of the stories are amusingly scatological, while others clearly establish the Machiguengan cosmogony. The Machiguengan people come into focus as a loose society of wanderers, "the men that walk," believing that their walking keeps the sun in the sky. In addition, the storyteller relates his own experiences as the link among the scattered Tasurinchis.

As the novel alternates between the narrator's account and the storyteller's tales, the two sequences, already linked by the photograph in Florence, begin to merge. The narrator describes his interest in Machiguengan storytellers and the unavailability of pertinent information. In the early 1980's, as host of a television program called *The Tower of Babel,* he ventured back into the jungle to report on the Machiguengans. There he encountered the Schneils, a husband-and-wife team of American linguists working with the Summer Institute for Linguistics. He had met them once before: It was Edwin Schneil who had first mentioned Machiguengan storytellers to the narrator. During this later visit, to the narrator's amazement, Schneil described an "albino" storyteller with a large birthmark on his face. In speaking with a Jewish coworker, the narrator also discovered that Saúl did not go to Israel as rumored. After his father's death, he disappeared.

In the following chapter, the storyteller relates how he found that vocation. He refers somewhat cryptically to his birthmark, his previous life elsewhere, his acceptance among the Tasurinchis, and his transformation from a studious listener to an itinerant teller of stories. It is strongly suggested, though not explicitly articulated, that the storyteller is Saúl Zuratas.

By the end of the novel, the narrator returns to the present moment in Florence, where he repeatedly visits the photography exhibit to view the singular image. He contemplates his friend's destiny, puts together the pieces of the puzzle he has been investigating, and decides for himself that the storyteller in the photograph is none other than his lost friend Saúl Zuratas, La Mascarita.

The Characters

The Storyteller is an extended meditation rather than a compelling dramatic narrative. Thus, the novel's characters are more strongly developed in terms of the ideas they hold and represent than in their human desires and interrelationships. Vargas Llosa seeks to particularize the larger struggle of indigenous peoples against the encroachment of modern, technological influence by focusing on two students, their ill-fated friendship, and their different interactions with a fascinating tribe.

As a stand-in for the author, the character of the narrator pulls the reader into the novel by blurring the separation between the real and fictional worlds. Clearly, the tribe described is a real tribe, and many of the people, places, and incidents evoked in the novel are authentic. The use of a semifictional narrator demands complicity, asking the reader to participate in the ideological discussions and to form an opinion about the Machiguengas.

In the narrator's chapters, the characters are not fully fleshed out with complex behavioral patterns based on personal, emotional responses to external situations. Saúl is kept at a distance; his father, Don Salomón, is referred to but not seen; and the Schneils are barely developed beyond expository purposes. Likewise, the university professors, the television crew, the missionaries, Machiguengan leaders, and many other minor characters seem only to exist to help elucidate the novel's central question.

In contrast, the characters in the storyteller chapters, though united by the common name of Tasurinchi, are of flesh and blood, with human desires and functions and clear links to land and nature. The storyteller himself conveys his fears and vulnerability, and in the stories he tells he creates a Machiguengan world that is vibrant with life and its own natural logic.

Thus, in his use of character, Vargas Llosa subtly supports an ideology that is central to the novel's debate. The Western narrator and his world are dry, fact-based, single-minded, and extremely impersonal and cerebral. The world of the storyteller and the Machiguengans is, conversely, rooted in visceral functions, emotions, physical acts and phenomena, and chance and improbability. In each half of the novel, one of the storytellers expresses how he has come to puzzle out his universe, but their methods, reflected in their characters and the worlds they portray, could not be more different. This difference provides ironic commentary on implicit assumptions about the civilization of "civilized" society and the primitiveness of "primitives."

Themes and Meanings

The Storyteller questions the basic values of modern Western culture by placing it in direct juxtaposition with the Machiguengans. Organizations such as the Summer Institute of Linguistics (a real entity) are charged with the disruption of natural prerogatives. In researching indigenous peoples of the Amazon, they appropriate native languages and ways while imposing Christianity, technology, and the Spanish language. Also implicit is criticism of the destruction perpetrated on precarious natural habitats such as the Amazon jungle. Vargas Llosa offers an evenhanded examination of these issues and effectively avoids sentimentalizing the plight of indigenous peoples. The questions, nevertheless, loom large over the novel.

Balance is a key element in *The Storyteller.* The alternating narrative voices balance one another, as do their respective cultures. Saúl and the narrator are balanced in their friendship and discussions. Saúl, the arrogant, impenetrable Jewish university student, contrasts sharply with the wise, humble, and candid Machiguengan storyteller that he allegedly has become. Machiguengan history is compared to Jewish history, with the storyteller recounting Biblical cosmology in Machiguengan terms. The narrator's journey into the heart of Machiguengan culture is placed in relief against the often-unwilling journey of Tasurinchi into knowledge about the world outside the Amazon jungle. For Vargas Llosa, transformation requires balance; the worlds of modern Peru and the traditional Machiguengans can only meet through slow and mutual accommodation and respect.

The novel is concerned with what is right. In the same way as Saúl and the narrator search intellectually for ethical ways of interpreting their world, the various Tasurinchis and the Machiguengan people as a whole strive to make the world right. Their entire cosmology makes sense of a natural world often riddled with contradictions, and they are aware of how human words and acts put natural elements and heavenly bodies out of order.

In such a world, the storyteller is essential as a preserver of order. Among a people whose mandate is to wander incessantly, the storyteller is an important link to the past, to the environment, and to the whole community. He is also the retainer and definer of the indigenous language (even if he, as suggested, is not a native speaker himself). Storytelling becomes a much larger cultural institution: It is the foundation of society.

The power of storytelling grows further when considered in the context of the novel as a whole. Vargas Llosa, through his narrator, sets out to learn about the Machiguengans, to create a stylistically viable language for them, and to tell their story as part of his own. In doing so, he highlights his own role as a storyteller in Latin American culture. His invocation of Franz Kafka and his reading of Dante in Florence place his present writing in the tradition of Western literature. At the same time, he is asserting not only the need for inclusion (rather than appropriation) of native history and culture, but also the speculative quality that such inclusion must take. Vargas Llosa cannot solve the mystery for certain: If the storyteller is indeed Saúl, he is inaccessible to his old friend. Machiguengan stories are inherently incompatible with Peruvian novels, so the storyteller chapters are by necessity inventions, and the coincidences—the birthmark and the recounting of Jewish history among them—are, by the rules of the game, not clues encountered in the narrator's investigation but rather manufactured results of an intellectual process. Thus, Vargas Llosa's efforts to inform and stimulate certainly succeed, but whether the two worlds do or can meet—and whether the elusive Machiguengan storyteller is indeed a transformed Saúl Zuratas—is a question that the reader, like the narrator, must in the end decide.

Critical Context

Vargas Llosa has always drawn from personal experience to document the injustices and uncertainties of life in modern Peru. His earliest novels, *La ciudad y los perros* (1962; *Time of the Hero*, 1966) and *La casa verde* (1966; *The Green House*, 1968), explore themes of repression and corruption in the military academy of his adolescence and a small jungle town of his youth. *Conversación en la catedral* (1969; *Conversation in the Cathedral*, 1975) is a panoramic portrait of Peru in the 1940's and 1950's under the dictator Manuel Odria. In these early novels, Vargas Llosa began to experiment with an interweaving, nonlinear narrative style.

His next two novels, *Pantaleón y las visitadoras* (1973; *Captain Pantoja and the Special Service*, 1978) and *La tía Julia y el escribidor* (1977; *Aunt Julia and the Scriptwriter*, 1982), incorporate humor and farce and draw on the author's knowledge of military life and the television industry. Both use the technique of incorporating fictional documentary material into the body of the novel.

With *La guerra del fin del mundo* (1981; *The War of the End of the World*, 1984) and *Historia de Mayta* (1984; *The Real Life of Alejandro Mayta*, 1986), Vargas Llosa returned to his serious, political writing, focusing on turn-of-the-century religious zealotry in Brazil and contemporary radicalism in Peru. For Vargas Llosa, writing is a political act; in 1990, the author ran unsuccessfully for the presidency of Peru. *The Storyteller*, not surprisingly, gives evidence of the political leader that Vargas Llosa has become, concerned with the larger issues confronting Peruvian government, society, and culture.

Bibliography

Alter, Robert. "The Metamorphosis." *The New Republic* 202 (January 8, 1990): 41-42. In this review, Alter focuses on the Jewish themes, the light characterizations, and the links to Joseph Conrad. He closely examines Vargas Llosa's craft in creating the style of the storyteller chapters.

Booker, M. Keith. *Vargas Llosa Among the Postmodernists*. Gainesville: University Press of Florida, 1994. A thorough examination of Vargas Llosa's works from a postmodern point of view. Includes a chapter entitled "Narrative, Metanarrative, and Utopian Fantasy in *The Storyteller*."

Castro-Klarén, Sara. *Understanding Mario Vargas Llosa*. Columbia: University of South Carolina Press, 1990. Castro-Klarén traces the thematic evolution of Vargas Llosa's oeuvre. The well-developed but sometimes dense chapter on *The Storyteller* examines the work's ideological underpinnings and the power of the storyteller chapters.

Dipple, Elizabeth. "Outside, Looking In: Aunt Julia and Vargas Llosa." *The Review of Contemporary Fiction* 17 (Spring, 1997): 58-69. Dipple argues that Vargas Llosa's *The Storyteller* and *Aunt Julia and the Scriptwriter* are examples of the author's tendency to separate reality and fiction, revealing that the main characters are a limited version of himself. However, Vargas Llosa belives that the representation of himself in his works is distorted by the warping of his own beliefs and obsessions.

Johnston, George Sim. "The Call of the Wild." *National Review* 42 (February 5, 1990): 56-57. Johnston's review is ultimately critical of the novel for its implausibility and incompleteness. He discusses Vargas Llosa's views of human morality, his sense of irony, and his European-style intellectualism.

Sommer, Doris. "About Face: The Talker Turns." *Boundary 2* 23 (Spring, 1996): 91-133. Sommer notes that Vargas Llosa's novel portrays moments of confrontation between Amazonian narratives and modern history, resolving such conflicts either through dismissal or identification with the other. She argues that when the Jewish anthropologist becomes the tribe's storyteller, the parallels between the Jews and the Indians as marginalized groups become more apparent.

Standish, Peter. "Contemplating Your Own Novel: The Case of Mario Vargas Llosa." *Hispanic Review* 61 (Winter, 1993): 53-63. Standish explores Vargas Llosa's use of metafictional devices in *Aunt Julia and the Scriptwriter* and *The Storyteller*. He maintains that Vargas Llosa's use of metafiction is chiefly digetic rather than linguistic, and reflects Vargas Llosa's preoccupation with the topic of storytelling.

Updike, John. "Writer-Consciousness." *The New Yorker* 65 (December 25, 1989): 103-104. Updike places Vargas Llosa in the postmodernist tradition of Italo Calvino, John Barth, and Vladimir Nabokov. He praises the author's inventiveness and the blending of the novel's real and imaginary worlds but bemoans the text's speculative quality and its lack of romance and sensuality.

Vargas Llosa, Mario. *A Writer's Reality.* Syracuse, N.Y.: Syracuse University Press, 1991. A collection of thoughtful and candid essays by the author, reflecting on his literary roots, his creative method, and his political beliefs. Although containing only a few references to *The Storyteller*, the volume is nevertheless a fascinating glimpse into the mind behind the novel.

Williams, Tamara. "*The Storyteller.*" *America* 162 (March 24, 1990): 298-299. Williams discusses Vargas Llosa's didactic and political purposes in the novel, enjoying the story as a quest for a lost way of life. She also examines how the novel reflects on the author as a storyteller and chronicler of his culture.

Barry Mann

STRANGERS ON A TRAIN

Author: Patricia Highsmith (1921-1995)
Type of plot: Suspense
Time of plot: The 1940's
Locale: Onboard trains, boats, and a plane; Texas, New York, and other states;
    Mexico and Haiti
First published: 1950

>   *Principal characters:*
>   GUY DANIEL HAINES, a twenty-nine year old architect
>   CHARLES ANTHONY BRUNO, an unemployed twenty-five year old
>   Harvard University dropout
>   MIRIAM HAINES, neé JOYCE, Guy Haines's first wife, murdered by
>   Charles Bruno
>   ANNE FAULKNER, a textile designer who is Haines's fiancee and then
>   second wife
>   SAMUEL BRUNO, Charles Bruno's wealthy father, murdered by Guy
>   Haines
>   ARTHUR GERARD, a private detective investigating Samuel Bruno's
>   murder
>   OWEN MARKMAN, Miriam Haines's lover

The Novel

Strangers on a Train is a psychological thriller. The novel's events take place over several months and seem to occur during the period of its composition in the 1940's. The story opens with Guy Haines, a young architect, traveling on a train from his home in New York City to meet his wife Miriam, who lives in Texas. They have been separated for three years, and Miriam is pregnant by another man. The negative emotions stirred in Guy when he thinks about her are countered by thoughts of the woman he now loves, Anne Faulkner, and by the hope Miriam will grant him a divorce. Guy is also hopeful he will soon hear he has been chosen to design a prestigious country club in Florida, a project that could make his name in his profession.

During the train ride, a stranger, Charles Bruno, engages Guy in conversation. Bruno, who lives with his parents on Long Island, New York, is devoted to his mother and hates his wealthy father. Sensing that Miriam could create trouble for Guy about the divorce and in his professional life, Bruno proposes that he and Guy exchange murders: Bruno will kill Miriam if Guy will kill Bruno's father. Each man would be able to arrange an alibi, and as they have met by chance, no one would be able to connect them to each other. Guy is sickened by the proposal and rejects it.

Eventually, however, the exchange of murders takes place. Learning that Guy is in Mexico, and without consulting him, Bruno goes to Texas and strangles Miriam. Guy suspects Bruno of her murder, but he does not report his suspicions to the police.

2408 Masterplots II

Nor does he confide in Anne, and when he wonders why, he thinks it is because of "some sense of personal guilt that he himself could not bear." After he receives a letter from Bruno, Guy's suspicions are confirmed, but he still does not report Bruno to the police.

Bruno steps up his contacts with Guy, in writing, on the phone, and in person, badgering him to keep his end of the bargain to which Guy had never agreed. Bruno also intrudes himself, more and more, into Guy's life, going so far as to show up uninvited at Guy's wedding to Anne. Finally, Guy does murder Bruno's father, but Bruno continues to insinuate himself into Guy's life until, on a sailing trip with Guy and Anne, he gets drunk, falls overboard, and drowns.

As time passes, guilt so torments Guy that he decides he must confess all and face the consequences. The only person he can think of who might have suffered because of the murders is Owen Markman, the man who had been going to marry Miriam. In a concluding chapter filled with ironies, Guy tells Owen about Bruno, explaining that "if not for me, Miriam would be alive now." But Owen does not consider Guy to be guilty of Miriam's death, and he tells Guy he himself had felt trapped by Miriam's pregnancy and was glad not to have had to marry her. When Guy goes on to confess his murder of Bruno's father, Owen says it is not his concern. Guy concludes that if Owen, representing society, does not care about the murders, there is no reason to turn himself in to the police. He then learns that his confession to Owen has been overheard by Arthur Gerard, the private detective hired by Bruno's mother to investigate her husband's murder. The novel ends with Guy giving himself up to Gerard.

The Characters

The minor characters in *Strangers on a Train* are types who function to underline themes and advance the plot: the supportive woman who begins to grow suspicious; the relentless detective; the man who is more interested in not getting involved than he is in justice. The main characters, Guy and Bruno, are the point of the plot, in that Highsmith uses her suspense story as a framework to explore their psyches and their increasingly entangled and emotionally complex relationship.

Highsmith's writing style is not especially notable. Occasionally she uses images to symbolize aspects of her characters, as when detective Gerard is described waggling his finger at, and so terrifying, a caged bird. Another example is the boil in the middle of Bruno's forehead, which symbolizes social and psychological realities: Something about him is noticeable to others and found to be unpleasant, something that he himself interprets as "everything I *hate* boiling up in me."

Highsmith also reveals character through action. One of the most memorable sequences in the novel involves Bruno's jubilant behavior on a merry-go-round, singing and shouting, as he stalks Miriam. Conversations, too, are important in providing insights into character, as when Bruno boasts to Guy about a gratuitous theft he has committed. When Guy tells Owen Markman that under certain circumstances anyone can be made to murder, the extent to which he has been influenced by Bruno is underlined; early on Guy had disagreed with Bruno's assertion that circumstances, and not temperament, are what cause a person to murder. "I'm not that kind of person," he had told Bruno.

Highsmith's most common and effective technique of characterization is her use of third-person-omniscient narration to report the thoughts and emotions of her protagonists, creating an effect akin to stream of consciousness, but with an important difference. As she notes in her 1966 book *Plotting and Writing Suspense Fiction*, "I have quite a bit of introspection in my heroes, and to write all this in the first person makes them sound like nasty schemers, which of course they are, but they seem less so if some all-knowing author is telling what is going on in their heads." The shift in point of view makes her murderers more sympathetic.

Themes and Meanings

Strangers on a Train raises the issue of why its protagonists murder, and it explores the theme of the double. Bruno's life is aimless and lonely. Murder, rather than making him feel guilty, fills him with a sense of accomplishment. When he decides to kill Miriam, he knows he cannot count on Guy's reciprocating, so he considers her murder to be motiveless, a "pure murder," and he is exhilarated by the idea. Yet the possibility occurs to him that, afterward, he might be able to persuade Guy to kill his hated father. Then again, Bruno may subconsciously hope the murder will establish a tie with Guy, on whom he has a crush. Someone who is bored and who has an Oedipus complex and homosexual longings does not necessarily commit murder. Ultimately, the murder of Miriam may be irrational, the act of a psychopath. Yet that raises the question of how it is that Bruno is a psychopath: are psychopaths born or made?

Guy's murder of Bruno's father is no less problematic. His life includes love and creative work, and murder fills him with tormenting guilt. At one point, he speculates that he and Bruno are each "what the other had not chosen to be, the cast-off self, what he thought he hated but perhaps in reality loved," and he thinks, "Nothing could be without its opposite that was bound up with it." Later, he thinks of himself as two people, one who is incapable of murder and another who is capable, whom he sees for an instant in the mirror "like a secret brother."

In the last chapter, Guy first thinks he committed murder because of temperament: "there had been that measure of perversity within him sufficient to do it." He then explains his act to Owen on the basis of circumstance: "Bruno broke me down with letters and blackmail and sleeplessness." Was Guy susceptible to Bruno because of a Bruno within; does everyone have a Bruno within; is everyone capable of murder?

In an interview with Diana Cooper-Clark, Highsmith told of her belief that heredity has more to do with the ability to murder than environment, and of her rejection of the idea that "everybody can be coerced into murder." Her novel raises the troubling issue but does not resolve it.

Critical Context

In *Plotting and Writing Suspense Fiction*, Patricia Highsmith reveals that her first published novel, *Strangers on a Train*, had its origin in the idea of two men exchanging murders. The resulting relationship established a precedent for many of her subsequent books, with their recurring pattern of "two men, usually quite different in make-up, sometimes obviously the good and the evil, sometimes merely ill-matched friends." Often, as in Bruno's crush on Guy, homosexual attraction is part of the relationship. *Strangers on a Train* is also typical of Highsmith's later writing in its focus on the criminal mind.

An influence on Highsmith was the writing of Fyodor Dostoevski. In *Plotting and Writing Suspense Fiction*, she cites his *Prestupleniye i nakazaniye* (*Crime and Punishment*, 1886) as evidence that the suspense genre can include works that are profound. The criminal's freedom in going beyond society's laws is an idea explored by Dostoevski and later by the French existentialists, whose writings have also been cited by critics as among Highsmith's influences. It is an idea that excites Charles Bruno, who relishes committing the perfect murder as the high point of his life. This is not to say Highsmith and her novel endorse such an idea. "Existentialism is self-indulgent," she told Diana Cooper-Clark, and she cautioned that the existentialist ideas in *Strangers on a Train* come from a psychopath.

Strangers on a Train, and the Alfred Hitchcock film of the same name (1951) based on the novel, made Patricia Highsmith famous. Later novels such as Stephen King's *Misery* (1987), with its psychopath's need to connect herself with the object of her hero-worship, and Thomas Harris's *The Silence of the Lambs* (1988), with its exploration of the mind of a serial murderer, have aspects in common with *Strangers on a Train*, but they differ from it in Highsmith's choice of criminals as her protagonists, rather than victims or detectives. The disturbing power of *Strangers on a Train* to challenge readers' moral predispositions and understanding of motives is, perhaps, its strongest claim to be taken seriously as literature.

Bibliography
Cochran, David. "'Some Torture That Perversely Eased': Patricia Highsmith and the Everyday Schizophrenia of American Life." *Clues* 18, no. 2 (Fall-Winter, 1997): 157-180. Analysis of Highsmith's fiction, including *Strangers on a Train*, as subversive of the dominant political and cultural assumptions of Cold War America.
Harrison, Russell. *Patricia Highsmith*. New York: Twayne, 1997. An introduction to the author and her work, with a chronology and a bibliography. Half of chapter 2 discusses *Strangers on a Train*, praising its psychological intensity and finding its existentialist themes impressive.
Highsmith, Patricia. "Patricia Highsmith: Interview." Interview by Diana Cooper-Clark. *The Armchair Detective* 14, no. 4 (Fall, 1981): 313-320. Highsmith delivers her views on a number of topics. She opines that existentialism is self-indulgent; that not everyone is capable of murder; and that the ability to murder has more to do with heredity than environment.
_____. *Plotting and Writing Suspense Fiction*. Boston: The Writer, 1966. Advice for authors in which Highsmith cites her own writings, including *Strangers on a Train*, to illustrate her points.

Klein, Kathleen Gregory. "Patricia Highsmith." In *And Then There Were Nine . . . : More Women of Mystery*, edited by Jane S. Bakerman. Bowling Green, Ohio: Bowling Green State University Popular Press, 1985. Argues Highsmith's crime fiction, beginning with *Strangers on a Train*, expands the genre's conventions by challenging "either/or" thinking and by suggesting that anyone is capable of murder.

Mahoney, Mary Kay. "A Train Running on Two Sets of Tracks: Highsmith's and Hitchcock's *Strangers on a Train*." In *It's a Print! Detective Fiction from Page to Screen*, edited by William Reynolds and Elizabeth Trembley. Bowling Green, Ohio: Bowling Green State University Popular Press, 1994. Argues that Hitchcock's film shifts the novel's focus on psychological analysis to a focus on action and suspense and de-emphasizes the novel's similarities between Guy and Bruno by transforming Guy into an innocent hero.

Jack Vincent Barbera

THE STREET

Author: Ann Petry (1908-1997)
Type of plot: Naturalism
Time of plot: The mid-1940's
Locale: Harlem, New York City
First published: 1946

>   *Principal characters:*
>   LUTIE JOHNSON, an attractive black woman in her early twenties
>   BUB, her eight-year-old son
>   JONES, the superintendent of the building in which Lutie rents an
>   apartment
>   MIN, a middle-aged woman who lives with Jones
>   MRS. HEDGES, a woman who operates a brothel on the first floor of the
>   building
>   JUNTO, a powerful white man attracted to Lutie
>   BOOTS SMITH, a bandleader who owes Junto

The Novel

The Street follows the foredoomed struggle of a young black woman to escape the street and to evade what the street threatens to do to her and to Bub, her young son. The street is 116th Street in Harlem. The time is the 1940's; World War II is not yet over.

Lutie Johnson has not come to the street by choice. Lutie had taken work as a domestic with the Chandlers, a white family in Connecticut. The job required that she live apart from Jim, her unemployed husband. In her absence, Jim took up with another woman. Unable to turn to her alcoholic father for support, Lutie has had to do the best she can for herself and her son Bub. At the moment, this means a low-paying job and a walk-up apartment on the top floor of a dismal building.

Three other inhabitants of the building play an important role in Lutie's story: Jones, Min, and Mrs. Hedges. Lutie senses at once the powerful lust of Jones, the superintendent. Her resistance generates in Jones a rage he takes out on Min, the most recent of a series of shapeless middle-aged women with whom he has lived. Min finally realizes that her only course is to leave him and to hope that some other man will take her. The repeatedly frustrated Jones is determined to get at Lutie somehow. He wins the trust of Bub, and when Jones's obsession with Lutie turns to hatred, he makes Bub his instrument in a plot to destroy her.

Mrs. Hedges takes an immediate, even protective, interest in Lutie, but her interest is not innocent. Lutie represents interesting possibilities: A nice white man is interested in her.

The white man is Junto, who operates the Junto Bar and Grill and a number of other enterprises in Harlem. He and Mrs. Hedges have been associates for a long time, ever since they met while both were picking through garbage. Junto has come a long way since them. He is now the power behind Mrs. Hedges's operations; he has powerful connections, and he knows what he wants. Ironically, Lutie's attempts to improve things for herself and her son make her vulnerable to Junto. Lutie has a fine singing voice, and when she is approached by Boots Smith, a bandleader, she dreams of a success that will take her and Bub away from the street. Lutie knows what Boots has in mind when he suggests that she should be "nice" to him, but she gambles that she will be able to handle Boots long enough to achieve independence by establishing herself as a performer.

What she does not know is that Boots is answerable to Junto. Not only does Boots owe much of his success to Junto, but it was also Junto who made it possible for Boots to evade military service in wartime. Although Boots is genuinely interested in Lutie—however limited and shallow that interest may be—he is unwilling to cross Junto.

Meanwhile, the influence of the street is working on Bub, and Lutie unwittingly reinforces that influence. Her pursuit of her goals leaves a frightened Bub alone at night, vulnerable to the false friendship of Jones. Moreover, her complaints about their poverty instill in Bub the notion that money is everything. After some hesitation, Bub agrees to make some money by assisting Jones in "detective work." In fact, Jones instructs Bub to steal letters from the mailboxes in the neighborhood, setting up the boy as a way of getting revenge on the mother.

Bub is arrested, and an unscrupulous lawyer tells Lutie that she needs two hundred dollars to pay for his services—although, in such a case, she does not need a lawyer at all. Desperate, Lutie asks Boots for help. He agrees, but when Lutie goes to his apartment she finds that Junto is there as well. The help she needs will be forthcoming only if she agrees to Junto's sexual demands. When Lutie refuses, Junto leaves. Defeated and angry, Boots attacks Lutie. When she hits him with a candlestick, Lutie is at first defending herself, but then she is striking out at all the forces that have conspired to crush her. She does not stop until Boots is dead.

In the eyes of the law, Lutie is sure, she has committed murder. With no one to turn to for help, she can only try to escape. This means abandoning Bub, the eight-year-old boy who is waiting for his mother to visit him in jail. Yet what hope can there be for Bub if he is saddled with a mother who has been branded a killer? On the train taking her to Chicago, Lutie hopes that Bub will remember that she loved him.

The Characters

In addition to being the protagonist, Lutie Johnson functions as the viewpoint character for much of the novel. Thus, readers come to know her in large part through her perceptions and the actions and reactions based on these. Readers see the street, the hallway, and the apartment through her eyes, and her dissatisfaction with what she sees reflects significantly on who she is. She is determined not to surrender to the street, but readers feel her anxiety and know how close she is to despair.

Other characters assume the role of viewpoint character for extended stretches.

Most of these characters are first seen through Lutie's perception of them, then through their perception of a world that includes Lutie. In Lutie's perception, Jones, the building superintendent, is frightening in the openness of his lust for her—and, indeed, her initial fears are justified by his attempt to rape her. Yet readers are also allowed to see something of how the world looks to Jones, and of the forces that have brought him to where he is. The result is not to make Jones a sympathetic character, but to suggest that one errs if one sees in him only the stock villain of melodrama.

Others function as viewpoint characters in the course of the novel. Of the principal characters, only Junto is excepted. Junto is depicted essentially on the basis of how others see him and in his effect on others. He protects Mrs. Hedges, as Jones finds out when he summons the law in an angry attempt to put her out of business. To Boots, Junto has given, and Junto can take away. Junto's desire for Lutie generates much of the action of the novel. Although Lutie manages to resist, this resistance forces her defeat.

The author also develops characters through comparison and contrast. Lutie, readers observe, has internalized the materialistic values of Mrs. Chandler, her white employer. Lutie's helplessness is shown in contrast to the varying, and ultimately unsatisfactory, sorts of resourcefulness represented by Mrs. Hedges and Min, each of whom might claim to be a survivor, but in a morally shrunken universe. Lutie is, by comparison, a morally vigorous character, but the negative power of the street is finally more than she can overcome.

Themes and Meanings

The Street is a novel about struggle and defeat. Lutie Johnson struggles against the limitations imposed upon her by circumstance, and she is destroyed in the struggle. Her defeat, when it comes, has about it an air of inevitability; readers respect her hopes but put no faith in them. Understanding the novel in which she appears may be a matter of understanding why a sense of hopelessness pervades a book that centers on a woman's hopes.

The novel begins with a description of the street. The author writes of the street as though it has a personality, and a malevolent one at that. The street works, consciously it almost seems, to defeat and destroy those within its influence. Moreover, readers know the street before meeting any human characters; when the humans are introduced, they are seen, as it were, in the shadow of the street. The result is to weaken the readers' sense of human moral agency.

When readers first meet Lutie Johnson, it is true, they are quickly made aware of the strength of her aspirations. At one point in the novel, Lutie half seriously compares herself to Benjamin Franklin, the great American model of the self-made man. He has served as a model for many ambitious young Americans, and Lutie dares to suppose he may serve as her model, too. She is determined to forge a better life for herself and her son.

Yet if readers know the strength of Lutie's aspirations, they also know the weakness of her condition. That Lutie has come to 116th Street is not a matter of choice. She finds herself in an environment that is ugly to her and, she is convinced, dangerous to her eight-year-old son because this is what her circumstances demand. Her hopes are not linked to any realistic positive options, not because Lutie is unintelligent, but because the narrowness of her situation allows little room for the creative use of intelligence.

Lutie's hopes are given a more specific direction when her talent for singing brings the promise of a career as a performer. Yet there is, from the start, something not quite real about this. Lutie's "discovery" is reminiscent of the mythology of fan magazines, and the life of a band singer, under the best of circumstances, seems far removed from the stability for which Lutie had been looking. As it turns out, Lutie's talent, although apparently genuine, presents Junto with an opportunity for manipulation. Her talent, then, becomes part of the causal chain leading to her destruction.

Her attractiveness to men is equally destructive in its consequences. It is this attractiveness that arouses the interest of Junto and that drives the obsession of Jones. Jones's obsession motivates the scheme that leads to Bub's arrest, and Bub's arrest forces Lutie to look for help, making her vulnerable to Junto. Finally, Lutie's attractiveness has made her desirable to Boots, and in rejecting Boots's advances, Lutie performs the action that finally destroys her. It is significant that the action does not arise out of any conscious decision; Lutie is simply striking out against all that has conspired in her defeat.

The structure of the novel, especially Petry's use of a series of viewpoint characters, forcing readers to see the world as it appears even to the least sympathetic of them, seems designed to suggest that these other characters are no more free moral agents than Lutie is. Even Junto, who embodies so much power, is driven by desires he seems incapable of understanding. The consistent portrayal of characters as driven or determined by forces, social and psychological, that they can neither understand nor control is among the defining features of the naturalistic tradition that the novel represents.

Critical Context

Ann Petry was not the first novelist to explore aspects of African American life in naturalistic terms. Richard Wright's *Native Son*, published in 1940, was a great predecessor. Part of the significance of Petry's achievement was her success in applying the naturalistic approach to the story of an articulate woman, in contrast to Wright's inarticulate moral drifter.

The significance of literary naturalism for the African American writer is plain. To see characters in terms of the forces that shape them, to define the distorting effects of negative social forces, offers a possibility of explanatory power in the depiction of African American life. It also provides the materials of a strong implicit indictment of white America, which has, after all, largely created and maintained the world writers like Wright and Petry depict. Lutie Johnson has a lucid perception of the ways in which white power works to limit the options of black Americans, even though this lucidity does not enable her to escape the effects of what she knows.

Yet it is no denigration of what Petry has achieved to point out that naturalism is but one option open to African American novelists, and that other alternatives will appeal to those writers for whom the portrayal of black people as victims is ultimately not enough. The folk imagination of Zora Neale Hurston, manifested in *Their Eyes Were Watching God* (1937), and the Transcendentalist impulse of Ralph Ellison's Invisible Man (1952) suggest other models, to which younger writers have responded. Petry's fine novel takes its place in an African American literary tradition the richness of which readers and critics are still learning to appreciate.

Bibliography
Clark, Keith. "A Distaff Dream Deferred? Ann Petry and the Art of Subversion." *African American Review* 26 (Fall, 1992). Clark claims that Petry's novel illustrates African American women's ability to succeed in America by circumventing the American Dream rather than allowing themselves to be isolated by racism, sexism, and classism. Two minor characters, Mrs. Hedges and Min, become powerful by taking positions considered inappropriate or sinful, thus subverting accepted conventions.
Gross, Theodore L. "Ann Petry: The Novelist as Social Critic." In *Black Fiction: New Studies in the Afro-American Novel Since 1945*, edited by A. Robert Lee. New York: Barnes & Noble, 1980. Gross sees Petry's concern as the oppressive details of ghetto life rather than black-white conflicts. Yet he comments that Petry does not let the reader forget that the white world has drawn the limitations and caused the bitter despair of black people.
Hernton, Calvin C. *The Sexual Mountain and Black Women Writers: Adventures in Sex, Literature, and Real Life.* New York: Anchor Press, 1987. Pays tribute to Petry's daring in depicting a black woman's killing of a black man because he is an oppressor; the novel looks forward to a later stage of consciousness in fiction by black women. Hernton naïvely treats fictional characters as if they were real people, with real histories beyond the books in which they appear.
Park, You-Me, and Gayle Wald. "Native Daughters in the Promised Land: Gender, Race, and the Question of Separate Spheres." *American Literature* 70 (September, 1998): 607-633. Park and Wald demonstrate how minority literature represents the boundaries between public and private spheres in the United States. They use both *The Street* by Ann Petry and *Maud Martha* by Gwendolyn Brooks to buttress their argument.
Pryse, Marjorie. "'Pattern Against the Sky': Deism and Motherhood in Ann Petry's *The Street.*" In *Conjuring: Black Women, Fiction, and the Literary Tradition*, edited by Marjorie Pryse and Hortense J. Spillers. Bloomington: Indiana University Press, 1985. Pryse takes Petry's reference to Benjamin Franklin to suggest that Deism figures significantly in the thematic and ideological implications of the novel. The discussion is stimulating, if a bit strained; Pryse seems prepared to make "Deism" mean whatever fits her argument.
Thomson, Rosemarie Garland. "Ann Petry's Mrs. Hedges and the Evil, One-Eyed

Girl: A Feminist Exploration of the Physically Disabled Female Subject." *Women's Studies* 24 (September, 1995): 599-614. Thomson contrasts the way heroines and villainesses are portrayed in children's literature: one as beautiful and virtuous and the other as ugly and wicked. She then argues that in the portrayal of Mrs. Hedges, Petry deviates from the conventional characterization of the handicapped woman, showing that she is neither vicious nor scheming.

W. P. Kenney

STRONG WIND

Author: Miguel Ángel Asturias (1899-1974)
Type of plot: Social commentary
Time of plot: The early twentieth century
Locale: An unnamed Latin American country, Chicago, and New York City
First published: Viento fuerte, 1950 (English translation, 1968)

> *Principal characters:*
> LESTER MEAD (COSI, LESTER STONER), the protagonist, a North American, a major investor in Tropbanana and an independent grower
> LELAND FOSTER, his wife
> ADELAIDO LUCERO, a worker on certain coastal banana plantations
> SARAJOBALDA, a witch
> RITO PERRAJ, a witch doctor

The Novel

    The antagonist in *Strong Wind* is Tropbanana, a North American fruit company. The novel begins when Tropbanana is establishing banana plantations on the Pacific coast of an unnamed Latin American country. Adelaido Lucero is one of many natives of the highlands drawn to work in the great enterprise of taming the tropical lowlands and carving plantations from them. He remains in the company town, marries, and rears his family there. He will work for the company all his life, but he buys land for his sons so that they will be able to be independent.

    Lester Mead, an American, also buys land, and he, along with Lucero's now grown sons, finds himself in conflict with Tropbanana. These independent growers prospered while the company bought their bananas at a good price. When the company decides to cut the price by more than fifty percent, however, Mead refuses to sell at a loss. He goes to Chicago to talk to the head of the company, but he fails to win any concessions for the independent growers.

    When Mead returns to the plantations, he suggests that the independent growers form a cooperative. The efforts of the members of the cooperative to preserve their independence from the company form the core of the novel.

    The company retaliates by taking over all the cooperative's markets and then has two of the cooperative members arrested during a demonstration of workers who are protesting against the company's policies. Mead finds that the only way to secure their release is through bribery: There is no legal recourse, and the company controls the press and the government.

    By the end of *Strong Wind*, neither the company nor the growers have won a clear victory. The growers still own their land and the company still controls its plantations. Yet the strong wind of the title has devastated the land and has claimed the lives of Lester Mead and his wife.

The Characters

Asturias is not primarily concerned with the psychological development of individual characters. Rather, the characters in this novel, through their actions and dialogues, represent the many types of people involved in the life on the banana plantations.

Adelaido Lucero is the first character introduced in the novel and it is his lifetime in the company town that provides the time frame of the novel. He is the prototype of his generation, which spends its lifetime in the service of the company. Lucero represents the experience, values, and beliefs of his people. It is around Adelaido Lucero that Asturias weaves the interactions of the major and minor characters of the novel.

Lester Mead, the American, is the most important character. Asturias first introduces him as Cosi, the vendor of sewing articles, known for his loud laugh, which people take as a sign that he is insane. Far from being a sign of his insanity, however, the laugh demonstrates his disdain for the accepted ways of doing things. He is known as Lester Mead in his role as independent grower and founder of the cooperative, and, at the end of the novel, he is revealed to be Lester Stoner, a major investor in Tropbanana. These three aspects of Mead, represented by his three names, are complementary. Cosi-Mead-Stoner is the nonconformist-idealist tempered by pragmatism.

Other characters are used by Asturias to present ideas through dialogue and actions rather than by narration from the point of view of the omniscient author. Leland Foster, Lester Mead's wife, is a character used in this manner. The reader learns Lester Mead's true identity as Lester Stoner at the same time that Leland learns it. Earlier in the novel, her first husband, John Pyle, explained to her the difference between those who created the plantations and those who succeeded these creators as managers. Roselia, Adelaido's wife, serves a similar function. Confiding in her, Adelaido expresses his desire to buy land for his sons and later his doubts about the value of Mead's methods in opposing the company.

Elsewhere, characters are spokespersons for attitudes and points of view that represent the entire range of Americans and native workers and growers in the town. Americans are seen socializing, drinking, and trying to escape the heat, while native workers are seen toiling through the heat. Tury Duzin, the American lesbian, serves as contrast to the family values held by the native workers. The workers are unable to defend their wives and daughters against the sexual advances and assaults of the Americans. Even the ancient Sarajobalda, the witch, the matchmaker who plies her trade with magic, is raped. Rito Perraj, along with Sarajobalda, represents the importance of belief in magic as part of the reality in which the local people live.

Themes and Meanings

The central theme of the novel is anti-imperialism. The plot revolves around the struggle of the local growers to maintain their dignity and independence in the face of the power of Tropbanana. By not naming a real place or company, Asturias has extended his attack to all monopolistic exploitation in all Latin America.

In this novel of the independent growers' struggle against the company, which initiates his Banana trilogy—the other novels in the trilogy are *El papa verde* (1954; *The Green Pope*, 1971) and *Los ojos de los enterrados* (1960; *The Eyes of the Interred*, 1973)—Asturias anticipates the rebellion of the workers which will occur in *The Eyes of the Interred*. Mead says that the members of the cooperative may not see the fruits of their struggle but that those who will follow them will benefit. Thus, the theme of the endurance of the people, the hope that eventually justice will triumph in spite of the odds, underlies the action of the novel.

Mead proposes changes in the company management to other stockholders in terms of educated self-interest. To protect their investment and guarantee a stable source of profits, they must curtail the excessive abuses of the company. He is not the pure idealist seeking only the welfare of the exploited; rather, he seeks the solutions that will benefit all involved, investors as well as workers and independent growers. The strong wind that takes the lives of Mead and his wife implies the inadequacy of these solutions. A greater force for change must blow through the plantations.

While he portrays many Americans who work for the company negatively, Asturias has not written an anti-American novel. The main character, Lester Mead, is an American who transcends stereotypes and struggles for justice and dignity for all people. Mead is portrayed as very human; he loves his wife and is drawn to a woman whom he meets in the capital. He rails against injustice, struggles with his frustrations, and cares for his friends.

In addition to the social themes that are dominant in the work, nature, myth, and magic are present as powerful forces throughout the novel. Nature is a force to be confronted, not merely a setting or background. The tropical coastlands must be put to the service of men, and nature must be respected. Myth and magic, so much a part of the lives of the native people, are also to be respected and put to the service of man. Sarajobalda, the witch, and Rito Perraj, the witch doctor, are sought out by the people for solutions to all manner of problems. Asturias affirms the importance of magic by having the strong wind, the force of nature, summoned by the magic of Rito Perraj. Man is not merely a social creature in contact with other men; man must maintain his relationships with nature and with the magical reality that surrounds him.

Critical Context

The work of Miguel Ángel Asturias was more widely known in Europe and Latin America than the United States prior to 1967, the year in which Asturias was awarded the Nobel Prize for Literature. Increased interest in his work then prompted the translation of *Strong Wind* into English in 1968. The other works of the Banana trilogy, which *Strong Wind* initiates, were translated soon afterward. *Strong Wind*, along with the rest of the trilogy, represents the height of Asturias's social concern. Although it is related to the other works in its shared characters and the common theme of anti-imperialism, *Strong Wind* can be profitably read without recourse to the trilogy.

Strong Wind has not received the critical attention accorded to Asturias's widely acclaimed first novel, *El señor presidente* (1946; *The President*, 1963) or *Hombres de maíz* (1949; *Men of Maize*, 1975). Less innovative and less concerned with myth than are his earlier works, *Strong Wind* represents Asturias's turn toward realism as a vehicle for social commentary. Much of the criticism of *Strong Wind* reflects the posture of the critic with regard to "committed" literature, literature written with a social purpose. Critics who value such committed literature fault *Strong Wind* for excessive allusions to myth and popular beliefs, which, they claim, dilute the direct impact of the novel's social message. Others attack the work as journalistic because its social theme overshadows the artistic elements.

Strong Wind is not limited to social realism. Because the social reality he presented is in intimate contact with nature and its forces, and because the people about whom he wrote attribute tremendous power to myth and magic, Asturias produced a novel of social realism, Magical Realism, and nature.

Bibliography
Callan, Richard. *Miguel Ángel Asturias*. New York: Twayne, 1970. An introductory study with a chapter of biography and a separate chapter discussing each of Asturias's major novels. Includes a chronology, notes, and an annotated bibliography.
Gonzalez Echevarria, Roberto. *Myth and Archive: A Theory of Latin American Narrative*. Cambridge, England: Cambridge University Press, 1990. A very helpful volume in coming to terms with Asturias's unusual narratives.
Harss, Luis, and Barbara Dohmann. *Into the Mainstream*. New York: Harpers, 1967. Includes an interview with Asturias covering the major features of his thought and fictional work.
Himmelblau, Jack. "Love, Self and Cosmos in the Early Works of Miguel Ángel Asturias." *Kentucky Romance Quarterly* 18 (1971). Should be read in conjunction with Prieto.
Perez, Galo Rene. "Miguel Ángel Asturias." *Americas*, January, 1968, 1-5. A searching examination of *El Señor Presidente* as a commentary on the novelist's society.
Prieto, Rene. *Miguel Ángel Asturias's Archaeology of Return*. Cambridge, England: Cambridge University Press, 1993. The best available study in English of the novelist's body of work. Prieto discusses both the stories and the novels, taking up issues of their unifying principles, idiom, and eroticism. See Prieto's measured introduction, in which he carefully analyzes Asturias's reputation and identifies his most important work. Includes very detailed notes and bibliography.
West, Anthony. Review of *El Señor Presidente*, by Miguel Ángel Asturias. *The New Yorker*, March 28, 1964. Often cited as one of the best interpretations of the novel.

Susan Spagna

THE SUICIDE'S WIFE

Author: David Madden (1933-   )
Type of plot: Tragic realism
Time of plot: 1968, from the time of Martin Luther King, Jr.'s assassination to
    Robert Kennedy's assassination
Locale: The fictitious university town of San Francisco, West Virginia
First published: 1978

> *Principal characters:*
>   ANN HARRINGTON, the protagonist, a housewife and the mother of
>   three small children; the suicide's wife
>   MARK HARRINGTON, her sensitive eleven-year-old son
>   MAX CRANE, a poet and former colleague of her husband, Wayne
>   Harrington

The Novel

The Suicide's Wife takes place in the fictitious university town of San Francisco, West Virginia. Ann Harrington, the protagonist, feels that this San Francisco is not the real San Francisco and that she is as fraudulent as is this counterfeit town. Indeed, much of the action of the novel takes place in Ann's tortured, lethargic mind rather than in the town proper.

Ann returns with Wayne, her English-professor husband, to his vacant family home in upstate New York for a nostalgic last look before it is sold. Tragedy strikes early the next day when Wayne disappears. Ann is sure that she has been abandoned and returns home alone. A few days later, her sister-in-law calls to tell her that she found Wayne sitting on the lawn in his favorite childhood spot, dead from a bullet to his head.

Wayne's death shakes Ann out of her complacent, ineffectual existence and forces her to reevaluate her life and redefine her reality. Through no choice of her own, Ann is thrust into an alien world where she is immediately branded with two distasteful labels: "widow" and "the suicide's wife."

Ill-prepared to take control of her life (she cannot even drive a car), Ann retreats into her own private world, where she is haunted by perverse sexual images and by her father's all-knowing admonitions. Her father, a drunken, abusive man, was stomped to death in an alley the year that she married Wayne.

Reared in a tough Polish ghetto in Pittsburgh, Ann did not end up in prison, as all her brothers did, but, just as tragically, she lost her persona at a very young age. When Ann was twelve years old, she relinquished her body to a gang of neighborhood boys. Never fully recovering from this traumatic incident, Ann finally felt important when she married her English professor and bore him three children.

To still the persistent voices and memories from her past and to avoid the probing questions and pitying glances from those in her present, Ann channels all of her energies into her home. She doggedly determines to get the house running efficiently. Since the house has not been properly cared for, there is much for Ann to do. In the midst of tragedy, Ann fixes the toilet, repairs the roof, tends to the washing machine, and, in fact, gets her house in working order. Unfortunately, Ann forgets to mend her family's emotional house.

Ann is gradually drawn into the real world by friends and neighbors who express genuine concern for her. As condolences continue to pour in, Ann's hunger and curiosity about her husband's life intensifies. She is besieged by feelings of guilt for not sensing her husband's deep depression. As she begins to probe into Wayne's life at the university, she uncovers some rather unsettling truths.

Wayne had not been respected by either his colleagues or his students, who regarded him as extremely boring and absolutely talentless. Although faculty members referred to him as a "sweet" man, none of them actually associated with him. Ann begins to realize that Wayne was as much a failure as she is.

Max Crane, a poet and a former colleague of Wayne, plays a critical role in Ann's growth and maturation. He forces Ann to confront her feelings about herself, her past, and her marriage to Wayne. He also poses the startling possibility that Anson Keller, a former student, may have been Wayne's lover and directly or indirectly responsible for Wayne's death.

Ann proceeds to look for evidence supporting or refuting these allegations, but the search is inconclusive. Astonished by how little she knew of her husband's life, she moves forward with renewed strength and determination. The turning point in the story comes when Ann and her son Mark venture out into the world after months of isolation. Soon after the two of them join a group of friends at the beach, Mark disappears. Ann's friends comb the waters for Mark, but to no avail. Terrified and hysterical, Ann keeps from gagging by putting her hand over her mouth. As the search continues, Ann glances around and sees Mark sitting on the hood of her car in the parking lot.

Ann loses the "good girl" self-control that she always exhibits and explodes violently at Mark. She hits him uncontrollably and vents all the emotions and feelings that she has suppressed through the years. Purged of the venom at last, Ann is finally capable of facing herself and those around her honestly and openly.

The Characters

Ann Harrington epitomizes the preemancipated woman, completely dependent on her husband. Had Wayne not died, this very ordinary woman would probably have remained trapped in her husband's shadow. Ironically, Wayne's "eminence" was merely a construct of Ann's—he was as empty a shell as she.

Madden conveys Ann's deep feelings of worthlessness by detailing a grueling childhood incident during which Ann submitted sexually to a gang of boys. Ann's apparent lack of shame reveals her well-developed defense mechanism. Madden implies that by cutting off and denying her true feelings, Ann has been able to minimize the painful experiences in her life.

Madden allows the reader to witness, partake, and rejoice in Ann's growth. The scenes in the driver's examination office are unforgettably written, sparse, yet vividly descriptive; the reader shares Ann's intense determination to pass her driver's test.

After teaching herself to drive in Wayne's battered old car, Ann feels confident enough to take the test. Unfortunately, she is tested by an arrogant, ignorant, sexist police officer who barks impossible orders at her. After her fourth attempt, the officer directs her to a secluded dirt road and tries to blackmail her into performing a sexual act. Her refusal to succumb to him marks a real breakthrough for Ann. She is no longer willing to use her body to attain what she wants. When she does pass the test, it is on her own terms, and the victory belongs not only to Ann but also to everyone who has ever been intimidated and exploited by someone with power and authority.

Mark Harrington is a sensitive, imaginative child who may be more like his mother than either of them realizes. When his father dies, Mark retreats into a private world of his own creation. Neglected by Ann, who is caught up in her own misery, Mark begins to write his father's biography. This, however, is no ordinary biography: Mark invents a wonderful life for his father—one in which Wayne takes on heroic proportions. Mark's fanciful story ironically excludes Ann. Indeed, Mark is openly hostile and antagonistic to Ann. His mother has been so preoccupied with her own problems that when he flunks the sixth grade, she is totally unprepared.

Mark's secretive and strange behavior escalates as the story progresses, culminating in a near tragedy when he disappears from Ann at the beach. For the first time since Wayne's death, Ann responds emotionally to Mark, and at last, he is able to express his feelings to her.

One of the most unusual characters in *The Suicide's Wife* is Max Crane. At first blush, Max appears to be the antithesis of Wayne. He is a good-looking, witty, successful poet who is popular with both his colleagues and his students. That he is a bit of a scoundrel and womanizer only adds to his mystique and charm.

Yet, as the reader learns, Max was inexplicably drawn to Wayne. At first, Max simply enjoyed feeling superior to the man whom the students branded "the most boring man on the face of the earth." Later, however, Max realized that the attraction was more complex. Wayne was the flip side of Max; Wayne's body image enhanced the image that Max had of his own body. Max became acutely aware, through Wayne, of the way other people affected him, physically and psychologically, and the way that he affected those around him. After Wayne's death, Max became fixated on the sound of his own heart—and on the fact that Wayne's heart no longer made any sound.

Max's attraction to Ann is based on his perverse interest in Wayne; through her, Max can continue to probe and analyze his alter ego. Nevertheless, Max plays a critical role in Ann's development and growth. Through Max, Ann discovers that she is ignorant not only about her husband's life, but also about her own life. Max's presence allows her to confront the ghosts from her past and face the truth about her present reality.

Themes and Meanings

The basic theme in *The Suicide's Wife* is that of death and rebirth. As a result of Wayne's death, Ann is reborn. Birth is always a painful process, and for Ann, the process is excruciating.

Surrounded by tragic events, both personally and nationally, Ann is forced to acknowledge her own feelings of loss and need. No longer having a husband to hide behind, Ann must at last find out who she is and where she belongs. Thrust into the world anew, she has two choices: accept the identity inflicted on her by other people or discover her own identity and everyone else be damned.

Ann consciously chooses to control her own destiny. She begins by rejecting the negative self-image which she has built over the years—that of a fat, dumpy woman whose only purpose in life is to serve others. Although feelings of helplessness overwhelm her at times, she continues to move forward, one small step at a time. She not only must overcome her own personal demons, but she also must do it in the South, in 1968—a time when women without men were creatures to be pitied and avoided.

Madden creates a situation that proves his thesis: Even during times of chaos and tragedy, personal growth is not only possible but also absolutely necessary for survival. The human spirit is indomitable and can be broken only when the desire to live diminishes.

From the war in Vietnam to the political and racial wars in the United States to the personal tragedies that befall all human beings, death and destruction hung like a cloud over everyone's head in 1968. Madden brilliantly weaves historical and local events into Ann's personal life. As she becomes increasingly aware of the political climate, Ann breaks out of her self-indulgent shell and starts identifying with and joining the real world. In one critical scene, Ann actually leaves her children sleeping in their beds and joins a student demonstration down the street.

Critical Context

As noted above, it is significant that *The Suicide's Wife* takes place in 1968, one of the most turbulent years in American history. The story goes full circle—it opens with the assassination of Martin Luther King, Jr., and ends with the assassination of Robert Kennedy. In between, the reader witnesses national rioting, student protests (in the United States and abroad), and antiwar demonstrations: "National events came at [Ann] like blows, made her flinch."

Television brought the tragic events of the day into everyone's living room. Not untouched by these catastrophic events, Ann also must cope with personal tragedies that affect her life directly: her husband's suicide, Mark's friend's sudden death, the collapse of the bridge connecting West Virginia with Ohio plunging cars, trucks, and a school bus deep into the Ohio River. In the midst of all this suffering and loss, Ann begins to realize that she can change her life; she is not doomed to a lifetime of failures.

The Suicide's Wife received mixed reviews from the critics. Some compared the novel favorably to Jean-Paul Sartre's masterpiece *Nausea* (1938), while others criticized it for being thin and laconic. Ann Harrington is obviously a character about whom Madden felt very deeply; the reader, too, is invited to share in her consciousness to an extraordinary degree.

Bibliography

Crowder, A. B. *Writing in the Southern Tradition: Interviews with Five Contemporary Authors.* Atlanta, Ga.: Rodopi, 1990. Includes an interview with David Madden.

Madden, David. "Interview with David Madden: On Technique in Fiction." Interview by Jeffrey J. Folks. *The Southern Quarterly* 25 (Winter, 1987). Madden discusses his writing strategies.

_____. "A Personal View: The 'Real Life' Fallacy." In *The American Writer and the University*, edited by Ben Siegel. Newark: University of Delaware Press, 1989. Interesting commentary by Madden on his views of writing.

Perrault, Anna H. "A David Madden Bibliography: 1952-1981" *Bulletin of Bibliography* 39 (September, 1982). Includes a brief biographical essay and listings of all works in every genre to 1982, including Madden's many short stories, as well as secondary sources. Reviews are conveniently listed with the works reviewed.

Prestridge, Samuel N. "An Interview with David Madden." *Mississippi Review* 6 (1977).

Walt, James. "Review of *The Suicide's Wife.*" *The New Republic* 179 (October 7, 1978): 39-40.

Deborah Lally

SUNDOWN

Author: John Joseph Mathews (1895-1979)
Type of plot: Psychological realism
Time of plot: The 1880's to 1930
Locale: Osage Indian country, near the Oklahoma-Kansas border
First published: 1934

> *Principal characters:*
>> CHALLENGE (CHAL) WINDZER, a mixed-blood Osage caught between cultures
>> JOHN WINDZER, Chal's optimistic father
>> CHAL'S MOTHER, a traditional Osage woman
>> COUSIN ELLEN, a stereotypically censorious white woman
>> BLO DAUBENEY, a foolish female college student whom Chal idolizes
>> RUNNING ELK, a friend whom Chal watches degenerate
>> JEP NEWBERG, a leading merchant
>> CHARLIE FANCHER, Chal's supercilious university pal
>> PROFESSOR GRANVILLE, Chal's friend and, later, flight instructor

The Novel

John Joseph Mathews's *Sundown* traces the disintegration of Chal Windzer's character. Chal is a mixed-blood Osage Indian torn by conflicts within Osage tribal values and confused by both the aggressiveness and the vices of the white Americans whom he encounters. The chronicle of Chal's life ends with his decline into boastful, passive dreaming, womanizing, and alcoholism. Chal becomes a sad caricature of the manhood exalted in the ideals of the Osage's warrior culture.

Chal's life of declining faith and growing insecurities unfolds through sixteen chapters. The first five of these cover his boyhood through his entrance into the university. Chal was born in the 1890's, when the great god of the Osage still ruled the land defined by the Caney and Arkansas rivers, centered on Pawhuska, near the Oklahoma-Kansas border. He enjoys an idyllic youth as part of an animistic culture. He interacts closely with prairie nature and leads a life nicely balanced between contemplation and action.

Even in boyhood, however, Chal's disillusionment is progressive. It is synonymous with his personal contacts with whites—merchants, teachers, Bible thumpers, government officials, and oilmen—drawn by opportunities to convert the "heathen," to exploit Indian lands, and to profit from the discovery and swift expansion of the Oklahoma oil fields after 1897. His disenchantment stems also from familial circumstances. His father is a sanguine white man with enduring faith in "the guv'mint" and his mother is a silent Osage woman who judges her son's character in the Osage way and sees little good in white culture.

As a mixed-blood, Chal also reflects a deep division with tribal ranks, one which had been confirmed by tribal councils in the 1860's and which thereafter consigned mixed-bloods to inferior position relative to full-bloods. In addition, by the time Chal reaches adolescence, the undreamed-of wealth accruing to the Osage from government annuities and (to a vastly greater extent) from oil royalties is wreaking its own havoc. Chal's youthful companions, like many Osage, lacking incentive and business acumen, become profligates. Chal's separation from them is widened by his entrance into the university, the subject of chapters 7 through 11.

Chal's university career has little to do with learning. Led on by his supercilious and patronizing "pal," Charlie Fancher, he succumbs almost immediately to the age-old frivolities: fraternities, football, cars, girls, drinking, and parties. Throughout these activities, he realizes that he does not fit; he is a curiosity, and he moves among people who smile with their teeth but not with their hearts. He is ensnared in a vapid, superficial world. Only his chance encounter with Professor Granville, a wise, understanding Englishman who represents what white culture could be like—but is not—affords a contrast to the inanities to which he has lent himself.

The American entrance into World War I offers Chal a way out when Granville suggests that Chal act on his plans to participate by joining the air service. He does so and wins his commission. More significant, in flying he finds a calling to which he is well adapted. He is reunited with Granville, who, having distinguished himself in the Royal Air Force, is Chal's flight instructor. Yet at war's end, despite his pride in his flying ability and his enjoyment of the notoriety brought to him by his commission, Chal finds little to do and resigns from the service. His father's death, meanwhile, has enriched him. He has no need to work, though he briefly toys with thoughts of business and investment. He watches the successful businessmen of his boyhood fail, however, and, with his own wealth in hand, he settles for a life of idleness. He spends his time driving through town in his "long, powerful red roadster," killing time with young people in the local drugstore, occasionally dating, and—as the years pass—succumbing to alcoholism. Chapters 13 through 16 are thus the final record of his decline, epitomized by his mother's silent judgment on his childishness and failure.

The Characters

Sundown is both a chronicle and a didactic exercise. Mathews's characters are thereby denied some of their potential dimensions so that the author can better convey his principal message: Namely that because of their values, the Osage are victims of the dubious concept of "progress" as embodied in white American society.

Chal, Mathews's mixed-blood protagonist, exemplifies the degradation that befell most American Indian cultures, unable as they were to maintain tribal integrity in the face of white incursions into their lands and values. Chal's heart looks in two directions. On the one hand, he profoundly enjoys and respects the fraternity with nature taught by the Osage's full-blooded elders; in a more specific way, he seeks to make his Osage mother proud of him within her traditional frame of reference. Yet on the other hand, he is drawn by the positive, confident, and assertive views of John Windzer, his white father, who doggedly persists in believing that the government will rectify the manifest injustices and dangers to which the Osage are exposed by the white people flooding into their midst. Chal is unsuited to function positively in either world, and he is confused by the attractions and repulsions of each.

While Chal's boyhood reactions to several white characters—merchants such as Jep Newberg and Mr. Fancher, teachers such as Miss Hoover, Christian do-gooders such as Cousin Ellen, and oilmen such as Osage Dubois—are negative, his serious distrust of whites comes after his entrance into the university. There he is taken in tow by Charlie Fancher, a know-it-all whom Mathews has created to emphasize the inanity and insincerity of wealthy, privileged white people. Lacking the substance to be genuinely bad, Fancher exposes Chal to continuous social exploitation. Fancher's female counterpart, the narcissistic Blo Daubeney, with whom Chal becomes infatuated, furthers his discomfiture in white university society by using him as a pawn in her dating and sexual gambits. Worse, Chal is soon abandoned to Fancher and Daubeney amid his growing disaffection with student life: Two of his boyhood Osage friends (like Chal they were recruited principally to play football) suddenly pack their trunks and depart for home.

The sole white character presented as engaging, strong, and admirable is Granville. Mathews uses him to underscore the perspective of Chal's mother—that white civilization had its virtues, but only at its European sources, before it was corrupted in its transition to America. Granville, the Englishman, is brave, gentle, courteous, and wise. He talks and smiles with his heart. Moreover, he leads Chal into his only positive experience in the white world: flying. Nevertheless, like all of *Sundown*'s characters, he tends to be a two-dimensional stereotype, the bearer of a heavy thematic burden.

Themes and Meanings

Mathews's objective, realized as far as his readers are concerned with some grace and a high level of interest, is to depict the victimization of a vulnerable American Indian culture by forces that a majority of non-Indian Americans historically have defined as progress. Repeated descriptions of the march of the oil derricks through Osage lands symbolically traces the flight of an arrow that lodges ever more deeply and fatally in the heart of Osage society.

As Mathews constantly reminds his readers, accompanying the inexorable march of the derricks came the white men who mined the earth. Whether motivated by good intentions aimed at bringing the Osage into conformity with mainstream American society or driven by witless adventuring and greed, their impact was devastating. During the latter part of the nineteenth century, as a consequence of intermarriages, whites had already divided the Osage among themselves. There were mixed-bloods, such as Chal, whose acceptance by full-bloods was at best grudging, however appreciative mixed-bloods were of the tribe's ways and the beauty of its perception of the world of the Osage gods. Children of intermarriage such as Chal were almost predestined to inferior status in the culture of each parent.

For the Osage, Mathews emphasizes, the fruits of white technological progress proved as catastrophic as did the planting of their personal seeds. Oil royalties appended to the annuities that the Osage already received from the federal government reportedly made them the wealthiest tribe in the world. In this regard, their situation differed dramatically from that of most American Indian groups. Most American Indians who clung to tribal customs were impoverished by contact with white society. The results of Osage wealth, nevertheless, were equally calamitous.

Mathews's descriptive powers evoke a sense of loss, a feeling that inevitable change is not necessarily for the better. The price paid for the Osage's share of progress was a loss of intimacy with the world of living things and sentient objects surrounding them. The fact that the choices between their traditional worldview and "the white man's road" confused and disillusioned many of the Osage reinforces Mathews's implication that white people too have frequently apprehended their losses and have often been confused and distraught by the many forks in the road.

Critical Context

Although *Sundown* is a semiautobiographical novel, its author did not follow the sad route of his protagonist, Chal Windzer. Mathews, like fellow Osages Clarence Tinker, Sylvester Tinker, and Maria Tallchief, distinguished himself in several ways. He was a pilot in World War I. Early in the postwar years, he was graduated from the University of Oklahoma and pursued study at Sewanee, the University of Oxford, and the University of Geneva. After a few years in ranching and real estate, he rejoined the Oklahoma Osage, became a tribal councilman, and was soon recognized as one of the Osage's principal spokespeople and their preeminent historian.

Publication of his *Wah'Kon-Tah: The Osage and the White Man's Road* (1932) brought him and the Osage national attention. It was the first university press book to be chosen as a Book-of-the-Month Club selection. (A paperback edition was republished by the University of Oklahoma Press in 1981.) Appearing two years later, *Sundown* was a literary plea for public acknowledgment of the Osage's fate and, by implication, of the plight of most American Indians. By the early 1930's, the Osages, like millions of other Americans caught in the grip of the Great Depression, had fallen on hard times, though they remained far less impoverished than most American Indians. The "Great Frenzy," the oil boom of the 1920's, had collapsed, and royalties had diminished to a trickle. A series of related and widely publicized murders, the "Osage Reign of Terror," deepened the pall over reservation life. However traumatic, these events posed opportunities for Mathews, since the entire nation was reexamining its traditional values.

Mathews's literary and historical skills, joined to the talents of others such as John Collier, an American Indian whom President Franklin Roosevelt appointed Commissioner of Indian Affairs, and Sylvester Tinker, helped to win substantial appropriations for Indian Emergency Conservation Work. Far more important, particularly since Mathews was keenly aware of his tribe's dissolution, were his contributions in setting the stage for passage of the Wheeler-Howard Bill, enacted in 1934 as the Indian Reorganization Act. Ostensibly repudiating past assimilationist policies, the act acknowledged the intrinsic worth of American Indian cultures and sought to reestablish tribal values and revitalize tribal life. To a considerable degree it was successful.

Meanwhile, Mathews continued with his Osage histories, which were completed in his beautiful and masterful *The Osages: Children of the Middle Waters* (1961), perhaps the finest American Indian history produced for any tribe.

Bibliography
Hunter, Carol. "The Protagonist as a Mixed-Blood in John Joseph Mathews' Novel: *Sundown.*" *American Indian Quarterly* 6 (Fall/Winter, 1982): 319-337. Author Hunter, herself a mixed-blood Osage, here analyzes the experiences of Mathews that encouraged him to create Chal Windzer. Hunter, a specialist in Osage mythology, brings interesting insights to bear on this aspect of Mathews's work. A useful perspective, especially since Mathews was himself an expert on Osage myths.
Mathews, John Joseph. "John Joseph Mathews: A Conversation." Interview by Guy Lodgson. *Nimrod* 16 (April, 1972): 70-75. A rare pleasure. Articulate as he was, Mathews tells little about himself on the record. This is a valuable dialogue because Lodgson interviewed Mathews after he had completed his major writings. Charming and revealing.
_____. *The Osages: Children of the Middle Waters*. Norman: University of Oklahoma Press, 1961. A beautiful and masterful study. Drawing on recollections that he coaxed from tribal elders, Mathews skillfully reconstructs the ethnohistory of his people. It is therefore a history written from an Osage perspective, but a balanced and objective one. The symbolisms embodied in it allow comparisons with Joseph Campbell's studies.
_____. *Talking to the Moon: Wildlife Adventures on the Plains and Prairies of Osage Country*. Chicago: University of Chicago Press, 1945. This was Mathews's own favorite among his writings, and it is a delight to read. It is based on memories of his boyhood among the blackjack pine, the red bank lands, and the prairie wildlife in the Oklahoma-Kansas Osage country. Reissued in paperback by the University of Oklahoma Press in 1979, the year of Mathews's death.
Warrior, Robert Allen. *Tribal Secrets: Recovering American Indian Intellectual Traditions*. Minneapolis: University of Minnesota, 1994. Compares and contrasts the treatment of American Indian sovereignty and survival in the works of two of the most acclaimed American Indian writers, Vine Deloria, Jr., and John Joseph Mathews. This study goes far beyond the assumption that representation of myths from the oral tradition is all there is to Native American literature.
Wilson, Terry P. "Osage Oxonian: The Heritage of John Joseph Mathews." *The Chronicles of Oklahoma* 59, no. 3 (1981): 264-293. This essay adduces all the reasons why Mathews, the distinguished warrior, intellectual, scholar, and tribal leader could serve as a role model for other American Indians. Not all of the Osage missed opportunities.
_____. *The Underground Reservation: Osage Oil*. Lincoln: University of Nebraska Press, 1985. An academic study that is well researched and well written.

Its background materials include Mathews's contributions, but it goes beyond them. Mathews concluded his study with the opening of the twentieth century, while Wilson updates through the 1970's. Good information on the Oklahoma land rush, the "Great Frenzy," "the Osage Reign of Terror," the Depression, and federal policies relevant to the Osage.

Clifton K. Yearley

SURFACING

Author: Margaret Atwood (1939-   )
Type of plot: Psychological realism
Time of the plot: 1969 or 1970
Locale: A wilderness area in Quebec, Canada
First published: 1972

>*Principal characters:*
>THE NARRATOR, an unnamed woman in her late twenties searching for her missing father
>JOE, the narrator's lover, who has come with her from the city
>DAVID, Joe's friend, who wants to vacation and make a film while the narrator looks for her father
>ANNA, David's wife, who is always worried about her appearance
>PAUL, a French Canadian local friend of the narrator's father

The Novel

Surfacing is divided into three parts of eight, eleven, and eight chapters, respectively. The time span of the novel is about two weeks, during which the protagonist is in the remote wilderness where she had spent her childhood. Her mother is dead of cancer, and her father is missing.

The protagonist tells her story in the present tense, as the action unfolds. Joe, David, and Anna plan to vacation while she checks on her father. From the moment they approach the small town on the other side of the lake, she begins to recall events and people from her childhood and to notice many changes. It is now a commercialized resort area appealing to American sportsmen. She speaks with Paul, a French Canadian who had contacted her because of his concern for her father, his longtime friend. With Paul's wife, Madame, who speaks only French, she experiences the same awkwardness she remembers when she and her mother would try to visit with Madame while her father visited with Paul. She goes to buy supplies for the group to take to the island and timidly tries a few French words to make her purchases; the people in the store mockingly imitate her accent. These opening scenes set up several continuing plot lines of the novel: the narrator's search not only for her father but for herself; her pondering of the loss of her parents and her years of not communicating with them; and her sense of alienation in a border area torn between French and English cultures and inundated with affluent Americans.

At the cabin, the narrator feels responsible for the others, feeding them, showing them how to fish, and taking them for hikes in the woods. The isolation leads to interpersonal conflicts. David and Anna continuously bicker and belittle each other. Joe, who seldom speaks, has decided that this is the time when he must force the narrator to tell him she loves him and will marry him. All three companions thus contribute to the strains on the narrator.

On a hiking trip, they find a dead heron hanging with a rope around its neck. The narrator assumes Americans have wantonly killed the bird just for the sake of killing. David sees it merely as something to add to his amateur film, "Random Samples."

The narrator believes her parents would not have approved of her life after she left home. Frequently, she recalls scenes from her marriage and divorce, and she slowly begins to admit to herself that much of what she wants to imagine about her recent years is false. There was no wedding; the scene she has in her memory is actually of the time her already married lover sent her to have an abortion. What her current lover, Joe, admires as her calmness she considers her numbness, an inability to feel.

The narrator finds strange stick-figure drawings that indicate that her father had discovered ancient Indian petroglyphs. Deducing that his most recent finds are on the rock edges of the lake but underwater, she repeatedly dives looking for them, but instead encounters dark limbs and open eyes. It is her father's body, weighted down by the camera around his neck, but she refuses to recognize it as such. That night, she pulls Joe outside on the ground and has urgent, impersonal sex with him.

When the others leave the island as scheduled, she stays behind. For the next few days, she abandons all forms of civilization. She leaves the cabin, eats only what berries or plants she can find, and attunes herself to the "native gods." In a kind of visionary madness, she sees something of her father, and she sees her mother in a characteristic pose, standing with her arms outstretched to feed birds. After flashes of insight into their lives and her own, she "surfaces" with the knowledge that she must protect the life that may be forming inside her. Perhaps that baby will be the first "true human." She hears Joe calling her. He has come back. She thinks she will try to trust him; but above all, she says, she must refuse to be a victim.

The Characters

The characters in *Surfacing* all contribute to the narrator's sense of alienation and victimization. David, a college communications teacher, is talkative but insensitive. Most characteristically, he imitates the sounds of movie cartoon characters. Egotistical and controlling, he forces Anna to strip for his film. He fancies himself clever and superior to others but is dependent upon his wife to reinforce this attitude. Anna shares the love/hate codependency, trapped in her marriage but constantly straining to please him. When the narrator opens the movie camera and throws all the film in the lake, Anna, rather than acknowledging female support, only says that David will be vindictive.

Joe, a potter who makes oddly mangled pots that no one buys, seldom says much, most often grunting responses, and the heavy hair on his back and body emphasizes the image of a primitive, animalistic man. He wants the narrator to say the words "I love you" and to marry him, a repeated refrain that indicates his insecurity. Once he has sex with Anna, perhaps intending to make the narrator jealous. David, in turn, tries to get the narrator to sleep with him, but she refuses. It is Joe she pulls to the earth, watching the moon over his shoulder in an almost primordial mating, and at the end of the novel, it is Joe who comes back to the island. He will not wait long, she thinks, and she is not quite ready to answer his call, but she will soon, because his very primitiveness indicates that he is not completely "formed," not totally corrupted by society.

Paul is a minor character but important as a representation of loyalty to a friend and the possibility of accord between unlike individuals. He symbolizes the diverse border culture and its problems; by extension, he shows that kindness and respect are qualities needed to change a greedy and violent global society.

The narrator and her interior thoughts form the center of the novel. She has no vocabulary or support to understand her lack of power in relation to males in a patriarchal society. She thinks of her first lover's insistence on the unwanted abortion; Joe's passive-aggressive urging for reassurance; David's uninvited propositions; her older brother's bullying threats in her childhood; her father's logic, which left no room for emotional needs. It was her mother who patterned for her a love of nature and a simple goodness but who herself was a victim of her husband's logic and often retreated to solitude.

In her own active retreat to solitude, the narrator shuns human artifacts and comes to see herself as a part of the cosmic spirit of existence. She watches a fish jump in the lake, which becomes the idea of a fish, life in many shapes and forms. She knows she cannot sustain her vision, but having known it, she can at least proceed with her life.

Themes and Meanings

Surfacing is a postmodern novel in that its ideological strategy is to rethink traditional views and question conventions. Its themes are numerous, virtually unlimited, one of the reasons it is the most widely written about of all Atwood's many works. Foremost is the portrayal of male/female relationships and the examination of power relationships of all kinds. It is also a psychological quest. Examining her life under extreme circumstances, the narrator experiences herself as part of a larger wholeness. The dead heron is thus more than itself; it is Christ crucified, the death of the cosmic harmony, humanity destroying the very nature of which it is a part. The feminist themes merge with the autonomy of the individual and the sacredness of life.

All the themes are interrelated. The narrator reclaims integrity as she acknowledges her complicity in the abortion rather than blaming everything on "him" or "they." The new life that is possibly growing in her will be given a chance to be more fully human than the violent actions of the historical past and present generations. The narrator refuses to relinquish her wilderness landscape to resort developers; it must be preserved for itself and its ecological system. Individuals must accept others regardless of differences and borders and languages that divide them. Artists must be allowed to and be willing to speak their truth and not be perverted into "random samples" of the bizarre and sensational. Rather than Canadians blaming Americans or children blaming parents, each person must accept responsibility, be compassionate, and work to find a third possibility beyond the dichotomous poles of "killer" or "victim." Such moral engagement demands actions that emerge from an understanding of the interconnectedness of all life.

Critical Context
Margaret Atwood is an internationally renowned writer whose work has been translated into more than twenty languages and published in dozens of countries. She has received numerous awards and honors for her poetry, novels, short stories, children's books, literary criticism, and nonfiction. Her work reflects her position as white, Canadian, and female, but she challenges these and all labels and the limitations they place on self-understanding and understanding others.

Surfacing was Atwood's second novel, and it is an outstanding example of her ability to use the written word to convey her beliefs and to argue the urgency of reexamining traditional ways of thinking. This questioning is consistent throughout her fiction, but the writing approach or genre she uses varies markedly from novel to novel: for example, the comic pathos of the first, *The Edible Woman* (1969), the dystopian future of *The Handmaid's Tale* (1985), and the historical novel based on an actual nineteenth century criminal case, *Alias Grace* (1996).

Surfacing can be read on many levels and thus appeals to diverse readers. It is a detective story, a psychological study of self-discovery, a realistic study of male-female relationships, an ecological tract, a sociological examination of power, a recasting of fairy tales in terms of modern sexual politics, and a philosophical discourse on the meaning of life.

Most significant is Atwood's aesthetic concern for language. The writing in *Surfacing* at first is flat and objective, as though the unnamed narrator is observing from the outside, unmoved by event. As the protagonist moves closer to what society would call madness, however, the language changes, just as it does again during her visions and during her return to face society. The writing is at times experimental, at others poetic. Always, it is compelling and powerful. *Surfacing* is a novel to read and re-read.

Bibliography
Christ, Carol P. *Diving Deep and Surfacing: Women Writers on Spiritual Quest.* Boston: Beacon Press, 1980. Discusses women's quests and spiritual awakenings. A chapter on Atwood is entitled "Refusing to Be Victim."
Hengen, Shannon. *Margaret Atwood's Power: Mirrors, Reflections, and Images in Select Fiction and Poetry.* Toronto: Second Story Press, 1993. Sees *Surfacing* as strong novel about female empowerment.
Howells, Coral Ann. *Margaret Atwood.* New York: St. Martin's Press, 1996. Gives an overview of facts about and characteristics of Atwood's writing. Considers *Surfacing* one of her Canadian signature works, chronicling postmodern malaise in a specifically Canadian context.
Nicholson, Colin, ed. *Margaret Atwood: Writing and Subjectivity.* New York: St. Martin's Press, 1994. Includes two lengthy essays on *Surfacing*, one arguing that the novel both invites and resists interpretation, remaining indeterminate, and the other that it is overtly existential in authorial intent.
Rigney, Barbara Hill. *Margaret Atwood.* Totowa, N.J.: Barnes and Noble Books,

1987. One chapter presents a clear summary of *Surfacing* and analyzes it in terms of borders and boundaries.

Rosenberg, Jerome H. *Margaret Atwood*. Boston: Twayne, 1984. An introduction to Atwood's works, with a chapter on *Surfacing* as a study in becoming truly human.

Wilson, Sharon Rose. *Margaret Atwood's Fairy-Tale Sexual Politics*. Jackson: University of Mississippi Press, 1993. An analysis of Atwood's use of fairy-tale motifs, with a detailed chapter on *Surfacing*.

Lois A. Marchino

SUSAN LENOX
Her Fall and Rise

Author: David Graham Phillips (1867-1911)
Type of plot: Social realism
Time of plot: 1879-1903
Locale: Southeastern Indiana; Louisville, Kentucky; Cincinnati, Ohio; New York City; London; and Paris
First published: Originally serialized in *Hurst's Magazine*, beginning June 1915; complete novel published in 1917

Principal characters:
>SUSAN LENOX, a young woman born out of wedlock
>FANNY WARHAM and
>GEORGE WARHAM, Susan's aunt and uncle
>RUTH WARHAM, the Warham's daughter
>SAM WRIGHT, Susan's first boyfriend
>JEB FERGUSON, the brutish sharecropper Susan is forced to marry
>ROBERT BURLINGHAM, a showboat operator
>RODERICK SPENSER, a newspaper reporter and aspiring playwright
>FREDDIE PALMER, a pimp
>GEORGE BRENT, a wealthy playwright

The Novel

Originally published in two volumes, *Susan Lenox: Her Fall and Rise* is the story of a young woman who struggles against hypocritical double standards, lapses into prostitution, and eventually finds her way back into respectable society. The story begins in Sutherland, a fictitious southeastern Indiana town along the Ohio River modeled after Phillips's hometown, Madison, Indiana. Susan Lenox's unmarried mother dies during childbirth without divulging her lover's identity. The lifeless baby does not respond to conventional methods of resuscitation, so the doctor holds her ankles and swings her around, forcing life into her tiny body. The infant's scream is the first of many times when Susan will boldly declare her existence.

Susan's aunt and uncle rear her alongside their own daughter, Ruth, two years older than Susan. Although Susan receives every advantage—clothes, education, refined upbringing—neither her adoptive family nor the townspeople forget her origins. No family wants their son to marry or even associate with Susan. Sam Wright shows interest in her when she is seventeen and even professes his love in order to gain her favor and steal a kiss. Naïve, Susan believes they will be married. The Warhams forbid the relationship because they want the young man for Ruth. One day Sam leads Susan into a cemetery, embraces her, and kisses her passionately. Someone sees them, and rumors spread until everyone believes that Susan has "fallen" like her mother. Not understanding the mechanics of sex, Susan acts guilty, assuming the kiss was the great sin about which the villagers are whispering.

To prevent Susan's reputation from contaminating their own daughter, the War-hams plan to send Susan away. Not wanting to leave Sam, Susan runs away to Cincinnati, hoping he will follow. Susan reaches the city safely, but the Warhams co-erce Sam to reveal her whereabouts. Within a day, George Warham and Sam's father bring Susan back to Indiana, but not to stay in Sutherland. Believing his family too good for the girl, Mr. Wright refuses Warham's request that Sam marry Susan. Fearing his ward's indiscretion will result in an unwanted pregnancy, Warham makes hasty arrangements to wed Susan to a brutish young sharecropper, Jeb Ferguson. Trapped without means of support, she cannot object. On their wedding night, Fergu-son forcibly takes Susan's virginity, horrifically exposing her to the realities of sex. When her husband falls asleep, the young bride flees.

Escaping towards the Ohio River, Susan meets Roderick Spenser, the son of an affluent northern Kentucky family. After loaning her enough money to get to Cincinnati, where he works as a newspaper reporter, Spenser promises to help Susan find work, but he sends her on ahead to avoid any impropriety. Realizing his family would disown him if they discovered his association with Susan, Spenser does not look for her when he returns to Cincinnati.

Susan reaches the river without incident and waits at an inn for a boat to take her upriver. After someone steals her money, Susan cannot pay her lodging bill, and she turns to a new acquaintance for help. Robert Burlingham, an older showboat operator dining at the inn, offers to let Susan sing in his show. Flattered, she joins his troupe. After teaching Susan the facts of life, one actress warns her, "don't drink" and "don't sell your body to get a living, unless you've got to."

When the showboat sinks while docked in Louisville, fatherly Burlingham takes Susan to Cincinnati to seek work. Burlingham falls ill, and Susan sacrifices all to pay his hospital bill, but he dies anyway. Alone and penniless again, Susan abandons her-self to a shadowy existence. She sings at a German beer garden, then moves to the poorest side of town, where she shares a tenement with a friend and works in a factory for less than subsistence wages. Disease, poverty, and frequent arsons plague the area. Eventually, the two girls became homeless. Starving, they head downtown to trade their bodies for food. After a week, Susan has a new wardrobe and one hundred dol-lars cash.

Less than a year has passed since Susan fled Sutherland. Finally able to repay her debt to Spenser, she tracks him down. They begin spending time together, and Susan becomes his mistress. Now understanding that a man of Spenser's class could not marry her, Susan does not suggest legitimizing their relationship. Tired of newspaper reporting, Spenser decides they should move to New York City, where he can pursue his real calling—writing plays.

The couple circulates freely in New York's artist community. Spenser, though, can-not sell his plays, and he grows despondent, drinks, and cavorts with other women. Jealous that Susan might seek similar diversions, he keeps her isolated until they eventually part ways. Susan seeks legitimate work and even obtains a high-paying job as a fur model, but when forced to "entertain" clients, she quits. Susan holds many jobs, but never for long, and keeps moving from tenement to tenement as her money runs out. Between jobs, she sells herself for food and rent money. For a while, she is exploited by Freddie Palmer, a politically ambitious young pimp, who constantly threatens to have Susan arrested if she does not prostitute herself and give him her earnings. Eventually, Susan finds the strength to escape.

Susan then encounters Spenser, drunk almost beyond recognition and very sick. While nursing him, Susan meets George Brent, a wealthy playwright who offers her a deal: He will provide Spenser with theater opportunities and pay Susan an allowance if she will become his pupil and learn to be a professional actress. The egotistical writer seeks to mold her into the perfect actress for his plays. When Brent unexpectedly goes to Europe, Susan refuses to continue accepting his money and seeks other employment. Desperate, she visits her old neighborhood and is immediately arrested by a policeman working for Palmer. The pimp gives Susan an ultimatum: She must either agree to be his wife or remain in jail. Susan agrees to accompany Freddie to Europe, where they can anonymously enter polite society. Dining at a posh restaurant before leaving New York, they meet Brent, who questions Susan's happiness and learns of their impending trip.

Brent follows the couple to Europe and befriends them. Freddie eagerly accepts this opportunity to enter elite society. Brent, however, has other motives and gradually convinces Susan to pursue her acting career in London. Freddie grows increasingly jealous as Susan begins falling in love with Brent. When Brent is called back to New York for a month, Freddie goes with him. After spending only six nights in New York, Freddie returns to Susan alone. A few days later, she learns that Brent has been murdered. Suspecting Freddie has arranged the crime, Susan confronts him. Heartbroken about Brent's death, Susan fears being on the streets again, but then learns Brent has left her his entire estate. Finally, Susan is free to live her own life without depending on others for money or respectability.

By preventing Susan from participating in proper society, the citizens of Sutherland ironically start her on a path that eventually fulfills their prophecy—that she will follow in her mother's footsteps. In fact, Susan goes farther than her mother, who had merely loved a man too much to reveal his identity to those who wanted to condemn him.

The Characters

Susan Lenox is a unique character among literature about fallen women. She is forced to sell herself, but she has the physical, moral, and intellectual strength to fight for survival. While most of his contemporaries kept their fallen women down, Phillips allowed Susan to rise back into respectable society. Her character is fully developed, perhaps too fully. Readers see every thought as she contemplates her actions. The novel's other characters, however, fall more into types—the spoiled boy toying with Susan, the bighearted swindler who befriends her, the roguish, discontented failure, and the generous benefactor who transforms Susan into a lady.

Themes and Meanings

Themes in the novel include illegitimacy, reputation, class, gender roles, marriage, poverty, and prostitution. Like his naturalist contemporaries Stephen Crane, Frank Norris, Jack London, and Theodore Dreiser, Phillips questions whether individuals can control their lives or if fates are predetermined. Phillips suggests that while external factors do limit choices, individuals are ultimately responsible for what they make of their situations. Rather than bemoaning determinism, Phillips instead turns his pen toward exposing those factors that impede Susan's progress. He enumerates low wages in her different occupations and exposes the vast economic gap between classes. In the box factory, Susan makes only three dollars per week, but wealthy men such as Brent spend thousands on new wardrobes. Rather than condemning prostitution as inherently evil, Phillips shows that poor women often have little choice if they want to eat and have a place to stay. In Cincinnati, when women from a wealthy neighborhood give charity to the poor, Phillips testifies that the money offered is really profit from the sweat of poor laborers. When Susan is arrested in New York, readers see that police often enable vice rather than prevent it. Things are not always what they seem, and a streetwalker might be a morally decent person.

Critical Context

Susan Lenox deserves reading mainly for its unique vision of prostitution through a female character's perspective. With its descriptions of Cincinnati sweatshops and vermin-infested tenements, the first half of the novel resembles the naturalistic fiction of Dreiser and Norris. However, in the second volume, plot is overshadowed by repeated attacks on double standards, poor housing, worker exploitation, and corrupt government. Like Upton Sinclair, Phillips used his fiction to expose injustice and was consequently labeled a "muckraker."

Exaggerated fiction of the time such as Reginald Wright Kauffman's *The House of Bondage* (1910) espoused the "white slave" myth, the idea that innocent young girls were trapped into prostitution and held against their will by evil pimps and madams. Phillips shows an entirely different view: Susan takes her first downward step because her family and neighbors expect it of her. Later instances of her prostitution are triggered by corrupt employers, poverty, and hunger, and even by altruism when she prostitutes herself to provide for sick friends. For Susan, prostitution is a last resort, into which society periodically forces her. While most "fallen woman" literature shows the heroine falling deeper and deeper into vice and degradation, Susan Lenox sells herself when necessary but rises, takes control of her life, and even prospers enough to live among New York's elite.

During his lifetime, Phillips was more widely read and respected than Theodore Dreiser, yet today his works are all but ignored. Of his more than twenty novels, only *Susan Lenox* receives much attention. After seven years of writing and revising what he considered his masterpiece, Phillips was ready to publish it when he met an untimely death, assassinated by a crazed reader that believed Phillips had slandered his sister in an earlier novel. Since *Susan Lenox* was published posthumously, Phillips did not have editorial control over the final work, and many revisions softened its content. Still, the work addresses difficult issues.

Bibliography

Filler, Louis. *Voice of the Democracy: A Critical Biography of David Graham Phillips, Journalist, Novelist, Progressive*. University Park: Pennsylvania State University Press, 1978. Urges readers to consider *Susan Lenox*'s merits as well as its flaws and excesses.

Marcosson, Isaac F. *David Graham Phillips and His Times*. New York: Dodd, Mead, 1932. Discusses how Phillips's experiences in Indiana and Ohio influenced *Susan Lenox*.

Ravitz, Abe C. *David Graham Phillips*. New York: Twayne, 1966. Biography and criticism. Discussion of *Susan Lenox* addresses important themes but oversimplifies the work in terms of other "fallen woman" novels.

Wilson, Christopher P. *The Labor of Words: Literary Professionalism in the Progressive Era*. Athens: University of Georgia Press, 1985. Discusses relationships between journalism, naturalistic fiction, and political muckraking, with a chapter on Phillips.

Geralyn Strecker

SUTTREE

Author: Cormac McCarthy (1933-   )
Type of plot: Impressionistic realism
Time of plot: The early 1950's
Locale: Knoxville, Tennessee, and the surrounding area
First published: 1978

Principal characters:

> CORNELIUS SUTTREE (also called BUDDY or SCOUT), the protagonist, a fisherman who lives near McAnally Flats in the slums of Knoxville, Tennessee
>
> GENE HARROGATE, the devious "country mouse" whom Suttree befriends
>
> ABEDNEGO (AB) JONES, the black proprietor of the local tavern
>
> LEONARD, a male prostitute
>
> HARVEY, a drunken junkman
>
> MICHAEL, an Indian fisherman
>
> REESE, a shellfish scavenger and patriarch of a large river family
>
> WANDA, Reese's daughter and Suttree's lover
>
> WILLARD, Reese's son
>
> BONEYARD,
>
> HOGHEAD,
>
> J-BONE, and
>
> BLIND RICHARD, other residents of McAnally Flats

The Novel

Suttree takes place during the early 1950's in the slums of Knoxville, Tennessee. Cornelius Suttree, who comes from a prominent family, has abandoned his wife and infant son and has chosen to live on a houseboat near McAnally Flats, among the drifters and derelicts of the town. He keeps himself alive by fishing in the filth of the Tennessee River, but his existence is apparently meaningless, given over to destructive drinking, fighting, and carousing. As the narrator explains in the introduction to the story, "We are come to a world within the world. In these alien reaches, these maugre sinks and interstitial wastes that the righteous see from carriage and car another life dreams. Ill-shapen or black or deranged, fugitive of all order, strangers in everyland." When the story begins, Suttree is an accepted part of this other world. He shares bottles, stories, and jail cells with the "ruder forms" that inhabit the region. They recognize that Suttree is different, has had opportunities denied them, but they never question his decision to live among them. To them, he is simply "old Sut."

There is no conventional plot line in Suttree's story. Rather, the reader follows him through apparently random experiences. The book is thus constructed in episodic fashion and depends on the cumulative effect of these episodes to develop its structure and identify its theme. Some characters come and go, touching Suttree only for the moment. Others, however, form a constant in his life, forcing him to come out of his self-imposed isolation and renew, in however meager a fashion, his connections with humanity.

Although the book is large and its contents rich and varied, several episodes do stand out as significant events in the sweep of Suttree's life. While in prison for having taken part, unintentionally, in a robbery, Suttree meets Gene Harrogate, a sly but often foolish country boy who later follows Suttree back to Knoxville to become part of the marginal world of the outcasts. Although Suttree tries to avoid being involved with Harrogate, he often finds himself drawn into the boy's mad schemes, and on occasion has to rescue the boy from his craziness. Other characters from McAnally Flats also place demands on Suttree's humanity despite his best attempts to deny them, and he forms special relationships with a number of the doomed inhabitants of the region. Among them are Ab Jones, a giant black man who fights constantly with the police; an old ragpicker, whose wisdom and stoicism Suttree admires; the Indian named Michael, who offers Suttree a quiet and dignified friendship; the pathetic catamite Leonard, who involves Suttree in a grotesque scheme to dispose of the decaying body of Leonard's long-dead father; the comic, bizarre family of shellfishermen who entice Suttree, despite his better judgment, away from Knoxville to the French Broad River with the promise of pearls and adventure; and the whore, who takes Suttree to live with her and employs him for a time as her moneyman.

Although Suttree's experiences are often horrible and degrading, the book ends with at least the possibility of hope. Nearly dying of typhoid fever, Suttree faces in his lengthy delirium the waste and cowardice of his life. When he recovers his strength and returns to McAnally Flats, he finds most of his companions either dead or absent. In his own houseboat, he discovers the rotting corpse of some unknown figure who has usurped his very home and identity. In death, however, there is new life, and Suttree leaves Knoxville, breaking with his past. His destination is unspecified. As he stands by the side of the road, a mysterious boy offers him a drink of water and smiles. Then a car stops for him without his making the effort to flag it. Both acts are, in one sense, minor, but they are also acts of grace.

The Characters

Cornelius Suttree is at all times the focus of this novel, but Cormac McCarthy gives the reader only a sketchy sense of how and why he has broken with his family, left his wife and child. Suttree is a lapsed Catholic born with a sense of guilt. His twin brother died in birth, and Suttree questions why he was chosen to live. "Mirror image. Gauche carbon. He lies in Woodlawn, whatever be left of the child with whom you shared your mother's belly. He neither spoke nor saw nor does he now. . . . He in the limbo of the Christless righteous, I in a terrestrial hell."

Although Suttree's parents are alive, he refuses to have anything to do with them. While at the University of Tennessee, he met and married a mountain girl by whom he had a son, but he has returned her and the child to her family. Near the beginning of the book, he learns that the child has died, but when he attempts to go to the funeral, he is attacked by his wife's mother, mad with grief, and then run out of town by the sheriff. His life is a series of self-imposed failures. He dooms himself, invites his own destruction as a kind of just punishment. He also gives of himself, however, and in doing so acknowledges his humanity.

The character that stands in opposition to Suttree is Gene Harrogate, the country boy who is put in prison for sexually molesting watermelons. Harrogate is a perverse and comic character, thoroughly dishonest and without common sense, a fool whose grandiose plans always end in ruin. He, in fact, may remind the reader of Sut Lovingood, the "natural born durn fool" of Southwest humor. Harrogate's most spectacular scheme is to find his way through the tunnels under Knoxville to a bank, and there to dynamite his way into the vault. Instead, he blows up a sewage retaining wall and is almost drowned by the muck that is released. Only Suttree notices his absence, and only Suttree spends time, day after day, in an attempt to find the boy lost in the darkness under the earth. It is, symbolically, a search for his dead brother, his dead son, his own soul.

Ultimately, Harrogate cannot be saved from his greed and stupidity. Despite Suttree's warnings, he attempts another robbery and is sent back to prison. Indeed, all of the characters Suttree comes in contact with seem doomed. While living with the family on the French Broad River, gathering shellfish and looking for pearls, Suttree has a romance with the oldest daughter, a girl named Wanda. Although Suttree is ashamed by his consuming lust for her, their relationship is the closest to a loving understanding that he has. When Wanda is killed by an avalanche of slate rock, Suttree once again returns to his isolated, self-enclosed world.

Suttree, however, is always surrounded by a large and intriguing cast of minor characters, ranging from the denizens of McAnally Flat, to the river family, to his own relatives, whom he visits on occasion. It is McCarthy's great achievement that he makes these characters seem real and distinct. In this novel, he creates and populates an original world, much as did Herman Melville in *Moby Dick* (1851), James Joyce in *Ulysses* (1922), and William Faulkner in *The Hamlet* (1940).

Themes and Meanings

Suttree is McCarthy's most complete study of the fugitive, the outcast suffering from a spiritual sickness that consumes his soul. McCarthy expresses this kind of isolation through a father-son motif that runs throughout his books. Suttree has broken contact with his father and has abandoned his own child. In McAnally Flats he has adopted others to fill these roles: the old ragpicker and, to an extent, Harrogate. Yet these relationships are poor substitutes at best. In a moment of rare candor after his son's funeral, when the sheriff has come to escort him out of town, Suttree tells the man, "No one cares. It's not important." "That's where you're wrong my friend," the sheriff answers. "Everything's important. A man lives his life, he has to make that important. Whether he's a small town county sheriff or the president. Or a busted out bum. You might even understand that some day. I don't say you will. You might."

By the end of the novel, Suttree has come to understand the importance of life and responsibility. The "water boy" who gives him a drink may well be his son in an act of forgiveness; the act of giving may be seen as a promise of grace. Indeed, there is a mystical quality to this final scene, as Suttree himself seems to disappear before the reader. The narrative voice shifts to first person, although it is not necessarily Suttree speaking. "Somewhere in the gray wood by the river is the huntsman and in the brooming corn and in the castellated press of cities," the voice says. "His work lies all wheres and his hounds tire not. I have seen them in a dream, slaverous and wild and their eyes crazed with ravening for souls in this world. Fly them."

Suttree does flee from the hound and the huntsman, but unlike Culla Holme in *Outer Dark* (1968) or Lester Ballad in *Child of God* (1974), there is hope for his eventual salvation. The corpse in his bed represents the death of one way of life. He has faced his past and seems ready to renew his existence in the world of the living.

Critical Context

McCarthy began work on *Suttree* early in his writing career, shortly after the publication of his first novel, *The Orchard Keeper*, in 1965. Although he put it aside to write two other shorter novels—*Outer Dark* and *Child of God*—it was clearly a story which challenged him, both in scale and in complexity. He drew heavily on his knowledge of Knoxville, where he grew up and attended school. Probably no other writer, not even Knoxville's native son James Agee, has better captured a sense of the city. *Suttree*'s realistic setting is in sharp contrast to the otherworldly atmospheres of his other novels, and the book reaffirms McCarthy's enormous and varied talents.

Suttree was critically recognized as a major work upon its publication, but, like McCarthy's other books, it was not a popular success. A densely textured novel, filled with rhetorical complexities and scenes of a disturbing and sometimes appalling nature, it was not a book to encourage easy admiration. Nevertheless, it remains a remarkable achievement, and a rewarding one for those willing to give the work the effort it deserves.

Bibliography
Aldrich, John W. "Cormac McCarthy's Bizarre Genius: A Reclusive Master of Language and the Picaresque, on a Roll." *The Atlantic Monthly* 274 (August, 1994): 89-97. Traces the evolution of McCarthy's fiction, from the publication of *Orchard Keeper* in 1965 to *All the Pretty Horses* in 1994. Offers brief analyses of *Outer Dark* and *Suttree*.
Arnold, Edwin T. "Blood and Grace: The Fiction of Cormac McCarthy." *Commonweal* 121 (November 4, 1994): 11-14. Arnold asserts that McCarthy's novels often explore the more negative aspects of the human condition in meaningful, religiously significant ways. He discusses several of McCarthy's works.
Arnold, Edwin T., and Diane C. Luce, eds. *Perspectives on Cormac McCarthy.* Jackson: University Press of Mississippi, 1993. This collection of ten essays explores the historical and philosophical influences on McCarthy's work, the moral center

that informs his writings, and the common themes of his fiction. Includes an extensive bibliography.

Jarret, Robert J. *Cormac McCarthy.* New York: Twayne, 1997. Jarret offers a detailed examination of all seven of McCarthy's works, including *Outer Dark* and *Suttree.*

Edwin T. Arnold

THE SWEET HEREAFTER

Author: Russell Banks (1940-   )
Type of plot: Psychological realism
Time of plot: The late 1980's
Locale: Sam Dent, New York
First published: 1991

Principal characters:
MITCHELL STEPHENS, a New York lawyer who specializes in
representing accident victims
NICHOLE BURNELL, a paralyzed teenage survivor of a school-bus
accident
BILLY ANSEL, a Vietnam veteran, widower, and father of twins killed in
the bus accident
DOLORES DRISCOLL, the bus driver who survives the accident, which
kills fourteen children

The Novel

The Sweet Hereafter dramatizes the emotional impact of a school-bus accident on
the injured survivors, the families of the victims, and the people of the small mountain
town of Sam Dent, New York. A multitude of lawsuits accuse everyone politically
connected with the town, the school board, or the school administration of responsibility for the accident, and the town of Sam Dent, initially united in its grief, is divided
by the litigation. In order to examine the cause of the accident, the author offers several perspectives of people directly involved with the accident.

Dolores Driscoll, the bus driver, says she that thought she saw a dog through the
snow-blinded windshield and swerved to avoid hitting it. How this slight movement
was sufficient to send the bus over a guardrail and down a steep incline until it rested
on a water-filled sandpit covered with thin ice is beyond her comprehension. Instead
of addressing the immediate circumstances, she relates her history of safe driving and
loving concern for each child boarding her bus. Influenced by her stroke-debilitated
husband, Dolores refuses to sue anyone.

The perspective of a grieving parent and the only witness of the accident is provided by Billy Ansel, who followed the bus every day to wave to his motherless children. However, deep in his thoughts, he noticed nothing different before the bus left
the road. Because of his Vietnam War experiences, Billy accepts death as inevitable;
therefore, he believes that no one was responsible for the accident. Believing the lawsuits are irrevocably dividing a formerly closeknit town, Billy urges the parents who
support one lawsuit—the Walkers, the Ottos, and the Burnells—to drop it so that healing can begin.

Another narrator, Mitchell Stephens, would seem to provide an outsider's objective
viewpoint, but his personal past and his professional interests as a lawyer soon obviate

that expectation. His expertise persuades some parents that greed is not the object of a civil suit; rather, the paying of damages will force those responsible to be more careful in the future and thus prevent repetition of accidents and further loss of life. Stephens blames contemporary society as a whole both for the bus accident and for his own daughter's drug addiction.

Beautiful, talented, fourteen-year-old Nichole Burnell, a paralyzed survivor of the crash, seems to be the most obvious victim and the one most in need of money to provide for her medical expenses. Although her father seems to dote on her, providing a ramp and a first-floor bedroom to facilitate her movement, flashbacks reveal his sexual abuse. Overhearing the respected Billy Ansel begging her parents to drop the lawsuit and feeling that her own family has also been divided by it, Nicole at her deposition falsely testifies that Dolores was speeding at 70 miles an hour at the time of the accident. Her testimony destroys any case against the state and school board.

Dolores Driscoll, unaware of Nichole's damaging false testimony, takes her invalid husband to the Demolition Derby held at the County Fair. The neighbors of a lifetime turn away from her and refuse to help her with the wheelchair. She learns about Nichole's deposition from a drunken Billy Ansel. However, when the car she formerly owned wins the competition, the townspeople respond positively and express their momentary forgiveness by carrying her husband down the steps. Although both victims and survivors of this tragic accident will live forever in the "sweet hereafter" of their shared grief, the author offers a brief reconciliation via the battered car's symbolic resurrection.

The Characters

Russell Banks makes characterization central to his theme in his examination of the impact of a trauma on the lives of ordinary people. Expressed in the first-person point of view, each narrative begins with a statement that immediately strikes a tone offering an important insight into the speaker's character. By using parallel treatment of the characters, the author highlights their differences, differences that explain—at least to the reader, if not to the other characters—their different reactions to the tragedy of the bus accident and their decisions either to support or reject the lawsuit.

Dolores Driscoll, the bus driver, begins, "A dog—it was a dog I saw for certain. Or thought I saw." The bewildered, anxious tone established by these contradictory words is continued throughout what sounds like a response to an interviewer's questions. The interviewer, though, is Dolores's conscience, responding to her own anxiety and to what she knows others must be thinking: that her negligence caused the accident. She provides a personal history of loving care for others: her sons, her invalid husband, the children on her bus. However, her last words describe the bus accident as she experienced it. Regardless of her refusal to accept responsibility for the accident, Dolores knows that fourteen children died in a bus she was driving.

Billy Ansel, a Vietnam veteran, a widower, the father of twins killed in the accident, and the only person to witness the accident as it occurred, believes it to have been unpreventable; he is angry with anyone who offers reasons for the accident, especially anyone who is pursuing a lawsuit. However, his description of himself as the strong, silent type is undermined by his withdrawal from society to drink.

Mitchell Stephens, the cynical, successful New York lawyer, has an angry tone that expresses his professional viewpoint: Someone has to pay for the pain suffered in life. Flashbacks to his own daughter's childhood are punctuated by her drug-addicted urgent pleas for money, explaining his feeling that the physical loss of a child may not be more difficult than the spiritual loss of one.

Nichole Burnell, the paralyzed teenaged survivor, introduces her account with an ironic statement: "The mind is kind, Dr. Robeson told me. . . ." The statement is ironic because while the doctor is referring to her inability to remember anything about the bus accident, her mind is obsessed with the memory of her father's frequent past sexual abuse. This ironic tone is maintained when, during a deposition to support her parents' lawsuit, she pretends to remember the cause of the accident. Even though Nichole knows that she is hurting her own financial future by undermining the lawsuit, she prefers vengeance against her father; he realizes her motive too late.

Themes and Meanings

Although *The Sweet Hereafter* is obviously exploring the various ways people deal with catastrophic loss, the novel is ultimately pursuing the universal questions underlying tragedy: Why did this accident happen? Who is responsible? If there are no answers to these questions, the world of cause and effect, of order and meaning, is threatened.

Russell Banks proposes all the obvious reasons for the accident—budget-driven civil officials and school board, a speeding bus driver, negligent bus maintenance— and then, through the various characters' accounts, eliminates them as causes. If there is a culprit, it is life itself.

Another effect achieved by the use of multiple narrators to tell the story of the impact of the accident on their lives and on the rest of the town is to heighten the reader's awareness of the inviolable nature of the individual. Indeed, after listening to their voices, the reader becomes aware of the reason for the lack of objective data in relating their view of the accident: The psychological histories of the narrators preclude objectivity.

The fourth narrator, the lawyer Mitchell Stephens, is the catalyst that tries to force those involved in the accident (bus driver, parents, child victim) to turn their anger and confusion into a force by pursuing a lawsuit.

The author softens the somewhat depressing themes and content of this novel by entitling the work *The Sweet Hereafter.* After being shunned by the townspeople and then cheered, Dolores Driscoll expresses the theme of trauma when she says: "All of us—Nichole, I, the children who survived the accident, and the children who didn't—it was as if we were the citizens of a wholly different town now, as if we were a town of solitaries living in a sweet hereafter. . . ."

The use of the metaphor of the Demolition Derby to inspire a change in the townspeople's feelings about the accused culprit, Dolores Driscoll, highlights the irrational behavior of people. On the other hand, the incident briefly restores the reader's confidence that people can love more quickly than they can hate.

Critical Context

Russell Banks's early postmodern novels—*Family Life* (1975) and *Hamilton Stark* (1978)—were followed by somewhat more conventional realistic ones, although *The Book of Jamaica* (1980) and *The Relation of My Imprisonment* (1983) continued to experiment with point of view and open endings. Although these early works received respectful critical reviews, they failed to attract the general readership. *Continental Drift* (1985), a finalist for the Pulitzer Prize in 1986, marked a turning point in Banks's writing career. With this realistic work, he created the ordinary characters struggling to make something of their lives who have since then constituted his literary signature.

Although Russell Banks initially read about an actual accident involving a school bus in the newspapers, these articles only provided a framework on which he could pursue some lifelong interests and themes. The child of a blue-collar family, the author personally experienced the difficult personal and economic challenges of the ordinary characters depicted in this work.

In an interview, Banks admitted to being "really interested in reinventing the narrator" because he believes the convention affords the writer a closeness to the characters and their stories that he does not otherwise have. This interest in experimenting with a narrator follows in the tradition initiated by Henry James, who believed the dramatic mode created by using a character's changing thoughts and feelings to be the most effective way of holding the reader's interest and providing psychological insights.

However, the central influence on Banks's theme that fate can be cruel regardless of a person's merits seems to be naturalism and its proto-authors—Theodore Dreiser, Frank Norris, and Stephen Crane.

Because these universal themes continue to challenge the human race, the artist in every generation must address them and express them in a style that will speak to the contemporary reader's sensibility. Both the critical and the general reader praise Russell Banks for fulfilling this need.

Bibliography
"All Lost Children." Review of *The Sweet Hereafter*, by Russell Banks. *Economist* 321, no. 7729 (October 19, 1991): 104. This review suggests the novel is concerned with both the physical loss of children in the accident and the moral loss of children's innocence represented by the drug-addicted daughter of the lawyer handling lawsuits against the civil authorities.
Banks, Russell. "The Search for Clarity: An Interview with Russell Banks." Interview by Trish Reeves. *New Letters* 53, no. 3 (Spring, 1987): 44-59. Banks remarks that although he does not see himself as a political activist, he tries to depict people of lower economic status as having as much complexity as the more affluent.
Cotter, James Finn. Review of *The Sweet Hereafter*, by Russell Banks. *America* 166, no. 15 (May 2, 1992): 391. Cotter asserts that the remote location and cold climate

of the town of Sam Dent mirror the lives of the townspeople after the bus crash.

Vandersee, Charles. "Russell Banks and the Great American Reader." *The Cresset* 53, no. 2 (December, 1989): 13-17. Although Vandersee is interpreting *Continental Drift* (1985) and *Affliction* (1989), his analysis of these two works clearly distinguishes Banks's overall artistic contributions to the American novel, for example, his historical approach linking the present with the past.

Wachtel, Chuck. "Character Witness." Review of *The Sweet Hereafter*, by Russell Banks. *The Nation* 253 (December 16, 1992): 786-788. As the title of his review suggests, Wachtel bases his evaluation of *Sweet Hereafter* on Banks's ability to create ordinary characters who are independent of literary models and social expectations.

Agnes A. Shields

SWEET WHISPERS, BROTHER RUSH

Author: Virginia Hamilton (1936-   )
Type of plot: Psychological realism
Time of plot: The 1970's
Locale: A large American city
First published: 1982

> *Principal characters:*
> TERESA PRATT (TREE), the protagonist, a sensitive fourteen-year-old
>   African American girl
> DABNEY PRATT (DAB), her mentally retarded brother
> VIOLA PRATT (MUH VY), their mother, a practical nurse
> BROTHER RUSH, Viola's dead brother
> CENITHIA PRICHERD, a homeless woman
> SILVESTER WILEY D. SMITH (SILVERSMITH), Muh Vy's business partner
>   and lover

The Novel

Sweet Whispers, Brother Rush is the story of a black girl in her early teens who must deal with poverty, isolation, overwhelming responsibility, disillusionment, and loss. That she survives and finally triumphs is the result of her own strength and, as she finally realizes, her mother's never-failing love for her.

Sweet Whispers, Brother Rush is divided into seventeen chapters. Although the novel is written in the third person, the voice throughout is that of the protagonist, Teresa Pratt. Sometimes she is identified as the narrator; often, however, the author presents Tree's thoughts in the first person or in fragmentary form. The matter of voice becomes particularly complex when, through the magic of the ghost Brother Rush, Tree travels into the past. Then she speaks and thinks as her own mother, a woman with two children, Tree and Dab, while at the same time never forgetting that she is really Tree, the fourteen-year-old observer. Though such segments demand close attention from the reader, they are essential to the plot; through these ventures into the past, Tree is led to important truths.

The book begins with Tree's falling in love at first sight with a well-dressed stranger she sees while she is walking home from school. Tree's life is not easy. She lives alone in a small apartment with her older brother Dabney, who is "slow" and often ill. Their mother Viola sometimes does not see her offspring for weeks at a time. Tree does not even know how to contact "Muh Vy" in case of an emergency, but has to hope that she will turn up when there is no food or money left. So far, Muh Vy always has.

Tree's glimpses of her "dude" serve to bring some excitement into a life of poverty, loneliness, and frightening responsibility. It is not until the stranger appears inside the Pratt apartment, standing inside a table, that Tree realizes that he is a benevolent ghost through whose auspices she can walk into the past. On her first journey, Tree sees the young woman her mother once was, and she discovers that the ghost is her mother's favorite brother. Just before Tree returns to the present, she sees Viola collapse after being informed that Brother Rush has been killed in an accident.

Obviously, Brother Rush is not just a creature of Tree's imagination. In the days that follow, Dabney also mentions being transported into Brother Rush's world, and Cenithia Pricherd, who is cleaning the apartment, sees the figure in the table so clearly that she falls into a dead faint.

On her ventures into the past, however, Tree is making some troubling discoveries. One is that her mother never loved Dabney but, in fact, abused him heartlessly. Another is that Brother Rush deliberately chose to die.

When Muh Vy appears, along with her likeable lover Silverster Wiley D. Smith, Tree is prepared to confront her mother with her knowledge. Muh Vy and Tree, however, have a more immediate problem: Dabney is desperately ill. After Muh Vy rushes him to a hospital, Tree gathers that Dab's illness is probably porphyria, which Viola knew had caused the deaths of her brothers and which is aggravated by the use of alcohol and drugs. When Dab dies, Tree blames her mother, and indeed Muh Vy admits that she had never even bothered to have Dab tested, much less to keep him away from the drugs that to some degree were responsible for killing him.

In the final section of the book, however, Tree comes to terms with her grief and with her anger. Silvester Smith's son Don helps her to accept the fact that all human beings are flawed—including her mother, who, despite her inability to love her son, does love Tree. While she misses Dab, Tree finds some consolation in his being freed from his misery. At the end of the novel, she looks forward to a future with new friends and a new family.

The Characters

Tree is the narrator, the protagonist, and, finally, the heroine of *Sweet Whispers, Brother Rush*. Tree voices almost all the opinions in the novel and describes every event from her perspective. Furthermore, Tree has many of the qualities one expects in a heroine. In a difficult situation, she displays intelligence, self-discipline, an admirable sense of responsibility, and a deep, uncomplaining love for both her difficult brother and her absent mother. Yet there is another side to Tree. When the homeless Cenithia Pricherd comes to clean up the apartment, Tree judges her harshly, summing her up as a lazy, greedy old woman. Clearly, in everyone except Dab, Tree expects perfection. Therefore, when she finds out the worst about her mother, she is at first unforgiving. Not until she learns to separate the sinner from the sin, to feel compassion for Muh Vy and for Cenithia, can Tree be considered a true heroine. Of all the characters in the novel, it is Tree who changes most drastically.

The alteration in Viola is less dramatic. While she does what she can to save Dabney, she cannot bring herself to love him. Yet she does love Tree enough to break the habit of a lifetime. When she admits that she abused Dabney and neglected both of her children, Muh Vy for once is facing facts instead of running away from them. She, too, has become a better person.

Unlike Tree and Muh Vy, most of the characters in *Sweet Whispers, Brother Rush* remain the same throughout the novel. As Tree learns more about others, however, her readers share her new perceptions of them. For example, Tree finds an explanation for Dab's increasingly erratic behavior, as well as an index to his pain, when she discovers that he is addicted to drugs. Similarly, when she sees Brother Rush throw himself out of the car, Tree realizes that the glittering "Numbers Man," who seemed so carefree, was actually suffering so much that he took refuge first in alcohol and eventually in suicide. Tree also discovers that Cenithia is not greedy but actually hungry and that she is not a ridiculous old woman but a person who is both brave and proud.

Unlike these characters, Silversmith and Don are exactly what they appear to be. From the moment Silversmith appears at the apartment door, Tree intuitively trusts the big man, who, she notices, is so careful not to misuse his physical strength. It is evident that he loves Muh Vy; it is also evident that there is room in his generous heart for her daughter. Silversmith's function in the novel is twofold. By joining with Muh Vy to make Tree's life better, he assumes the role of the father for whom Tree has yearned and thus makes it possible for the book to end on a hopeful note. At the same time, the qualities united in his nature—strength and tenderness, respect for others and a sense of responsibility—make him a paradigm.

Don Smith, too, is important to both plot and theme. At Dab's funeral, when Silversmith is preoccupied with Muh Vy, it is Don who moves to console Tree, thus establishing a friendship that enables her to move out of her isolation. In addition, Don can be seen as a model for other young black men. The boys on the street corner, and even Tree's beloved Dabney, see girls as sexual prey, to be used and thrown away. In contrast, as he proves when he takes Tree on her first date, Don sees them as fellow human beings. Thus, like his father, Don is presented as an ideal.

Themes and Meanings

Sweet Whispers, Brother Rush is a story about growing up. Although Tree's situation is unusual, her uncertainties are not. Like all girls of her age, she is troubled about relationships with parents, with siblings, and with the opposite sex. In her parents' absence, she yearns to be part of a real family; when her mother is revealed as less than perfect, however, Tree distances herself and rejects Muh Vy's love. Similarly, while she has always made allowances for her brother, Tree is not happy about his sexual promiscuity, which seems no different from the behavior of the boys on the street corner, whose catcalls somehow make her ashamed of her own gender.

What makes this story so different from most young adult novels is that instead of rebelling against the standards she has been taught, the protagonist clings to them too rigidly. In the process of growing up, Tree must learn to temper two good qualities she possesses, her capacity for devoted love and her strong sense of resonsibility, with compassion for those who are deficient in those virtues. It is easy to idealize an absent mother; it is more difficult to forgive one who is present, admitting what seem like unforgivable faults. Fortunately, Tree already has some experience in accepting imperfection; what she must learn is to extend the tolerance she displays in her relationship with Dabney to others, like her mother, who are not so obviously flawed.

Finally, *Sweet Whispers, Brother Rush* emphasizes the importance of dealing honestly with the past. After Muh Vy's rejection and mistreatment of Dabney is revealed, it is obvious to the reader, though perhaps not yet to Tree, that Muh Vy's feelings of guilt are the reason she sees her children so infrequently, just as her habit of denial is the reason she has suppressed her memories of her brothers' deaths. It is interesting that the past, in the person of Brother Rush, chooses to approach Tree, rather than Muh Vy herself. One might say that, after all, this is a young adult novel, with a young adult protagonist. Yet it is more significant that by having Viola redeemed through her daughter, Virginia Hamilton has expanded the theme of responsibility. It is not just the obviously afflicted who merit concern, she suggests; everyone in a society or in a family has an obligation to everyone else.

Critical Context

Few writers for young readers are better know than Virginia Hamilton, who for decades has been delighting her public as well as winning high praise from critics. Among her many successful books are *The Planet of Junior Brown* (1971), a finalist for the National Book Award and a Newbery Honor Book, and her best-known novel, *M. C. Higgins, the Great* (1974), which won both the National Book Award and the Newbery Medal. After completing *The Gathering* (1981), the third work in a science-fiction trilogy, Hamilton returned to realism with *Sweet Whispers, Brother Rush*, another Newbery Honor Book.

While she writes in a genre that has fixed conventions—for example, the absence or the relative unimportance of parents, the focus on a young protagonist who functions as a savior, and the inevitable happy ending—Hamilton is not enslaved by custom. She places her characters in unusual situations; one thinks of M. C. Higgins, perched on a bicycle at the top of a pole, keeping watch over his mountain domain; of the time-travelers in *The Gathering* who are trying to rescue an unhappy computer; and of Tree, walking through Brother Rush's mirror into another world. Hamilton avoids the use of stock characters as religiously as she eschews humdrum plots. Each of her characters is distinctive, and many of them are memorable, in part because Hamilton often has them reveal their thoughts in poetic language, reflecting the rhythms of black dialect. Critics agree, however, that it is not her technical skill but her powerful imagination that keeps Virginia Hamilton at the top of her genre.

Bibliography
Farrell, Kirby. "Virginia Hamilton's *Sweet Whispers, Brother Rush* and the Case for a Radical Existential Criticism." *Contemporary Literature* 31, no. 2 (Summer, 1990): 161-176. A detailed analysis from a psychological perspective. Farrell argues that the novel has the same appeal as popular romances. By minimizing the protagonist's mother and killing off all the black males except two unrealistic, idealized characters, the author fulfills the fantasies of young black female readers.

Guy, David. "Escaping from a World of Troubles." *The Washington Post Book World*, November 7, 1982, pp. 14. A lucid explanation of the ghost's significance in Hamilton's work. While the reviewer notes the effectiveness of this device, he believes that the formula of the young adult novel prevents the author from expressing her profoundest visions. Comments on her use of black dialect, which, though realistic, may confuse some readers.

Hamilton, Virginia. "Talking with Virginia Hamilton." Interview by Yolanda Robinson Coles. *American Visions* 10 (December/January, 1995): 31-32. Hamilton credits her family as being the main source of her stories and storytelling skills. In this interview she compares her calling as a storyteller to the griot's role in African American culture. This interview provides valuable insight into her work as a whole.

Heins, Ethel L. Review of *Sweet Whispers, Brother Rush*, by Virginia Hamilton. *Horn Book Magazine* 58, no. 5 (October, 1982): 505-506. Despite occasional "lapses into obscurity," Heins comments, Hamilton is a superb writer, "daring, inventive, and challenging to read." With characteristic deftness, she creates a believable ghost, whom she then uses to reveal past history. The reviewer praises Hamilton for creating characters who are "complex, contradictory, and ambivalent."

Mikkelsen, Nina. *Virginia Hamilton*. New York: Twayne, 1994. In this first book-length study of Hamilton's work, Mikkelsen presents a biographical portrait of Hamilton, and then proceeds to analyze her fiction, biographies, folklore collections, and fantasy. In-depth literary criticism of each of Hamilton's books is offered, including *Sweet Whispers, Brother Rush*.

Paterson, Katherine. "Family Visions." *The New York Times Book Review*, November 14, 1982, pp. 41, 56. Asserts that unlike some of Hamilton's other novels, this book catches a reader's attention from the very first and keeps it to the last page. Paterson also remarks on the "unique black light" that Hamilton casts upon such conventional subjects of young adult fiction as the quest for identity, the perils of membership in a family, and the death of a loved one.

Trites, Roberta Seelinger. "'I Double Never Ever Never Lie to My Children': Inside People in Virginia Hamilton's Narratives." *African American Review* 32 (Spring, 1998): 146-155. Discusses the racial issues that lie at the heart of Hamilton's books, especially how those issues relate to the impact of exclusion and inclusion in society at large. Hamilton acknowledges the influence of the Black Power movement and Malcolm X on her books, reflecting the importance of African American culture on American history.

Rosemary M. Canfield Reisman

THE SYSTEM OF DANTE'S HELL

Author: Amiri Baraka (Everett LeRoi Jones; 1934-   )
Type of plot: Autobiographical fiction
Time of plot: The indistinguishable past and present
Locale: The literal Inferno of the Ghetto, the psychological Hell of the narrator's experience
First published: 1965

Principal character:
THE NARRATOR, the author's persona

The Novel

The System of Dante's Hell is a loosely arranged prose poem, autobiographical insofar as it presents projections drawn from its author's experiences. Baraka chooses to call it "Dante's Hell" because he believes that what has caused him to "sin," what has enchained his spirit, derives essentially from the Western intellectual and artistic tradition in which he received his education. These have left him somewhere between black and white cultures, accepted by neither and estranged from both.

Western culture attracts him intellectually, yet it morally damns him. The inscription on his Hell's Gate is, therefore, appropriate: "You love these demons and will not abandon them," a counterpoint to Dante's "Abandon all hope, you who enter here." Baraka abandons as well the structure of Dante's first canto, shifting the order of Dante's circles, redefining the sins of Dante's poem, and breaking away for "fast narratives" when it suits his purpose. *The System of Dante's Hell,* accordingly, owes only nominal homage to Dante's *Inferno.*

It is Baraka's fear that he subconsciously enjoys his "damnation," which drives him away from structured narrative. The "anarchy" of his text matches the frenzy that he feels. He begins by questioning what most would consider self-evident, asking for any gesture which can prove to himself his own existence. He desires only the ability to move and perceive his own movement. In this he resembles John Milton's fallen angels in *Paradise Lost.* Like these (though unlike the pilgrim Dante) he is incapable of true contrition, primarily because he views his sins as not of his own making. He clings to the habits which have brought him pain, and though he desires goodness, he feels only self-disgust: "I am left only with my small words . . . against the day. Against you. Against. My self." He indicts those he has loved, those who have "seduced" him with words: James Joyce, Marcel Proust, T. S. Eliot, William Butler Yeats, Ezra Pound, e. e. cummings, William Carlos Williams, and Dante.

Disjointed narrative and fractured syntax become an attempt to escape Western literary conventions; these are deliberately antiliterary rather than his personal adaptation of "stream of consciousness." He says that his gift with words allowed him to share early the street-corner jiving of the "bigboys" on his block. The "bigboys," how-

ever, did not understand the nuances of his language. They appreciated only the pro-
fanity.

Even so, his desire for Western intellectuality makes him at once the seducer and
the seduced. A good example of this appears in the eighth ditch of *The System of
Dante's Hell*, that of the fraudulent counselors. Here, "46," a "smooth faced" black
youth, meets his literally opposite number, "64." In this dialogue, a homosexual seduction, the youth sucks the "thots" of the elder, who identifies himself as "The
Street." Soon "46" sells his body (what he values least) for the intellectual wares that
"64" offers. Moral and intellectual isolation and bodily and intellectual violence make
the narrator a self-torturer (ironically like Arthur Rimbaud or Charles Baudelaire),
one whose punishment forever requires him to repeat his sin.

The rugged "journey" in this eventually leads the Narrator to "The Bottom," a place
of "wordless energies . . . where the colored lived." This is the region of the heretics,
the sinners that Baraka considers the most unredeemed. Even here, the Narrator is
torn between black and white worlds. In this "fast narrative," the Narrator, stationed at
a Louisiana Air Force base, travels to a red-light district. His guide (his "Vergil") is an
Air Force buddy who has been there before. The Narrator feels simultaneously attracted and repelled by the noise, the common atmosphere, and by Peaches, a prostitute who continues his "education."

After spending the night with Peaches, acceptance of those who live in "The Bottom" pleases him; even so, the Narrator can hardly wait to return to his white, Air
Force world. He leaves so hurriedly that he forgets (perhaps on purpose) his uniform
cap. Here, then, is his dilemma; the Narrator finds himself caught between two hells,
unable to achieve the release which will allow him to mediate between his Eliot-like
"wasteland" and his stereotyped vision of the black world, one of violence and promiscuous sexuality. He remains "the unseen object, and, the constantly observed
subject."

The Characters

The characters of *The System of Dante's Hell* are basically types or projections of
the author's experience. They float in and out of the narrative, rarely with any delineation, except insofar as they contribute to the Narrator's self-portrait. Sometimes the
associations that they hold for Baraka are intensely personal, but the Narrator does not
feel obliged to share these associations with his readers. For example, "powell" is a
lawyer, "pinckney" a teacher. Does Baraka intend references to leaders of the black
community? Does he desire to disparage them or their professions by spelling their
names with the lowercase? Why does he consider simply naming their professions
sufficient character description? There is no certain way to answer any of these
questions.

Sometimes the persons mentioned form a kind of syllogism. For example, Baraka's
definition of "PROSPEROUS" (Baraka uses uppercase) is Dolores Morgan, who had
had an illegitimate child. Calvin Lewis is the incarnation of "PRIDE" because he
"gave it to her." "Michael" is the result, at a beach in the warm tide. It is impossible to

analyze such characters since they are the author's typology, foils for presenting the Narrator. Accordingly, the cumulative effect of such passages is to suggest the Narrator's point of view rather than to provide a more traditional "narrative point of view." They indicate the Narrator's way of thinking rather than explicating his thoughts.

After seven circles of such characterizations, the novel becomes more traditionally narrative with the "DRAMA" of "46" and "64" discussed above. The seduction that the "DRAMA" presents describes the Narrator's severed personality. It is both literal homosexual seduction and "seduction by language." Two "fast narratives" follow. In the first, called "The Rape," the Narrator and a group of middle-class black youths that he leads decide to kidnap and rape a worn and drunken black woman who happens by. The Narrator does not really want to carry this through, but he wishes to prove his worthiness to lead. When the woman tells the youths that she has venereal disease, they toss her from the moving car. The Narrator's warring personality emerges again here as does the theme of self-directed black violence. Peaches and the Air Force buddy, who appear in the "fast narrative" which follows, remain types, though they are more detailed because of the more extended narrative in which they appear.

Themes and Meanings

The principal theme of *The System of Dante's Hell* is the quandary of the black intellectual educated according to Western values and traditions. Baraka believes that such a person finds himself in a hell not of his own making, one of middle-class values which estrange him from his origins and make him an imitation white. Such an individual can be articulate by white standards, even brilliant, but he loses his black heritage as a result. He stands between two worlds which he simultaneously loves and hates, a hated curiosity to both.

As a vehicle for its theme, the novel's first half abandons traditional narrative and substitutes a series of disjointed reflections, impressionistic and intentionally neither completely in "black English" nor in "white" stream of consciousness. To have preferred either would have undercut Baraka's thesis that his Narrator is caught between two worlds. Baraka's spelling, capitalization, and syntax remain absolutely his own.

Baraka preserves Dante's gyres, the circles which contain the various sins that his Narrator sees. While some of these are Dante's classifications ("THE INCONTI-NENT: Lasciviousness," "The Diviners," "Thieves"), those who inhabit these circles are condemned by Baraka's (or the Narrator's) judgment, not that of Minos. Moreover, he feels no obligation to maintain the order of Dante's classifications. He tells the reader that his own heretics belong at the lowest of the circles, logically, for these have been unfaithful to their own origins.

Critical Context

The System of Dante's Hell appeared under the author's given (Baraka would say "slave") name, Everett LeRoi Jones. This is significant, since Baraka's adoption of a

Muslim name just a year later, in 1966, represents one way in which the author has attempted to deal with the difficulty that his novel presents but never resolves. Baraka chose his new name carefully. Imamu signifies a Muslim poet-priest; an honorific title rather than a name per se, it implies that artistic creation is concomitantly a religious act. (Baraka subsequently dropped this title.) Amiri implies a warrior-leader and transcends the "slave name" Jones. Baraka is a gift or blessing—in the author's case, a conversion from his intellectual Western and Christian background to another intellectual and religious tradition, Eastern and Muslim. His name change therefore implies that Baraka had continued to deal with and, at least on one level, resolve the problem his Narrator considers unsolvable.

Baraka's novel drew considerable fire from critics upon publication. Most considered it largely unreadable; others gave cautious approval to the "fast narratives." Even so, the book exists, not for its readers, but for its author. It is a work that Baraka had to write, one from the depths of his experience. Though it may seem to its readers at times offensive or outrageous, it is the work of a profoundly original mind, of a man who has seen "the dark night of the soul" and survived.

Bibliography
Baraka, Imamu Amiri. *The Autobiography of Leroi Jones*. Rev. ed. Chicago: Lawrence Hill Books, 1997. Baraka updates and restores the original text of his autobiography, which recounts his life, political transformations, and writing career. Valuable insights into the influence of the Beats and the Black Arts movement on Baraka's writing as well as an overview of his social and political views.
Benston, Kimberly W., ed. *Imamu Amiri Baraka (LeRoi Jones): A Collection of Critical Essays*. Englewood Cliffs, N.J.: Prentice-Hall, 1978. Critical and interpretive essays on Baraka's novel, his poems, and his plays.
Brown, Lloyd W. *Amiri Baraka*. Boston: Twayne, 1980. Brown provides a critical and interpretive study of Baraka, with a close reading of his major works, a solid bibliography, and complete notes and references.
Dieke, Ikenna. "Tragic Faith and the Dionysian Unconscious: An Interfacing of Novelist Baraka and Friedrich Nietzsche." *Black American Literature Forum* 24 (Spring, 1990): 99-116. Dieke explores the convergence of Nietzsche's metaphysical thought and Baraka's voluntaristic vision in *The System of Dante's Hell*. Dieke concludes that for Baraka and Nietzsche, the final goal of life is not attained through the abolition of striving and suffering, but through its overcoming.
Draper, James P., ed. *Black Literature Criticism*. 3 vols. Detroit: Gale Research, 1992. Includes an extensive biographical profile of Baraka and excerpts from criticism on his works.
Reilly, Charlie, ed. *Conversations with Amiri Baraka*. Jackson: University Press of Mississippi, 1994. A collection of interviews with Baraka by various interviewers, including Maya Angelou and David Frost. The interviews chronicle Baraka's evolving political views over three decades and include many references to his literary career and to his individual works.

Woodard, Komozi. *A Nation Within a Nation: Imamu Amiri Baraka, the Dynamics of Cultural Nationalism, and the Politics of Black Power, 1966-1976*. Chapel Hill: University of North Carolina Press, 1999. Although this book focuses on Baraka's political involvement and commitment to black nationalism, Woodard's study is useful in understanding how Baraka's urban politics inform his career as a poet and novelist.

Robert J. Forman

TAR BABY

Author: Toni Morrison (Chloe Anthony Wofford, 1931-   )
Type of plot: Social realism
Time of plot: The 1970's
Locale: The Caribbean, New York City, and Florida
First published: 1981

   Principal characters:
      WILLIAM "SON" GREEN, an uneducated African American man
      JADINE "JADE" CHILDS, a well-educated African American model
      VALERIAN STREET, a retired white businessman
      MARGARET STREET, Valerian's wife
      SYDNEY CHILDS, Jade's uncle, the Streets' butler
      ONDINE CHILDS, Jade's aunt, the Streets' cook

The Novel

   The tar baby in Morrison's title is Jade, an intelligent black woman, orphaned and Paris-educated, who at twenty-five stands poised between two worlds. The world into which she was born is that of her aunt and uncle, Sydney and Ondine Childs, servants to the affluent Streets. Impressed by Jade's unique abilities, the Streets have provided the wherewithal for her to study art history at the Sorbonne. Jade functions socially both in the world of the Streets and the world of the Childses.

   Tar Baby, a polemical novel, projects Jade's two worlds effectively. Although legitimately a member of each world, Jade sometimes wishes that race were not a part of her social context. She wants to be accepted for the person she is inside. Much of the book is—on the surface, at least—concerned with Jade's attempts to establish her identity.

   Isle des Chevaliers, the Caribbean island on which most of the novel is set, is a mystical place named for a shipload of legendary blacks who were struck blind at their first sight of the island. They were not sold into slavery, as had originally been intended, but were left to wander the island, as their descendants still do. The setting is idyllic yet ominous; spirits lurk in the deep jungle foliage.

   Valerian Street and his wife, Margaret, a former beauty queen two decades his junior, came to the island from Philadelphia. Valerian has retired from his lucrative candy manufacturing business. Their faithful servants, Sydney and Ondine Childs, accompanied them to Isle des Chevaliers, Sydney as butler, Ondine as cook. The two, however, are not enthralled at being separated from their roots. Sydney dreams often of his native Baltimore. The Childses are exemplary servants. Their relationship is warm and touching.

   Into this harmonious setting comes Son, the protagonist, a street-savvy black who has fled the United States after murdering a woman. Son, homesick and disheartened, sneaks off his ship shortly before Christmas and is borne by the currents to Isle des Chevaliers. He steals food from the Streets' kitchen.

When Son is caught, Valerian, rather than having him arrested, invites Son to eat at his table, where Jade and Son interact uncertainly. Son is not Jade's kind of black. To begin with, his skin is much darker than hers. He is unschooled. He believes that whites and blacks can work together, but—reflecting attitudes Morrison's own father possessed—he clearly thinks that blacks and whites should not eat, live, or sleep together.

Son and Jade become antagonistic to each other. Each obviously sees in the other something magnetically attractive yet inherently threatening. Their mutual attraction, however, prevails, and soon the two are openly enamored of each other.

Jade perceives her primitive roots in Son—what Morrison elsewhere calls the "true and ancient properties" of her race. Jade is to Son the fulfillment of his dreams, the tar baby that attracts him hypnotically but that can trap and destroy him utterly.

Shortly after Christmas, Son and Jade go to New York, where they cohabit for several months. They then journey to Florida, where Son was reared. During this trip, Jade realizes that she cannot be Son's "woman" in the dominating way he demands. Son knows he cannot accommodate Jade's way of life, where color lines are muted, where black and white commingle on equal terms.

Son pursues Jade when she returns to Isle des Chevaliers. In the novel's epilogue, however, Son is on the far side of the island, stumbling in the overgrown foliage, seeking the blind horsemen, the distant progeny of the original black settlers, who will help him renew his roots and escape the charms of the tar baby who has nearly robbed him of his manhood and ethnicity.

In the end, Valerian Street's way of life is eroded when he learns that his wife has abused their child, a secret Ondine has kept from Valerian and Sydney for many years. Sydney and Ondine essentially take control of l'Arbe de la Croix, Valerian's ironically named, idyllic estate, upon which the unrelenting tropical jungle encroaches steadily.

The Characters

Valerian Street, a good businessman who grew rich in the competitive world of manufacturing, married Margaret, recently crowned Miss Maine, when he was in his mid-thirties. Margaret was more a trophy than a wife. Valerian, more liberal and sensitive than the stereotypical cigar-chomping American businessman, accepts his servants' orphaned niece as a surrogate daughter. Valerian, however, does not realize that some blacks toward whom he directs his liberalism—notably Son and Sydney—do not share his egalitarian views of race and class. In the end, Sydney is more the master of l'Arbe de la Croix than Valerian can be; Son, having made his statement, flees the socially disordered household he has disrupted.

Margaret Street married too young. Her youth and beauty attracted Valerian and her major effort now is to preserve the fast-fading youth and beauty that first made her attractive to him. It is a losing battle. Margaret is terrified of Son, probably because he represents a smoldering, primitive sexual force that simultaneously attracts and repels her. Margaret apparently has no society outside her life with Valerian. She tried early in their marriage to establish a social equality, a camaraderie, between herself and Ondine, but Valerian discouraged it.

Sydney Childs has pride and dignity. He loves his wife deeply and touchingly. He massages her throbbing feet, but refuses to wear slippers when his bunions ache because he considers himself a first-rate butler who cannot be first-rate in slippers. Sydney is reminiscent of the title character in James Barrie's *The Admirable Crichton* (1902), the resourceful, highly competent butler, capable of taking over but—understanding class distinctions—willing to only when dire necessity makes it unavoidable.

Ondine Childs demonstrates the special bond that exists among women. She is Margaret's confidante, a role in which she proves herself completely trustworthy. She has not shared Margaret's darkest secret with anyone, including her husband. Ondine is the quintessential black matriarch. She and Sydney are, in essence, more capable of running l'Arbe de la Croix than the Streets are. Race, class, and gender are the major factors that keep Ondine in the kitchen for most of her life rather than in the drawing room, where, given Jade's opportunities, she might have landed. Ondine, like her husband, has inherent dignity and native intelligence.

Jadine Childs exemplifies the new black. Well-educated, refined, intelligent, upwardly mobile, the twenty-five-year-old Jade holds the world in the palm of her hand. She wants to overcome her blackness not because she is ashamed of it but because she believes that race is not a relevant factor in determining the worth of people. Her own accomplishments bespeak her contention. Jade, nevertheless, is drawn to the unschooled, primitive Son, who represents the pulsating call of the ancestral past.

Morrison's father might well have been the inspiration for Son's father. In racial matters, Son thinks the way Morrison's father thought. He distrusts whites and believes in the separation of the races. Son's attraction to Jade is perhaps based psychologically upon his desire to tame her, to return her to her racial roots. Jade attracts Son physically, but more as an object to be controlled and tamed than as someone with whom to share his life.

Two minor characters are also significant: Gideon, the yardman, and Thérèsa, the partially blind maid, both of whom function as a sort of chorus. Although free, they are treated like chattel—ostensibly free, but slaves nevertheless.

Themes and Meanings

In *Tar Baby*, Morrison broaches the most pressing human conflicts in American society: rich versus poor, male versus female, black versus white, primitive versus civilized, old versus young. Most of the novel evolves against a backdrop of a primitive jungle that must be trimmed constantly to keep it from encroaching on and ultimately consuming the cultivated enclave the Streets occupy.

Morrison uses her characters to represent a similar conflict. Son represents the primitive, Jade the cultivated. Morrison's question is more whether the primitive should be tamed than whether it can be tamed. Her question is an essential one that goes beyond matters of race. It causes one to question how thick and durable is the socially accepted veneer of cultivation that defines society. The jungle, left unchecked, will reclaim everything in its path.

Morrison also considers the theme of ultimate worth. The Streets are richer than the Childses and are acceptable in venues where the Childses dare not tread, but are they better than their servants? Jade, left unattended, could have led the life her aunt and uncle led. She could have spent her life in a kitchen preparing meals for white people. Given Jade's opportunities, could not Sydney and Ondine be the social equals of the Streets—or even their social superiors?

The Streets, by rescuing Jade from such a fate, prove that native ability, when nurtured, can bring people to high levels of accomplishment. The question remains, however, of whether someone like Jade can function in the environment that her accomplishments have finally won for her. She wishes that she could be judged by her inner self rather than by her pigmentation. In the end, however, it is unclear whether she judges herself according to her own criteria.

Morrison deals with the universality of human needs and emotions. She uses metaphors related to feet to reflect the similarities of all people: Son loses his shoes when he jumps ship; Sydney suffers from painful bunions, Valerian from aching corns; Sydney massages Ondine's sore feet as an act of love; Sydney refuses, because of professional pride, to wear slippers on the job; Jade returns to Paris wearing high-heeled boots. The human condition is universal, but as society is structured—perhaps immutably—inequalities exist: This is what Morrison implies by this metaphor.

Tar Baby is presented from multiple viewpoints. Every character represents an individual point of view, and the two minor characters, Gideon and Thérèsa, represent the perspective of the native inhabitants of Isle de Chevaliers. Using a multiple viewpoint enables Morrison to heighten the conflict on which *Tar Baby* focuses. The introduction of Gideon and Thérèsa allows Morrison to articulate points of view that none of the major characters can represent convincingly but that require airing—if for no other reason than to lend credibility to Son's final retreat into the briars.

Critical Context

Reared in Ohio, Toni Morrison was in her thirties when the race riots of the 1960's raged. By then, she held a bachelor's degree in English from Howard University and a master's degree from Cornell University, had taught at two universities, had married, had borne two sons, and had been divorced. By the end of the 1960's, she had taken a position as an editor at Random House. The events of the 1960's affected her deeply, even though she was not an activist.

Nevertheless, the social changes of the time had implications for all African Americans, causing Morrison to think hard about what it means to grow up black in America. Her first novel, *The Bluest Eye* (1970), is about a young black girl who longs to have blue eyes. Morrison's *Sula* (1973) and *Song of Solomon* (1977) explore some of the social problems Morrison pinpoints so sharply in *Tar Baby.*

Along with obvious matters of racial prejudice and stereotypes, Morrison's novels are concerned with black women's roles in male-dominated societies. Her works also focus on the social and economic questions of the poor in a society that is clearly affluent—one that is, paradoxically, equal yet glaringly unequal.

The social context of *Tar Baby* is enhanced by Morrison's choice of setting. Isle des Chevaliers is at once romantic and decadent, appealing and appalling, comfortable and terrifying, foreign and familiar. Despite its distance from the United States, this Caribbean island provides a microcosm that obviously represents the United States and that presents—often in exaggerated form—the most pressing social problems of Morrison's homeland.

Jade, in broad ways an autobiographical character, suggests many correspondences to Morrison's own life and to the adjustments she had to make as a member of a racial minority during a time of racial transition. Jade is, at least partially, on the road to becoming what Morrison became in society: a black woman, bright and educated, who could function well in the white world. Both have shaken loose their bonds of blackness in a segregated society and, by virtue of sheer intelligence and talent, have flourished in the broader social context. The inner conflicts that Jade experiences are conflicts with which Morrison had first-hand familiarity.

Bibliography

Aithal, S. Krishnamoorthy. "Getting Out of One's Skin and Being the Only Person Inside: Toni Morrison's *Tar Baby.*" *American Studies International* 34 (October, 1996): 76-85. Aithal asserts that Morrison's self-definition is radically different from the stereotype of the rest of the black community, and her novel helps blacks to relate to contradictory ideologies. Offering insight into both black and white identities, Morrison helps readers to empathize with her characters and suggests that the acceptance of black identity is a key to integrity.

Baker-Fletcher, Karen. "*Tar Baby* and Womanist Theology." *Theology Today* 50 (April, 1993): 29-37. Baker-Fletcher argues that Morrison's novel considers the theological anthropology of black womanhood in a way that supports a womanist theology of the community. Morrison depicts womanhood as a sacred and nurturing experience that links black women's strengths and weaknesses to a narrative based on African and African American experiences.

Bloom, Harold, ed. *Toni Morrison*. New York: Chelsea, 1990. This 247-page book has an introduction by its editor and extensive contributions from more than a dozen scholars of Morrison's work. The overall assessments are useful in placing Morrison within her literary context. The essays that deal directly with *Tar Baby* are thoughtful, sometimes profound.

Duvall, John N. "Descent on the *House of Chloe*: Race, Rape, and Undaunted in Toni Morrison's *Tar Baby.*" *Contemporary Literature* 38 (Summer, 1997): 325-349. Duvall acknowledges that *Tar Baby* is considered a marginal work in the context of Morrison's canon and receives less critical attention. Yet he argues that it is an important novel because it carries forward themes from her previous works. He explores the theme of feminine identity in the black community as portrayed by Morrison and suggests that the protagonist can become self-reliant by reconciling the conflicts between gender and racial identity.

McKay, Nellie Y., comp. *Critical Essays on Toni Morrison*. Boston: G. K. Hall, 1988. All the essays in this collection will be useful to readers interested in Morrison. Of particular note is Craig H. Werner's "The Briar Patch as Modernist Myth: Morrison, Barthes and *Tar Baby* As-Is." This piece considers Morrison in the light of modern critical theory.

Pereira, Malin W. "Be(e)ing and 'Truth': *Tar Baby*'s Signifying on Sylvia Plath's Bee Poems." *Twentieth Century Literature* 42 (Winter, 1996): 526-534. Pereira compares and contrasts the description of the life of a queen of soldier ants in Morrison's novel to the description of a queen bee from Plath's bee sequence in her poem "Ariel." Pereira contends that although the queen bee in Plath's poem has been interpreted as a symbol of the female self, Morrison's revision of Plath's queen bee reveals this self to be white, "constructed in part by the fear and repression of blackness."

R. Baird Shuman

TARZAN OF THE APES

Author: Edgar Rice Burroughs (1875-1950)
Type of plot: Adventure
Time of plot: 1888
Locale: Northwest Africa, Baltimore, and Wisconsin
First published: 1912 in *All-Story Magazine*; 1914 in book form

Principal characters:
> JOHN CLAYTON, LORD GREYSTOKE, an aspiring young English civil
> servant
> ALICE, his pregnant wife
> TARZAN, their son, reared from infancy by apes
> KALA, Tarzan's adoptive mother
> KERCHAK, king of the tribe of apes
> TERKOZ, a bullying ape
> JANE PORTER, a young American woman
> PROFESSOR ARCHIMEDES Q. PORTER, her father
> SAMUEL T. PHILANDER, Professor Porter's friend
> WILLIAM CECIL CLAYTON, heir apparent to Lord Greystoke
> LIEUTENANT PAUL D'ARNOT, a French naval officer
> ROBERT CANLER, Professor Porter's creditor

The Novel

Tarzan of the Apes was the first of twenty-four Tarzan novels that Edgar Rice Burroughs wrote over the course of three decades. Most of this introductory novel describes Tarzan's upbringing in a tribe of African apes and his self-education in written English, but it ends by telling a little of his entry into the world of civilized humankind.

The novel begins with a storyteller's disclaimer about having gotten the story from an unspecified man who had Colonial Office records to verify the tale. Burroughs then turns to third-person narration, first through the point of view of Tarzan's father, then largely through that of Tarzan himself.

John Clayton, Lord Greystoke, boards a ship for British West Africa with Alice, his bride. He saves a burly sailor from the brutal captain. When the crew mutinies, the grateful sailor makes sure that the Englishman and his wife are not killed, but he abandons them in a wilderness harbor with all of their luggage and a few supplies. The site has a river mouth for water, and John and Alice gather and hunt to live well after their supplies run out. Although not a tradesman, John builds and furnishes a log cabin with a clever door latch for protection against wild beasts. Their son is born there. A year later, Alice dies, and Clayton is killed by an ape, Kerchak.

Among the attacking apes is Kala, a female whose own baby has died. Finding the now-orphaned, hairless white baby, she takes it up as her own. After ten years, the relatively puny and slow Tarzan—"white ape" in their tongue—begins to mature in both body and brain. Although he knows nothing of his connection with the cabin, it fascinates him. When he discovers how to open the cabin latch, he finds many books, including a brightly illustrated alphabet. The "bugs" on the pages fascinate him, and in time he teaches himself to read them. He also finds a sharp hunting knife and, when a huge gorilla attacks him, he accidentally discovers the knife's usefulness. With it, he gains status as the tribe's greatest hunter and fighter, eventually becoming king of the tribe.

When a tribe of native humans migrates into the apes' territory and one of them kills Kala, Tarzan tracks him down and avenges his "mother." He goes on to harass and terrify the black tribe, as an unseen god who causes the disappearance of their arrow stockpiles, other items, and occasionally warriors.

Kingship curtails Tarzan's liberty. As his intelligence and knowledge grow, he drifts away from the apes. After fighting the bully Terkoz but sparing his life, the motherless Tarzan leaves the apes.

When a ship appears in the harbor, Tarzan gets his first sight of humans with white skin like his own. After the mutineers ransack the cabin, Tarzan writes a note warning against further harm: "Tarzan watches." They leave behind five passengers, including Jane Porter, and Tarzan almost immediately falls in love with her.

Unseen, Tarzan spears a sailor to save William Clayton's life. Later, he wrestles a lion to save Clayton again. Back at the cabin, he kills a lioness that is attacking Jane there. The oblivious Professor Archimedes Q. Porter and his friend Samuel T. Philander are lost in the jungle, stalked by another lion, and Tarzan saves them, too. Their savior had never before heard spoken English and thus cannot speak or understand it, so all believe he cannot be the "Tarzan" who had left the note.

Seeing the ship leave, Professor Porter laments the loss of the treasure chest for which he had mortgaged his estate. When the mutineers see a pursuing French ship, they return to shore and bury the treasure so they will not get caught with it. Tarzan alone sees this, digs up the chest, and reburies it elsewhere.

One day, Tarzan hears Jane's screams as Terkoz abducts her. He tracks them down and kills the ape. Jane falls in love with her rescuer. Meanwhile, the French patrol ship lands in the harbor. A French party searches for the missing Jane; meanwhile, Tarzan returns her to the cabin.

Native warriors capture and torture Lieutenant Paul d'Arnot, but Tarzan rescues him and nurses him back to health. After d'Arnot has tried speaking several languages to him, Tarzan fetches a pencil and writes an English message. He explains why he does not understand spoken human language; d'Arnot teaches him to speak his own language, French. Meanwhile, Professor Porter finds that the buried treasure is missing and decides to leave on the French ship. When Tarzan and d'Arnot return to the cabin, they find two notes from Jane, one explaining their plans and the other expounding her love for Tarzan.

With help from d'Arnot, Tarzan goes to America to find Jane. Robert Canler, Professor Porter's creditor, demands to marry Jane, but she puts him off. Tarzan suddenly arrives and rescues her from a forest fire; he then cows Canler and gives Professor Porter his treasure. Jane nevertheless agrees to marry William Clayton.

The Characters

The characters in *Tarzan of the Apes* are largely stereotypes of the elements found in any adventure story—action hero, villains, romantic heroine, romantic opposition, and comic distractions.

Tarzan, of course, is the principal action hero. He is much stronger than most men and more highly skilled as a fighter. These traits come naturally to one who grows up in a world in which survival requires him to make up for the differences between his body and those of the animals around him. He also exhibits great intelligence, inquisitiveness, and moral rectitude, and he uses these traits to overcome his physical inferiority among the jungle animals.

Villainy is well-distributed, providing an ever-changing set of challenges to his growing abilities. The child Tarzan has the apes Kerchak and Tublat to harry and torment him and his adoptive mother Kala. The adolescent Tarzan has the bully Terkoz to worry about. The newly independent Tarzan has to combat the natives who kill Kala and later torture d'Arnot. After being introduced to civilization, he has Canler to counter. Subsequent novels continue to provide him with scores of varied villains with which to contend.

There are two heroines, the ape Kala, who adopts Tarzan and protects him through the early years when he is puny and retarded relative to all the surrounding youngsters, and Jane, the romantic heroine for the last half of *Tarzan of the Apes* and the rest of the many Tarzan novels. William Clayton provides the honorable romantic opposition, while Professor Porter and Jane's servant are the comic distractions.

Themes and Meanings

Two important precursors of the Tarzan stories were the legend of Romulus and Remus, who were suckled by a she-wolf and later founded Rome, and the tale of the boy Mowgli, who is reared by wolves and taught by a bear in Rudyard Kipling's *The Jungle Book* (1894). Burroughs read the classics as a student, but he rarely read fiction as an adult. He wrote in 1931 that the Roman story had led him to wonder just what kind of person would develop "if the child of a highly civilized, intelligent, and cultured couple were to be raised by a wild beast" with no human interaction. He had often played with this idea.

Kipling published the Mowgli stories nearly twenty years before Burroughs invented Tarzan, and Burroughs noted, "The Mowgli theme is several years older than Mr. Kipling. It is older than books. Doubtless it is older than the first attempts of man to evolve a written language." Tarzan, Mowgli, and Romulus and Remus all explore the conflict of heredity and environment. Tarzan, especially, also compares the vices of destructive human civilization with the simpler honesty of animals. Burroughs liked to speculate on how heredity, environment, and training affected a child's mind, morals, and physique, so he spawned a child for whom the civilized environment was stripped away, heredity was strong, and the opportunity for self-training remained.

Throughout the book, Kipling reminds the reader of the heredity factor. When Tarzan kills his first lion and roars his animal roar, Burroughs tells readers, "And in London another Lord Greystoke was speaking to his kind in the House of Lords, but none trembled at the sound of his soft voice." Much later, with Jane, he performs

a stately and gallant little compliment . . . the hall-mark of aristocratic birth, the natural outcropping of many generations of fine breeding, an hereditary instinct of graciousness which a lifetime of uncouth and savage training and environment could not eradicate.

Tarzan constantly shows himself capable of learning and of using his new knowledge to improve his lot, from working the cabin latch to absorbing the nuances of civilization from d'Arnot.

Everywhere in the Tarzan series, readers see the theme of human greed, hypocrisy, and deceit versus the natural order and justice of the jungle. In *Tarzan of the Apes*, both sets of mutineering sailors are almost totally lacking in admirable qualities. "Perhaps I hoped to shame men into being more like beasts in those respects in which beasts excel men, and these are not few," Burroughs wrote.

All this is not to deny that a major part of Tarzan's appeal, both to the author and to readers, is simple escapism. As Burroughs said, the series was his own escape from unpleasant or humdrum reality.

Critical Context

Burroughs never visited Africa. Born in Chicago, he drifted through life as a U.S. cavalryman, Oregon gold miner, Idaho cowboy, Utah railway policeman, and small businessman. Inspired by writers such as H. Rider Haggard, he took up writing and sold the first "John Carter of Mars" serial to a magazine in 1911. He then conceived and sold another series about an Englishman reared by apes. These two series gave Burroughs a comfortable living for the rest of his life.

Burroughs sold his *Tarzan of the Apes* serial to a magazine in 1912, and two years later he sold it to a book publisher. He continued writing Tarzan stories, among others, until 1941. He was the first American writer to become a corporation; his San Fernando Valley ranch, Tarzana, became a town. More than twenty-five million Tarzan books have been sold in at least fifty-six languages.

Bibliography
Farmer, Philip José. *Tarzan Alive: A Definitive Biography of Lord Greystoke*. Garden City, N.Y.: Doubleday, 1972. A detailed biography of Tarzan as a real person, neatly explaining the series' inconsistencies. Includes a five-generation family tree relating Tarzan to Sherlock Holmes, the Scarlet Pimpernel, Doc Savage, Nero Wolfe, Lord Peter Wimsey, and Bulldog Drummond.
Fenton, Robert W. *The Big Swingers*. Englewood Cliffs, N.J.: Prentice-Hall, 1967. A somewhat superficial discussion of Burroughs and his stories.

Holtsmark, Erling B. *Tarzan and Tradition: Classical Myth in Popular Literature.* Westport, Conn.: Greenwood Press, 1981. Analyzes Burroughs's novels and their characters as deriving from the literary traditions of classical antiquity.

Lupoff, Richard A. *Edgar Rice Burroughs: Master of Adventure.* New York: Ace Books, 1968. A good study of the man who created Tarzan, John Carter, and other series.

Porges, Irwin. *Edgar Rice Burroughs: The Man Who Created Tarzan.* Provo, Utah: Brigham Young University Press, 1975. An extensive biography of Burroughs and analysis of his works, published on the hundredth anniversary of his birth. Includes many photographs of Burroughs, story drafts, magazine covers, and the maps and character lists that helped him to preserve continuity within his series.

Vidal, Gore. "Tarzan Revisited." *Esquire* 60, no. 6 (December, 1963): 193, 262, 264. Review and commentary on the Tarzan novels.

J. Edmund Rush

TATTOO THE WICKED CROSS

Author: Floyd Salas (1931-   )
Type of plot: Social realism
Time of plot: After World War II
Locale: Golden Gate Institute of Industry and Reform, a prison farm in California
First published: 1967

Principal characters:

AARON D'ARAGON, a fifteen-year-old boxer and gang leader sent to the boys' prison farm for fighting

BARNEYWAY, a former gang member and Aaron's good friend, also in prison

BUZZER, a large black youth who is brutal and vengeful

RATTLER, a follower of Buzzer

JUDITH, Aaron's girlfriend

BIG STOOP, a brutal giant, the commanding officer of the prison farm

THE PRISON CHAPLAIN, a Protestant minister

The Novel

Floyd Salas's *Tattoo the Wicked Cross* takes place in a boys' prison farm. The novel is divided into ten parts. As Aaron D'Aragon enters the prison, he sees its sign: GOLDEN GATE INSTITUTE OF INDUSTRY AND REFORM. The prison looks almost like a cemetery, and the entrance resembles the "pearly gates" of heaven. Aaron has been sent to prison for gang fighting. The story encompasses approximately six months and shows the changes that Aaron goes through during that time. He changes from an idealistic, religious youth who believes in God and honor to one who learns that to survive he must change and learn a different code of honor. He learns that in prison there is a code that must be followed: One does not snitch, and one takes care of oneself.

Aaron is apprehensive when he arrives at the prison. His good friend Barneyway is in prison, and Aaron is looking forward to seeing him. Part 1 is titled "Dead Time," referring to the stage of a prison sentence during which an inmate is not yet acclimated to prison life. Aaron is placed in a cell with a limited view of the prison and other inmates. He hears people but cannot see them, and his food is brought to him. While in this cell, he discovers that someone has carved a heart with the message RICHIE DE LA CRUZ + EVA, Richard of the Cross and Eve. Along with the heart is a pachuco cross with three lines, suggesting rays of light emanating from it. From his initial contacts with other inmates, he learns about prison and also learns he must be cautious, especially when inquiring about his friend Barneyway.

In part 2 "Buddies and Bad Actor," he learns that Buzzer rules the prison ruthlessly and brutally and that he sodomizes whomever he wishes. When Aaron learns that

Barneyway is one of Buzzer's victims and has become a "queen," he becomes determined not to be a victim.

In the third through eighth parts, Aaron learns of the brutalities occurring in the prison and must make decisions about how to respond. Aaron's family visits him and encourages him to do what they believe is right. They tell him to avoid trouble and do his time quietly. Aaron's girlfriend, Judith, gives him hope in a seemingly hopeless brutal place.

Aaron finds himself in a dilemma: How can he live up to his ideals and beliefs if he is beaten and sodomized by Buzzer? Aaron does not want to be a hapless victim like Barneyway. He wants vengeance but cannot seek it while remaining true to his Catholic faith.

Judith appears for one of her visits with a tattoo on her cheek. Because she has a tattoo, Aaron now views her as lost, no longer the ideal pure person who gave him hope. His faith was already slipping because he was angry with God for taking his mother; now his girlfriend has been taken away from him.

Part 9 prepares the background for the final chapter. Aaron is in the prison hospital recovering from a savage beating and rape by Buzzer and his gang. He is aware that he has been beaten badly but knows that he fought bravely. At this point he does not know that he has been "gang banged." When he is told, he does not feel anger; he only feels shame. He is asked for the names of the people who jumped him. He says he does not know. Barneyway visits Aaron, and Aaron says he must make sure that Buzzer does not bother them again. It is then that he decides he must have revenge.

Buzzer and his gang attack Aaron again. Hot with anger, he remembers that there is poison in the supply room to feed Buzzer and his gang. He pours the white powder into the soup. Buzzer dies a horrible death in the chapel, but Barneyway also dies of poisoning.

Tattoo the Wicked Cross ends with part 10, "Good Time." Aaron's revenge does three things for him: He has gotten back at Buzzer, has earned the respect of his fellow inmates, and will finally be left alone. He is a mass murderer, but because he is a minor, he is not sentenced to the gas chamber or a state prison. He will remain in the institute doing "good time," remaining on his best behavior.

The Characters

The story is told from Aaron's perspective. Aaron is the most developed of all the characters. He must pit his survival skills against the other youths and against the prison itself. He is an individual with convictions. His interior monologues let the reader know how he feels about his prison experience. Initially, he is cautious in his contacts with other prisoners. No matter how he feels inside, he does not let others know his inner feelings. His introspection and analysis of his circumstances moves the story along briskly.

Barneyway, Aaron's friend, has succumbed to prison life and become a "queen" as a result of Buzzer's brutish force. Although Barneyway is not the same forceful person he was outside prison, Aaron still wants him as a friend. He finds it painful to see what has happened to Barneyway. Barneyway's characterization shows the reader what happens to some youths in prison and the kind of adaptation sometimes necessary to survive.

Buzzer shows how cruel a person can become when there is nothing holding him back. Prison rewards Buzzer for his large size and lack of a conscience. The most developed characteristics of Buzzer are his cruelty and ruthlessness. He has acquired precisely those characteristics that the prison tries to eliminate. There is no pretense of rehabilitation for him. Buzzer's almost unchecked power is seen each time he comes into the reader's view. He is evil personified.

Although Rattler can strike and kill, and although he is sly and slick, he is only a follower of Buzzer. Rattler's role is essential in that he represents those who are loyal to power; Buzzer is the power.

Judith, Aaron's girlfriend, personifies influences outside the prison. Outsiders represent hope for those inside. Aaron loses hope after seeing Judith's tattooed cheek. She is no longer a symbol of the purity and virtue possible in the outside world.

Big Stoop, the commander of the institute, represents the brutal power of the institution. He provides the connection between the ultimate power of the institution and the inmates. He also represents the militaristic power of the state.

The prison chaplain represents false hope. It is through the chaplain's inaction that the reader learns what kind of person he is. He is supposed to, but does not, provide spiritual hope for the inmates. He proves to be a lackey for the prison, informing on the "flock" to the authorities.

Themes and Meanings

Tattoo the Wicked Cross is a complex novel with many themes and meanings. Ostensibly it is about what happens to a fifteen-year-old delinquent, Aaron D'Aragon, while in a boys' prison farm. The prison is supposed to teach him to be a "good citizen," to reform. Aaron and the other boys in prison have a different code of ethics, the ethics of the streets. Salas shows the reader that prison is a dehumanizing place, one that offers corruption instead of the promised rehabilitation. When Aaron enters prison, he is an "innocent" boy who still has beliefs and a sense of right and wrong. He soon realizes that he cannot hold on to his ideals. His good friend Barneyway is also in prison, and Aaron is eager to see him. He remembers Barneyway as a tough gang member but Aaron soon learns that he was not tough enough to withstand the brutality of Buzzer. Barneyway falls victim to Buzzer and thus to the system that created this cruel person.

Another theme is the loss of faith. Aaron tries to pray as he has been taught and tries to remain true to his Catholic faith. When he is beaten and violated by Buzzer and his gang, a dilemma develops. How can he remain true to his faith, which does not allow retaliation? How does one remain nonviolent in a violent world? Aaron finds it impossible to abide by his old moral code and makes a decision to take vengeance on his tormentors. Aaron poisons his tormentors, forsaking his faith and becoming a mass murderer.

The outside world and the visitors who once gave him hope have changed. Judith, his girlfriend, was once a symbol of purity and virtue, of love and goodness. Aaron sees her differently when she tattoos her cheek. She is now a symbol of fallen feminine perfection, no longer the biblical symbol that bears her name, "the praised one." She is also not the symbolic heroine of the apocryphal Book of Judith. Aaron becomes angry with God for taking away his mother and for allowing Judith to fall from purity. Even the death of Buzzer has religious overtones. Buzzer dies in the prison chapel, at the altar. It is ironic that Buzzer, the one who torments and "crucifies" Aaron, is now the crucified.

In the kind of prison system in which Aaron is placed, the murders elevate him. As a killer, he will be respected by his peers. Salas asks whether this is the kind of system in which youths should be placed.

Another main point made in the novel is that society destroys its "innocent" children under the guise of helping them. If these children are to be rehabilitated, this will not be accomplished by placing them in dehumanizing prisons with dehumanized authorities and dehumanized inmates. The result will be tragedy. Salas makes his point by chronicling the changes that the main character goes through during his first six months in prison.

Critical Context

Tattoo the Wicked Cross is an important novel because it deals with universal themes of honor, faith, good and evil, survival, and identity. Much of the fiction by Latinos and Chicanos during the 1960's deals with their experiences with authority figures such as the police, the church, schools, and parents. Fiction of that period also addresses issues of poverty, insufficient social and health services, lack of education, and discrimination. Although Salas's novel touches on some of these concerns, he has concentrated on the environmental factors that send young people to prison and what happens to those youths while they are incarcerated. Salas's novel speaks eloquently and graphically about the injustices of the penal system, especially as it concerns youthful offenders. Placing them in prisons does not rehabilitate them; it corrupts them. It turns youths into incorrigibles unfit for society.

Salas's book gives the reader a glimpse of the penal system that destroys youth. He speaks from some of his own experiences in a youth camp. Since publication of his books, there has been a movement to treat youthful offenders with an eye toward rehabilitation rather than punishment. Perhaps Salas's book has influenced some members of the penal and judicial system.

Tattoo the Wicked Cross, Salas's first published novel, set him apart from other Latino and Chicano writers of the time. The novel set the tone of his writing, which rebelled against the literary world. Two other works that show his rebellious bent are the novels *What Now My Love* (1969) and *Lay My Body on the Line* (1978). He writes about issues that concern him, even though the resulting works may not readily find publishers. He remains true to himself and to his art.

Tattoo the Wicked Cross was honored with the Henry Joseph Jackson Award and

Eugene F. Saxton Fiction Fellowship. The novel was reissued in 1981, and it was translated into French in 1969 and into Spanish in 1971. Salas's recognition as a writer goes beyond the sphere of Latino and Chicano writing, but his works are becoming part of the canon of Latino and Chicano literature.

In addition to writing Latino fiction, Salas has also published poetry and numerous essays on the craft of writing. In 1986, he edited *Stories and Poems from Close to Home*, a collection of writings by San Francisco Bay writers, and in 1992 he published *Buffalo Nickel: A Memoir*, an autobiography that reads like a novel. Although his roots are Latino, of Spanish stock, he has not limited his writings. He has contributed much to Latino literature, but his writings are truly contributions to the wider American literature.

Bibliography

Bruce-Novoa, Juan. *Chicano Authors: Inquiry by Interview*. Austin: University of Texas Press, 1980. In the introduction, Bruce-Novoa examines the position that Salas's novels hold within Chicano literature. The book as a whole offers a good perspective on Chicano literature and the concerns of Chicano writers.

Haslam, Gerald. *Forgotten Pages of American Literature*. Boston: Houghton Mifflin, 1970. The section titled "Viva La Raza: Latino American Literature" offers a good commentary on Salas's work within the framework of Chicano literature. Haslam discussed the problem of placing a Spanish American writer with Chicano writers even though the main character in *Tattoo the Wicked Cross* is depicted as a Chicano.

McKenna, Teresa. "Three Novels: An Analysis." *Aztlán* 1 (Fall, 1970): 48-49. McKenna's analysis includes three writers: Richard Vasquez, Raymond Barrio, and Floyd Salas. Her analysis includes Salas's *Tattoo the Wicked Cross*, which she sees as concerning rites of passage. She also does an analysis of language use to show Aaron D'Aragon's inward perception. A good analysis for the reader who wishes to see how Salas uses language to develop the character.

Salas, Floyd. *Buffalo Nickel: A Memoir*. Houston: Arte Publico Press, 1992. An eloquent and revealing autobiographical account that centers on the relationship Salas had with his brother, Al. Discusses his various fictional works, including the highly acclaimed *Tatoo the Wicked Cross*.

_____. "An Interview with Floyd Salas." Interview by Gerald Haslam. *MELUS* 19 (Spring, 1994): 97-112. This informative interview with Salas explores his background, the cultural and social influences on his writing, his literary style, thoughts on boxing and fighting, family relationships, and insights into his works. Although *Tatoo the Wicked Cross* is not specifically discussed, this article offers a solid overview of Salas's career.

Shirley, Carl R., and Paula W. Shirley. *Understanding Chicano Literature*. Columbia: University of South Carolina Press, 1988. Chapter 3 briefly discusses sixteen Latino writers who have had considerable influence on the contemporary Latino novel. The chapter gives the reader a quick overview of the place of Salas's work within Latino literature.

Tatum, Charles M. *Chicano Literature.* Boston: Twayne, 1982. In the introduction to chapter 5, "Contemporary Chicano Novel," Tatum offers a brief historical overview of Chicano literature since 1959. Part of Tatum's discussion includes *Tattoo the Wicked Cross.* His comments center on the personality of Aaron D'Aragon, the inner conflicts of nonviolence as taught by his religious beliefs, and his survival in the brutal prison system. The book provides a synopsis of the Chicano novel and its development.

Marcus "C" López

TELL ME THAT YOU LOVE ME, JUNIE MOON

Author: Marjorie Kellogg (1922-   )
Type of plot: Social issues/romance
Time of plot: The 1960's
Locale: A small town and a seaside resort somewhere in the United States
First published: 1968

> *Principal characters:*
> JUNIE MOON, a young woman with a disfigured face and disfigured
>   hands
> ARTHUR, a young man with a progressive neurological disease
> WARREN, a paraplegic
> MARIO, their friend, the owner of a fish store

The Novel

When Junie Moon, Warren, and Arthur decide to set up housekeeping together after being released from the hospital, it is because no one else wants them. This arrangement of convenience soon becomes a strong, three-way emotional reliance, however, when the three "freaks" move into a ramshackle house on the edge of town. Marjorie Kellogg's short but richly textured first novel chronicles their brief life together as a trio of outcasts united against a cold and unaccepting world.

All three main characters are profoundly and permanently disabled. Junie Moon has had acid poured over her face and hands by a sexually disturbed assailant, leaving her hideously disfigured. Warren, a paraplegic confined to a wheelchair, has been unable to walk since being shot during a hunting trip in his adolescence. Only Arthur, though, faces the prospect of impending death. His terminal disease, which has baffled the countless doctors who have tried to diagnose it, makes it difficult for him to control his movements. His spasms are getting more severe, his seizures more frequent as the novel opens.

Approximately one-third of the novel takes place in the hospital where the three meet. Along with Minnie, Junie Moon's terminally ill roommate, they provide the only color in the hospital's bleak and depressing landscape. The patients' lives are punctuated only by medicine calls from the authoritarian head nurse, Miss Oxford, and by Grand Rounds, a comic ritual during which overbearing doctors and sycophantic interns poke and prod the patients, asking predictable questions but never waiting for answers.

Only Binnie Farber, their sympathetic social worker, takes their communal living proposal seriously. The three seem unlikely housemates: They bicker constantly, the only thing they have in common being the fierce determination to start life anew outside the hospital. Warren finds them a house on the edge of town, which, though run-down and ill-equipped, has a certain charm: It is overshadowed by a vast banyan tree, and the trio's closest neighbor is the tree's resident owl, who views their arrival with territorial jealousy. Also spying on them is Sidney Wyner, who lives next door; a hateful, troublesome meddler, Sidney spends much of his time watching them through the hedge.

Adjusting to their new living arrangement is not easy. The two men disagree constantly, and the wisecracking Junie Moon can do little to mediate. Warren is lazy and imperious, Arthur distant and uncooperative. Being self-conscious about their various disabilities, the three seldom leave the house. Junie Moon's ravaged face, only partially hidden by her sombrero, horrifies the townspeople. Their only real adventure comes when Warren, always attractive to and attracted to good-looking people, brings home Gregory, a beautiful young heiress. Gregory takes them to her home, a castle on the side of a hill, but the visit turns out badly when Junie Moon and Arthur come upon Gregory sadistically forcing Warren to try to walk.

Slowly it becomes apparent that Junie Moon and Arthur are falling in love, though neither of them knows quite how to go about it. Arthur, ashamed of accepting welfare, tries to get a job, partly to impress Junie Moon. He is almost hired by Mario, a gentle bachelor who owns a fish store, but Sidney Wyner phones Mario to tell him that Arthur is a sodomist. Dejected, Arthur disappears. Junie Moon enlists Mario's aid and mounts a search. Arthur later turns up at the house, accompanied by a stray dog.

The novel's final movement begins when Mario decides that the three housemates need a vacation and lends them his truck to drive to the seashore. At Patty's Hideaway, an expensive seafront hotel, Warren convinces the management that they are dignitaries traveling incognito. All three find a measure of contentment on their holiday: Warren spends the three days with Beach Boy, a beautiful cabana attendant who pampers him and takes him to parties; Junie Moon and Arthur begin to realize the extent of their love and indulge in a reciprocity that neither has ever before enjoyed.

The vacation ends when it is realized that Arthur is dying. They drive nonstop from the seashore back home, Arthur's condition deteriorating all the while. He dies in Junie Moon's arms under cover of the banyan tree, as content as he has ever been in his miserable life. Warren, Junie Moon, and the dog move in with their new friend Mario, who has long been lonely in his large and empty house.

The Characters

Tell Me That You Love Me, Junie Moon, a novel in which little "action" occurs, derives its success largely from the deftness of Kellogg's characterizations of the three "freaks." Each carries the emotional baggage of a complex and painful life, and the ways in which their complicated psyches clash and harmonize comprise the main subject matter of the book. Because much about each character (including such secondary characters as Mario and the dog) is recounted by the omniscient narrator, the reader knows much more about them than they know about one another, which lends their interaction poignancy and humor.

Arthur is the most sympathetic character of the three, and he is also the most fully developed. Since he speaks little, much of what the reader knows about him comes from the narrator's account of his early life. Unjustly sent to an institution for the feebleminded at an early age (he is by far the most intelligent of the trio), he has been ignored and misunderstood all his life. His first love, the cook at the mental institution, publicly humiliated him; his parents moved away without telling him. Arthur is a character of superior intellect and sensitivity who has faced a lifetime of rejection because of his inexplicable disease. His stream of consciousness is more frequently rendered than are Warren's or Junie Moon's, and this added insight enables the reader to see Arthur as he sees himself: as a potential lover but also as a desperately ill man.

The other half of this unlikely romantic pair is Junie Moon, a tough, cynical, often maddening character, as angry and undemonstrative as Arthur is gentle and sensitive. Junie Moon has had a long and sordid romantic history: Jesse, the man who poured acid on her face and hands after forcing her to disrobe and uttering obscenities to her, was only the worst of a reprehensible lot. She has seldom if ever known love. Like Arthur's, her parents left without a trace, which has hardened and embittered her. Yet Junie Moon's sense of humor and her refusal to indulge in self-pity give her an unmistakable appeal—both Arthur and Mario are attracted to her. Nor is she completely without compassion. Her behavior toward Minnie, her terminally ill roommate, is touching without being maudlin: Against Warren's wishes, Junie Moon arranges for Minnie to spend the day at their home, providing the old woman with a brief respite from the hospital. Her coarseness and her ability to laugh at herself are often frustrating to those around her, but they allow Junie Moon to survive in a hostile world.

Warren has little to recommend him. Spoiled and petulant, he is a manipulator who pouts when his wishes are thwarted. Abandoned in infancy by his beautiful young mother, Warren was reared by his biochemist grandmother and by Guiles, the only person, male or female, whom Warren has ever loved (toward the end of the book, he dubs the beautiful Beach Boy "Guiles"). Warren is secretive about his homosexuality—the "accident" which has left him crippled was no doubt the result of a failed proposition. Still, he, like Junie Moon, is a survivor who has done what he must to cope, and he has an undeniable flair for overcoming the obstacles erected by an obstinate and bureaucratic society.

The minor characters serve rather too obviously as "normal" counterparts to the protagonists. The sympathetic Nurse Holt and the stuffy Miss Oxford counterbalance each other, as do the intolerant Sidney Wyner and the kindly Mario. One of the most compelling of the novel's characters is the dog, a promiscuous stray with a history and a viewpoint all his own. The human characteristics given both the dog and the owl add humor and charm to this fablelike story of rejection and belonging.

Themes and Meanings

Tell Me That You Love Me, Junie Moon is a story about finding a place to belong. All three of the protagonists are, like the dog who later joins them, strays. Junie Moon's parents, anxious for an opportunity to be rid of an unmarriageable daughter, abandon her when she is assaulted. Arthur, also deserted by his parents, has grown up in a state mental institution. Warren, though loved and cared for by Guiles and by his grandmother, has never even seen his mother or his father. The house under the banyan tree is the first real home any of them has ever known, and their often antagonistic behavior toward one another can be seen as an attempt to establish the sort of family relationship that has been denied them in the past. Since no one cares about them, they decide to care about one another. In this novel, "home" and "family" are created, not inherited, and even secondary characters such as Minnie and Mario illustrate the advantages of chosen kin over blood kin.

Though it is primarily concerned with personal relationships, this is also a novel with social vision. Junie Moon, Arthur, and Warren are "freaks," unwanted and misunderstood by the world of the healthy and the complacently "normal." A well-meaning shop clerk is so horrified by Junie Moon's face that he sells her a red wagon at a ridiculous discount; even the tolerant Mario denies Arthur a job because of one of Sidney Wyner's lies; the rich and eccentric Gregory victimizes Warren, treating him as a sadomasochistic plaything. The normal characters in this novel reveal dark and sinister undersides, while the freaks—though far from being the sentimentalized martyrs that a less talented writer might have made them—display depths of intellect and feeling such as Sidney Wyner and Miss Oxford have never known.

Junie Moon, Warren, and Arthur insist on their right to exist outside the hospital. In that they overcome enormous difficulties in reaching their goal, they are heroes. Their wit, their vanity, and their very real need for one another make them above all else human beings—human beings whose handicaps are only a bit more apparent than those of other people.

Critical Context

Tell Me That You Love Me, Junie Moon was Marjorie Kellogg's first novel, and it created a tremendous sensation when it first appeared in 1968. Critics praised it almost unanimously, and it became a best-seller. Kellogg's second novel, *Like the Lion's Tooth* (1972), also deals with a trio of outcasts, in this case emotionally disturbed children. The author's astonishingly accurate portrayal of hospitals and mental institutions and her sure understanding of the bureaucratic mentality are in part explained by her professional experience as a hospital social worker. Also a newspaper writer and a playwright, Kellogg wrote the screenplay for Otto Preminger's unreleased 1970 film adaptation of *Tell Me That You Love Me, Junie Moon.*

Many critics have found affinities between Kellogg's fiction and the novels and short stories of the Southern women writers Eudora Welty, Flannery O'Connor, and Carson McCullers. With its emphasis on the grotesque, its hypersensitivity to emotional nuance, its eerie nonrealism (most characters have no surnames; the date is unspecified, as are the location and the name of the town), and its use of a romantic triangle of sorts, *Tell Me That You Love Me, Junie Moon* does indeed seem heavily influenced by such Southern gothic tales as McCullers's *The Ballad of the Sad Café* (1951). Kellogg shares with these writers the ability to illuminate lives that far too often go unnoticed by the healthy and the sane.

Bibliography
Fox, Paula. *"Tell Me That You Love Me, Junie Moon*: A Second Look." *The Horn Book Magazine* 60 (August, 1984): 496-498. A re-examination of the novel.
Kozol, Jonathan. "Like Three Pawnshop Balls." *The New York Times Book Review* 73 (October 6, 1968): 4. A prominent early review.
O'Connell, Shaun. Review in *The Village Voice* (February 6, 1969). O'Connell compares Kellogg to writers Eudora Welty, Carson McCullers, and Flannery O'Conner in her treatment of "freaks" that questions the idea of "normal." He comments on the stylistic problems with the novel which he calls "artful, but artificial."
Price, Martin. Review in *The Yale Review* 58 (Spring, 1969). Describes *Tell Me That You Love Me, Junie Moon* as "brilliantly clever" and observes the undercurrent of black comedy.
Stern, Daniel. "Love Among Life's Wounded." *Life* (October 4, 1968). Stern is impressed with the many dimensions of the characters and sees the novel as a reflection of the madness of contemporary life.
White, Edmund. "Victims of Love." *The New Republic* 159 (November 23, 1968): 38. White finds the book superior to most of its contemporaries, but a bit overly crafted.

James D. Daubs